THIRD WORLD 89/90

Second Edition

Editor

Jeffrey M. Elliot
North Carolina Central University

Jeffrey M. Elliot is professor of political science at North Carolina Central University. He received his Bachelor of Arts degree in 1969 and his Master of Arts in 1970 from the University of Southern California, and his Doctor of Arts from the Claremont Graduate School in 1978. In 1985 he was awarded an honorary Doctor of Humane Letters degree from Shaw University, and in 1986 California State University, San Bernardino, established The Jeffrey M. Elliot Collection, a permanent archive of his published works. He is the author of 58 books and over 500 articles, reviews, and interviews. His work has appeared in more than 250 publications, both in the United States and abroad, and has been nominated for numerous literary awards. Recent book titles include: *The State and Local Government Political Dictionary* (ABC-Clio, 1987), *The Trilemma of World Oil Politics* (The Borgo Press, 1987), *Fidel Castro: Nothing Can Stop the Course of History* (Pathfinder Press, 1986), *Urban Society* (The Dushkin Publishing Group, 1986), *Black Voices in American Politics* (Harcourt Brace Jovanovich, 1985), *The Presidential-Congressional Political Dictionary* (ABC-Clio, 1984), and *Tempest in a Teapot: The Falkland Islands War* (The Borgo Press, 1983). A freelance journalist, he has conducted over 350 interviews, among them: President Jimmy Carter, Nobel Prize winner Bishop Desmond Tutu, Cuban President Fidel Castro, Zairian President Mobutu Sese Seko, UNITA President Jonas Savimbi, Contra leader Adolfo Calero, and Jamaican Prime Minister Michael Manley. In addition to his academic duties, he serves as Distinguished Advisor on Foreign Affairs to Congressman Mervyn M. Dymally (D-Calif.) and as editor of the *Journal of Caribbean-American Studies* and *Journal of Black Political Studies*.

Cover illustration by Mike Eagle

Annual Editions

A Library of Information from the Public Press

The Dushkin Publishing Group, Inc.
Sluice Dock, Guilford, Connecticut 06437

The Annual Editions Series

Annual Editions is a series of over forty-five volumes designed to provide the reader with convenient, low-cost access to a wide range of current, carefully selected articles from some of the most important magazines, newspapers, and journals published today. Annual Editions are updated on an annual basis through a continuous monitoring of over 200 periodical sources. All Annual Editions have a number of features designed to make them particularly useful, including topic guides, annotated tables of contents, unit overviews, and indexes. For the teacher using Annual Editions in the classroom, an Instructor's Resource Guide with test questions is available for each volume.

VOLUMES AVAILABLE

Africa
Aging
American Government
American History, Pre-Civil War
American History, Post-Civil War
Anthropology
Biology
Business and Management
Business Ethics
China
Comparative Politics
Computers in Education
Computers in Business
Computers in Society
Criminal Justice
Drugs, Society, and Behavior
Early Childhood Education
Economics
Educating Exceptional Children
Education
Educational Psychology
Environment
Geography
Global Issues
Health
Human Development
Human Resources
Human Sexuality
Latin America
Macroeconomics
Marketing
Marriage and Family
Middle East and the Islamic World
Nutrition
Personal Growth and Behavior
Psychology
Social Problems
Sociology
Soviet Union and Eastern Europe
State and Local Government
Third World
Urban Society
Western Civilization, Pre-Reformation
Western Civilization, Post-Reformation
Western Europe
World History, Pre-Modern
World History, Modern
World Politics

Library of Congress Cataloging in Publication Data
Main entry under title: Annual Editions: Third world.
1. Underdeveloped areas—Periodicals. I. Elliot, Jeffrey M., *comp.* II. Title: The Third World
ISBN 0-87967-794-5 303.4′4

Second Edition

Manufactured by The Banta Company, Harrisonburg, Virginia 22801

Editors/ Advisory Board

Members of the Advisory Board are instrumental in the final selection of articles for each edition of Annual Editions. Their review of articles for content, level, currency, and appropriateness provides critical direction to the editor and staff. We think you'll find their careful consideration well reflected in this volume.

EDITOR

Jeffrey M. Elliot
North Carolina Central University

ADVISORY BOARD

STAFF

Rick Connelly, Publisher
Ian A. Nielsen, Program Manager
Brenda S. Filley, Production Manager
Lynne Chapman, Editor
Addie Kawula, Administrative Editor
Cheryl Nicholas, Permissions Editor
Charles Vitelli, Designer
Jean Bailey, Graphics Coordinator
Shawn Callahan, Graphics
Lynn Shannon, Graphics
Libra A. Cusack, Typesetting Coordinator
Juliana Arbo, Typesetter
Diane Barker, Editorial Assistant

To The Reader

In publishing ANNUAL EDITIONS we recognize the enormous role played by the magazines, newspapers, and journals of the *public press* in providing current, first-rate educational information in a broad spectrum of interest areas. Within the articles, the best scientists, practitioners, researchers, and commentators draw issues into new perspective as accepted theories and viewpoints are called into account by new events, recent discoveries change old facts, and fresh debate breaks out over important controversies.
Many of the articles resulting from this enormous editorial effort are appropriate for students, researchers, and professionals seeking accurate, current material to help bridge the gap between principles and theories and the real world. These articles, however, become more useful for study when those of lasting value are carefully *collected, organized, indexed,* and *reproduced* in a *low-cost format*, which provides easy and permanent access when the material is needed. That is the role played by *Annual Editions*.
Under the direction of each volume's *Editor*, who is an expert in the subject area, and with the guidance of an *Advisory Board*, we seek each year to provide in each *ANNUAL EDITION* a current, well-balanced, carefully selected collection of the best of the public press for your study and enjoyment. We think you'll find this volume useful, and we hope you'll take a moment to let us know what you think.

Traditionally, the study of international relations has focused primarily on East-West relations—that is, the post-World War II struggle between the Soviet bloc countries and the West. This collection of readings examines the social, political, and economic status of the recently emancipated Third World nations of Africa, Asia, the Middle East, South and Central America, the Caribbean, and the South Pacific.

Annual Editions: Third World seeks to define, explain, and analyze the myriad issues and problems facing the developing world—a widely divergent group of states that defy sweeping generalization. An intelligent examination of the Third World demands an interdisciplinary approach, one that welds the analytical tools of the political scientist, historian, economist, and sociologist. Such issues as institutional stability, economic development, human rights, environmental protection, ethnic strife, regional cooperation, and national security require this interdisciplinary perspective.

The readings explore sundry topics of current interest and controversy. The selections are written by knowledgeable and recognized scholars, journalists, and practitioners. In selecting the articles, I have placed special emphasis on accuracy, readability, objectivity, and currency. In addition, I have eschewed readings that are overly abstract or empirical, lack focus or definition, fail to ask basic questions or raise critical issues, or ignore or misinterpret the conventional literature on the developing world.

Obviously, the Third World is a complex topic, one that cannot be adequately covered in any one book. I have attempted to include those articles that treat, in a systematic and comprehensive way, major questions about the developing world. Most of the selections are fresh, current analyses. I do not agree, nor will you, with all the views expressed in this collection—but no one will read this volume without acquiring new insights and valuable perspectives that can enrich his or her understanding and appreciation of the challenges and opportunities of this vital part of the world.

While this anthology treats much of the information traditionally covered in introductory courses in international relations, comparative government, foreign policy, and area studies, my primary goal has been to draw the reader into the great controversies and debates surrounding the future of the Third World. To this end, I hope that this collection will stimulate rather than inhibit creative thinking, and that it will spark further study and discussion. I owe a special thanks to Ian Nielsen, program manager of the *Annual Editions* series, who played an important part in the creation of this volume and provided many perceptive comments and suggestions.

Jeffrey M. Elliot

Editor

Contents

Unit 1

Understanding the Third World

Seven selections examine what is meant by the term "Third World." The topics covered include poverty in the Third World, the condition of structural dependency, Third World conflict, and Soviet policy in the Third World.

The concepts in bold italics are developed in the article. For further expansion please refer to the Topic Guide and the Index.

Unit 2

People, Power, and Leadership

Four articles examine some of the leaders who are important in the Third World. Included are interviews with President Mobutu Sese Seko of Zaire, Jonas Savimbi, rebel leader in Angola, and Ferdinand Marcos, ex-ruler of the Philippines, and his wife Imelda.

Unit 3

Stability, Crisis, and Revolution

Seven selections discuss the current state of crisis in the Third World. The areas considered include Nicaragua, El Salvador, the Arab world, India, and South Africa.

Unit 4

The Limits of American Power

Six selections examine the limits of American power. Considered are American policies toward the Third World, with specific attention to U.S. policy toward Third World dictatorships, the failure of U.S. foreign aid, U.S. policy in El Salvador, U.S.-Asian relations, and the current U.S. relationship with South Africa.

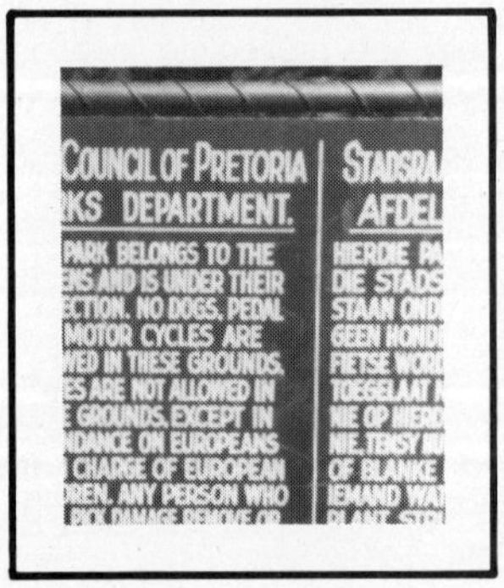

Unit 5

Human Rights and Democratic Rule

Six articles discuss the current state of human rights policy in the world.

Unit 6

Easing the Debt Crisis

Seven articles examine the impact of the debt crisis on the Third World. The selections consider the ethics of international debt, swapping debt responsibilities, the consequences of defaulting on debt, and the positive effects of available funds on Third World nations.

Unit 7

A World in Change

Nine selections consider how our world is changing. Topics include the long-term effects of malnutrition, the rising "Fourth World" of refugees, the growth of the Third World arms industry, the role of narcotics in world terrorism, and the effect of corporate crime on the Third World.

The concepts in bold italics are developed in the article. For further expansion please refer to the Topic Guide and the Index.

Topic Guide

This topic guide suggests how the selections in this book relate to topics of traditional concern to students and professionals involved with the study of the Third World. It is very useful in locating articles which relate to each other for reading and research. The guide is arranged alphabetically according to topic. Articles may, of course, treat topics that do not appear in the topic guide. In turn, entries in the topic guide do not necessarily constitute a comprehensive listing of all the contents of each selection.

TOPIC AREA	TREATED AS AN ISSUE IN:
Malnutrition	2. Second Thoughts About the Third World 38. The Hidden Malice of Malnutrition 46. Where the Future Begins
Mandela, Nelson	8. When Leaders Fall
Marcos, Ferdinand & Imelda	11. Imelda and Ferdinand Marcos
Mexico	35. Will the Planet Pay the Price?
Middle East	14. The Arab World
Mozambique	17. The RENAMO Menace 18. South Africa and Its Neighbors
Mozambique National Resistance (RENAMO)	17. The RENAMO Menace
Namibia	18. South Africa and Its Neighbors
Nationalism	1. The Third World 2. Second Thoughts About the Third World 3. "We Are Told . . ." 4. Ethnocentrism and Third World Development 5. Third World War 7. Gorbachev's New Politics
Nicaragua	13. Do the Sandinistas Want Democracy?
Noriega, Manuel	23. The Panama Perplex 29. Hugo Spadafora's Last Day
Overpopulation	2. Second Thoughts About the Third World 3. "We Are Told . . ." 4. Ethnocentrism and Third World Development 6. Industrial Development 40. Refugees: A Fact of Life?
Palestine Liberation Organization (PLO)	14. The Arab World
Palestinians	14. The Arab World
Panama	23. The Panama Perplex 29. Hugo Spadafora's Last Day
Philippines	25. The Human Rights Imperative
Poverty	2. Second Thoughts About the Third World 3. "We Are Told . . ." 12. A Pioneering Democracy Struggles 35. Will the Planet Pay the Price? 38. The Hidden Malice of Malnutrition

TOPIC AREA	TREATED AS AN ISSUE IN:
Reagan, Ronald	23. The Panama Perplex
Refugees	5. Third World War 39. The "Fourth World" 40. Refugees: A Fact of Life?
Religious Fanaticism	14. The Arab World 16. Collective Violence in India 30. Along the Streets of Tehran
Religious Freedom	15. Ayatollah Realpolitik 18. South Africa and Its Neighbors
Sandinistas (Sandinista Revolution)	13. Do the Sandinistas Want Democracy?
Savimbi, Jonas	10. Savimbi: Warrior Poet
Somalia	26. What Price Political Prisoners?
South Africa	8. When Leaders Fall 9. Mobutu Sese Seko 10. Savimbi: Warrior Poet 18. South Africa and Its Neighbors 24. Rancor Aside, Trade Ties Grow 25. The Human Rights Imperative 27. South Africa: Where Did the Story Go?
South Korea	28. Babies for Sale
Soviet Foreign Policy	7. Gorbachev's New Politics 19. Policies Toward the Third World 25. The Human Rights Imperative
Succession	12. A Pioneering Democracy Struggles
Technological Revolution	46. Where the Future Begins
Terrorism	16. Collective Violence in India 17. The RENAMO Menace
Union for the Total Independence of Angola (UNITA)	10. Savimbi: Warrior Poet
United States Foreign Policy	15. Ayatollah Realpolitik 19. Policies Toward the Third World 20. The U.S. and Third World Dictatorships 21. Five Myths About the Third World 22. Quagmire in the Making 25. The Human Rights Imperative
Zaire	9. Mobutu Sese Seko
Zimbabwe	18. South Africa and Its Neighbors

Understanding the Third World

The term "Third World" is typically used to describe the over 100 economically underdeveloped and developing nations in Asia, Africa, and South America. It can be distinguished from the First World (the United States and its industrialized allies) and the Second World (the Soviet Union and its East European partners). In recent years, the United Nations has employed the term "Fourth World" to identify those countries with an extremely low annual per capita income. Unfortunately, nomenclature in this area is quite imprecise; the Third World is also referred to as the South, the poor countries, the underdeveloped nations, and the less developed, or developing, nations.

Most Third World nations (which now include over one half of the world's population) have achieved independence since World War II. Generally, these countries are poor, weak, and unstable; they produce primary and semifinished products; and their population growth precludes sustained economic progress (as measured by living standards in the industrialized world). The developing nations represent a majority in the General Assembly of the United Nations. To maximize their influence in this body, they have formed a caucusing bloc, called the Group of Seventy-Seven (G77), in order to shape the agenda and call attention to their special concerns. Although many Third World nations meet regularly to discuss common problems, unified action is difficult to achieve because of the diversity and complexity of these problems. Most developing countries participate in the Nonaligned Movement.

Over the last several decades, these newly independent nations have struggled to improve their standards of living and eliminate the debilitating poverty and misery of past centuries. Since achieving independence, the nations of the Third World have made enormous strides in achieving self-determination, equality, and dignity. However, economic progress has proven more elusive. Many Third World peoples continue to practice subsistence agriculture, deprived of the modern tools they need to increase productivity. In addition, many of these countries lack the political machinery, social structures, and cultural traditions required of industrialized nations. Despite countless initiatives, a majority of these nations have failed to realize sustained economic growth.

Unfortunately, the economic challenge is not the only obstacle facing the developing world. Many Third World countries are still wrestling with the problem of nation-building—that is, attempting to build viable political institutions that meld the various tribal, religious, racial, and linguistic interests of the nation. This is no mean feat. In many cases, public attitudes are parochial and particularistic; formidable barriers prevent integration and assimilation. Many Third World nations are plagued by deep disunity, engendered by a host of competing values, beliefs, and traditions.

The developing world also must wage a concerted campaign to stem the population explosion. Although this problem is not universal in the Third World, it does affect many nations. For those countries, it has prevented significant economic growth. Obviously, a nation cannot spend huge sums on industrial development if it is unable to feed, clothe, and shelter its people. Many of these countries have attempted to reduce their fast-rising populations by initiating birth control campaigns, often with minimal success. The problem has reached epidemic proportions in some Third World countries, where the population has continued to double every 20 years.

Clearly, economic growth is not solely dependent on the development of industry. It is not enough simply to build new factories or dams or steel mills. The developing world must redefine many of its social, political, and economic beliefs. Indeed, modernization requires the complete transformation of the entire society. To achieve this objective, nations must rethink their beliefs on such matters as economic competition, savings, investments, profits, and economic growth.

Unless the Third World solves these and other problems, it is likely to face unprecedented chaos, disorder, and violence, not to mention instability, insecurity, and dependence. As these nations wrestle with the problem of nation-building, they must develop the conditions necessary for economic growth. In many ways, the battle for independence pales by comparison. To survive, Third World nations must promote both agrarian and industrial development. They must not only be able to feed their burgeoning populations, but must devise new ways to produce the goods and services necessary to achieve modernization. The clock is ticking away. The future demands bold action; anything else will invite catastrophe.

Looking Ahead: Challenge Questions

Why is it so difficult to define the Third World politically?

Has independence significantly improved the quality of life in the developing world?

What are the most common sources of conflict in the Third World?

Why is sovereignty a major obstacle to peace in the developing world?

Is underdevelopment a problem indigenous to the Third World?

To what extent, if any, is poverty in the developing world the result of overpopulation and colonial exploitation?

Why is the Third World so susceptible to fluctuations in the international economy?

How does ethnocentrism affect Third World development?

How is agriculture tied to the growth of Third World nations?

Do shifts in Soviet pronouncements about the developing world signal a retreat from established policy?

How has Soviet strategy changed in the Third World?

The Third World

David W. Ziegler

David W. Ziegler, Professor of Political Science at Western Washington University, received his M.A. and his Ph.D. degrees from Harvard University. He also has received Fulbright, Danforth, and Woodrow Wilson Fellowships.

The concept of sovereignty, as developed in Europe in the seventeenth and eighteenth centuries, was until recently applied only to the most powerful states, most of which were located in Europe. The rest of the world, lacking sovereignty, could therefore legitimately be "discovered" and then "claimed" by these powerful states and added to their own territory. It was only with the League of Nations in the 1920's and 1930's that some inroads were made on the traditional view that the non-Western world was territory in which the inhabitants had no legitimate claims of their own. The League provided for what it called "mandates" in some areas of the world. Although the effect on the inhabitants of mandated territories was not very different from colonial rule, the presumption was that the major power in charge of the mandate would not rule indefinitely but only as long as it took to prepare the people for self-government. This system provided some hope for the future, but it did little to change the day-to-day realities. In 1935, 70 percent of the world's population was still under the control of Western governments.[1]

RISE TO PROMINENCE

It was only with the foundation and growth of the United Nations that a significant number of non-Western states began to play an important role in world politics. The UN Charter mentions as a basic principle the self-determination of peoples. Although in its first years the membership of the UN was confined to just about the same countries that had composed the League of Nations, this balance began to change as former colonies acquired their independence. The year 1960 marks an important turning point. In that year sixteen newly independent African states were admited as members of the UN. The number of such states has continued to grow, and at present they make up more than half of the states of the world.

The term often used to describe these new states is remnant of Cold War thinking. In the bipolar conception developed in the 1950's, states belonged to the world of the United States and its allies or to the world of the Soviet Union and its allies. The remaining countries were said to make up the *Third World*.

DEFINITION OF "THIRD WORLD"

People use the name "Third World" as though it referred to a coherent group of states—much in the way "the Soviet bloc" refers to centrally planned economies ruled by Marxist-Leninist parties with close ties to the Soviet Union. But Third World is a label lacking precision. Both Sweden and Switzerland were neutral states, yet they were not considered Third World countries. The Third World countries were said to be located in Asia, Africa, and Latin America, but that area includes Taiwan, Israel, and South Africa, which were not considered part of the Third World. Most Third World states were poor and struggling with problems of economic development, yet so were Greece and Turkey, both members of NATO. In short, Third World is a residual category, where we put what is left over.

Efforts to define Third World positively—as the membership of some group—are more useful. In political terms, the most significant such group is the Non-Aligned Nations. President Sukarno of Indonesia called the first conference of states wishing to avoid involvement with the major powers at Bandung in 1955. Six years later, Sukarno, along with Nehru of India, Nasser of Egypt, and Tito of Yugoslavia, turned it into a permanent organization, with twenty-five members. The movement grew to almost one-hundred members, with yearly meetings of foreign ministers and summit conferences of heads of state every three years.

Yet divisions within the movement began to appear in 1975, when it added to its membership North Korea and North Vietnam, states that were by any reasonable definition not non-aligned but members of the Soviet bloc. Internal divisions appeared in 1978 as some of the original members tried to resist attempts by Cuba, Angola, and Vietnam—all of whom had pacts with the Soviet Union—to take consistently pro-Soviet positions on foreign policy issues. A summit conference in Havana in 1979 was dominated by Castro, with only minor concessions to the more traditional aims represented by Tito, the last of the original founders to attend. The final declaration of the Havana Conference included numerous attacks on the United States—for example, for its colonialism of Puerto Rico—but none on the Soviet Union. The unity of the movement and the influence of Castro as its chairperson received a sharp setback, however, in early 1980, when half of the membership in a United Nations vote condemned the Soviet Union for its invasion of Afghanistan.

The disunity of the Non-Aligned Nations illustrated a basic

feature of the concept of the Third World. Despite the desire by many members of these states to think of themselves as a unified group, they are beset by serious differences. Even if alliances with major powers are discounted, the political differences among these states are very great. Saudi Arabia, which has a conservative monarchy, is a member; so is its radical neighbor South Yemen. In fact the only ideology they share is that of nationalism, but because nationalism stresses the particular state, it tends to divide and not to unite.

The emphasis in the 1950's and 1960's was on defining the Third World politically. Recent years have seen more emphasis on economic condition as a defining characteristic. Thus, the twenty-four wealthy states known as "industrially developed market economies" are members of the Organization for Economic Cooperation and Development (OECD). States modeled on the Marxist-Leninist ideal of a "centrally planned economy" are members of the Council for Mutual Economic Assistance (CMEA). The remaining states are members of the Group of 77, a somewhat misleading name that was taken from the actual number at the time of its formation in 1964 but which today comprises well over one-hundred states. Because the most prominent OECD countries are in the northern hemisphere—United States, Japan, Western Europe—and many of the Group of 77 are in the southern, they are sometimes referred to as the North and the South. (The CMEA has tried to attract little attention, claiming that whatever poverty exists in the poor countries is the result of imperialism and so they share no responsibility.)

An economic definition of the Third World is not particularly helpful. At the one extreme are countries with suddenly very high incomes per capita because of oil wealth—Saudi Arabia, Kuwait, United Arab Emirates. At the other extreme are countries so poor they are often put in a separate category of "Fourth World." Over 1 billion people live in countries where the per capita income is under $220 a year. These are countries with no natural resources and a growth rate of under 1 per cent a year—enough to add only two dollars to each person's yearly income.

In between the oil-rich and the low-income are the "newly industrialized" countries—South Korea, Brazil, India, Mexico. In some ways these countries are much closer to the OECD countries than they are to other members of the Group of 77. They have no interest in the cancellation of debts, for example, because much of the high growth rate they have achieved (an average in 1979 and 1980 of 5.5 per cent) results from international loans. Defaulting on loans or having them cancelled would deprive them of loans in the future to sustain their growth rate.

The differences among countries generally considered Third World—whether defined politically or economically—are so great that we cannot reasonably speak of the Third World as a unified actor in international politics.

THIRD WORLD INFLUENCE ON WAR AND PEACE

The participation in international politics by over one-hundred new states in Asia, Africa, and Latin America poses two obstacles to peace. On the one hand, it has vitiated some of the traditional approaches to peace. On the other, it has been the source of many new conflicts.

. . . The extent and force of international law have been seriously restricted by the anti-colonial revolution promoted by and working to the benefit of these states. Legal principles of long standing, such as freedom of the high seas or immunity for diplomats, are disregarded in the name of anti-imperialism. Likewise the focus of international organizations such as the United Nations has been shifted away from issues of war and peace toward support first of liberation from colonial rule and then economic development.

The gap between the Third World's new aspirations and traditional ways of conducting international relations is a source of conflict. It widened particularly in the 1960's and 1970's, as people's attitudes in one group of states—above all our own, but also many of the states of Western Europe—were moving in one direction while the people's attitudes in the Third World were moving in another. Many of the states in the Third World had been part of larger, multinational political units, usually colonial empires. As these empires ended they were replaced by more numerous, smaller states.

At the same time, many people in long-established states were calling for a broadening of horizons beyond the nation, for seeing problems in global terms, for viewing ourselves as travelers on "Spaceship Earth." Among many young people patriotism came to be seen as old-fashioned. Proposals to reinstitute the draft were greeted by students holding signs proclaiming, "Nothing is worth dying for." National barriers seemed less important to Europeans, as more states joined the European Community.

These trends were not mirrored in the Third World. The opposite was more likely to be the case. States jealously defended their sovereignty. Young people seemed to find many issues worth dying for, as they joined armies to liberate unredeemed territory (Somalis in the 1970's), to aid other members of their national group (Turks in 1974), or expel foreigners from their land (Iranians in the 1980's). While the United States worried about the proper way to deal with an increase in illegal aliens, the government of Nigeria one day simply announced the forcible expulsion of all foreigners without work permits. According to the Nigerian government's own estimate, 2 million aliens were deported.

Many states have tried to remove foreign influences in a process called *indigenization.* Joseph Mobutu changed the name of his country from the "Congo" to what he saw as the more native name "Zaire," then changed his own name to Mobutu Sesu Seko. In Libya and Iran street signs in English or even ones using the Latin alphabet have been removed, leaving only signs in Arabic script.

Sometimes attempts by international organizations to implement policies were vigorously resisted in the name of sovereignty. Out of sensitivity to the charge that they were not managing their affairs as well as they had been under colonial rule, states tried to cover up health problems, even if the latter were not the result of government policy. Most African states denied for a long time that they had any cases of acquired immune deficiency syndrome (AIDS), despite an international obligation to report all cases to the World Health Organization; exercising their sovereignty they routinely denied visas to reporters investigating AIDS. Ethiopia expelled foreign doctors who reported cases of cholera after the government had denied that such cases existed.[2] Many other states objected to the austerity measures demanded by the International Monetary Fund (IMF) as a condition for loans to support collapsing economies; blame for the resulting rise in cost of living was placed on the IMF, not their own countries' mistaken policies, and governments were tempted to repudiate the IMF rather than face down rioters.[3]

We have seen repeatedly how sovereignty is a major obstacle to peace. The increase in the number of states enamored of it and glorifying it multiplies the obstacles to international agreement and cooperation.

SOURCES OF CONFLICT WITHIN THE THIRD WORLD

The Third World is an important source of conflict quite apart from great power interests. One study has put the total deaths from 1945 to 1967 resulting from violence within and among these countries at 7,480,000.[4] If we add to that the deaths from only two of the conflicts that have occurred since 1967—the Nigerian civil war (2 million deaths) and the Pakistan civil war (500,000 deaths)—we already exceed the number of battle deaths of World War I. With violence of such magnitude, the disputes are worth looking at for their own sake, but in addition they frequently have repercussions in international politics. After looking at the origin of many of these disputes, we shall see why their effects spread so far.

Conflict in the Third World has been attributed to a number of factors—the desire to acquire modern industrial technology, resentment at higher standards of living in economically developed countries, colonial exploitation in the past, and racial discrimination in the present. Important as these may be, they are overshadowed by another source of conflict: national sentiment.

The word "nation" is often inappropriately used (as in the name the United Nations), and so it is necessary to first define carefully what we mean. By *nation* we mean a distinct ethnic group that is clearly set off from its neighbors by such features as a separate language, separate customs, and separate traditions. One important feature of a nation is that you have no control over which one you belong to—you are born into it. Nationality is sometimes called a "primordial tie," a primary bond as opposed to second-order ties or associations. You can choose to join the Audobon Society or the Democratic Party or the Free Will Baptist Church; you can also choose to quit these associations if you desire. The element of choice is absent from a primordial tie.[5]

Conflict resulting from nationalist and other primordial ties is not limited to the Third World. Canada's problems with Quebec and Britain's problems with Northern Ireland are conflicts that have their origin in primordial ties. But it is in the Third World that the problems are most severe. For in the Third World the conditions that facilitated secondary or associational ties are becoming weaker and the conditions that activate primordial ties are becoming stronger. The British Empire, like other colonial empires, was an association. Although membership in it was not always strictly voluntary, no group was excluded because of a primordial trait. Nigerians and Indians alike were free to embrace Anglican or Catholic Christianity, learn English, study at Oxford, and participate in whatever other privileges were extended to British subjects. But Nigeria and India were themselves composed of many ethnic groups. These groups united to free themselves of British rule, but once the British left, the primordial ties reasserted themselves. In Nigeria 250 different languages are spoken; in India the number is 1,652. With the British imposing English on the entire country, it was possible to have a uniform school system and a common government language. With the departure of the British, the question of what language would be used for instruction and government business became a hotly contested political issue.

It is precisely those developments to which we refer as modernizing and progressive—such things as increased industrialization, improved means of communication, and higher standards of education—that increase the importance of primordial ties. This is so because all these developments mix together people from different groups who previously had no contact with each other. By increasing contact you increase the possibilities for conflict. We might take the case of Nigeria. Suppose several Ibo-speakers from the east take advantage of a new highway to travel north to the part of Nigeria inhabited by Hausa-speakers. Perhaps they open a shop there to sell products newly imported from Europe or Japan, such as sewing machines. The Ibos are likely to be Christians and offend the Muslim Hausas by raising and eating pigs (which are forbidden to Muslims). The language of trade between Ibos and Hausas may be English but among themselves the Ibos use their own language, which arouses suspicions among the Hausas that the Ibos are saying things about them, making fun of them, plotting to cheat them. This example is not a hypothetical one. It was precisely such movement by the Ibos and such hostility that it aroused that it led to a massacre of 50,000 Ibos in northern Nigeria in 1966. Another 1 million Ibos were driven out. They fled back to the east and demanded their own state as the only sure source of protection, an event that led to a bloody and ultimately unsuccessful civil war.

It was precisely the modern developments such as better roads and imported sewing machines that generated this conflict. In the past diverse ethnic groups had little contact with each other. Colonial rule by the British set in motion the process by which the groups came in contact, although the British also were able to prevent tensions from erupting into violence. When the British departed, the process continued, now without any effective central control.

PRIMORDIAL TIES AS A SOURCE OF CONFLICT

The experience of the Ibos in Nigeria illustrates what many people have come to believe, that security for an ethnic group can be found only when that group controls its own state. With thousands of ethnic groups in the world and only about 150 states, it is clear that not all groups control their own states. The most obvious problem is that one state may include many ethnic groups.

But this is not the only problem. In some places states' borders cut right through the territory inhabited by an ethnic group. Sometimes the group so divided is only one of many; this is the case in many African countries where the boundaries were drawn by European colonial powers with no concern for local inhabitants. In other cases the group divided by a state boundary makes up the entire population of each political unit—in other words, a single nation is divided into several states. It was this condition that led to the German wars of unification in the nineteenth century. A century later the division of Vietnam and Korea caused wars for the same reason.

Even though these few cases have been the source of international conflict, they are far outnumbered by the cases in which one state embraces many nations. Only fourteen states (or fewer, if you treat Germany, Vietnam, and Korea each as one), about 10 per cent of the world's states, are homogeneous in ethnic makeup. In another 40 per cent, one ethnic group is dominant, making up 75 per cent or more of the population. But, as Cyprus showed, this is no guarantee of peace; although the Greeks made up more than 80 per cent of the population, the Turks were not willing to submit to rule by them. The problems are even more acute in those states in which no one group makes up even as much as half the population. Almost 30 per cent of the states of the world fall into this category. Nigeria is one example; India and Pakistan are others.

The conflicts generated by ethnic questions within such states are a threat to international peace because they frequently spread beyond the borders of a single country. There are a number of reasons why this happens. When one nation is divided among several states, the issue is by definition international. When one ethnic group finds itself divided between two states, efforts by the group to ignore the border may provoke international disputes. This has been the case when Somali nomads ignored the borders between Somalia and the neighboring countries of Ethiopia and Kenya that cut across their traditional grazing land.

Another reason why conflict spreads is that ethnic ties are valued so highly in the world today that actions taken to support members of one's own ethnic group are considered justification for violating the basic principle of noninterference in the internal affairs of a sovereign state. India felt justified in entering Pakistan's civil war in 1971 because the massacre of Bengalis in Pakistan could not be tolerated by the Bengalis in India. The internal governance of Rhodesia and South Africa is a major concern to black African states; support for guerrillas seeking to overthrow regimes in these countries is not seen as illegitimate. The conflict over Israel has been escalated into a world conflict by primordial ties: Countries as distant as Morocco send troops to fight because of solidarity with other Arabs. American Jews translate their solidarity with Israel into active pressure on the United States government for greater commitment to Israel.

NATIONALISM AND WAR

In states that have been established for a long time, primordial ties are often weaker. Many Latin American states have been independent for over a century and in their populations nationalism is the primary emotion. (In states only recently independent, however, ethnic ties are still major factors. Guyana, a British colony until 1966, is split between groups originating in Africa and ones from the East Indies.) Conflicts between states in Latin America have been made more difficult to solve by intense nationalist feelings and in some cases have led to war. In 1969 El Salvador and Honduras fought over a disputed border. Argentina and Chile have gone as far as mobilizing troops over disputed islands in the sea south of Argentina. Argentina, to most people's surprise, landed troops on islands claimed by them in 1982. The British, who ruled the islands under the name of the Falklands, underestimated the intensity of nationalist feeling that led the Argentines to challenge a superior military power.

The war in the Falklands illustrates how conflicts in the Third World draw in other powers. The British felt directly challenged because of political claims for British protection by the people living on the Falklands, most of whom were of British origin. (Had the islands been uninhabited, the British would have turned them over to the Argentines years ago.) Sometimes outside powers are drawn in in less direct ways. Third World states may actively seek the support of major powers in their quarrels. India actively solicited the support of the Soviet Union in its quarrel with Pakistan. Pakistan in turn sought support from both China and the United States. Thus the war between India and Pakistan in 1971 over an essentially ethnic issue became a potential confrontation between the major powers.

The conflict between India and Pakistan also appears to have been the major motivation for first India and then Pakistan to try to acquire nuclear weapons. In 1974 India exploded a nuclear device that it termed "peaceful." In the absence of any clear-cut need for such a device or any subsequent use of nuclear technology for peaceful purposes, the impression remains strong that India was interested mainly in demonstrating its potential to acquire nuclear weapons. Pakistan's prime minister certainly perceived such an intent, because he declared, "We will eat leaves and grass, even go hungry, but we will have to get one."[6] By April 1979 Pakistan's program was so advanced that the United States government cut off all aid to Pakistan under the provisions of a law requiring such termination to countries acquiring nuclear weapons.[7]

NUCLEAR PROLIFERATION

The Indian explosion of a nuclear device in 1974 was important for three reasons. It was the first acquisition of nuclear capability by a country in over a decade (China's had been the most recent, in 1964). It was the first by a country not generally considered a great power (all other acknowledged nuclear states were permanent members of the Security Council). And it was the first nuclear device built with fuel diverted from power reactors. This last feature was the most alarming. A standard 1,000-megawatt thermal power reactor of current design produces over 200 kilograms of spent fuel a year, enough to make forty small nuclear explosives. With over 200 such reactors operating in more than forty-two countries, the potential for the spread of nuclear weapons to more countries is very great.[8]

Reaction to the Indian explosion illustrates again the essential lack of cohesion in the Third World. Although most of the Third World states adhered to the Non-Proliferation Treaty of 1968 (and thereby made it possible in the first place), when India exploded its nuclear device in 1974, Pakistan was the only member of the Third World to criticize India in the subsequent United Nations General Assembly. Some of these states may have been contemplating nuclear programs of their own; there is evidence that Iraq and Argentina were. Others may have been reluctant to criticize so prominent a member of the Non-Aligned Movement; they may even have enjoyed the technological triumph of what was once called a "backward nation."

But these feelings of solidarity among members of the Non-Aligned Movement have generated anxieties in states not accepted by the Non-Aligned Movement and not fitting comfortably into any grouping. Such states are sometimes called "pariah" or outcast states and many of them are considered the most likely to acquire nuclear weapons of their own—for example Israel, South Africa, Taiwan, South Korea. Although not normally considered Third World states, these states are geographically in the middle of the Third World and have Third World states for neighbors.

The proliferation of nuclear weapons to Third World states makes the Third World an even more serious source of international conflict. The use of such weapons in local or regional quarrels would quickly turn such quarrels into world crises. In another round of war between India and Pakistan or between Israel and its Arab neighbors, one can imagine the losing side resorting to nuclear weapons in desperation. Had Argentina possessed nuclear weapons when it was fighting Britain for the Falkland Islands, it might have been tempted to use them to save its position or even as an emotional reaction to the British sinking of one of their ships.

In response to evidence that Pakistan was building nuclear weapons, the United States suspended military aid; India, feeling more directly threatened, considered stronger measures. In 1982 United States intelligence officials suspected that India was developing a plan for a preemptive air strike to destroy the Pakistani facilities.[9] Israel carried out such a strike against Iraq in 1981, and although that strike did not escalate into war, an Indian strike against Pakistan could have. The Israelis struck against a small program, still far from completion, and evidently were completely successful. An only partially successful strike against an extensive program might provoke the target state to retaliate with whatever nuclear weapons remained.

Some analysts have speculated that some of Pakistan's weapons could find their way into the hands of Libya's President Muammar Qaddafi, perhaps in return for his financial support. Some of Qaddafi's public statements suggest he would be more willing to use such weapons against his avowed enemies, particularly Israel, than many other leaders would be. Or Qaddafi might transfer such weapons to a terrorist group, putting that group beyond the control of any state.[10]

We might recall the arguments of those who advocate a balance of terror. According to this line of thought, the possession of nuclear weapons by Third World states might make war less likely just as nuclear weapons have restrained the United States-Soviet rivalry. The argument has some merit but is not completely comforting. The United States and the Soviet Union have ample arsenals, not just a few weapons they would be tempted to use or lose. They have had years to consider carefully the implications of such weapons and to devise doctrines that try to deal with the complexities. They have invested in control devices to prevent unauthorized use. Neither the United States nor the Soviet Union is plagued by the problem common to most Third World states—military coups or takeovers by rival factions within the military.

The internal problems of Third World states are the most common cause of conflict in the world today. Tension between the superpowers occupies the attention of many people, but the actual fighting and dying occurs in countries such as Cambodia, Iraq, and Chad. In the older states, the conflicts generated by primordial ties have been largely settled. This has been the result not of superior wisdom or inherent virtue but simply of the relatively long time these countries have had to work on the problem. In some cases the problem was solved by the creation of separate states. Norway and Sweden became separate countries in 1905, for example. In other cases ethnic minorities were subdued by military conquest, as happened in the English wars against the Welsh and the Scots. In 1945 the Poles adopted an equally drastic measure against the Germans, expelling 10 million Germans from the territory they claimed as the Polish state. But even in the older states, not all conflicts over ethnic issues have been settled. The British have been struggling with the Irish for hundreds of years, and it appears that they will continue to do so for many more. With such struggles just beginning in many parts of the Third World, we can expect conflict there to continue for a long time to come.

NOTES

1. Grover Clark, *A Place in the Sun* (1936), cited by Harold Isaacs, *Idols of the Tribe* (New York: Harper & Row, 1975), p. 6.
2. Lawrence K. Altman, "In Africa, Problems Change But the Frustrations Go On," *The New York Times*, December 10, 1985, p. Y18.
3. It is generally accepted that the government of Sudan was overthrown in 1985 because it tried to implement austerity measures demanded by the IMF.
4. Robert D. Crane, "Postwar Ethnic Cultural Conflicts" (1968), cited by Isaacs, p. 7.
5. There is some disagreement about terms. "Primordial" is used in approximately this way by Clifford Geertz, "The Integrative Revolution: Primordial Sentiments and Civil Politics in the New States," in *Old Societies and New States*, ed. Clifford Geertz (New York: Free Press, 1963), especially pp. 109-119. See also the definition by Walker Connor, "The Politics of Ethnonationalism," *Journal of International Affairs*, Vol. 27, No. 1 (1973), p. 2n.
6. Donna S. Kramer (Congressional Research Service), *Nuclear Energy: The Threat of Pakistan Going Nuclear*, Issue Brief No. IB 79093, October 23, 1979.
7. U.S. Senate, Committee on Governmental Affairs, Subcommittee on Energy, Nuclear Proliferation, and Federal Services, *Nuclear Proliferation: The Situation in Pakistan and India: Hearings*, 96th Congress, 1st sess., May 1, 1979.
8. Walter Marshall, "On Plutonium Fears," *The New York Times*, April 18, 1978, p. 33.
9. Leonard S. Spector, *Nuclear Proliferation Today* (New York: Vintage, 1985), p. 48.
10. Steve Weissman and Herbert Krosney, *The Islamic Bomb* (New York: Times Books, 1981).

Second Thoughts About the Third World

Thomas Sowell

Thomas Sowell is a fellow at the Hoover Institution at Stanford University. This article is excerpted from his book, The Economics and Politics of Race, *published by William Morrow.*

What is popularly called the Third World is larger than the first world of affluent nations (western Europe, the United States, Canada, Australia, and Japan) and the second world of communist-bloc countries combined. Most of the human race lives in the Third World. In that sense, it is an immensely important reality. In another sense, however, the Third World as a concept is a creature of vague and inconsistent definition—lumping together countries that are highly disparate in economic, cultural, political, racial, and ethnic terms. Poverty is supposed to be the defining characteristic of the Third World, but substantial geographic regions and social classes in the Third World are far from poor, and some whole countries in the Third World are closer to the living standards of western Europe than to those of other third-world nations. Sometimes the Third World is defined racially, with the white nations being rich and the nonwhite poor. But nonwhite Japan has a higher per capita income than Great Britain, the Soviet Union, and various other nations of eastern and western Europe, as well as such predominantly white South American countries as Brazil and Argentina. Saudi Arabia and Kuwait likewise have higher per capita incomes than various white nations. Moreover, when the Third World is conceived in terms of people rather than nations, it so happens that it contains more whites than blacks.

While the boundaries of the Third World are difficult to define with both meaningfulness and precision, it remains true nevertheless that substantial regions of the world, substantial numbers of nations, and substantial proportions of the human race live at economic levels that would be considered poverty in western Europe, the United States, or Japan. The reasons for this poverty, possible ways of alleviating it, and the prospects for achieving prosperity in the Third World are therefore important concerns.

Because poverty is one of those things that is simply the absence of something else—wealth, in this case—special care is necessary in analyzing it. Other concepts that are simply the absence of something else—baldness, or a vacuum, for example—refer to an absence of things that occur spontaneously in nature. Wealth does not occur spontaneously in nature. Its presence, rather than its absence, requires explanation—especially since most of today's wealthy nations were poor nations only a few centuries ago. The real question is—what confluence of circumstances produced the fortunate conditions that a relatively small part of the human species enjoys today? To what extent can these peculiar combinations of historical circumstances be analyzed, recreated, or grafted onto other societies?

But before even considering these crucial questions, it is necessary to deal with other views so widely and insistently propagated that they are certain to haunt any discussion in which they are not specifically addressed. It is widely believed that overpopulation and/or colonial exploitation explain third-world poverty, and that transfers of tax money from more prosperous nations are essential, not merely for dealing with episodic emergencies, but for promoting economic growth among the poorer nations. All these views require careful scrutiny.

Too many people?

ONE OF the oldest explanations of poverty, both domestically and internationally, is overpopulation. Even before Malthus's *Essay on the Principle of Population* in 1798, others had argued that families and nations could have too many children to prosper. Malthus's extrapolations of supposedly geometrically growing population and arithmetically increasing food supply did much to dramatize and fix in the public's mind the concept of overpopulation—*before* there was any census data or other hard evidence in most of the countries of the world. Using similar extrapolations, one could show that if the temperature has risen a few degrees since this morning, a continuation of this trend would have us all burned to a crisp before the end of the month. The question is whether such reasoning should be the basis for alarm, analysis, or public policy.

To get some idea of how crowded the planet is in actuality, imagine that every man, woman, and child on earth were placed in the state of Texas. There are 4,414 million people in the world and Texas has 262,134 square miles of land area. That works out to approximately 1,700 square feet per person. A family of four would thus have 6,800 square feet—about the size of a typical middle-class American home with front- and backyards. In short, every human being on the face of the earth could be housed in the state of Texas in one-story, single-family homes, each with a front- and backyard.

What of the teeming masses of the poor that we see and hear so much about, crowding the streets of Calcutta or the slums of Puerto Rico? It should be noted, first of all, that *rich* people are never called "teeming masses," no matter how many of them there are per square mile. Wealthy Park Avenue–type neighborhoods have concentrations of people that compare with slums around the world. The more general question of crowded cities has little to do with total population or "over"-population, relative to the land area of a country. From an economic standpoint, crowding is what cities are all about.

Many of the features of a city—the variety and scale of businesses, amenities, and entertainments—are economically feasible only when drawing on a large population as customers and workers. There may be ample land in a country whose cities are crowded—or "over"-crowded, to those who do not like it. When the population of the United States was half of what it is today, its cities were *more* crowded than now.

When Irish, Italian, and Jewish immigrants were packed five or ten to a room in the slums of New York, one could travel through a hundred miles of open countryside in America without seeing a living soul (and still can today). To many well-meaning observers, it seemed obvious that the urban poor should spread out. But the immigrants wanted the jobs and the other features of a city, including the companionship of other people from a familiar culture in a strange land. Numerous efforts to get them to relocate in the countryside failed, and the few who did go often either failed as farmers or found themselves unable to cope with the isolation or other features of agricultural life. Even the Jews who became successful in an urban setting failed totally in farming communities in America and Argentina. The poverty and crowding of various immigrant groups in the urban slums had nothing to do with any lack of land in America.

Internationally as well, there is little or no relationship between poverty and population density. There are high-income, low-income, and medium-income nations with high population density, low population density, and medium population density. Ethiopia has almost the same number of people per square mile as the United States (sixty-one and sixty-five, respectively), but averages just over a hundred dollars in annual per capita income. Singapore has more than 10,000 people per square mile, and its income per capita is more than thirty times higher than that of Ethiopia. Prosperous Japan, with an income higher than that of many European nations, has more people per square mile than India, one of the poorest nations on earth.

An argument could be made that it is not land but arable land that is most relevant, since deserts and mountains may have little economic significance. But while this seems plausible, the deserts of Kuwait and Saudi Arabia contain the petroleum that puts them among the wealthier nations of the world. However, even if one were to use arable land as the standard, that would change no fundamental conclusion. Japan, for example, compares even more unfavorably to India on the basis of arable land than of land in general, but it is India that has famines. Similarly, famine-stricken Ethiopia has many times more acres of arable land per capita than Singapore or Great Britain.

Nor has the growth rate of population had the dire economic consequences in history that it has in theory. For example, between the 1890s and the 1930s, Malaysia was transformed from a sparsely populated country of hamlets and fishing villages into a nation with cities and modern economic development. While its population rose from one and a half million to about six million people, this much larger population had both a higher standard of living and greater longevity. Hong Kong and Singapore have also had rapid population growth since 1950, along with increases in real income. As for the Western world, its population has quadrupled since the mid-eighteenth century, while real income per capita has risen fivefold. Much of this increase in Western living standards took place while its population was growing faster than in today's Third World.

NATURAL resources are another concept so familiar as to *seem* to require no definition. Yet this is a slippery and treacherous notion. For example, a large and alarming literature proclaims that we are running out of natural resources in general, or some specific resource (like petroleum) in particular. By simplistic extrapolation, that would seem to be inevitable, just as such extrapolations would also lead us to be alarmed about running out of space or being burned to death by rising temperatures.

A natural resource is something occurring in nature that *we know how to use* for our purposes. Our knowledge is as integral to the concept of a natural resource as the physical thing itself. An inventory of natural resources two centuries ago would not have included uranium or hydroelectric power, because no one knew how to use such things. Once natural resources are seen in this light, it no longer follows that there are fewer natural resources with the passing centuries.

In some ultimate sense, natural resources are finite, just as land is finite. John Stuart Mill, as a young man, once worried that, because of the finite number of musical notes, we were "running out" of music; at that point Brahms and Tchaikovsky had not yet been born, and jazz not yet conceived. But many natural resources may become obsolete—superseded by better alternatives—long before they are physically exhausted. In practical terms, we will never run out of them.

Differences in wealth among nations bear little relationship to differences in natural resources. Japan has no petroleum and imports most of the natural resources needed to produce its large industrial output. Yet it has a much higher per capita income than Mexico, which has abundant minerals, fertile soil, large petroleum deposits, and rivers capable of producing much hydroelectric power. The Japanese simply have high levels of skill, discipline, organizational capability, and other traits that enable them to outperform Mexicans economically, whether the two groups are in their respective homelands or both in California, where they have been for a similar period of time and where they began in very similar occupations.

The natural resources of a given nation are likewise utilized very differently by different groups of people. All the things that were natural resources to Europeans existed in the western hemisphere before Columbus, but the indigenous populations—misnamed "Indians"—had not used those resources to achieve the economic and technological level of the Europeans, as indicated by the fact that the latter succeeded in forcing them off their lands, often against a numerical superiority of brave and resourceful Indians. In Argentina, some of the finest wheat-growing land in the world did not prevent the Argentines from *importing* wheat for generations, until a new set of peoples from different cultures and with different values and skills turned it into one of the world's great exporters of wheat. In southeast Asia, the Malay peninsula contained rich tin deposits long before the Chinese arrived to develop them, but the native Malays did little with these deposits. The same story could be repeated, with local variations, for much of Africa and the Middle East.

A BEST-SELLING scare book, *The Population Bomb*, says on its cover: "While you are reading these words, three children are dying of starvation—and twenty-four more babies are being born."

As a propaganda device, juxtaposing two striking phenomena can successfully insinuate that there is some cause-and-effect relationship between them, however little logic or evidence there may be to support this conclusion. Famines have had no demonstrable relationship to the number of children in the world, or to the number being born. Because famines often involve a race between relief supplies being distributed through a primitive area and the ravages of hunger, people die of starvation and disease while there are food surpluses in the world, or even in their own country. But the idea that we are running out of food enjoys a certain plausibility that has kept it going for two centuries, despite overwhelming empirical evidence against it.

When Malthus first wrote on population at the end of the eighteenth century, there was extremely little hard evidence on the subject. As data became available in the nineteenth century, they showed that in fact the food supply was growing faster than the population. This has continued to be true in the twentieth century, even at the height of the "population explosion" hysteria. Like most data, these have fluctuations over time, so that those who have a vested interest in hysteria—which sells both books and political programs—can point to such things as a 2 percent decline in the world's food supply from 1965 to 1966. But, as against this one-year "trend," food per capita is generally higher today than a century ago, when there were far fewer people on Earth.

Overpopulation hysteria is both philosophically and politically congenial to the outlook of those who see the world's problems in general in terms of the foolish many needing to be directed by the wise few, like themselves. India, for example, instituted a massive compulsory sterilization program in 1975–1977 in which hundreds of thousands of people were "sterilized against their will, often brutally and in insanitary conditions." Many Western officials and intellectuals are likewise calling for "strong leadership" to control population growth in less developed countries. This leadership almost invariably means various degrees of authoritarianism wielded by the Westernized elite against the general populace.

Deficiencies of food, ranging from malnutrition to famine, are often more a result of political policies than of population size. Many third-world nations forbid the use of tractors, harvesters, and other agricultural machinery, on the dubious assumption that machinery reduces jobs. Famines have been produced (in sixteenth-century Belgium) and exacerbated (in eighteenth-century India) by price controls. Fortunately, the nineteenth-century authorities in India learned from the catastrophe of a century earlier, and met a new threat of famine in 1866 by following opposite policies:

> *Far from trying to check speculation, as in 1770, the Government did all in its power to stimulate it. . . . In the earlier famine one could hardly engage in the grain trade without becoming amenable to the law. In 1866 respectable men in vast numbers went into the trade; for the Government, by publishing weekly returns of the rates in every district, rendered the traffic both easy and safe. Everyone knew where to buy grain cheapest and where to sell it dearest and food was accordingly brought from the districts which could best spare it and carried to those which most urgently needed it.*

An economically effective policy like this could be followed, without fear of political repercussions, because India was ruled by British colonial officials. It was also the era when laissez-faire economics had its widest acceptance. Today, it is difficult to imagine an elected government letting a market operate freely during a famine—amidst inevitable charges by their political opponents that prices were "unconscionable"—even if they knew that that was in fact the fastest way to get the famine over with and save the most lives.

The role of imperialism

Decades after the decolonization that began with the end of World War II, the economic and political aftermath of imperialism remains an important factor in world history, and the causes and effects of imperialism remain matters of controversy.

Although imperialism is thousands of years old, there have been many attempts to create special theories for the imperialism of the capitalist era or of European nations. These theories require scrutiny, not only for the question of their validity, but also as clues to the kind of thinking that shapes policies and attitudes in the Third World and elsewhere. Finally, the actual effects of imperialism must be examined, as well as its enduring legacy—in the West as well as in the less developed world.

One of those whose name is often invoked in discussions of imperialism is Karl Marx. But the actual writings of Marx and Engels reveal a very different view of imperialism from that of latter-day Marxists. While Marx found much that the British did in India "brutal," "sickening," and "actuated only by the vilest interests," he nevertheless concluded that the net effect of introducing Western economic advancements would be to bring India out of a "stagnatory" and "vegetative" kind of life. Marx had no romantic view of less developed countries: "I share not the opinion of those who believe in a golden age of Hindustan." In a similar vein, Engels regarded the introduction of European civilization as a step forward for the colonial peoples:

> *All these nations of free barbarians look very proud, noble, and glorious at a distance, but only come near them and you will find that they, as well as the more civilized nations, are ruled by the lust of gain, and only employ ruder and more cruel means. And after all, the modern* bourgeois, *with civilization, industry, order, and at least relative enlightenment following him, is preferable to the feudal lord or to the marauding robber, with the barbarian state of society to which they belong.*

Although these Marxian writings have been a source of embarrassment to some latter-day Marxists, they are consistent with the general Marxist view that (1) what matters is not people's subjective motivations but their objective effects, and that (2) particular social systems—including slavery, capitalism, and imperialism—may be "historically justified" during particular eras, even though they may be superseded later by better systems.

As the passing decades failed to produce either the increasing misery of the proletariat or the decisive crisis of the capitalist system predicted by Marx, he and Engels used imperialism as an explanation of how these phenomena had been postponed. These passing remarks of Marx and Engels later became the cornerstone of V. I. Lenin's theory of imperialism. Lenin's message can be summed up in his own words. In the era of "the parasitism and decay of capitalism," a few powerful imperialist nations "plunder the whole world" and "out of such enormous *super-profits*" they bribe their own workers and labor leaders. While thus keeping the workers quiescent, imperialism also disposes of surplus capital—"the prodigious increase of capital, which overflows the brim," in Lenin's words, and which would otherwise lead to internal economic crises in capitalist nations, according to Marxist theory.

Like the brilliant propagandist that he was, Lenin inundated the reader with statistical data on *things that were not at issue*—that capitalist industry was growing, that banks had large and increasing deposits that they invested in many places—and then glided swiftly from these facts to conclusions that had neither empirical nor analytical support. However, if developed industrial nations were simply investing in other developed industrial nations—shuffling their capital around among themselves—then the whole scenario of net outflows of capital from capitalist nations to avert "crisis" would collapse like a house of cards. The United States, for example, invests more in Canada than in all of Asia and Africa put together—and it invests more in Europe than it does in Canada. Moreover, investors living in the Third World often prefer investing in the

United States or Europe to investing in their own countries. Western investments are often an overwhelming proportion of all investments in a poor country, but may nevertheless be a very small part of Western investments worldwide.

The end of the colonial era after World War II has led to, among other things, voluminous writings on *neo*colonialism. According to this literature, imperialism has merely changed its form, not its substance. Under neocolonialism, according to African leader Kwame Nkrumah, a newly independent state with "all the outward trappings of international sovereignty" continues to have "its economic system and thus its political policy . . . directed from outside." This means "control of nominally independent Third World countries by giant financial interests" in the West. Like its Leninist predecessor, this literature tends to document to the hilt things that are not the least bit at issue—that there are large exports and imports, or many overseas branches of American banks. Mundane economic facts—that most of the razor blades sold in France are American-made—are given sinister interpretations, when they are simply what would be expected on the basis of Adam Smith's 200-year-old writings about the international division of labor. A high proportion of cameras sold in the United States are made in Japan, but no one considers the United States a colony of Japan.

Running through most modern theories of imperialism and neocolonialism is the old notion of the mercantilists, that one country's enrichment is another country's impoverishment. According to neocolonialist theory, the "conflict between the rich and the poor has now been transferred on to the international scene." Thus the "fabulous profits" of Western capitalism show "the enrichment of one side of the world out of the exploitation of the other." As in most uses of the word "exploitation," the term is not defined concretely. Somehow the neocolonial theorist has determined a "fair price"—a feat that has eluded economists for centuries—and knows that third-world countries are paid less than that for their labor and raw materials.

Whatever the factual or intellectual inadequacies of neocolonialist theory, it serves some very important political and psychic functions. It explains—even if incorrectly—why the economic collapse of capitalism that Marx so confidently expected within his lifetime has still not occurred a hundred years later, without even raising the possibility that Marx might have been fundamentally wrong in his analysis of the situation. It explains why the capitalist employees who were supposed by Marxists to become progressively more miserable over time seem on the contrary to be progressing from generation to generation. Above all else, it explains for those in the Third World why their economic performance is so far below that of Western nations, for reasons that reflect no inadequacies on their part but only moral deficiencies on the part of others. In short, it is the perfect political explanation, however little economic sense it makes.

The legacy of empire

In one respect, Marx was quite correct: what matters in a cause-and-effect analysis of history is not people's subjective motivations but the actual results. In Engels's words, "what each individual wills is obstructed by everyone else, and what emerges is something that no one wills." What emerges from imperialism is thus not a question of the greed of some or the corruption of others but of concrete consequences of highly complex interactions.

It is necessary to begin with the conditions that existed in third-world countries before the imperialists came—conditions that made them vulnerable to conquest in the first place. To say that colonialism or neocolonialism is what *prevents* development in a third-world nation because of "external forces which have a vested interest in keeping it undeveloped" is to beg the question as to why it was undeveloped for centuries before the imperialists arrived.

Much of sub-Saharan Africa, North and South America, and southeast Asia consisted of small, tribal societies living at a relatively primitive level of organization and technology. For example, "almost no African community south of the Sahara managed to harness draft animals to pull plows and wagons until European newcomers introduced these new methods of traction in the nineteenth and twentieth centuries." The precolonial technology of the region was incapable of using wind or water power for milling grain. Tribal warfare, military raids, slavery, and serfdom were widespread throughout the area. Literacy was unknown outside of Ethiopia. Similar conditions existed in the western hemisphere in pre-Columbian times.

Not all parts of the colonized world were primitive, nor did the coming of Western civilization always represent progress in all aspects of life. But by and large European colonialism brought to the Third World what Roman imperialism had brought to Britain in the first century A.D.: (1) a reduction or cessation of internal fighting that had plagued these regions for centuries, holding back economic and social progress; (2) a unified system of law as a framework for stable expectations and the security and individual planning that law makes possible; (3) features of a more advanced system of technology and organization; and (4) contact with a wider world, enabling creative potential to emerge from the restrictions of insularity. Nowhere did these benefits exist unalloyed. Everywhere they were mixed with the arrogance, insensitivity, and often brutality that have marked conquerors of virtually every race and culture.

The net balance of European impact on the Third World may never be totaled in all its psychic, cultural, social, and political dimensions. The record of oppression is long and often ghastly—both before and after the imperialists came. European oppression was by no means unique in kind or degree, and the spread of this particular oppression cannot be assumed to be a net increase of oppression in the world. There was certainly no Eden before. On the central issue of economic exploitation, however, the empirical evidence is somewhat more clear. Those parts of the Third World that have had the most extensive, pervasive, and diversified contacts with the Western world have generally achieved much higher standards of living than those regions that have remained relatively untouched by Western civilization. Aborigines in the jungles and deserts of Africa, Asia, or South America have yet to approach the economic level of those native peoples who live in the ports, mining towns, or cash-crop areas that developed under Western auspices.

The enduring and fervent belief in imperialism as the cause of third-world poverty is difficult to understand in terms of empirical evidence. But this belief is much more readily understandable in terms of the high psychic and political costs of believing otherwise. Those costs are high not only to some people in the Third World, but also to those in the West whose whole vision of the world depends on seeing poverty as victimization and themselves as rescuers—both domestically and internationally. Many such people assume a stance of being partisans of the poor. But even to be an effective partisan of the poor, one must first be a partisan of the truth.

Escape from poverty

ECONOMIC development is difficult to define and measure, much less plan and execute. Statistical uncertainties, illusions, and deceptions are especially likely in measuring the economic progress of a third-world country that is in the process of shifting from agricultural to industrial output, paying market prices for services that were formerly provided outside the market (child care, for example), and channeling an increasing proportion of its resources through government monopolies of one sort or another. The fact that a rising share of the nation's goods and services now pass through statistical checkpoints does not mean that there is a correspondingly larger amount than before, when much of this same activity took place informally, without money changing hands or being recorded on the government's books. Conversely, much saving and investment by peasant farmers in third-world countries may go entirely unrecorded, either because of secretiveness on the part of peasants, or because of the practical difficulties of the government's keeping track of innumerable peasants and their many small repairs and improvements on their farms, or their larger or smaller amounts of fertilizer, seeds, seedlings, or other materials set aside for the coming year's crop. Investments in the form of planting materials or improved irrigation ditches may completely escape the attention of the government's statisticians in the capital city, and would be virtually impossible to quantify if they did know about them.

The bias toward preoccupation with individually large and striking investments, to the neglect of individually small and unimpressive investments—which may in the aggregate be of far greater economic consequence—is due not only to statistical difficulties but also to political bias. As Adam Smith noted two centuries ago:

> *The proud minister of an ostentatious court may frequently take pleasure in executing a work of splendour and magnificience, such as a great highway, which is frequently seen by the principal nobility, whose applauses not only flatter his vanity, but even contribute to support his interest at court. But to execute a great number of little works, in which nothing that can be done can make any great appearance, or excite the smallest degree of admiration in any traveller, and which, in short, have nothing to recommend them but their extreme utility, is a business which appears in every respect too mean and paultry to merit the attention of so great a magistrate.*

Uneconomic steel mills built in third-world nations have become a symbol of this attitude. So are national airlines that operate in the red when there are plenty of existing international airlines capable of handling the same volume of traffic at lower cost. This approach, aptly termed an "investment fetish," has been seconded by international organizations that have been impressed by grandiose plans, strikingly visible demonstration projects, and rhetoric—that is, by things that impress the eye and ear, rather than things that actually produce economic results. The extent to which plausibility has replaced performance in discussions of economic development in the Third World may be illustrated by an example of successful development that should have been very unsuccessful, according to prevailing theories:

> *How would you rate the economic prospects of an Asian country which has very little land (and only eroded hillsides at that), and which is indeed the most densely populated country in the world; whose population has grown rapidly, both through natural increase and large-scale immigration; which imports all its oil and raw materials, and even most of its water; whose government is not engaged in development planning and operates no exchange controls or restrictions on capital exports and imports; and which is the only remaining Western colony of any significance? You would think that this country must be doomed, unless it received large external donations.*

This country is, however, the British colony of Hong Kong, which has a per capita income more than five times that of Malaysia, the Philippines, Indonesia, Burma, or Thailand—just to compare countries in the area. In the postwar world, Hong Kong's population increased more than sevenfold, nearly half being refugees. Despite low tax rates—a 15 percent maximum on personal income—the Hong

Kong government has had budget surpluses in thirty-one of the thirty-four years from 1945 to 1980. Hong Kong's population is 98 percent Chinese. This is not only another example of the productiveness of the overseas Chinese; it also fatally undermines the "exploitation" explanation of the prosperity of the overseas Chinese, because there are only 2 percent of non-Chinese who might conceivably be exploited, and many of these are the British who control the colony. More broadly, Hong Kong underscores the point that the "human capital" in the general populace is crucial to economic development.

The actual material wealth brought to a region has in many cases played a relatively small role in economic development, compared with the human capital that was brought. Poverty-stricken Italians immigrated to poverty-stricken Argentina in the nineteenth century and made both the country and themselves more prosperous. Chinese immigrants with little more than the clothes on their backs have entered southeast Asia—often on foot—and proceeded to create economic advancement for both the native populations and themselves. Germans too poor to pay their passage to eighteenth-century America nevertheless, after years of unpaid work as indentured servants, went out to the undeveloped frontier and built prosperous farming communities up and down the great valleys of the eastern United States.

Much of the poverty, stagnation, and even retrogression found in third-world countries is not the result of an inevitable "vicious circle of poverty," for which dramatic aid programs or draconian domestic policies are the only cures. Indeed, a substantial part of the current efforts of the rulers and governments of such countries often consists of repressing, impeding, or even driving out of the country those who possess the human capital to develop it. The massive deaths on the high seas of southeast Asia of the "boat people" were not only a moral horror and a human catastrophe but also an economic insanity, destroying vast amounts of human capital desperately needed in that region of the world. It made sense only politically.

Less dramatic examples and policies also indicate massive destruction of, or impeding of the operation of, human capital. South Africa has, at various times in its history, forcibly forbidden the use by black Africans of various skills they have acquired, and has put positive barriers in the way of their further acquisition of such skills. Jews have been hounded from one country to another in Europe and the Middle East, often to the economic detriment of the country they left and the economic benefit of the country to which they went. Idi Amin's brutal expulsions of the East Indians from Uganda and the Nigerians' slaughter of the Ibos were part of a similar pattern.

2. Second Thoughts About the Third World

ONE FORM of human capital emphasized by many third-world countries and the international agencies advising them is formal education. While this can be beneficial, it by no means follows that every increment of schooling is more beneficial than alternative uses of the same resources, whether viewed economically or socially. Desperately needed technological, organizational, and entrepreneurial skills tend to be neglected in favor of literary education.

Agricultural science, for example, tends to be neglected even in predominantly agricultural nations of the Third World. In Nigeria, more than 40 percent of the jobs for senior agricultural researchers have been vacant at one time. In Senegal, it was 1979—a generation after independence—before agriculture was taught at the university level, although the University of Dakar had thousands of liberal-arts students. In Malaysia, where the Malay college students are concentrated in the liberal arts—mostly Malay studies and Islamic studies—many end up working for the government after graduation, for they lack skills that would have a value in the economy. Nor is Malaysia unique. In India three quarters of college graduates work for the government, and a leading authority on Africa describes African education as "a machine for producing graduate bureaucrats." Indonesian youth likewise turn after graduation toward bureaucratic careers, despite the warning of Indonesian novelist Ananta Toer that "we must get rid of the silly idea of wanting to be government clerks."

Burgeoning bureaucracies are more likely to be impediments than contributors to economic development. They are, for example, a major factor in many African nations' declining ability to feed themselves. Yet in many third-world countries the alternative to enlarging bureaucracies in order to absorb college graduates without economically meaningful skills is to let them become unemployed, discontented, and politically dangerous.

The very phrase "foreign aid," which has become so familiar through repetition, is one which—in the words of a distinguished development economist—"disarms criticism, prejudges the effects of the policy and also obscures its realities and results." In short, whether the political process of transferring wealth from Western taxpayers to third-world government officials aids or hinders economic development in the Third World is an empirical question rather than a foregone conclusion. Using the phrase "foreign aid" is no more justified a priori than calling it "foreign hindrance." Whether it is an aid or a hindrance is a question of fact in each specific case. Calling the transferring organizations "development agencies" is likewise begging the central question. They are in fact transfer or donor organizations, and the actual effect of their donations is precisely what is at issue. For example, Africa has lost its historic ability to feed itself precisely during the era when the phasing out of donations to Latin America has caused donor agencies to "smother Africa with project aid."

"Foreign aid" is in fact often used by third-world governments to (1) acquire arms to be used principally in suppressing political critics and movements within their own country; (2) persecute racial and ethnic minorities, especially those who are more economically productive or entrepreneurial, such as the overseas Chinese; (3) cover deficits caused by the inefficiency or irresponsibility of the recipient government, thereby enabling it to remain in power longer by insulating it from the consequences of its own actions. Moreover, international transferring organizations tend to want recipient governments to be more activist or *dirigiste* in planning and controlling the economy—a process that may or may not prove beneficial, in the Third World or elsewhere—and their control of vast funds enables them to impose experiments and preconceived schemes from which the aid-organization officials suffer no damage, even if these schemes should prove catastrophic to third-world peoples. Moreover, the failure of these schemes or the waste of funds in general will not embarrass any given donor nation, since multilateral transfers are administered from a fund to which many nations contribute and for which none is responsible. The chief benefits of multilateral grants, from the standpoint of the recipient governments, is that they are less likely to carry restrictions or preconditions designed to ensure economic efficiency or responsible financial policies.

Tanzania is a striking example of the effects of international wealth transfers through multilateral agencies. It has received more "foreign aid" per capita than any other nation. Its output per worker has *declined* 50 percent over a period of a decade; it has turned from an exporter to an importer of maize; nearly half the more than 300 companies expropriated by the government ("nationalized") were bankrupt by 1975, with many of the remainder operating at a loss. As the economy has declined, government bureaucracy has grown by 14 percent per annum, doubling in less than a decade. Tanzania's ruler, Julius Nyerere, has repeatedly been unopposed in "elections," and his political prisoners run into the thousands—many tortured, according to Amnesty International. International wealth transfers to the Nyerere regime have not proved to be "foreign aid" to Tanzania.

The Tanzanian example illustrates another important point—the political importance of professed *intentions*, as contrasted with demonstrable economic or other *results*. Despite a despotic rule and economic declines, Nyerere remains one of the most revered African leaders, especially among Western intellectuals. Nyerere has expressed many noble intentions and humanitarian goals, even as he has jailed or executed his critics, uprooted vast portions of the Tanzanian population at gunpoint, and mismanaged nationalized industries into bankruptcy, while producing widespread hunger in a country that was once an exporter of food. Conversely, the very phrase "multinational corporation" immediately evokes negative feelings, because their *intentions*—to make a profit for themselves—are not nearly as noble as those expressed by Nyerere, and it is often the intentions rather than the results that count politically.

Multinational corporations may themselves engage in expressions of altruistic intentions toward third-world countries for public relations purposes, but no one is deceived, and such statements may in fact increase cynicism toward the multinationals. If they were in fact engaged in altruistic behavior, they would be violating the confidence of the stockholders who entrusted their savings to the corporations for the purpose of gain rather than philanthropic donation.

The real basis for judging the impact of multinational corporations on third-world countries is in terms of results. When the multinational corporations pay higher wages than those prevailing in a third-world country, this is criticized as promoting "the interests of the small number of modern-sector workers against the interests of the rest by widening wage differentials." When multinational corporations fill some local consumer need, this is criticized because it means "inhibiting the expansion of indigenous firms" who might have served the same market, even if they had never done so before. In short, multinational corporations are blamed for a pervasive reality of the human condition—that benefits have costs. Such economic *results* as higher wages for third-world workers, or new or cheaper products for third-world consumers, are politically unacceptable, because the *intentions* that produced these results are morally suspect. But when looked at systemically, instead of by intentions, it is hardly surprising that an economic organization like a multinational corporation is more effective in economic decisions, while political leaders who make disastrous economic decisions are more effective in gaining political acceptance and even admiration. Conversely, the political failure of multinational corporations is evident from the fact that their very name is anathema to many.

"We are told...we must have more of the disease."

Michael Manley responds to Thomas Sowell

Thomas Sowell's wide-ranging account of the Third World, of poverty, and of the problem of development ["Second Thoughts About the Third World," previous article] provides much useful analysis that, unfortunately, leads to a surprisingly simplistic conclusion. Mr. Sowell writes with a disarming lucidity and is clearly blessed with one of those facile minds that can put eggs beside oranges with such skill that the unwary reader may find himself concluding that they are both the issue of the hen, or perhaps both a species of citrus.

The article does make two contributions to our understanding that are of real value. First, Mr. Sowell's demolition of the ancient Malthusian bogey about overpopulation is as timely as it is devastating. Other readers were probably as startled as I to learn that all the 4.4 billion people in the world could be fitted into the state of Texas in families of four with 6,800 square feet per family. The reminder that this is the space claimed by the average U.S. middle-class family for its bungalow and yard was a delightful touch.

Second, the description of the countries of the Third World, emphasizing their extraordinary racial, cultural, economic, political, and historical complexity and diversity, is a useful reminder to those third-world advocates who underestimate their task by retreating into a romantic oversimplification of reality. It is equally a reminder to those third-world critics who dismiss the Third World as a kind of garbage dump of lazy louts tyrannized by fast-talking despots.

I take issue on two levels, however, both with Mr. Sowell's analysis and his implied conclusion.

"Second Thoughts" "smudges" history by ignoring historical process, preferring to look at existing situations as a basis for the making of comparisons and the drawing of conclusions. The underlying historical forces that may explain the difference between the per capita incomes of Hong Kong and Tanzania in 1983 are conveniently ignored. And the conclusions toward which Mr. Sowell directs us are unforgivably superficial. He would have us believe that successful capital accumulation, low income taxes, and a budget surplus in Hong Kong are enough to determine the answer to the huge and complex challenges of genuine nation-building for the majority of mankind.

Mr. Sowell contends that imperialism is both inevitable and beneficial. It is inevitable because the groups with more advanced cultures are stronger than those at a more primitive stage of development. And it is beneficial for precisely the same reason. Accordingly, imperialism was a civilizing influence, bringing in its wake superior technological and social skills.

The multinational corporation, as the most advanced form of overseas investment capital, is thus represented as a good thing because the corporations themselves tend to pay higher wages than most local industries and expose native populations to the most advanced methods of production.

Finally, Mr. Sowell relies heavily on a "human capital" theme. The Asiatic work ethic comes in for honorable mention. A comparison between the performance of Japanese and Mexican migrants to California entirely favorable to the Japanese is alleged. The author is too sophisticated to make a blatantly racist point. However, a racist conclusion is conjured out of a carefully selected set of comparative examples and left dangling. There it tantalizes the reader with the thought that where the right racial stock is present and properly exposed to the civilizing benefits of imperialism and multinational corporations, all will be well. Left unanswered, of course, is the rather sad question: what is going to happen to the rest of us who, not being Asiatic (or was it WASP? or Aryan?) are unable to take full advantage of all these skills?

At the risk of being accused either of being rhetorical or of making

Michael Manley is the former prime minister of Jamaica.

"We Are Told . . . We Must Have More of the Disease," by Michael Manley, *Harper's*, December 1983. Reprinted by permission.

excuses, I would like to suggest that an understanding of the Third World does not best arise from a superficial apology for modern imperialism but rather from a somewhat closer study of its history and nature.

Modern imperialism undoubtedly owes its origins to impulses similar to those that led to earlier examples of conquest and domination of one people by another. As it evolved, however, it was to be distinguished by a number of unique features. Never before was so vast an area of the earth's surface to be conquered by such a comparatively small group, the people clustered along the Atlantic coast of Europe and in the British Isles. Of even greater importance was the fact that the imperialist process increasingly became the creature of the burgeoning capitalist system at the centers of imperialist power.

The normal social evolution of any group of people involves the production of their basic needs in the first instance. In due course, surpluses in the production of one group provide the basis for exchange with some other group. This in turn lays the basis for trade and makes possible the later development of specialized production, international finance, the international division of labor, and so on. All of this takes place, however, within the context of a society that produces first for itself and later for exchange.

Modern imperialism reversed all of this. For the first time, vast areas of the globe were exploited to produce not for their own population but for the needs of their conquerors. The new factories of Britain and Europe needed raw materials. A taste for sugar was acquired at the tables of the families that owned the factories. Meanwhile, colonies had economies dominated by huge plantations with a single purpose: production of cotton, sugar, perhaps rubber.

Mr. Sowell will doubtless tell us that the Africans, Indians, Jamaicans, and Latin Americans were lucky to have the chance to grow those commodities and certainly lacked the capacity to produce all that cloth so efficiently before the imperial masters passed their way. What he has not confessed is the ruthless distortion of the normal economic process that was involved in the transaction.

For the first time in the history of mankind, we witnessed the phenomenon of a society forced, literally at gunpoint, to export everything that it produced and to import everything that it consumed. Furthermore, the economic process ensured that every single wealth-creating, technology-requiring economic activity, after the moment of reaping the commodities, was controlled by the colonizing power. Imperialism evolved into a vast "factory" of wealth, of training, of know-how, of confidence, of the capacity to control the environment for the people who made up the imperial powers.

Mr. Sowell will undoubtedly argue: "To the victors go the spoils." He might assert, further, that it was the inventiveness of the European that created the technology in the first place. That is true. But it ignores the fact that the apparatus of exploitation was kept in place by three supporting pillars. There was, first, the military power, which made possible the conquest at the outset. Second, there was the political system, varying with the imperial power, but always designed to ensure the controlled administration of the conquered territory and its absolute subservience to the interests of the imperial authority. Finally, there was the increasing cultural penetration that follows closely on the heels of conquest and that spreads through the control of the political process and the institutions that result.

The imperial process had a common, central objective. But it was not applied in a common situation, nor did it always employ identical methods. Latin America involved the uneasy coexistence of growing numbers of people of Spanish or Portuguese origin with a large and surviving indigenous Indian population. In North America the European conquered the local population, eventually reducing it to a state of herded impotence. On the other hand, in the Caribbean islands, the indigenous population was wiped out, to be replaced by the African slave. I was relieved to observe that Mr. Sowell did not include this last in the category of those who benefited from imperialism.

Inevitably, the interaction between the imperial forces and the indigenous population reflected the variety of the elements in the mixture. Although the process had a common purpose, it could not have a uniform outcome. However, there were certain common results. I will list these as follows:

1. Imperialism produced and continues to produce a substantial net source of wealth for the imperial powers. This provided an important source of investment capital for the industrial revolution and later for a significant margin in the standard of living of European, and eventually of North American, people.

2. It led to the comparative distortion of the economies of the colonial countries, with a heavy emphasis on the export-import content of their economies and the artificial restriction of economic activity to the simplest level.

3. Taking up Mr. Sowell's point that poverty is comparative, we must note that the imperial process is associated with, if not the cause of, vast disparities in wealth between the conqueror and the conquered.

4. By the middle of the twentieth century there was a common determination to shake off the yoke of external domination and to struggle for national independence. In due course, more than one hundred new nations have been born as a result of the drive for decolonization and the determination to end the political domination of one people by another.

Now, man is currently perplexed by the question of how to create social viability in the countries that shared the common experience of imperial domination and now occupy their corner of the earth as independent nations.

Mr. Sowell does more than hint that the answer to the question is to be found in the experience of those countries that have, like Hong Kong, opted for a particular path of development. This is the path of industrialization by invitation and is characterized by a vigorous policy of attracting private foreign capital in the greatest possible quantity in the fastest possible time. Small countries with rapidly growing GNPs are compared with large countries with declining GNPs. Resource-rich countries are compared with resource-poor countries. Hong Kong is the winner of the resulting sweepstakes because it is small, resource-poor but rich. Ergo, Hong Kong is the model for all seasons.

No regard is paid to the fact that Hong Kong is a unique corner of the world existing in very special and highly artificial circumstances. The fact that it has put those circumstances to effective use in the context of goals that we must assume the Hong Kong people accept for themselves tells us nothing more than the fact that the particular goals are attainable in those highly particular circumstances. To compare Hong Kong with Tanzania, even by implication, is an insult to the intelligence as gross as Mr. Sowell's despicably dishonest references to Tanzania's president.

It is common to view development solely in terms of structures and productive capacity. Certainly, productive capacity is an indispensable element in and objective of the development process. However, the concept in which development and material things are absolutely equated is dangerously misleading. High levels of productivity are indispensable to the creation of wealth, but they do not of themselves guarantee that wealth is equitably shared even by those whose labor is directly involved.

I would suggest that a society is developed to the extent that it can define widely shared objectives for itself and demonstrate the means to realize those objectives. It is safe to assume that most people would prefer to have larger rather than smaller real incomes; that they would prefer to live in comfortable rather than uncomfortable homes; that they would aspire to high- rather than low-quality education for their children; that they would prefer to have a job rather than not have a job. But it may be that they would also prefer to feel they are a part of a system that gives them a sense of belonging, of significance in their own land; that they would prefer to feel that they have power over rather than feel powerless in their own environment; that they belong to a society that cares for its sick and its old and its very young; that they are a part of a community that uses the political process to engineer social equity.

When one examines a little more closely the experience of those countries that have experimented with the model of development adopted by Hong Kong, Singapore, Taiwan, South Korea, Puerto Rico, Chile, Brazil, and so on, one is struck by a number of things. In the first place, not one of these countries has been able to carry out the development process in the context of free institutions. The only exception is Puerto Rico, and that experiment is stalled in disaster, with an unemployment rate of 24 percent and rising in spite of exporting millions of people to the U.S.

The other countries involved have either controlled political systems, emasculated trade unions, or both. Mr. Sowell's bias shows like a petticoat beneath the hemline of his argument when he assaults Nyerere's Tanzanian experiment with inaccurate statistics, without so much as a glance in the direction of Pinochet's Chile or the military rulers of Taiwan, Lee Kuan Yew's highly controlled democracy in Singapore or South Korea's farcical excuse for one. As for the implied racial argument, "Poor Man's Burden" does not explain what conclusion we should draw from the legendary efficiency of the German people by comparison with the rather different accomplishments of "lesser" creatures such as Italians and Irishmen.

Surely the truth is that different societies at different stages demonstrate particular characteristics. It is a fatal fallacy, and typical of Mr. Sowell's static mode of analysis, to look at these characteristics at a point in time and universalize them as if they were part of some collective advantage or disadvantage in the genes of the group. For example, employers in the Caribbean are notorious for complaining about the comparative inefficiencies of local labor. That same labor, transplanted as migrants to North America, commonly outproduces the natives in the U.S. Their genes have not been altered by the short flight from Kingston to Miami. What has altered is their motivation. The results, in terms of productivity, provide a dramatic contrast. But they are the same human beings.

The problem with Mr. Sowell's model is that heavy dependence on foreign capital as the sole engine of development tends to reinforce all of the deficiencies with which the average third-world country begins. Dependence, more than any other word, defines the typical third-world condition—the structural dependence of economies designed to serve the interests of another center of economic power.

Now we are told that to solve a problem that is delineated by dependence itself, we must have more of the disease. What is more, we are told that the amount of private investment capital available in the world at any given moment (which has by itself proved unable to provide equitable and widely shared development in the countries where it is invested) can suddenly, as if by magic, encompass the whole Third World and sweep it along in a universal embrace of prosperity.

The truth is that no one can prescribe the solution to another man's crisis. Mr. Sowell has written an interesting commentary, even an entertaining one from a particular point of view. On the other hand, if we understand the real nature of imperialism and the true challenges of development in the Third World, we need to consider three things. What set of world arrangements would best facilitate third-world development? And the corollary question: would such a set of arrangements be inimical to the interest of developed nations? And what internal arrangements should third-world countries make for themselves the better to promote their development possibilities?

This article cannot examine the arguments in favor of that set of arrangements for the world economy that are proposed by the Third World and described as the New International Economic Order (NIEO). Suffice it to say that in our experience the terms of trade, the operations of the multinational-corporation system, and the present organization of the international financial institutions create a distinctive bias in favor of the more developed nations.

Let us create an equitable economic environment, including financial institutions that are sensitive to the particular needs of developing economies. Let us also give to those institutions the means to supply working capital for those who are willing to plan intelligently and implement honestly. Natural selection will provide its own answer for those who do not try. At present, there are countless millions of people in scores of young nations who are making valiant efforts to develop themselves. All too often, however, they are like people trying to get from the first to the second floor of a building where there is only a down escalator. If those people try very hard, they find that they do well to remain in the same place.

Each nation must find the path to development for itself by the same process of trial and error adopted by the developed countries throughout their own histories. The United States has built a remarkable civilization from its great fertile plains, its superb range of natural resources, from the energy of waves of highly motivated migrant people, and from a free-enterprise model well tailored to the mood of people escaping from the suffocating tyrannies of Europe. That represents a set of factors as extraordinary and as peculiar to a moment of history as those applying in the Hong Kong of today. The Scandinavian countries, it is arguable, have produced equally viable economies with a qualitatively superior social order. Both are success stories judged by ordinary criteria today. Which should be the model for the Third World?

The answer to that question can only be found in the dynamics of each society, which reflect its history and what its people have made of it. The challenge to third-world leadership is not to imitate models but rather to evolve political processes that can first define widely shared objectives and then mobilize people to attain them. In this, local savings, individual productivity, the work ethic, entrepreneurial initiative, sound administration, just laws, and humane social arrangements all have their place. All will need to be supplemented with external capital both public and private.

The Third World identifies itself as those countries that were at one time or another marked by modern imperialism. Their search must be for the internal political process that is uniquely a product of their own experience, which can best guarantee everything from the work ethic to humane social arrangements. To the extent that the developed countries can understand this and help to provide an equitable opportunity for those with the will to try, they will help guarantee a world in which all will prosper because its benefits will be more widely shared and its economic growth more securely underwritten.

Ethnocentrism and Third World Development

Howard J. Wiarda

Howard J. Wiarda is professor of political science at the University of Massachusetts at Amherst; a research scholar at the American Enterprise Institute for Public Policy Research in Washington, D.C.; and a fellow of the Foreign Policy Research Institute. Among many books, he has written Ethnocentrism in American Foreign Policy: Can We Understand the Third World?

That body of literature focusing on political development has come under severe attack. Once the dominant paradigm within the discipline, the political development approach has been strongly criticized in various ways. Among these is the charge that political development heretofore has been conceived in almost exclusively Western (Northwest European and North American) terms. That is, that the categories and understandings of extant political development are derived ethnocentrically from the EuroAmerican experience and have little or no relevance to the non-Western world.

This charge is serious from several vantage points. First, it has major implications for the Third World: whether the development process is universal, whether Third World nations are but pale and retarded versions of the Western model, whether they will repeat the experience of the early developers, or whether they will fashion an indigenous model of development—or some blend of the Western and the indigenous. Second, it has important ramifications for the social sciences, with most of their concepts based on the Western developmental experience which may or may not be relevant to the Third World. Third, it has important implications for the foreign assistance donor nations—chiefly the United States but increasingly those of Western Europe—concerning the relevance of the developmental models and programs they seek to export to the Third World.

This article explores the problem of ethnocentrism in the study of political development. It is part of a larger project examining both Western and non-Western theories of development. This work suggests that the models of development most familiar in the literature are all derived from the Western experience, of a particular time and place, and therefore have but limited relevance to today's Third World nations. The study emphasizes the efforts of various Third World areas to devise indigenous models of development or to blend these with the Western and presumably more universal models. It suggests that Western foreign assistance programs, largely based on the older ethnocentric understandings, have seldom been successful; yet it concludes pessimistically that because Western policymakers, regardless of party, generally lack the comprehension and knowledge base to understand the Third World on its own terms, in its own language, and in its own cultural and institutional terms, the mistakes of the past are likely to be repeated.

In other papers and publications I have dealt with the ethnocentric assumptions of the social sciences, as well as the effort by Third World leaders to articulate and fashion an indigenous developmental model. In one paper I considered this issue as it affects human rights and United States human rights policy; in another, the revived effort to export democracy abroad; in still another, the ethnocentrism of United States economic assistance programs, expectations regarding the political role of the middle class, the armed forces and "professionalization," and the model of trade unionism the United States has tried to implant abroad.

I concentrate here on a series of other, but closely related, development assistance efforts: agrarian reform, community development, the United States-sponsored law and development program, and family planning. All of these programs derive from the same ethnocentric assumptions; together they form a social and political history (a pathology?) of developmentalism. I touch briefly on the common intellectual and programmatic assumptions of all these efforts, as well as Third World attempts to devise their own developmental paradigms. The theme

Published by permission of Transaction Publishers, from *Society,* Vol. 24, No. 6, September/October 1987, pp. 55-64.

and cry of "let us do it our way" is now becoming a global chorus. I also deal with the politics of the developmentalist approach and why it will be such a difficult paradigm to change or supersede.

I conclude that the often misguided and misdirected developmentalist programs analyzed here grow chiefly out of naiveté and wrong assumptions, not from venality, malevolence, or even "imperialism." American development assistance programs are generally based not on evil scheming but on good intentions gone awry for various reasons. I question as to where, other than their own experiences, Americans could conceivably have derived their developmentalist models. I fault them here for their biases and ethnocentrism, but realistically it seems unlikely that any model other than their own could have been used. Additionally, the Third World lack of understanding of the United States is often at least as great as our malcomprehension of them. Here I concentrate on the latter theme, but the former also requires attention.

Misguided development programs grow chiefly out of naiveté and wrong assumptions.

Development and Developmentalism

The literature of development and the practice of developmentalism, as an approach to alleviate underdevelopment, were uniquely American phenomena—although scholars and political leaders from other areas also accepted and participated in the formulation of this paradigm. It was uniquely American in that it was extremely, perhaps excessively, optimistic; it derived from the American experience of development (including Lockean liberalism and pluralism); it was largely written by Americans; it reflected a long American "missionary" tradition to bring the benefits of our civilization to other lands; and it became an integral part of American foreign policy toward the Third World, particularly Latin America.

The development literature and developmentalism were not just some abstract intellectual formulations confined to the academy. Rather these ideas had both direct and indirect impacts on policy. Through the incorporation into the Kennedy administration of intellectuals associated with developmentalist themes—such as Walt W. Rostow, McGeorge Bundy, John Kenneth Galbraith, Adolph Berle, Arthur Schlesinger, Jr., and Lincoln Gordon—the ideas of developmentalism were often translated directly into policy. Indirectly this body of literature also had a major impact: as developmentalism became something of the leitmotiv of the 1960s, the thing to do, and the basis for United States policy toward the Third World, the ideas of the leading theorists of development were gradually infused into the bureaucracy. This came about by the developmentalist intellectuals attending the almost endless conferences that agencies such as the U.S. Agency for International Development (AID) and the Department of State organize, and by the widespread dissemination of the intellectuals' ideas through the universities and among university-trained technocrats of development. Just because a government bureaucrat did not know specifically that it was Walt Rostow's or Seymour Martin Lipset's ideas that he was implementing is hardly sufficient reason to deny the immense impact on United States foreign assistance programs that these ideas had for a long time, and that they continue to have in many government circles today.

Two themes particularly command our attention here. The first is the need for a social and political history of the idea of development itself, tracing its rise in the 1950s and 1960s, its gradual decline in the 1970s and 1980s, and the reasons for this decline. The second involves a history of the rise and fall of various developmental panaceas—agrarian reform, community development, infrastructure development, family planning, basic human needs, the democracy agenda, and private sector initiatives—that have been proffered by the developmentalist school over the years. Such a history would examine the often fickle elevation and then abandonment of these ideas, their intellectual and political origins, and their fate when tested against the hard realities of Third World and non-Western areas.

Agrarian reform in the Third World is part of a larger scheme to promote economic development, build a stronger middle class, and, from the point of view of its United States sponsors, reduce or eliminate the appeal of radical groups. Agrarian reform must thus be looked at in the broader context of the United States effort to fashion a Marshall Plan-like assistance program for the Third World, one component of which was designed for the rural sector. Walt W. Rostow's significantly titled *The Stages of Economic Growth: A Non-Communist Manifesto* served as a key volume in providing the intellectual rationalizations for such an effort. Rostow argued that the stages of economic growth (such as "preconditions for take-off" and "take off") outlined in his book were universal, that all societies (including those of the Third World) went through the same processes, that the United States was the most advanced nation and therefore provided the model for others, that the United States should assist the Third World in its growth, that the funds thus generated would trickle down, that by our assistance a middle-class society would be created that looked just like our own—stable, moderate politically, socially just, and so on. I have dealt critically with the Rostow arguments in other writings. Here, I hope to show that agrarian reform was simply one aspect of a much larger assistance program which had at its base a definite political agenda.

I favor agrarian reform under the proper circumstances and am supportive of the other social assistance programs discussed here: community development, law and development, and family planning. My purpose is not to attack these programs as such but only to discuss the context out of which they emerged and the particular biases of United States official efforts in these areas. I seek not to tear these programs down but to provide a basis to refashion and foment them in ways that make them culturally and socially relevant to the societies in which they are applied and that enable them to take hold and have more lasting effects than they have in the past.

Agrarian reform, as part of a broader United States assistance program, was viewed as an extension of the Rostow analysis to the Third World countryside. It was aimed, especially in Latin America, at creating a rural middle class where none had existed before. According to much lore and popular literature, the Latin American countryside was characterized by immensely large landholdings, latifundia, and dominated by a rapacious oligarchy more interested in exploiting the peasants and using land as a symbol of social status than for greater production. By dividing up this land, the argument maintained, the back of this quasifeudal system could be broken, the oligarchy destroyed, and a new class of medium-sized rural landholders created. Because they would own their land and thus have a stronger stake in their own futures, these new middle-class family farmers would be loyal to the system and would no longer be prey to the appeal of either fascism or communism. Agrarian reform was seen as the rural counterpart to what overall United States economic assistance a la Rostow was designed to create in urban areas: a prosperous middle class that could serve as a bastion of democracy, stability, and anticommunism.

Agrarian Reform

As a form of social engineering, agrarian reform originated in the postwar United States occupation of Japan and in the nationalist occupation of Taiwan. Initially, virtually everyone involved in the agrarian reform programs promoted by the United States in Latin America had first learned their lessons through experience in Japan and Taiwan. Indeed, Japan and Taiwan served as the models for the programs in Latin America. Scholars are still discussing whether and to what degree the programs in Japan or Taiwan may be termed "successes." I concede that the successes in these two countries outweigh the failures, but, aside from that, we must have doubts about the applicability of the Japanese or Taiwanese "models" to Latin America, where conditions are entirely different. Far more open space exists which gives agrarian reform less immediacy; there is no occupation army to enforce the program as there had been in Japan and Taiwan, and (although I hesitate to use the term) the Latin American ethos, behavior patterns, social structure, and attitudes toward land are different than those of the two Asian nations. The contrast is so great that we can doubt the feasibility and appropriateness of transferring a Japanese or Taiwanese model to a set of societies in Latin America.

While the "model" and experience of those active in the agrarian reform movement came from Japan and Taiwan, the real example, as might be expected from Rostow's analysis, was the United States. Agrarian reform in Latin America and other Third World areas derived from an idealized version of the American family farm. That farm was medium-sized—neither too big (latifundia) nor too small (minifundia); it was managed by self-sufficient yeoman farmers who were educated and used the most modern techniques. These farmers were civically conscious, active participants in local government and town meetings; they were politically moderate, not subject to the appeal of radical ideologies of Left or Right. Although the foreign experience of the early agrarian reform practitioners was in Asia, the real model was in the United States: the American midwest or the New England family farm.

Whether or not the American farm and farmer was portrayed accurately, whether the family farm was really the rock of stability it was imagined to be, or even whether the family farm has any future in America—all serious concerns—we must question the applicability of this model to Latin America and other Third World areas. Upon close examination, the differences between the United States and these other areas are more significant than the similarities. The social structure is entirely different (there is no rural middle class in most of Latin America), class and ethnic differences are large, economies are different (capitalist versus neomercantilist), and political structures are different. These differences are so pronounced that it is far-fetched and beyond the realm of possibility to expect a North American rural structure to ever be transplanted into Latin America.

The United States' effort to bring agrarian reform to Latin America and the rest of the Third World was born of the cold war and launched in the wake of the great fear following the Cuban Revolution that all of Latin America was about "to go communist." Agrarian reform was in part a cold war strategy initiated in some desperation and without its prospects and possibilities having been thoroughly thought through. The arguments seemed so plausible: American technology and funds would help the Latin American nations to achieve democracy, development, and stability through the reform of the rural sector. At the time, no one paid much attention to the impossibility of the United States transferring its institutions to societies where they did not fit, or could fit only imperfectly. John F. Kennedy was in office, the United States was at the height of its power and influence, optimism and hope ran high, Vietnam and Watergate had not yet occurred, and the United States still seemed to be both policeman and inspiration to the world. Only later would we come to see why the program not only did not work but could not work.

Agrarian reform was not just a program the Latin Americans could take or leave; rather, the adoption of an agrarian reform law was the condition by which a country qualified for Alliance for Progress assistance. Hence most of the Latin American countries dutifully enacted an agrarian reform law. Since their hearts were not really in it, or not fully committed, or because they soon developed other priorities, relatively little agrarian reform was ever implemented. Some peasants received titles to land under the program; this was usually accompanied by presidential helicopters, expansive media coverage, and great celebratory outpourings. But in no country was the structure of rural life fundamentally affected by the United States-inspired agrarian reform efforts.

There are various forms of agrarian reform. The one at which the United States is most successful involves technical assistance, farm credits, agricultural extension, and the like. None of these involve changing the pattern of ownership; instead they provide aid to those who already own land. We must also distinguish between an agrarian reform carried out for economic purposes versus one carried out with social or political goals in mind. The conclusion of the experts is that in general agrarian reform does not make sense economically because production falls, at least initially, as a result; whether agrarian reform makes much sense sociologically or politically is more difficult to decide. It could be argued that agrarian reform has helped buy the United States some time and perhaps some limited stability in Latin America, but the revolutions in Nicaragua and El Salvador as well as ferment in a number of other countries seem to indicate that it may not have been enough.

Eventually the United States itself lost interest in agrarian reform—except in emergency cases such as El Salvador. The results were generally disappointing; the Latin American governments were not cooperative; and other agendas came to the fore. Agrarian reform was the great developmentalist panacea of the 1960s; by the 1970s there were other concerns.

Overall, pervasive ethnocentrism characterized many aspects of the United States' efforts to export agrarian reform. This is evident by: (1) the political agenda and cold war considerations that undergirded the United States agrarian reform efforts; (2) the strong influence on these programs of the Japanese and Taiwanese experiences which had little relevance for Latin America; (3) the implicit reliance on the United States family farm model, as if that could be transferred to Latin America; (4) the heavy grounding of these programs on United States political assumptions; and (5) the naiveté and lack of knowledge or sophistication about Latin America of so many of the United States officials and technicians involved in the program. It is small wonder that the program produced only limited results.

Community Development

The social and political history of community development is remarkably parallel to that of agrarian reform. Both programs flourished with considerable romance and pizzazz in the early 1960s. Both emerged as major public policy agenda items during the era of Camelot, the presidency of John F. Kennedy. Both were products of what has been called the "Peace Corps mood" of those times—that is, the urge not just to study development but to bring its agreed-upon benefits to less-favored lands. By the end of that decade both programs had faded. They did not entirely disappear. There are still some true believers, although they are a dwindling number and without the levels of enthusiasm and support that characterized the earlier halcyon and optimistic years.

The community development programs of the 1960s grew directly out of the United States programs of the same name and era. In Latin America and elsewhere in the Third World a large share of the program was carried out by American Peace Corps volunteers. In addition, there was a cottage industry of community development experts—all trained in the United States, deriving their models from the United States, and often closely connected with the United States civil rights movement and other forms of political activism. In those Latin American countries where there was little or no community development, the United States proceeded, as it did with agrarian reform, to create a special agency to administer the program within the host country government structure.

Again, I add a cautionary note: I have nothing against community development; indeed I tend to favor such programs. The problem is not community development but rather the models used and the appropriateness of these in a non-Western, partially Western, or Third World context.

Community development was the special preserve of the Peace Corps, and considerable literature developed out of that experience. Some of this literature even had more ambitious general and theoretical pretensions. In their training programs, Peace Corps volunteers "majored" in community development. Most of the volunteers, in those early days, had been liberal arts students as undergraduates; they often lacked necessary technical expertise or experience. What they meant by "community development" was often rudimentary: building latrines, digging ditches, aiding various self-help projects and what was called "organizational literacy." The latter referred to the basic organizational principles of running a meeting; talking in order; contacting a local official or congressman; forming a cooperative; or lobbying local authorities for housing materials, well-drilling equipment, sewers, roads, and electricity.

These Peace Corps activities were generally harmless enough and sometimes something positive was accomplished. In the long run, the advantages of Peace Corps service were probably greater for the volunteers themselves (in learning a new language and culture) than for the host community. The model with which the volunteers had to work was a major problem.

That model was derived almost entirely from the United States experience. The kind of community-based, grass-roots, self-help programs the Peace Corps sought to initiate came from the North American experience; they were grounded in the tradition of the New England town meeting and local self-governance. They were based upon a liberal, Lockean, Jeffersonian notion of direct and participatory democracy that had almost no basis in Latin America. The historical base of the Latin American systems is not Lockean; it is derived from the organic monism and unity of Saint Thomas and Francisco Suárez. Lockean liberalism is a relatively recent implant in Latin America, and in most countries it remains a minority strain.

The other major problem pertained to the structure of Latin American local government. Local government in Latin America is patterned after the French system. Almost all power is concentrated in the central state and its agencies. Local governments have almost no independent authority. They have almost no power to tax, to set policy, or to initiate new programs. Activities which in the United States are administered at the local level—concerning schools, utilities, health care, police, water supplies, sewers, and so on, the activities with which Peace Corps volunteers were trained to assist—are in Latin America handled not at the local but at the national level. The national government and its ministries determine educational policy, health policy, and so forth. Even if the Peace Corps volunteers could convince local authorities that they needed roads or well-drilling equipment or virtually anything else, the local government had no funds, no authority, no requisitioning power to get any of those things done. The result was a great deal of unhappiness and disillusionment on all sides.

Agrarian reform was in part a cold war strategy initiated in some desperation.

The response took various forms. To overcome these bottlenecks, the United States helped create in several Latin American countries a national Office of Community Development that would help organize and facilitate development activities. These agencies were almost 100 percent United States agencies: staffed, funded, and largely run by the United States or by nationals trained in the United States—so much for self-help. To compound the problem, these offices tended to serve as agencies for even further centralization in countries already highly, some would say overly, centralized. In many instances they took away the already slight residual power that had been located at the local level.

The Peace Corps volunteers were also frustrated. In some notorious early cases they all but completely took over the local communities to which they had been assigned. At least one was elected mayor of his town—a perfectly rational step from the point of view of local townspeople who felt they would get more for their community that way, but unacceptable to Peace Corps officials who rightly pointed out to this particular volunteer that he was there to help at the local level, not to take over the place. Many volunteers put to work the lobbying and political organizational skills they had learned in the United States by leading demonstrations, marching on town hall, or leading delegations to the capital city to push for their particular projects. Again, Peace Corps officials had to suggest that such activities, heretofore largely unheard of in Latin America, were not what they had in mind by "community development." After considerable comings and goings, many volunteers ended up teaching English at the local level—a useful contribution, but one far removed from the more grandiose designs of community development theory.

I do not mean to imply that either the Peace Corps or community development are bad ideas. Their accomplishments have been many and significant. I do maintain that the model was flawed, perhaps mortally so, from its inception. It was: (1) based upon a set of liberal-Lockean United States political perceptions and understandings about participatory government that had little basis in Latin America; (2) grounded on the model of a decentralized political system that was different from that of Latin America's centralist tradition, and (3) responsible for producing the opposite effect from that intended—greater centralization, often at the expense of local units. By the end of the 1960s, the community development panacea had also run its course.

Law and Development

Compared with the others, the American-sponsored program on law and development in Latin America was modest. Nevertheless, it was cut from the same cloth as the ones I have discussed, and it exhibited all the familiar biases. For this program, we already have James A. Gardner's thorough, well-researched, scholarly study, *Legal Imperialism*, that recounts its social and political history.

In a manner remarkably parallel to that of a myriad of other United States-conceived programs fashioned in the early to mid-1960s, the law and development program was an effort to bring to bear American legal expertise and ways of doing things for the benefit of Third World development. In part it reflected the aspiration of American lawyers to get in on the same travel and consulting opportunities as economists, sociologists, and political scientists; more fundamentally it reflected the belief among lawyers that they too had major contributions to make to Third World development.

Unfortunately, American concepts and models underpinned and defined the program. The model used was an idealized vision of law and the lawyer—pragmatic, omnicompetent, problem-solving—in United States society. No attention was paid to Latin American law or legal precepts. These were swept aside as "traditional" in favor of the new American conception. The program was also strongly conditioned by cold war considerations and a strident anticommunism. It was bolstered, as were the other programs I have discussed, by a Marshall Plan-like vision, as well as the confidence that we could do it. As Gardner, the foremost student of this program, has written, it was inept and fatally flawed from the beginning.

The program relied exclusively on an American conception of legal culture: It was based on and tried to implant an American system of legal education; it used the case method; it was grounded in American legal thought; it employed the Socratic dialogue of United States law schools; it taught the adversarial approach of American law; it was pragmatic, issues-oriented, and problem-solving. The United States model that these legal advisers sought to export contained a benign view of the state—that it was or would be liberal, pluralist, developmental, impartial, and progressive—which soon ran head-on into the authoritarian statism of Latin America.

The program was initiated on the basis of American notions of political democracy, liberal capitalism, and non- or anticommunism. There is nothing wrong with these values; the question is one of their relevance to Latin America. United States lawyers would presumably help engineer freer and more democratic societies in Latin America, as—in their own eyes, at least—they had done in the United States. They viewed Latin America as not having viable institutions of its own and hence as a social laboratory for a United States-based program of law-and-development assistance. As in other programs, it was a missionary call that went out, a particularly American one. The program, having as its goal the advancement and implanting of a particularly American legal model, was, as Gardner put it, a "tropical New Deal."

Community development was the special preserve of the Peace Corps.

According to Gardner, the American lawyers and law schools who were part of the law and development program in Latin America were poorly equipped by training or background for their assignments. Typically they had no understanding of the local language, customs, or law. They were culturally unaware, sociologically uninformed, and ethnocentric—consistently viewing Latin America in the self-image of the United States. They found, apparently to their surprise, that the goals and methods they brought with them from the United States, and which they assumed to be universal, were not necessarily shared in the Third World. They found the local legal cultures to be resilient and resistant to change. Many apparently lacked the tact to deal with their local counterparts. Relying on an American legal system and methods which they carried abroad with almost crusading zeal, and often inept and insensitive in dealing with local practices they—or at least the program's administrators—soon discovered that the model used was wrong and inappropriate. The overall result, by common consensus of both the host countries and the program's United States administrators, was failure.

The Latin American legal tradition was entirely different from that of the United States, being based on a code or civil law tradition, not on a common law tradition as in the United States. Most of the United States lawyers involved in the program knew that, but they were not aware of the full implications, of the wide-ranging ramifications of this distinct jurisprudential tradition. At a most basic level, it is doubtful whether this tradition in Latin America is even compatible with a law-and-development orientation. The Socratic method is of doubtful utility in a system based on rote memorization. The use of cases is not appropriate in a context in which the role of the judge is to find the applicable provision of the code, not to induce a general principle from a series of cases. The system of law school training in Latin America and even the role of the law school teacher is entirely different than in the United States. In Latin America there is little judicial review. Rather, as in the French system, these are administrative states, bureaucratic states that are grounded on a system of state positivism, not American-style separation of powers and interest-group pluralism. Prior to plunging headlong into the field, there were almost no preparations, no grounding in Latin American law, no studies of the implications of bringing an American legal system in contact with an undeveloped Roman-Iberian one. As a result, the program had what one author calls "unexpected vulnerabilities" even in those countries of Latin America (for example, Colombia) that were most democratic and therefore closer to the American system.

Three aspects of the law and development program especially command our attention. First, although neither the Latin American governments nor their lawyers or law schools especially wanted the program, the American government brought it anyway. Law and development was like many United States programs then and now: it was grounded on the notion that "we [North Americans] know best," not "they [Latin Americans] know best." Latin Americans not only had different expectations of the program, but they knew from the beginning that it would not work in their context. Bringing in a program anyway that was considered folly, and was known in advance not to work—by the locals if not by the Americans—seems the height of insensitivity.

Second, this program closely complemented and reinforced other United States ideas about foreign aid. It was entirely grounded in the American experience, with little reference to Latin American realities. It viewed Latin American realities with considerable disdain, its legal institutions as a "problem to be overcome." Since Latin America's history had been, by common consent, a "failure" and its institutions unresponsive and "dysfunctional," these could be cavalierly and precipitously discarded in favor of a presumably better model. Attempting naively and ethnocentrically to recast Latin America in the United States mold, and without any consideration for the possible viability of indigenous institutions, the program was bound to be a failure, as proved to be the case. The strong criticisms, even the language, leveled by critics seems equally applicable to the other programs I am describing.

Third, the program had a not very thinly disguised political agenda. Although small in comparison with other programs, it was neither harmless nor "benignly neutral." The program was to be, along with a number of others promulgated in this period, an agency of advanced, even radical change. It was designed to break down the existing legal system of Latin America and to substitute another, more "progressive" one for it. The notion that we and our assistance programs, however well-intentioned, should sweep away another country's (actually a whole set of countries') legal system and replace it with our own presumably better one would seem to be arrogant, misguided, and shortsighted.

Family Planning

Family planning was to the late 1960s and early 1970s what agrarian reform and community development had been in the earlier 1960s; the great panacea that would solve all of Latin America's problems. Impressionistically, I believe there were, and are, more true believers in family planning than in agrarian reform. Among certain cadres, family planning and population control are believed in with fervor and quasi-religiosity. Such attitudes may be useful when recruiting new supporters for the programs envisioned, but in foreign policy that can easily become a formula for disaster.

The language I use here in describing family planning and population control activities is sometimes biting and caustic, but I am sympathetic to family planning. To the extent that these are effective and well-run programs reflecting the desires of the local population, I am supportive of them. The problem here as elsewhere is not family planning or the activity per se but the particular model used by the United States to export it.

We do not as yet have a social and political history of family planning programs comparable to the one available on law and development. We need an insider account by someone in the Ford Foundation, the Population Council, the Population Crisis Committee, or the U.S. Agency for International Development, by one of those dozen or so key persons who has been influential in designing and implementing population policy over the last quarter-century.

The most successful early family planning programs in which the social engineering of the population control experts was put to work may have been those in Taiwan. A significant decline in birth rates began there in 1951 and, after a brief interruption, continued from 1955. Many of the giants in the family planning/population control community first earned their spurs by studying the Taiwanese model. Other places where efforts to reduce fertility have attained at least the appearance of success include Puerto Rico, Jamaica, Singapore, South Korea, and Thailand. The model of these programs has been carried over to the rest of Latin America.

I say the "appearance of success" because it is not clear whether the decline in the birth rate in these societies was due to the actual program to induce smaller families or to broad, "natural" changes in the society itself. It is clear that the societies from which the "population model" (like the agrarian reform and other "models") derives may not be representative of the Third World. Taiwan, Puerto Rico, Jamaica, Singapore, South Korea, and Thailand have a number of characteristics in common that may make them atypical of much of the developing world. All are relatively small, homogeneous, stable, and generally well administered, so that the substantial financial assistance from the United States government and the population agencies could be put to good use. These countries are also among the most advanced of the developing nations, typically already transitional to a developed economy rather than truly underdeveloped. Nor could it be said that Jamaica with its high literacy rate and Westminister political institutions, or Puerto Rico with its special relationship (and outlet for surplus population) to the United States, are at all typical of Latin America. As demographer and population expert William Peterson has written in *Population*, Taiwan is not India and Puerto Rico is not Mexico or Brazil. Nevertheless, despite its ill fit, this is the model that served as the basis for the family planning programs in Latin America.

Family planning was seen as the great panacea that would solve all of Latin America's problems.

These programs have been designed, launched, inspired, funded, and in large part administered from the United States; but considerable pains have been taken to disguise that fact. Much of the funding has been channeled through third-party agencies to disguise the extent of United States involvement. Various fronts have been set up to make it appear, particularly in the early stages, as though it is a private association that is supporting the program, not the United States government. But when an agency receives, directly or indirectly, 90 percent to 95 percent of its funds from AID, we are probably safe in considering it a front agency. Care has also been taken to find local doctors and concerned citizens in the countries affected so as to provide the appearance of local control, even though the funding and much of the direction may come from outside.

An elaborate scenario has been worked out to bring family planning and population control to the Third World through a somewhat secretive, furtive, and back-door route. First, a group of doctors are found, usually gynecologists and health care specialists, who receive specialized training in the United States and begin to talk about and publicize population-related topics: abandoned children, illegal and dangerous abortions, crowding, population growth rates that exceed economic growth, and so on. They provide a climate conducive to family planning activities. Then, typically, a private family planning association is formed consisting of these same doctors, demographers, and interested persons. United States aid is provided, usually funneled initially through private agencies. A pilot program of family planning clinics is begun; more publicity is generated; and a lobbying effort is begun with the government. In the third stage, the government, through its health or social assistance ministry, is persuaded to take over a program of family planning that is already in existence and to incorporate it into its nationwide system of maternity and child health care. This third and final step makes the program also eligible for large-scale foreign assistance, from AID, the United Nations, the Pan American Health Organization (PAHO), and other donors. At that stage the program is, presumably, well established, on its way, and on its own. These furtive and often secretive strategies have often generated resentments in the Third World and made the population programs objects of suspicion or hostility.

While these maneuverings were under way to establish a population program, in accord with a model imported from the outside, no one had bothered to check with Latin American countries to see if they wanted family planning, or wanted it all that much. My argument is complicated by the fact that survey data indicate Latin Americans do, overwhelmingly, want to limit family size, to have fewer children. Moreover, most influential groups in society—the army, the elites, even the church or some sectors of it—now see the need for some form of family planning. The problem is that they often see the issue in different terms than the population control donor agencies. The "population problem" in Latin America is variously defined from country to country, but it is usually put in terms of dealing with the problem of abandoned children, of illegal and often dangerous abortions, of resettlement of population and colonization, of squaring population growth with social and economic growth and ensuring that the former does not outstrip the latter. These Latin American concerns most often are barely given lip service by the donor agencies, whose overriding concern has been to limit population growth. It is not family planning per se that is at issue; rather, it is the particular model used and the insensitivity of the major population agencies to the wishes of Latin Americans. Unless population programs are carried out in accord with the wishes of the host countries, they are unlikely to produce successful results.

At this stage there are so many problems with the population programs that I can only list some of them here. First, the model may not be appropriate: what worked in Taiwan or even Puerto Rico is unlikely to work in Peru or Colombia. Second, the three-stage plan for population policy development can be and has been, in various countries, short-circuited and stalled at any one of several points; there is nothing inevitable or unilinear about the model. Third, while population growth rates are falling in Latin America, we are still not sure—as we are still not sure for Taiwan itself—whether this is due to natural causes (rising literacy, better education, urbanization, greater numbers of women in the work force) or to the efforts of the family planning agencies. Resolving that issue before plunging further ahead would seem to be an important task.

Fourth, there are major problems with the population agencies responsible for carrying out these programs. Their accounting method often leaves much to be desired; some have been guilty of doctoring population statistics to suit their own purposes; they have sometimes presented misleading information to the United States Congress and to AID; and some have been guilty of violating if not the letter then probably the spirit of United States law. Whatever one thinks of the legislation, there are now clear legal guidelines prohibiting the use of United States government funds in support of abortion services; yet some of the population agencies have continued to provide abortion information and equipment—although under pressure from Washington they have been discouraged from direct involvement in actual abortion services. In addition, a key problem has been that the population agencies are full of globalists and generalists, and their knowledge of particular regions such as Latin America has often been minuscule. Indeed, since the population problem is global and the solutions universally applicable, in their view, they see no need to acquire specialists or expertise in specific cultural or geographic areas.

Fifth, and most importantly, there is the true believer syndrome. The population issue is defined differently in Latin America, but it is difficult to convince the population control advocates that such differences are important and should be given serious consideration. They see the population problem as a world problem demanding immediate and emergency measures, and they see it as unidimensional: too many people. Since it is an emergency problem, they feel that time and energy should not be wasted paying serious attention to cultural differences across continents or to the nuances of individual nationalistic preferences. It is hard for these population true believers to comprehend that once the demographic facts are presented all right-thinking people would not see the solution in the same terms. They, in short, already know all the answers. They may give some limited attention to the broader and more intricate Latin American views of the problem, but first and foremost their conception is with global population control. They may even be right, but it is unlikely that they will ultimately win the war in Latin America without seriously taking into account Latin Americans' own perceptions and definitions of the problem. These are increasingly nationalistic, assertive, and resentful of outsiders who tell them what to do.

In the case of population policy it is not so much an American model that is being exported, although Americans have been the chief agents involved. Ironically, although Americans have served as the architects of the program, the United States itself has no national population policy—and could not conceivably pass such a program through Congress—yet we insist that Latin American countries adopt one as a condition of foreign aid largess or, it is strongly suspected, World Bank subsidies. Inspired by the United States, it is nevertheless a global model that is being exported, a perception of spiraling population growth that must be checked at all costs worldwide through the use of a plan of action universally applicable and emanating from the United States. It cannot possibly work. As sociologist William Peterson concludes in *Population*:

> Those [population] analysts in each social discipline who have attempted to transcend the bounds of a single case have very often erred on the side of too facile generalization, and repeatedly we have been put to the task of freeing our thoughts from one or another monistic bond—in earlier generations racial or geographic determinism and, more recently, their economic or demographic analogues. How much of a guide is the past development of advanced countries for mapping the future modernization of presently backward areas? In some overall sense, obviously; the world is becoming more homogenous, and it is just this metamorphosis that we mean by modernization. But to assume the details of the process must follow a known course, or that the homogenization must eventually eliminate all fundamental differences, is to commit the most egregious error of comparative analysis.

In general, ethnocentrism is strong in virtually all aspects of United States foreign policy toward the Third World. All these programs are based on and derive from the peculiarly Western experience with development and are of limited relevance to the Third World. They are based on particular and special experience with development, of a particular time and period, whose economic, sociological, and political laws may not apply to the Third World—or may apply only partially and incompletely.

Whether we are discussing agrarian reform, community development, law and development, or family planning/population control, or referring to other contexts of economic development strategy, military modernization, the democracy agenda, human rights concerns, trade unionism, or any one of countless other programs, the problems have been remarkably parallel. They were all born of a particularly Western experience with development, were based on Western assumptions about the modernization process which were then overgeneralized to the rest of the world, and have not adequately taken into account local and indigenous institutions and ways of doing things.

We may understand why this is so, why we use our own models to understand other areas of the world, why our ethnocentrism is so pronounced; but we must also be aware of the consequences of such ethnocentrism. By this time the policy failures have been so numerous and the Third World resentments engendered so strong that the notion of "let us do it our way" is becoming widespread. The Third World is increasingly inclined to reject the models and recommendations imposed as suggested by the West and is more and more searching for and asserting indigenous models and institutional arrangements more attuned to their own preferences, histories, and ways of doing things.

A long time must pass before policies based on the developmental assumptions of the past will change. These assumptions are strongly entrenched in the foreign assistance bureaucracies; and we know that a policy consensus on these or any other issues once arrived at is difficult to alter. Change will be difficult because these assumptions about agrarian reform, community development, the role of the middle class, and so on are closely associated with the history, culture, and ethos of the Western countries. They are embedded deeply in our educational system, our values, and our civic consciousness and ideology; and these will not be changed quickly or easily. They are part of a powerful social science tradition which sees the Western nations as most "developed" and leading the way and providing the example for the "less developed countries" to follow.

Change will be difficult to achieve because the more nuanced and less ethnocentric ideas I have suggested may be too complex for nonspecialist policymakers and the general public to grasp. I do not say this in a condescending or patronizing fashion but with the frank realization that in political Washington it is the image, the brief phrase, the lowest common denominator that usually counts in policymaking; the substance of the whole argument is often too complicated to get across. It is hard enough to get a consensus in Washington on such programs as agrarian reform and family planning; to say now that these programs will require far greater refinement and diverse adaptations to distinct local conditions is too

Population control has been brought to the Third World through a secretive, furtive, and back-door route.

difficult to convey to lawmakers or the public—and it may have the political side effect of scuttling the whole program or making it impossible to pass through Congress. For these and other reasons, it will likely take considerable time, perhaps a generation, for the changes I have suggested to reach fruition, for us to become less convinced that our own particular model is universal, and for us to take seriously the efforts of various Third World peoples to chart and institutionalize their own developmental routes.

The implications of the trends I have discussed are that the already developed donor nations will have to considerably reorient their assistance programs if they are to succeed in the Third World of the future. They will have to genuinely, not just with lip service, pay attention to local wants and aspirations. They will have to come to grips with models of development different from their own Western one. Far better and more thoroughly than in the past, they will have to learn the language, culture, and institutional procedures of various Third World areas.

The Third World is searching for and asserting indigenous models of development.

They will have to accept the notion now widespread in the Third World that "they know best" instead of the older one that "we know best for them." They will have to empathize and listen seriously for the first time and be prepared to support some of the Third World notions of development as distinct from the Western one. In the Islamic world, in Africa, Asia, and Latin America the sense is now well-nigh universal that the Western models, in their several varieties, have not worked very well, and therefore a social science model of development more attuned to local ways will have to be created. Strenuous efforts are now under way in various areas of the Third World to fashion such indigenous models or to achieve a better blend and fusion between imported and indigenous ones.

It is likely that this will be the next great innovative frontier in the social sciences and in development and foreign assistance research and theory. The foundations, various think tanks, and some within the academy—to say nothing of the Third World itself—are all moving in this direction. It is time for political development theory also to rethink its earlier premises and assumptions, all based strongly on the Western experience, and to move toward greater cultural relativism and an understanding of the Third World and the various parts thereof, on its own terms rather than through the prism of the earlier Western experience which fits the Third World only partially and incompletely. Once this new revolution in the social sciences and in development theory has taken place, it may be that the foreign assistance programs emanating from the Western nations can also be reoriented.

Four major questions come immediately to mind: (1) Are there still universals in the development process and, if so, what are they and how do we go about implementing and bringing about their more positive ends and features? (2) How do we make wise decisions in our foreign policy if not from the matrix of our own being and experience of what we understand to have been good in that experience? (3) Where do we draw lines in terms of the limits of the cultural relativism implied here—that is, once we are agreed that Hitler and Bokassa are unacceptable, what do we do about the tougher cases: Pinochet, South Africa, Zia, the Ayatollah, and Central America? (4) Suppose we heed the admonitions I offer, and then find that there are no Third World models of development worth hanging our hats on; what then do we do—not just intellectually but also from the point of view of policymakers who must make the decisions and carry our policies for these countries?

If past experience is any guide, it will likely take at least ten years (we are already half way through the generation change I referred to, marking a move away from the earlier development literature) before these newer models of development are reflected in more realistic assistance programs, reflecting a more accurate portrayal (as distinct from a wishful one, which far too often constituted the older approach) of Third World realities and institutions. It is, nevertheless, important to begin making the case now, both for educational purposes and because we may still hope to convince policymakers—hard though that is—that the success of their development programs must finally depend on their being adapted to the realities of distinct Third World areas. Success, after all, ultimately reflects the bottom line of American commitment to such programs.

READINGS SUGGESTED BY THE AUTHOR:

Bendix, Reinhard. "Tradition and Modernity Reconsidered." *Studies in Society and History* IX (April 1967).

Gardner, James A. *Legal Imperialism: American Lawyers and Foreign Aid in Latin America.* Madison: University of Wisconsin Press, 1980.

Inter-American Foundation. *They Know How . . .: An Experiment in Development Assistance.* Washington, D.C.: Government Printing Office, 1977.

Nisbet, Robert A. *Social Change and History: Aspects of the Western Theory of Development.* London: Oxford University Press, 1969.

Packenham, Robert. *Liberal America and the Third World: Political Development Ideas in Foreign Aid and Social Science.* Princeton: Princeton University Press, 1973.

Veliz, Claudio. *The Centralist Tradition in Latin America.* Princeton: Princeton University Press, 1980.

Wiarda, Howard J. *Ethnocentrism in Foreign Policy: Can We Understand the Third World?* Washington, D.C.: American Enterprise Institute for Public Policy Research, 1985.

Third World War: The global conflict over the rights of indigenous nations

BERNARD NIETSCHMANN/*CULTURAL SURVIVAL QUARTERLY*

The Third World War has already begun. It began when new states tried to take over old nations. It began in the hills north of India and Burma in 1948. Burma moved its army into the homelands of the Karen and Shan people and India started its military invasion of the Naga nation. The Third World War is now being fought on every continent except Antarctica. It has killed millions of people and forced massive dislocations of indigenous peoples. It encompasses most of the groups who are accused of being terrorists. And each year it widens to new areas, states, and nations.

The Third World War is being fought on different fronts with different means and for different goals than the previous two world wars. Conventional war between armies of opposing states is rare in this age; nuclear arsenals discourage direct military confrontation between today's superpowers. The nature and geography of global war has changed. The new world war is focused on the Third World, and pits state governments against guerrilla insurgencies and indigenous nations. Most of these wars are over territory, resources, and identity, not ideology.

In this war, military occupation is called economic development, resistance is called terrorism.

The roots of most of today's wars and tension areas are partially obscured by our obsession with East-West and North-South political divisions and by the preponderance of state-sided interpretations and explanations of world events by journalists and academics. Nearly all media and academia are anchored in the world's centralized states. Their tendency is to consider struggles against the state to be illegitimate or invisible.

The Third World War is hidden from most people's view because the fighting is against peoples and countries that are often not even on the map. In this war territorial invasion is called "national integration," occupation is called "economic development," and resistance is called "terrorism."

In almost every newspaper and television news program, the terms state, nation, and nation-state are used interchangeably. This is not just a harmless semantic matter, but a major distortion that fogs our understanding of international events.

Nations are geographically bounded territories of a common people. A nation is made up of communities of people who see themselves as one people on the basis of common ancestry, history, society, institutions, ideology, language, territory, and (often) religion. Nation peoples clearly distinguish themselves and their countries from other people and countries—both adjacent and distant. The existence of nations is ancient.

Today there are between 3,000 to 5,000 nations in the world. No directory, atlas, or encyclopedia exists that lists or describes all or even most of the world's nations. Some are very small in population and area—several live on just a few acres. Other nations are huge, with populations in the millions—such as Kawthoolei, in South Asia, with its 4.5 to 5 million Karen people, larger than 48 percent of the member states in the United Nations, or the Oromo nation in East Africa with more than 20 million people. Unlike a state, a nation does not require a central military-political bureaucracy to exist.

A state is a centralized political system that is recognized by other states and that uses a civilian and military bureaucracy to enforce one set of institutions, laws, and sometimes language and religion within its claimed boundaries. This is done regardless of the presence of nations within its boundaries that may have pre-existing and different laws and institutions. States commonly lay claim to many nations that may not consent to being governed by an imposed central government in the hands of a different people. Although most central governments assert

From *Utne Reader,* November/December 1988, pp. 84-91. Excerpted with permission from *Cultural Survival Quarterly* (September 1987), 11 Divinity Avenue, Cambridge, MA 02138.

that their state is made up of one common people, more than 95 percent of the world's 168 states are multinational, that is, composed of many nations, some unconsenting. These 168 states assert sovereignty over the world's 3,000 to 5,000 nations and peoples, all of the continents, 40 percent of the oceans, and even the lower reaches of space. States range in size from the republic of Nauru, with a population of 10,000, to Belize and the Bahamas with 200,000 each, to states such as Indonesia, which stretches across 3,000 miles, 13,700 islands, and 300 nations.

A nation-state—a common people with a common historical territory governed by an internationally recognized central political system—is a rarity these days. Thus only a few of the world's states really are nation-states: Iceland, Western Samoa, East Germany, North and South Korea, and a handful more.

Nations without a state make up the Fourth World of internationally unrecognized nations. This Fourth World comprises the nation peoples and their countries that exist beneath the imposed states of the West (First), East (Second), and Third worlds. Nation people consider themselves to be members of distinct nations by virtue of cultural and territorial heritage; they may not consider themselves to be citizens of some intruding state government made up of other peoples from other places. Fourth World nations may be surrounded, divided, or dismembered by one or more international states. The Fourth World encompasses most of the world's nations, about a third of the world's population, and approximately 50 percent of the land area. Nation peoples may be industrialized

The Third World War began in the hills north of Burma in 1948.

(Latvians, Estonians, Catalans), or live from hunting and marketing (Inuits), herding (Samis), agriculture (Shan), ranching (Western Shoshone), or commercial and subsistence fishing (Haida).

Nation peoples may not recognize a state's assertion of sovereignty. Many Irish do not consider themselves part of Great Britain; Catalans of Spain; Palestinians of Israel; Mayans of Guatemala; Tamils of Sri Lanka; Pathans of Pakistan or Afghanistan; Kurds of Syria, Turkey, Iran, Iraq, or the USSR; Miskitos of Nicaragua or Honduras; Tigrayans and Oromo of Ethiopia; Sami of Norway, Sweden, Finland, or the USSR; Western Shoshone of the U.S.; Shuswap of Canada; Haida of Canada or the U.S.; the peoples of South Moluccas, East Timor, and West Papua of Indonesia. These are not exceptions, but examples of one of the most important geopolitical facts of our times: Almost all of the distinct peoples in the world live in nations that do not want to be ruled by state government.

Many nation peoples are militarily resisting annexation and absorption by state regimes that would strip them of their nationality, land, and resources. Palestinians will not become "ethnic Israelis," Kurds will not become "mountain Turks," and Oromo will not become "Ethiopian." To do so would erase their nationality, history, and country.

To defend their nations from being annihilated, many peoples have taken up arms and are carrying out what are the world's longest wars. The very thing they are fighting for—the survival of their nation and nationality—is usually the focus of distortion and

Many Irish do not consider themselves part of Great Britain; Palestinians of Israel; Mayans of Guatemala; Shoshone of the U.S.

misrepresentation by most journalists and academics. Nation people are almost always misidentified as either members of the very state they are fighting against (Oromo are called "Ethiopian rebels"), or by the propaganda terms used by the invading state (the Burma government refers to the five million Karen as "terrorists"). Pick up a newspaper or a newsmagazine or turn on a television news program and try to find out the nationality of the peoples shooting at each other in Ethiopia, Sudan, Angola, Afghanistan, Indonesia, Burma, Bangladesh, Nicaragua, Guatemala, or in any of the rest of the world's wars. Nation peoples are rarely identified by their own names; instead, they are referred to as rebels, separatists, extremists, dissidents, insurgents, terrorists, tribals, minorities, or ethnic groups.

How can a people be an ethnic group in its own nation? Are Palestinians an ethnic group in Palestine? Are Karens an ethnic group in Kawthoolei? How can the Miskitos be separatists if they never consented to joining the Nicaraguan state, even before the Sandinista revolution? How can the Sahrawi people in North Africa be rebels because they resist the Moroccan invasion? When asked by a Sandinista leader if the Miskito people would accept special status as a Nicaraguan ethnic group, Miskito coordinator Brooklyn Rivera replied, "Ethnic groups run restaurants. We are people. We have an army. We want self-determination."

The concept of an ethnic group is embedded in our state-biased way of thinking. An ethnic group is a population that maintains its own cultural identify in another nation. Individuals, and even majorities of a people, may leave their nation—by force or choice—to live in a new country in which they have no historical land or national territory. But a nation people living within its own territory is not an "ethnic group" or a "minority." Sikhs may be an ethnic group in London, but not in Punjab (Khalistan); Samis may be a minority in Oslo or Stockholm, but in Samiland (also known as Lapland) they are a people. A people does not automatically become a minority or an ethnic group because its nation is invaded. The French, Poles, and Dutch did not become "minorities" during the German occupation.

States define nation peoples as ethnic groups and minorities as a tactic to annex their identities in order to incorporate their lands and resources. Whereas "a people" has internationally recognized rights to self-determination, subsistence, resources, and national territory, an ethnic group or minority does not.

Almost none of the world's more than 3,000 distinct peoples are recognized internationally. Their existence, territories, and defensive struggles are largely invisible. Instead, multinational state populations become internationally recognized as "peoples" and "nations" even though they have none of the characteristics.

An unintentional result of World War II was the uprooting and eventual replacement of European colonial rulers in Africa, Asia, and the Pacific. The war shattered the seeming invincibility of colonial powers. Anti-colonialist forces used the right of self-determination to justify ousting foreign rule. Within three decades the number of states more than doubled, from 72 to 156 (168 in 1987). Artificial states were formed from artificial colonial territories. Artificial "peoples" were also formed.

A shell game was played globally. The concept of a people and a nation was fast-switched with that of an ethnic group and a state. Peoples were re-categorized as ethnic groups, and ethnic groups were recast as peoples. For example, the autonomous Karens and their nation were termed a Burmese "hill tribe," whereas the Burman people—only one of a dozen nations in the British-created state of Burma—became the ruling regime of the mythical "Burmese people."

Instead of decolonization, Fourth World nations got recolonization, with brown and black colonial rulers instead of white. They got rid of occupation forces who were from distant places only to be invaded by occupation forces from nearby places.

After World War II the nature of global conflict changed. The vast majority of individual wars today—which together make up the Third World War—are between states and nations. Of the approximately 120 ongoing wars, 72 percent (86) were state-nation conflicts. Wars between states account for less than 3 percent, and between states and rightist or leftist insurgency movements 15 percent. About 10 percent of the world's conflicts are nations fighting nations and insurgencies fighting nations.

The present global war is fought largely by the Third World. Out of 120 conflicts, 98 percent (118) are in the Third World and 75 percent (90) are between Third World states and Fourth World nations.

The Third World War is more a conflict over territory, not over ideology. The common denominator is a nation's resistance to state expansion. Most of the states at war with nations are carrying out military invasions to annex territory and resources under the guise of national integration, nation building, border security, economic development, social progress and eradication of communists, mercenaries, bandits, or terrorists.

Facing absorption and subjugation at the hands of the state, many nations have no other choice than to militarily resist the state invasion. The goal of most nations is to regain or maintain local control over their territory, resources, peoples, and communities. Military and political means are mobilized to achieve autonomy. The common tactic is to use widespread hit-and-run ambushes and small-scale attacks to geographically entangle the state's military and to make the occupation as costly as possible. Meanwhile, international political support and arms supply may be sought.

Territorial autonomy for nations would end most wars. *Autonomy* is the umbrella term for various territorial and political solutions to territorial conflicts between states and nations. Of the nations at war today, about 60 percent seek an autonomous territorial and political relationship with the invading state, 15 percent are divided between autonomy and independence, and 25 percent want independence.

To carry out their invasions or to defend against them, both states and nations seek outside support from superpowers and regional powers. Most national resistance forces follow the philosophy that "the enemy of my enemy is my arms supplier." And the superpowers broadcast this message"The enemy of my enemy will be supplied with arms."

However, the U.S. and the USSR are more likely to support governments of recognized states and political insurgencies than indigenous peoples because the geopolitical return is greater. The U.S. does supply YATAMA (the Miskito, Sumo, and Rama nation resistance in Nicaragua) because it is fighting the Sandinistas. But more characteristic is the U.S. military assistance to Indonesia's government, which is fighting West Papua's OPM and East Timor's Fretilin resistance forces. Similarly, because Morocco is a staunch U.S. ally in a strategic and otherwise anti-U.S. region, King Hassan II's 12-year, million-dollar-per-day war against the Sahrawi Republic (Western Sahara) is heavily supported by the U.S.

The USSR is just as inclined as the U.S. to support the state sides in wars because of geopolitical gains that come from alliances with internationally recognized governments. China militarily supports more autonomy-seeking nations than either the U.S.

More than 85 percent of the world's 168 states are composed of more than one nation.

or USSR, including the nine-nation anti-Burman resistance.

But a nation's armed resistance is likely to continue despite a cutoff or switch in outside military assistance. For example, Africa's longest and most diversified wars occur within the area claimed by Ethiopia. Combatant forces include those of the Ethiopian state, guerrilla insurgencies, and several nations. The multinational Eritrean forces have fought against territorial incorporation by Ethiopia since 1961. Before 1974, when Ethiopia was ruled by U.S.-backed emperor Haile Selassie, the USSR provided military assistance to Eritrean resistance forces. But when the Marxists-led Dergue nation took control of the state, the USSR and KGB abandoned Eritrean forces and backed the new government. Nevertheless, Eritrea still resists. Because of situations such as this, many nations are learning to switch-hit to obtain support from both the right and the left.

State-nation wars are as dirty, vicious, and destructive as conventional wars between states. Almost every state- occupation army uses military forces to kill or capture nation combatants and to crush civilian support. Common occupation tactics—misidentified as "counterinsurgency"—include arbitrary arrest to intimidate nationalist opposition, control of food and medicine to make the people dependent upon the occupation regime, and destruction of villages and forced relocations to "drain the sea to strand the fish" (deprive nationalist guerrilla forces of information, shelter, recruits, and food).

The current conflicts that comprise the Third World War have taken approximately five million lives—combatants and civilians. In fact, civilians are often targeted rather than being simply by-product casualties of fighting between combatants.

In the present world war, indigenous nation populations are seen by many Third World state governments as a hindrance. Often already overpopulated, states are after more land and resources, not more people. If a nation resists absorption into an occupying nation or state, then the alternatives are straightforward: Destroy them or force them to flee to become other countries' problems.

The Third World War produces almost all of the world's refugees. Displaced by invasion, war, hunger, and politics, the majority of refugees are from Fourth World nations.

The Third World War will likely continue because almost all states still believe that it is in their interest to occupy the world wall to wall.

The Third World War is under way because many Fourth World nations are fighting to protect their own peoples and territories from military occupation by invading states. No matter what journalists and foreign policy experts tell us, these Fourth World nations have their own goals, leaders, fighters, and internal support. Fourth World nations don't have to wear uniforms, carry a flag, mint currency, send a team to the Olympics, or defend their lands and identities, which have already stood the tests of both time and bombs. Recognizing the existence of these ancient nations will help us understand the world today and lay the groundwork for peace tomorrow.

The Third World War is hidden from most people's view because the fighting is against countries that are not even on the map.

Industrial development –

A NATURAL GROWTH IF ROOTED IN AGRICULTURAL DEMAND

Anthony Mutsaers

Anthony Mutsaers *has worked in FAO's Investment Centre for the last ten years. He wrote this article while on external training as a visiting scholar at the University of California at Berkeley in 1987.*

The Third World agricultural development system — the myriad of bilateral donors, governmental and non-governmental, the network of multilateral donors (the UN specialized agencies, especially the World Bank and FAO), their respective multiple domestic power bases, and on the recipient side, Third World governments and their ministries — represents a politically diverse and complex set of well-established bureaucracies. Any change would require a broad-based consensus among all parties concerned that current means and approaches are not reaching proposed objectives. In fact, experience shows that nothing less than a serious crisis in the attainment of objectives is required to shift donor policies toward Third World agriculture.

In the early 1970s, the most important example of such a crisis was the events leading up to the World Food Conference of 1974. The Conference was primarily the result of the realization that in too many countries population growth continued to exceed growth in food production and that little or no progress was being made on the "poverty" front, a message which at that time was powerfully delivered in the form of a series of devastating famines, especially in Africa, and to a lesser extent in Asia. These famines were well publicized on television in all developed countries. The additional severe oil shock at this critical moment paralysed non-oil-exporting less developed countries (LDCs). They did not initiate any corrective action, and the scene was set for a major new policy.

These world events were reacted to by an unlikely coalition of the US Secretary of Agriculture, Earl Butz; US Secretary of State, Henry Kissinger, and a "rebel" Third World faction within FAO which formulated the position that famines and financial shocks necessitate "National Food Self-Sufficiency" through increased domestic food production by the developing countries. Butz felt that one way to reduce costly US farm support programmes would be by shrinking US grain imports by LDCs through increasing LDC food production. Kissinger supported the idea of a conference to soften the blow from the oil shock to non-oil-exporting LDCs. In turn, this US and LDC coalition was instrumental in generating the support of OECD and Arab oil-exporters.

The resulting World Food Conference of 1974, the first and probably the last of its kind, was attended at the highest level by more than 150 countries. It created, among other items, a US$1 billion "International Fund for Agricultural Development" (IFAD) with the specific aim of assuring national food security, especially for the poorest of the poor.

Given the subsequent dubious record of the LDC agricultural sector, it now seems that the crisis of 1974 has not been adequately addressed, the Conference's good intentions notwithstanding. In fact, the situation has actually deteriorated, particularly in Africa. With regard to per caput food production, between 1974 and 1984 of 23 "low-income African countries" (1984 population 260 million) only two (population 12 million) saw per caput food production exceed population growth. Four witnessed no growth (population 76 million) and in 17 (population 172 million) population growth rates exceeded food production growth. In all eight "medium-income African countries" (population 188 million), population growth exceeded food production growth. In Asia, exactly the opposite occurred.

Reprinted from *Ceres*, March/April 1988, pp. 42-48. CERES, the FAO review on agriculture and development.

…y in Nepal did population growth …xceed food production growth, whereas in Bangladesh and Pakistan, the two rates were equal. In all other countries, but especially in China, there was net per caput growth in food production. In Latin America, only Brazil and Honduras showed an improvement out of the eight countries in the region. It is estimated that all in all in 44 out of 65 countries (representing the bulk of LDC population, China excluded) population growth exceeded food production growth.

Tripled dependence on imports. This poor performance is reflected in the overall figures for food imports and public debt. Low-income and medium-income African and middle-income Asian countries doubled and tripled their dependence on cereal imports between 1974 and 1984, in the middle-income African countries up to 80 kg per caput. The levels of agricultural exports dropped dramatically. Financially the African and Latin American countries have increased their external public debt about tenfold and face severe repayment problems. Public budget deficits rose as a result of the phenomenal rise of the expenditure on public administration and defence and the related investments in parastatals.

When it comes to poverty, statistics are confusing and vague. The World Conference on Agricultural Reform and Rural Development (WCARRD) papers of the 1987 FAO Conference suggest that absolute poverty diminished in Asia and the Near East, changed little, if at all, in Latin America, and worsened in Africa. Still, about two-thirds of the world's poor are in Asia. In total, these numbers (high estimate) increased from 460 million in 1969/71 to 512 million in 1983/85. WCARRD econometric analysis shows a close correlation between poverty and per caput food production, suggesting that increasing per caput food production is a priority item for economic development.

There are problems however. WCARRD population projections show an increase in the rural population of the developing countries by 162 million between 1980 and 1985. Of this total, 96 million were added to the agricultural population, but only 12 million hectares of additional land was brought under production, which suggests that farms are getting smaller all the time. At the same time, 66 million were added to the rural population, of which, according to ILO, only 25 per cent could find employment. In brief, the rural areas are increasingly characterized by fragmented farms and rural landlessness, the manifestations of poverty.

The future prospects, at least in the medium term, for improvement in both per caput food production and poverty, are worse than ever. Africa was poorer in resources in 1985 than it was a generation ago in 1960. The Near East saw cuts in public expenditures and food subsidies. Non-oil-exporting countries fared badly, with slackening emigration, decline of remittances, and dwindling financial and import capability. The economic crisis was most severe in Latin America considering the devaluations, inflation, public budget cuts and lower employment wages.

African and middle income Asian countries doubled and tripled their dependence on cereal imports

It is clear from these data that most developing countries are now even less prepared to cope with providing food self-sufficiency and eradicating poverty than they were at the time of the World Food Conference.

There appears little hope that Official Development Assistance (ODA) will fill the gap. Between 1974 and 1984 net annual disbursements of ODA to agriculture from all sources increased only from $7.1 billion in 1978 to $8.0 billion in 1983. Africa's share during this period increased slightly, from 24 per cent to 26 per cent of the total. External private financial flows to agriculture took a nose-dive, especially in Africa and Latin America, and now represent about 15 per cent of the ODA total and are almost exclusively in the agro-industrial manufacturing sector. Nor are there any reasonable chances for major increases in foreign aid flows, given the difficult economic situation in the OECD countries. IFAD's replenishment struggle, placing in doubt for some time the very survival of the Fund which concerns the poorest of the poor, is an all too clear manifestation of this reality.

All this suggests that we are once again facing a grave crisis and that the time has come to look at the possibility of doing more with the available means, of reviewing the efficiency of established ways instead of simply crying for more money. Solutions for survival are now up to industry. Creative development is the word.

The role of agriculture and the rural sectors in the development process. If the food self-sufficiency and poverty problems of the rural sector are to be resolved, LDC governments must be provided with powerful arguments to legislate and enforce policies favourable to agriculture and to the rural sector as a whole and, probably, as part of this policy, to increase significantly agriculture's share of the total investment budget.

Powerful reasons are required because well-embedded historical beliefs have left conscious or even subconscious biases against agriculture, the "traditional" sector, as opposed to the industrial and mining, or "modern", sectors. The inclusion of these two words "modern" and "traditional" are ingrained in the economic development literature for the industrial and agricultural sectors respectively. Together these two words sum up the widespread attitude, in the developed and developing world alike, toward the two sectors.

In the early history of the developing world, the development of the agricultural sector development consisted in the colonial power's strategy of limiting the Third World to the role of supplier of cheap raw materials for its own highly successful industrial development. Undoubtedly, this strategy goes far to explain the urgency with which many newly independent LDCs embraced industrial development as the principal road to their economic salvation. Since these were agricultural societies, such a strategy required the exploitation of agriculture to provide surplus labour and cheap food to keep down industrial wages as well as various forms of agricultural taxation to generate the necessary capital surpluses. Typically, export-oriented cash crops were favoured over domestic food-crop production, as these both generated foreign exchange and allowed for easy taxation in the form of export taxes.

To stimulate further industrial development and generate the necessary financing, the countries undertook expansionary monetary and fiscal policies (including heavy foreign borrowing) and adopted various related policies to protect "infant" industries through import controls favouring industrial capital and intermediate inputs and food.

As artificially high profits were thus generated in the industrial sector, resources shifted out of agriculture in search of higher returns. Since the expansionary policies usually led to inflation levels higher than world levels, the currencies became overvalued, thus penalizing agricultural exports while lowering the domestic cost of imported industrial sector imports. Cheap imported food lowered farmgate prices for locally consumed agricultural output, while prices of locally produced protected farm inputs rose. The terms of trade turned sharply against agriculture.

The preference for industrial development over agricultural development, however, was more than a simple reaction to colonialism or a result of the belief that industrial development ensured economic growth and modernization.

There was also the issue of access to capital and entrepreneurship. Industrial development is to a large extent predisposed toward private capital and private entrepreneurship. The growth of the industrial and mining sectors requires a minimum of public investment in research, infrastructural support, or marketing. These sectors come essentially as self-contained and sustained private investment packages. Likewise, the investment in the actual production technology itself, the factory, the mine, is essentially private. In contrast, in the agricultural sector, all these activities are, to a large extent, public. If one reviews official IMF, World Bank, or OECD statistics on the sectoral breakdown of foreign private investment, the agricultural sector is conspicuous by its absence.

Then there is the issue of technology. The agricultural sector was dependent on unpredictable nature: there was the need to manage large numbers of producers, widely scattered geographically, with the related problems of access and communications; agricultural technology was dependent on local research and local conditions. It may be understandable that most of the countries considered it safer to depend on industry, safely confined within factory walls in one or a few cities, with known well-established technologies based on long and proven history in the developed world, and run essentially by an independent, self-financing dynamic private sector.

Africa was poorer in resources in 1985 than it was a generation ago in 1960

Furthermore — and these considerations may possibly be the most important — urban aspects of industrial development have obvious political advantages. Given the nature of the democratic base of many LDC governments, satisfying the more vocal, physically concentrated urban population with industrial employment, cheap food and, last but not least, "modern" imported consumer goods, is overriding.

Then there is the actual record of success of such early Newly Industrialized Countries (NICs) as Japan, the Republic of Korea, the City States (Singapore, Hong Kong), Taiwan province, and, to a lesser extent, Malaysia with their industrial policies. Right now, these serve as role models for many aspiring LDCs, although the possibility of following their examples may currently be very much curtailed.

In these successful exporting countries, the industrialization base was laid in the early 1950s and 1960s, during a period of import substitution. Import substitution creates the first experience with satisfying consumer demand and mass production behind protective barriers. Once domestic demand is satisfied, the industry is prepared to enter international markets.

Strong supporters of export-led development strategies feel that entry in the world export market gives the domestic economy a leanness and an international know-how (technical and managerial skills) and most important, the discipline that comes with a demanding competitiveness of succeeding in such markets. Such characteristics, they reason, are why countries with an export-led strategy, like Korea or Japan, survived the international financial and oil crises. They simply exported themselves out of the crises.

These countries, on the whole, also pursued a more benign policy toward agriculture. The terms of trade were not against agriculture; exchange rates and export taxes did not discourage agricultural exports. Taxation was not excessive and did not discourage agricultural growth. At the same time, public investment budgets for the sector remained high. There were strong policies to assure asset distribution (effective land reform) and to introduce rapid technological change.

Countries like Brazil, the Philippines, Turkey, and Mexico, dominated in the 1960s and early '70s by import substitution policies, did not, by definition, have the export capacity to generate the necessary foreign exchange to avoid the financial crises. The problems of these countries at that time were that reliance on import substitution policies behind comfortable import barriers led to inefficiency, overcapitalization, and managerial laziness, and, as it involved an overvalued domestic currency, an overall misallocation of resources within the economy which was subsequently combined with capital flight. A related negative was that incentives for import substitution, through foreign exchange rationing, increased the cost of imports, making exporting less profitable. The agricultural sector, with the greatest possibilities for exports, suffered most.

Although, since the middle 1970s, these countries have begun to turn toward a balanced, or even export-promotion, policy, shedding many of the structural problems created by excessive import substitution, they experienced a very high entry cost. The adoption of the export-led strategy leads to major increases in foreign borrowing in the early periods for imports of intermediate and capital goods; only late in the development process does industry become a net contributor of foreign exchange. These late blooming Newly Industrialized Countries (NICs) were thus caught in the double bind of having to support high levels of imports without the necessary compensating export levels and with diminishing access to external financing.

A related major problem for these countries was, and still is, that the current world trade environment, with protectionism on the rise, compares unfavourably with the expanding world free trade picture of the 1970s when the early NICs made their entries.

Alain De Janvry suggests an inward looking change in policy for future aspiring countries: "Given this context of export skepticism and much more orthodox trade and price policies resulting from stabilization efforts, it is clear that expansion of the domestic market to generate final demand for industry will have to play a much greater role than in the previous three decades.

"In an open economy with industrial export skepticism, imperfect substitution between domestic and imported capital goods, binding foreign savings, and significant import substitution possibilities in agriculture without necessary protectionism, productivity growth in agriculture becomes an important new source of economic reactivation."

In fact, in Japan, between 1914 and 1965, 58 per cent of GDP growth (increasing 28-fold during this period) was generated through domestic demand. Studies carried out on Turkey, Korea, and Yugoslavia found that domestic demand accounted for between 63 and 95 per cent of GDP growth. Such considerations now inhibit the wholehearted adoption of an export-led policy on behalf of aspiring newcomers.

Only late in the development process does industry become a net contributor of foreign exchange

---

An inward-looking orientation would not necessarily imply a total exclusion of the role of exports. Even in the examples cited there remains a critical role for the export sector, but such an orientation rather suggests that a major development thrust would be to activate domestic production for the domestic market. In the agricultural sector this still leaves substantial scope for improving the competitiveness of agricultural exports (especially in Africa), which may have positive spill-over effects for the production for the local markets. World Bank studies show that the development of cash-crop production raises the quality of farming in general (largely thanks to improvement in the input/output system) and thus benefits food crops as well.

The relationship between agricultural and industrial growth. There are other sobering statistics which suggest that an industrial export-led strategy often involves the neglect or exploitation of agriculture because such a strategy ignores the capacity of the agricultural sector to generate industrial demand.

A recent publication, "Investing in Development" (Baum and Tolbert) neatly ranks, with stunning results, about 50 countries by their bias against agriculture (measured by the extent of price distortion) and the related annual GDP growth rate, the domestic savings income ratio, and the annual rate of agriculture and others, as summarized in the table.

As the distortion increases, agricultural and GDP growth rates fall, along with domestic savings. The World Bank, in its 1986 *World Development Report*, finds a perfect correlation between the industrial growth rate and the agricultural sector growth rate for most of 41 countries, the exceptions being the exporters of oil and minerals. In all other cases, low agricultural growth rates correspond to low industrial growth rate and vice versa. The report concludes, "Agriculture's intimate connections with growth and the wider economy mean that the costs of discrimination against agriculture are not borne by farming alone."

All this suggests that foreign aid should probably be oriented strongly in favour of pro-agricultural policies. It is interesting to note, however, that aid-flows by themselves appear to have a limited effect on agricultural development. Many countries depend heavily on aid; in fact, donors dominate the operating and investment budgets of many African countries and some smaller Asian countries as well. Yet in countries where cereal production growth far exceeds population growth, like China, India, the Republic of Korea, and Indonesia, aid per caput varies from $1 in China to $4 in Indonesia. On the other hand, in low-income food-deficit African countries, aid per caput varies from $20 to $30 per year and up to $70 in Somalia. While it may be true that the food-deficit countries would have done worse without aid and that the food-surplus countries could have done even better with aid, it follows that aid does not appear to be essential to agricultural growth.

Agricultural demand led industrial growth (ADLI). The inward-looking development strategy, as presented by Adelman or Mellor does not, like the previous industrial import-substitution policies, depend on creating artificial import barriers. Rather it hinges on the development of the agricultural sector and on the demand which a prosperous agricultural sector would generate.

Adelman puts the case as follows:

- Prosperous farmers would require large volumes of inputs from the industrial sector: fertilizer, insecticides, weed-killers, water pumps, agricultural tools and equipment, creating effective domestic demand and employment in these sectors.
- Increased agricultural production calls for increased agro-industrial processing operations, further strengthening industrial output and possibly exports.
- A prosperous rural sector would create a lucrative market for locally made industrial products and related employment. Urban consumers demand more imported goods.
- Demand for rural transport and construction and related materials would increase.
- Per unit of output, the technology of agricultural development, especially of small owner-operated farms, is much more labour-intensive than industrial development technology, and conversely much less capital-intensive. That is, it increases employment and lowers the need for capital, both foreign and domestic.
- Agricultural development requires much less in imports, also per unit of output, than industrial development, since it uses traditionally locally available resources.
- A strong, healthy agricultural sector would produce surplus for exports, which would provide foreign exchange for agricultural inputs.

To assure emphasis on labour-intensive technology and a reduction of imports per unit of output, emphasis should be on small- and medium-scale agriculture, as large farms and mechanized government farms usually use imported capital-intensive inputs. Smaller farmers are also more likely to consume local products, including clothing, footwear, and simple consumer durables (bicycles, sewing machines) than larger farmers who might prefer motorcycles and automobiles with a higher import component.

Adelman gives figures to support these arguments. Working with a Computable General Equilibrium (CGE) model for the Republic of Korea, he shows that, with agriculture contributing 50 per cent to GDP and industry 25 per cent (a typical LDC situation), and an industrial-demand multiplier of income originating in agriculture of 1.4 per cent, a 3 per cent agricultural growth rate would generate a 8.4 per cent industrial output growth rate.

Emphasis should be on small and medium-size agriculture

Mellor makes essentially the same point by suggesting that the introduction of "technological change" would generate the necessary agricultural growth, and that the resulting increased agricultural production could (a) substitute for imports, (b) be absorbed domestically through accelerated growth in employment and thus purchasing power (in the backward and forward linkage industries serving agriculture), or (c) as a third possibility, be sold on international markets. This resulting increased agricultural income would generate demand for low capital intensity and industrial sector goods and services. Either increased agricultural exports or import substitution would generate or free the foreign exchange to sustain the import of intermediate inputs.

The policy is attractive in that it addresses both agricultural production and the question of near and complete landlessness (agricultural labourers) in the rural areas, by absorbing the rural poor in the backward and forward linkages of the agricultural service sector. It is a sensible recognition of the close interdependence between the agricultural and rural service sectors. The FAO and World Bank literature contains overwhelming evidence that agricultural growth is extremely limited not only by lack of adequate infrastructure, especially roads which affect market costs and producer prices, but also by inadequate and untimely supplies of appropriate fertilizer, improved seeds, and chemicals; easily accessible banking or savings and loan services; appropriate equipment and tools; by inadequate repair and maintenance facilities, improper on-and-off farm storage facilities, underdeveloped wholesale and retail activities, related product advice, and a lack of access to consumer goods. A well-developed agricultural service industry would certainly be one of the most reliable ways to increase agricultural production and raise rural employment. Intensive market penetration would assure high volumes of input supply and output marketing, which would place these goods and services at the disposal of even the smallest farmer, that is, the poorest farmer. Monopolistic profit making would disappear once there is a large, thriving, competitive sector which will try to reach even the smallest farmer, now very often neglected or not reached by the integrated rural development projects, which often benefit larger farmers.

An agricultural development policy such as ADLI could provide the necessary framework for an agriculturally oriented development process which emphasizes food self-sufficiency considerations and poverty elimination. For such a policy to be implemented, the country and the donor community would need to agree on and execute a programme that would:

- Avoid an overvalued exchange rate.
- Adjust effective protection for industrial goods.
- Avoid subsidies and pricing policies which favour larger farmers and cre-

ate instead agricultural input/output price ratios conducive to owner-oriented farm surplus production.
- Keep interest rates sufficiently positive to attract and assure rural savings.
- Keep a balance between urban/rural wage differentials.
- Price infrastructure at true costs to allow for cost recoveries and infrastructural growth.
- Avoid inflation rates inducing capital flight.
- Increase the public budget investment share of agriculture to about 25 per cent of the total.
- Target the ADLI programme to small owner-operated farmers.

Mathematical modelling is now sufficiently advanced for economists to develop acceptable Computable General Equilibrium (CGE) models which would reflect existing base-year conditions on which the specifics of such future alternative development strategies as outlined above could be realistically simulated. This would provide local and donor policy-makers with a view of what the possible sectoral growth, equity, (employment) public revenue and expenditure, and balance of payments implications are of a variety of agricultural and other policies.

To institutionalize such a capability would require a reorientation for ministries of planning, which are often involved in the preparation of medium-term plans, including lists of projects for up to five years in the future. Such plans in practice reduce at best to "shopping lists" for donors, but have otherwise limited impact. The projects are usually too general and too superficially identified and, in many cases, obsolete after some years, to be considered as serious investment proposals.

A more suitable division of labour would be for such ministries to emphasize macro-policy analysis frameworks within which various sector strategies and investment proposals of the technical ministries may be evaluated.

A stop-gap measure would be the organization of working seminars with participating local governments, donor representatives, and concerned UN agencies. The necessary quantitative framework could be provided by the academic community. Various universities have at their disposal well proven computerized general equilibrium models — CGE models — which can create realistically any variety of quantitative scenarios regarding various industrial/agricultural policy adjustment (exchange rates, taxes, etc.). The model would generate quantified scenarios proposed by the participants on a variety of variables selected by them for discussion among them. Through various iterations, this process could lead, eventually, to an impartial consensual macro policy formulation.

Conditions for a successful adoption of ADLI. Assuming that the intersectoral issues raised above would be addressed at the macro national planning level, there looms large the specific agricultural-sector constraints which currently obstruct the successful implementation of ADLI. There is first the question of the availability of a suitable technology which could be easily and quickly absorbed by the farmer; there are the problems of overcoming current institutional constraints and the question of the management of a greatly improved agricultural support industry (the input-output system). There is, above all, the question of finance. Additional investment funds will have to be generated to set the whole system in motion; increased exports may help, but would most likely not suffice. The second half of this article will address these issues and outline alternative solutions in the next issue.

There exists currently in the rural areas a substantial pent-up demand for additional inputs

Issues of agricultural technology. ADLI would require a substantial absorptive capacity of technology to create the rapid and efficient growth required. Given the well-known difficulty development projects have in motivating farmers to adopt new technology, this absorptive capacity is often seriously questioned. In response, one should first consider that there is by now sufficient evidence to indicate that farmers respond positively to new technology, provided the incentives are right. Considering risk and other factors, farmers require substantial safety margins in order to invest in new technology. With a positive macro policy toward agriculture, which would improve on the existing farm cost/benefit ratios, one may expect increased demand for inputs at existing levels of technology. In fact, there are many indications that there exists currently in the rural areas, a substantial pent-up demand for additional inputs and improved marketing services. The post-Second World War succession of projects, in combination with mass communications and rural-urban migration, has familiarized the majority of the farmers, even in the most backward areas, with the benefits of fertilizer, pesticides, and other inputs.

Even with the division of most countries into donor coordinated integrated rural development projects, and the myriad of other donor projects, only a fraction of the small farmers are benefiting from reliable access to extension and related input supply and output marketing facilities. It is a fallacy to think that one or even several successive projects suddenly transform a backward primitive shifting-cultivation agricultural area into a modern, high-tech farming community. The typical project can do just so much; everything takes time. If an IRD project can assist 30-50 per cent of the farming community, it already has accomplished a lot.

The situation generally deteriorates, even for the privileged, when the project is terminated or scaled down, or underfunded or mismanaged, all likely events. In all of these cases, the end result is that the government is unable to maintain the project's standards, and often the situation quickly breaks down to pre-project conditions, including the total breakdown of the project-supported input supply/output servicing.

All this implies a substantial disequilibrium in the agricultural sector, that is, there is a substantial input supply and related servicing absorptive capacity in the short to medium term at existing levels of technology. To continue to generate demand beyond this period would require the generation of a consensual technology, generally accepted by the epistemological society of experts. Given that the introduction of new technology, is, to a very major extent, a donor affair, substantial improvement in donor coordination would be required to reach the point where ADLI could be based on such a consensual technology.

For example, there are very few homogeneous agro-ecological areas for which agronomists agree on a scientific "technical package". Agronomists associated with agricultural investment project identification, preparation, and appraisal are often put in a situation where they simply put together a package based on long-term personal experience, which, while representing the best of the state of the arts, does lead to the situation where recommendations for the technical package vary from one agronomist to another, from one committee of agronomists to another committee, from one organization to another.

Thanks to the creation of the Consultative Group on International Agricultural Research (CGIAR) (a network of internationally financed international research systems and regional research stations; IITA, in Nigeria, ICRISAT in the Niger, and WARDA in Côte d'Ivoire), and other efforts in the Sudan, one may expect improved crop varieties to come along. Already, there have been, for the African continent, Asian rice green-revolution-type breakthroughs in hybrid palm oil in West Africa, cotton in the Sahel, and maize in East Africa. However, in all too many project identification missions, regional research is not always replicated at a national level; and if it is, there are still the applied research experiments to be done for the specific sub-agroecological zone in question, and the on-farm trials.

Summarizing this point, on the donor side, it is not that the multitude of different development experiences and opinions among organizations and within organizations is bad in and of itself. On the contrary, the donor community has benefited from a very rich, very fruitful learning experience. The core of the problem is that very little of this experience is shared; each donor applies only a fraction of what is potentially available. Technology remains too compartmentalized and confined within the learning curve of each actor. There is too little cross fertilization, obstructing severely the rapid development and adoption of new technology for agricultural growth.

GORBACHEV'S NEW POLITICS

SOVIET THIRD WORLD POLICY

FRANCIS FUKUYAMA

Mr. Fukuyama is a senior staff member of the Rand Corporation.

Now that Mikhail Gorbachev has been General Secretary of the Communist Party of the Soviet Union (CPSU) for nearly three years, it is possible to make some judgments about the degree to which his policy toward the Third World differs from that of his predecessors, particularly Leonid Brezhnev. Gorbachev has frequently surprised Western observers by speaking in a very different way about the entire Soviet policy agenda. He has stated on numerous occasions that for him domestic policy has priority over foreign policy, and that to carry out his ambitious domestic reform program, he needs peace and the lowering of international tensions. In the realm of foreign policy, he and his lieutenants have been proclaiming the need for "new political thinking" about problems of international security and global order. The "new political thinking" at this point consists of some concrete changes, notably in Soviet approaches to arms control, and a great deal of rhetoric about the mutuality of security, economic and environmental interdependence, the impermissibility of war in the nuclear era, and the like. In a recent article that was presented as a letter to the Secretary General of the United Nations, Gorbachev touched upon all these themes:

> Objective processes are leading to a situation in which our complex and diverse world is becoming increasingly interrelated and interdependent. It increasingly needs a mechanism that is able to responsibly discuss the world's common problems at a representative level and to be a place of joint search for a balance of the various and contradictory but real interests of today's community of states and nations.

In view of this new rhetoric, has Soviet policy in the Third World changed? I would argue that Gorbachev does have a fairly well-defined Third World policy already in place, a policy whose theoretical justification has been developed systematically in the 1980's, and whose implementation is by now evident. The core of this policy is a shift to the "right" in the traditional language of communism: future initiatives are likely to be directed toward strengthening ties with geopolitically important Third World states, even if they are capitalist-oriented, rather than helping to power self-proclaimed Marxist-Leninist regimes, the "left" policy pursued in the 1970's under Leonid Brezhnev.

Yet, the Soviets will have to deal at the same time with the legacy of the late Brezhnev years, when Moscow made commitments to weak, troubled Marxist-Leninist states like Angola, Afghanistan, and Ethiopia. The shift in Soviet preferences with regard to clients has not thus far meant, and is not likely to mean, the abandonment of allies from the earlier generation; rather, the old list of friends will be overlaid with a new one. Overall Soviet policy in the Third World will therefore seem quite eclectic, with a broadening of Soviet ties to a heterogeneous collection of states around the globe. This type of shift or tactical adjustment is

From *Current*, June 1988, pp. 15-24. Originally from "Patterns of Soviet Third World Policy," by Francis Fukuyama, *Problems of Communism*, September-October 1987. Reprinted by permission.

nothing new in Soviet foreign policy, and in fact represents only the tenth and most recent period in an alternating cycle of left- and right-wing strategies pursued since 1917.

PERIODS OF SOVIET FOREIGN POLICY

Samuel Huntington has recently written that Soviet policy in the Third World has gone through two phases or waves in the postwar period (corresponding to the tenures of Nikita Khrushchev and Brezhnev), interspersed with three periods of American assertiveness. This periodization is correct as far as it goes, but in looking at the entire course of Soviet history, one finds that policy toward the colonial regions and later the Third World has in fact gone through ten shifts, of which Gorbachev's turn to the right is only the most recent.

The defining feature of Soviet policy has been an alternation between what have come to be known as "left-wing" and "right-wing" strategies. The distinction between left and right revolves around the issue of the appropriate choice of allies in the quest for communist power or Soviet influence. In left-wing periods, communist parties have tended to eschew alliances of any sort, concentrating instead on maintaining their internal orthodoxy and discipline. Right-wing periods, by contrast, have been ones of broad alliance between communist parties and other sympathetic noncommunist groups. In the case of the colonial/Third World, these have been local "bourgeois" nationalists, national liberation movements, and other "anti-imperialist" groups.

NATIONALISM

The issue of allying with local nationalist elites has been a subject of contention in Soviet and world communist circles practically since the Bolsheviks came to power in 1917. It was raised explicitly at the Second Comintern Congress in 1920 when a young Indian Marxist, Manabendra Nath Roy, criticized Lenin's draft theses on the national and colonial question. Roy argued that Lenin's general endorsement of national liberation movements led by the middle class in the colonial world would serve only to establish capitalism in these areas and would ultimately lead to a betrayal of communists and the revolution. Roy stated that such groups as the Chinese Kuomintang and the Indian National Congress were inherently untrustworthy and should not be seen as vehicles to advance the interests of world communism.

This tactical debate has never been fully resolved. Indeed, the whole of Soviet foreign policy from 1917 to the present can be seen as an alternation between left-and right-wing policies (see Table 1). Although the labels for many of these periods are drawn from Soviet domestic politics, they correspond to distinctive phases of policy toward the developing world as well. The years immediately following the October Revolution were ones of revolutionary enthusiasm, when Bolshevik leaders hoped for the immediate establishment of communism in Europe, and particularly in defeated Germany. The Bolsheviks sought to undermine the almost universally hostile capitalist states of the West (particularly Great Britain) by promoting colonial revolutions. They staged a Congress of the People of the East in Baku in 1920, creating an infrastructure within the Comintern to control the newly-established communist parties in countries like China and Indonesia, and even organizing an army in Tashkent to invade northern India.

This initial left-wing period, when hopes for instability in the capitalist world and imminent communist revolutions were high, was followed by three more left phases prior to Stalin's death in 1953. During the so-called Third Period from the Sixth Comintern Congress in mid-1928 through the beginning of the Popular Front period in 1935, the Comintern advised local parties to jettison bourgeois nationalist allies in favor of a go-it-alone insurrectionary policy that led to abortive uprisings in China, Indochina, and Brazil. In the brief interlude when the Nazi-Soviet Pact was in effect, from 1939 to 1941, communists in the developing world

Table 1: Ten Periods of Soviet Third World Policy

	Dates	Orientation	Characterization
1.	1917–1921	Left	War Communism
2.	1921–1928	Right	New Economic Policy (NEP)
3.	1928–1935	Left	"Third Period"
4.	1935–1939	Right	Popular Front
5.	1939–1941	Left	Nazi-Soviet Pact
6.	1941–1947	Right	Wartime alliance
7.	1947–1952	Left	Zhdanovshchina
8.	1954–1964	Right	Khrushchev's opening to "bourgeois nationalists"
8a.	1964–1972	Right	Moribund Khrushchevism
9.	1973–1982	Left	Support for Marxist-Leninist vanguard parties
10.	1982–	Right	Andropov-Gorbachev policy

adopted obstructionist tactics to impede the war efforts of their West European colonial masters. Finally, there was the left period associated with the name of Andrey Zhdanov, dating from the founding of the Cominform in September 1947 and lasting approximately to the 19th CPSU Congress in November 1952. With the onset of the cold war, Third World communist parties once again broke with their bourgeois nationalist allies. Acting without broad support, the parties in Indonesia, Malaya, the Philippines, Burma, and India launched bids for power and failed, while the Chinese communists came to power, and the North Koreans invaded the South.

These left-wing periods were interspersed with three right-wing ones in which the Soviets put off hopes for the immediate revolutionary seizure of power by local communist parties and adopted a longer-term strategy of building influence through the cultivation of alliances with noncommunists. The first of these periods of retrenchment is dated in conventional histories on the Comintern from 1924 (after the failure of the uprisings in Germany during the Ruhr crisis), although it actually began in 1921 with the signing of the Anglo-Soviet trade agreement—Moscow's first effort at détente with the West. The Comintern ordered its affiliated parties to form united fronts with the major bourgeois nationalist groups of the day—such as the Chinese Kuomintang, the Indian National Congress, the Sarekat Islam in Indonesia, and the Wafd in Egypt. Later right-wing shifts tended to occur at times when Moscow wanted good relations with the West, and involved the formation of broad alliances with noncommunist groups, as in the Popular Front period in the mid-1930's or when the wartime alliance with the United States and Britain was in effect, 1941–45.

POST-STALIN FLUCTUATIONS

Though this periodization of Soviet foreign policy through 1953 is relatively conventional, fitting the post-Stalin years into the traditional left-right framework may seem strange to many. Nonetheless, these categories are still useful for understanding Soviet foreign policy, at least its policy toward the Third World. Khrushchev and Brezhnev did not use Stalinist terms like "right-wing opportunist," "united front from below," or "class against class," but the issue of whether and how closely to ally with bourgeois nationalists, socialists, and other sympathetic anti-imperialist groups has been and remains to this day a very live and open question. The old Lenin-Roy debate is still being carried on today in a somewhat, but not totally, different vocabulary.

Khrushchev, for example, dramatically expanded Soviet influence in the Third World by adopting what was essentially a right-wing policy of support for "bourgeois nationalist" regimes. Nasser's Egypt, Nehru's India, and Sukarno's Indonesia, the very states that Moscow had spurned as "imperialist lackeys" in the left-wing period after September 1947, figured prominently in his foreign policy initiatives. Like Lenin, who was willing to write off the fledgling Turkish Communist Party in the early 1920's for the sake of smooth relations with Kemal's Turkey, Khrushchev maintained alliances with Nasser of Egypt and Qassem of Iraq even while these leaders were persecuting local communists. The choice for the Soviets was a familiar one: the right-wing policy brought broadly-based Soviet political influence, but at the cost of a significant dilution of local communist strength. Moscow's influence in the Third World grew impressively during this period, but Khrushchev's policies also led to the undertaking of large and poorly thought-out commitments to such countries as Cuba and Egypt.

The period between Khrushchev's ouster in 1964 and the late Brezhnev years—labeled 8a in the table—is difficult to define in left/right categories. Soviet policy was a mixture of caution with regard to revolutionary expectations, and hard-nosed assertion of military power as seen in the Soviet navy's ever broadening deployments and the dispatch of 20,000 air defense troops to Egypt in 1970. This period might be considered one of "moribund Khrushchevism," that is, one of the continuing support for bourgeois nationalists but without Khrushchev's enthusiasm for the project.

In one sense, all Soviet policy since Stalin has been "right-wing," because it has all but abandoned the orthodox but generally weak communist parties, and worked instead almost entirely with "revolutionary democrats." Nevertheless, it can be argued that by the mid-1970's, Soviet policy had moved leftward relative to the Khrushchev era. The exact dating of this turn is more difficult to specify since the break with past policy was not nearly as trenchant as under Stalin: even in his "left-wing" period, Brezhnev continued to support traditional nationalist clients like India, Syria, and Algeria. However, Brezhnev's policy distinctly emphasized support for self-proclaimed Marxist-Leninist national liberation movements or regimes, and made efforts to help them evolve into formal Marxist-Leninist vanguard parties. This shifted the center of gravity of support away from the nationalist governments to the Marxist-Leninist regimes. The same rationale that had motivated earlier Soviet shifts from right to left also motivated Brezhnev. Alliances with the bourgeois nationalists in the 1960's and early 1970's had been disappointing because, from the Soviet perspective, they proved unreliable and insufficiently anti-imperialist. Moscow therefore turned to groups that were, if not necessarily orthodox communist, at least more ideologically sympathetic.

We are currently in a tenth period of Soviet policy, characterized by a classical shift to the right as seen in Moscow's cultivation of large, geopolitically important Third World countries. As did Lenin in the early 1920's, Stalin during the Popular Front period, and Khrushchev in the 1950's, the new Gorbachev leadership has come to recognize that political power lies not with narrowly based Marxist-Leninist groups in the Third World, but with powerful nationalist states such as Mexico, India, and Argentina. Thus, the best strategy for expanding Soviet influence in the world may be the "opportunist" one of allying with the existing national governments, irrespective of their ideological coloration.

THEORETICAL BACKGROUND

The Gorbachev shift in policy must therefore be viewed against the background of the Brezhnev policies and the Soviet reassessment of them. Soviet activism in the Third World in the mid-1970's rested on the belief that Moscow could secure and protect its influence in the Third World by espousing the cause of Marxist-Leninist regimes, helping them to form vanguard parties, and thereby institutionalizing, so to speak, those states' good relations with Moscow. This "second generation" of clients would, the Brezhnev leadership hoped, be less preoccupied with their own nationalist agendas and more willing to collaborate with Moscow than were the "first generation" of postcolonial leaders in the 1950's and 1960's. At the same time, it was hoped that the new clients would become less vulnerable to coups and other political setbacks. In contrast to the arms-length policies pursued in the 1950's and 1960's, the Soviets worked actively together with their Cuban and East German allies in the late Brezhnev years to restructure the internal political systems of countries like South Yemen, Afghanistan, and Ethiopia along orthodox communist lines.

EXPORTING REVOLUTION

However, the project of exporting Soviet political and economic structures to the Third World did not work out well. By the early 1980's, there was a general recognition in the Soviet theoretical literature that earlier hopes for strong clients and lasting influence resulting from the promotion of Marxist-Leninist vanguard party-states were not being realized. Though the new generation of Marxist-Leninist allies willingly cooperated with Moscow both politically and militarily, they themselves were not doing well. They tended to be economically backward, even by Third World standards, and this condition was made worse by the "premature" introduction of such socialist "measures" as collectivization of agriculture and wholesale nationalization of foreign property. Due to their small domestic political base and ideological narrowness, many of these regimes were perceived as illegitimate by sizable segments of their own populations; several, including those in Angola, Mozambique, Afghanistan, Cambodia, and Nicaragua, faced internal guerrilla insurgencies. Rather than having the need for Soviet military and economic assistance taper off when the Marxist-Leninist regimes came to power, in many cases the need for assistance grew substantially over time, to the point of making the Soviet Third World "empire" a non-negligible drain on Soviet resources.

Even though disillusionment with the Marxist-Leninist vanguard party-state became more or less universal among Soviet specialists on the Third World by the mid-1980's, few suggested alternatives to this policy. An important exception was Karen Brutents, a deputy head of the CPSU Central Committee's International Department since the mid-1970's. Initially responsible for the Middle East and Latin America, Brutents has probably held the portfolio for the rest of the Third World as well since the retirement of Rostislav Ul'yanovskiy. Brutents differed from many of his colleagues in never manifesting particular enthusiasm for Marxist-Leninist vanguard parties. Throughout his academic career, he was consistently skeptical about the possibility of building genuinely socialist institutions in backward countries. In a series of articles written in the early 1980's, Brutents argued in favor of shifting Soviet emphasis away from countries that are ideologically correct but small and weak to geopolitically important Third World nations with "objective" anti-imperialist potential, including those that are capitalist-oriented. Even before Brezhnev's death, Brutents pointed out "the solid base for the Soviet Union's growing cooperation with those liberated countries where capitalist relations are developing but which pursue a policy of defending and strengthening national sovereignty in politics and economics." He noted the Soviet Union's growing links with non-Marxist-Leninist countries like India, Brazil, and Mexico, and suggested that it was they and not the socialist oriented Ethiopias, Afghanistans, and Angolas which ought to be the focus of Soviet attention. In 1984, he further amplified this thesis. Pointing to the existence of significant contradictions between many capitalist-oriented Third World states and the West, he observed: "As long as it does not reach the monopolistic stage, even the development of capitalist relations in the liberated countries does not nullify [these contradictions] and does not directly contribute to consolidating the positions of imperialism. . . ."

PRAGMATISM

Although Brutents's views were not in vogue in the late Brezhnev years, his ideas have found a better reception under Gorbachev. The International Department, which succeeded the Comintern as the organization for promoting the world revolutionary process, has traditionally been a home for hard-liners. Such figures as Boris Ponomarev and Ul'yanovskiy were quite sympathetic in the 1970's to a policy of promoting Marxist-Leninist vanguard parties—and relatively insensitive to the effects of such a policy on US-Soviet relations. But Ponomarev, who was an official of the Comintern until its dissolution in 1943 and became head of the International Department soon after its creation, finally retired in February 1986. Later that year, the other deputy responsible for Third World affairs, Ul'yanovskiy (whose career also started in the Comintern in the 1930's) retired. Ponomarev was replaced by Anatoliy Dobrynin, the former ambassador to the United States and a career foreign ministry official whose background and life experience have been very different from his predecessor's.

Another Soviet official who has written about the importance of the non-Marxist-Leninist Third World has been Aleksandr Yakovlev. Yakovlev, who was head of the Institute of the World Economy and International Relations (IMEMO), was promoted by Gorbachev in 1985 to the Propaganda Department in the Secretariat of the CPSU Central Committee. He was made a candidate member of the Politburo at the January 1987 Central Committee plenum and a full member at the June 1987 plenum. He is reportedly one of Gorbachev's closest advisers and the party secretary with main responsibility for implementing the policy of *glasnost'*.

Gorbachev's foreign policy initiatives reflect Yakovlev's thinking in many ways. The latter's interest in the major states of the Third World evolved while at IMEMO, which concerns itself with the overall strategy of Soviet foreign policy. IMEMO has argued that there are numerous intercapitalist contradictions of which the Soviet Union can take advantage. Rather than focusing narrowly on US-Soviet relations, as was often done while Andrey Gromyko was foreign minister, Yakovlev has suggested a multipolar strategy through which the Soviet Union could broaden its range of contacts and cultivate important capitalist allies of the United States in Western Europe and Asia. During Gorbachev's first two years as General Secretary, there has in fact been considerable diplomatic engagement with states like France and West Germany, and Foreign Minister Eduard Shevardnadze has visited Tokyo, something not done by Gromyko since the mid-1970's. The Soviet Union has also launched several initiatives aimed at improving Sino-Soviet relations, among them Gorbachev's major address on Asian security delivered in Vladivostok in July 1986.

Yakovlev's general thinking led him to espouse the same policy toward the Third World as does Brutents. In a recent article, Yakovlev stated:

> Among the consequences engendered by the operation of the law of unevenness in our age is the appearance of sufficiently strong young national capitalist states—the "newly industrializing countries"—which are at the same time both the object and agent of economic expansion. They—for instance, Brazil, Argentina, and Mexico—have their own monopolistic groups, in certain cases capable of entering the struggle against the "old" industrial empires. . . . One must suppose that in the historically foreseeable future, the centrifugal trend—toward the growth of interimperialist contradictions and the further splintering of the centripetal capitalist world of the postwar decades—will actively resist the centripetal forces.

Yakovlev and Brutents in effect favor a return to a Khrushchev-like policy of cultivating ties with important Third World states and de-emphasizing implicitly support for states ruled by Marxist-Leninist vanguard parties.

The approach received official sanction in the new party program adopted at the 27th CPSU Congress in February 1986. The program states:

> The practice of the USSR's relations with the liberated countries has shown that there are also real grounds for cooperation with young states that are traveling the capitalist road. These grounds include a common interest in the preservation of peace, the strengthening of international security, and the termination of the arms race. They include the sharpening contradiction between the interests of the peoples and the imperialist policy of *diktat* and expansion. They include the understanding by the young states of the fact that political and economic ties with the Soviet Union facilitate the strengthening of their independence.

Clearly, therefore, the Soviet Union ought to be neither inattentive to the Third World nor accommodating to American and Western interests; rather, it should anticipate and take advantage of the "contradictions" between the West and the newly industrializing countries. Interestingly, the party program devotes only one brief paragraph to the socialist-oriented countries—the very same self-proclaimed Marxist-Leninist regimes that had been ritualistically celebrated in earlier pronouncements by Leonid Brezhnev.

IMPLEMENTATION OF THE NEW LINE

Moscow's new emphasis on large, geopolitically important states appears therefore to be a carefully thought-out policy direction and certainly one of the most clearly heralded. By now, the practical implications of the policy are evident in a variety of regions around the world, nowhere more so than in India. India, of course, has been favored by the Soviets since the mid-1950's, but under Gorbachev, India has received by far the greatest amount of Soviet attention; it was the only country of the Third World, besides Afghanistan, to be specifically referred to in Gorbachev's address to the 27th party congress in 1986. Rajiv Gandhi visited Moscow in May 1985 as one of Gorbachev's first foreign guests, and Gorbachev returned the visit in late November 1986; this visit was his first to a Third World or Asian country. Gorbachev clearly views India as the centerpiece of his policy toward the developing world. In his address to the Indian parliament, he said:

> To me personally, it is quite obvious that much of what we call new political thinking manifested itself internationally for the first time in relations between the Soviet Union and India. And the fact that differences of sociopolitical system and ideology and our national, cultural, and other distinctions have not hampered our dialogue is extremely important as a guiding example for others.

Since the visit, Soviet leaders speaking in other Third World countries have repeatedly referred to Soviet-Indian relations as a kind of "model" for Moscow's ties with developing countries.

In the course of these meetings, the Soviet Union and India agreed to a series of wide-ranging economic and military interactions, including Soviet credits equivalent to US$1.4 billion in May 1985, a four-year trade agreement in November 1985 and another one in November 1986, and an agreement announced in July 1986 under which India would manufacture MiG—29 aircraft. This is not to suggest that the Soviet-Indian alliance has been without problems. The Soviets have had a difficult time balancing their bilateral trade with India, in view of declining Indian demand for Soviet machinery and the drop in world oil prices that began in the mid-1980's. But the Soviet Union has remained the largest customer for Indian exports while India is one of the biggest buyers of Soviet arms.

BUILDING BRIDGES

India is not the only Third World country on Gorbachev's agenda. In October 1986, Soviet Foreign Minister Shevardnadze visited Mexico City. Shortly thereafter, the Soviets announced plans for the General Secretary to visit Mexico, Brazil, Argentina, and Uruguay, the very countries cited by Brutents and Yakovlev as targets for Soviet diplomacy, sometime in 1987. The Mexican Foreign Minister Bernado Sepulveda Amor was given a lavish reception in Moscow in early May 1987. He was received by Gorbachev personally, even as the Libyan foreign minister was allowed to pass through Moscow with relatively little fanfare. The Mexicans have endorsed various Soviet international positions on Central America and on the total elimination of nuclear weapons. Although Gorbachev's visit to South America was delayed by other more pressing matters, Shevardnadze, in late September 1987 journeyed to Brazil, Argentina, and Uruguay.

Evidence abounds of heightened Soviet interest during the past three years in the capitalist-oriented parts of the Third World. The area in which the Soviet Union has undertaken the most visible initiatives is the Middle East. Moscow established diplomatic relations with Oman and the United Arab Emirates in September and November 1985 respectively. Although the process of normalizing ties with the conservative states of the Persian Gulf was set back temporarily by the January 1986 civil war in South Yemen, the Saudi oil minister visited Moscow in early 1987, and rumors persist that the establishment of Soviet-Saudi diplomatic relations is imminent. In March, Moscow promptly rescheduled a large tranche of debt to Egypt which was to come due later in the year, inviting comparisons between Soviet generosity and the behavior of Egypt's Western creditors like the United States and the International Monetary Fund, which have pressed Egypt for various internal reforms. The Soviet Union has been edging closer to reopening ties with the predominant military power in the Middle East, Israel, as well. The first official contact was made in Helsinki in August 1986. In April 1987, Gorbachev made the pointed assertion in a dinner for Syrian President Hafez al-Assad that the absence of diplomatic relations between Israel and the USSR "cannot be considered normal," and a Soviet consular delegation arrived in Jerusalem in July.

Moscow's most remarkable initiative, however, came in the Persian Gulf in the summer of 1987. The Soviets promptly responded to Kuwait's request to protect its tankers threatened by Iran in May 1987 by agreeing to permit Kuwait to charter three Soviet-flagged tankers to transport its oil. But Soviet diplomacy was low-key and nonconfrontational and sought to maintain its balance between Iran and Iraq. Moscow was also able to capitalize on the American heavy-handed response to the Gulf situation which included tilting fairly openly toward Iraq and sending a large naval task force into the Gulf in answer to a parallel request from Kuwait for protection of its tankers. While continuing to support Iraq with weapons and voting in favor of UN Security Council Resolution 598 urging a ceasefire in the tanker war, the Soviets kept their bridges open to Tehran by not supporting a second resolution, mandating sanctions against Iran. The Iranians, not wanting to be isolated from both superpowers simultaneously, invited Soviet Deputy Foreign Minister Yuliy Vorontsov to Tehran in June, August, and October. In the course of these visits, the two sides discussed a number of economic projects including a new oil pipeline and a railroad link with the USSR. Moscow was thus not only able to meet the Kuwaiti request for reflagging, but to use the opening as leverage to actually *improve* relations with Tehran at the same time. Should Iran and Iraq for their own reasons decide to settle the conflict, Moscow will be in a very good position to play the role of mediator.

The USSR has also been very active in building bridges to members of the Association of Southeast Asian Nations (ASEAN), despite Soviet commitments to Vietnam. There has been an upsurge in bilateral visits between Soviet officials and their counterparts in Malaysia, Indonesia, and Thailand. Indonesia's economics minister Ali Wardhana visited Moscow in October 1984; in July 1985, Anatoliy Zaytsev, in charge of the Soviet Foreign Ministry's Southeast Asia bureau, headed the first of several Soviet delegations that have visited Bangkok; and Yakov Ryabov, a deputy prime minister, visited Kuala Lumpur in November 1985. The Soviets have been expanding economic ties and have tried to capitalize on the ASEAN trade disputes with the United States and on fears of the People's Republic of China. In early March 1987, Shevardnadze made a visit to Australia and Indonesia, and the foreign ministers of Thailand and Malaysia were hosted at the Kremlin later in the year.

In contrast, Moscow's treatment of some of the Third World communist states has been less diplomatic. For example, the speech given by Yegor Ligachev at the 6th Congress of the Communist Party of Vietnam in Hanoi can only be described as brutally frank. This party congress, held in December 1986, was marked by a remarkable degree of self-criticism on the part of the Vietnamese themselves; nonetheless, Ligachev said that the Vietnamese party:

> . . . is concentrating the attention of communists on existing problems, boldly revealing the miscalculations that have been committed, and restructuring its organizational and cadre work in accordance with the requirements of transformations in the socioeconomic sphere. All its activity is taking place in an atmosphere of responsible criticism and self-criticism and of observance of the principle of looking the truth in the face. This is characteristic of a truly Marxist-Leninist party. V. I. Lenin used to say that "the party of the revolutionary proletariat which is strong enough to criticize itself openly can call error and weakness by their names without beating around the bush."

There have been considerable recriminations between Moscow and Hanoi in recent years over the latter's mismanagement of the Vietnamese economy and the squandering of the annual Soviet subsidy valued at US$1–2 billion. However, the Soviets have not cut their subsidy but have raised it by approximately 50 percent over the next five years. Nonetheless, the Soviets are clearly unhappy with the performance of the Vietnamese economy and the costs of aiding it.

A comparison of India and Vietnam is instructive when trying to understand the motives for Moscow's right-wing shift, because the two are in many ways respectively prototypes of the "bourgeois nationalist" and the Marxist-Leninist state. Moscow's interest in Vietnam is obvious: the latter has provided concrete payoffs in the form of basing rights at Danang and Cam Ranh Bay, and serves as an ally and counterweight to the People's Republic of China. Vietnam is, moreover, officially classified as a "socialist" country by the Soviets, and therefore of special ideological significance; it and Cuba are the only two Third World countries that are full members of the Council for Economic Mutual Assistance.

The benefits offered by India are much less tangible. India has consistently refused basing rights to Moscow and is almost certain to do so for the foreseeable future. Although nonaligned and reasonably anti-Chinese, India has proven over the years to be fully independent of Moscow in its political and economic dealings with the outside world. Nonetheless, for the Soviet Union, India has advantages over Vietnam in several respects. First, bilateral Soviet-Indian trade is quite considerable and does not represent a disguised Soviet subsidy like Moscow's trade with many Marxist-Leninist countries, including Vietnam. In return for military technology and industrial machinery the USSR imports substantial quantities of Indian textiles and consumer goods.

Second, India is highly influential in the Non-Aligned Movement. While Vietnam has totally isolated itself from ASEAN and the rest of Asia by its militaristic policies in Cambodia and elsewhere, India remains in very good standing with most of the Third World.

Third, there is tremendous stability to the Soviet-Indian relationship. Moscow's ties with New Delhi have lasted now for well over 30 years. Moscow can be confident that the Indian government is unlikely to be overthrown by a coup or displaced by a guerrilla movement.

Fourth, India can be relied upon to take the Soviet side on numerous East-West issues, including the Strategic Defense Initiative (SDI) and arms control, and to exercise a certain moral suasion supportive of Soviet positions in such forums as the United Nations. Vietnam, of course, takes pro-Soviet positions as well, but carries very little weight in the international community. India, moreover, can be anti-American and anti-Chinese without embroiling Moscow in dangerous conflicts with either of those powers.

Finally, there are specific political issues on

which Moscow hopes to gain Indian good will, particularly Afghanistan and Cambodia. It is important to bear in mind that India is in a position to help the Soviets solve problems; it is not a source of problems as the Marxist-Leninist regimes of Vietnam or Afghanistan are.

Although Soviet-Indian relations are by far the best-developed, Moscow can hope to achieve similar relationships by cultivating better ties with Mexico, Brazil, and Argentina. Bilateral trade with Argentina is already substantial (though largely one-way). Moreover, Moscow can hope to develop its influential friends among these large Latin American countries without having to subsidize yet another faltering economy or risk a confrontation with the United States.

It should be noted that the Soviet emphasis on big Third World states should not be regarded as evidence of a passive Soviet policy. The policy envisioned by Brutents and Yakovlev is in fact a very active one that seeks to build new and, in some instances, stronger ties with states that have grievances against the United States and the West—indeed, to play upon those grievances and to exacerbate them where possible. At the same time, the nature of Moscow's relationships with these countries will tend to be political and economic rather than military. The Soviets will make greater efforts to line up these influential developing states behind Soviet positions, and expand bilateral economic links, particularly in raw materials and intermediate technologies.

The new Soviet policy at this point consists largely of statements of purpose and of a series of accomplished or planned visits by Soviet officials. Nonetheless, the level of Soviet diplomatic activity during the thirty-plus months of the Gorbachev administration is impressive and suggests that further, more dramatic initiatives can be expected.

THE OLD AGENDA

Moscow's new initiatives have not canceled its commitments to the clients acquired in the Brezhnev years, including the self-proclaimed Marxist-Leninist states. Although these commitments may seem onerous as Soviet economic managers start casting about for investment funds, they are hardly heavy enough to justify taking the political risk of outright retreat in countries where Moscow has become significantly involved. Thus, the old agenda is still very much a part of Soviet Third World policy, and Moscow dedicates ever-increasing sums of money to established clients. As noted above, despite Ligachev's criticism of Vietnamese management, the Soviet Union increased its subsidy to Hanoi. Syria reportedly had its approximately $15 billion debt rescheduled during a visit by Hafez al-Assad to Moscow in April 1987, in addition to receiving commitments for supply of more advanced weapons. Nicaragua and Libya have both received new commitments for arms supplies during Gorbachev's tenure as General Secretary, the latter getting SA–5 long-range missiles in December 1985. These missiles were fired at US aircraft in the Gulf of Sidra in March 1986, thereby touching off the sequence of events leading to the US retaliatory raid on Tripoli the following month. The Soviets and Cubans helped to organize the third major yearly offensive in Angola against Jonas Savimbi's UNITA in the spring of 1987, based on substantial promises of military aid made in 1983–84. There are also reports that the USSR is again providing Mozambique with counterinsurgency aid.

Soviet behavior in Afghanistan should provide a good test of how far-reaching the changes in Soviet Third World policy are. There is accumulating evidence of growing disenchantment with the occupation of Afghanistan on the part of both the public at large and Soviet elites. Certainly there have been various kinds of negative social consequences. On the military front, the provision of qualitatively better US military assistance to the Afghan mujahedin, including portable Stinger anti-aircraft missiles, has caused the rate of Soviet equipment losses to go up considerably over the past year and one-half. The Soviets have repeatedly stated their intention to withdraw and have dropped many hints privately that they are prepared to do so imminently, provided they can find an appropriate face-saving formula to mask their abandonment of the People's Democratic Party of Afghanistan (PDPA). Notwithstanding these hints, the much-touted withdrawal of six regiments announced in Gorbachev's Vladivostok speech in July 1986, and the unilateral ceasefire undertaken by the PDPA regime in December of that year, there is as yet no real indication that the Soviets are prepared to withdraw. Indeed, Soviet military operations have increased substantially in scope and effectiveness with each summer offensive. The frequency and violence of Afghan Air Force cross-border attacks into Pakistan also increased early in 1987.

Finally, the Soviet collective security system has continued to grow. The most recent self-proclaimed Marxist-Leninist state to sign a Declaration of Friendship and Cooperation with Moscow was Benin. Mathieu Kerekou, the chairman of Benin's People's Revolutionary Party, journeyed to Moscow for the signing in November 1986. It seems that the traditional agenda is not being jettisoned, especially when it can be executed with low visibility and few costs. There have been persistent reports of Soviet deliveries of money and weapons to the communists in both the Philippines and Chile. Soviet support for the New People's Army in the Philippines, which evidently began in 1984–85, has been disguised by using middlemen such as the Vietnamese.

CONCLUSION AND PROJECTIONS

CHARACTERISTICS

The manner in which Moscow is implementing its policy toward the Third World under Gorbachev points to several characteristics of Soviet foreign policy in general. The first is the striking continuity of tactical issues facing Kremlin leaders. In this, the tenth phase of Soviet foreign policy, the Brutentses and Yakovlevs echo their counterparts in the Stalins and Bukharins of the 1920's. Similarly, those in the International Department who advocated support of Marxist-Leninist vanguard parties in the 1970's repeated many of the arguments of such early leftists as M. N. Roy, Georgiy Dimitrov, or even Lev Trotskiy. Soviet policy toward the developing world has thus had a cyclical character, with the shortcomings of one line inclining Soviet leaders to try the opposite. Just as Soviet experiences with Chiang Kai-shek and Kemal Atatürk in the 1920's led them to espouse the likes of Li Li-san or Qu Qiu-bai during the "Third Period," so the Brezhnev leadership sought to replace the Sadats and Siad Barres of the 1970's with such leaders as Abd al-Fattah Ismail and Mengistu Haile Mariam. Both left-and right-wing policies have advantages and defects, and neither can totally satisfy Soviet policy requirements for both influence and reliability. Hence the constant reappearance of the same tactical issue.

The second characteristic is that the role of ideology in defining Soviet foreign policy objectives and in providing political instruments for expansion has been steadily declining in the postwar period. The changes already brought about by Gorbachev have further accelerated that decline. Whatever the real-world implications of the "new political thinking," the old ideological language of Marxism-Leninism and vanguard parties is now seldom heard, and those who use that idiom seem strangely out of place in the current milieu.

The third characteristic of Soviet foreign policy that has special bearing for the Third World is that Moscow no longer has at its disposal a world communist movement through which it can work and to which it can give orders with a reasonable expectation of compliance. The Soviet leadership cannot announce a single "line" applicable to all parts of the world as it did earlier through the Comintern and the Cominform. The Third World Marxist-Leninists are dealt with almost entirely separately from the European communists. Simply stated, the Soviet Union does not have the option of issuing and enforcing a single line because international communism has not recovered and is unlikely to recover from the splits with Yugoslavia in the 1940's and with China in the 1950's and 1960's. Furthermore, the loyalty of some recently acquired allies is rather suspect; even such seemingly close allies as Vietnam cooperate with Moscow on the basis of political calculation rather than fealty to the socialist "homeland." Third World Marxist-Leninists are also a rather weak group. Only Cuba and Vietnam are ruled by "orthodox" communist parties and hence qualify as genuine socialist countries in Soviet eyes. The groups governing such countries as Angola, Ethiopia, and Afghanistan are but pale imitations of the Chinese or Indonesian communist parties of the 1920's and 1930's, being at a much more primitive level in terms of both party organization and ideological self-understanding.

DOMESTIC LIMITATIONS

In addition to these external constraints on Moscow's implementation of Third World policy, there are domestic limitations to a full-scale commitment to and implementation of the principles of the tenth period. Primary among these are the ingrained attitudes found in the military and such party bodies as the International Department, which militate against accepting a new agenda. While the departure of Ponomarev and Ul'yanovskiy from the International Department and the events surrounding the firing of Defense Minister Sergey Sokolov and Air Defense Minister Aleksandr Koldunov suggest some diminution of these forces, there are still powerful groups devoted to the old agenda. The internal institutional drama is far from being played out.

Finally, the continued tenure of Gorbachev and the vitality of his economic reform program are necessary for the effectiveness of the right-wing shift. Without an economic revitalization of the Soviet Union, it is difficult to see how its relations with such countries as Mexico and Brazil or the ASEAN states could develop very far. Military goods and services remain the Soviet Union's area of comparative advantage in competing with the West for the favor of Third World countries. But the large and relatively stable newly industrializing countries do not need the package of internal and external security assistance offered by the Soviet Union and its bloc allies. Indeed, Brazil competes with Moscow in selling arms to Third World countries. In the absence of a much more thoroughgoing internal economic reform, the Soviets will remain relatively poor at offering technology, markets, and other economic benefits. Furthermore, the Soviet leadership seems to have decided against offering substantial quantities of economic assistance.

Moscow's relations with New Delhi or Buenos Aires will therefore never become as close as its ties with Vietnam or Angola.

All of this indicates that disappointment with the new policy must inevitably set in. The question remains, then, whether there will be calls for a return to greater ideological orthodoxy and support for self-proclaimed Marxist-Leninists. Will there be a return to Soviet interventionism in the Third World in the manner of the late Brezhnev period? In sum, will there be a swing back to the left in the next, the eleventh, phase of Soviet policy toward the Third World? Of one thing we can be relatively sure: the Soviet Union is likely to remain an expansionist power with far-flung military and political interests all over the Third World. Indeed, the Brutents-Yakovlev strategy of Soviet policy is also expansionist and hostile to American interests. But the rationale for this expansionism is likely to become less ideological. The Soviet Union will still seek influence and will still worry about its prestige and commitments, but more in the name of protecting its interests as a great power than as the carrier of a messianic, universal ideology.

People, Power, and Leadership

Third World leaders have much in common with the leaders of the industrialized world, yet some facets of their jobs are unique. Unlike most Western heads of state, many leaders of developing nations face persistent attacks on their legitimacy—that is, they lack a popular mandate or broad-based support. Some leaders seized power, others manipulated the election process, others intimidated the electorate, and still others prohibited, harassed, or imprisoned rival candidates. In many cases, this was accomplished through force or threat of force, thereby denying the voters a meaningful say in the selection of their leaders.

Unit 2

Additionally, most Third World leaders face severe social, political, and economic problems, and are forced to manage with extremely limited resources. Indeed, widespread poverty and illiteracy, coupled with the lack of a viable industrial base and few economic alternatives, compound their problems and make it difficult, if not impossible, to solve them.

Furthermore, leaders in the developing world confront myriad cultural, religious, and ethnic problems that undermine national unity and jeopardize the success of official policy. In these countries, the leaders are forced to walk a delicate line between opposing groups, wary of initiating any action that could trigger a major social explosion. Many of these leaders are compelled to share power—both formal and informal—with sundry other figures, many of whom have vastly different perspectives.

Moreover, many Third World leaders face numerous institutional problems, such as the lack of a clearly defined political infrastructure and an unresponsive bureaucracy, plagued by divisive partisan wrangling, pervasive corruption, undefined rules and procedures, and contempt for democratic rights. As a result, these heads of state, however well-meaning, lack the ability to implement their agendas.

Frequently, Third World leaders are also prisoners of the policies and practices of the superpowers and are helpless to steer an independent course. Indeed, in some instances, they function as satellites; their rhetoric and actions must reflect the goals and objectives of those nations upon which they depend for political, economic, and military support. Clearly, these leaders are prevented from formulating policy, expressing dissent, or establishing alliances that may be in the best interests of their peoples.

Obviously, heads of state in the developing world are extremely limited in their ability to solve such pressing problems as hunger, poverty, illiteracy, disease, pollution, and war. They know that they will inevitably arouse both internal and external opposition if they adopt a policy that threatens the ruling elite or a major ally, whose support they need to maintain their position. Thus, many Third World leaders are forced to operate in an untenable situation, one that precludes autonomy and independence.

Somewhat paradoxically, many Third World peoples expect more from their leaders, while denying them the authority and flexibility they require to perform their duties. In many developing nations, the people expect their leaders to produce instant results, even when objective reality would appear to make such changes impossible. When the new leader fails to produce the desired "miracles," he or she quickly becomes the object of derision and scorn—the target of a potential purge, coup, or revolution. Clearly, winning office is only part of the problem, perhaps the easiest part. Far more difficult is the challenge of governing a Third World nation.

Looking Ahead: Challenge Questions

What are the main problems of leadership succession in the Third World?

What conditions are most likely to lead to the demise of authoritarian regimes?

How valid is President Mobutu Sese Seko's defense of Zaire's one-party system?

To what extent, if any, does fostering a "cult of personality" help or hurt Third World development?

Would the passage of the Dellums' bill lead to major reforms in Zaire?

In what sense, if any, does Jonas Savimbi's UNITA represent a clear example of the Reagan doctrine?

How valid is Savimbi's defense of South African assistance?

What special problems does a guerrilla organization, like UNITA, face in fighting a war against an established government?

According to President Ferdinand Marcos, what role, if any, did he play in the Aquino assassination?

How do the Marcoses justify their wealth and extravagance?

Does Marcos appear to understand the reasons for his fall from power?

When Leaders Fall: Succession Systems in the Non-Industrialized World

Michael Nacht

Michael Nacht is the Dean of the School of Public Affairs at the University of Maryland. Author of The Age of Vulnerability: Threats to the Nuclear Stalemate *(Brookings, 1985), he is currently editing a volume on forceful regime change in developing countries.*

The problem of leadership succession in the non-industrialized world is among the most vexing issues facing both students of political development and the policy-making community. Despite the considerable efforts of many leading scholars over a sustained period of several decades, there is no single coherent theory that provides a persuasive explanation for the dominant causes of leadership change in developing countries. In the absence of a theoretical or conceptual framework, much policy-making in the United States and elsewhere concerning the nature of regime change and regime stability is understandably guided more by *ad hoc* predilections than by evidence and analysis.

Consider first the nature of the overall problem. According to reasonably reliable statistics (see for example the annual *World Development Report* published by the World Bank), there are 128 nation-states with populations in excess of one million (this includes all UN and World Bank members; additionally, there are thirty-four nations with populations of less than one million that are UN and World Bank members). Of these 128 states, the Soviet Union and seven others are classified as "East European non-market economies;" each is ruled by its respective communist party whose leaders have, without exception, selected the general secretary of the party who is the *de facto* head of state and head of government. Nineteen states are classified as "industrial market economies," ranging in gross national product (GNP) per capita from Spain and Ireland (less than $5,000) to the United States and Switzerland (greater than $15,000). Each of these states has a democratic political system with regularized and legitimized forms of political succession that are determined at the ballot box. This leaves 101 countries, almost all of which are located in Asia, Africa, and Latin America. Thirty-six are classified as "low-income economies" (GNP per capita less than $400); forty are "middle-income economies" (between $450 and $1700); and five are "high-income oil exporters," all located in the Middle East/Persian Gulf region.

The low-income group includes a few communist or "totalitarian" regimes (e.g., Vietnam, Kampuchea, China) and one democracy (India); all others are "authoritarian" regimes led by civilian or military leaders who remain in power until they are forced out by others, unguided by any form of legitimized political succession process. The middle-income group includes communist regimes in the Democratic Republic of Yemen, Nicaragua, Angola, Cuba, North Korea, and Mongolia; and democratic governments in the Philippines, El Salvador (arguably), Jamaica, Colombia, and Costa Rica. Virtually all the others are ruled by an authoritarian form of government. Among the upper-middle-income countries there is one communist regime (Yugoslavia), and democracies of various forms in Brazil, Portugal, Uruguay, Mexico, Venezuela, Argentina, Greece, and Israel. Finally, all five of the high-income oil exporters are authoritarian.

Although there are many cross-currents running through these data, there is one central tendency: the richer the group of nations, the greater the percentage of democratic regimes (with the exception of the five high-income oil exporters). The vast majority of the states in Asia and Africa as well as many in Latin America are ruled by authoritarian regimes.

In overall perspective, there is a second general pattern: regimes of particular types are succeeded most often by regimes of the same type. This pattern is most pronounced among totalitarian regimes: no communist government, once having seized power, has ever relinquished authority to a non-communist regime. With only slightly less consistency (the Turkish *coup d'etat* in 1980, for example),

From *Harvard International Review,* February/March 1988, pp. 6-7, 31. Reprinted by permission.

Democracies and totalitarian regimes tend to be more stable than authoritarian ones.

democracies also tend to perpetuate themselves. Authoritarian regimes exhibit the least consistency in terms of political succession. Some, such as Bolivia, have experienced a consistent pattern over many decades of one authoritarian regime replaced by another. What is striking since 1970, however, is the number of authoritarian regimes that have either been replaced by communist systems (e.g. Vietnam, Cambodia, Nicaragua, Angola) or have shifted to democratic systems (Philippines, Greece, Spain, Portugal, Brazil, Argentina, and several other South American states). South Korea now appears to be ready to join the group of states to make the transition from authoritarianism to democracy.

What leads to the demise of authoritarian regimes? There appear to be several indicators of difficulty. These include:

A protracted economic downturn after extensive economic improvement: If a nation has only known deep poverty, then poverty *per se* may not be a grievance against the regime. Extensive economic improvement, however, generates significant changes in expectations among the populace. A protracted economic downturn then stimulates intense disillusionment that is often channelled into a commitment to forceful regime change.

Ideology of opposition: Different societies have different expectations as to what is acceptable in terms of regime behavior. In the case of the Shah of Iran, for example, he was hounded because of his blatant irreligiosity and the fact that he was thought to have been installed by the Central Intelligence Agency. The central grievances against Marcos of the Phillippines were, first, the belief that a return to democracy in a country that had previously experienced it was not feasible under his rule, and, second, that the levels of corruption had exceeded the accepted norms of Philippine society.

The state of civil-military relations: In most cases a regime change cannot be effected in an authoritarian system without the support of the uniformed military who have the weapons to determine the success or failure of the change. Senior military officials less often promote change because they are usually part of the ruling elite and enjoy the benefits of their position. What is crucial, therefore, are the political allegiances of the second- and third-echelon military who do not share in the material rewards offered by the regime. In the Philippines, for example, the opposition of recent military academy graduates to the Marcos regime and to the "overstaying generals" was a key ingredient in the regime's demise.

Relative attitudes toward corruption and repression: In the vast majority of non-industrialized countries there is extensive corruption (perversion of behavior for private gain) and repression (removal of political opponents). Their presence thus tells us little about regime stability. What is more significant is the rate of change of these characteristics and whether they reach levels that are unacceptable based upon the norms of the society.

The role of external actors as agents of change: In the modern world virtually no nation lives in isolation from the world community. Great powers such as the United States and the Soviet Union as well as regional powers such as

France and China sometimes adopt explicit policies of military and economic aid to foster regime change or to forestall it. Sometimes the suspension of economic assistance by the World Bank or the International Monetary Fund can have profoundly destabilizing effects on a politically fragile regime in the non-industrialized world. This, for example, was the case in Cuba in 1958.

The issue of corruption is especially relevant both to regime change and to the stability of the successor regime. Recent research has revealed that several common assertions concerning corruption are false: that corruption always tends to destabilize regimes; that corruption alone can induce a forceful regime change; and that there is no corruption in socialist countries. What has been found is that corruption needs to be disaggregated into a number of discrete aspects to assess its effect on political stability. These include answers to the following questions:

- Has the scale of corruption deviated significantly from accepted norms?
- Are powerful rivals to the regime excluded from the rewards of corruption?
- Are military officers other than the top leadership excluded from the rewards of corruption?
- Do groups excluded from the rewards of corruption reflect deep social, ethnic, or geographic cleavages in the society?
- Is the overall economic condition perceived as being severely damaged because of corrupt practices?
- Have the rewards of corruption been reduced in the face of a major economic downturn?
- Has corruption undermined the ability of the armed forces to protect the nation from threats to its security?
- Has corruption undermined external support for the regime?
- Has criticism of corruption stimulated increased repression by the regime against these critics and other groups?
- Is corruption a rallying cry for opposition groups?
- Is the leadership vulnerable to the criticism that its corrupt practices are antithetical to the moral basis of its authority?
- Has a catalytic event (e.g., a political assassination, a major natural disaster) exacerbated corruption or its effects?
- Does the pervasiveness of corruption increase at higher levels of the power structure?
- Are the demands of pressure groups for material rewards not being satisfied by corrupt practices?
- Is the elite too large to be fully rewarded through corrupt practices?

By systematically addressing these questions, one can assess the extent to which corruption would tend to stabilize or destabilize a regime. In the case where corruption is a major grievance against the regime, the successor regime would be expected to remedy these conditions. If the new leadership in turn is found to adopt similar practices, it would also be vulnerable to the same criticism. The Aquino regime, for example, swept into power on the promise of restoring democracy, improving the economy, dealing with the insurgency, and reducing corruption. Subsequent difficulties experienced by the regime have related to the inability to address the second and third conditions effectively. If, in addition, it is found that extensive corruption is practised at the highest levels, then this regime could meet the fate of its predecessor. In South Korea, on the other hand, corruption has not been a central grievance. The absence of democratic reform has been the principal rallying cry. Corruption is only likely to surface as a major issue if the successor to President Chun suspends democratic practices or deals ineffectively with economic or national security issues.

These considerations lead to the following overall conclusions:

- A system of leadership succession is greatly influenced by the political history of the society. A nation with a totalitarian or democratic system is likely to have established institutional, legal, and coercive safeguards to ensure that successor regimes maintain the same type of political system. Authoritarian regimes are more vulnerable to systemic change because of the lack of institutionalization and political legitimacy of the current system.
- A particular system of leadership succession is likely to be sustained if the successor regime redresses the central grievances that brought about the original regime change.
- Ideology and the national experience are pivotal factors in establishing the process of political succession. Societies that have experienced democratic procedures, that practise economic pluralism, or that have well-developed economies, are more likely to turn toward democratic modes of political succession. □

Mobutu Sese Seko: "I Have a Clear Conscience"

Jeffrey M. Elliot and Mervyn M. Dymally

Sitting astride Africa's mid-section and bordering nine other countries, Zaire has an importance that is both strategic and symbolic. Its size – roughly equal to the United States east of the Mississippi River – its rich natural resources and its firmly pro-Western policies have ensured continuous financial and political backing from western Europe and North America.

But enthusiasm for that support has recently been tempered by questions about the nature of Zaire's government. The conservative Washington, D.C.-based Heritage Foundation says Zaire "is one of America's most consistent allies in Africa" but calls President Mobutu Sese Seko a "corrupt Third World strongman."

Mounting criticism of continuing U.S. aid to Zaire recently prompted Representative Mervyn Dymally (D-CA.), who currently chairs the Congressional Black Caucus, and Dr. Jeffrey M. Elliot, a writer and political scientist from North Carolina Central University who advises Dymally on foreign affairs, to visit Zaire, where they spent ten days traveling with Mobutu. For the third installment in our series on Zaire, we present the following excerpts from their conversations.

JEFFREY M. ELLIOT: According to Amnesty International, your government has, over the past two decades, either ordered, approved, or condoned myriad human rights violations, including detention without charge or trial, imprisonment of political opponents, torture and ill treatment of prisoners, extrajudicial executions, and illegal surveillance and extortion. How can you justify such flagrant abuses?

MOBUTU SESE SEKO: First, let me say, I appreciate your candor. I can say, however, without equivocation, that I have a clear conscience. Most political outsiders view human rights in the context of a multi-party system. They demand that I institute such a system, which I refuse to do. Africa's history and traditions will not permit a two-party system. Nowhere in this continent have there been two chiefs in one village: a majority chief and an opposition chief. Dating back to ancestral times, there has been only one chief. In the United States and Europe, it is commonly accepted that enlightenment emanates from the clash of ideas. In Africa, we follow an ancestral policy in which, when a problem arises, we rally around the leader and work out a solution. Zaire is a shining example of this policy in action. For this reason, we have become the most stable country in Africa.

President Mobutu Sese Seko Jeffrey Elliot

In Zaire, freedom of expression, which is guaranteed by the Constitution, is respected. During my tenure as president, I have struggled hard to restore peace, unity and security. My efforts are based on a firm belief in human rights. To demonstrate my commitment, and to quash the baseless charges against my country, I established a high-level department on human rights, which reports directly to me. You will not find a similar department anywhere in Africa. Moreover, I urged Amnesty International to return to Zaire. Their delegation spent eight days here this past November. They conducted a thorough investigation, during which time they spoke to everyone they requested to see. In the end, they left satisfied. Later, the Association of African Lawyers which, like Amnesty International, is deeply concerned with human rights issues, and whose current chairman is a Senegalese, requested my permission to establish a branch in Zaire. I immediately approved the request.

Let me ask you a question: How many of Africa's 50 independent states have a multi-party system? Of these 50, how many can boast a better re-

Reprinted by permission from *African News,* Vol. 29, No. 5, March 7, 1988, pp. 4-14.

cord than ours? Zimbabwe, for example, experimented with a multi-party system, but was forced to abandon it and return to a one-party system. Ask Zimbabwe's socialist president, Robert Mugabe, why it failed. His answer should prove instructive.

When I took power in 1965, I inherited the Belgian system – a system that was totally corrupt. At the time, the Belgians had established Catholicism as the official state religion, relegating Protestantism, Kibanguism, and Islam to second-class status. That act was a direct assault on religious freedom. Although I am a devout Catholic, I abolished religious inequality and placed all religious denominations on an equal footing. I did so in order to serve freedom and justice.

MERVYN M. DYMALLY: But Amnesty International maintains that hundreds of political prisoners have been arrested, detained or imprisoned, often without ever being charged or tried. Do you dispute these accusations? If so, why do you think they persist?

MOBUTU: I wonder if a head of state should swear, but if anyone can cite the name of a single political prisoner, supported by hard fact, who is presently in any Zairian prison, I will immediately resign. As far as Amnesty International is concerned, I indicated that they were in Zaire last November at the invitation of the special department that oversees human rights and civil liberties. They left satisfied, and so am I. Without overstating the case, I am convinced that Amnesty International's attitude towards Zaire has changed markedly as a result of their investigation.

ELLIOT: Your opponents contend that the government does not respect the fundamental rights of workers. There is no freedom of association with respect to independent trade unions; collective bargaining agreements are not guaranteed; working conditions are abysmal; purchasing power has plummeted; and unemployment is at a record high. How can your government be described as anything but anti-worker? Don't these facts speak for themselves?

MOBUTU: They would if they were true, but they're not. In fact, they bear no resemblance to the truth. The truth is, my government recognizes fundamental worker rights, a fact acknowledged by our membership and participation in the International Labor Organization. The National Union of Zairian Workers (UNTZA), a federation of several

Amnesty International:

"We Remain Concerned"

Excerpts from "Zaire: Amnesty International Concerns Between January 1987 and January 1988."

In October 1987 an Amnesty International delegation visited Kinshasa at the invitation of the State Commissioner for Citizen's Rights and Freedoms, Maitre Nimy Mayidika Ngimbi. It seemed ... that most complaints made to the department during 1987 had concerned miscarriages of justice and administrative problems, rather than serious violations of human rights, and that it did not yet have the capacity to investigate abuses committed outside Kinshasa.

Despite the establishment of the Department for Citizen's Rights and Freedoms and the disbanding of the military security service in 1986, the security forces' powers of arrest and detention nevertheless remained unchanged, particularly those of the two main security services, the National Documentation Agency (AND) and the Military Action and Intelligence Service (SARM), which had replaced the service disbanded in 1986. Both these two services retained powers to detain prisoners incommunicado without charge or trial for as long as they considered necessary.

During 1987 the AND detained both prisoners of conscience and other political prisoners incommunicado for several months or more. In the first half of the year, they included prisoners of conscience detained on account of their non-violent opposition to the government. Later in the year detainees held for long periods included some accused of espionage. ... Other military and paramilitary units empowered by law to detain suspects for only a few days nevertheless exceeded their powers and kept detainees in custody for periods of weeks or months. ...

By March 1987 more than 40 UDPS supporters arrested in 1985 and 1986 were restricted under administrative banishment orders. ... The formal procedures for banishment, which are contained in a 1961 decree-law and which include a regular review by a special committee, were not observed. ...

Cases of the torture of political prisoners were not reported in Zaire in 1987 on the same scale as in previous years, but detentions by the armed forces in Kivu region were reportedly accompanied by beatings and sometimes torture. The main area concerned was in northeast Kivu region, between Beni and the Ugandan border, where the presence of an armed opposition group was reported on a number of occasions between November 1986 and July 1987. ... Further arrests occurred during 1987 and the level of violence in the area by mid-1987 caused several thousand villagers to leave their homes and seek refuge in Uganda. ...

During the first half of 1987 Amnesty International appealed for the release of all those detained or banished on account of links with the UDPS and also called for the lifting of restrictions imposed on prisoners of conscience arrested for different reasons. ...

Lisa Peterson of Amnesty International's Washington office told Africa News *that, while the human rights organization welcomed improvements in communication between itself and the Zairian government and in Zaire's human rights record, "we remain concerned."*

earlier independent and Christian trade unions, is active on the international scene, affiliated with international labor organizations, and enjoys close relations with your AFL-CIO. Collective bargaining agreements – approximately 600 – are guaranteed. While working conditions may fall short of Western standards, they are much better in the organized sector represented by UNTZA than in the informal sector. No labor leaders are presently in detention, and several former leaders who have disagreed with union policies are now free and pursuing their personal interests.

DYMALLY: Despite several presidential amnesties to Zairian political exiles, reports persist that many of your critics have been subjected to detention and/or arrest. Are you prepared to welcome home all of your political opponents, both those in the United States and abroad, with the promise that they will not be harassed or imprisoned?
MOBUTU: Absolutely. In fact, tens of thousands of Zairians who fled the country during or after the rebellions of the 1960s and the Shaba events of 1977 and 1978 have already returned to their homeland. They know they are welcome – that Zaire belongs to them, not to President Mobutu. If you meet any of them in the United States or Europe, assure them that they have my word; that they may return home without fear. Those who are most qualified will certainly find jobs. That is a national priority, not simply mine.

Corruption

ELLIOT: According to top officials of the International Monetary Fund (IMF), Zaire is plagued by "uncontrollable corruption" and the "illegal outflow of wealth from the country." The IMF charges that money for improving farms, roads and agricultural projects has been diverted into personal use by government officials. In one speech, you yourself called bribery "the Zairian illness." If this is true, why hasn't your government punished the guilty parties and adopted strong measures to prevent future corruption?
MOBUTU: Your last quotation is inaccurate. I never stated that bribery is "the Zairian illness." I once condemned corruption, but I never described it as my country's illness. To be accurate, I stated – while expressing New Year's wishes to my officers – "We keep hearing about corruption, without knowing who is corrupt and who is corrupting."

At the time, I was specifically referring to you – the Americans and Europeans – who taught us the art of corrupting. When you come to Zaire to sell your products, you tell our officials, "It costs $800. But for you, I'll set aside $200 per piece. That would amount to one million dollars – all yours." That is corruption, and you introduced it. You are therefore unfit to educate us on public morals, since you have yet to address the same ethical concerns in your respective societies.

Corruption is not a Zairian problem; it is a world problem. Take the Lockheed case, for example, which involved high-ranking government officials in the United States, Germany, and Japan – and ultimately President Jimmy Carter. No, the sole purpose of these rumors is to spoil the good name of Zaire. If our critics were honest, they would point the finger at those nations which are most guilty of corruption. We all know which are the most corrupt nations in Africa. Unfortunately, for diplomatic reasons, I can't cite them.

> *If anyone can cite the name of a single political prisoner, supported by hard fact, who is presently in any Zairian prison, I will immediately resign.*

DYMALLY: Your critics argue, with strong conviction, that Zaire's security forces have, over the past two decades, engaged in wanton corruption. Doesn't this reflect a failure of leadership?
MOBUTU: Although some abuses and lack of discipline among low-level security personnel may occur from time to time, major efforts have been made since 1985 to improve security force conduct. For example, regular police roadblocks have virtually disappeared. While incidents of extortion are reported on occasion, the practice is not condoned by the government and the perpetrators are increasingly brought to justice. Practices introduced during the colonial period, when security forces under Belgian control employed harsh measures, are presently being corrected.

DYMALLY: Your critics contend that you are fabulously wealthy, with an estimated personal fortune of $5 billion, which includes 11 palaces in Zaire and numerous villas in various European countries. How did you accumulate such enormous wealth? Isn't your lifestyle incongruous with the abject poverty that plagues Zaire?
MOBUTU: Although this question has been raised – and answered – many times, I will respond to your inquiry with total frankness. My conscience is clear. I challenge the existence of these alleged international financial experts – who frequently choose to hide under the cloak of anonymity in order to spread false propaganda against me. Who are these financial experts? These reports emanate from the press. Why do they persist? Frankly speaking, some reporters have been manipulated by questionable interests. Who are these interests? In truth, I have been singled out for attack because I am a nationalist. Moreover, I am intransigent on the subject of nationalism. In 1967, for example, I nationalized the *Union Miniere*, today known as Gecamines, making it the exclusive property of the Zairian people. Ironically, from that date on I became the object of scorn and derision, as I was widely considered to have pilfered Gecamines' profits in order to enrich myself, even though its finances are closely monitored by company auditors. Yet, its balance sheet bears no budget titles suggesting my involvement in its financial operations. Let me repeat: Gecamines is the exclusive property of the Zairian people.

When I assumed power, my

budget was called a "dotation"– a special presidential fund. However, unlike other presidential funds, mine is known and is subject to parliamentary approval. Every year I submit a budget proposal which must be approved by Parliament. At times, it has voted to disapprove various presidential requests. This year, without my requesting a raise, Zaire's elected representatives voted to increase the presidential fund, after assessing the uses to which it was put. Thus, my budget is officially known by the Parliament and the people.

In the past, when I went to Europe, I stayed in sundry hotels. However, my European friends repeatedly advised me, "Mr. President, your security is not assured when you reside in such hotels. We strongly urge you to purchase several homes, as your security is of the utmost importance. You should own your own homes, where you can guarantee your security. Look at such and such head of state. He has proper security. By the way, if Zaire can afford to spend so much on your security when you travel abroad, then buying homes should not prove exhorbitant." The very friends who gave me this advice are the same ones who disseminated the false rumors about the myriad castles and villas I am supposed to have. These are typical of the kinds of intrigues and conspiracies to which I have been subjected.

Clearly, I would be lying if I said I do not have a bank account in Europe; I do. I would also be lying if I said I do not have considerable money in my account; I do. Yes, I have a fair amount of money. However, I would estimate it to total less than $50 million. What is that after 22 years as head of state of such a big country?

As for my alleged fortune, do you recall the remark which a Belgian once made to one of his country's top-ranking officials? The man who made the remark has been my subordinate for over 20 years, first in the army, and now at the Presidency. He was asked a similar question about my finances, to which he replied: "From the way things are going, I am afraid for this man. He has a large family, with many children. If he dies, he will do so in misery. He has spent his money building chapels, temples, cathedrals, schools and clinics. Patients who could not be treated at home were flown to Europe or the United States. That is how he has spent his money."

Besides, of Africa's 50 independent countries, can you name one leader – just one – who can boast of having spent as much of his own money to benefit so many people? No, I have a clear conscience. I am an honest man. I have not pocketed one dollar of the people's money.

Finally, my so-called fortune has proven extremely beneficial to many African causes. An American journalist should be sent to Mozambique, so that that country's president, Joaquim Chissano, could tell him how helpful I have been to that nation's freedom fighters. The former president, Samora Machel, was likewise aware of my assistance. Thanks to my alleged fortune, I sent trucks, jeeps and officers to train Mozambique's army in Tanzania, while arms and ammunition were sent day and night via our pilots. On Mozambique's independence day, 3,000 Mozambique soldiers marched into that country through Tanzania, all of whom were clad in helmets, boots and uniforms supplied by Zaire.

The same alleged fortune has proved extremely helpful to the security of my neighbors and other African states. It enabled me to train five battalions of paratroopers – two for Burundi, one for Rwanda, one for Togo and one for Benin. It also enabled me to train 250 Mauritanian commando-paratroopers, as well as to help Chad score a crushing victory over Qaddafi. We trained five battalions in Zaire, and a sixth is presently being trained. All of this has been done without publicity, very much unlike France, the United States, Great Britain, Japan or Canada, who would typically follow up such good deeds with self-serving press releases.

Moreover, when Mauritania, Senegal, Mali, Cape Verde and Guinea were hit by a drought, for two years running I sent them checks drawn on the Bank of Zaire to help them to ease the crisis. This was done quietly and without fanfare. Similarly, when Sekou Toure's Guinea was hit by an earthquake, I sent a check for one million dollars to help them as a sister nation. They were the ones who made it public. Last year, when yet another African country, Cameroon, suffered a gas explosion, I sent them $200,000, as well as doctors and 20 soldiers who delivered tents and medicines worth over $200,000.

That is how I have used my alleged fortune – to strengthen the security of African countries and to lessen the plight of disaster victims. We have not done this because Zaire is rich; we are no richer than any other African nation. No, we want to teach our fellow African citizens the noble art of sharing.

During 22 years as head of state, I have never disclosed such inside information to anyone, for my mother taught me never to brag about my deeds of kindness to others. Because your question was so searching, I decided to be forthright and to open my mind to you, not for the pride of it, but in order to lay out the facts.

ELLIOT: Still, after over 20 years of your rule, the evidence reveals little improvement in the quality of life for the average Zairian. Indeed, the ordinary Zairian earns one-tenth of what he or she earned in 1965 before your government took power. It has been reported that half of the children die before the age of three, and one-third of those who survive past the age of three will die of malnutrition. Are you fighting a losing battle? Can the present situation be reversed? Is there reason for optimism?

MOBUTU: The statistics and criticisms you cite, which have been published by *The Washington Post*, come from the Belgian press. They stem from the kind of dishonesty and unfairness that you would expect to find, given our checkered historical relationship.

There is, however, a major difference between the People's Republic of Zaire, my fatherland, and many other African countries. Let's go back to 1960 to 1965, a period I know quite well. At the time, Zaire was in complete ruins, following the most destructive civil war ever fought in Africa. Schools, churches, ports, roads and ferries stood in ruin. When I took power in 1965, my priority was to launch a massive reconstruction effort, whereas other African nations, such as the Ivory Coast, Gabon and Morocco began by building on what the colonial powers had left behind. This is an important difference, both from a social and economic standpoint. I rebuilt schools, bridges and hospitals throughout the country. I also repaired damaged tracks and replaced both broken engines and railroad cars. The projects culminated in the construction of the Inga Dam and the conveyance of hydroelectric power, which spans a distance of over 2,000 kilometers, from Inga to Shaba. In addition, I opened a much-needed maritime company, the Zairian Maritime Company, as well as Air Zaire. Reconstruction took a long time.

Meanwhile, I still had to deal with the problem of terrorism. For nearly a year, I left the capital and assumed residence in Shaba province in order to conduct the war. These obstacles should be considered when assessing my record. The rehabilitation program, coupled with the war against terrorism, cost Zaire billions of dollars and plunged my nation into debt – one that now totals $5.1 billion.

My friend, when you criticize me, please do not cite the foreign press, for these articles originate from Belgium. I can produce copies of all of them from my home library. There is not a grain of truth in any of them, for their sole purpose is to spoil the good name of Zaire. I hold nothing against the Belgians, or Belgium, for that matter. I simply cannot harness my nationalistic pride. It is only natural for me, as an unabashed nationalist, to resist any attempt by another country smaller than mine to interfere in our internal affairs, even if by a historical misfortune they once colonized us. I will never live to see that happen again. I place the interests of my country first; everything else comes after. I might sound like an unprogressive leader, but before criticizing Zaire, compare it with other African countries. In my view, we have made enormous progress.

I would be lying if I said I do not have a bank account in Europe; I do. I would also be lying if I said I do not have considerable money in my account; I do. However, I would estimate it to total less than $50 million. What is that after 22 years as Head of State of such a big country?

ELLIOT: Granted that you have made considerable economic progress, most experts insist that the economy of Zaire remains fundamentally weak and vulnerable. Indeed, many observers contend that the Zairian people are deeply resentful of their economic plight – the "pauperization of the masses," as one analyst put it – but that they have been frightened into silence. Specifically, what measures have you initiated to improve the economic plight of the average Zairian?

MOBUTU: As you know, Zaire, like many other sub-Saharan African countries, has experienced slower economic growth and deteriorating terms of trade since it won its independence in 1960. However, we are among those few nations fortunate enough to have benefited from a prolonged period of civil stability and peace, which has provided our people with relative physical security for the past 20 years.

Since 1982, I have initiated several major economic reforms which have increased business confidence in Zaire's future and have had a positive impact on the overall standard of living. Owing to the elimination of exchange and price controls, parallel markets have virtually disappeared and profits now accrue to legitimate marketers and small farmers, thus encouraging more regular supplies to markets. As a result, the supply of both foreign and domestic goods in Zaire's markets has noticeably increased, eliminating the periodic shortages that used to occur.

Moreover, improved fiscal controls since 1983 insure that key industries like mining now receive the foreign exchange and local currency they need to operate and to maintain their productive capacity, thus providing continued employment for Zaire's industrial workforce. In addition, improved fiscal and monetary policies have reduced rates of inflation and currency depreciation, and have encouraged a modest re-

A welcoming ceremony for President Mobutu Jeffrey Elliot

sumption of business investment. Although there have been setbacks in the external environment, the reform program has survived and conserved its momentum, leading to realistic hopes of progress and real growth in the medium term.

The population-to-physician ratio improved from 79,620 to one in 1960 to 14,780 to one in 1980. These figures compare favorably to those of other sub-Saharan countries.

Health Care

DYMALLY: Many experts argue that your government has done little to improve health care in the country. For example, isn't it true that your government has not built one new hospital since 1965? They point out that in 1965, Zaire had at least two hospitals in every city. Today, less than 50% of these hospitals are functioning at 80% capacity. Of the five hospitals in Kinshasa, only two are accessible to the general public. Why does your government tolerate such a situation? Isn't this reason enough for action?

MOBUTU: First, I must take strong exception to the statistics you've cited. They're simply not accurate. I suspect you obtained them from *The Washington Post,* which, as I stated earlier, simply parrots whatever the Belgian press reports. These sources are completely unreliable.

Let's talk facts. At independence, Zaire had one of the most extensive infrastructures in Africa, with more than 400 hospitals. The current need is not to build new hospitals but to make the existing ones more functional. A few hospitals have been constructed, such as the one at Goma. With the help of foreign assistance, construction is nearing completion on a new hospital in Kinshasa.

During the pre-independence era, there were always two "hospitals" in each administrative zone – one for the Europeans and one for the Africans. This "double standard" was abolished and the expatriate clinics have been closed and/or converted into other service establishments, such as health centers. Today, there are several public hospitals in Kinshasa, including Mama Yemo, Kinoise, Kintambo, University Clinic, Ngaliema and Kimbanseke. My goal is to create 22 urban health zones and hospital centers, which will make health care more universally available.

As for the doctor-to-patient ratio, according to international sources, the ratio of patient-to-nurse-to-doctor has improved greatly since 1960. The population-to-physician ratio improved from 79,620 to one in 1960 to 14,780 to one in 1980. The population-to-nurse ratio improved during the same period from 3,510 to one to 1,920 to one. These figures compare favorably to those of other sub-Saharan countries. This past year, Zaire graduated about 1,700 nurses; in 1988, the number is expected to increase to 2,400. Those are the facts.

DYMALLY: Like many other African nations, Zaire faces a serious AIDS epidemic. It has been reported that one out of seven women is infected with the disease. What steps, if any, have you taken to meet this crisis?

MOBUTU: Once again, your statistics are inaccurate. In fact, the AIDS virus is estimated to be present in approximately 6% to 8% of the urban population. Still, there is ample reason for concern. Although we have a lower incidence of AIDS than many of our neighbors, we have nevertheless vigorously addressed the AIDS problem. In this regard, we have initiated an aggressive information campaign aimed at educating the general population about the dangers of the disease. In a country of marginal literacy, this program have been innovative and creative in its approach, and has included: 500,000 leaflets warning of the dangers of the disease and the best ways to avoid it have been distributed; two episodes of the nation's most popular television show have addressed the AIDS problem, and several documentaries have been broadcast; a song about the dangers of AIDS by a widely popular singer has been recorded; newspaper and radio accounts of AIDS and question-and-answer columns and programs have been produced; churches and other organizations have been used to spread the word at services and special meetings; and 100,000 copies of a comic book has been published, which tells the story of a businessman who ignored warnings about promiscuity and caught the disease, passing it on to his family and friends.

In addition to these preventive measures, Zaire is presently collaborating with the international medical community, including the Pasteur Institute of Paris and the United States Centers for Disease Control, in an effort to find a cure for the disease.

Only recently, a team of Zairian and Egyptian doctors announced promising findings with a new drug known as MM1. During a six-month study of 39 AIDS patients, 12 of the 19 members of the test group survived and showed definite signs of improvement in their immunological responses, while all 20 of the control group died. A new study is presently underway, involving a larger group of patients, in order to verify the initial results to determine if MM1 is indeed a cure for this deadly disease.

ELLIOT: Many analysts charge that Zaire's socioeconomic infrastructure has broken down due to neglect by the nation's leaders. Your once extensive road network is now covered with bush. Eighty-three percent of the people live without electricity and telephones, many in mud huts. Do you dispute these statistics? If not, why haven't you attempted to correct the situation?

MOBUTU: Despite the assumptions implicit in your question, the road system in Zaire has shown some improvement in recent years. Before 1960, the rural road network was maintained by forced labor under the Belgian colonial administration. During the civil disturbances from

1960 to 1965, bridges were blown up and roads mined, closing thousands of kilometers to vehicular traffic. At the same time, trucks became bigger and heavier and contributed to the rapid deterioration of fragile dirt roads, particularly during the rainy seasons. Starting in 1972, however, I created a National Roads Office that has been increasingly effective in improving road maintenance. Despite funding problems, this department has reopened some of the roads that were closed during the 12 years following independence, and is presently maintaining 30,000 to 40,000 kilometers a year.

Two years ago, American military aid amounted to the equivalent of 21 jeeps and assorted spare parts for our aircraft.

Debt and Foreign Policy

ELLIOT: In order to resolve the debt crisis stemming from the $5.1 billion you said Zaire now owes, you signed an unprecedented agreement with the International Monetary Fund, which your critics contend will produce deepening poverty and misery among the Zairian people. Why did you agree to such stringent IMF demands? How long can Zaire hold out without the danger of civil disorders – or worse?

MOBUTU: First, I deserve credit for having limited Zaire's foreign debt to $5.1 billion, irrespective of our nation's wealth. Not long ago, I asked an eminent professor of international economics to evaluate the percentage and likely impact of this debt as compared to Zaire's known wealth. He concluded that it represented less than 2.5% of our national wealth. Clearly, $5.1 billion is modest when measured against the staggering debts of other African countries – for example, $8 billion, $12 billion, $19 billion, $26 billion, $40 billion. In addition, these nations owe their foreign debts to private international banks, while only 5% of Zaire's foreign debt is due private international banks. The remaining 95% results from financial assistance and government loans granted by friendly countries, including the United States, France, Great Britain, Belgium, Canada and Japan. Thus, no one could claim that Zaire would be endangering the international banking system if it failed to repay its debts. For instance, we owed $40 million to Canada, but they chose to cancel it.

Let me discuss our agreements with the International Monetary Fund. These agreements were signed at the end of 1982. Up until 1986, Zaire had fully complied with the terms of the agreement with her international partners, including the World Bank and the IMF. In October, 1986, the Central Committee of our national party (the Popular Movement of the Revolution), met to evaluate the austerity measures imposed by our partners. It found that those measures had been extremely costly to Zaire.

The assessment showed that Zaire had, for four years (1983 to 1986), disbursed $1.9 billion toward the payment of our credits. Meanwhile, over the same period, we had received only one billion dollars in foreign assistance. In other words, Zaire had become a net exporter of $900 million of hard currency, as compared to what we had received. This upset many Central Committee members, who subsequently ordered my government to discontinue the austerity program.

We are prepared to fulfill our commitments as best we can, but this must not involve austerity measures intended to make the Zairian people suffer. The Central Committee also placed a 20% limit on any payments from export earnings. That is, if we receive one billion dollars in export earnings, we should pay back no more than $200 million.

DYMALLY: Many African leaders, yourself included, have been extremely critical of American foreign policy, particularly as it concerns Africa. In your view, is the Reagan policy doomed to failure? If so, why?

MOBUTU: First, it is not my place to dictate United States foreign policy in Africa. However, present policy does not enhance the image of a great power like the United States. For example, recent statistics on American aid to Africa reveal that Egypt receives over one billion dollars, followed by Morocco and Tunisia, which receive hundreds of millions of dollars. Yet, famine and misery have exacted a heavy toll on several African countries south of the Sahara. How do you explain this disparity? How can you justify the billions of dollars given to North Africa, while many of the neediest countries receive next to nothing?

I don't mean to criticize your government's policy; I am merely pointing out certain facts. Unfortunately, the situation is not likely to improve, what with President Reagan's recent announcement that American aid to the Third World would be cut by 20%. The International Monetary Fund has, as you know, created a special fund estimated to total $11.5 billion over the next three years. This fund was intended to help ease the crisis in the developing world, especially Africa.

U.S. Aid to Zaire

Military:

Fiscal Year
1984: $7 million
1985: $7 million
1986: $7 million
1987: $4 million
1988: $3 million

Economic (Development Assistance, Economic Support Fund, food aid):

Fiscal Year
1984: $40 million
1985: $54 million
1986: $62 million
1987: $56 million
1988: (approximately) $55-$60 million

Source: U.S. Department of State

The major participants in this partnership include the World Bank, the International Monetary Fund, France, Great Britain and Japan. The United States refused to participate. What explanation can you give for its refusal?

ELLIOT: As you know, Rep. Ronald V. Dellums (D-CA), has introduced legislation to withdraw military aid and put controls on economic aid to Zaire by the United States. How do you respond?

MOBUTU: Does Zaire, in fact, receive military aid from the United States? In my view, such legislation only complicates our present relationship. You know all too well that American military aid is, for the most part, negligible. Two years ago, it amounted to the equivalent of 21 jeeps and assorted spare parts for our aircraft. If that is the extent of your aid, how would we suffer if it were curtailed?

Since independence, Zaire has been a dependable ally of the United States. However, we are paying dearly for our friendship. Indeed, time after time, the United States has invented myriad excuses for denying us aid – human rights violations, South Africa, corruption, etc. These charges are completely unfounded.

In all sincerity, I believe that those African countries which are inclined toward a Marxist-Leninist ideology, with close ties to the Soviet Union and its Eastern Bloc allies, are treated far better than is Zaire, which has opted for close ties with the West. For us, it has been a virtual sea of troubles. I expressed this same view to Vice President Bush, when he visited Zaire. In reality, Zaire receives little if any aid from the United States. How are we repaid? With ingratitude and criticism. Bush himself acknowledged that America's strongest critics are always rewarded, while their faithful friends are always poorly treated.

Let me cite a case in point – namely, the August, 1975 OAU summit, which was held in Kampala under the auspices of Ugandan President Idi Amin. President Jaafar Numeiry of Sudan introduced a virulent motion aimed at the Western powers. Although I am not paid by these nations to defend their interests at the OAU, I strongly opposed Numeiry's motion, not wanting the OAU to be regarded as ideologically anti-West or at the disposition of the East. President Numeiry again took the floor and lambasted me, stating, "He [Mobutu] can't speak up. He is a servant of the United States, a puppet of the West." This caused an uproar. The motion was then put to the floor for a vote. Almost everyone else followed my lead, and the motion was defeated. Two years later, President Numeiry chased out the Russians and his Eastern allies from Sudan and opened his doors to the United States. Since then, Sudan has been a yearly candidate for $100 million in American economic assistance.

In answering your question, I am making a great effort to choose my words carefully, for when I recall that trying incident, I am tempted to break all ties with your country. Numeiry insulted me, condemned you, and then reversed his stand, only to be rewarded with $100 million each year for additional aircraft, cannons, etc., while Zaire hasn't received a cartridge. At the same time, the United States has been fulminating a variety of problems in Zaire under the pretext of human rights violations, political corruption, South Africa and the like. If I have, against all odds, decided to remain a faithful friend to the United States, it is because in politics one must be courageous. Political courage cannot be defined as doting after a great power in the anticipation of future aid; what matters most to me are friendship and faith. That is the true meaning of courage.

ELLIOT: Isn't it true that Zaire has, at the urging of the CIA, allowed the Kamina Base to be used to provide covert American aid to Jonas Savimbi's rebels in Angola and that you have provided direct assistance to Savimbi?

MOBUTU: No. You know very well the geography of Africa. If you examine a map of Africa, you will discover that Angola stretches 2,600 kilometers along our southern frontier. This boundary line is controlled by the legitimate ruling government of Angola. Everyone knows that for aid to reach this land-locked country, it must pass through South Africa or some other country, but not Zaire. Any aid that we might provide would inevitably fail to reach Savimbi, who is well off to the south – indeed, less than 20 kilometers from Angola's southern border with South Africa.

Not long ago, I officially requested that the chairman of the Organization of African Unity

Traditionally clad dancer performing for the president's party. Jeffrey Elliot

Mobutu Takes Charge

On June 30, 1960, the Belgian Congo became independent. Within weeks, army mutinies and the attempted seccession of Katanga - now Shaba – province combined with domestic political rivalries and foreign intervention to create what came to be known as the "Congo Crisis." (United Nations Secretary General Dag Hammerskjold was killed in a plane crash during an attempt to mediate that conflict.)

From the beginning, the then Joseph Desire Mobutu was a major player. Three months after independence he ousted President Joseph Kasavubu and Prime Minister Patrice Lumumba, who was later killed under mysterious circumstances. Mobutu returned the government to a civilian administration but remained powerful as head of the armed forces.

He seized control again in a coup on Novermber 24, 1965, and has ruled Zaire ever since.

(OAU) appoint several military experts to improve the surveillance system at Kamina Base. They would be paid by OAU member states – although Zaire would be prepared to shoulder all of the expenses – and would be charged with the responsibility to examine the contents of every aircraft that lands or takes off. Although this approach would run contrary to current military practice, it would go a long way toward monitoring any possible violations.

DYMALLY: The Organization of African Unity has, for many years, supported a boycott against Israel. Yet, Zaire was the first African country to renew diplomatic relations with Israel that were severed during the 1973 Middle East War. At the same time, you have openly criticized Israel before members of Congress and castigated Israel for its Palestinian policy. How do you explain this seeming contradiction?
MOBUTU: No contradiction exists. I view Israel as a friend, but this does not imply that I am slavishly obliged to endorse her policies. Even within Israel, where the government has hitherto enjoyed the complete backing of the people, voices of disapprobation regarding her West Bank policy can be heard. Thus, we are friends with Israel, but we have voiced strong opposition to those actions that we deem unjustifiable. Therefore, no contradiction exists. The United States supports Israel 100%. Yet, you recently criticized her West Bank policy, but are still friends. We view our relationship much the same way.

ELLIOT: In recent years, you have expressed strong opposition to Libyan President Muammar Qaddafi and his efforts to expand his sphere of influence. How serious is the Libyan threat in the region?
MOBUTU: First, my goal is not to oust Qaddafi as head of state. Rather, I oppose many of his policies aimed at his sister countries in Africa, including Zaire. His occupation of Chad, for example, is in direct violation of one of the major clauses of the OAU Charter, which prohibits the occupation of one African country by another. The Charter recommends that all disputes be settled through peaceful negotiations.

Obviously, Qaddafi has resorted to military occupation for the simple reason that Libya is far more powerful than Chad. While Zaire is also less powerful, it still condemns Libya, both verbally in international forums and through its unconditional support for an independent Chad. Our position is consistent with the OAU Charter, which calls for non-interference in the internal affairs of other countries.

In this regard, I decided to brave Qaddafi's threats by intervening in Chad. This may be called the "right of interference," since Zaire does not share a common boundary with Chad. We are merely close friends. I do not expect praise for my position; it is a question of justice. Unfortunately, I have become a target, and wherever I travel in Europe I am heavily guarded. We are aware of, and are closely monitoring, Zairian Libyan-trained terrorists seeking to destabilize our country. Regardless of the personal consequences, I will not haul down my flag or retreat from Chad. Recently, we dispatched 3,000 paratroopers to Chad. Since that time, we have lost 22 of our best young men.

DYMALLY: Many critics have argued that consistency is not your most prominent trait. You speak of the need for African "authenticity" and for Africans to cast aside the bonds of "neocolonialism," yet Zaire is one of white-ruled South Africa's top African trading partners. How do you square this apparent inconsistency?
MOBUTU: Your question makes me laugh. But, please don't think that I am laughing at you. You are an American, a citizen of the United States. You are fully aware that your country enjoys diplomatic ties with South Africa, as evidenced by the existence in Washington and in Pretoria of your respective embassies. My situation is quite different. We are drawn together by one simple fact: the transportation of our minerals through the Southern Road to our land-locked country. That is the extent of our relations. By the way, are Western journalists unaware that all European countries have embassies in South Africa – that they engage in economic trade and military cooperation?

Don't forget, Zaire is hemmed in, and is required to use the Southern Road, which transports 25% to 30% of our minerals. The national port simply cannot accomodate more than 40% of our imports or exports. The remaining 60% is transported by the Southern Road or the Tanzanian Road. Therefore, our relationship with South Africa is, strictly speaking, a matter of survival. Moreover, it is not a gift from the South African government; we are billed for using their railway.

Obviously, my policy has drawn

sharp criticism. However, consider those other African nations that cannot survive without South Africa; nothing is said about them. Zaire is the only scapegoat. That is my response.

ELLIOT: As far as South Africa is concerned, do you support President Reagan's policy of "constructive engagement"? Do you favor stronger sanctions or direct military intervention in South Africa?
MOBUTU: Let's not go too far afield. If only the actions recommended by the United Nations were implemented to the letter, and with the full backing of the Western powers, we would not be where we are today. Clearly, the great powers are playing games in South Africa.

DYMALLY: According to your critics, you bear direct responsibility for the death of former Prime Minister Patrice Lumumba, who was arrested by your troops and flown to Katanga, where, it is believed, he was killed by Congolese or Katangese troops. Indeed, some observers maintain that you were part of a CIA plot to assassinate Lumumba. What role, if any, did you play in the collapse of the Lumumba government and the subsequent assassination of Lumumba himself?
MOBUTU: As a black leader in your country, you are obviously sensitive to the plight of Africa and its peoples. However, your interest in Zaire's internal affairs is consistent with your nation's treatment of African countries as a whole. It seems to me that you are here in search of a scapegoat, as reflected by your probing questions concerning human rights, Savimbi, South Africa and now Lumumba. In some ways, I feel that I am on trial. In any event, let me respond.

First, I was not a high-ranking government official in 1961; I was in charge of the armed forces, not the Head of State. I don't wish to criticize my predecessor, President Kasavubu, but it was he who ordered Lumumba's arrest and his subsequent transfer to Lubumbashi in Shaba province, where he died.

When Lumumba was assassinated, I was in Kinshasa, carrying out my duties as chief of staff of the army. I was as surprised as anyone when the news of his death was reported. Since I wasn't there at the time, I don't know exactly what occurred. Neither do I know President Kasavubu's motives for transferring him to Shaba province. I don't know who assassinated Lumumba, and thus can't be of much help. To repeat: I wasn't the head of state; I was a soldier. I did not initiate policy; I merely executed orders from above. Besides, Lumumba's transfer was not within my jurisdiction. Nonetheless, I was, and remain, implicated in Lumumba's assassination because I was a member of the ruling government.

Let me try to shed some light on the actual sequence of events. In January, 1961, the period in which Lumumba was transferred and later murdered, the troops that were stationed in Shaba province, then known as Katanga province, were not under my command. This absolves me of the charge that "It was you, the army officers, who gave the orders." I had no control over the troops in Shaba, but was under orders from the government to suppress the secession. Thus, I held no position of power, either politically in Kinshasa or militarily in Katanga, to be held accountable for anything.

Why did I begin my answer with such a prologue? It appears that some people in your country would like to tie economic and military assistance to African countries to events such as this. Liberia is a case in point. As head of state, I shouldn't criticize another nation. However, you force me to give you an example. If you calculate American aid to Liberia, dating back to when Samuel Doe took power up until 1987, you would find that it is double that of Zaire's. Why don't you question Doe on his predecessor's assassination? Liberia receives far more aid, but is not asked such questions; we receive virtually no aid, and can't live in peace. How can you compare Zaire's president, who did not murder his predecessor but merely removed him from power, to someone who brutally murdered his predecessor? [Note: Mobutu refers here to his overthrow of President Joseph Kasavubu in 1965.]

Until his death, for example, President Kasavubu enjoyed all of the privileges due an ex-president: a full salary, cars, etc. When he died, he was given full military honors at his funeral. Thus, how can you compare these two cases?

Today, you can still see the small home President Kasavubu left in Kinshasa, and in which his widow and family resided. In my view, it wasn't dignified for the wife of an

A ceremonial dancer greeting foreign dignitaries Jeffrey Elliot

ex-president, so I decided to erect a more spacious home for her and her family. All of Kasavubu's children, who survived him, studied in Europe at my expense. His eldest son, a veterinary surgeon, is presently working closely with me; his daughter is a member of the Central Committee; and his wife is earning a salary equivalent to a full cabinet minister. Where else can you find a similar situation in Africa? It would be instructive if you could meet and talk to Mrs. Kasavubu, so that you could learn the facts first-hand.

As for Lumumba, his son, a virulent critic of my government, and one who fomented rebellion in Europe, is slated to return to Zaire within a fortnight. Go to Cairo, where Mrs. Lumumba has taken up temporary residence, and ask her whether she has received help from President Mobutu, what favors I've done her. I would like you to act as an intermediary in securing her return home, either through the intervention of a journalist or a friend. I am prepared to finance the mission.

The widow of Liberia's former president, William Tolbert, is presently residing in New York. Ask her if I have been helpful to her and her son, a law student in New York, whenever I visit there. Ask her son whether I have provided him with financial assistance? Ask him how many times he has visited Zaire? Ask him how President Mobutu received him? These are facts that shouldn't be overlooked, although, of course, I don't mean to blow my own trumpet.

ELLIOT: Your opponents insist that you are extremely egotistical. Indeed, a Zairian presidential hymn includes the words: "Today, we are going to admire the Guide Mobutu. If you see him, admire him. If everyone sees him, let them admire him. The country is called Zaire." Why have you so attempted to personalize Zairian politics? Aren't there dangers in establishing a government based on the cult of personality?

MOBUTU: Believe it or not, there is no "cult of personality" in Zaire. It exists only in the minds of our critics. Zaire is not France, Great Britain, Denmark or the United States. Zaire is Africa in miniature. The customs and traditions you have witnessed over the past week do not even represent a quarter of what is tribal, authentic Africa. Since becoming head of state, I have supported a policy of cultural revival, in the hope that Zairians will rediscover themselves and their heritage.

Believe it or not there's no "cult of personality" in Zaire. It exists only in the minds of our critics.

Ambassador [Nguz a] Karl-i-Bond, for example, comes from a tribe in Shaba province, which has dedicated a song to its paramount chief. The song is called "Ndjalelo", which means "Hail to the Chief." In that tribe, the chief appeared only once a year, and when he did the event was celebrated for days on end, sometimes up to a week.

I am unable, however, to disappear for a year; I must be visible every day. The paramount chiefs of that province decided to dedicate the song to me, stating, "He is more popular and more successful than was any emperor in our history." That is how I came to be honored with the song "Ndjalelo," which is now sung not only when I visit Shaba province, but whenever I salute the army.

This reverence has never been imposed on the people. It emanates from deep within them, and it is a demonstration of their personal loyalty. Yet, this treatment is far short of what our African traditions require of the people. Therefore, when the Zairian people pay tribute to me as their chief, they are simply following their authentic, indigenous traditions.

DYMALLY: Finally, at age 57, you have survived it all: coup attempts, invasions by Katanganese rebels, defections by your highest officials. To what do you attribute your longevity – your survival? What explains your remarkable durability?

MOBUTU: The answer is quite simple. My support over the past 22 years has come from the Zairian people – their loyalty and their love. Beyond that I can't say more. That relationship, viewed on a somewhat formal level, is one of complete loyalty. Although I am the boss, when I meet the troops, they regard me more or less as a comrade, particularly the paratroopers. As you know, I was a paratrooper myself. Among the military pilots, I am considered to be one of theirs. Since the army issues from the people, it is a reflection of their faith and confidence. My political survival is that simple.

I cannot judge myself, only the people can. For a country as large as Zaire, the leader must know his job, and must be accepted by the people. I know I am doing my job – that I am responding to the people's needs. Thus, I shouldn't brag about it. The people are the ultimate judge.

I've never had any illusions about the people's loyalty and faith, for there are clear signs and these signs do not mislead.

You might have heard rumors, for example, about my so-called illness and alleged death, which surfaced recently when I was out of the country. When I returned to Zaire and the people discovered that these rumors were baseless, I was accorded an unprecedented welcome by the Kinshasa population.

According to the media, of that city's 3 million inhabitants, 2.5 million men, women and children flooded the streets to give me a triumphant welcome. Neither me, nor a visiting statesman, had ever before received such a welcome. That is a clear sign – an unmistakable sign – of the people's affection. I will not belabor the point.

I have an idea. Let's drive to the university in my car, without a bodyguard, and without notice. I'll just bring my hat. Don't leave me for a second, so you won't think it was pre-planned. Let's try this experiment. It will reveal, most clearly, how I am viewed by the people.

Savimbi: Warrior Poet

Struggle To Free Angola Is Not A 'One-Man Show'

Richard Lessner

Richard Lessner, Arizona Republic *editorial writer, spent eight days in July with Jonas Savimbi's Union for the Total Independence of Angola rebel forces fighting that country's Soviet- and Cuban-supported Marxist government. Lessner visited Jamba, Unita's provisional capital and military training base in the remote bush country of southeastern Angola, and the main supply and logistics center at Likuwa. Lessner met with many of Unita's top political and military leaders, including Savimbi himself.*

Jonas Savimbi is the founder, president and military commander of Unita. A self-described Angolan nationalist, Savimbi believes the Reagan doctrine can succeed in this part of Africa, where his rebel organization is building a state within a state as evidenced by an extensive education system with schools in the bush.

Some of the key points made by Jonas Savimbi during his interview with *The Arizona Republic*:

On charges that the South Africans have joined forces with Unita in fighting—*"Never have South Africans fought with Unita. We have captured many Cubans and Soviets, but where are the South Africans? Why hasn't Luanda in all these years captured at least one South African?"*

On turning to the People's Republic of China for assistance—*"We went to the Chinese for help in fighting the Portuguese when no Western nation would come to our assistance. If the Chinese or North Koreans will give us guns to get the Portuguese out of Angola, good. The Clark Amendment frightened off our new African friends who were afraid to face the Cubans and Soviets alone without U.S. support . . ."*

On support provided by the South African government—*"If our receiving South African support creates problems for the MPLA, we say fine. If South Africa wants to use us to make trouble for the MPLA, we are happy to oblige. But that doesn't mean we support apartheid."*

On his role as leader of Unita—*"If Unita were a one-man band, it would have collapsed by now . . . I do not believe in a one-party system, not because that's what Americans want to hear from Savimbi, but because that's what I believe. If I come into Luanda and become a dictator, I will have failed."*

On the outlook for this year in the field—*"This time I am confident because of the U.S. support. Our morale is high and the MPLA's is very low. Now we have nothing to fear. Now their planes and tanks are running from us. For every $1 in U.S. aid we are destroying $100 in Cuban and Soviet equipment."*

Jamba, Angola—He is perhaps the most charismatic leader in sub-Sahara Africa today.

Flamboyant, articulate, intense, a passionate nationalist, a political poet, an organizational and military genius capable of inspiring simultaneously nearly fanatical loyalty among his followers and profound loathing in his enemies—Jonas Malheiro Savimbi is the founder, president and supreme military commander of the National Union for the Total Independence of Angola (Unita).

In a wide-ranging 90-minute-long interview with *The Arizona Republic* in his bush headquarters in remote southeastern Angola, Savimbi discussed Unita's history since Portugal unceremoniously quit its former colony in 1974; the subsequent civil war and sundry cease-fire accords among the three anti-colonial factions competing for political supremacy; the United States' withdrawal from Angola in the wake of the Vietnam debacle; the 1976 invasion of Cuban and Soviet troops, which turned the military tide against Unita and drove Savimbi's forces into the bush; his organization's controversial links to the Republic of South Africa; Savimbi's all-pervasive personal dominance of Unita; the return of the United States under Ronald Reagan; and Unita's current military prospects as nearly 45,000 Cubans and 2,500 Soviet advisers and officers launch another dry-season offensive aimed at destroying the irrepressible Savimbi.

Along with the Afghan *mujahideen* and the Nicaraguan *contras*, Savimbi's Unita represents the clearest expression of the Reagan doctrine—the extension of more than just moral and diplomatic support to anti-communist "freedom fighters" resisting the expansion of Soviet military power exercised directly or through surrogates. The doctrine endorses the ideas of a clear victory of democratic values worldwide, and support for forces fighting to shrug off Marxist rule. . . .

Many in the United States view Unita as a pawn Pretoria manipulates to keep Angola destabilized, using the continued presence of Cubans and Soviets here as a pretext for retaining a military presence in Namibia (South West Africa). Moreover, the People's Movement for the Liberation of Angola government in Luanda regularly charges that South African forces fight alongside Unita. . . .

South Africa did invade Angola during the 1975 civil war on the assumption, which proved erroneous, that the pro-Soviet MPLA could be defeated with relative ease. Another incursion occurred in 1981. Savimbi charges the South Africans had no more, or less, right than the Cubans to be in Angola.

Nevertheless, Unita does receive logistic support from South Africa, a fact for which Savimbi is unapologetic. Although making his opposition to apartheid clear, Savimbi says he will take whatever help he can find from any quarter in order to drive the Cubans and Soviets out of his country.

Recounts MPLA Betrayal

Savimbi delights in recounting how Unita, as one of the three anti-Portuguese opposition movements, agreed to share power with the MPLA, and was betrayed by the Cuban invasion. With the passage of the Clark Amendment in 1976 prohibiting U.S. aid to Unita, Savimbi turned to the only source of support left to him: South Africa.

"We went to the Chinese for help in fighting the Portuguese when no Western nation would come to our assistance. If the Chinese or North Koreans will give us guns to get the Portuguese out of Angola, good. If not for the Clark Amendment, we wouldn't have had to turn to South Africa for support against the Cubans. The Clark Amendment frightened off our few African friends who were afraid to face the Cubans and Soviets alone without U.S. support, so what were we supposed to do?

"If our receiving South African support creates problems for the MPLA, we say fine. If South Africa wants to use us to make trouble for the MPLA, we are happy to oblige. But that doesn't mean we support apartheid."

Savimbi says Unita received no direct support from Pretoria until 1981. Today, he claims that the only direct support South Africa supplies Unita is cost-free diesel fuel for its trucks, transshipment facilities through that country or Namibia and some short-term credit.

Picking up a can of Coke, Savimbi brandishes it about to drive home a point: "Unita purchases supplies in South Africa, for which we are criticized. But if we were to buy Coke from Zambia or Zaire, it would change nothing since their Coke is also produced in South Africa.

"Why is it all right for Zambia and Zaire to buy from South Africa and not Unita? Who down here—name them!—doesn't have economic relations with South Africa?" Savimbi asks rhetorically, noting that the economic influence of South Africa is pervasive and inescapable in the region, something which his American critics often fail to appreciate.

Another common criticism often leveled is that Savimbi is an unreliable ally, a political chameleon, changing color to suit his needs and audience. He and the leadership cadre of Unita received guerrilla warfare training in the People's Republic of China in 1965, but now he makes a great show of being democratic and Western in his outlook.

"I was never a Marxist," he says. "I was trained in China simply because no one else would help us. I wanted to fight for the freedom of my country, and only the Chinese offered to help. But we studied guerrilla warfare tactics, not ideology."

Savimbi is fond of saying the Chinese taught him how to conduct a guerrilla war and how *not* to run an economy, rejecting a collectivized statist approach in which truck drivers become civil servants. He makes much of the fact that by past colonial experience—Portuguese is still the common language of the country—Angola has always been a westward-looking country and not a part of the Eastern bloc.

Savimbi's eclipsing presence dominates Unita. His face and revolutionary slogans are ubiquitous in the Unita-controlled parts of Angola. In Unita schools children sing, "I have a friend and his name is Savimbi." Is Unita a one-man show, and is Savimbi just another black African dictator-in-waiting giving lip-service to democratic ideals until he has seized power? . . .

"Look, we're not fighting the Portuguese anymore. We're fighting a superpower, in the whole country, from Cabinda in the north to the Namibian border in the south; from Zaire to the Atlantic. We have to be organized and diversified. We have a collective leadership.

"I can't be a dictator. I am an intellectual. Intellectuals want debate, discussion. Democracy *is* debate. I don't want to go back. The little I have learned took a long time, and I don't want to lose it. I want people of equal or superior ability around me.

"I do not believe in a one-party system, not because that's what Americans want to hear from Savimbi, but because that's what I believe. No one party can express all views. It's impossible!

"If I come into Luanda and become a dictator, I will have failed."

Another reason some Americans are reluctant to support Savimbi is the perception that Unita represents another lost cause, another jungle quagmire, that Unita cannot win. In an interview with *The Arizona Republic*, Unita Vice President Jeremias Chitunda called this the self-defeating "myth of Soviet invincibility."

"To accept this view only hardens Soviet resolve," Chitunda said. "We must continue to raise the ante. Let the message go forth: the Soviets are being humiliated in Angola."

Savimbi makes the same point. After more than a decade in the bush, and after more than $1 billion in Soviet military aid and the introduction of 45,000 Cuban troops, the MPLA is no closer to victory and Unita is stronger than ever. . . .

With revocation of the Clark Amendment in 1985, $15 million in covert U.S. aid went to Unita last year, mostly in the form of sophisticated anti-aircraft missiles and anti-tank weapons along with U.S.-supplied training. Is Savimbi satisfied with the current levels of U.S. aid?

"This time I am. This (year's) offensive will be a very big show. We are waiting for them," Savimbi said with a broad smile and a clenched fist. "This time I am confident because of the U.S. support. Our morale is high and the MPLA's is very low. Only their air and armor superiority allowed them to make progress in 1985. Now we have nothing to fear. Now their planes and tanks are running from us. Their air power is useless. If they dare to use it, it is lost. For every $1 in U.S. aid we are destroying $100 in Cuban and Soviet equipment."

Savimbi is counting on the Russians' inability, despite the high stakes involved, to keep up their financial commitment to Luanda indefinitely. Sooner or later, he believes with an apparently unshakable faith, the MPLA will be forced to negotiate with Unita. If, he cautions, the United States sticks by him and continues to keep up the military pressure. . . .

Savimbi believes that MPLA President Jose Eduardo dos Santos cannot ask for a Cuban-Soviet withdrawal even if he wished it, for the Soviets are in charge in Luanda. Nor can Luanda afford to send the mercenaries home, Savimbi asserts, because Unita could win an outright military victory over the MPLA in short order. Thus Savimbi is unworried by Crocker's diplomatic initiative—which the undersecretary himself described as "a waste of time"—simply because there is nothing on which Luanda is prepared or able to concede.

Oil Paying Luanda's Bills

For now, Luanda is paying for its Cuban mercenaries and Soviet tanks with proceeds garnered from the U.S. Gulf-Chevron oil operation in Cabinda. The United States remains Angola's largest trading partner. Arizona Sen. Dennis DeConcini introduced a Senate resolution last month calling for an embargo against the U.S. oil companies in Cabinda, a measure which was defeated 68–31. Nevertheless, in the wake of Crocker's unproductive visit to Luanda, the Senate voted to revoke Angola's favored-nation trading status. The measure, which requires House approval, would dramatically reduce the level of Luanda's exports to the United States.

While he would not say so outright, it is apparent that Savimbi doubts the utility of a total embargo. While it is no small irony that American-run oil fields are guarded by Cuban troops, and that U.S. oil company revenues subsidize the war against the rebel organization Washington is supporting, Savimbi knows that several European oil companies stand ready to step into Cabinda should Gulf-Chevron be forced to suspend operations. . . .

"The American public must pressure Chevron. It is contradicting U.S. foreign policy. Cuban imperialism should not be acceptable to any Americans, including Chevron. The Cubans must go! This is not only a Reagan idea, but is an American idea. Cubans out of Angola!"

Unita Builds Society in Exile

Unita controls the southeastern one-third of the country, and carries out guerrilla operations against MPLA, Cuban and Soviet installations throughout Angola. Unita is the *de facto* government in this part of the country, providing a total social infrastructure—political, economic and police authority, health, education and welfare systems. Unita strives mightily to achieve the impression that here is more than just a rag-tag band of guerrillas, but rather a whole society, a government in exile with a fixed territorial base inside the country and a supportive population waiting to assume power.

This impression is reinforced from the moment a visitor steps foot in "Angola Libre," but getting here is not easy. A treetop-level flight over Botswana and the Caprivi Strip of Namibia—with the South West Africa People's Organization active in the Caprivi, pilots take no chances at finding a stray SAM-7 anti-aircraft missile—ends at a dirt airstrip carved out of the bush. Inside a grass hut a Unita official solemnly asks to see your passport, you are required to fill out immigration forms and your bag is cleared through "customs."

From the airstrip it is a two-hour-long bone-rattling jeep ride to Jamba, Unita's provisional capital and main military training base, and another full day's travel to the logistical center here in Likuwa. There are no roads worthy of the name in this part of Angola. Drivers of big four-wheel drive Toyotas and Land Rovers attempt to follow rough tracks through knee-deep sand, but mostly they make their own roads by slashing and crashing through the brush, startling elephants and scattering antelope.

This territorial base is what sets Unita apart from the other examples of the so-called "Reagan doctrine." Unlike the Afghan *mujahideen* who rely on refugee camps in Pakistan or the Nicaraguan *contras* who depend on their sanctuaries in Honduras, Unita has a secure base within the country. Moreover, Savimbi has learned well the bitter lesson of past betrayals and abandonments, and now stresses the principle of Unita's self-sufficiency. From sewing uniforms for the troops to repairing captured Soviet trucks and weapons, Unita strives to rely as little as possible on external support.

Civil War Wrecks Economy

Angola is an immense country—twice the size of Texas—with a population of 6.5 million. It is, by African standards, sparsely populated with a density of only 8 people per square mile. Rich in rivers, water sources and arable land, Angola fed itself and was a net exporter of food until a decade of civil war and the Marxist government's massive military buildup wrecked the economy. In the vast southeastern third of the country, Unita is responsible for nearly half the population, 3 million people. In the region, Unita provides:

- Seven central hospitals, 60 regional hospitals and 600 clinics. There are, however, only four doctors and 112 technicians for the entire population.
- Unita operates three orphanages for boys (girls are placed with families so that they may learn domestic skills). In the capital of Jamba the orphanage cares for 700 boys under age 17, while two other facilities have 1,500 and 2,000 orphans in them.
- Stressing the importance of education, Unita's territory boasts seven high schools with 95 teachers and 2,000 students; 951 grammar schools with 232,620 students and 4,800 teachers; and an adult literacy program with 23,000 enrolled.
- A ministry for information operates a shortwave radio station—"the enemy is fighting not only with bullets, but also with information"—which broadcasts six hours a day in Portuguese and nine native dialects.

Savimbi places great emphasis on the importance to a guerrilla movement to gain and retain the support of the population as a base of operations, a principle he learned from his military education in the People's Republic of China. Officials angrily reject MPLA charges that Unita troops commit atrocities against the civilian population, or that Unita controls its occupied territory through terrorism.

Basically a cashless society, Unita has three main sources of hard currency for purchasing the weapons, food, clothing, trucks and other materiel that cannot be produced internally: two sawmills cut hardwood for export; several diamond mines lie within Unita-controlled areas; and ivory is collected for export. These sources, along with private contributions and fund-raising efforts in Europe and the United States allow Unita to maintain its armed forces and logistic base.

The war between Unita and the MPLA has two aspects. Along the frontier between the government- and Unita-controlled areas, the fight is very much a conventional conflict. An estimated 45,000 Cuban combat troops support the MPLA's 80,000-man army. In addition, there are in the country 2,500 Soviet advisers, officers and pilots; 2,500 East Germans; and 2,500 North Koreans. . . .

In 1986, the Soviet Union supplied the MPLA with an estimated $1 billion in military material. While the MPLA is dependent on heavy columns of armor and massive air cover, Unita is a typical guerrilla force armed with light, easily portable weapons. It resorts to heavy weapons only when they are captured from the government's forces and abandons them quickly if they become liabilities. Otherwise, they are modified or repaired for use by Unita's forces. . . .

Unita's logistical requirements, even for its conventional brigades, are much lighter than those of the MPLA and the Cubans. Unita cannot afford to put heavy, unanticipated demands on its tenuous logistics and transport systems. The movement of materiel in this part of Angola is a torturous process. Just to reach the front near the town of Cuito Cuanavale requires nearly five days of extremely difficult travel by heavy truck from Jamba. . . .

Experienced American military observers say Unita's forces are well-trained and equipped, highly motivated and competently commanded. The delay in this year's dry-season offensive, which was just getting underway in mid-July, might be due to the reportedly low morale among MPLA troops and new fears of Unita's improved anti-aircraft and anti-tank capabilities. . . .

Unita was founded by Savimbi in 1966. It was one of the three opposition guerrilla organizations fighting Portugal for the independence of Angola. When a cease-fire was signed in June 1974, it was expected the three groups would share power. The Alvor Conference in January 1975 negotiated an agreement for free elections, a pact the MPLA almost immediately renounced. Soviet advisers and Cuban troops began landing in Luanda in January 1975 in support of the MPLA's drive to forge a one-party Marxist dictatorship, and by the summer of that year civil war had broken out.

Savimbi has a slogan that appears tacked to trees and hung in posters all over Unita-controlled Angola: "Unita is the key to Angola; Angola is the key to Africa; Africa is the key to the West."

The Soviet Union has been expanding into the Third

World since the early 1960s. In southern Africa its objectives have been consistent over time: to separate the West from its sources of vital raw materials. According to the U.S. Bureau of Mines, the Soviet Union is not dependent on southern Africa for a single, nonfuel strategic mineral. The West, however, is. The United States depends on South Africa for between 41 percent and 99 percent of its supply of such critical minerals as vanadium, cobalt, manganese, chromium and platinum. . . .

"Angola is obviously a long-term Soviet objective. Soviet power is here because of the long absence of the United States from the region," said Jeremias Chitunda, Unita vice president. "But Angola has become a much more serious problem than what (the Soviets) expected.

"Perhaps they regret the West didn't stand up to them in 1975, then they wouldn't be bogged down in this current quagmire. Only two people in the world still think the MPLA can win an outright victory over Unita: Fidel and Raul Castro."

Indeed, despite the United States' withdrawal from Angola in 1975, epitomized by the Clark Amendment which prohibited U.S. covert aid to Unita, Savimbi has done very well on his own. Unita is militarily stronger today than ever. The MPLA, however, apparently still retains hopes of defeating Unita. Despite a reported manpower shortage—defectors report forced conscriptions of children as young as 12 into the armed forces—low morale and widespread desertion, the MPLA is preparing to launch yet another drive on Unita's logistical base and provisional capital. Unita intelligence has tracked hundreds of Soviet supply flights from Luanda to areas around Menogue, Huambo, Bie and Luso.

A Chance For Success

If the Reagan doctrine—the rolling back of Marxist gains and the advancement of democratic values—has any chance of succeeding anywhere in the world it is probably here in Angola. A standard negotiation procedure of Soviet client states is to achieve international recognition and establish the regime's legitimacy, and thereby gain time to defeat the internal armed opposition. The need for legitimacy is why communist insurgencies like that in El Salvador plead for negotiations with the government, while as yet insecure Marxist governments like that in Luanda refuse even to recognize the existence of internal opposition.

Thus far the MPLA has sought to gain U.S. recognition without making any concession to Unita. In July, Chester Crocker, undersecretary of state for southern African affairs, met for two days with the MPLA leadership in Luanda. Even though the State Department has been reluctant to provide U.S. military aid to Unita and has long sought a diplomatic settlement to the Angolan war, Crocker left Luanda disillusioned, saying the meetings were a waste of time, that the MPLA had nothing new to offer and still refuses to negotiate with Unita or agree to free elections. Luanda is demanding a total embargo of Western aid to Unita in exchange for a protracted withdrawal of Cuban and Soviet troops. President Jose Eduardo dos Santos has also stated that the Cubans will stay in Angola as long as apartheid remains in South Africa, although what one has to do with the other is unclear. Meanwhile, the Soviets continue to improve and expand their naval and air bases in Angola.

The psychological and political implications of a Soviet-Cuban defeat in Angola would be staggering. The reverberations of a Third World humiliation here would bring the virtual collapse of Soviet influence all across the African continent, and a loss of prestige worldwide.

Few believe Unita can win an outright military victory so long as the MPLA has the hard currency earned from the U.S. oil operations in Cabinda to pay for Cuban troops and Soviet materiel. But with the renewal of American military assistance funneled through Zaire, especially the lethal Stinger anti-aircraft missile, military experts expect Unita to hold its own in this part of Angola.

As for Savimbi the military leader, he remains cautious, yet optimistic. Savimbi the Angolan nationalist believes that sooner or later, the Soviet imperialists will grow weary and go home. Savimbi the poet says,

Don't cry my golden baby,
Don't cry my love.
The days of the Cuban intruder are numbered.
The flowers will bloom anew
When the land will smile again.

PLAYBOY INTERVIEW: IMELDA AND FERDINAND MARCOS

a candid conversation with the former president and first lady of the philippines about tyranny, revolution, betrayal, love—and those shoes

On a good day, Ferdinand Marcos rises with the sun, does a few stretching exercises and gazes out at his domain: a couple of acres of grass and flowers in the hills of Honolulu, with a decent view of Diamond Head.

His wife, Imelda, wakes up a few hours later and prepares for her day: tending the rows of dark-red bougainvillaea she's planted, pottering about in her garden—an assemblage of clay pots with plants from the homeland enclosed by a mesh of chicken wire. She then plans the day's main events—lunch and dinner. The rosary beads she fingers keep her constant company.

Theirs is a classic study in bathos—how the mighty have fallen. For 20 years, they ruled supreme as the president and first lady of the Philippines. Elected president in 1965, Marcos declared martial law in 1972 in the face of what he called "lawless elements" and the Communist-led insurgency and effectively turned his country into his own personal fiefdom. For 14 years, he consolidated his rule, resisting calls for fair elections, confident in his support by successive U.S. Governments, which were always eager to have a firm ally securing the two giant U.S. military bases in the Philippines. As martial law stretched into the Eighties, there were increased reports of systematic looting of the public purse and more and more disregard for human rights.

Meanwhile, Marcos had named Imelda first governor of Metro Manila; she assumed vast control over the city's life. Always obsessed by "beauty," she determined to leave her mark by gutting slums and erecting a huge cultural center in Manila, where she could entertain such famous friends as George Hamilton, Cristina Ford and Ronald Reagan. She also made the most of her position by jet-setting around the globe and meeting world leaders (Qaddafi, Castro, Mao, Kosygin, the shah, the Pope, to name a few), sometimes negotiating in her husband's stead. Her lavish taste for the finer things in life, the huge—some said obscene—amounts of money she spent on furs, jewelry and shoes, and her reputation for dealing harshly with perceived enemies earned her the title in the world press of Steel Butterfly.

"An enchanted fairy tale" is the way Imelda Marcos likes to describe her political and marital union with her husband. The fairy tale began to sour quickly in 1983, when the Marcoses' major opposition leader, Benigno Aquino, returned from exile in the United States and was assassinated moments after his commercial flight landed in Manila. Although Philippine army troops had been on hand to meet him, under the command of Ferdinand Marcos' military chief of staff, General Fabian Ver, Marcos maintained that a Communist gunman had somehow made his way through the ranks and shot Aquino. International opinion said otherwise; Marcos was pressured into ordering a special court to investigate the matter. The middle class of the country took to the streets in an unprecedented display of opposition, which was covered by international television.

When Ver was officially acquitted and reinstated to his army post, the political pressure from the United States—the Reagan Administration having been a particularly staunch supporter of the Marcos regime—and the daily demonstrations in Manila led Marcos to call for a quick election. His opponent was Aquino's widow, Corazon, and her campaign pledge to rid the country of corruption led to a mass movement. An international team of observers, including a delegation from the United States Congress, was dispatched to watch the polling places in the February 1986 election. The reports of vote fraud were unambiguous: Marcos was the reported winner, but the election was rigged.

The pressure at home and from the U.S. continued unabated. Demonstrations increased. President Reagan dispatched his friend and advisor Senator Paul Laxalt to tell Marcos of U.S. concerns. Still, Marcos resisted. But within two weeks of the election, a key player, defense minister Juan Ponce Enrile, switched sides. He joined with Corazon Aquino to engineer a bloodless revolution. Ferdinand and Imelda Marcos, along with an assortment of family members and staff, were forced to flee the Malacañang Palace in the middle of the night, leaving half-eaten dinners on the table. After a stopover in Guam, they ended up in Honolulu. There they have been "marooned"—Imelda Marcos' word—ever since.

Aside from gardening and stargazing, the Marcoses spend a lot of time trying to avoid appearances before two American grand juries convened to investigate their finances—and those of the Philippines, since they were intertwined for more than 20 years. The Marcoses' reported wealth—his salary as president was less than $6000 a year—is in the billions and is supposed to include real estate in Manhattan, entire corporations, countless foreign bank accounts.

Although they insist, as did General MacArthur, that they will return to the Philippines, many observers feel that their "retirement" in Hawaii is appropriate. Both Marcoses grew up while the Philippines was an American protectorate; and when they reminisce about the past and talk about the present, the tone of the conversation is almost that the Philippines, after all, is the 51st state—more American than America. Both have the ultimate colonial mentality.

Still, their desire to return, however far-fetched, seems sincere. Their eyes fill up when they talk of it, in impassioned speeches, in poetry, in bursts of song. Reclaiming their power in the Philippines is something they consider their divine destiny. PLAYBOY *sent West Coast–based free-lance writer* **Ken Kelley** *and* San Francisco Examiner *reporter* **Phil Bronstein** *to Honolulu for a week to conduct the "Playboy Interview" with the deposed couple. Here is Kelley's account:*

"I asked Bronstein to be my co-interviewer because he's been covering the chaotic Philippine scene for the past five years and knows Filipino politics on both sides of the Marcos fence. Most important, I knew that Ferdinand and Imelda Marcos trusted him to give a fair depiction of their predicament, even though some of his reports about them in the Examiner *were quite scathing. He was the first reporter in the palace the night the Marcoses fled.*

"I also knew that PLAYBOY *had tried to interview Marcos while they were still in power, only to have the deal fall through at the last minute. And, indeed, this one almost did, too: After the session had begun, Ferdinand began waffling about whether or not he wanted to go through with it. He was persuaded by Bronstein to carry on, perhaps aided by the reporter's spirited piano playing to accompany Imelda's versions of 'Sentimental Journey' and 'Don't Fence Me In.'*

"Some of the old forms were followed. We drove up to chez *Marcos and waited a good half hour before being admitted—beefy security guards shuffled about, but here the hired help were watching 'Wheel of Fortune' on a TV set in the vacant garage.*

"Duly admitted, we waited an hour or so before Ferdinand Marcos emerged, impeccably attired in his pinstripe-wool suit. The temperature was around 90 degrees, and he didn't even sweat a drop. He did *appear to have a lot of trouble walking. He teetered and tottered about, one step at a time.*

"I figured we would be lucky to get an hour out of him. Wrong. We interviewed him for several hours in his living room; and as we talked, he became rejuvenated and would vigorously gesticulate when trying to emphasize a point—it was a remarkable transformation. So much so, in fact, that Imelda Marcos, who had arranged the daily lunch spread, one o'clock on the dot, was waving her hands in obvious displeasure—'Get in here now' motions.

"Eventually, we did.

"We ended up spending seven hours around that immense table, a piece of wood that seemed ten yards long. Ferdinand—'Mr. President,' as he prefers to be called—sat at the south end of the table with Bronstein and his mike, while I sat at the other end zone with 'Ma'am,' Imelda's official appellation, my tape recorder running.

"It was a fascinating interplay. Bronstein was at one end, I was at the other; and although we'd have a lot of uninterrupted one-on-one discussion, Imelda has a finely tuned ear. And a strong voice. Occasionally, while talking with me, she'd interrupt the Bronstein-Ferdinand conversation to interject her own opinions, to which her husband would sometimes reply with exasperation.

"Talking with Imelda Marcos is like talking with the Filipina version of Maria von Trapp—she sings *her point of view so often, songs from Broadway classics to nursery rhymes she'd learned as a child. She does it to make her point in a light way. Her husband, on the other hand, likes to lighten things up by telling lawyer jokes; having been one for so long, he knows them all, and so does everybody he's telling them to, and the staff cracks up because he's telling a joke—he's* Marcos, *after all. But when you boil it down to sheer entertainment value, Imelda wins hands down. She plays her living room with gusto.*

> *"There was fraud on both sides. But* mine *was not massive."*

"During our luncheon session, the conversations were repeatedly interrupted by calls from the Philippines. Some were taken in the dining room, some just outside; but Ferdinand's and Imelda's responses could be still heard. His voice was much more low-key; hers, much more animated. 'Now you make sure that you get your act together, combine all the liberation forces, make sure that the Moslems and the Christians get together and we'll free the country and become one nation again,' she shouted at one point. It was not just for the benefit of the reporters' ears. Ferdinand and Imelda Marcos desperately want to return. And that was the topic with which we began our conversations."

PLAYBOY: Mr. President, if you were somehow to return to power in the Philippines, what would be the first thing you would do?

FERDINAND: Immediately stop the corruption taking place under Madame Aquino.

PLAYBOY: The same corruption that many feel drove you from office in the first place?

FERDINAND: That is the popular perception, encouraged by the media. What is never mentioned is that Madame Aquino's family has been one of the largest landholders in the Philippines for centuries.

PLAYBOY: How would you stop this alleged corruption?

FERDINAND: Arrest everybody engaged in it. Madame Aquino doesn't have the nerve to do that.

PLAYBOY: So if you went back into power, you would arrest Mrs. Aquino on corruption charges?

FERDINAND: No, I would just prevent her people from participating in all the enterprises they are engaged in. Like Peping Cojuangco [Aquino's brother]. *He* should just be anesthetized. [*Laughs*]

PLAYBOY: Speaking of corruption, your old friend former defense minister Johnny Ponce Enrile, who helped stage the revolt against you, said he committed fraud for you during the last presidential election, the one you claim you rightfully won.

FERDINAND: Come on! Come on! He doesn't have the guts to commit fraud. He is a guy who always orders somebody else to do the dirty work.

PLAYBOY: Don't you concede it was possible that there was fraud during the elections?

FERDINAND: Yes. There was fraud on both sides. But *mine* was not massive. In the last weeks, my opposition was using greenbacks to buy votes. We have the sworn statements of some of these people.

PLAYBOY: Did you give these statements to the team of U.S. observers that charged your side with voter fraud?

FERDINAND: The team didn't really bother. One gentleman—I won't name him—visited one election precinct, then went to the bar and made up stories about us.

PLAYBOY: Thinking back about your downfall, do you now think you relied on people who betrayed you? How did you know whom to trust?

FERDINAND: It came down to a choice between bad and worse.

PLAYBOY: Meaning?

FERDINAND: Meaning General [Fidel] Ramos or General Ver. How can you choose? One guy, Ramos, is a weakling, and his people are traitors. The other, Ver, would give his life for you—but he's too rough. He kicks people—things like that. Like Patton.

IMELDA: [*Speaking at the other end of the table*] I used to tell him, "The palace is a snake farm."

FERDINAND: Still, I think the first lady and I acquired an instinct in determining who can be trusted. We flatter ourselves in believing we have been largely right.

IMELDA: Our instincts? Well, remember, *he*'s a very linear thinker—very precise, logical, one, two, three. But I think very . . . *woman*, very holistic. So sometimes he thinks I'm dumb and spaced out.

PLAYBOY: What's an example?

IMELDA: I'll tell him this or that guy is no good. He'll say, "Wanna bet? His credentials are this, that, fantastic; he comes from Harvard or wherever." I'll say, "Funny, but he just doesn't look right."

PLAYBOY: And you always mistrusted Enrile?

IMELDA: Yes, and I'm sorry I was proved right.

PLAYBOY: Mr. President, Mrs. Marcos says you are rational and logical, yet others say you are superstitious. Don't you believe in special numbers and carry a talisman?

FERDINAND: I am not superstitious. But I do believe in clairvoyance. I believe in extrasensory perception. I believe in telepathic messages. I get the idea to watch out for a particular fellow—he may have a pistol in his pocket, ready to shoot me.

PLAYBOY: Does your clairvoyance tell you anything about a possible return?

FERDINAND: Yes. I have that feeling. God, or the Big Guy up there, my guardian angel, tells me. I keep asking, "Give me a sign if I can return."

PLAYBOY: Any signs so far?

FERDINAND: So far, the sign has been "Don't move yet."

PLAYBOY: What about the move you made in January, when there was a private jet waiting for you at Honolulu Airport to fly you back to rally your supporters just after an attempted coup?

FERDINAND: No, no, wait a minute. Let's clarify this. There was someone representing this fellow who made inquiries to us here, but we never got in touch with anybody—except when they were already here and sent word they were available [*laughs*] if we wanted to use them. I said, "After all this hullabaloo, how can I accept your offer? I'm not going to be shot down in the middle of the Pacific. That's not the graveyard I choose!"

PLAYBOY: You mean because the matter had become so public?

FERDINAND: Yes, all the hubbub that was created. But back to your question: Do I believe in the spiritual, in the effectiveness of, well, communicating with your God? Yes. And I believe you will have to make an accounting to Him after death. Say you'd killed so-and-so. I would have to say, "Yes, Lord, forgive me." If I *did*. Like, for instance, He would probably ask me, "Weren't you a participant in the conspiracy to kill Benigno Aquino?" And, of course, I'd tell Him, "You know better than that, Lord, because I was sick; I wasn't even working at the time it happened. I really ripped into the office of security."

PLAYBOY: Does that mean you still believe in the lone-assassin theory—that the gunman, Rolando Galman, managed to penetrate all the airport security that your friend and military chief of staff General Fabian Ver had set up?

FERDINAND: I don't "believe." I *know*.

PLAYBOY: Yet you announced that theory even before your own investigators had concluded their study.

FERDINAND: That was because the American Ambassador and the State Department people were pestering me, along with my other critics.

PLAYBOY: What would you have done with Aquino if he had not been murdered?

FERDINAND: Bring him back to prison! Because he already had a death sentence over him, there was no need to assassinate him. All you had to do is bring him back to prison and let the execution take place.

PLAYBOY: You mean you would have killed him anyway?

FERDINAND: Throughout my 20 years in office, I executed only one prisoner—a heroin dealer who took pride in having destroyed the lives of so many Filipinos. Aquino, though, he was a sly one. He kept calling me to see if he could negotiate his way into the government. He even tried to do that a couple of months before he came back.

IMELDA: *I* ran against Aquino [in congressional elections]. He was no threat to the president and me. I beat Aquino by more than 1,000,000 votes.

PLAYBOY: But, Mrs. Marcos, he was in *jail* at the time.

IMELDA: Well, my God! That was the most romantic place to be in! I would like to be in jail when I'm running for office. No, my conscience is clear on Aquino. After [the assassination], people suspected me of conspiring with General Ver, but I'd be surprised if I've spoken ten sentences to the general in the past 20 years. In fact, when I called him, he would be terrorized.

PLAYBOY: Mr. President, wasn't Aquino's assassination the turning point for you? If he hadn't been killed, wouldn't you still be in Malacañang Palace?

FERDINAND: His assassination just added to the resolve of the U.S. embassy to try to knock me out. It was [former U.S. Ambassador to the Philippines Michael] Armacost, I think, who masterminded the whole thing. But, look, he's now number three in the State Department. Let's not pick a quarrel with him. We have enough enemies.

PLAYBOY: The first lady is signaling us that it's time to eat.

FERDINAND: Well, she's the mistress of the house. In the Philippines, we say that once the lady of the house has spoken, you say, "Amen."

[*There is a break for lunch, during which Mr. and Mrs. Marcos agree to keep taping the interview. Mrs. Marcos has laid out a buffet lunch.*]

IMELDA: You know, these are all my recipes. I don't make the food myself, but they're all from my family tradition. Let's see—why don't you sit down next to me.

[*Mrs. Marcos is at one end of the table, the president at the other.*]

PLAYBOY: Mrs. Marcos, do you feel a bit of cabin fever, overseeing the running of a small compound here in Hawaii, instead of the glory you once commanded?

IMELDA: No, because I feel that this is just an *intermission* in my life. I don't have as much to do as I did when I was in my country, but I feel very happy. I have my garden to tend to. My bougainvillaeas are blooming, and I feel hopeful.

One of the things for which I pat myself on the back is that I have not missed my possessions. It would be wonderful if I could see them once in a while, but I have a good memory. Malacañang Palace will always stay with me.

PLAYBOY: Still, to go from dining with heads of state to gardening—it must bother you.

IMELDA: What bothers me more is that the press has got it all wrong. My husband, a great humanist, is called a tyrant! A great dict——uh, I mean a great democrat is called a dictator! *That* bothers me. Fighting for the Philippines is like fighting for America, because we are one in spirit. And yet you leave the Philippines, this jewel of a country, in the hands of a coconut!

What bothers me even more is that being here in America, the most beautiful country in the world—oh, why do you let Japan outsmart you, beat you?

Let me show you something. [*Gets up, goes out of the dining room and returns*] Look at this—what's this?

PLAYBOY: It looks to us like Uncle Sam in a clown outfit——

IMELDA: It *is*! Uncle Sam as a clown, and when you wind it up, it has a music box underneath that plays *God Bless America*. This is what American kids buy now. What a disgrace to us Americans——

PLAYBOY: *Us* Americans?

IMELDA: [*Laughs*] I can't believe I said that, us. [*Knocks on her temples*] Can you imagine, me being an American? But you see what I am saying—in America, this is what is being offered to American kids for playthings. Look at this one, too.

PLAYBOY: It's a sort of G.I. Joe with a walrus head and long tusks holding a bazooka.

IMELDA: That's what it is. [*Detaches bazooka and fingers it*] These walrus fangs—that's what they painted on our pictures in the Philippines after Cory Aquino took over, all over the place, fangs everywhere on the posters of me and the president. [*Turns over toys*] Let's see where these things were made—I knew it! Japan. The country saved by America after it tried to destroy America—they turn around and do this thing to America, and America just gobbles it all up. It's so terrible. Children, American children, are buying Japanese toys that ridicule America.

PLAYBOY: Why do you have these items, then, if you're so disgusted by them?

IMELDA: My grandchildren wanted some

toys, and someone bought them. If I were a policeman, I'd shoot them down, these symbols of America. My friends in the Philippines tell me that they're now making Cory Aquino dolls that look like those horrible rag dolls—what do you call them?

PLAYBOY: Cabbage Patch Kids?

IMELDA: Yes, those. And they're ugly. All the time I was in the Philippines, they never made a doll of *me*. I guess it's not my fault, because I'm not ugly.

PLAYBOY: Whereas Mrs. Aquino is?

IMELDA: No comment. [*Laughs*] I just believe in beauty. Take PLAYBOY, for instance. PLAYBOY really shows beautiful women in a way they can be admired. Some people call it pornographic, but I don't think so. I think PLAYBOY shows the beauty of the female body. Goya did the same thing a century ago. Americans have always admired beauty, and I admire Americans because of that. But—look at these toys! This is not beauty!

PLAYBOY: We recall that you had something of a problem with naked pictures of yourself way back when——

IMELDA: Yes, I got into trouble during the 1965 election. Somebody mounted my face on naked pictures. I was so furious—they were very naked, very ugly bodies. If they had used Marilyn Monroe's body, then I would have had no problem. I might even have ordered some. [*Laughs*]

But, again, I just don't understand why, when you have the most beautiful country in the world, you let other countries outsmart you.

PLAYBOY: What would be a better system?

IMELDA: There should be only one leader. Too many cooks spoil the broth! You have the Congress, a very strong Congress; you have the Justice Department——

PLAYBOY: You mean the Judiciary——

IMELDA: Yes, that. And then you have the President, and then you have a fourth—the *media*! Who think of nothing but perceptions.

PLAYBOY: Mr. Marcos began with a system like ours. You had in the Philippines the *Batasang Pambansa*, your own congress——

IMELDA: Yes, and that is why Marcos changed it. Originally, it was like yours, but it did not work, because we were all spread out—7150 islands. So Marcos changed it to a parliamentary system.

FERDINAND: Excuse me, you're wrong. The reason was that in the old days, the congress system ended up with some congressmen blackmailing the president when the president tried to—well, systematize the expenditure of public funds. Why? Because a lot of the congressmen were collecting bribes.

IMELDA: I didn't know this.

FERDINAND: If we hadn't stepped in, the entire system would have collapsed.

IMELDA: And as the days went by, it would have——

FERDINAND: Please hold on! Instead of the simple martial law we declared, the alternative would have been the commander in chief's taking over the entire government.

PLAYBOY: Of course, your critics charge that that's exactly what you did.

FERDINAND: You must understand that I was also protecting my life and the life of my family. After the 1969 election, two American gunmen were caught in an attempt to assassinate me.

IMELDA: And they were hired by——

FERDINAND: Hold it! They were hired by Eugenio Lopez, Sr., and many other of my enemies. Many of them confessed. Even when Eugenio came to the Malacañang Palace to confess and apologize—he was coughing all over the place—I just said, "You didn't need to come here. I know what's going on. Furthermore, the lies you have spread about me and my wife——"

IMELDA: The president and myself——

FERDINAND: Hold it, hold it! Lopez apologized to me. He said, "I had nothing to do with the assassination plot, but I admit that the information I published about your wife was fabricated." [U.S. press reports tell a different story: A member of a prominent family, Eugenio Lopez, Jr., was imprisoned without formal charges for two years, while his family refrained from public criticism of the Marcos regime and turned over more than $400,000,000 worth of holdings—including a newspaper and a broadcasting network—to Marcos' relatives and supporters. In 1974, Lopez Sr., then dying of cancer, visited the Marcoses at the palace, but his son was not released. Lopez Jr. then went on a hunger strike, and his family spoke out against Marcos. It was not until 1976 that Marcos first charged Lopez Jr. with attempted assassination.]

IMELDA: The worst things he'd published were stories that I was stupid! And that I hadn't grown up across the street from where General MacArthur had his headquarters—that I grew up in a little shop. Can you imagine that?

PLAYBOY: Why were you called stupid?

IMELDA: I went to a Benedictine convent for my entire education. And in this yearbook that you'd autograph for your classmates, I would miss an E or an I or whatever. At least I wrote some words.

FERDINAND: She was also the student-council president.

IMELDA: That's not the point—a psychiatrist came to look at how I wrote, and he said, "She thinks faster than she can write." I always mistake words when I write, even today.

[*Marcos leaves to take a phone call.*]

PLAYBOY: Earlier, we were talking about the betrayal by Enrile——

IMELDA: On the *day* we arrived here, knowing exactly that the main culprit of the coup was Johnny Ponce Enrile—J.P.E., Marcos called him. Can you imagine that—calling your enemy——

PLAYBOY: Who had been your friend for 20 years?

IMELDA: Exactly. But Marcos said, "You take over the prime ministership of the parliament and I will support you." Imagine! Mrs. Aquino did not offer the prime ministership to J.P.E.!

PLAYBOY: Did that make you angry? That your husband had——

IMELDA: I was very angry. All of us were in a state of shock. This man Enrile, the one who caused all of these problems—it was so terrible. We suffered all these indignities when we left. We were dumped into a C-141, were all on top of each other; there was no opening in the airplane, and we could barely breathe, and it went from so cold to so hot—it was a plane meant only for cattle! So on the day, the very moment, we arrived in Hawaii, he put in a call to J.P.E., saying he'd support him.

PLAYBOY: And how did you react?

IMELDA: I said, "You are insane!"

[*Marcos returns to the room in time for that remark.*]

PLAYBOY: Mr. President, what do you think?

FERDINAND: Take her, take her, please. [*Laughs*]

IMELDA: I'm serious. Mrs. Aquino abolished the constitution, abolished the parliament—and they talk about Marcos as a dictator? Marcos as oppressive? Marcos, a tyrant? Mrs. Aquino, do you think that if you destroy Marcos, the Philippines will flourish? If Marcos was the problem, OK; he's out. Why do you have to spit at him, curse him, kick him?

This woman, Aquino, she is *satanic*. In the name of God, she used God to package communism, these crazy things.

PLAYBOY: Mr. President, if you do not succeed in going back, how do you think history will remember you?

FERDINAND: I cannot answer that yet. There are several scenarios.

PLAYBOY: Meaning you still hope to return?

FERDINAND: Let's put it this way: History is not through with me yet. I still believe that justice, no matter how slowly, it grinds. But it grinds exceedingly well.

PLAYBOY: Well, let us put it this way: When you hear your wife refer to you as honest, generous, loving and the most wonderful man on earth, do you believe her?

FERDINAND: [*Pauses*] I am a full man.

IMELDA: No, you're a whole man.

FERDINAND: Right, I'm a whole man.

PLAYBOY: Which means?

FERDINAND: Most of the Third World people have lost the values that made them a whole man—the perception of dignity, the true meaning of freedom and the willingness to fight for that freedom.

IMELDA: Can I grab your pen for a minute? I can draw it for you, to show what I mean. [*Takes pen and draws circles, squares and other shapes*] We're talking about the whole man—body, mind and spirit. You give the body what is good and makes him healthy [*draws circle*]. Give the mind the truth to make him educated [*draws stars over the circle*]. And then, when everything is in harmony, he is whole and starts to smile [*draws a smiling face over the other drawings*]. And if you take off one part of that, the picture will look like a crocodile, and we are *not* content with that. We want fulfillment and happiness to make a truly happy face. If he has an unhappy face, it's this [*draws an upside-down heart*]. Mind, body and spirit—and we all have a happy face!

PLAYBOY: Is this semeiology a way of expressing a, what shall we say——

IMELDA: I call it a theology. It's a little presumptuous, but it is correct. I made a theology toward a new human order, using symbols. And I call it Seven Portals to Peace. [*Takes pen in hand again*] Here I'm going to use only the numerical symbols of one and zero. Number one, how does the children [*sic*] draw a tree? Zero and one. See? As long as there is one tree on the planet, there will be infinity to bring about ecological order. [*Keeps drawing*]

Number two, as long as there is one woman—this is the sex symbol of the woman—and one man, the phallic symbol, there you have it: woman and man. So there will be infinity and there will be a human order. Are you following me?

PLAYBOY: We're trying. Please go on.

IMELDA: Number three, as long as you're not thinking of the dollar and going in circles for the dollar like a porcupine, man will be the center, and man will flourish, the dollar will go around and there will be an economic order. Using only zero and one! Zero, zero, zero, zero, zero. And man is the center. And here's number four—I always say the problem is also an opportunity. I don't solve problems. I recycle problems into assets.

PLAYBOY: Of course, your financial assets, many of which are being held, have been of great interest to the U.S. media.

IMELDA: That's my problem. I have an American mind; I'm honest and open. That's what my problem is and the problem of America is—we tell everything.

PLAYBOY: You haven't told everything to the courts about your assets.

IMELDA: My dear, I *will* survive. Assets——

PLAYBOY: Such as, of course, the shoes in your palace closet——

IMELDA: At least there were no *skeletons* in my closet, no? [*Laughs*] People forget. In the Philippines, shoes are now 60 pesos a pair—that's three dollars. And this business of my having 3000 pairs of shoes—even if I'd had 10,000 pairs of shoes for 20 years, that's only $30,000. Many people spend a lot more than that in ten years.

The thing is, I was promoting anything that was Filipino—I was the first lady; remember that.

PLAYBOY: Did you wear only Filipino shoes?

IMELDA: Well—I was not always parochial, let's say. [*Laughs*] But I did wear a lot of Filipino-made shoes. Look at these, for instance. [*Takes shoe off right foot*] This is Oleg Cassini, franchised in the Philippines, and it was made in two hours. [*Holds up shoe for inspection*] In Italy, the shoes would have taken two days to make. Two *days*!

PLAYBOY: Yes, but if they'd been made in Italy, they wouldn't have rubber soles, as yours do, would they?

IMELDA: They still stand up for wear. The point is, by making these shoes, we were able to give jobs to our people. Shoes were not even my weakness.

PLAYBOY: What was?

IMELDA: [*Laughs*] I'm certainly not going to say it out loud for PLAYBOY; are you kidding? Seriously, my weakness was trusting people I shouldn't have trusted.

FERDINAND: One thing about her shoes—she lost a shoe on a state visit to China, because so many people were bugging her. Later, when the media publicized the 3000, we joked that we should have taken them all along on that trip.

IMELDA: I got along the rest of the day in China with one shoe by wearing a long gown. But when I got back to the hotel, I threw that shoe away. Then, a few days after we got back to Manila, the Chinese ambassador came to call. He had with him the shoe I had thrown away!

The moral is, never throw shoes away, because they will catch up with you. [*Laughs*]

PLAYBOY: President and Mrs. Reagan made their own state visit to Bali last year. Were you disappointed that you didn't get to speak with them in person?

IMELDA: [*Pauses*] No, I was happy that we got to speak with them on the phone. We were grateful that they remembered to call, that they took time to speak with us. I had spoken with Mrs. Reagan during the final days in Manila.

PLAYBOY: Really? You spoke with Mrs. Reagan on the phone during that period?

IMELDA: Yes. On the day the palace was under attack by rockets, she said to me, "Come, Mrs. Marcos, I invite you to the United States." The Reagans were very sweet and wanted us to be their guests. I had to say that I would be the *last* to leave my country. Unfortunately, the Reagans were then fed lies by bureaucrats. But I surely appreciated their humane concern.

PLAYBOY: Has it ever occurred to you, now that the Reagans have their own troubles with the Iran/*Contra* crisis, to call up Nancy Reagan and return the favor—tell her to just hang in there, that sort of thing?

IMELDA: Yes, I feel there will be a time for all of that, but I don't want to be presumptuous. They're smart enough to do this thing right, and what President Reagan did has a moral foundation to it.

PLAYBOY: Selling arms to Iran has a moral foundation?

IMELDA: You just cannot argue with me about it—President Reagan did what he did because he wanted to protect America. Reagan's number-one oath is to protect America. And the system would not help, so he had to go an illegal way. But it was morally right!

And, of course, I understand what it is like to be in distress. Last year, just before Thanksgiving, we were getting so congested in our home here—people were getting hotheaded with each other, wounding each other, hurting each other; it was like everybody had his own foxhole. So then some of our people came and said, "Mr. President, we are leaving; we can't stand this anymore; we're up to here." [*Points to neck*]

PLAYBOY: A mutiny?

IMELDA: A mutiny. So the president said, "Gentlemen, this situation reminds me of my namesake, Ferdinand Magellan." He said, "When Magellan and his crew had not seen land for many months as they were circumnavigating the globe, Magellan went before all of his men and said, 'Gentlemen, today we are no longer ordinary mortals. We have just turned into gods. And let us thank the Lord for this great privilege of having been so deprived, so humiliated, and given all these indignities, because these are all instruments for heroism and greatness.'

"And I promise you," said Marcos, "that this is one fight no one will lose—even if we fail, we fail as martyrs for freedom." There were three or four minutes of silence; then everybody stood up and saluted Marcos and said, "We're sorry, sir." I have never seen the president in a more glorious and shining moment than then.

When I saw this, I had to go and embrace the president. I said, "Hallelujah, this is *something*!" And ever since then, things have been fine with our staff.

PLAYBOY: You think of yourselves as gods, then?

IMELDA: Yes, because we are on a divine mission.

PLAYBOY: Which is?

IMELDA: To return to the Philippines to reclaim our destiny.

FERDINAND: We are part of the achievement of being a god. That is what we are about now. An ordinary mortal would not be able to stand it. All of our statements now have to prove that we have not gone back to being ordinary mortals.

IMELDA: And even if we fall——

FERDINAND: We'll fall as martyrs for the cause; we'll fall with honor.

PLAYBOY: You've said you would do anything to keep the "flame" alive——

IMELDA: The flame of freedom!

PLAYBOY: What, exactly, does that mean?

FERDINAND: I'm willing to die! If necessary. But I don't think that may be necessary. . . . I will not be surprised if by the time this appears in print, we are enjoying the Manila sunsets.

[*Marcos leaves to take a phone call.*]

IMELDA: After you've been deposed, after a leader has fallen, he's suddenly ugly, a crook. Somoza! The shah! Everybody! You know who was the first to call us when we got here? The shah's widow.

But, again, why did Marcos proclaim martial law? Because the Communists were already pounding on the gates of Malacañang Palace and in congress. Did Americans realize why we did it? No!

PLAYBOY: What Americans did hear were the many allegations by human-rights groups, such as Amnesty International, of the terrible things the Marcoses had ordered done to people——

IMELDA: Human rights! Human rights! How about human *right*? We chose to be with America, not the Communists, and that's why we're now being crucified!

PLAYBOY: You keep invoking the Deity. Do you think God has something special in mind for you?

IMELDA: Yes. I think He *has* something special in mind for me. This has been too much of a preparation. And I don't just believe in God—I make God *real*. I want to be surrounded by what is beautiful. I want to do beautiful things.

FERDINAND: [*Returning to the table*] My doctors have been telling me to take my nap. I said I had an interesting interview with PLAYBOY. They asked, "Are they making you the centerfold?" [*Laughs*] Maybe we should send them the immigration commissioner's picture.

IMELDA: They can't use your picture; I don't want you to look too healthy now. You'll be forced to sit down before the grand jury in Virginia [about alleged misuse of U.S. Government funds]. [*Laughs*] Me, I recycle everything—even being in jail would be very positive for me if they called me to a grand jury.

FERDINAND: I do not want to go home that way. [*Laughs*]

IMELDA: Andy, tell them about your bitterest enemy.

FERDINAND: You're talking about the guy who tried to turn me into a *queer*, which I'm not and don't intend to be!

PLAYBOY: A homosexual political enemy?

FERDINAND: We won't mention his name.

PLAYBOY: Yet enemies of Marcos had real reasons to fear you, didn't they?

IMELDA: OK. What so terrorizes a lot of people in the Philippines who would fight against Marcos is that, always, all of Marcos' enemies somehow go and get sick, or something terrible happens. [*Laughs*] From time immemoriable [*sic*].

FERDINAND: Unfortunately, my enemies are slowly dying away. And so the game is not as exciting as it used to be. I am surprised at the way they are disappearing from the scene.

PLAYBOY: Some people charge that, over the years, *you* have been responsible for some of their disappearances.

FERDINAND: Let them say what they want. It's not true.

PLAYBOY: What if something terrible were to befall Cory Aquino?

FERDINAND: The Communists will probably try to kill Madame Aquino and blame it on me. It's in their blood.

PLAYBOY: It's in their blood to kill Cory?

FERDINAND: What do you mean, Cory? Everybody! All the leaders of every party, including ours. All *she* did was release from jail the 441 most prominent Communist leaders our government had spent years trying to track down! The way the Communists are conducting themselves, even if Madame Aquino survives the elections, she will not last the year.

[*The interview resumes in the living room.*]

PLAYBOY: Let's talk about the hours before your downfall. Why didn't you try to mount a counterattack with troops loyal to you?

FERDINAND: I could have had the Malacañang Palace bombed. I could have done a number of things to ward off the attackers. But I had another plan. I was going to cut off all the palace's utilities and then infiltrate the defense building—friends of Enrile's are also friends of mine. So I called him and said, "Let's stop this foolishness." Enrile promised me he would try to work it out; but by that time, I suspect, Cory was already in touch with him—through the Americans.

PLAYBOY: Why do you suspect that?

FERDINAND: Because I received a threat that the Marines would be used against me. The U.S. Marines! I got a formal note—unsigned—from I won't say whom, but it was a high-ranking U.S. official. [Marcos has elsewhere named former Ambassador Stephen Bosworth as the official who threatened him. Bosworth denies this.]

PLAYBOY: How did you respond?

FERDINAND: I said, "You show me this note, but signed by President Reagan, and I'll surrender to you." I mean, if President Reagan was declaring war on me—what the heck! I surrender! I face reality! I'll go to the President and say, "I'm your prisoner; what's happening?" [*Laughs*]

PLAYBOY: Yet it seems clear that the order for you to step down came from the President.

FERDINAND: I seriously doubt it. It was the diplomatic-level people at the U.S. embassy. The policy there was to get Marcos out. There was a U.S. Senator there whose 24-year-old daughter felt insulted because there was a party she wasn't invited to attend. [State Department sources say that no one of that description was in the U.S. embassy at that time.] I talked with President Reagan later and I think he was unaware; he was misled.

PLAYBOY: And the assassination of Aquino, as we have discussed, was crucial.

FERDINAND: The Aquino assassination added to the resolve of the U.S. embassy to try to knock me off. But I'm not going to fault anyone. All I know is that somebody from a Senator's office [presumably that of then-Senator Paul Laxalt, who served as go-between during that period] called and said, "You'd better get out of there. Even gunboats will be used against you." So I immediately issued an order that if any American gunboat came into Manila Bay, or if the Marines landed, no firing. [Laxalt denies this and says that Marcos was "terrified" by reports of gunboats, which Laxalt checked out. Laxalt then called Marcos to assure him that there was no such threat.]

PLAYBOY: So, in effect, Senator Laxalt told you that you had to cut and run.

FERDINAND: No, he never said those words to me. In fact, I do not know what Laxalt's memory is, but the truth is that I did *not* talk with him before the events that ended in my departure from the Philippines. I talked with him afterward. [Laxalt says this is not true and that he and Marcos spoke several times before his departure.] If he had ever said those words to me, I would have said, "May I talk to President Reagan?"

PLAYBOY: And what would you have said to your old friend President Reagan?

FERDINAND: I would have said, "You know you're ordering the use of American troops and violating the law. You are supposed to submit this to the Congress within 90 days."

But the President did not know what was happening to us. I know this because he stopped off in Honolulu last year, on his way to Bali, and he gave me the impression that he did not know. It was all underlings. The same type of underlings that, in my case, I say stole so much money from the Philippines.

PLAYBOY: Since you bring it up, do you know what your net worth is?

FERDINAND: Yes. But I'm not about to tell you. [*Laughs*] The true answer is yes and no. My net worth is covered by the documents I have, and I am ready to show them at the proper time. My enemies say I have deposits in the Bahamas, in Panama.

Now, I'd like to see those, because I don't have any paper on those.

They claim I'm worth—how much? Thirty billion? I say, "Show me the paper, and we can split it. You take 29 billion, give me one billion and let's say goodbye like friends." But they have to find it first! And not in pesos—in American dollars! [*Laughs*]

IMELDA: You remember *The Wall Street Journal* had stories that either the money didn't exist or Marcos was smart to have hidden it so well. Which was it, Andy?

FERDINAND: Well——

IMELDA: You were smart! [*Laughs*]

[*Mrs. Marcos leaves for a while.*]

PLAYBOY: Earlier, when you talked about America, and when Mrs. Marcos referred to "us Americans," it seemed as if your history is so tightly intertwined with U.S. history——

FERDINAND: Look, I learned the Gettysburg Address before I could read. We were under the U.S. educational system. But my grandfather headed the revolutionary forces and fought to the death!

PLAYBOY: Against the Americans?

FERDINAND: First against the Spanish, then against the Americans. So I knew about American history through his stories, and I was fascinated by American heroes—Teddy Roosevelt, all the guys my grandfather fought. I guess I was always fascinated by America.

PLAYBOY: So you grew up in an essentially American way.

FERDINAND: Yeah, with hopes of going to Harvard, only I was ordered into the military. But I had, I remember, a yellow convertible, a Chrysler fireball, all kinds of other cars. I lived the bachelor existence.

PLAYBOY: A pretty lavish one, too. You had some early success as a lawyer, didn't you?

FERDINAND: Yes, I was earning a good living, because I had a reputation for having represented myself successfully before I got my law degree.

PLAYBOY: What case was that?

FERDINAND: I was accused of murder. In '39. The guy testifying against me as an eyewitness was someone I'd never seen before. I jumped on him right in court and started to choke him. I was strong and forgot myself. I was actually in jail when I took my bar exam and, of course, everyone said, "He'll never be able to concentrate and take the exam." But I am the type who can put aside tensions and worries, and I took the exam, passed it and began handling big cases right away. Although I specialized in corporate law, I decided to practice some criminal law, for the sake of the criminals who had been in the penitentiary with me.

Anyway, when you're a lawyer in the Philippines, you're automatically considered presidential material. One of my first cases was that of a *bon vivant* charged in a gold-mining scam. *He* was living quite the bachelor life.

PLAYBOY: Unlike yourself? Didn't you say you led a fast life—cars, ladies?

FERDINAND: God, we're returning to sex! I try to avoid it. The answer is yes and no. There's a saying in the Philippines, "You can be hungry in the eyes but no further than that." My greatest fear was that someday I might wake up and discover somebody I was not in love with beside me in bed. I was afraid I would go crazy and shoot myself. So I promised myself I would never have an affair to the extent that a woman could, well, corner me into a shotgun wedding. So I kept window shopping. But when I met Imelda, I was swept off my feet. I proposed to her in the first 30 minutes.

PLAYBOY: What persuaded you?

FERDINAND: First, I made her stand up to find out how tall she was. She was about my height, and I said, "I guess you'll do." I told her I felt bells, I smelled roses, I could quote poetry the whole night through—I had never felt like that about any other woman.

PLAYBOY: And you did not even kiss her until——

FERDINAND: The altar. She was very circumspect and had a chaperon before we were married. Our wedding was in '55, and I was running for congress, and she started having these migraine headaches. [Both were involved with others at the time of their wedding, which was in 1954, and Marcos was already a congressman.]

We went to the doctors and they told me the headaches were caused by my desire to become involved in politics. They said, "Either you give up politics or she will not be able to perform normally as a wife."

So I said to Imelda, "I'll give up politics. I'll practice law, write books and amass a fortune—part of which I could put into a foundation for the poor." But she cried, "I cannot make you give up your life's ambition! Everyone says you will run for president in 20 years!" I beat them by nine years, by the way—I ran for president 11 years later. But basically, she said, "I'm going to be a politician's wife."

PLAYBOY: Then it must have hurt when, over the years, she was portrayed as the ultimate dragon lady.

FERDINAND: Of course. She was not anything like that. She was not ambitious. She was not grasping.

PLAYBOY: Then why is the world's perception of her the opposite?

FERDINAND: Because she did not bother to explain herself—I had to do it. In the early days, she was always afraid of appearing before a crowd—until I got her to sing. She'd always been a good singer. When she was a kid in the Benedictine convent, she lived right across the street from General MacArthur's headquarters, and he used to have her come over and sing for his staff.

PLAYBOY: And you then began to sing together as a campaign trademark, right?

FERDINAND: Yes. Before I knew it, she was also delivering speeches.

PLAYBOY: And——

FERDINAND: And she stopped having migraine headaches. [*Laughs*]

[*Mrs. Marcos rejoins the interview.*]

PLAYBOY: We've heard that there is an interesting story about your first public appearance as a singer. What year are we talking about?

IMELDA: Oh, don't ask me this! It was 1944, and I was singing at a garden party in the MacArthur compound. I sang a song—*God Bless the Philippines*—and Irving Berlin, who was there, heard me. He came up to me and embraced me and said, "Dear girl, this song is *God Bless America!*" I said, "No, this is *God Bless the Philippines.*" He said, "*I* composed this song, and it's *God Bless America.*" I said, "There's no difference, because America and the Philippines are the same." He said, "No, no, no. Almost the same but not really the same; this song is really meant for America." So Irving Berlin went off into a little corner and stayed for a while. He came over to me and said, "I must have a piano." So he went to our house right across the street and played a new song. "I have this new song for you," he said—*Heaven Watch the Philippines.* "You'll learn this," he said, "and tomorrow there's going to be a big show I'm going to present. You'll premiere this in front of 40,000 men." So the next day, I sang it in front of the entire Eighth Army, with General MacArthur and Admiral Nimitz and Admiral Halsey, and I had a backup chorus of 200 soldiers! You should have seen me! [Irving Berlin, 99, says he composed the song in 1945, not 1944, and "definitely not" for Mrs. Marcos. Pentagon sources say that it is highly unlikely that such an event took place during that period.] This is how I first became public—I was ten or 12 years old. [*Laughs*] I still do love to sing, but I don't get much of a chance anymore.

PLAYBOY: Perhaps you could sing a song or two for us. We'll play the piano.

[*Phil Bronstein, one of the two interviewers, sits down at the piano.*]

IMELDA: Well . . . all right. Let's start with *Sentimental Journey*—do you know it?

PLAYBOY: We'll try.

IMELDA: [*Gives a rousing rendition*] "I'll be counting every mile of railroad track that takes me back./Never thought my heart could be so yearny,/[*Slowly, then more upbeat*] Like a child in wild anticipation./. . . [*Breathy voice*] Never thought my heart could be so yearny./Why did I decide to roam?/Got to take the sentimental journey, sentimental journey hommmmmmmmmme."

PLAYBOY: Bravo.

IMELDA: Now let's try *Don't Fence Me In.* [*Sings with great gusto*] "I want to ride to the ridge where the West commences,/ Gaze at the moon till I lose my senses. . . ./ Don't fence me in. [*Winds up*] Oh, baby, now, don't fence me in. Don't you fence me in!" [*Applause*]

PLAYBOY: Do you have a secret desire to be on Broadway?

IMELDA: I do have an offer to do a show. It's called *Aloha.* It has seven beautiful songs, and it's the story of Hawaii. In it, the queen, Alika, comes out beautifully dressed in her *lei* and grass skirt and long hair—my hair is long, anyway. But the nice part is, my first public appearance will be with beautiful things in my hair, wearing a grass skirt—and without shoes! [*Laughs*] I'm going to make money on those shoes, you know. How is that for recycling a problem into an asset?

PLAYBOY: Is there a singer whom you particularly admire?

IMELDA: Elvis Presley. He was ahead of his time, because he had deep feelings. He had the privilege of deep feelings because he was deeply loved by his mother, Gladys. He was able to appreciate deep, profound beauty in sounds. And he started a musical revolution. They say all revolutions start from love.

PLAYBOY: Including the Aquino revolution?

IMELDA: No! That was started in vengeance!

PLAYBOY: Your own love story was pretty special, according to President Marcos——

IMELDA: Yes, it was made in heaven. I've been so blessed. Our life is a fairy tale.

PLAYBOY: Yet the rumors persist about extramarital affairs. Yours, for instance, with George Hamilton.

IMELDA: Well [*pauses*], at *least* he's good-looking, isn't he? I'm in good company, because he's got one of the most beautiful women in the world as his girlfriend, Elizabeth Taylor. We are beautiful women, beautiful people. Why does the press lap up all this stuff? Because we are *all* beautiful people. But George Hamilton and I were never more than good friends.

PLAYBOY: Then, too, there has been much publicity of late about your husband's alleged affair with a starlet, Dovie Beams de Villagran, a former B-movie actress who claims she was once his mistress.

IMELDA: [*Laughs*] Wait a minute! I know better. I have a special sensitivity about these things. You can tell when they're playing hooky. We're too close. I would be able to tell if he was with someone else.

[*Mrs. Marcos leaves for a while.*]

PLAYBOY: Mr. President, your own health became the topic of speculation through the last years of your presidency. There were reports that you were a candidate for a kidney transplant. Is that true?

FERDINAND: I was ready for a transplant, yes. But when I came to the U.S. in 1982 and the doctors saw the results of my kidneys' performing, they laughed me off the operating table. I said, "Be frank with me; do I need one?" Because I might have had to give up my duties as president, and I said I would have to settle my affairs and would like to die in the Philippines—or, better yet, live in the Philippines. They said, "Don't worry."

PLAYBOY: Kidney dialysis is a procedure that many people cannot afford. Yet when the Aquino forces took over the palace, they found seven dialysis machines.

FERDINAND: That's right, seven. When a doctor friend of mine was asked why I would need seven dialysis machines, he said I probably had seven kidneys. [*Laughs*] The truth of the matter is, we were preparing for a battle, so we were setting up an emergency hospital. The first wounds in battle are usually those that affect your kidneys. That's why they were there.

PLAYBOY: There was also a stir raised on American TV when a video of your own version of a Jane Fonda workout was broadcast. Was it to show people in the Philippines that you were healthy, despite the rumors?

FERDINAND: To be frank, I did not intend for it to be shown in the Philippines, though it was. I wanted it as a record of how I was feeling. Somebody apparently got hold of it and sold it.

PLAYBOY: How could that happen?

FERDINAND: That's like asking how someone can tap my phone—but they do. The telephone company even told me so. I wrote a letter to the State Department complaining, but to no avail.

PLAYBOY: Let's talk briefly about some of the world leaders you've met. Can you give us some thumbnail sketches of the greatest—Mao Tse-tung, to start?

FERDINAND: I admire all leaders who attain their objective, no matter what their politics. I appreciated Mao because it was always said that no one would ever be able to unite China. He did. He probably killed more people than were lost in World War Two, but at least he kept to his objective—until the last few years. He wiped out Chiang Kai-shek.

PLAYBOY: Did Fidel Castro impress you?

FERDINAND: Yes, very much. A flamboyant person. He impressed me in this sense: He's one of the leaders who believe that in war, as in love, deceit is acceptable. [*Laughs*]

PLAYBOY: And Margaret Thatcher?

FERDINAND: Her? The Iron Lady? Don't they say she's the best man in England? [*Laughs*]

PLAYBOY: Didn't you say, when Mrs. Aquino ran against you, that it was beneath your dignity to run against a woman?

FERDINAND: Oh, no! Not all women are *that* incompetent!

PLAYBOY: Yet didn't you have Mrs. Marcos negotiate the Tripoli Agreement with Muammar el-Qaddafi in 1977, when you were seeking to have him cease funding the Moslem rebels on the Philippine island of Mindanao?

FERDINAND: Yes, Mrs. Marcos had been over in Libya for a few days, and I talked with Qaddafi through her efforts. In 15 minutes, we had reached an agreement through the persistence of Mrs. Marcos.

PLAYBOY: Wasn't she threatened by the P.L.O. during that trip?

FERDINAND: Yes, they were going to bomb the plane she was on. And so all the *macho* soldiers, including Ramos and Enrile, abandoned her and took another plane back to Rome. She stayed on the plane, on the theory that the P.L.O. didn't kill women. I said, "Knock on wood," because they *had* killed women.

[*Mrs. Marcos rejoins the interview.*]

IMELDA: So, what are we talking about here?

PLAYBOY: World leaders and your role in dealing with some of them.

IMELDA: Who?

PLAYBOY: Qaddafi.

IMELDA: Oh, *him.* You know, I really went out of my way to be friends with Qaddafi. The stories I could tell! But I will tell you this: I think he has a real problem because he was spoiled by his mother—whom I met and who is a wonderful lady—but it's this whole Arab *macho* thing.

PLAYBOY: Mr. President, is there one achievement you're proudest of during your 20 years in office?

FERDINAND: Yes. Getting rid of this slavish colonial mentality in the Philippines. Converting a people to learn their own past, to stand up for themselves. None of that whining, beggary, mendicant posture.

PLAYBOY: Do you think the people appreciate that?

FERDINAND: Why do you think they cling to these ideas even after I'm gone? It's only because of me. Those young kids—they're not just fighting for Marcos but for what he may have taught them. I was a symbol. Those in their 20s knew no other president except me. They knew Marcos as a guy who could crack jokes, who could demystify the complicated philosophy of life. He could quote Rousseau and explain it—which no one had ever done.

IMELDA: That was one reason the U.S. was so fascinated by us, as well. When we were elected, we were called the Kennedys of the Far East. I remember that *The New York Times*, *Life*, *Time*, *Newsweek* covered us. I even had my own articles in *Reader's Digest.* Because we were fighting for the same thing America stands for. This estrangement now is just an interlude, an intermission. Wait till the second time around. It's going to be a big, big love affair. [*Sings*] "Love is lovelier the second time around. . . ."

PLAYBOY: Yet your reputation now, both in the U.S. and in the Philippines, is of your wealth and extravagance in a poor country——

IMELDA: What the president and I see in the Philippines is not what you see. When you go to the Philippines, you see poor people. You must remember how poor they were yesterday.

PLAYBOY: Still, your own extravagance——

IMELDA: I always believed there was no extravagance in good taste. There was no extravagance in what I did and bought for my country. I lost my mother, the prime giver of love, when I was nine. We were poor. Then, years later, when I was able to give, I was crucified for it. If you want to be intimate with poverty, be a poor relation. And I was. I came from a third-class province of a Third World country to become leader of the country for more than 20 years, to travel in all the major corridors of power in my time. Isn't *that* something?

PLAYBOY: When you sang *Don't Fence Me In,* we couldn't help feeling that you were singing that your soul *does* feel fenced in, living in exile.

IMELDA: It's a divine birthright to live and die in one's country. I never willed and desired to be born in the Philippines—it was just destiny.

PLAYBOY: If you got the opportunity, would you go back to the Philippines without President Marcos?

IMELDA: The president is no longer here in mind and spirit—this is only the shell of a man. He's physically in Hawaii, but his mind and heart are in the Philippines.

PLAYBOY: Yes, but if he had to stay here—let's say for health reasons—and you had the chance to go back by yourself, would you go?

IMELDA: Yes, oh, yes, I would. Right at this moment, I'd go home. It's the only place I'm obsessed with. Thirty-five years ago, I went to Manila with a youthful face, a dream and five pesos in my pocket. This time, I will not go home even with a face, because I've been deprived of my honor and my dignity. I'll go back with five pesos and make *billions and billions* of dollars, because what I do comes from the heart and the brain—I've got both.

PLAYBOY: Mr. President, we'll be winding up now——

FERDINAND: Did I tire you? Did I bore you? As long as I did not bore you.

PLAYBOY: Not at all. But one more question: something we alluded to before. You said you're not yet ready to say what your place in history will be. But how would you want your epitaph to read?

FERDINAND: I don't . . . what's the lawyer's epitaph? HERE LIES A LAWYER——

IMELDA: WHO LIES NO MORE.

FERDINAND: WHO LIES STILL.

PLAYBOY: Your epitaph, Mrs. Marcos?

IMELDA: One word: LOVE.

PLAYBOY: And *your* place in history?

IMELDA: I just want to be in heaven.

Stability, Crisis, and Revolution

In assessing the root causes of most Third World conflicts (e.g., those in Nicaragua, El Salvador, South Africa, Lebanon, and the Philippines), one is left with myriad unanswered and perhaps unanswerable questions regarding rights, responsibilities, claims, and blame. These questions include, among others: Did the government achieve power legitimately? If not, who speaks for the people? Does the head of state possess sufficient authority to rule? If not, how does this affect the decision-making process? Do the people enjoy true freedom? If not, is real freedom possible? Are democratic rights respected? If not, is the government justified in limiting individual freedom in order to promote unity, stability, and peace? Is the government capable of solving basic social problems? If not, who is? Is war inevitable? If not, why do nations continue to expand their military arsenals? Is economic progress possible? If not, what factors preclude success?

In any society, there are two systems of government—the myth system and the operational system. One part of the myth system consists of the stories that people like to tell one another. Some of these stories are romantic tales that have been handed down from generation to generation to glorify a nation's history. Another part of the myth system is dictated by political theory, idealism, and even by a healthy fear of such persistent human vices as greed, corruption, and nepotism. When the myth system deliber-

Unit 3

ately refuses to take account of these human failings, it represents the political equivalent of whistling past a graveyard.

The operational system describes how things actually work. The myth system and the operational system cannot be the same for two important reasons. First, people wish to take bribes, help their relatives, further their economic interests, gratify their vanity, and work as little as possible. Second, the myth system always reaches for the ideal, which means that there will probably be design defects in the myth system's plan which will make it impossible to construct a truly functional government according to the myth. Yet, the myth system affects the operational system in a constructive way. It provides a standard by which the operational system can be judged; deviations from the myth's ideals arouse guilt and shame among those in the operational system.

The divergence between the myth and operational systems is important to bear in mind when studying Third World governments. Indeed, there is an inherent tension between what political theory tells the people ought to happen in their society and what actually occurs in the day-to-day operations of their government. For example, the Nicaraguan people love democracy—having long been denied it—but are willing to support a regime, at least temporarily, that endorses democratic rights while limiting individual freedoms.

According to the myth system, the developing nations, like other countries in the industrialized world, routinely denounce the evils of international violence. Indeed, the myth system requires governments to eschew armed conflict in favor of peaceful negotiations. Yet, the operational system demonstrates the unreality of such claims in many Third World countries. Despite the fact that sanity and survival would seem to dictate peaceful solutions to international problems, many developing nations continue to wage brutal wars with dire political consequences.

The myth system tells us that war is bad—that it should be avoided at all costs. But is it always bad? It depends on a country's objectives. In the case of some Third World nations, it may actually rescue a country from economic depression, reduce unemployment, or enable a despot to silence the opposition. At times, war is initiated to promote national sovereignty, territoriality, and strength. It may also foster such national goals as unity, cohesion, and stability. In most cases, the proponents of war are far more organized, influential, and vocal than those who advocate peace. War fever can easily be mobilized by economic, ideological, dynastic, political, and other sources of international conflict.

The supreme challenge of any real government is not to design an ideal system based on unrealistic theoretical assumptions, but rather to meld political institutions and human nature—with all their vices and imperfections—so that they work together more or less acceptably. Analyze the international crises explored in this unit in the context of the myth-operational system—that is, probe beneath the official pronouncements, with an eye to understanding what makes the engine run. In this regard, remember that politics is the study of power: how to get it, how to keep it, and how to use it. Unfortunately, this definition often describes the relations of nations as they battle for the real-world advantages of power, influence, and authority.

Looking Ahead: Challenge Questions

What, if anything, can Salvadoran President José Napoleón Duarte do to rescue his country from economic ruin?

Could the Duarte regime survive without continued American support?

Do the Sandinistas believe in democratic rule?

Is it likely that the Sandinistas will honor the peace process and institute the agreed-upon reforms?

Why is the Arab world plagued by disunity and discontent?

What explains the lack of political and democratic rights in many Arab states?

Is it possible for the Arab world to combine economic efficiency with social justice and a reasonable degree of democracy?

Is Iranian society, as is often said, immune to reason and restraint in its conduct of foreign affairs?

To what extent do ideology and religion dictate Iranian life?

What steps, if any, can be taken to moderate the Iranian government and improve the present international climate?

Why has individual and collective violence increased in India in recent decades?

How will this violence affect the future of Indian society?

Is violence inevitable in modern-day India?

What explains the widespread hunger and violence in Mozambique?

How serious is the threat posed by RENAMO?

What impact will the future of Mozambique have on the future of southern Africa?

Does South Africa pose a threat to its neighbors?

What, if anything, can or should be done to reduce South Africa's influence in the area?

A Pioneering Democracy Struggles with Disillusion

SUMMARY: Despite continuing U.S. aid — about $1.3 million each day — and the efforts of a young democratic government, El Salvador is a nation in trouble. The list of hurdles President Jose Napoleon Duarte must overcome is daunting: a labor force crippled by widespread unemployment, a business sector dissatisfied with recent austerity measures, a political opposition fearful of single-party rule, and a communist guerrilla movement intent on economic sabotage.

Three years after the nation's widely trumpeted presidential elections, El Salvador's citizens are still groping for political routine.

The country's legislators meet in a parking garage, the devastating October earthquake having rendered their old hall unsafe. They debate the issues of the day sitting at blue-topped desks, flanked by Datsuns and aging Chevrolets. In this atmosphere political accommodation remains elusive. "We in the opposition parties have little democratic maturity," says Hugo Barrera, who last year formed his own party on the right. "We still tend to view each other as enemies rather than as part of a democratic [government]. This is a problem."

There are other problems. Despite military strength that more than tripled from 1981 to 1986, the nation's once horribly bloody civil war (an estimated 62,000 dead) drags on with little promise of settlement. The communist guerrilla groups making up the Farabundo Marti National Liberation Front (FMLN) battle on. One-third to one-half of the population is unemployed. For the rest, inflation is high and economic morale low. Austerity tax measures instituted last year have eroded much of the government's popular support.

The ruling Christian Democrat government has seen its efforts at negotiating with the rebels fail, and President Jose Napoleon Duarte has seen his daughter Ines kidnapped and held hostage by the rebels for more than a month before being released. The nation's right wing considers Duarte little different from the communists the army is battling. And the military, largely recovered from its appalling reputation as a haven for murderers in the earlier part of the decade, is increasingly testy over Duarte's inability to provide services to the countryside where the guerrillas are fighting and over the ruinous political infighting that wracks the political system.

Duarte himself calls the situation a "prerevolutionary spiral" and compares the current political climate to a "typhoon."

The ramifications of this disorderly state of affairs are immense, both for U.S. policy in Central America and for the region as a whole. After three democratic elections in the midst of civil war, U.S. officials were trumpeting the "historic" growth of democracy in the region. In the forefront was El Salvador, fledgling proof of the system's success and a viable political alternative to totalitarian Nicaragua. From 1979 to 1986 some $2 billion in U.S. military and humanitarian aid went toward ensuring that claim. But as the attentions of the U.S. government and public have shifted to the efforts of the anti-Sandinista rebels in Nicaragua, the long-term outlook in El Salvador remains far from certain. The oldest new democracy in the region is also the most troubled. "We're witnessing a maintenance mode," says one U.S. analyst, "and you cannot consolidate a democratic regime on a maintenance mode."

JOHN ANDERSON JR. / INSIGHT

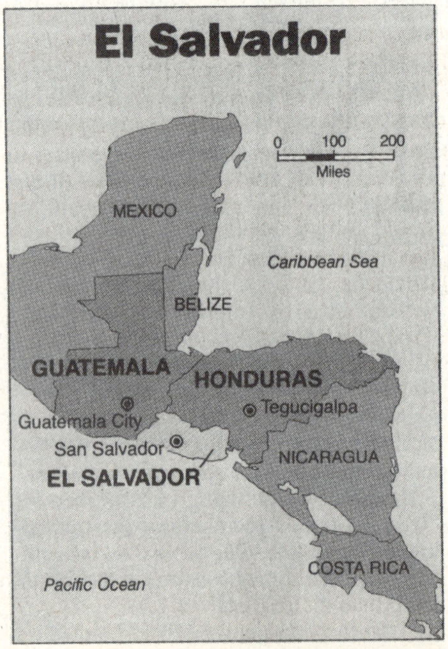

One thing is certain: Democracy in El Salvador has raised substantially the level of public complaint. This is no small accomplishment. As recently as five years ago, speaking one's mind could result in a bullet to the temple from a death squad made up partially of off-duty military men, or assassination by the guerrillas.

Thirty miles west of the capital, Felipe Serrano ponders the nature of Salvadoran democracy, scratches his neck and spits. Fifty-eight years old, he "works the land," a euphemism around the village of Panchimalco for dirt farming. Serrano's actions are slow, his voice rasping. Wearily he waves the flies away from his head, explaining how he has worked the same *mansana* (an area less than an acre) of land for the past three decades. He notes that since the 1984 election, the price of burials has risen tenfold. "Free enterprise," he says. "Now everyone has to pay."

He had planned to vote for Duarte but spent election day in bed with rheumatism. The village went heavily for Roberto D'Aubuisson Arrieta (who has been linked to death squad activity) and the right-wing ARENA party, something Serrano does not now regret. "Nothing has changed here,"

"A Pioneering Democracy Struggles with Disillusion," by Adam Platt, *Insight*, May 18, 1987, pp. 10-14. Reprinted by permission.

he says. "The poor have had no aid. It was promised to us but nothing was given."

His land produces roughly 700 pounds of corn a year, much of which is spoiled by animals and insects. Two sons help him. Another, age 24, has had polio since childhood and must be spoon-fed. "The military government was better; there is no comparison," he says. "We will try to vote for someone else who might help us. That is the only hope."

Equally blunt opinions of Duarte are offered at the country's annual beauty contest in the capital, San Salvador. "The man is a dictator," says a coffee industry lawyer sitting at one of the front-row tables. "When it comes to laws he does whatever he wants to." He will not give his name because "this government will come back after you." He is 47 years old, wears gold-rimmed glasses and a brown synthetic weave suit and fingers a glass of whiskey. "Country girls," he explains, motioning to the stage of the Sheraton hotel where hopefuls from the 14 departments, or provinces, totter about in evening dress.

"Duarte is a disaster. Economically I am feeling the disaster." On this point the lawyer is rabid. World coffee prices plummeted last year to nearly half the 1985 levels. The crop regularly accounts for some 60 percent of Salvador's foreign exchange earnings. Six years ago, the government nationalized its export, buying coffee from local producers and selling it abroad.

Wary of what they call Duarte's statist intentions and worried that he will nationalize the coffee business altogether, coffee growers have stopped reinvesting in their crops and income is expected to drop further this year. "We have no confidence in what this man is going to do," says the lawyer, "so everyone is protecting what they have left."

The president takes the news calmly. "Democracy," Duarte tells an **Insight** reporter during an interview in his office, "is the management of conflict. . . . Sometimes [people] overdo it. They go overboard." The previous day, demonstrators marking the seventh anniversary of the assassination of El Salvador's Archbishop Oscar Romero had marched on the presidential palace. That, the president says, further shows the system's success. "This is strengthening democracy in this country. I am showing that the government is liable and has to accept criticism."

Complaints from the private sector, says Duarte, are to be expected. "They want to regain power, to go back to the good old days when they had everything and the people had nothing." The populist tone in his words refers to the oligarchic past, when a notorious group of 14 families owned nearly every square inch of El Salvador and had the rest of the populace for their sharecroppers.

The presidential palace in the suburbs of San Salvador sits along the fault line of the October earthquake. The whitewashed, sprawling building sustained some damage, and as Duarte holds forth in his second-floor study the sounds of masonry work drift up from the courtyard below. The war, he says, "is a political war, an ideological war. If one side wins the people, it wins the war." The economy is "unbalanced," due in some measure to the "rightist opposition," which has prevented the government from implementing certain programs. "We're still at the edge of night," says the president, "but as an overall dimension I am moving. That is the important thing."

Others are more succinct. "Picture the shuttle Challenger on the launchpad, early morning on Jan. 27, 1986," says one U.S. academic, "just one freezing night away from disaster." With U.S. attentions having shifted toward the Nicaraguan rebels, El Salvador, say experts, remains the most volatile and politically tenuous country in Central America.

The military gains made by the government in the past three years are no cause for celebration, they say. "The idea is the guerrillas aren't going to win tomorrow so we don't have a problem," says Richard Millett, professor of history at Southern Illinois University. "I think we have a problem. I think Duarte's in political trouble."

U.S. officials argue that the process of "democratic self-determination," as laid out by the authors of the Kissinger commission report in January 1984, is proceeding as well as can be expected in El Salvador. They point to the marked drop in human rights violations (from a staggering high of 5,331 violations in 1981 to 261 last year, according to State Department estimates) and the new professionalism of the military as evidence of a basic stability. They emphasize that events outside El Salvador's control, such as the ruinous earthquake and the fall in world coffee prices, have played a large part in the country's economic misfortunes.

None doubts, however, that U.S. aid, pumped into the country at the rate of nearly $1.3 million daily, is crucial to the maintenance of any gains. "It probably would not last without U.S. support," says one U.S. analyst. The military, he says, would be "less firm in its commitment" without an ample supply of U.S. dollars. "You have not reached the point of democracy in El Salvador being irreversible, and you will not for three or four more presidential elections. There are still people around who would do away with the system, to get rid of an unpopular president."

In January right-wing businessmen secretly petitioned members of the military to remove Duarte. The rebuke by the military surprised some observers in the capital more than the request.

That the president survived points to a relative sea change in the political environment. Duarte's political opponents, after excoriating the Christian Democrats for freezing them out in National Assembly debates, invariably point to the next elections, for the assembly in March 1988 and the presidency a year later, as their means of revenge — not to a military coup or some other means of taking power. "We hope that after the elections there will be change," says ARENA Vice President Caulderon Sol. "We hope that Washington will respect the will of the people."

Washington, publicly, seems pleased. "The progress has been encouraging, considering their history and considering the economic difficulties they are laboring under," says former National Security Council staffer William J. Perry. Democracy in Central America remains, he says, a relative term.

For much of the country's population it is only a concept, constrained by age-old social structures and by the institutionalized power of the military. Echoing U.S. officials in Washington and El Salvador, Perry points out that the United States was an aristocratic republic until Andrew Jackson's presidency in 1829. Democracy, he says, takes time to evolve.

Democracy as it has developed in El Salvador, says political scientist Enrique Baloyra at the University of Miami, has been successful in its initial tactical goal: to undercut the radical left politically. Consolidating these gains through political compromise and consensus, however, has proved more difficult.

The Christian Democrats and the right have been publicly at odds since 1972, when members of the oligarchy conspired with the military to steal the presidential election from Duarte. Duarte's running mate in that election, officially won by Col. Arturo Molina, was Guillermo Ungo, now leader of the FMLN. (Ungo joined the communist front in 1979.)

Duarte, who was nearly killed by Molina supporters and spent the next seven years in exile in Venezuela, accuses the right of wanting, as he puts it, to "recuperate their power." He returned to power as the figurehead in a reformist military coup in 1979. He left office in 1982 when the first election failed to give his party a majority but won handily in 1984.

Bringing these two sides together in a democratic environment has proved problematic from the beginning. "This [Reagan] administration to a degree wanted to use the metaphor of the prisoner's di-

> "Our main export, coffee, is now sold abroad by politicians. Who knows what they sell it for, or how much they keep for themselves."

lemma," says Baloyra. "Reconciliation is possible as long as the two antagonists focus their attentions on a common enemy. [U.S. policymakers] tried this with the Christian Democrats and the right wing, and it didn't work."

Differences have surfaced most prominently over the management of the economy. In January 1986, with a massive budget deficit and a gross national product that has fallen steadily since the beginning of the civil war in 1979, Duarte further devalued the national currency, the colon; placed taxes on gasoline and transportation; and tightened credit in the state-owned banks.

"The Christian Democrats tried to solve the country's economic problems politically," says Victor Steiner, president of the El Salvador Chamber of Commerce and Industry. In so doing, he says, "they have taken El Salvador into a very socialized economy." Caulderon Sol of ARENA agrees. "Our main export, coffee, is now sold abroad by politicians. Who knows what they sell it for, or how much they keep for themselves. With this new capacity to manipulate, the corruption in El Salvador is terrible."

The fight has moved into the courts. A war tax that was proposed in December by the Christian Democrats was ruled unconstitutional by the right-wing-controlled Supreme Court of Justice. According to the Salvadoran Constitution, the tax money cannot be devoted to a particular purpose unless war has been declared. The judges pointed out that El Salvador was not officially at war but in "a state of national calamity."

This unsettling brush with taxation, which was read as further evidence of Duarte's statist motives, led to a general strike in the private sector. On Jan. 22, some 85 percent of the capital's businesses closed down. The strike was called, according to Steiner, to demonstrate to Duarte that "we feel this is the wrong way to go." Others see a deeper motivation. "They just don't trust Duarte," says one foreign analyst in San Salvador. "They're sure he has plans to do them and their interests in."

According to Baloyra, there is an added element of personal pique in the conflict. "These people have a long historical record of political success behind them," he says of the strikers. "They thought they would never be abandoned. They thought they would always be the favorites of U.S. administrations, and they have not reconciled themselves to the idea that Reagan deserted them and the U.S. came down for Duarte."

Duarte responded to the strikers by calling a demonstration of his own. Government estimates put the Feb. 7 turnout at 70,000, but U.S. Embassy sources in El Salvador say the number was substantially lower. Whatever the numbers, Duarte's stance toward his opponents has been less than conciliatory.

"He is a man who holds grudges," says Dagoverto Gavidia, a San Salvador architect who worked with the president when Duarte was pursuing a career as an engineer. "He has held grudges all his life. He does not feel he can trust the people that did not help him when he needed help."

Whatever the personal dynamics, most analysts agree that the economy will not recover without private sector support. The bulk of the capital that left El Salvador when the civil war began has not returned. For more extreme members of the old order, confidence will be lacking as long as Duarte remains in power.

But many middle-class and upper-middle-class professionals, the backbone of a developing democracy, say they are simply confused, that the government has given mixed signals on economic policy and that Duarte himself has done little to help matters.

"We have made some steps forward," says Jose Rolando Vasquez, a gas station owner in the capital. "Certain things were not permitted before. Now you can talk freely, you can oppose the government and express your opinions." Like many Salvadoran professionals he sees human rights and the war as secondary to the country's economic problems. "Politically, right battles left. The government has no clear idea of how to work for the people." The country, he says, "needs a plan of action, and we haven't seen one." And what of government corruption, historically the bane of all reformers in Central American history? "We have no proof, but it is generalized in our environment."

Gavidia says that although bribes have long been a part of the construction business his "payments" under the Christian Democrats have been higher than ever. "Politicians here don't have a long life. They're like football players: They have to earn a lot while they can and they know it."

Political opponents say corruption runs hand in hand with Christian Democratic plans to build a one-party democracy along the lines of the Partido Revolucionario Institucional in Mexico (which has held power since 1929). Late last year 27 opposition legislators went on strike, protesting perceived attempts by the ruling party to usurp control of the election commission over the heads of the opposition, a charge Duarte vigorously denies. "We believe that the Christian Democrats are trying to get reelected," says Hugo Barrera, leader of the Liberation Party. "All of their work up to now has been toward this goal, and not toward solving the economic and social problems of the country."

The strike, which ended last month, froze legislation requiring a two-thirds majority vote. The principal political casualty was the national state of emergency, in effect since 1981 and subject to renewal every 30 days. Laws allowing military and security police more leeway in the capture and questioning of suspected guerrillas lapsed.

This is one of the few instances in El Salvador of politics interfering with the military's ability to prosecute the war. Most analysts say that as long as the two remain separate, and as long as the army is not solely dependent on the civilian government for its funds, military commanders are unlikely to take the same interest in Salvadoran politics as before. "The private sector used to have some influence, but that was a long time ago," says one colonel in San Salvador. "Now even they are aware that the army cannot favor any single political movement."

The military has certainly prospered under the Duarte government, growing to the present troop level of 57,000. During the past three years, official U.S. military aid to El Salvador has hovered near $120 million, roughly the amount of the annual military budget. The Christian Democrats have pushed the army on human rights reforms but have had little success in rectifying abuses as has Argentina. "The military used to see the people as their enemies," says Samuel Maldanado, head of the Salvadoran Communal Union, the largest peasant union. "This is less true today, but there are still things done outside the law."

The law, however, is a tenuous business in El Salvador. Even the most fervent government supporters say the justice system is a shambles. Since the earthquake, judges and prosecutors have operated from tents. As a rule, say local analysts, most are underpaid and undertrained and got their jobs through political patronage. Many judges work in the afternoon as lawyers, and until recently police traveled by public transport to investigate crimes. Law enforcement depends more on confessions than other evidence.

"We cannot continue living with the judicial system we have now," says Maldanado. "This system offers no solution, no hope of finding justice for the guilty who have committed so many murders in this country." The $9.2 million U.S. Judicial Reform Project begun in 1985 so far has had little effect. "It's harder to reform the judicial system in El Salvador than it is to change the military," says one U.S. official. Human rights organizations counter that, as in the past, the real test of Salvadoran rule of law will be the extent to which the military chooses to obey it.

Meanwhile, the war continues. Says Barrera: "There is no Salvadoran — political, military, civilian — who can say when this war will end." The 62,000 people who have died in the conflict represent more than 1 percent of the entire population. U.S. Embassy estimates put the combined force of the five rebel groups at 6,000, half the total boasted during the early 1980s. Unable to sustain a full-blown military offensive, the rebels have concentrated on economic sabotage, interspersed by the kind of concentrated hit-and-run attack that killed 69 government soldiers and one U.S. military adviser in El Paraiso March 31.

Salvadoran government officials say that with the rebels no longer an immediate military threat, the war is now "90 percent political." "The only time these conflicts end overnight is when one side defeats the other militarily," says Duarte. "That is not my policy." More important, he says, is wooing the populace, proving again that the government can deliver services as well as protection.

A combined civic-military program called United to Reconstruct has been under way in 14 conflict zones. Designed to demonstrate government competence and goodwill through relief and health services, the program has had more success in some of the departments than others. "It very much depends on who the local authorities are and who the minister is of the ministry involved as to how effective it is," according to one Washington analyst. "The military sees this as an important program. They think this is a political war and it's not going to be won militarily, and they're unhappy that there's so much inefficiency in some of the ministries."

Services or no, the vast majority of the Salvadoran population is clearly fed up with the conflict. Christobal Paz has spent the last three of his 24 years at a ramshackle relocation camp in Santa Tecla, 20 kilometers outside of San Salvador. "I see no reason behind the war," he says, "only suffering." He left his home in the department of Usulutan after government soldiers killed his father and torched their farm. He contends that they were driven away by the general fighting, that he has no interest in politics, that he is "neutral." He did not vote, nor does he hold much promise for his country's form of government. "Democracy," he sneers. "It's just politics."

Such disillusionment is perhaps the greatest threat to Duarte's government and to the nascent democracy he heads. "The goal is to win the people," he says. "I have to win a political battle using democracy as an instrument, not only a goal."

— Adam Platt in San Salvador

Do the Sandinistas Want Democracy?

Nicaragua at a Crossroads

Horst Bieber

DIE ZEIT

In only a few months, the peace process has softened Nicaragua's Sandinista regime more than seven years of the Contra war have done. The White House, having been rebuffed in its bid for continued aid to the Contras, argues that only constant pressure will force the Sandinistas to put their power at risk by agreeing to hold democratic elections. The Democratic congressional majority fears that a continuation of Contra aid would interfere with the peace process—or even destroy it. These conflicting views converge on one basic question: Can the Sandinistas be trusted to fulfill their promises about peace and pluralism—or will they break those promises as soon as pressure from the Contras lets up?

That question will not be answered quickly. For the time being, the war will drag on. The Contras still have enough funds from previous American payments, as well as enough weapons, to hold out for another few months—if, that is, the Contra mercenaries do not simply give up on what looks like a lost cause and go their separate ways.

Managua, at any rate, is not counting on a quick end to the fighting; the Sandinistas are calling for untiring vigilance. The Contra leadership, too, promises that it will never put down its weapons. This is chin-up propaganda for its own troops; on the other hand, it stems from the real fear that the Contras might be excluded from the political negotiations that have just begun.

But by mid-year at the latest, the military situation will have eased to such an extent that the Sandinistas will no longer have any arguments to support their hard-nosed position. Oscar Arias, president of Costa Rica and father of the peace plan, is gleefully counting on this, welcoming the American decision to end Contra aid, and calling on Moscow to stop sending military aid to Daniel Ortega's regime. In 1987, Soviet aid to the Sandinistas was an estimated $505 million—far more than the U.S. payments to the Contras.

Arias has the logic of the peace plan on his side—as well as the hopes of other Central American countries that are afraid of the Sandinista military power. Consciously or unconsciously, Arias also is taking aim at a fundamental principle of the Sandinista regime—one that is both its strength and its weakness: the decision of a poor country to turn to a kind of military socialism that subordinates development to defense, and that needs external and internal enemies to warrant this policy.

When the Sandinistas first appeared on Nicaragua's political scene, they had a completely different profile. In July, 1979, when President Anastasio Somoza fled the country because Jimmy Carter had decided to let him fall, the Sandinistas were part of a coalition with the bourgeois opposition. That coalition had agreed on the principles of pluralism, neutrality, and a mixed economy, but the Sandinistas quickly departed from the original program. Their model was—and remains—Cuba.

After Ronald Reagan became president in January, 1981, he immediately warned that he would stop the onset of communism in El Salvador. The Sandinistas, who overestimated their power, declared themselves in favor of international solidarity for all revolutionaries, with the predictable result that by the end of 1981 the Contras had found a patron in Washington.

Nicaragua's civil war prevented an imitation of the Cuban model. It created military socialism with its attendant interdependence between the party, the army, and the police. The social costs and political rigidity that emerged from military socialism quickly became apparent. The church, the industrialists, the middle class, and the nonruling parties turned their backs on the Sandinistas.

A state of emergency, press censorship, and the suspension of important constitutional rights all pointed in a dif-

From the liberal weekly "Die Zeit" of Hamburg.

By Horst Bieber, *Die Zeit*, Hamburg. Reprinted from *World Press Review*, April 1988, pp. 12, 14.

ferent direction from the freedom that the revolution had originally promised. The Sandinista regime began to dig in its heels, justifying its bunker mentality by pointing to its enemies at home and abroad. In spite of economic misery—inflation, unemployment, and shortages of consumer goods—the regime was able to win a loyal following as the defender of Nicaraguan national sovereignty—but only at the risk of making this slogan into an empty shell for a hungry nation.

Debates within the circle of the *comandantes* did not come into the open for a long time. Only in mid-1987 did it become clear that such debates had been going on. President Ortega's decision to put his signature to the Guatemala peace plan has not met with approval everywhere.

Arguments are rife. The president praises free elections, another *comandante* declares that the Sandinistas will never give up their power. The president expresses his willingness to negotiate with the internal Nicaraguan opposition; his colleague, Minister of the Interior Tomás Borge, orders the arrest of the opposition. One *comandante* smiles scornfully and promises that the closed-down opposition newspaper *La Prensa* will resume publication only over his dead body; at the same time, the president is having coffee with the newspaper's publisher after having announced that the ban on the paper has been lifted.

These differences of opinion delineate three camps within the Sandinista leadership. The realists concede that the war will have to be brought to an end through negotiations. If it means pluralism, free elections, a mixed economy, and less power for the Sandinistas, they are ready to pay that price. President Ortega represents this group.

The hawks, a second group, do not want any deviation from current policy, even if it means that the war will drag on. As a logical consequence of this position, they will remain dependent on Soviet assistance—which is beginning to ebb, and which Soviet leader Mikhail Gorbachev intends to reduce even more. This position is represented by the minister of the interior.

A third group seeks a middle road—yes to concessions, but only when that is unavoidable. The existing system must be salvaged to whatever degree is possible. This group is responsible for the contradictory, hesitant behavior of the Nicaraguan government, because Ortega is forced to negotiate with this group every time he wants to initiate a new liberalization.

It is an open question who will have the upper hand when the military pressure lets up. The Sandinistas are aware that they are losing popular support even as an end to the misery of war appears tantalizingly close. The general sentiment is, "We have made enough sacrifices. Now it is time for you to exploit the opportunity at hand."

An internal struggle for power is beginning. It is the Soviets who will determine whether the struggle reaches major proportions. If the Kremlin decides to reduce drastically its military assistance, the hawks in Nicaragua will have to capitulate. They have learned that Cuba manages to survive only by virtue of Moscow's assistance.

It was a mistake for the superpowers to blow up the conflict in Nicaragua enough to make the country an East-West battlefield, incurring the requisite costs for aid. Washington and Moscow could have agreed long ago to reduce their level of involvement. As Fidel Castro told Daniel Ortega at their latest meeting in Havana, it is easy to begin a war, harder to win it, and almost impossible to make use of victory once it is achieved.

The Arab World: Its Own Worst Enemy

Unable to agree, much less unite

The Economist

Consider a riddle. The Arab East—the area from Egypt in the west to Iraq in the east—holds 110 million people and half of the world's proven oil reserves. Its warm and inventive people speak a common language (Arabic) and most profess a common religion (Islam). Its governments say they believe in Arab unity and belong to an organization (the Arab League) designed to promote it. The Arabs ought to be strong. Why are they so weak?

Outsiders could once afford to consider this question merely intriguing. No longer. The Arab East has become a zone of chronic instability with a bad habit of drawing foreign powers into its troubles. Yet it is one whose inner workings the outside world understands only dimly.

Arabs exult in the memory of the 7th and 8th centuries, when they built an empire from Persia to the Pyrenees. After their empire collapsed, the Arabs spent four centuries under the repressive hand of the Ottomans. Most Arabs did not rule themselves again until after World War II. Since then, a handful of Arab countries have bobbed to riches on a flood of oil, but wealth has not yet removed a brooding sense of national failure.

Feeding their sense of failure is the Arabs' bitter, losing contest with Israel. In the 1930s and 1940s, the Arab nations were determined to prevent the founding of a Jewish state in Palestine. They fought the first of five wars with Israel in 1948. Yet, in May Israel will celebrate its 40th anniversary as a state.

The men responsible for the Arab revolt against Turkey in World War I wanted the Arab East to flower into a single nation with its capital in Damascus. Arab unification was the hope with which Gamal Abdel Nasser, the Egyptian president who became the Arabs' greatest modern hero, filled an entire generation in the 1950s. The dream fades a little with every passing year. The borders sketched in the sands by the departing French and British colonial powers have turned out to be remarkably durable, but in Arab hearts the idea of unity lingers mischievously on.

If not unity why not cooperation? Their common culture and language, together with their growing military power and immense oil wealth, ought to have made the Arab states into one of the world's great power blocs. They have not, because with rare exceptions Arab countries have not learned how to integrate their economies or coordinate their foreign policies.

Arab attempts to combine have been thwarted by geography. Physically, the region is dominated by two vast countries. In Saudi Arabia, 14 million people (average annual income per person: $11,000) live comfortably on an underground ocean of oil. In Egypt, some 51 million people (average annual income per person: $1,100) scrape a dusty living out of the sliver of land that borders the Nile.

Saudi Arabia, a conservative monarchy, is fringed to the south by two bone-poor countries, both of which call themselves the only real Yemen, and one of which considers itself a marxist republic. To the Saudis' east lie the glittering oil states of the Gulf. (In Qatar, the average annual income per person is $16,500.) Kuwait has armed forces of about 13,000; next-door Iraq has more than 600,000. The Iraqis' northwestern neighbor is Syria; tucked into Syria's armpit is the shambles of Lebanon; south of Syria is the vulnerable little monarchy of Jordan.

A perverse imbalance of wealth, population, and military power is a poor recipe for neighborliness. So is a bewildering variety of political beliefs. Some Arab governments (Syria, Iraq) are militantly secular; others (Saudi Arabia) claim their mandate from the Koran. Some (Egypt, Jordan) depend for military protection and economic support on the U.S.; others (Syria, South Yemen) are Soviet clients. Little wonder that some Arabs fear one another more than they fear outsiders.

The foreign policies of the Arab East are guided mainly by the internal troubles of leaders whose people are still searching for a full sense of nationhood. Only when they have acquired one will this turbulent region shed the burdens of the past and settle peacefully into the community of nations.

The governments of the Arab East nations face a stubborn problem. Their people feel tugged between two differ-

From the newsmagazine "The Economist" of London.

ent loyalties—a general one toward "Arabism," and a narrower one to their region, clan, or religious sect. Loyalty to the state sometimes comes a poor third.

A wretched proof is the disintegration of Lebanon. The delicate Lebanese National Pact, which tried to freeze political power in proportion to the balance of religious groups in the 1930s, might have limped on a little longer if the country had not also become the playground of warring Palestinians, Israelis, and Syrians. Still, most of Lebanon's poison was brewed at home, in the refusal of the Maronite Christian minority to share power with the Moslem majority. The Maronite tribe could not grip Lebanon's flag tightly enough to prevent the illusion of nationhood from collapsing under the weight of hatreds.

No other Arab state has made the mistake of letting central authority become so weak that armed enclaves have sprouted in its midst. Some, though, have come perilously close. In 1970, when armed Palestinians threatened to shake King Hussein's hold on Jordan, he launched the ugly civil war that disarmed them. In 1982, when opposition by Islamic extremists began to pose a serious threat to Syria's President Hafez al-Assad, he unleashed his army on the rebels, killing thousands of civilians.

Governments throughout the Arab East suffer from the Lebanese disease. Because they draw their support from a narrow segment of the population, they are still struggling to establish their political legitimacy.

An improbable example is the Hashemite Kingdom of Jordan, an oasis of tranquility in the Middle East. King Hussein has been in his job for an uninterrupted 35 years. But the Hashemites have shallow roots in Jordan. Britain invented the place in 1921 as a reward for help received from King Hussein's grandfather, Abdullah, in World War I. While the king survives, Jordan's internal stability looks secure—but its national identity is still in question. More than half of Jordan's citizens consider themselves Palestinians. They accept the king's authority, serve in his army, fill important positions in his cabinet, and dominate commerce—but they are reluctant to relinquish their Palestinian identity.

Partly as a result of such divided loyalties, Arab rulers still lack self-confidence. That is the key to understanding why they govern in the way they do. Democracy has not flourished in the Arab East. Fearful of change, most Arab governments have created closed societies in which dissent is smothered and civil liberties are widely abused.

Egypt lets it people cast their votes, but does not bother much about counting those votes. The conservative monarchies of the Arabian peninsula talk about participation but mean only that citizens can have access to a *majlis*, an open house where the ruling families will listen to their complaints. Jordan has a parliament without powers; political parties are prohibited. Syria and Iraq are dominated by one party, with a strong whiff of Stalinism.

Excuses for this dismal situation abound. Democracy, government apologists earnestly explain, is a foreign notion that does not belong in the Arab East. Islam, Western scholars intone, has a tradition of authoritarianism. These things may be true, but wherever they are given the chance, Arabs show themselves as eager as people anywhere else to have a voice in the way they are governed.

Not all governments of the Arab East are equally oppressive. A few islands of freedom exist. Kuwait has a "freeish" press and a parliament with a handful of real powers. By abolishing censorship and allowing opposition parties to organize, Egypt has made a move in the democratic direction. Such steps go some way toward meeting the clamor of a growing educated class for broader participation in political life, but there is a long way to go.

In Syria and Iraq liberalization is painfully slow. Innocent Iraqis are liable to be questioned, detained, tortured, and even executed without being properly charged or tried. Amnesty International has said that there is routine use of torture in Syria and in the parts of Lebanon under Syrian control.

Saudi Arabia is no democracy, but power is dispersed through the many branches of the royal family, and shared with a Western-educated government technocracy and with the country's influential religious leaders, the *a-ima*. The Saud family has made it a rule to consult widely on all big decisions, and to insure that the kingdom's oil wealth gives all social classes a stake in the regime. This has helped the government keep a firm grip on power without having to resort to the repressive practices of Iraq or Syria.

Jordan considers itself one of the most Westernized Arab states, but its monarchy is more traditional than Saudi Arabia's. King Hussein's personal powers are virtually unlimited. There have been no elections to Jordan's toothless parliament for four years. Government-controlled television is used mainly for propaganda. The nominally independent newspapers are shamelessly muzzled.

The king has remained popular. He uses his power sparingly. Jordan's *mukhabarat*, the secret police, manages to go about its business with delicacy. Jordanians who step out of line—by, say, attending unauthorized meetings of a banned writers' association—are less likely to be bullied in a police station than to receive a gentle warning over the telephone.

King Hussein has an advantage. Jordan (without the West Bank) is a pocket handkerchief of a country with fewer than 3 million people. Maintaining order in societies as complex as Iraq (16 million people) or Syria (11 million) is obviously harder. Yet the most ambitious experiment of the Arab East is taking place not in some tiny Gulf state but in Egypt, a country with one of the least efficient economies in the Middle East and with a society under mounting pressure from Islamic fundamentalism.

The colonels who seized power in Egypt in 1952 had no time for democracy. President Nasser ran Egypt through a single ruling party, the Arab Socialist Union (ASU). In 1976 President Anwar Sadat introduced a hint of political pluralism by allowing the ASU to split into competing "forums," which later became separate political parties. This experiment was short-lived; after Egypt's food riots of 1977, political liberties were curtailed. By the time of his assassination in 1981, Sadat had arrested most of the country's opposition leaders.

Under President Hosni Mubarak, political reform has started moving cautiously forward. Elections, as ever, are rigged. But newspapers are free to criticize the government, and the distribution of seats in parliament has begun to give a slightly more accurate reflection of sentiment in the country.

Autocracy, when it is efficiently administered, has its advantages. Egypt has had only three presidents in more than 30 years. King Hussein of Jordan, President Saddam

Hussein of Iraq, and President Assad of Syria among themselves have notched up well over half a century as heads of state. This stability is in marked contrast to the chaos of the 1950s, when the Arab East seemed at times to have a military coup every other weekend. It is also the sort of stability that brings dangers.

Today's Arab leaders have survived as long as they have primarily because they have mastered the art of controlling their armed forces. They know that if there is a danger to their regimes, it is less likely to come in the form of a popular rebellion than as a coup by disgruntled officers. Keeping officers gruntled is expensive. A happy army is generally one whose officers receive the weapons they think they need and the pay, privileges, and respect they know they deserve.

Virtually all Arab countries maintain large and expensive armed forces. These burgeoning armies are not just an economic burden. In the absence of democratic institutions, they have become the place where much political life of the Arab states takes place. All too often the maneuvers that matter in the Arab world are not cabinet reshuffles or party realignments but the juggling of the sectarian balance inside elite army units and the formation and dissolution of rival Praetorian guards.

Many Arab East countries owe the stability of the past decade to the emergence of a handful of remarkable leaders who have learned to dominate their armies by winning the allegiance of senior officers. Unless an equally shrewd generation of leaders is waiting in the wings, or the Arabs suddenly acquire the habit of democracy, there is danger that the 1990s will see much of the Arab East fall into the hands of military juntas.

Military situations are largely domestic matters. On the international level, a major dilemma for Arab East countries is Israel, whose existence "is like a dagger that has severed the Arab world and dismembered it," in the words of Kamel Abu Jaber, a professor of political science at the University of Jordan. Nearly half a century of conflict with Israel has driven a wedge between "moderate" Arab states that are willing to make peace with Israel on reasonable terms and "radical" states that are not.

Many Arabs consider the six-day war of 1967 the seminal event of modern Arab history. At the end of that war, Israel had captured the Sinai peninsula and Gaza Strip from Egypt, Jerusalem and the West Bank from Jordan, and the Golan Heights from Syria. This was more than a military defeat. The *naqba*, or disaster, brought the ideology of Nasserism to an abrupt and crushing end.

The 1967 war insured that, in Arab eyes, Israel would be blamed not only for the injustice done to the Palestinians but also for thwarting Arab hopes of restoring their ancient greatness. When Egyptian and Syrian armies did much better in their surprise attack on Israel in 1973, this was enough for the Egyptians to remove the taint of 1967. Within six years President Sadat had signed his peace treaty with Israel. Even so, the old dream of forging the Arabs into a single nation never really recovered from the blow.

Why, if the struggle against Israel is so significant in the Arab East, have the Arab countries found it so difficult to act together? A case in point is their relations with the Palestine Liberation Organization (PLO), a movement that they believe they ought to support but that they are frequently tempted to exploit in pursuit of their own national advantage. An elegant example: In 1983, Syria's President Assad supported a mutiny within the PLO in the hope of dislodging Yassir Arafat and bringing the organization under Syrian control. Egypt's President Mubarak, spotting an opportunity to prove himself a good Arab and to edge Egypt out of its post-Camp David isolation, promptly gave Arafat a royal welcome in Cairo.

Clearly, the Arabs have been unable to unite against Israel. Nor is there evidence of a united Arab stand against Persian Iran in its bitter war against Arab Iraq. Israel and Iran have presented the Arabs with their biggest geo-strategic challenges. In each case, a powerful Arab state has blocked the emergence of a common front—Egypt by its peace with Israel, and Syria by remaining friendly with Iran and hostile to Iraq.

The Arab East has two worries about the Gulf war. Threat number one, an Iraqi military collapse followed by Iran's revolutionary armies sweeping deeper into the Arabian peninsula, appears unlikely. The exhausted Iranians would need time for recuperation, and they know that taking their war further inside Arab territory would run the risk of goading the U.S. into military action in defense of the Gulf's oil.

Most Arab states worry more about threat number two. Unlike Israel, Iran poses a challenge to the internal authority of Arab rulers. The Iranian revolution claims to hold a message for all Moslems. Return to Islam, Ayatollah Khomeini says to the Arabs, and you will rediscover your former greatness—just as we Iranians did when our revolution of 1979 swept away the Shah and defied the mighty Americans.

This message disturbs the Arab regimes. From their point of view, Islam is an awkward religion. It recognizes no distinction between religious and temporal power, and it is hostile to nationalism. Moslems are supposed to belong to an *umma* (a single community of believers) united under the sacred law (the *sharia*), not to separate national jurisdictions with a hodgepodge of secular laws.

Most Arab governments have a long and bloody history of doing battle with Islamic extremists who want either to impose full *sharia* law or, better still, to replace their secular governments with an Islamic theocracy. These groups insist on their right to use violent means in pursuit of their righteous ends. But Islamic extremists who have tried to fight the full power of the state have generally lost, mainly because Arab governments have shown few qualms about responding to their actions with massive force.

Sooner or later, the Arabs are going to have to choose between government by men and government by God. Their choice may turn out to depend on the power of money as much as on the power of ideas. For the past decade and a half, Arab governments have relied on oil wealth to buy their way out of political difficulty.

They have had plenty of cash. Oil exports have earned the Arab states $1.5 trillion since the oil shock of 1973. That party is now over. In 1981 Saudi Arabia earned nearly $120 billion from oil; in 1987, $22 billion.

In the years of plenty, countries like Egypt and Jordan, which have little or no oil to export, did the next best thing by exporting people to take the jobs their oil-rich neighbors would not take. This has done more than any number of pan-Arab bureaucracies to tie the economies of the region closer together. Some 500,000 Jordanians—about 50 percent of the country's workforce—work in the Gulf, as do more than 2 million Egyptians. Their remittances home have become an indispensable source of foreign exchange.

Doomsayers who expect hard times in the Gulf to bring Arab governments tumbling down are almost certainly wrong. What may be true is that the Arab East has begun to enter a period in which unfamiliar economic forces rather than familiar political ones will pose the main threat to the survival of regimes.

In Saudi Arabia, for example, the government is already finding it difficult to meet the aspirations of all those who expect admission to universities, and of graduates who expect comfortable jobs in government service. In 1986 university admissions were cut by a third. At some point, unmet expectations will begin to erode loyalty to the regime.

Saudi Arabia's problems fade into insignificance compared with those of Egypt, which is beset by a foreign-exchange famine. Its ability to pay for its imports and to service its external debt has been damaged by a slump in remittances from workers in the Gulf and by disappointing oil revenues. Experts predict that the Egyptians will be lucky if their economy manages a growth rate of even two percent a year.

Few predictions about the Arab world come out right. But there is a case for believing that Egypt's fate will provide the best clue to the shape of the next decade in the Arab East. By its sheer size, by the weight of its history, and by the fact that it is the Arab East's only true nation, Egypt is condemned to be the dominant force in the Arab world.

It is tackling the big question for the Arab East—how to combine economic efficiency with social injustice and a modicum of democracy. If Egypt's experiment survives, other Arabs may accept the fact that the separate states into which history has divided them are not going to wither away. In this future, the legitimacy of governments will depend more on their behavior at home than on crusades abroad. It is a future that might work.

AYATOLLAH REALPOLITIK

Henry Precht

HENRY PRECHT, *director of Iranian affairs at the State Department from 1978 to 1980, is president of the Cleveland Council on World Affairs.*

The American consensus on Iran is persistent and clear: The leaders in Tehran are crazy, blindly ideological, resistant to international law and opinion, and virtually impossible to deal with. And the bad news only gets worse from this wild bunch. The *New York Times*, for instance, reported in its August 29, 1987, issue that militants were taking over Iran's foreign policy. If the prevailing analysis is correct, the United States and its Western and Arab friends are right to quarantine this threat to stable, rational order. But is it correct? Is there any hope for refashioning a relationship with a country once considered so important to America's security and well-being? Is the ideological barrier on both sides too dense to penetrate? What will it take to bring the United States and Iran closer? How might making, or not making, the effort affect U.S. interests in the region?

There are several defects in the prevailing consensus. One is ignorance. Iranian society and politics have always seemed a black hole for American officials, journalists, and, to a lesser extent, academics. If little was known about the internal dynamics of Shah Mohammed Riza Pahlevi's regime and its opponents, almost nothing is known about the current leadership. Another defect is that American labels—liberal and conservative, fanatic and moderate—are ill-chosen for Iranian politics. Differences exist on many issues and among many political personalities. A conservative on economic policy may be radical on social standards and ambivalent on foreign policy. Finally, the American view is contorted by emotions over Iran's revolutionary excesses and continuing confrontations. Toward the United States, Iran displays equal or greater ignorance, conceptual difficulties, and emotional obstacles.

How sound is the American consensus? When the United States launched its policy of providing naval escorts to Kuwaiti oil tankers in the Persian Gulf in July 1987, experts predicted that Iran would retaliate with terrorism. Perhaps it will someday. But one reaction from Tehran was to assist in freeing a West German hostage in Lebanon. Another was to receive—respectfully this time—U.N. Secretary General Javier Pérez de Cuéllar when he went to Tehran in his second attempt at persuading Iran to accept a U.N.-sanctioned cease-fire in its 7-year-long war with Iraq. After the July 1987 deaths of rioting Iranian pilgrims in Mecca, analysts feared an Iranian blow at Saudi Arabia. It may yet happen. But while words from Tehran have been harsh, retribution has been nonexistent. Perhaps if Americans read the Iranian record with the calm geopolitical interest of a Soviet or Turkish analyst, the former client might seem less mad, more insecure and inexperienced, less ideological, and more pragmatic.

By most accounts, the Islamic fundamentalist revolution, now fused with the Iran-Iraq war as a source of mobilization, shows no sign of relaxing its grip on the Iranian public. Ideology counts with the masses. Yet despite a decade of external and internal conflicts and the new and harsh rhetoric, a continuity in the conduct of international relations does link the old and new regimes. Thus the maxim is borne out that a country's geopolitical situation eventually must prevail over its ideology. An Islamic nationalism rooted in the national interests of Iran outweighs an ideology of Islam as a world revolutionary movement. This turning inward is the natural consolidation of a mass movement, accelerated by the exigencies of

Reprinted with permsision from *Foreign Policy,* 70, Spring 1988, pp. 109-128.

war. It also derives from the strictly national origins of Iran's Islamic movement. Since taking power the movement's leaders have found it necessary to pursue basic economic and security objectives with states whose policies they deem abhorrent—Turkey and the USSR, as well as France, Great Britain, and Saudi Arabia—until events in the latter three countries forced what probably will be a temporary reversal of Tehran's tack.

The revolutionary regime's process of settling down has moved haltingly, though more steadily in foreign affairs than in domestic life. Barring additional shocks and provided the right incentives, the trend toward pragmatism can build strength. Realistic decisions will be required to assert interests and shelter vulnerabilities in a difficult war and later in a difficult peace. While the power of ideology will persist, its sway will be progressively limited to issues that are fundamental to the regime's legitimacy as the Islamic defender of the oppressed—and that primarily for home consumption. To the confusion of outsiders, symbolism in the service of ideology will cloak the development of a realistic policy serving national interests. Although Washington should be able to deal with such a regime, success will require a generous supply of patience and skill—qualities the United States has not always shown toward Near East radicals.

The first step in understanding Ayatollah Ruhollah Khomeini's brand of foreign policy is to restudy the shah's. The shah's diplomacy was grounded on the U.S. commitment to counter any external threat too great for him while facilitating the building of a stronger Iran. The partnership was never exclusive; the shah made sure he had useful links to other states, including the USSR.

Three other principles also shaped the shah's policies. First was the basic need to protect Iran's external and internal security. By 1977 money, autocracy, and key friendships seemed to have made Iran safe. The achievement of security allowed the pursuit of a second principle, the projection of Iranian prestige. The shah aimed beyond forcing the development pace of a backward country. He would show his country and the world that Iran now counted. But when the oil balloon deflated in the late 1970s, the shah fell because he had no ideological safety net. Finally came the principle of preserving the beneficent conservative state—preferably a monarchy—as the best defense against communism. While realistic enough not to advocate the export of monarchy, the shah clearly preferred the company of rulers who did not carry their own bags.

The shah's foreign policy, then, was not so different in content from other countries' foreign policies. What set it apart were the heavy reliance on the United States and the conservative, elitist ideology. A revolution turns things upside down, and Khomeini put into play the opposite ideas: doing without the United States and glorifying the concept of the oppressed man.

With the revolution's success, opposition to the shah found that it was united only on that achieved goal. In those early days Khomeini's was the only authoritative voice, and even his words lacked consistency. The revolution was possessed by its victory. It was not a moment for nuance or for attention to the effect of ill-considered words on nervous, nonrevolutionary listeners. A predisposition abroad took every Iranian utterance as a dire threat to the West or its regional friends. The embrace of Khomeini and Palestine Liberation Organization (PLO) Chairman Yasir Arafat made the front pages of newspapers and magazines, not the new regime's help to Israeli embassy staff in safely departing the country. Outsiders still rely on the most radical rhetoric in interpreting Tehran. When Iran's president, Hojatolislam Ali Khamenei, warned "our friend" Kuwait in 1986 not to allow Iraq to use the island of Bubiyan for military purposes, the foreign press heard him threaten invasion. But Iran did not invade and for some months continued to seek improved relations with Kuwait.

Despite outside perceptions, greater coherence in foreign affairs began to develop in 1984. In August of that year, when hijackers flew an Air France jet to Tehran, the regime was swept by a bitter internal debate over how to react. The decision went against the hijackers. A few days later Khomeini denied Iran's involvement in the incident and also criticized the state radio for suggesting that Iran supported planting mines in the Red Sea. Later in 1984 Khomeini ended another debate by approving diplomatic relations with all states except Israel, South Africa, and the United States.

Several factors have advanced the creeping systematization of Iran's foreign policy. The regime has been successful in eliminating its internal competition. Debate is much freer than in the old days, but it centers on details like land reform and not fundamentals like the regime's Islamic identity. When debate takes a more threatening turn, as it did over the covert purchases of U.S. arms, it can be muzzled. In addition, the regime has faced varying external threats throughout its existence, and that danger tends to force agreement. And as with all governments, a maturing process takes over despite the pressures of extremists. Maturity does not require officials to wear ties, but it leads them to learn from past experimentation. Having shouted slogans outside ministries in their formative years and inside in their early governing days, officials have learned that leadership demands something more. Perhaps they themselves now hear shouts outside to which they must respond with practical measures.

Defensive Nationalism

Foremost among the Khomeini regime's guiding principles is its rigid insistence on independence—above all, on the complete end of any dependence on the United States. In good part that stood at the heart of the revolution. A pure Islam will protect the country, and Iran's independence will keep Islam pure. Implementing this principle has meant virtually eliminating foreign debt and earnestly seeking economic self-sufficiency. Iran will not borrow and fall into the "abyss of dependence," as Prime Minister Mir Hussein Mousavi told the Tehran Trade Fair in August 1986.

If this principle accurately describes a nationalistic purpose for the Islamic republic, it weakens the thesis that Tehran aspires to create a larger Islamic polity. That inspiring concept elevates political rhetoric as a distant goal. Extremist factions do hold this universalistic outlook. But nowhere is it reflected in the practical actions of the leadership. Their commitments rarely go beyond the historical national borders. Although they would deny loudly that they are "Iran Firsters" with new language and different tactics, the current leaders follow much the same nationalism as their predecessor. Historically, Iranian nationalism has been defensive, not jingoistic; it has not embraced serious irredentist claims or a desire to absorb outsiders. Like the shah, today's rulers want Iran to be respected as a model and to exercise great influence in the region. But their immediate agenda is political and economic independence at home, not dominion abroad.

The second principle is intrinsic to the first: "The predominant requirement is to safeguard the Islamic Republic," as Khomeini acknowledged in February 1986. The great sacrifices of the revolution and the war are not to be risked by ill-considered actions. The republic deals with the USSR despite loathing its policies toward Moslems. It has bought arms from Israel and the United States. Buying security, however, does not mean selling out independence or ideology.

For more than 7 years the principle of national security has called for winning the war with Iraq, not merely ending it, which is the Iraqi objective. The insistence on victory is both pragmatic and ideological. Strategically, Iran wants to assure that a totally defeated Iraq, with its leadership removed, will be unable to resume hostilities in the future. The Iraqi threat to Iran's western border—both from direct aggression and from trouble-making ethnic Kurds and counterrevolutionaries—finally must be squelched. The regime that set out to destroy the Islamic republic cannot be trusted; it must be eliminated. The shah thought he had achieved security on his western border through the 1975 Algiers accord and through military deterrence. Khomeini is taking a more drastic and costly approach to the same pragmatic goal.

Ideology also keeps Iran fighting. The pursuit of total victory is in part pure, vengeful rage against what Tehran considers an impious ruler, reputedly backed by the United States, who dared attack a truly Islamic government. Uncompromising religious fervor mobilized people against the shah and sustains support for a long, costly war. People give their all because they know that there will be no compromise before the sacred attainment of victory.

Another factor in prosecuting the war is peculiar to Iran's politics. Khomeini set the original war aims—Iraq's withdrawal from Iranian territory, reparations, and the removal of Iraqi President Saddam Hussein. The first is essentially achieved and the second is negotiable. But the last is the sticking point. Will the man who has never compromised on a demand of crucial importance yield on requiring a regime change in Baghdad? While some statements from Tehran have seemed to soften this demand, Khamenei told the U.N. General Assembly on September 22, 1987, that the most important goal of the three war aims remains "to punish and remove the aggressor." Iran's insistence on U.N. condemnation of Iraqi war culpability seems to be a way of discrediting Hussein both internationally and with his own people. Acceptance of an interim cease-fire cannot be excluded if Iran is offered a face-saving device and if economic pressures become insupportable, but real peace for Tehran will require removing Hussein. The regime has invested too much in blood and fervor to abandon that demand and still survive at home.

The third—and unique—foreign-policy principle is the promotion abroad of Iran's homegrown Islamic ideology as a catalyst for oppressed peoples to overcome what it regards as arrogant and impious rulers. Iran stands with the masses, especially when they are Moslem—and not just Shiite Moslem—as in Lebanon and with Palestinians, but also when they are not, as in South Africa. This principle is the most loudly celebrated and carries great influence over policy. Yet ideology seems increasingly subject to qualification and interpretation in the mix of foreign-policy choices. Pursuit of Islamic goals is not immune to calculations of opportunity costs. Tehran supports Damascus despite its repression of the fundamentalist group Moslem Brotherhood because Syrian support is crucial in the war. But it also shows preference for the Eritrean Moslems rebelling against the Marxist revolutionary regime in Addis Ababa because Ethiopia has relatively little importance. When Saudi police shoot Iranian pilgrims in Mecca, the careful pragmatic policy toward Riyadh seems overtaken by the national outcry, but the actual response is to avoid further trouble.

The ayatollah's regime has found a way to maintain fidelity to the revolution's ideals while protecting the country through pragmatism: It cautiously selects opportunities for actively promoting Islam and generally remains more rhetorical than active. Thus Iranian leaders repeatedly have explained that the revolution's universal goals are to be achieved by Iran's inspirational role and not by its active interference in other states' affairs. The model is the revolution—carried out by the Iranian people themselves without outside help and, indeed, in opposition to powerful foreign forces.

If Americans read the Iranian record with the calm geopolitical interest of a Soviet or Turkish analyst, the former client might seem less mad, more insecure and inexperienced, less ideological, and more pragmatic.

To a large degree Iranian policy is reactive. Positions are taken after Tehran observes how it is regarded in other capitals. This does not mean that an "oppressor" state can redeem itself simply by offering sweet words and cake or that "usurpers" can ever be redeemed. With most states, however, uncritical words and pleasing actions can bring eventual rewards, especially when Tehran sees that its own interests are being served. The reverse—such as perceived insults from the British and French—can produce a severe reaction.

The test of foreign-policy principles lies in their application to neighbors and more distant states. A review of Iran's diplomacy reveals the ascendancy of pragmatism. Two neighbors—Turkey and Pakistan—should fare poorly by the Islamic republic's standards. Turkey, although it has mellowed the secularist policies of its first president, Mustafa Kemal Atatürk, has long been for Iran's clerics the example of what an Islamic state should not become. (Khomeini himself was exiled there in 1964 but soon departed for Iraq.) Turkey was the model for the shah and remained a close friend of his son. Moreover, the closure of Iraq's pipeline through Syria made Turkey a major shipping point for Iraqi oil. Finally, Turkey is a NATO member with U.S. bases on its soil.

As strong as these arguments are, the other side of the ledger is more persuasive for Tehran. Turkey actively has solicited good relations since the Khomeini regime's first days. Ankara fears problems with its Islamic activists and its Kurdish minority; good relations with Iran might help to keep those elements in check. Turkey benefits from both the transit trade to and from Iran and its own trade with Iran. Turkey is preoccupied with Greece and the USSR, so it needs a peaceful border with Iran. Iran's outlook on these points is similar. It wants the trade, the peace, and the trouble-free relationship offered by Turkey, which, after all, maintains a large, tough army. Above all, Turkey is Iran's principal link to the West. Iran's relations with Turkey offer the clearest evidence of the rewards for those who treat Tehran with the respect it craves.

Turkey is joined with Iran and Pakistan—just as in the days of the Central Treaty Organization—in a formal economic association. For Iran, the economic linkage with Pakistan is not compelling. Yet it overlooks Pakistan's close association with the United States for the sake of more overriding concerns—Iran's land route to the east, the welfare of Pakistan's large Shiite population, and the need for peace on the border where Baluch tribes have been manipulated in the past.

Policy toward Afghanistan has long been a function of policy toward the Soviet Union. Then Prime Minister Mehdi Bazargan's government, which ruled in a 9-month interregnum between the shah and the ayatollah in 1979, ignored U.S. warnings of danger resulting from the Soviet invasion of Afghanistan. While Khomeini and his associates regularly condemn Soviet repression of Moslems, Iran's concrete role is equivocal. Actions lag behind rhetoric. Aid to the rebels is necessarily limited by the war with Iraq. The few resources that can be spared are channeled to Shiite groups. Even if funds were available, planners in Tehran would see much risk in a more active involvement in the fighting. More refugees could be generated to add to Iran's already heavy burden of 2 million Afghans. Indeed, significant Iranian help to Afghan rebels could bring Soviet retaliation. The fighting has spilled over the border before, and Iran has only one effective alternative to Soviet pressure—the ideologically impossible answer of turning to the United States.

Iranian language against the Soviet Union on other issues has also been fairly tough but, as with Afghanistan, not always reflected in action. Each country is wary of the other, but neither is looking for trouble. Iranian religious broadcasts are heard in the Soviet Moslem republics apparently without exciting too much concern in Moscow, and Iran tolerates sporadic propaganda from the north. The Soviets moved quickly to recognize the new reality in Iran: Their ambassador was one of the first and most frequent to call on Khomeini. Their posture of waiting out the revolution and suffering abuse stoically has begun to pay off. In 1983 the Iranians smashed the communist Tudeh party and expelled 18 Soviet diplomats. Now that chapter is closed and a page turned with the Soviet-Iranian agreements in 1986 and 1987 on oil and gas exploration and the reopening of a gas pipeline. Under these agreements, Soviet technicians are to return to Iran. And some years hence Iran may export oil by means of the pipeline. Economic ties also have grown closer than at any time since 1978.

But income probably counts less than political leverage. Iran wants the Soviet Union to work to end the Iran-Iraq war on terms Iran can accept, or at least to restrain itself in augmenting Iraqi strength. (The Soviets resumed military aid to Iraq in 1982 after Iran muscled Iraqi forces from its territory.) For several decades the Soviet military threat to Iran has meant more to Washington than to Tehran, which has not deployed major forces to the north or seriously planned for a Soviet assault. Iran's pragmatic wooing was set back in 1987 by Moscow's policy toward Arab gulf states: The USSR leased three oil tankers to Kuwait. Limited damage to Soviet shipping from a patrol boat attack and a mine served as Iran's dignity-protecting response in May. The Soviets swallowed hard and, helped by the U.S. Navy's move into the Persian Gulf, have more than patched up relations. Moscow continues to work patiently for a long-term rapprochement; and Tehran, fearing U.S. aggression, reciprocates.

The war with Iraq is the primary platform for expression of the three Iranian principles of independence, security of the state, and promotion of Islam. Tehran's stated aim of avoiding harm to Iraqi civilians derives from its limited capabilities and its hope that the Shiite majority in Iraq will rebel against the "irreligious" Baghdad regime. No greater "export the revolution" drive has been launched from Tehran, but the response from Iraqi Shiites thus far has been virtually nil.

Criteria for Good Relations

Iran's attitudes toward the gulf states essentially are determined by their aid to Iraq, their oil policies, and their military cooperation with the United States. These issues override Tehran's evident distaste for regimes that are the antithesis of the Iranian model. Timid on Israel, attracted by the "sinful" allure of the West, with immensely wealthy rulers of "oppressed" Moslems, these vulnerable states would seem ripe targets of the "revolution for export." That was the case judging by earlier threats from Iranian extremists and the residual perception of some gulf politicians and outsiders. Tehran was blamed for a 1981 coup attempt in Bahrain and the Kuwait bombings of 1986 and 1987. It denied both. The 1986 Mecca pilgrimage became not only a stage for Khomeini-style propaganda but also a destination for explosives. The responsible individual was arrested and later executed in Tehran on other charges. The 1987 violence in Mecca seems to have been a tragic accident. It conflicted with current policy in both Tehran and Riyadh; neither capital could have desired the resulting damage to relations.

In about 1984 Iran shifted to a soft policy toward its gulf neighbors. Unable to force its will on them, Tehran tried reducing its stridency. In 1982 Khamenei had denounced the gulf state monarchs as "greedy pigs . . . sheikhs who have spent their whole life plundering your wealth. . . . We will destroy all the dwarfs." But 3 years later the line was different: "We have friendly feelings towards Gulf neighbors . . . have begun to establish more sincere relations. They have welcomed them." A consistent theme in Tehran's message during the years of soft policy toward the gulf Arabs was its reiteration that it sought to serve as the inspiration for revolution rather than to export the revolution by force.

Abu Dhabi was a leader in the dialogue. Fearful Kuwait, closely linked to Iraq, antagonistic in the Organization of Petroleum Exporting Countries (OPEC), and a target of pro-Iranian terrorism, suffers the worst relations. Iran might have resumed its place in the January 1987 meeting of the Islamic Conference Organization had the gathering not been held in Kuwait. The Gulf Cooperation Council (GCC)—formed of peninsula states deeply concerned about an aggressive Iran—for a time benefited from an Iranian perception that its own threats, albeit largely empty ones, were making the regimes nervous and increasing the possibility that the Arabs might invite the United States to assume permanently the old British role of protector. Tehran is not apt to test U.S. power. Despite the anti-Iran resolutions adopted at the Arab League and GCC summit meetings in December 1987, Tehran will resume work on receptive gulf neighbors to invite the U.S. military back "over the horizon."

The Mecca incident dramatically set back Tehran's previously successful diplomacy toward Riyadh. Since 1984 both sides had avoided being carried away by the war's occasional spillover—whether in the mutual restraint following the Saudi downing of two Iranian F-4 fighter planes in 1984 or in the war on shipping. When Saudi Arabia and its friends took the lead to drive down oil prices, Iran interpreted the policy as intended to weaken the republic in its war with Iraq and sent warnings across the gulf. But those broadcasts always held out the expectation that the Arabs would see their true interests and act in time to avoid a clash. The soft Iranian line worked. As Iran played the statesman in OPEC rather than the renegade, the atmosphere became more businesslike and helped produce agreement to limit production. Whether Iran can get back on a positive track in OPEC with Saudi Arabia is a crucial question for Iran's economy and war effort.

Acceptance of an interim cease-fire cannot be excluded if Iran is offered a face-saving device and if economic pressures become insupportable, but real peace for Tehran will require removing Saddam Hussein.

The list of countries that Iran regards as truly close friends is quite short. It includes Algeria, Libya, and Syria, as well as selected liberation movements. Each relationship is burdened by conflicting interests. Syria, for one, shares hostility toward Iraq, closed its pipeline to Iraqi oil in exchange for cut-rate Iranian oil, and serves as the gateway to the Shiites in Lebanon. It is tactically dear to Iran. But tension in the relationship does not bode well for the future. When in 1986 Iranian deputies grouched about Syria's delay in paying for oil, Damascus murmured about restoring ties with Baghdad. That blew over, but Syria will remain obliged to tend to its anti-Israel policy and to the Arab subsidies it receives, much of them from GCC countries. Tehran can only fret when Syrian President Hafez al-Assad and Hussein meet someday.

Algeria, like Syria, has been tough on its Islamic opposition but sports excellent revolutionary credentials and, as a hard-pressed oil and gas producer, a similar outlook on OPEC. Islam-respecting Libya gets high marks as the region's most unrelenting enemy of the United States, as a radical oil producer, and, like Syria, as a source of weaponry. Yet there is tension in the relationship. Its flamboyant leader, Colonel Muammar el-Qaddafi, is not fully acceptable to Iran's conservative mullahs. Moreover, he has never explained the disappearance of Lebanon's Shiite leader, Iran-born Musa Sadr, during a trip to Libya in 1978.

Liberation movements rate automatic distinction in Iranian rhetoric, provided they maintain uncompromising anti-oppressor credentials. The PLO, it seems, fell from esteem as Arafat turned soft and anti-Syrian. Condemning him for cooperating with Jordan's King Hussein on the future of Palestine, Ayatollah Hussein Ali Montazeri, Khomeini's designated successor, declared, "What has been taken by force must be retrieved by force." The more intransigent Palestinians remain in good grace but must take second place to the radical Shiite group Hezbollah (Party of God) operating in Lebanon against Western interests. The Lebanese struggle appears to receive more Iranian assistance than any other movement, including the Shiites in Afghanistan. It is not clear whether the aid comes from official entities or from private groups. The fuzzy distinction illustrates the still prevailing revolutionary fluidity in Tehran and underscores the problem for government spokesmen: They condemn terrorism but endorse liberation struggle. The conceptual predicament is not unique; the entire region suffers from it.

Among the growing group of favorably regarded states, those with revolutionary origins make Tehran most comfortable. Religion helps but is not always decisive. Iran preferred the Christian rebels in Sudan to the regime of Jafar Nimeiri, which applied Islamic law but whose ties to the United States and Egypt were fatal. The new regime in Khartoum has done better: Tehran has forgiven its uncollectible debts.

Those countries that provide war materiel have a special place among the helpful countries but, owing to sensitivities about their links to the United States or the USSR, gain little public recognition. The two Koreas are prime examples. Arms supplies apart, Tehran has two criteria for good relations. First, does the state have an antirevolutionary record? China was hurt by then Communist party Chairman Hua Guofeng's visit to the shah during the massive 1978 demonstrations and its subsequent failure to make amends to the republic. But it is now redeemed as the leading purveyor of arms to Iran, including Silkworm missiles deployed along the gulf. Second, can economic benefit be had without political strings? In this vein, Australian meat and Japanese technology do not threaten Iranian independence.

Until 1987 Britain and France were doing nicely because of persistent efforts to get back on track with Tehran. According to Hojatolislam Hashemi Rafsanjani, speaker of Iran's parliament, France's treatment of Iran was "worse than what the American Government did to us," and only its past hospitality to Khomeini saved it from a break in relations.[1] France supplied arms to Iraq, fought the Shiites in Lebanon and Qaddafi in Chad, owed Iran $1 billion from a loan the shah made, and sheltered antirevolutionary activists. In 1986 France moved to meet Rafsanjani's demands by expelling Massoud Rajavi, leader of the largest Iranian opposition group, the People's Mujahedeen, and by agreeing to repay the loan. But when a suspected terrorist took refuge in Tehran's embassy in Paris, the ensuing crisis derailed the patched-up job until a deal was worked out in December 1987 for the release of two French hostages in Lebanon and the expulsion from France of Mujahedeen activists. Britain has experienced a similar roller coaster relationship with Iranian sensitivities.

Two countries on Iran's blacklist, Israel and South Africa, are forever fixed as "lesser Satans." It is inconceivable that these two governments, which in Tehran's eyes fuse oppression with usurpation, could construct a relationship with Iran, even with the most adroit effort. South Africa is spared by distance from becoming an active target. The destruction of Israeli power, however, ranks second after victory over Iraq on Tehran's agenda. The Iranian slogan "The road to Jerusalem leads through Baghdad" foretells that after the war more active enmity—though not official armed forces—will be focused on the Zionist state.

The two "usurpers" apart, it is possible in the right circumstances for Iran to repair its relations with others on its current blacklist, including America. Among Arab governments, Jordan, Egypt, and Morocco are especially despised because of their close links to the old regime, their firm ties to the United States, their softness toward Israel, and their inability to affect Iran's well-being as a major oil producer can. Another key factor in Iran's foreign relations is also at work in these three cases—the personalization of politics. "Hussein, Hosni, and Hassan" have been regular targets for Khomeini's personal scorn. It is impossible to imagine that the republic could form a connection with the two monarchs who were close friends of the shah. But President Hosni Mubarak's Egypt is different. An important player in the war, Egypt could experience Iran's pragmatic diplomacy if the right opening appeared.

Beginning a Healing Process

Then there is the "Great Satan." The United States has everything going against it: its past with the shah, the searing experience of the hostage crisis, the years of mutual suspicion and accusations, and its pro-Iraq, anti-Iran tilt in the gulf war. What might motivate better relations? From Iran's perspective, America is a great power and cannot be ignored by a state that aspires to influence beyond its borders. In the future the United States could be useful for a classic power balance if the USSR should threaten. But if the USSR continues present policies, Iran is unlikely to worry about a Soviet threat. After all, Iran safely ignored the threat from the United States during the hostage crisis without turning to the USSR for support.

More important for Iran than political dialogue will be what the United States can offer Iran through commercial channels. Spare parts and new machines, training, and new techniques are needed in every sector of Iranian life—whether in the military where the Pentagon set the foundation under the shah or in agriculture and medicine where Americans did relatively little but are respected. Khomeini has called training impressionable Iranian youth in foreign universities the greatest danger to the republic. But many technocrats took such training and kept their purity; they will want the benefits American universities can offer for Iran's development. Their model is Japan, a modern state that preserved its culture while modernizing. Also, many Iranians are attracted to the basic "goodness" of the American people, despite hostile official policies. Khomeini and Montazeri each has endorsed relations with Washington on a new basis. Rafsanjani has said that "Iran has not sworn to be crossed with the U.S. until doomsday . . . provided that Washington deals with Iran as an independent country and gives up unreasonable expectations."[2] Re-

---

[1] *Foreign Broadcast Information Service*, "*Hashemi-Rafsanjani Meets with French Official*," Daily Report: South Asia, *1 April 1985*, *12*.

[2] *Foreign Broadcast Information Service*, "*Majlis Speaker on Conditions for Future U.S. Ties*," Daily Report: South Asia, *10 February 1986*, *12*.

fashioning a relationship will mean difficult changes on both sides. The impact of a change on the war is the primary consideration for Iran, as terrorism and regional destabilization are for America. Because of the personality factor on both sides real progress probably will have to wait for leadership changes in Washington and Tehran. Whenever the healing process begins, it will—and should—be a long time building.

Such a healing process will require four policy components. First, if a new relationship is to have a chance, the war with Iraq must end or be approaching a conclusion. Otherwise, demands for arms and suspicions of hostility will distort all business. Washington's first step should be to become truly neutral: No assistance should be delivered to one side that is denied to the other. Ending America's tilt toward Iraq will send a significant message to Iran. It will, of course, be even more significant and unsettling to the Arabs. Thus Washington also should bolster external security for the gulf Arab states; Congress should support reasonable military supplies and a moderate U.S. presence. To foster internal stability the United States should show greater activity and balance on Arab-Israeli issues. And for longer-term security and stability, the United States should begin to think with Iraq's friends about a realistic peace. Minimally, that will mean publicly conceding Iran's right to compensation as the victim of aggression. It may require identifying those funds and possibly organizing a peace-keeping force on the border. The consequences for the regime of Saddam Hussein will be severe. But the alternatives to the dread change in Washington's position are the remote hope that Tehran will yield on its demand for Hussein's removal or the destabilizing attainment of that outcome through an Iranian victory or internal upheaval in Iraq.

The second component in rebuilding a relationship is to demonstrate public U.S. acceptance of the revolution—something Iran's leadership has sought since February 1979. Measures to accomplish this could include:

• progressively reducing the U.S. military presence in the Persian Gulf as the war ends and avoiding a blatant anti-Iran label on forces that stay;

• treating Iran as a normal state, which would include not expecting special treatment from Tehran, showing sensitivity to Iran's independence, and avoiding the old temptation to manipulate and seek special favors. In return, Washington should insist on normal state behavior from Iran;

• avoiding identification with any faction to dispel the inevitable suspicion of U.S. plotting against the revolution, although some will see proper contacts with the government as favor for one faction or the other;

• tidying up the multitude of long-delayed business from before and after the hostage crisis, including accelerating the work of the Iran-U.S. Claims Tribunal; and

• after the war—and only then—responding slowly and cautiously to the abiding Iranian interest in spare parts and support for military hardware.

The third component in rebuilding relations would be cautiously to encourage private groups, such as exporters, banks, oil companies, and educators, to test and develop connections with Iran. The commercial linkage will be crucial. Ending the administration's trade embargo early in any negotiations will ease Iran's belief that Washington opposes a relationship based on sovereign equality. Official relations are likely to require first a foundation of commercial confidence.

Finally, the American public must be prepared step-by-step for any change toward Iran. Administration rhetoric should be mellowed, but Iran would also have to do its part. If a new relationship is to succeed, Iran must get a tighter grip on its unrestrained factions and make clear that terrorism is not official doctrine. The United States should demand not that Iran be purer in this respect than other governments it deals with, but that there should be minimal standards, such as cooperation on freeing American hostages held in Lebanon.

With or without a U.S. relationship, what policies and behavior can be anticipated from the Islamic republic in the years ahead? Under Khomeini's authoritative hand, Khamenei, Mousavi, Rafsanjani, and Montazeri have functioned as a team before while holding power. Their differences appear to be tactical and personal. When Khomeini dies, those differences could become sharper, or the present leadership collectively could face an internal challenge. In the past Khomeini's authority, his street power, and the state apparatus have defeated opposition. If there is conflict in post-Khomeini Iran, the role of the Revolutionary Guards and the army will be decisive. Will they remain in the barracks, oppose the regime, or fragment among power centers? In such a struggle, any group that labels itself moderate to gain U.S. support will be demonstrably desperate and not a major contender. But the same fierce independence also will block any faction from successfully drawing in the Soviet Union.

Whatever situation evolves, it seems certain that the revolution will not be rolled back. A new regime may have a different complexion, but if it is to rule with some popular consent it will have to follow precepts closer to the present regime's than to the shah's. The primary ideological values of the revolution cannot be ignored by any group that is serious about popular support. The United States must learn to live with this fact.

Under any conceivable regime ideology cannot ignore the pragmatic requirements of Iran's geopolitical position. Therefore, realism will generally govern, except where the regime's legitimacy is at stake. On vital questions of the war and postwar recovery, ideology should yield to pragmatic solutions. Leaders will try to restrain wilder elements. Safeguarding the state by developing its economy will necessitate a diplomacy designed to refurbish Iran's image and win supportive friends.

The war's outcome is the great uncertain but determinant factor for Iran's relations with its regional neighbors and the United States. Two possibilities may safely be excluded: The war will not last forever and, if the United States does not become more involved, Iraq will not win it. Thus two endings are possible: The war may close with no clear victor or Iran may succeed. On the basis of the war's course to date—slow, halting, but sustained Iranian progress despite supply shortages and economic pressures—eventual Iranian victory seems likely unless a negotiated deal satisfactory to Tehran is cut.

If Iran completes a smashing victory, the message to regional Islamic groups will be compelling, and much stronger than it was when the shah was deposed. The groups themselves are much stronger now, and Islamic Iran remains a latent model. Iran will have proved the efficacy of faith in a religiously defined struggle. The exultation in Tehran will be sobered, at least privately, by the weighty problems of the immediate postwar period. The regime will need to set its mind to the difficult tasks of delivering an economic peace dividend, repairing the devastation, arranging increased oil-export levels with OPEC, demobilizing and engaging the energies of the victorious fighters, and coping with heightened dissension that may follow the war's end.

But the call from the region's admiring "oppressed" peoples will be hard to resist. Even without making speeches or sending agents, the Iranian leadership will become the heroic symbol for Islamic activists whose governments inevitably will suspect Iranian incitement for any trouble. In this confused and explosive atmosphere, the reactions of Islamic groups, regional governments, and Iranians will profoundly shape the region's politics. Pragmatists in Tehran will have a hard time reassuring the region of Iran's good-neighborliness and controlling their country's hotheads. Iranian-inspired instability will pose a likelier danger than invasion from Iran's conquering but exhausted army. And military containment of Iran will have little value in conditions of growing regional hostility toward the United States.

However, if the war ends through an accord that gives Tehran its basic demands and nothing extra, the regime and the region are more likely to turn inward to deal with urgent postwar demands. The celebration in Tehran may not drown out such questions as Why did we suffer? and What has this regime done for us? The need for realistic answers at home will overrule extremist demands for new adventures abroad. Clearly this outcome is much to be preferred by the regional states, despite the short-term pain of negotiating an end to the war that will hurt Iraq.

A new American relationship with Iran will not weigh decisively in a negotiated conclusion to the war. America has lost that stature and cannot realistically aspire to regain it. But Washington can exert modest influence by helping to reduce Tehran's sense of siege, isolation, and abiding Western hostility. Ending the war in the context of Iran's acceptance by its former enemies—especially the Great Satan—would offer it incentives to return to normal state behavior. The patient course taken by West Germany, the Soviet Union, Turkey, and others should be instructive to the United States. They have succeeded on their own terms with the Islamic republic and helped in small ways to prod a return to the world community.

There is ample reason for the United States to work for an end to the war and to begin the slow, painful process of reconnecting with Iran. More than the American future with Iran is at stake. Regional stability will be threatened if the conflict runs its unguided course. Iran is no longer a "crazy" country. For good or ill, its diplomacy has become increasingly adept; it cannot be ignored on the regional scene. The encouraging tendency in Tehran toward inward-looking, practical policies will be overtaken by a refired ideology if Iran emerges from the war feeling victorious, but bitter and alone.

Collective Violence in India

GEORGE J. BRYJAK

The land of Mahatma Gandi, the champion of nonviolence, is no stranger to the misery, death, and destruction brought about by collective violence. India became an independent nation in the midst of one of modern history's most savage and gruesome struggles. Along with India's freedom in August 1947 came the creation of the state of Pakistan, a geographically divided nation most of whose population came from the Punjab region of the Indian subcontinent. With this partition approximately 7 to 8 million Hindus and Sikhs found themselves residents of a new country that was predominantly Muslim. An estimated equal number of Muslims were now part of a state that was overwhelmingly Hindu. In a desperate attempt to become citizens of societies comprised primarily of members of their own religion, millions of people embarked on one of the greatest migrations in history.

During this chaotic mass exodus of people, centuries-old hostilities between Hindus and Sikhs on one side and Muslims on the other erupted into a bloodbath of major proportions. As Khushwant Singh notes, "By the summer of 1947, when the creation of the new state of Pakistan was formally announced, ten million people—Muslims and Hindus and Sikhs—were in flight. By the time the monsoon broke, almost a million of them were dead, and all of northern India was in arms, in terror and in hiding."[1]

Although the magnitude of the atrocities of 1947 and 1948 has not yet been repeated, there has been an increase in the rates of individual and collective violence. As India struggles to modernize, it is beset by a growing number of problems and internal conflicts that are being settled by violence in the streets. This paper examines collective violence in India, attempts to explain why it is occurring with increased frequency, and considers how these ongoing conflicts will affect Indian society in the future.

India is a land of tremendous diversity. A nation with a population of approximately 762 million people in 1985, India may well be the most heterogenous country in the world. It is a society inhabited by people of different races, religions, linguistic groups, and cultures. Besides the Hindu majority who comprise 83 percent of the population, there are significant numbers of Muslims, Sikhs, and Christians. The constitution officially recognizes sixteen major languages; Indians speak over sixteen hundred regional dialects. The people range from taller, relatively fair-skinned Punjabis in the north to the shorter, darker Dravidians in the south. Indians have an acute sense of regionalism and are quick to identify themselves as residents of a particular state or geographic area. They can choose from a multitude of opposition parties, although Rajiv Gandhi's Congress Party is the country's dominant political organization. Indian society is divided hierarchically into five major castes and thousands of subcastes that affect both Hindus and non-Hindus.

Sociopolitical diversity continues to be a major source of conflict in contemporary India. This conflict usually occurs between members of the following groups: caste Hindus and untouchables; Hindus and Muslims; Hindus and Sikhs; Muslims and the police; Marxists and Maoists; union members and the police; the army and the police; untouchables and the police; and farmers and the police.[2]

Accurate statements about these trends of collective violence are difficult to make for at least two reasons: (1) accurate data on the frequency of group violence, especially in rural areas, are scarce; and (2) the definition of *rioting* used by the Indian police includes a wide range of behaviors. The Indian penal code defines rioting as "the use of violence by a group of five or more people"—thus, a skirmish between a small number may be reported in the crime statistics as a riot. "Two or three men may fight and when the police come implicate a number of witnesses so as to discredit their testimony and spread the blame. The police then record a riot case not a case of assault or an affray."[3] Riot statistics, therefore, can be somewhat misleading as they do not really reflect the magnitude, duration, or seriousness of collective violence. Nevertheless, these statistics are useful in pointing out general trends of collective disorder over long periods of time.

Table 1.—Riots in India

Year	Actual no.	Per 100,000 pop.
1953	20,529	5.5
1954	22,777	6.0
1955	23,609	6.1
1956	24,700	6.2
1957	23,750	5.9
1958	24,942	6.0
1959	26,987	6.4
1960	26,890	6.3
1961	27,199	6.2
1962	29,096	6.5
1963	28,114	6.1
1964	32,693	7.0
1965	32,940	6.9
1966	34,696	7.1
1967	42,447	8.5
1968	45,801	8.9
1969	55,796	10.7
1970	68,331	12.8
1971	64,114	11.5
1972	65,781	11.7
1973	73,388	12.7
1974	80,547	13.7
1975	67,241	11.2
1976	63,675	10.4
1977	80,081	12.9

Adapted from: B. R. Nayar (1975), *Violence and crime in India—A quantitative study* (MacMillan Co. of India Ltd.); *Crime in India 1977* (1981), Faridabad: Government of India Press.

The publication of Indian crime statistics lags at least four years behind the time offenses occurred. For example, *Crime in India 1977* (similar to the *FBI Uniform Crime Reports*) was not published by the Government of India Press until 1981. An examination of statistics for 1953–77 indicates both an increase in the absolute number of riots and the rate of this behavior as

From *Asian Affairs—An American Review*, Summer 1986, pp. 35-55. Reprinted with permission of the Helen Dwight Reid Educational Foundation. Published by Heldref Publications, 4000 Albemarle St., N.W., Washington, D.C. 20016.

expressed in cases per 100,000 population. Table 1 shows that the riot rate increased slowly in the thirteen-year period between 1953 and 1966, climbing from 5.5 to 7.1. The rate jumped to 8.5 in 1967 and then to 10.7 in 1969. Between 1970 and 1977, the riot rate vacillated between 11.5 and 13.7. While the rate has fluctuated, the overall trend is clear: riot activity in India is increasing.

A Typology of Collective Violence

David Bayley, a specialist on crime and the Indian criminal justice system, constructed a useful typology for categorizing and analyzing riots or collective violence in India. The following discussion utilizes an adapted version of this typology and owes much to its conceptual framework.[4] Three categories of collective violence exist—violence of remonstrance, violence of confrontation, and violence of frustration. Each of these may vary along the following seven dimensions: (1) occasion; (2) target; (3) catalytic agent; (4) organization; (5) duration of growth; (6) participants; and (7) location.

Violence of Remonstrance

The violence of remonstrance culminates from the efforts of a group of demonstrators to bring attention to a particular point of view, usually in the form of a set of perceived or experienced grievances. Participants are most likely to be members of formal groups with an organizational hierarchy, who possess the necessary skills and resources to mobilize members and make their dissatisfactions known to officials or government agencies. This form of violence increasingly occurs in the countryside because of rising social awareness, literacy rates, and proliferation of rural-based or rural-oriented political parties; it is not spontaneous but erupts after prolonged periods of agitation or demonstration. Since the targets are government officials (or other authority figures), violence is often tactically precipitated by the police. After marching on a government office and demanding to see officials, for example, demonstrators may become impatient and rowdy. They may cross police barricades or fail to disburse when ordered to do so. The police may then respond by attempting to arrest group leaders, push back the demonstrators, or control the crowd. Some demonstrators may not move, may refuse to let their leaders be taken away, or may commence an attack on the police. Isolated clashes between the police and a few demonstrators can quickly grow from a small fracas into a full-scale violent confrontation.

Incidents of violence of remonstrance have occurred frequently in the state of Punjab where the majority of India's 15 million Sikhs reside. Sikhism, a religion founded by Guru Nanak in the fifteenth century, has a long and proud military tradition. Sikhs view themselves as a unique people, and some of them have attempted to establish an independent political state since 1947. The desire for an autonomous homeland to be called Khalistan (derived from the concept of *Khalsa*—a chosen race of soldier-saints), along with a number of other economic, social, and cultural grievances, has pitted Sikhs against their Hindu neighbors, the local police, and the federal government over the past few years.

Prior to the armed forces' storming of the Sikh Golden Temple in Amritsar in June 1984, demonstrations, protests, and acts of terrorism had been common in Punjab. In the summer of 1981, after a fundamentalist Sikh leader was arrested, police clashed with demonstrators who demanded his release. Unable to disperse or control the protesters, the police fired into the crowd and killed thirteen people. Over seven hundred arrests were made as violence spread to other cities and towns within the region. In March 1983 in an effort to draw attention to their demands, Sikhs set up roadblocks on numerous major highways throughout the state. When police attempted to clear these roadways, the protesters resisted violently. In the aftermath of these confrontations, 20 people were killed, approximately 400 policemen were injured, and over 1,000 people were arrested. At the conclusion of an eighteen-month period ending in April 1983, 140 people had been killed as a result of violence in Punjab. Most of these deaths were the result of clashes between demonstrators and the police.[5]

India is a land of scarcity and poverty, and any substantial increase in prices or decrease in government subsidies is likely to result in demonstrations. In November 1980 Punjabi students were protesting the increase in bus fares when eighteen policemen (for some undetermined reason) suddenly charged their ranks and "mercilessly" beat many of them.[6] Layoffs and strikes (especially in Bombay and Calcutta) often result in confrontations between angry union members and the police. Newspapers regularly report the numbers killed and injured in these confrontations, but unless the casualties have been unusually high such stories are not considered newsworthy and are relegated to back pages.

Violence of Confrontation

Unlike the violence of remonstrance where a group's feelings of injustice and anger are directed toward an authority figure, the violence of confrontation results from the conflict between two groups of private citizens over an issue. These factions are usually informal, comprised primarily of friends, relatives, neighbors, and/or members of the same caste, religious, linguistic, or regional group. Tension and latent hostility between two groups may simmer for long periods before exploding into violence. The police are not the catalyst of violence; rather, the rival group's behavior triggers conflict.

Violence of confrontation is both a rural and an urban phenomenon. In rural areas personal relationships are stronger and lend themselves more easily to intense partisanship. Another contributing factor is the relatively small number of police and other formal agents of social control who normally monitor and diffuse the tension between rural groups and keep the conflict to a nominal level of violence if fighting does break out. Sporadic incidents between two rival groups can be drawn out over extended periods as a momentary victory in a particular confrontation by one group results in vengeful feelings and a strong determination to get even by the other.

Violence of confrontation, however, occurs more often in the cities where many different groups occupy a crowded, deteriorating environment. India's largest cities are especially heterogeneous in their ethnic composition. According to the 1971 census, 31.8 percent, 16.9 percent, and 16.3 percent of the residents of Bombay, Calcutta, and Bangalore, respectively, are interstate migrants as defined by their last place of residence.[7] It appears that as long as they attract people from all corners of the subcontinent, India's largest metropolitan areas will be potential centers of violence of confrontation.

The caste system, which ranks people in a rigid hierarchy and prohibits individual mobility, has been the source of much violence of confrontation. This stratification system has withstood the challenges of reformers and abolitionists since the time of Buddha, some twenty-five hundred years ago. It was, however, affected by the adoption of the Indian constitution in 1950, which officially abolished discrimination on the basis of untouchability. In an attempt to integrate the untouchables (or *scheduled castes*, as they are now often called) into the mainstream of economic and political life, the union government has instituted a type of affirmative action program. Under various facets of this program, a designated number of seats and/or jobs are "reserved" for untouchables in schools, professions, and government positions. Many "caste" Hindus, however, have been and continue to be outraged by such a policy. Confrontations between untouchables and caste Hindus over these programs have been frequent and often violent. In the state of Maharashtra the two groups have also fought over land rights, agricultural wages, and the renaming of a state university after a prominent untouchable leader.[8]

After caste Hindus attacked national banks, police stations, and schools to demonstrate their displeasure at the government's policy of admitting a set number of untouchables into medical school, thirty thousand untouchable textile workers went on strike in Ahmadabad (the capital of the state of Gujarat) in 1981 to demonstrate their support for the reservations. When the mill finally reopened a few days later, the police had to be summoned to control fighting between caste Hindus and untouchable workers. These confrontations occurred intermittently for almost three months and resulted in the deaths of forty people.[9]

During the spring and summer of 1985 Gujarat was once again the scene of intercaste confrontations. This latest wave of violence erupted after the state government announced that it was raising the admission quotas for "backward classes" in medical and engineering schools from 10 percent to 28 percent.[10] Backward classes are those who—although not outside the caste system (outcastes, i.e., untouchables)—are very poor and often despised.[11]

Untouchables (who comprise approximately 14 percent of India's population) and tribal non-Hindus (who make up another 8 percent and would also benefit from this upward adjustment) welcomed the new government figures. Upper-caste Hindus, however, were furious, and antireservation protests began almost immediately. Joining caste Hindus in their opposition to preferential treatment for backward castes were farmers already disgruntled by untouchable reservations. These protests soon turned violent as the antagonistic groups battled each other for four months. Two hundred and twenty-four people were killed, hundreds more injured, and at least ten thousand had their homes destroyed as a result of the fighting.[12] In the midst of these intercaste confrontations, Hindus and Muslims began killing one another. Unable to control the hostilities, local authorities called in the army, and curfews were established in Ahmadabad.[13]

The recent Gujarat antireservation riots are the most serious among thousands of confrontations that occur each year between upper-caste Hindus and untouchables.[14] Most of these incidents take place in rural areas and rarely come to the attention of government officials. Upper-caste policemen often oppress untouchables who are struggling for their constitutional rights.[15]

The most costly incidents in terms of lives lost and property destroyed are those clashes that the Ministry of Home Affairs refers to as "communal violence." This type of confrontation takes place between two or more ethnic, linguistic, and/or religious groups. Table 2 shows the growing number of confrontations and casualties resulting from incidents of communal violence between 1976 and 1980. Communal confrontations increased from 169 in 1976 to 421 in 1980, while the number of people killed rose from 39 to 372 during this period.

Table 2.—Communal Violence in India

Year	No. of incidents of communal violence	No. of persons killed	No. of persons injured
1976	169	39	794
1977	188	36	1,122
1978	230	110	1,853
1979	304	261	2,379
1980	421	372	2,691

Adapted from: The Economic and Political Weekly (1981), Bisharif, 9 May: 1.

While Hindus and Sikhs battle each other in northern India, Hindus and their traditional Muslim rivals maintain an uneasy peace that is at times punctuated by episodes of extreme violence. One such incident occurred in the industrial city of Jamshedpur in 1979. In an attempt to avoid a Hindu-Muslim confrontation during an upcoming religious celebration, the police arrested 150 (whom they considered) religious fanatics. During the course of the celebration, a procession was stopped by Hindus who demanded that one of their priests be released from police custody. An argument between the officers who refused to release the priest and the Hindus who wanted his release soon turned into a shouting match between Hindu and Muslim onlookers. This exchange led to stone-throwing that escalated to hand-to-hand combat. The Hindus then stormed into Muslim neighborhoods and responded in kind. Before the police could restore order, over one hundred people had been killed.[16]

In an April 1984 speech in Bombay a leader of a radical Marathi organization likened India's Muslim population to a growing cancer that had to be surgically removed. Such highly inflammatory remarks not only increased religious tensions in Bombay but began to polarize Muslims and Hindus in a number of coastal cities north of India's largest industrial center. In the city of Bhiwandi—with a "delicately balanced" population that is 45 percent Hindu and 55 percent Muslim—Hindus prepared for an upcoming religious festival by flying saffron-colored flags. Not to be outdone, Muslims began to display their traditional green flags wherever possible. Bhiwandi's heightened religious consciousness erupted into a week-long riot that quickly spread south from one city to another. In Bombay alone 100 people were killed, and the widespread carnage ultimately claimed the lives of 230 people. Fire is especially treacherous in poor, densely populated urban areas, and in one Bhiwandi neighborhood 27 people trapped in their homes burned to death. Only the army's intervention prevented a higher death toll.[17]

Perhaps the most brutal incident of confrontational violence occurred in the eastern state of Assam during the winter of 1983. The "agony of Assam," as Indira Gandhi referred to these hostilities, was not specifically a matter of religious, ethnic, or cultural differences. Instead, all such elements were to be found in a situation that has its roots in the economy of colonial India.[18] Since the British discovery and cultivation of tea as a cash crop in the early eighteen-hundreds, millions of people (mostly Bengali Hindus and Muslims) have migrated to Assam.

The indigenous people of Assam have deeply resented the continual invasion of their homeland.[19] Under British rule they were powerless to keep the migrants out, and the constitution of independent India provides for the unimpeded movement of all citizens. The federal government's reluctance to stem the tide of people crossing into Assam illegally from Bangladesh has caused the population to escalate. It is surprising that Assamese hostility toward migrants and the non-Assamese resentment at being labeled as outsiders (even though some have lived and worked in the state for generations) has not erupted into violence more frequently. Some of the more recent conflicts, however, such as the Assamese Disturbances of 1960, the anti-Bengali riots of 1972, and the violent protest of 1980 that prompted Mrs. Gandhi to place the state under federal law for one year were but minor skirmishes compared to the death and destruction that ravaged the state in 1983.

Tensions in Assam reached a boiling point with the coming of spring elections. The Assamese believed that if the immigrant populations were to become citizens and vote, then the indigenous Assamese would be overrun politically. The most recent wave of migrants and the Bengali Muslims felt that if the Assamese could prevent them from voting, then they would eventually lose other rights as well as their land. Under such a political climate, it seemed inevitable that legislation would be introduced demanding the expulsion of some or all of the nonindigenous population. Despite numerous protests, strikes, and boycotts on the part of the Assamese and threats of further violent disruptions, Indira Gandhi decided to go ahead with the scheduled elections. Hundreds of thousands of immigrants would not be disenfranchised.

With the Assamese determined not to permit state elections to proceed under these conditions, violence continued until the situation deteriorated into India's worst communal fighting since partition. In one incident alone, Lalung tribesmen massacred over one thousand Bengali Muslims (mostly women and children) who were unable to flee. The killing, however, was not confined to Assamese versus Muslims. Apart from Assamese Hindus killing Bengali Muslims, "Assamese Muslims killed Bengali Muslims, Assamese Muslims killed Bengali tribals, tribals killed Assamese Hindus, tribals killed Bengali Muslims, tribals killed tribals, Bengali Muslims killed Bengali Hindus, older assimilated immigrants killed recently arrived ones, and all the local peoples killed Nepalese and Biharis."[20] In a nightmare of fear, hatred, panic, and confusion "every community killed every other community."[18] When the slaughter was over, approximately four thousand people lay dead, many of them killed in a most barbaric way. People were hacked to death by machetes, shot through with arrows, and impaled on spears. Bodies were decapitated and thrown into a river. When the police and some of the seventy thousand troops (that Mrs. Gandhi had dispatched to Assam) arrived, they found bloated buzzards sated on human flesh.[21]

To the terrible loss of life resulting from this communal fury can be added the high economic price India must pay for its internal warfare. Besides destroying a substantial amount of property, in 1980 protestors successfully blockaded the movement of oil from Assam to other Indian states, forcing the government to spend nearly 100 million dollars a month for additional imports. The transport of jute and other forest products was also temporarily halted, depriving India of much-needed funds derived from the export of these materials.[22] Since granaries were a prime target of arsonists, and farmers missed one rice planting because of the chaos, Assam was threatened by a substantial food shortage.

The agony of Assam is a bitter example of the magnitude of brutality that can result from communal conflict. Although the level of heterogeneity and political and cultural strife that exists in Assam is not indicative of the situation in most of India, there are a number of northeastern states with similar problems. In 1980 in the small state of Tripura 383 "foreigners" were killed (unofficial estimates were in the thousands) in clashes between local tribesmen and immigrants from Bangladesh. A number of villages were burned, and 30,000 people were forced to seek food and shelter in relief camps.[23]

Violence of Frustration

The final form of collective violence results from frustration and occurs when people perceive themselves to be in a situation they find unendurable. In some cases the police are the catalyst for this form of violence. Some impersonal event usually sets in motion the people's anger and frustration. Once the crowd begins engaging in aggressive action, it becomes opportunistic and may lash out randomly, in some cases destroying everything in its path. Participants are not usually organized, although impromptu leaders may emerge from the crowd's more vociferous, forceful members. Participants may or may not know each other, but they are brought together because of some common interest or event that suddenly turns violent. The violence of frustration is an urban phenomenon often associated with the disadvantages and irritations of living in a poor and crowded city.

One of the bloodiest riots in India was a spontaneous uprising that took place in the city of Moradabad in 1980. To celebrate the conclusion of the holy month of Ramadan, Muslims gathered for prayer at a local mosque on the outskirts of the city. A disturbance began after someone noticed that a pig had strayed into the mosque. When nearby police refused to retrieve it, some members of the crowd accused them of purposefully allowing the pig to enter the mosque. Before long the crowd became angry and began throwing stones at a stall where a number of policemen were seated, and the outnumbered officers retaliated by firing into the crowd. Police reinforcements arrived shortly and the shooting continued. By this time the swelling crowd retreated toward the city, chanting: "Kill the police!" Upon reaching a small substation, they beat up all of the officers, stole the available weapons, and set the station on fire. One policeman trapped inside was burned alive. News of the Moradabad incident quickly spread, and rioting broke out in eighteen other cities in the region. A large contingent of paramilitary forces had to be brought in to restore order. On the following day, Hindus began attacking Muslims and burning their shops. A riot of frustration initially targeted at the police—accompanied by the destruction of property—had turned into a Hindu versus Muslim confrontation. The final toll of death and destruction was extremely high: estimates of the number killed ranged from 250 to 300. The number of injuries was in the thousands, with nearly all of the casualties being Muslim.[24]

Indira Gandhi's assassination by her two Sikh bodyguards on October 31, 1984 resulted in some of the worst rioting in India since the time of independence and partition in 1947. The Hindus' rage at the death of their "mother" exploded in an all-out attack on Sikhs in many parts of Delhi. Sikhs were savagely beaten, shot, and in many cases burned to death. Within a week of Gandhi's death, two thousand people (mostly Sikhs) were killed in the capital city, and another five hundred died as a result of riots in five neighboring states.[25] The army (which was not called in until the second day of rioting) did not gain control of the situation in Delhi until Mrs. Gandhi had been cremated on November 3, three days after her death.

According to Pran Chopra of New Delhi's Center for Policy Research, Indira Gandhi's death triggered violence rooted in "class antagonisms taking shelter under religious coverings."[26] Chopra argues that the rioters were members of Delhi's lowest economic class, many of them rural-to-urban migrants only recently arrived in the capital city. Their victims were often members of a Sikh business caste, financially well-off by Indian standards. The prime minister's death provided them with both a cover and an excuse to vent their frustrations and hostilities toward a class of people whose economic prosperity they will probably never experience. If Chopra is correct, this type of violence will no doubt increase as Indian cities swell with poor migrants who have little if any chance of achieving upward mobility.

The Hindu-dominated police are often accused of facilitating intergroup violence by remaining passive when Hindus are the instigators of, and/or have the upper hand in, communal confrontations. Sikh leaders, for example, charged that during the Delhi riots following the assassination of Mrs. Gandhi, the police could have prevented much of the killing and destruction but chose not to do so. According to some reports, Delhi police officers actually took part in the looting of Sikh-owned businesses.

At other times the police themselves have instigated collective violence. On one occasion during the Gujarat violence some policemen joined in the rioting, siding with untouchables, and even led the mob that destroyed the offices of a local newspaper.[27] During the antireservation riots in Ahmadabad the police were stoned by demonstrators and local residents for more than a week. In apparent retaliation, the police charged into a group of people and were "absolutely ruthless in their attack." According to one account, the police beat and molested women, broke water pipes in a residential neighborhood, and ransacked some homes.[28]

In August 1982 roaming groups of Bombay police burned buses, sabotaged railway signals, and managed to block almost all road and rail traffic in and out of the city. As a result five people were killed and sixty-seven policemen were fired. A similar, although less serious, incident in the state of Haryana resulted in the dismissal of almost four hundred officers. The possible reasons behind this violence are thought to be low pay, long hours, poor benefits, and few chances for promotion. Prospects for advancement are especially dismal, "with about 75 percent of all personnel retiring in the rank at which they were recruited."[29] Bayley believes that, "for better or worse, the lower ranks of the police are now prepared to emulate the tactics of militant labor. They will strike and they will organize." It also appears that they will engage in collective violence if and when they deem such action necessary. Police may also be opting for the least dangerous alternative regarding their own safety in attempting to keep two groups of people from killing each other. Rather than taking a more defensive posture and just trying to keep opposing groups separated, police may press the attack themselves. Although this tactic may or may not be effective in stemming the tide of collective violence, it will certainly facilitate the mistrust and disdain that many Indians already have for the police.

Modernization and Collective Violence

Explanations for the increase in rates of collective violence in India are to be found in its effort to modernize. After a society undergoes an internal political revolution—or gains independence from a colonial power, as in India's case—it must begin to find solutions to a series of complex problems. Unfortunately, political autonomy does not necessarily translate into a dramatically improved standard of living for the people of a recently independent nation. The new government must being to deliver on the promises it made during the struggle for power. Although the majority probably does not expect immediate changes in the country's major institutions, it does expect that substantial improvements in the overall quality of life will come about in a reasonable amount of time. It has now been thirty-nine years since India became independent, and even though the standard of living has improved for some, as far as many Indians are concerned, it has not improved fast enough or gone far enough.

The paradox of India's political situation is that whereas Mrs. Gandhi's popularity was high, a substantial number of urban Indians were not satisfied with the state of the nation. A quarterly opinion poll—conducted in fifteen urban areas by the India Market Research Bureau between September 1980 and July 1982—indicates that between 57 percent and 59 percent of those surveyed were satisfied with Mrs. Gandhi's performance in office. At the same time, between 64 and 67 percent of those interviewed believed that overall "things are going badly" in India.[30] Dissatisfaction was the highest in the large industrial cities of Bombay, Ahmadabad, Madras, and Bangalore, with between 76 and 85 percent of the respondents stating that conditions were "bad." Perhaps Mrs. Gandhi's popularity was a major reason why there were not substantially more protests, strikes, and violent confrontations. It is quite possible that if Rajiv Gandhi does not prove to be as popular as his mother, and social and economic conditions do not improve to the satisfaction of more urban residents, India will experience a rather tumultous period characterized by significant social and political unrest.

The belief that India's leaders have not been able to bring about a more favorable economic climate has been accompanied by the realization that some segments of society, especially the cities, have prospered greatly and will continue to do so. Mrs. Gandhi commented on the poor's changing self-perception: "The rich are richer, just as the richer countries are getting richer. But that doesn't mean that the poor are getting poorer. What is happening is that they see their poverty—even though it is an improved situation—with much sharper eyes. Before they tolerated it; today they say, 'Why shall I tolerate it?' "[31] As education advances farther into the countryside and the number of literate people increases (in 1981 only 36 percent could read and write), more Indians will be liberated from the ignorance of their isolated existence. The number of dissatisfied people who reside in India's 600,000 villages will grow.

Not the least of India's problems and a factor related to collective violence is the number of people who inhabit the subcontinent. A nation of 762 million, India has a growth rate of 2.23 percent per annum. This rate, relatively modest when compared to other third world countries, translates into a population increase of over 15 million people a year. Demographers estimate that at this rate, India will surpass China to become the most populous nation on earth not too far into the twenty-first century. Thus a substantial amount of economic growth is negated by the needs of a rapidly expanding population. Even the world's richest nations would be hard-pressed to increase their standard of living if they had to meet the needs of so many more people.

These factors, coupled with an extremely heterogeneous society whose many rival groups have a long history of communal conflict, are responsible for the collective violence seen in India today. As India continues to modernize and traditional values and centers of power are challenged, many mutually hostile groups are likely to become even further polarized. Untouchables, for example, seem determined to exercise their rights as guaranteed by the constitution and by the Untouchability (Offenses) Act of 1955. Caste Hindus, however, who have dominated and exploited the outcastes for three thousand years, appear equally determined to maintain their position of superiority. Each victory that untouchables gain will no doubt be countered by caste Hindus who have shown little, if any, reluctance to engage in violent reprisals against scheduled castes. This same bleak scenario can be extended to Hindu-Muslim relations, as well as to the multi-ethnic, religious, and linguistic groups that inhabit the northeastern states. All are competing for political power and for the paucity of resources: land, housing, and jobs in one of the word's poorest countries.

Feelings of pride in one's religion, ethnicity, language, and way of life that once led to an independent India now have the potential for not only impeding modernization, but also for causing widespread death and destruction. In the aftermath of colonial independence, nationalist movements have emerged in the third world, as people reject the many arbitrary internal and external political boundaries established by the colonial powers.[32] The preindependence cohesiveness and internal solidarity of many new nations is being replaced by regional loyalties and identification at the ethnic, religious, and linguistic level. In a society as large and diverse as India, the results of this phenomenon can be devastating. Bridging the gap from the traditional to the modern world is problematic enough for a basically homogeneous society where there is general agreement on national goals and priorities. For a country as heterogeneous as India, this transition may be impossible.

Collective Violence and Revolution

With a growing number of dissatisfied, angry people engaging in demonstrations, protests, and collective violence, the question arises as to why this anger and frustration is not aggregated into an organized opposition movement targeted at the state and/or union movement. From a Marxist perspective, one might imagine that even in a society as heterogeneous as India it is only a matter of time before all those who are dissatisfied with the current state of affairs are galvanized into an opposition force whose aim is to topple the Congress Party and the federal government. There are, however, a number of reasons why these widespread outbursts of collective violence in India have been and probably will continue to be unorganized and fragmented.

1. As Huntington notes, people can be too poor to engage in ongoing revolutionary activity. "The slum dweller lives on a low margin; the payoff that counts is in the here and now. He who is concerned with eating is unlikely to be concerned about revolting."[33] Almost anyone can engage in sporadic episodes of collective action and violence. Revolutionary politics requires the time and energy that the most downtrodden segments of Indian society simply do not have.

2. Between 1970 and 1975 approximately 45 percent of India's urban growth was a function of rural-to-urban migration.[34] These relatively recent arrivals are probably still comparing their lives in urban India to the intractable poverty and despair of those who continue to toil in the countryside. Although it is difficult to comprehend, the typical poor urban migrant—even the pavement dweller—is in a superior economic position (with chances for advancement) compared to many of his rural counterparts. Unless conditions in the city seriously worsen, the urban poor will most likely remain politically passive, content with the realization that they have broken the cycle of helplessness that exists in rural India.

3. Based upon his study of nineteenth- and twentieth-century France, Charles Tilly argues that incidents of collective violence do not correspond to the pace of urban growth. He notes: "If anything, the correlation runs the other way: rapid urban growth—less collective violence."[35] He observes that rates of collective violence increase a number of years after peak periods of urban growth. There is, in effect, a gap or lag between the migrants' arrival in the cities and their disruptive action. Rural peasants new to the city simply do not possess the skills and level of organization necessary for concerted collective action, especially revolutionary activity. Tilly's findings and interpretation are consistent with the "marginality perspective" that emphasizes the traditional attitudes of rural-to-urban migrants and the lack of political participation on the part of low-income urban people.

4. In a pluralistic society—like India—where people tend to think of themselves foremost as members of a particular caste, religious, ethnic, or language group, feelings of anger and frustration emanating from economic and social problems (that would usually be directed at the government) are often aimed at another group. A significant number of Indians think of their society in terms of a zero sum game where one group's gains are believed to result from another group's losses. This widely held belief mitigates a good deal of hostility that would otherwise be directed against the government because of its inability to oversee or create opportunities that permit more upward mobility for a significantly larger number of people. The sometimes vast cultural and social differences existing among the multiplicity of Indian subcultures (that have hindered communication and coordination and made modernization even more difficult) may pose organizational problems that potential revolutionary groups find difficult—if not impossible—to overcome.

Similarly, the social and economic gradations existing within any class in India will make it extremely difficult to generate a class-based revolutionary movement. Classes in India are superimposed on a caste system that in itself is comprised of thousands of *jati*, or subcastes. These jati are typically local groups each having a particular occupation or profession. Jati (which do not usually cross regional boundaries) are hierarchically arranged within the five major castes. These are (in descending order of status): brahman; kshatriya; vaishya; sudra; and outcastes, or untouchables. While members of different jati within a particular caste may occupy the same economic position—a mason and basketweaver, for example—they do not consider each other as social equals and thus they act accordingly. Any feelings of "class consciousness," in the Marxist sense, will have to overcome this fundamentally divisive feature of the caste system. Joshi observes that in the Gujarat riots of 1981, "The conflict was not between owner and laborer, but between 'Untouchable' and non-Untouchable laborer."[36] Because they loathe being associated with and possibly suffering some of the abuse now reserved for untouchables, nonuntouchables may be fearful of aligning themselves politically with any of India's more than 100 million outcastes. The poor and dispossesed may share the same economic position in society, but they still view one another as superordinates and subordinates in a complex system of status differentiation that places extreme importance on ritual purity and pollution.

Violence and India's Future

Whereas some or all of the aforementioned reasons may preclude the possibility of a forthcoming national revolutionary movement taking hold in India, they do not necessarily diminish the chances for future widespread collective violence. Asghar Ali Engineer, for example, believes that politicians from all levels exploit the heterogeneity of India, which further polarizes its many antagonistic groups. In their drive toward public office, "Politicians conduct aggressive campaigns on the basis of caste and communities."[37] Office-seekers exacerbate their supporters' feelings of hatred and bitterness by reminding them of previous tensions and conflicts. The elation of a previous victory is celebrated anew, while the stinging memories of a past defeat are painfully resurrected and experienced again. Such political strategy can only increase the likelihood of future confrontations.

If Tilly is correct, India's most difficult days of social protest and collective violence are yet to come. Along with their increasing "relative deprivation," the children of rural-to-urban migrants will acquire the skills necessary to engage in concerted political action that may subsequently become violent. The children of this migrant generation may not be as easily satisfied as their parents and will take little comfort from the fact that they are better off than the majority of people in rural India. As young adults they are more likely to focus their attention on the lifestyle of their neighbors and coworkers rather than dwelling on the extreme hardships of rural peasants (which they have never experienced). While the luxury of the successful urban middle classes is visible on a day-to-day basis, the misery of the past, as related by their parents, is difficult for the young to understand. When this second generation of urban poor becomes sufficiently disenchanted with prospects in urban India, they might engage in incidents of violence of frustration and remonstrance. Tens of thousands of urban slum dwellers could take to the streets so as to demonstrate their displeasure with existing social and economic conditions. Demonstrations protesting escalating food prices, for example, could easily trigger similar protests leading to violence of remonstrance and massive civil disobedience across the country.

Controlling nationwide civil disturbances could prove to be a formidable task almost certainly requiring substantial military intervention. Prolonged disorder might force the federal government to impose martial law or enact emergency measures similar to those Mrs. Gandhi utilized for twenty months between 1975 and 1977. Rajiv Gandhi has already stated that unless violence and terrorism can be controlled, he will impose a state of emergency in India.[38] The suspension of some basic civil rights under emergency conditions could result in further demonstrations, which in turn would invite an even stronger militaristic posture by the government.

India has problems similar to those of many of the world's poor. On the one hand, a rapidly expanding urban population demands employment opportunities, adequate housing, and a variety of educational, health, and sanitary services that are not now being provided. The problem of housing alone in urban India is of catastrophic proportions. One social scientist estimates that as many as 22 million people—one-fifth of India's urban population—live in substandard housing.[39] Slums are increasing at 8 percent per year in large urban areas, approximately twice the rate of total population growth in these cities. In Calcutta, for example, one out of every three people lives in the city's approximately three hundred registered slums, and pavement dwellers number in the hundreds of thousands. This housing shortage only enhances the possibilities for collective violence, as members of different ethnic groups compete with one another for living space as well as for jobs. "Moving into an area that was formerly defined as the territory of one particular group according to the traditional divisions in the plural society city, as well as moving into an occupational area that was formerly monopolized by a particular ethnic group, is interpreted in the social consciousness as invasion and leads to defense reactions."[40] The likelihood that urban housing conditions will substantially improve and reduce this competition for living space is doubtful because of the reluctance of private investors or the government to commit the large sums of money necessary to a nonproductive segment of the economy.[41]

On the other hand, conditions in rural India are even more deplorable as an increasing number of peasants see their land holdings dwindle and disappear. Half the farms in India now occupy less than one-tenth of the total agricultural area.[42] The proportion of landless rural people soared from 24 percent in 1961 to 35 percent in 1971.[43] The population of rural India in 1961 was 360 million. By 1978 that number had increased to 499 million, of whom 239 million were below poverty level and 130 million well below that level.[44]

The tremendous increase in the number of rural inhabitants is a function of natural population growth resulting from an excess of births over deaths and new technology. The number of people living in poverty in rural India is not only a function of growth due to natural increase but also a function of change and the decline of economic conditions in the countryside, which has resulted in a large albeit fluctuating rate of rural pauperization (see Figure 1). If this poverty continues, it will provide even more people with the motivation to relocate to the cities. If only 1 percent of the 239 million people in the countryside who live below the poverty line moved to the cities each year for the next ten years, India's urban areas would have to absorb an additional 23,900,000 people during the next decade—over and above the population increase attributed to natural increase.

The problem of collective violence is not confined to the cities, however. The slaughter in Assam demonstrated that large-scale confrontations occur in the countryside as well. Pluralistic rural areas in Assam as well as other

Figure 1.—Changes in the Incidence of Rural Poverty in India (1956–57 to 1977–78)

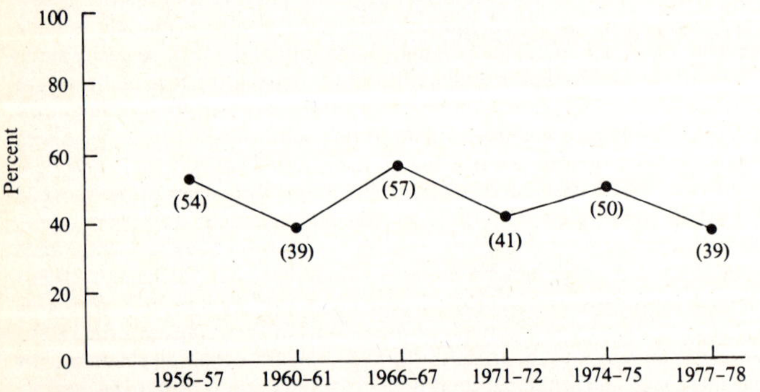

Adapted from: J. W. Mellor, and G. M. Desai (1985), Agricultural change and rural poverty: A synthesis, in *Agricultural change and rural poverty: Variations on a theme by Dharm Narian*, edited by Mellor and Desai (Baltimore: Johns Hopkins Press): 192–211.

regions of the Indian countryside may be just as prone to intergroup hostilities as highly diverse urban areas. India's untouchables, who reside primarily in rural areas, have been the particular targets of violent behavior. These *Harijans*, or "children of God," as Gandhi called them, are being beaten to death, robbed, raped, and even burned alive in record numbers. In 1975 over six thousand such incidents were reported to authorities, with the number climbing to eighteen thousand (about fifty per day) in 1980.[45] The actual number is probably much higher as many, if not most, of these rural atrocities go unreported. In many cases the untouchables' greatest enemy are members of the local police and gangs of *goondas* (thugs) who are under the employ of local landowners. When untouchables resist attack, they run the risk of even more brutal and oppressive treatment. The potential for a large number of casualties resulting from collective violence is even higher in rural areas than in the cities. Once the fighting and killing begins in the countryside, it is very difficult for a small police force to maintain control. By the time the army or additional police can be brought in, the loss of life and number of injuries can be quite extensive.

Although it seems apparent that rates of collective violence will increase in the coming years, the impact these incidents as a whole will have on Indian society is much less clear. Dilip Hiro, an Indian journalist and author, foresees intermittent "periods of advances" by leftist parties in his country's political future. These advances, he argues, will be followed by a period of "repression and setback as the dominant classes manipulate the political form of the state from liberal democratic to authoritarian or semi-authoritarian. . . ."[46] While some form of successful leftist revolution in the not-too-distant future seems a remote possibility, the likelihood that these political challenges (along with an increase in the other forms of collective violence we have examined) could result in the emergence of a less democratic society—as Hiro predicts—is more realistic. We may witness a gradual erosion of some fundamental freedoms in the world's largest democracy as the government implements whatever measures it deems necessary to maintain order and stability, especially in the cities.

Large segments of the urban middle and upper classes may not oppose any movement aimed at curtailing freedoms guaranteed by the Indian constitution but instead may welcome these changes. These people may be quite willing to accept a government that would utilize increasing amounts of force in order to keep the cities free of protests and collective violence if they can be assured that their economic advantages and relatively comfortable lifestyles will be preserved. It would not be the first time the affluent classes exchanged a democratic form of government for a repressive one that permitted them to maintain their positions of wealth and status.

NOTES

1. K. Singh (1956), *Mano majra* (New York: Grove Press): 1.
2. This list is not exhaustive and represents only the more significant groups who have engaged in collective violence.
3. D. H. Bayley (1969), *The police and political development in India* (Princeton: Princeton University Press): 247.
4. Ibid.: 249–284.
5. T. Marshall (1983), 20 killed as Sikhs fight India police, *Los Angeles Times*, 5 April.
6. *The Economic and Political Weekly* (1981), Sources of violence, 17 January: 44.
7. P. Visaria, and L. Visaria (1981), *India's population: Second and growing* (Washington, D.C.: Population Reference Bureau, Inc.).
8. M. Weiner (1980), *India at the polls, 1980: A study of the parliamentary elections* (Washington, D.C.: American Institute for Public Policy): 19. For an examination of scheduled caste politics see: A. Béteille (1965), *Caste, class, and power* (Berkeley: University of California Press); also O. M. Lynch (1968), The politics of untouchability: A case from Agra, India, in *Structure and change in Indian society*, edited by M. Singer and B. Cohn (Chicago: Aldine Publishing Company). An excellent series of articles on scheduled castes can be found in *The untouchables in contemporary India* (1972), edited by J. M. Mahar (Tucson: University of Arizona Press).
9. B. Joshi (1982), Whose law, whose order: 'Untouchables' social violence and the state in India, *Asian Survey*, July: 676–687.
10. R. Tempest (1985), India's college, job quotas reignite old caste hatred, *Los Angeles Times*, 28 April.
11. R. G. Revankar (1971), *The Indian constitution—A case study of backward classes* (Rutherford, NJ: Fairleigh Dickinson University): 183.
12. *Los Angeles Times* (1985), 21 July.
13. A. Kumar (1985), Continuing violence, *India Today*, 31 May: 38–39.
14. *Economist* (1984), Murders most foul, 26 May: 38.
15. *The Illustrated Weekly of India* (1983), Brutalizing the police, 27 March: 8–10.
16. *Economist* (1979), The fires of faith, 21 April: 91.
17. C. Kapoor (1984), Nightmare at noon, *India Today*, 15 June: 8–14.
18. The English took steps to create a tea industry in the fertile soils of Assam. The small, indigenous, relatively prosperous population was not overjoyed, however, at the prospect of toiling for low wages in the extremely hot and humid junglelike terrain. Outside labor, therefore, was needed to work the plantation, and after an unsuccessful attempt to settle Chinese coolies in the area, the British were forced to look elsewhere for manpower. Utilizing a system of contract labor, tribal people from the highlands of South Bihar were brought to Assam. To administer their new and thriving enterprise, the British encouraged the migration of Bengali Hindus recently educated at missionary and government colleges. A relatively small number of people—the Marawaris from the state of Rajasthan—also made their way to Assam. The Bengali Hindus and Marawaris were to form the backbone of a growing professional class. The turn of the twentieth century witnessed the beginning of a steady stream of Muslims from the neighboring state of Bengal into the area. With partition in 1947 and the Pakistani civil war that resulted in the creation of Bangladesh in 1972, millions of people crossed the international border into Assam. Of the 20 million people who reside in Assam today, approximately 48 percent are migrants or the descendants of migrants. One of the fastest growing states in India, the population of Assam increased by 24.7 percent between 1971 and 1981.

For an excellent overview of the sociopolitical history of Assam, see M. Weiner (1978), When migrants succeed and natives fail: Assam and its migrants, in *Sons of the soil* (Princeton: Princeton University Press): 75–144.

19. Ibid., 131: "The Assamese blame the British for giving the Bengalis a head start, Muslim politicians for encouraging Muslim migrations and Bengali Hindus and Marawaris for using their superior economic positions to prevent Assamese from effectively moving up the occupational and economic ladder."
20. *Economist* (1983), All against all in Assam, 19 March: 63–64.
21. *Newsweek* (1983), An Assam massacre: Bad blood for India, 7 March: 38–40.
22. *Economist* (1980), Peace, perhaps, 9 August: 33.
23. S. Wolpert (1982), *A new history of India* (New York: Oxford University Press): 411.
24. K. Gandhi (1980), Anatomy of the Moradabad riots, *The Economic and Political Weekly*, 13 August: 1505–1507.

25. R. Santhanam (1985), The crucial probe, *India Today*, 31 January: 50.
26. R. Tempest (1984), Anger at "rich" linked to riots after Gandhi's death, *Los Angeles Times*, 16 November.
27. *Economist* (1985), Auction politic, 25 May: 36.
28. A. Kumar, and R. Mendon (1985), State of siege, *India Today*, 15 May: 24–33.
29. D. H. Bayley (1985), The police and political order in India, *Asian Survey*, 23(4):484–496.
30. *India Today* (1982), An unending paradox, 31 July: 17–18.
31. T. Szulc (1982), What Indira Gandhi wants you to know, *Parade*, 25 July: 4–6.
32. State boundaries in India, however, were redrawn in the 1950s primarily on the basis of language.
33. S. P. Huntington (1968), *Political order in changing societies* (New Haven: Yale University Press): 280.
34. K. Newland (1980), City limits: Emerging constraints on urban growth, (Washington, D.C.: Worldwatch Paper 38).
35. C. Tilly (1974), The chaos of the living city, in *An urban world*, edited by C. Tilly (Boston: Little, Brown & Company): 86–109.
36. Joshi, note 9.
37. A. A. Engineer (1983), The politics of communalism, *The Illustrated Weekly of India*, 23–29 October: 16–21.
38. *Los Angeles Times* (1985), Gandhi warns terrorists, 8 July.
39. H. Spodek (1985), Squatter settlements in urban India: Self-help and government policies, *Economic and Political Weekly*, 3–10 September: 1575–1587.
40. H. Evers (1975), Urbanization and urban conflict in Southeast Asia, *Asian Survey*, September: 775–785.
41. B. Roberts (1978), *Cities of peasants: The political economy of urbanization in the third world* (Beverly Hills: Sage): 148.
42. J. Loup (1983), *Can the third world survive?* (Baltimore: Johns Hopkins University Press): 114.
43. P. Harrison (1979), *Inside the third world* (New York: The Harvester Press): 80.
44. S. Guhan (1980), Rural poverty: Policy and play acting, *The Economic and Political Weekly*, 22 November: 1975–1982.
45. O. Ilhau (1981), Converting India's untouchables, *World Press Review*, December: 58.
46. D. Hiro (1979), *Inside India today* (New York: Monthly Review Press): 290.

THE RENAMO MENACE

Hunger and Carnage in Mozambique

AUGUSTUS RICHARD NORTON

AUGUSTUS RICHARD NORTON, *an associate professor of social sciences at West Point, recently returned from a fact-finding mission to Mozambique.*

SAMORA MACHEL

MAPUTO

JUST ABOUT the only foreigners arriving on international flights to Mozambique these days are missionaries, aid officials and technicians, diplomats, and a few businessmen. Despite the natural beauty all around, no one comes to take in the views—for good reasons: Hunger and disease are everywhere, transportation is arduous at best, and an ongoing South African-backed insurgency has wrecked the economy and made horrific violence almost a commonplace. Indeed, the problems afflicting this former Portuguese colony are as formidable as those facing any country on earth.

Surprisingly, entry formalities at Maputo's airport are handled with reasonable efficiency, especially compared with many other airports in the Third World. You might be delayed a few minutes while immigration officers leave their posts to pick up their daily food rations, but that is not hard to excuse—even self-important civil servants have to eat. Baggage is given a cursory inspection, and no one bothers to ask for the mandatory inoculation certificates, scarcely of great moment in a state under siege.

The route from the terminal to downtown Maputo circles around the austere concrete tomb of President Samora Machel, whose Soviet-crewed jet plunged to the ground in South Africa last October under circumstances that are still murky. The monument is ringed with pieces of the wreckage from the Tupolov 134A aircraft that Mozambique charges strayed off course and crashed as a result of South African tampering with ground-based signal beacons. Pretoria strongly denies the accusation.

The highway itself is in rather good condition. Flanking it, though, are ramshackle dwellings that provide a foretaste of the absolute deprivation prevailing throughout the country. And in contrast to the bustle characteristic of the developing world, you are struck by an eerie quiet as you drive along, a reflection not only of the tiny number of motor vehicles relative to the population but of an economy that is dying.

Mozambique's capital is remarkably well-kept. While some buildings are in disrepair, overall one gets the impression that an effort is being made to avoid the architectural decay so often found in Third World capitals. The city is spacious and its design is not at all unappealing, offering some lovely postcard vistas of the Indian Ocean. Yet this is small compensation to residents, for their money has scant buying power and, like the airport officials and people outside the capital, they depend on daily food rations to subsist. Everything, down to such basic items as cooking oil and soap, is apportioned by the government.

Shop windows that appear to announce merchandise within are usually little more than clever displays of yellowed posters promoting name-brand perfumes, cosmetics and aftershaves, Jantzen sportswear, and fashionable Italian shoes—all of which have been out of stock for years, in many cases since Mozambique won its independence from Portugal in 1975. What few goods are offered for sale are of low quality, and have mostly been made in China. Prices are steep for Mozambicans, whose currency, the metical, was devalued by 90 per cent against the dollar earlier this year (a move interpreted in international financial circles as a sign that the government is serious about dealing with the country's economic problems).

The metical is not even accepted at the Polana Hotel, a majestic reminder of the recently concluded colonial period. The hotel caters to foreigners, including a large number of South African businessmen. In its dining room the beer served more often than not comes from South Africa, and the rand will do as hard currency throughout Maputo.

GRIM AS conditions are in the capital, life here nevertheless represents the bright side in a nation where the per capita income has fallen to $140 per year, one of the lowest in the world. During the 1983-84 drought, the effects of which linger, some 100,000 people in the countryside died of starvation; today "hunger is general," an aid official declared.

In Inhambane, one of Mozambique's 10 provinces, 652,000 of the 1.1 million people are said by the government to be threatened by severe food shortages. Official estimates for the country as a whole, generally accepted by international aid representatives, indicate that 4.5 million out of a total population of 14.4 million are at risk. Roughly 2 million have been displaced, driven from their villages by the ravages of hunger or by armed marauders, ranging from free-lance bandits to anti-government guerrillas.

In some inaccessible locations people are literally without clothes, usually because there is no cloth for barter and nothing to barter with anyway. Raiding parties also steal clothing, as well as food and tools, leaving villagers with nothing except ugly wounds and corpses to bury. It is now fairly common to see grain sacks or rags converted into crude attire. In the northern province of Niassa, where there are not enough gunny sacks to go around, naked residents have reportedly painted "clothing" on their bodies.

Maputo lacks the means to relieve the ubiquitous suffering. The national treasury is broke, and as Prime Minister Mário da Graça Machungo noted in September, Mozambique's meager projected export earnings of $85 million from cashew nuts, sisal, prawn, and fish will not even be adequate to meet the interest due on international loans (payments on the principal have been rescheduled). The trade balance has deteriorated from a deficit of $65 million in 1981 to $542 million in 1986. Over the same five years export earnings fell steadily from $281 million to $79 million, largely because of disturbances caused by the insurgency. Another $30 million in foreign exchange will be lost when Mozambicans working in gold mines in South Africa are repatriated in May 1988.

Some 30 different aid organizations are currently represented in Mozambique, working with admirable efficiency to stem the growing misery. But despite pledged donations approaching $1 billion, massive food shortages are expected to persist through the next year.

The challenge is not merely securing food and other relief supplies, it is also distributing them. Mozambique, a country twice the size of California with a 1,535 mile-long coastline, has only about 16,000 miles of roads. Since barely one-sixth of them are paved, the movement of goods from Maputo in the far south to the rest of the country is difficult. Moreover, there is a drastic shortage of vehicles, with no more than one truck or bus for every 600 people. (Government officials candidly note that CARE, equipped with 300 trucks, runs the best transport system in the country.)

In several cases delivering relief supplies turns out to be much more expensive than obtaining them. The United Nations Development Program, for example, must airlift food to Zambezia, a province hit hard by both drought and fighting, and this raises costs ten-fold. Important supply routes are often incredibly convoluted and tedious: Many provisions are sent by rail from Harare,

UNLOADING RELIEF SUPPLIES

the capital of Zimbabwe, to the Mozambican port of Beira, a distance of 340 miles. From Beira they are sent by ship to Nacala, Mozambique's northern port, and then by rail to Nampula, whence they are distributed by truck. That food convoys are always vulnerable to attack by rebel gangs further complicates delivery.

There can be little doubt that Mozambique's difficulties are in significant measure the direct consequence of its unhappy experiment with State Socialism. The inefficiencies inherent in central economic planning did particular harm to the agriculture sector: State farms, communal villages and agricultural cooperatives only succeeded in exacerbating the plight of an already poor country.

An early, albeit tacit, admission of failure came in 1980 with the denationalization of retail trade. Since 1983 in particular, the government's ardor for Marxist solutions has cooled considerably. The rhetoric may still be heard on occasion, but the ideology no longer shapes economic policy as it once did. Under pressure from harsh reality as well as the World Bank, Mozambique has begun to discover the merits of the free market.

Recently steps have been taken to introduce the market mechanism into the agricultural system: Farmers are now allowed to sell their produce directly, rather than through state-operated cooperatives at controlled prices. Prices are still high relative to meager incomes, however; even in those exceptional areas where rural security is good, persistent drought conditions and the lack of seeds and tools combine to keep productivity very low. In one roadside market outside Maputo less than a pound of tomatoes costs the equivalent of $1.25, and a handful of small fish about the same.

If the government has in the past pursued an unfortunate model, one is prone to be skeptical that the situation would be very much better had inspiration been sought from Adam Smith instead of Karl Marx. Following independence, the Portuguese who had manned the bureaucracy and run the economy departed en masse—taking their technical and managerial expertise with them. In 1974, when Lisbon agreed to concede sovereignty to Mozambique, there were 250,000 Portuguese colonists in the country; a year later, around 25,000 remained. At that time well over 90 per cent of the native population was illiterate. Fewer than 10 Mozambicans had a college education, and only a couple of them were versed in economics. Not a single Mozambican had serious training in agronomy, the country's agrarian economy notwithstanding. To say Portugal left Mozambique poorly prepared for self-government would be a gross understatement.

The indigenous authority that emerged at independence was really a pair of parallel structures: the party arm of the Front for the Liberation of Mozambique (FRELIMO), the organization that dominated the struggle against Portugal, and a more-or-less conventionally organized government, which FRELIMO is constitutionally empowered to delimit and direct. Both party and government extend from national to local-level bodies.

Major political figures often hold office simultaneously in the party and government, and the leader of FRELIMO serves as president of the republic. The People's Assembly—constitutionally defined as the ultimate locus of state power—is clearly subordinate to the President and Council of Ministers, who together call the tune in Mozambique.

Despite the authentic-sounding titles of many of the government agencies, job-holders are, as one bureau chief complained, usually more interested in getting a watch and a car than in doing much work in the public interest. The pattern of government operations is one of general ineptitude—officials are disarmingly frank to admit—punctuated by occasional bursts of competence. Fortunately, an exceptionally able official, Prakash Ratilal, has been charged with coordinating relief efforts.

STILL, THE postindependence government might have muddled through, were it not for the insurgency that has been active almost continuously over the last 12 years. The FRELIMO regime made significant progress in health care and education, reducing illiteracy to 86 per cent and building a network of simple clinics. But these gains have been wiped out by the destruction of roughly 2,000 schools and 25 per cent of the health clinics, mostly at the hands of anti-government forces.

The rebels, part of a movement called the Mozambique National Resistance (MNR or, more commonly, RENAMO), are estimated variously to be from 5,000 to 25,000 men strong. The overwhelming majority of the membership is Mozambican, although black Africans from other countries are allegedly involved, and former Portuguese colonists (many of whom fled to South Africa at independence) seem to play a major role as well. Some of the RENAMO leadership has been drawn from a cadre of disaffected FRELIMO adherents, particularly speakers of the Shona dialect from Manica and Sofala provinces, who resent the party's domination by elements from the Maputo area.

RENAMO was adopted by Pretoria in 1980, when the originally Rhodesian-created force was orphaned by the fall of Ian Smith's white-controlled government and the creation of Zimbabwe. South Africa furnishes the movement with supplies and intelligence, trains its members, and at times directs its operations. RENAMO is widely—and I believe, accurately—viewed as one of the instruments employed by Pretoria to destabilize its black neighbors, to maintain their economic dependence on South Africa, and to discourage the Front Line states from supporting opponents of apartheid.

Through the fortunes of geography, Mozambique's three major west-east rail lines are important outlets to the Indian Ocean and potential alternatives to South Africa's rail network. The Southern African Development Coordination Conference (SADCC)—comprising Mozambique, Angola, Botswana, Lesotho, Malawi, Tanzania, Swaziland, Zambia, and Zimbabwe—has therefore initiated a plan to develop the Beira rail corridor as an economic lifeline free from Pretoria's manipulation.

If Mozambique can stay reasonably stable and keep its rail system fully operative, states like Zimbabwe and Zambia might be able to achieve their declared goal of economic autonomy from South

Africa. The Harare-Beira line, though still functioning at less than capacity, is now carrying about 15 million tons of cargo a year that was previously shipped via South Africa, including much of Zambia's copper exports. While South Africa has not, through RENAMO, succeeded in disrupting the Beira corridor, it has fomented plenty of chaos in the effort.

In 1984 South Africa and Mozambique concluded a pact obliging Pretoria to cease backing RENAMO in exchange for Maputo's withdrawal of support from the anti-apartheid African National Congress—the Nkomati accord. After the signing, however, RENAMO attacks in Mozambique escalated. In 1985 the South African Foreign Minister conceded that his country had "technically violated" the accord, and that elements within South Africa were continuing to help the Mozambican insurgents. Senior U.S. officials have stated, as recently as June 1987, that South Africa is still aiding RENAMO. Mozambique, by contrast, is widely credited with having kept its side of the agreement, and has emphasized its intention to go on doing so.

Although RENAMO spokesmen in Lisbon and Washington strive to depict their organization as spearheading an anti-Marxist uprising against the Maputo regime, the movement's style of operation is wholly inconsistent with the goal of winning popular support. On the contrary, RENAMO assaults seem calculated to intimidate, frighten and horrify the populace, further burdening an already overloaded government in the process. In addition to destroying bridges, rail lines, electrical pylons, schools, and medical dispensaries, the rebels target civilians. Noses and ears are often lopped off with machetes, and there have been incidents in which lips have been severed and women's breasts slashed. The most serious RENAMO massacre occurred this past July in the city of Homoine, where as many as 424 people were murdered. Such atrocities can only earn the abhorrence of Mozambicans.

Mozambique's Army is incapable of dealing with the guerrilla threat. It is critically short of almost everything, including radios and trucks. Thus, even when the Army receives timely warning of an insurgent strike through its dreadfully poor communications system, it frequently lacks the transport necessary to move soldiers to the scene of the action. Delays of one or two days are not uncommon, and, as one African diplomat noted, "the Army may never show up." When deployed, soldiers frequently lack rations, not to mention shoes and clothing.

Well-placed local officials acknowledge that the Army is inefficient, underpaid, underfed, inadequately supplied, poorly trained, and sometimes undisciplined. In fact, RENAMO has no monopoly on banditry: Army elements (and run-of-the-mill criminals) have conducted their share of looting, maiming and killing. One of the major issues of discussion during the recent parliamentary session was the establishment of a tribunal system to deal with military crimes. The Army's problems have been publicly addressed by President Joaquim A. Chissano, too, and there is a program in place to improve its operational effectiveness. In an attempt to trade quantity for quality, the Armed Forces are actually being brought down in size.

JOAQUIM CHISSANO

HERETOFORE the key factor in turning back RENAMO has been not the Mozambican Army, but the 10,000-12,000 soldiers of the highly regarded Zimbabwe Army deployed along the strategic Beira corridor. Tanzania has also placed as many as 2,000 men in Zambezia province, the agricultural heartland of Mozambique, and a small contingent from Malawi guards parts of the northernmost rail line. The Front Line nation troops are enough to stave off disaster and buy the Maputo regime some time, but they are inadequate to defeat RENAMO.

The support Mozambique has been winning from a number of European governments is therefore particularly important. The country is now the number one recipient of British aid, which includes training for Mozambican officers and soldiers. Italy, Sweden, Norway, Denmark, Iceland, and Portugal are also all heavily involved in what has become an international undertaking, and the United States provided $75 million in emergency assistance in the fiscal year that ended on September 30.

A number of Mozambique's benefactors have come to realize that in a country where the most serious problem besides hunger is the inability of villagers to defend themselves, the distinction between humanitarian aid and security assistance blurs: Until the public safety is assured and development projects are safeguarded, the suffering will not be ameliorated. This, for example, was the conclusion of the Commonwealth countries at their meeting in Vancouver last month, attended by Mozambique as an invited observer. At the end of the session, Commonwealth leaders agreed to set up "an enhanced program of coordinated assistance" to help Mozambique meet its security needs.

The stakes here extend beyond one country alone to the whole southern part of the continent. If South Africa's campaign to destabilize the FRELIMO government can be thwarted, the likely upshot would be economic autonomy for the Front Line nations through linkage with a peaceful and developing Mozambique. Pretoria would then be forced to reach an enlightened accommodation with its no longer pliant neighbors, and would feel increased pressure to set in motion meaningful reforms at home. Failure to turn back the RENAMO threat, on the other hand, would bolster South African domination of the region. It would also imperil the survival of millions of Mozambicans, who deserve a chance to live.

South Africa And Its Neighbors

South Africa's menace to the well-being of black people is not limited to the territory within its borders. Its neighbors have felt its heavy-handed pressure.

ROLLINS E. LAMBERT

The Rev. Rollins E. Lambert *is the adviser on African affairs for the United States Catholic Conference in Washington, D.C.*

Apartheid in South Africa is intolerable to the black people of that nation. Many of their leaders have called on the international community for increased pressure on Pretoria to dismantle the system, which has for decades been imposed on the black majority by the white minority. Such international pressure is mounting, but its outcome is very much in doubt. The Afrikaners, the controlling white descendants of Dutch settlers, have a strong traditional tendency to resist pressure and, in fact, to counteract it with pressures of their own making. Hence the announcement recently, after the Commonwealth leaders agreed on some sanctions, that Zambia and Zimbabwe will be made to suffer restrictions and impediments to their vital commerce through and with the Republic of South Africa.

South Africa's menace to the well-being of black people is not limited to the territory within its borders. Also involved are Namibia (South West Africa), Lesotho, Swaziland, Botswana, Zimbabwe, Mozambique and Angola. All of these countries have felt the heavy hand of South African pressure in their efforts either to establish independence, as in the case of Namibia, or to achieve economic stability, as in the case of Zimbabwe and Mozambique, or even to maintain civil peace, as in the cases of Angola, Mozambique and Zimbabwe.

South Africa's armed forces occupy, or have occupied, parts of Angola for years, as they attempt a two-fold objective: First, to hit the bases of the South West Africa People's Organization (SWAPO), the main organization working and fighting for the independence of Namibia; second, to prevent the establishment of a settled government in Angola.

When the Reagan Administration took office, it said that Namibia's independence would be a priority in its southern African policy. Shortly thereafter, however, it added a "Catch 22" proviso: Cuban forces would have to leave Angola as a condition of South Africa's withdrawal from Namibia. More recently, the Administration has backed moves in Congress to provide covert military assistance to Jonas Savimbi, leader of the National Union for the Total Independence of Angola (UNITA), the main dissident guerrilla force in Angola. This means, of course, that the Government in Luanda, the Angolan capital—the one recognized by most of the world community—is called upon to dismiss the Cuban support forces at the same time that the United States and South Africa are supplying arms to Savimbi, whose objective is to overthrow the Government. There seems to be a lack of logic here.

The Catholic bishops of Angola wrote in a Feb. 27, 1986, pastoral letter: "We Angolans are celebrating 10 years of independence, unhappily 10 years with arms in our hands. As if this were not enough, the specter of war keeps growing larger, a fratricidal war which goes on destroying the nation. Even foreign armed forces make our land a battlefield. We are decimated physically and morally. The fine flower of our youth goes on falling on the combat front. And many announced victories are the victories of death and destruction."

There are other tolls of war: Railroads cannot run, roads are unsafe for transport, schools and health facilities are

From *America*, February 21, 1987, pp. 148-152. Reprinted with permission of America Press, Inc., 106 West 56th Street, New York, NY 10019.

closed or destroyed. All the usual horrors of war have been prolonged because South Africa and the United States have preferred a military solution to a negotiated peace.

The people of Namibia, too, are victims of South Africa's continued occupation of their country. South Africa's defense force (S.A.D.F.) is the largest on the African continent, but SWAPO's guerrillas continue to harass it and SWAPO continues to exert strong political attraction for the people of Namibia. Reports of murder, torture and other forms of brutality perpetrated by the S.A.D.F. make their way to the outside world almost daily.

Addressing the U.S. Secretary of State's Advisory Committee on South Africa on June 3, 1986, Bishop David W. Preus, the presiding bishop of the American Lutheran Church, summed up the situation in these words: "The churches and the vast majority of people in Namibia see no threat whatsoever in the presence of Cuban troops in Angola. They see no reason why we should allow South Africa to justify brutal occupation of their land because of events which don't concern them....As far as the Namibian churches are concerned, there are now two countries responsible for the occupation of Namibia: South Africa and the United States."

Bishop Preus was only echoing an April 1986 declaration signed by all the major churches in Namibia, including the Catholic Church, in which they unanimously resolved "to reject the unholy alliance between the United States and the Republic of South Africa in their attempts to bypass the United Nations Security Council Resolution 435 by linking the independence of Namibia to issues that are totally extraneous, such as the withdrawal of Cuban troops from Angola." They went on to reaffirm that the resolution is "the only peaceful and democratic way of achieving internationally recognized independence for Namibia."

As far back as 1976, the U.S. Catholic Conference's Committee on Social Development and World Peace urged "that the United States raise for discussion in the U.N. Security Council the threat to world peace created by the Republic of South Africa by its internal policy of apartheid and its occupation of Namibia with a view to imposing international economic sanctions against that nation until substantial changes have been made." The committee also recommended "that the United States recognize and enforce the decree of the U.N. Council for Namibia for the protection of the natural resources of Namibia against exploitation by South Africa during its illegal occupation of that territory." Only in the recently concluded session of 99th Congress were steps in this direction taken: Sanctions were passed—unilateral, not international—which include Namibia, and an effort was made by Representative Pat Schroeder (D., Colo.) to protect Namibian resources; her bill did not reach the House floor.

On the other side of the continent, South Africa's surrogates continue to batter Mozambique's economy, inflicting death and destruction on the people of that struggling country. In 1984, South African authorities signed the Nkomati accords with the Mozambican Government. Both parties agreed not to sponsor or permit attacks against the other to be planned and executed from their territory. According to published accounts, Mozambique has faithfully observed the pact, but South Africa's support of Mozambique Resistance Movement guerrillas continues to the present. Attacks have been launched, not only along the border where the two countries meet, but also in the central heartland where agriculture and rail and sea transport are essential to the development, if not the survival, of the nation.

The long war has resulted in barbarous executions, massacres and the destruction of houses and goods of defenseless populations.

The Mozambican Government estimates that the six-year-old guerrilla war has already left at least a half million displaced persons, with another 300,000 having fled to neighboring countries, particularly South Africa and Zimbabwe. On Oct. 8, 1986, the South African Government announced that it will prohibit the importation of Mozambican workers into South Africa, in reprisal for guerrilla attacks on South African troops along the border between the two nations. This means that nearly 69,000 men will be out of work in the near future and will add their presence to the already stricken economic scene in Mozambique.

Like their brother bishops on the other side of the continent, the Mozambique Catholic bishops have pleaded for an end to violence and war. They asked "those who finance or support in some way this cruel war," including "the West and East blocs," to stop giving military help. Such aid only prolongs the war and endangers more lives. The long war, the bishops said in their pastoral letter of May 31, 1986, has resulted in "barbarous executions in the presence of young people and children, massacres and the destruction of houses and goods of defenseless populations."

What is the point of South Africa's military adventures across its borders, and its economic pressures against its neighbors? There is a great deal at stake.

Perhaps foremost is the bad example that would be given to the black majority in South Africa if black-ruled nations manage to be successful in promoting peace and development for their peoples. South African blacks are led to believe that only white rulers can run a country properly. Their own education is carefully inhibited by the Government so that few of them can aspire to positions of authority. To see Mozambique, Zimbabwe or Angola successful would tend to dispel the myth of black inferiority.

Second, South Africa has ambitions to be the economic

center of the subcontinent and, by its economic power, the dominant component in the region. Colonial history tends to make any alternative improbable: South Africa is highly developed industrially and commercially. It has the railroads and seaports needed to distribute imports and collect exports; the other nations limp in comparison. But the neighbors have not capitulated to this South African dream. Wanting as much independence as possible, they have formed the Southern African Development Coordinating Conference (S.A.D.C.C.), a collaborative and cooperative venture aimed at reducing South Africa's dominance. South Africa's way to prevent S.A.D.C.C. from achieving its goals has been to destabilize its neighbors so that the exploitation of labor and natural resources can continue under white control. It has not hesitated to use sanctions against unruly neighbors, but protests vehemently when other nations impose sanctions on South Africa itself. Mozambique is a special target since the principal alternative routes for the landlocked nations—Zimbabwe, Zambia, Botswana and Swaziland—are over Mozambique's railroads to its seaports. Meeting in Harare, Zimbabwe, in October 1986, the heads of the front-line states expressed the fear that South Africa is planning military actions against them, using its own S.A.D.F. instead of concealing its aggression by using surrogates and mercenaries. With inflation running at 18 percent, with its currency, the rand, having lost half its value in the past year or so, with internal unrest continuing, what better diversion could the South African Government offer its people than a war?

South African blacks are led to believe that only white rulers can run a country properly.

For the South African Government and its supporters, and for many Americans as well, the central fact about southern Africa is the presence of Marxist-Leninist governments and Soviet-supported liberation movements. Angola, Mozambique and Zimbabwe openly adhere to Marxist doctrine and practice; Namibia's leading liberation movement, SWAPO, receives much of its backing from the Communist bloc; South Africa's African National Congress (A.N.C.) admits that a number of its leadership people are Marxists but firmly denies that its policies and programs are directed from Moscow. It should be noted that support also is provided by some non-Communist governments, particularly in Scandinavia.

Looking to history, one can easily understand why a close relationship exists with the Communist bloc: The liberation movements in the three independent countries—Angola, Mozambique and Zimbabwe—as well as SWAPO and the A.N.C. looked in vain for help from the West. Members of the North Atlantic Treaty Organization (NATO) were not inclined to offend Portugal, a NATO member, by backing independence movements in Portuguese colonies. The white minority Government in Rhodesia had strong political and economic ties to Britain and the United States.

Since independence, Marxist ideology has not prevented the new governments from maintaining satisfactory relations with the West. The Angolan Government is described by American business people as a good partner. Zimbabwe has lagged behind its promise to redistribute land because it has respected the productivity of farms and mines owned by whites, whether Zimbabwean or foreign. Angola has indicated its willingness to deal with Western business enterprises, but the internal turmoil created by guerrilla activity has been a deterrent to all economic activity.

Looking to the future, one would expect that all three nations, as well as a majority-ruled South Africa and an independent Namibia, would find far more incentive to cooperate with western Europe and North America than with the Soviet bloc. They need markets for their agricultural and mineral produce. Eastern Europe offers little hope in this area. They need development assistance in the form of technology and finance; the Soviet Union is not known for being useful in these areas.

A realistic American policy, then, should recognize the possibilities for constructive relationships with the nations and organizations in southern Africa. These possibilities include an emphasis on respect for human rights when they are seriously violated. Once peace and a modicum of prosperity are established, African governments might well be persuaded to permit more freedom to their people than they are willing to allow when warfare or guerrilla activity prevail.

U.S. policy in southern Africa over the years—not just the Reagan years—has clearly failed. Namibia is still not independent. Apartheid has been modified, but the black majority are still totally excluded from political power at the national level. Under recent decrees, freedom of speech and association, freedom of movement and freedom of the press have been suppressed with more force than ever before.

What new policy steps might be envisioned to produce real development in Namibia and South Africa itself? What might restrain South Africa's violent treatment of its regional neighbors? Let me suggest several actions.

1. The United States and other North American, European and Asian governments should support S.A.D.C.C., not only with money, but also with technology appropriate to its plans and priorities.

2. Mozambique should be provided with the military

equipment necessary to deter unauthorized South African overflights and attacks.

3. The United States should discontinue any support of UNITA in Angola.

4. Instead, the United States should encourage and support efforts in the Organization of African Unity and/or the United Nations to mediate a political peace in Angola. The United States, by supporting UNITA, has forfeited its possible role as an "honest broker" in the region. Perhaps a disinterested country such as Spain could fill that role. Spain never had more than minuscule colonial activity in Africa; its king has a reputation for conciliation as well as for firmness, and he clearly believes in constitutional democracy.

5. The United States should drop its demand that Cuban withdrawal from Angola accompany South African withdrawal from Namibia. If peace is successfully mediated in Angola, the need for Cuban military forces will disappear and the Government would be happy to be relieved of their expense.

6. Pressure for the independence of Namibia according to U.N. Resolution 435 should be redoubled. A definite time should be set for completion of the necessary intervening steps, with no excuses accepted. This was nearly accomplished in the past, but South Africa found convenient excuses for stalling.

To see Mozambique, Zimbabwe or Angola successful would tend to dispel the myth of black inferiority.

7. Preparations, coordinated with other friendly countries, should be made to alleviate deprivation in the region—deprivations that may arise from South Africa's reprisals or the predicted effects of U.S. and European sanctions against South Africa. Airlifts should be provided for such critical items as medicines, and transport by land or sea for food, petroleum products and other commodities.

The problems of southern Africa are multiple and complex. The United States and other nations should not be expected to solve all of them. Nevertheless, the United States and the international community can work toward the basic objective—peace. With freedom from South Africa's aggression and with internal conciliation, the people of the region and their governments can get down to the critical business of growing food for themselves, educating their children, providing health care and moving into the channels of development that will enhance the living conditions of all. Without peace, none of these objectives is possible.

South Africa is highly developed industrially and commercially; the other nations limp in comparison.

There is one problem that would remain to be solved: apartheid in South Africa itself, and the consequent efforts of the A.N.C. to bring about the downfall of that system by acts of sabotage, guerrilla warfare and other forms of intimidation. The solution to this problem lies squarely with the South African Government and its supporters. As long as they refuse to negotiate with the authentic black leaders to plan for a new dispensation, there will be no peace in South Africa. The urgency of the situation is well described by the Southern African Catholic Bishops' Conference in their May 2, 1986, statement: "The system of apartheid has caused so much suffering and so much harm in human relations in our country for so long and is now being defended, despite some reforms, with so much repressive violence that people have had to resort to the strongest possible forms of pressure to change the system. It seems that the most effective of nonviolent forms of pressure left is economic pressure."

The U.S. Congress and other nations are moving in the direction of such pressure, with some sanctions already legislated or promised. It is up to the South African Government to decide if and when that pressure will be increased or withdrawn.

The Limits of American Power

Many Americans believe—and correctly so—that United States foreign policy is, at times, both difficult to explain and difficult to predict. In their view, American policy lacks coherence and consistency, which undermines unity at home and support abroad. Legislative-executive conflict, political discord, the absence of clearly defined goals, and numerous legal vagaries all contribute to the foreign policy maze that continues to baffle both pundits and lay citizens alike.

To understand foreign policy-making, it is necessary to possess sufficient information. In some cases, however, the problem is not a lack of information but too much information. Still, possessing information alone is not sufficient; to understand the contradictions and nuances of the policy-making process, one must ask the right sorts of questions. In this regard, it may prove useful to posit several alternative models that have been developed by political scientists to assess foreign policy decisions.

The most widely accepted approach is the strategic or rational model. According to this approach, state leaders can be viewed as "solitary actors," seeking to advance their objectives in the international arena. This action-reaction model attempts to explain each response as a rational calculation to counterbalance a move by the other side. Like all models, it has strengths and limitations. Its principal advantage is its simplicity, in that it permits one to analyze foreign policy decisions with a minimum of complexity. On the other hand, it understates the impact of sundry domestic and international actors. In addition, it assumes a level of rationality that is rarely present in the formulation and implementation of foreign policy decisions.

The second approach is the decision-making model, which is considerably more complex. This approach focuses on myriad internal and external factors that shape foreign policy choices. It places special emphasis on the weight assigned to the determining factors by official decisionmakers. Its salient advantage is that it underscores the significance of the human factor—that is, the motivations of official policymakers, the flow of information among them, and the impact of various alternatives on their decisions.

The bureaucratic politics model not only examines the major players in the foreign policy process, but highlights the role played by top bureaucrats who are involved in the process. It is based on the assumption that, in many cases, important decisions are influenced by high-level bureaucrats, who frequently possess greater expertise than the elected politicians who actively solicit their advice and assistance. Additionally, these bureaucrats are intimately involved in the implementation of foreign policy directives and, like all bureaucrats, can choose to implement a policy, do so reluctantly, or refuse to act at all. The primary limitation of this model is the tendency to overestimate the role of bureaucrats in the policy process.

The adaptive approach attempts to analyze foreign policy decisions by examining the ways in which nations respond to the opportunities and constraints imposed by their international environments. This model maintains that official state actions are often defined by the environment in which the states function. Clearly, the adaptive capacities of states differ, based both on their desire to act and their ability to do so. In reality, a state's ability to act is, to a large extent, the product of its political allegiances, geographical position, and military strength.

Finally, the incremental decision-making model views foreign policy decisions as an ongoing series of small forward steps, each based on the actions that preceded it. It challenges the rational-actor model, arguing that the lack of certainty and information, combined with the large number of foreign policy actors, preclude comprehensive rational calculation. Rather than weighing every possible option, top decisionmakers tend to concentrate on those alternatives that reflect past policy.

As you read the following articles, consider the above models. These approaches will help you to define a policy, evaluate its strengths and weaknesses, identify key actors, and suggest viable alternatives. Remember, however, that foreign policy defies simple explanation—it is rarely the product of any *one* model. Moreover, foreign policy is the result of numerous domestic and international considerations, any one or a combination of which may bear heavily on the action taken. And keep in mind that American foreign policy can rarely be explained in terms of good guys and bad guys; nations tend to act on the basis of self-interest, even if that means signing a pact with the devil.

Looking Ahead: Challenge Questions

Why should the United States be concerned about the Third World?

When, if ever, should the United States intervene to affect political conditions in the developing world?

Should the United States adopt a conciliatory noninterventionist posture toward the Third World, as a means of reducing the risk of American military involvement in that part of the world?

Would a policy of benign detachment restore honor and

Unit 4

consistency to American foreign policy in the developing world?

According to Ernest Lefever, what are the five main myths that surround U.S. policy toward the Third World?

How does Lefever define America's role in the Third World?

Has the United States succeeded in developing a viable counterinsurgency force in El Salvador?

What lessons should future presidents learn as a result of America's experience in El Salvador?

In what ways, if any, have recent events in Panama affected the fabric of that country?

Why has U.S. policy in Panama been condemned by most Latin American governments, including many of America's closet allies?

Did President Ronald Reagan act wrongly in his efforts to force the removal of Panamanian strongman General Manuel Noriega?

Despite their public protestations, why have most black-ruled nations in Africa secretly attempted to expand their trade ties with South Africa?

In what ways, if any, have South Africa's black neighbors undermined the effectiveness of Western sanctions against that country?

What does South Africa hope to gain by expanding its economic presence in the region?

Policies Toward the Third World

Seyom Brown
Brandeis University

To those people in the huts and villages of half the globe struggling to break the bonds of mass misery, we pledge our best efforts to help them help themselves, for whatever period is required—not because the Communists may be doing it, not because we seek their votes, but because it is right.
—John F. Kennedy (Inaugural Address, January 20, 1961)

United States policies toward the so-called Third World—the nonindustrialized countries outside of Europe, most of which are former colonies of one or another of the European powers—are ostensibly for the purpose of furthering the development of economically underdeveloped or politically fragile countries. Presumably, special United States help or intervention is required by many of these countries for them to tend adequately to their people's material needs and to maintain internal peace and independence from foreign domination.

But *why* should the condition of such Third World countries be of major concern to the United States? The answers encountered in the policy community range from narrow self-interest concerns to universal imperatives to alleviate the suffering of others wherever in the world they might reside. Each answer has its own rationale and generates its own objections.

NATIONAL SELF-INTEREST RATIONALE

United States government programs to help other countries develop economically rarely obtain congressional majorities to fund them unless a convincing case can be made that the United States itself will benefit from such a diversion of the taxpayers' money from domestic programs. This condition often is satisfied by Buy American provisos stipulated by Congress on financial credits extended to countries that need money to purchase equipment, technology, or experts for their economic development projects. Such strings, of course, are not possible to attach to U.S. contributions to international development agencies, such as the World Bank or regional development banks, nor are they appropriate to attach to U.S. loans to governments to help them balance their budgets and pay off existing foreign debts.

In cases where immediate or quick payback through purchase of U.S. goods and services is inappropriate, other—indirect—benefits to the United States usually have to be demonstrated to gain congressional approval of a foreign assistance program. These indirect benefits to the United States can be economic, political, or both.

Straight grants, concessionary loans, and associated economic assistance to particular developing countries or to multinational regional development banks often will be championed as important stimulants to the economic growth of the recipients; and purportedly, the resulting economic growth will provide new markets for U.S. products and new opportunities for U.S. investments, including the location of subsidiaries of multinational corporations. These types of benefits to the United States private economic sector were a large part of the rationale in President Reagan's 1982 Caribbean Basin Development Initiative.[1] Though philosophically opposed to heavy reliance on market distorting mechanisms such as government-to-government loans at concessionary interest rates, free enterprisers such as Ronald Reagan and his economic advisers are willing to resort to them temporarily because they provide seed money for generating an initial development cycle. Then, the loans can, presumably, be eliminated as the potential for growth in the aided countries begins to attract private investment.[2]

Often the economic self-interest rationale for foreign assistance is less direct, focusing on the effects of the economic aid on the political conditions within the recipient countries—conditions that are thought to be inhibiting what would otherwise be a profitable market for U.S. products and a stable source of inputs for U.S. industrial processes. The political disorder that disrupts normal commerce is attributed to the resentment of the poor alienated masses who have lost all hope of improving their lives within the system and thus can be mobilized into radical revolutionary movements willing to use violence to topple the existing order. Progress in economic development is a necessary precondition, so the argument goes, for the minimum public order, which in turn, is the precondition for a degree of economic development that will allow for mutually profitable commerce with the United States.

The political self-interest rationale for the United States helping economically disadvantaged countries has two facets: (1) To the extent such help does indeed relieve economic conditions that otherwise would lead to widespread despair, alienation, and susceptibility to radical revolutionary mobilization, the opportunities for the Soviet Union and its friends to make easy gains among the world's poor will be reduced; and (2) To the degree that U.S. economic aid is perceived by recipients as essential to their development efforts, the United States will gain gratitude that can be cashed in, so to speak, for at least informal commitments by the recipients not to become client states of the Soviet Union or for political support (perhaps in votes in international agencies) on issues of importance to the United States. From some recipient governments, particularly those that want financial or other help in building up their military establishments, the quid pro quo for United States aid can be base rights and servicing facilities for U.S. aircraft and naval vessels, permission for the U.S. to operate intelligence gathering stations, or a formal mutual security alliance.

WORLD-INTEREST RATIONALE

A broader national-interest rationale, sometimes called enlightened self-interest, holds that the United States will fare best in a world community where countries not only respect one another but assume some responsibility for one another's well-being, especially in cases of dire need.

A minimum starting point toward such a world community, it is argued, would be for the United States to accede to the request of developing countries that each affluent country devote some specified fraction of its annual gross national product (GNP) to improving the lot of poor countries—without political or economic strings attached. (The standard figure asked by the coalition of developing countries is seven-tenths of one percent of an industrial country's GNP).

In a more elaborate and generous gesture, the United States could embrace the philosophy and something like the general program of action put forward by the Brandt Commission in 1980:* The Brandt Commission argued that a major effort by the more affluent countries to cooperate with the poorer nations in reducing the gap between the rich and the suffering poor was required in the interests of world survival:

> Continued rapid population growth in the next century could make the world unmanageable; but that growth can only be forestalled if action is taken to combat poverty in this century. Much the same is true for the biological environment, which is threatened with destruction in many countries as a direct result of poverty—though in others as a result of ill-considered technological decisions and patterns of industrial growth. These problems—nuclear weapons proliferation is another—can only be solved by North and South acting in cooperation, and their mutual interests in doing so are only too obvious. The conquest of poverty and the promotion of sustainable growth are matters not just of the survival of the poor, but of everyone.[3]

Specifically, the United States would endorse and contribute to raising at least $8 billion annually for a special fund to overcome food deficits in poor countries through a broad program of increased food production and agricultural development. The United States would resist pressures from special industry and labor groups for protection against Third World products. The United States would support the use of the reserve assets of the International Monetary Fund (IMF), principally the Special Drawing Rights, to help developing countries with their financial problems. The United States, in addition to meeting the 0.7 percent target for official development assistance, would support certain forms of automatic international taxation to raise funds from those with great wealth to be transferred to the world's poor. (The Brandt Commission, in some of its most controversial proposals, suggested taxes on international trade, especially on arms exports, and taxes on users of the international "commons" areas—the ocean beyond national jurisdiction, the atmosphere, and outer space.) And the United States would be more responsive than it has been to price-stabilization agreements with the producers of basic commodities subject to devastating fluctuations in the international market.

The United States would also attempt to promote a more cooperative relationship with developing countries by allowing them more decision-making weight in international institutions affecting their welfare, such as the IMF and the World Bank and by moving more in the direction of one-nation-one-vote arrangements in new institutions, such as those being set up to regulate the exploitation of minerals on the deep seabed.[4]

The Brandt Commission's recommendation for global negotiations, including periodic summit meetings among world leaders, to move toward the more "equitable world order" envisioned in its report, would be responded to positively, not begrudgingly in the manner of the Reagan administration, if this basically generous and accommodating approach to Third World demands for a restructured global political economy were to become United States policy.

Some Americans agree with Willy Brandt that "What is now on the agenda (and should be supported) is a rearrangement of international relations, the building of a new order and a new kind of comprehensive approach to the problems of development."[5] But clearly, not all Americans agree.

The Case Against a Policy of Apolitical Generosity

Three kinds of objections to generous foreign assistance programs are raised in public and internal government debates over the ways and extent to which the United States should attempt to help the world's poor. The first, which can be called *economic nationalism,* emphasizes the need to tend to problems at home before devoting resources to the welfare of others. The second, the *conservative realpolitik* stance, is fearful of disruptions to the global political and economic status quo that are resulting from the unrealistic expectations and demands stimulated by the notion that there should be a global social-welfare approach to the world's poor. The third kind of objection, argu-

*Willy Brandt, the former chancellor of the Federal Republic of Germany, at the suggestion of World Bank President Robert McNamara, appointed a commission of distinguished persons in 1978 to study the international issues arising from the economic and social disparities of the world and to recommend remedies. In addition to Brandt, the members were Edward Heath (Conservative prime minister of the United Kingdom, 1970-1974), Olaf Palme (prime minister of Sweden, 1969-1976), Peter G. Peterson (United States secretary of commerce, 1972-1973), Eduardo Frei Monyalva (president of Chile, 1964-1970), Adam Malik (vice president of Indonesia, 1977-1978, and minister of foreign affairs, 1966-1979), Layachi Yaker (minister of commerce of Algeria, 1969-1977), Antoine Kipsa Dakoure (minister of commerce of Upper Volta, 1970-1976), Rodrigo Botero Montoya (minister of finance of Colombia, 1974-1976), Lakshmit Kant Jha (Indian ambassador to the United States, 1970-1973), Haruki Mori (Japanese ambassador to the United Kingdom, 1972-1975), Joe Morris (Canadian labor leader and chairman of the International Labor Organization Governing Body, 1977-1978), Abdlatif Y. Al-Hamad (prominent Kuwaiti economist), Khatijah Ahmad (prominent Malaysian banker and economist), and Katherine Graham (publisher of the *Washington Post*).

ing from the premises of *classical economics,* holds that the best path for increasing everyone's well-being lies in a free international market, the emergence of which is retarded by the market-distorting effects of artificial affluent-to-poor resource transfers.

Economic nationalism. Nationalistic objections to substantial programs of special assistance to economically disadvantaged countries are of two sorts: (1) those stressing that charity begins at home; and (2) those concerned over the presumed loss of U.S. profits and jobs that could result from giving the disadvantaged countries special subsidies and privileges to compete in the market.

In a domestic United States political and economic environment dominated by demands to cut down government expenditures and reduce taxes on personal and corporate incomes, the popular saying that charity begins at home has greater consequences for foreign assistance programs than it normally does.

Even in the relatively good economic conditions of the 1950s and early 1960s, policymakers advocating increased resource transfers to the disadvantaged countries had great difficulty in convincing their fellow Americans that it was just as important to spend the United States taxpayers' money on helping the poor in India and Peru as on helping the poor in Harlem and Appalachia. Therefore, during this period, the cold war rationale of competing with the Soviets for influence in the Third World was invoked to justify foreign resource transfers. Economic development assistance was subordinated to or made an adjunct of "security assistance," and claimants in the United States government for such resources for foreign assistance programs competed with one another to demonstrate the country or region within their bureaucratic responsibility would "go communist" or align with the Sino-Soviet bloc if the United States failed to come to its aid.

In the early 1980s, the burden of proof carried by the advocates of foreign development assistance became heavier than ever. Public funds for this purpose were harder to come by than at any time since the end of World War II. This meant that political merit criteria would push aside most other considerations in the allocation of scarce resources, and the definitions of political merit would be narrowly drawn to virtually exclude that which did not add to U.S. power in its global rivalry with the Soviet Union.

Conservative realpolitik. International disorder, chaos, disruptions in the normal functioning of the global economy, and opportunities for the Soviet Union and other opponents of the United States to fish in troubled waters are the likely results, from the conservative perspective, of giving in to demands to share wealth and power with the Third World. The inequality of nations, it is argued, is not a superficial condition imposed on the world by a few selfish and venal leaders, but rather it is the product of a long and profound process of historical evolution of the nation-state system itself. The nation-state system is structured around the norm of autonomous national political economies, each sovereign over its own resources, and an orderly system of trade and bargaining between the nation-states, sustained by the great powers. To grant the argument being pushed by Third World leaders and their supporters in the more developed countries that the affluent and powerful nations have a duty to share their wealth and power in the name of global social justice is to undermine the legitimacy of the evolved international order before the groundwork for any viable alternative world order has been laid. Such action will stimulate unrealistic demands, which will have to go unmet and which in turn, therefore, will intensify the frustrations and anger of the have-nots and prevent the reasoned discourse and moderate policies necessary for international peace and security.

The conservatives are particularly adamant in opposing attempts by developing countries to democratize the structure of international institutions, such as the International Monetary Fund, the General Agreements on Tariffs and Trade, the International Maritime Consultative Organization, and the International Telecommunications Union, set up to ensure an orderly functioning of the international economy and commerce. Decision-making weight in these bodies characteristically rests with those countries with the most real resource power in the economic sector to be regulated. Moves in the direction of a one-country-one-vote decision process in such institutions will, according to conservatives, make for irresponsible decisions and will simply drive away the holders of real resources whose participation in any case is voluntary. Similar objections are raised to proposals to give developing countries more power in the allocation and approval of loans by the World Bank, which gets most of its resources from affluent governments and private corporations. If the World Bank's Board of Governors no longer represents the contributors when it sets the terms on loans, then the sources of the Bank's assets will dry up because the contributors will either revert to bilateral negotiations with recipients or form new multilateral lending consortia under the control of the donor countries.

This basic conservative stance was reflected in the Reagan administration's efforts to alter the Law of the Sea treaty provisions subjecting deep seabed mining and mineral exploitation to regulation by a thirty-six-nation council in which the United States, Japan, West Germany, Britain, and France could be outvoted by a combination of Third World and Warsaw Pact countries. The Reagan administration, in voting against the treaty in the spring of 1982, indicated it could not accept a seabed council weighted against those countries with the heaviest investments in seabed mining.[6]

Classical economics. A third kind of objection to generous international income redistribution policies normally finds expression in the Treasury Department and among a large portion—perhaps a majority—of academic economists at American universities. The classical economists want to remove most man-made barriers to the free exchange of goods in the international market. From their point of view, anything that prevents individuals from buying as cheaply as possible and selling to the highest bidder anywhere in the world is unjust. International free trade—or as close an approximation to it as possible—supposedly will result in the greatest good for the greatest number of people. It will induce procurers to locate where the factors of production (natural resources, labor, capital, managerial capabilities) can be obtained most efficiently and therefore result in goods that can be sold more cheaply. Everyone benefits. According to the classical theory, this basic free market process will tend toward a global distribution of production, and thus income earning capabilities, on the basis of the comparative advantage of various societies in providing factors of production more efficiently for certain kinds of products. This dynamic, in turn, will produce a specialization of production by particular societies and presumably therefore provide each of them with secure sources of income.

Ronald Reagan has been a devotee of the classical economic notions and has stated that they are the official premises of his administration's economic policies toward developing countries: "The societies which have achieved the most spectacular broad-based economic progress in the shortest period of time . . . believe in the magic of the marketplace," he told the Board of Governors of the International Monetary Fund and the World Bank. "My own government is committed to policies of free trade, unrestricted investment and open capital markets."[7]

Any program to correct the flow of trade and investments (and their rewards in the form of income) that naturally occurs in the free market is, by these lights, considered to be a harmful distortion of those processes that eventually will stimulate the most economic development. Large-scale official development assistance, concessionary loans and debt forgiveness, and any form of international taxation are prime examples of such distortive mechanisms and must be opposed.

Responding to Specific Economic Demands[8]

The various philosophical stances toward social justice claims of developing countries can be seen in debates in the United States policy community over how to respond to many of the specific demands put forward by the Third World coalition at successive meetings of the United Nations Conference on Trade and Development (UNCTAD) and at Special Sessions of the United Nations General Assembly (especially the sixth and seventh Special Sessions of 1974 and 1975).

On commodity agreements. The case for assuring that developing country producers of basic commodities (mostly agricultural products and other raw materials) receive minimum or floor prices, or for indexing the prices of such commodities to the international market prices of industrial goods, rests on claims of fairness as well as United States self-interest. It is grossly inequitable, so the argument goes, that poor countries with economies highly dependent upon export earnings from one or a few basic commodities should be thrown into sudden and severe depressions because of a slackening of international demand for these commodities or a decline in real earnings in relation to goods they must import. The more diversified economies of the affluent countries are better able to absorb demand and price changes in particular sectors. (Indeed, most of them subsidize their own vulnerable sectors, like grain farmers, with price supports and government purchasing arrangements.) Simple fairness, therefore, requires international guarantees to poor countries against disastrous export-income losses that are no fault of their own. Some participants in the U.S. policy debates over providing special protection to the disadvantaged commodity producers also grant the argument of many Third World people that the industrial countries bear a special responsibility for redressing the existing disparities because it was they—the former colonial imperialists—who allegedly forced a specialization of one or a small number of primary products on their colonies in previous centuries. The U.S. self-interest argument for commodity price-stabilization schemes merely emphasizes the connection between having reliable markets for U.S. exports in the Third World and providing the developing countries with assured means of earning what they need to pay for U.S. goods. Surely, it is argued, guarantees of an equitable relationship between industrial prices and prices for primary commodity imports couldn't *hurt* the United States economy.

Objections to commodity agreements center on both their desirability and their practicality. According to the orthodox free traders, everyone loses over the long run by making purchasers of any goods pay more than they would if prices were allowed to reflect supply and demand. Especially where price declines reflect the entry into the market of new producers, the development of more efficient means of production, or the use of better substitutes, efforts to prop up commodity prices are unfair to the consumers—many of whom may also be poor. Artificially pegging the price of raw rubber to the price of automobiles and other manufactured goods, for example, will only increase the costs to everyone, rich and poor alike, of getting from place to place; and, the marginal increases are likely to hurt the poor more than the rich. Moreover, it is argued, such artificial pricing arrangements will either feed on themselves, by attracting even more producers into a particular commodity line and thus requiring even heavier controls on prices (most likely in the form of production quotas), or else they will collapse when the number of new producers extends supply beyond the point where restraining competitive selling underneath fixed prices is feasible.

Another type of objection challenges the relevance of commodity agreements to the global rich-poor gap. Those who produce commodities for exports, it is pointed out, are not necessarily poor. Most of the large industrial countries are also raw material producers and exporters. Furthermore, within the poor countries themselves, the exporting sectors are the most affluent and resistant to income redistribution policies and other social reforms in their own societies. More often than not, their profits are reinvested in banks and corporations outside of their own countries; and sometimes, as in the so-called banana republics of Central America, they operate in cahoots with foreign-owned multinational corporations to keep control of the economies and political systems of their countries.

On tariff preferences. Discrimination in favor of the products of developing countries by allowing them duty-free or low tariff entry into the United States market is one of the ways that these countries and advocates of their cause within the U.S. see to help them earn foreign exchange and diversify their economies. Some preferences were granted by the European Community and Japan in 1971 and then by the United States in 1975. The European countries have extended trading privileges in the Common Market to their former colonies, while denying them to other countries. Similarly, the United States, in President Reagan's Caribbean Basin Development Plan, favors a subset of developing countries willing to cooperate with the United States in political as well as economic matters affecting the hemisphere.

Objections to the extension of tariff preferences come not only from particular industry and labor groups that fear their products will be undersold, but also from supporters of the Most Favored Nation (MFN) principle of the General Agreements on Tariffs and Trade. In the eyes of many, MFN is the heart of the GATT system of nondiscriminatory trade in that it states that all nations shall have access to a country's market equal to the most favored nation. Without such a rule, the world economy would evolve into rivalrous trading blocs antithetical to the goal of universal free trade. But advocates of tariff preferences for developing countries cite the long tolerance of the United States for European Economic Community (EEC) trading arrangements that discriminate against nonmembers—especially during the years of post-World War II reconstruction of the European economy—as a precedent for compromising with GATT principles when an important world-order objective is served thereby.

An official development assistance. Support for the proposition that affluent industrial countries should appropriate 0.7 percent of their gross national product to development assistance for disadvantaged countries (as recommended in various UN resolutions and the Brandt report) is very thin in the United States policy community and probably even thinner on the part of the general public. The small minority that argues for such an obligatory donation takes its stand largely on the premise that the world has become an interdependent community and on the ethical postulate that in a community the affluent are duty bound to help the poor. Some geopolitically oriented public officials, while not wanting to be tied to any specific percentage of GNP, regard official development assistance as a useful tool of foreign policy because it provides the government with leverage that is lacking in resources transferred through the private sector or through multilateral institutions.

Those who advocate a generous response to the needs of disadvantaged countries worry that bilateral foreign assistance will be used primarily to pressure recipient countries to conform to United States foreign policy objectives. In order to gain congressional majorities, the sponsors of foreign aid legislation must often accept a variety of rides to their bills, ranging from Buy American provisions, to human rights stipulations, to guarantees against expropriation of U.S. corporations. Economic development functions of the resource transfers more often than not are subordinated to the particular hobby horses of congressmen whose votes are required. Rather modest levels of transfers are burdened beyond their carrying capacity with the result that few if any of the hoped-for effects—least of all economic development—are realized; and, neither the United States as donor nor the recipient countries are satisfied. Instead it is just as likely that both sides become increasingly disenchanted, if not bitter, with each other.

Because government-to-government development aid is tempting for the donor country to use as a lever on the recipients, many developing countries would prefer to receive help from international institutions; and the constituency in the United States policy community championing selfless assistance to developing countries tends to support such a funnelling of aid through multilateral rather than bilateral arrangements. Yet not all developing countries want to compete equally against each other for the limited funds of international and regional banks. Some countries, particularly those that are favored military and ideological allies of the United States (like Guatemala or Thailand), are anxious to preserve their position as the preferred beneficiaries of any U.S. generosity. And the congressional and administrative backers of particular allies are equally desirous of keeping direct control of the resource transfers so that they can be used as rewards to those foreign regimes presumed to be most supportive of U.S. policies.

Thus, even controversies over basic types of official development assistance—multilateral versus bilateral—are, at base, debates over the extent to which the United States should be pursuing a long-term, politically neutral strategy of helping developing countries, as opposed to a more politicized strategy of attempting to affect immediate international alignment and ideological character of Third World countries. Equally important decisions on if and how much a particular country should be helped are infused with these controversies over the basic purposes of foreign assistance as well as arguments over whether the countries are politically and economically worthy of aid.

On debt and balance-of-payments relief. There is controversy over how to respond to the fact that, even with the availability of low interest loans and other concessionary resource transfers, many a developing country is unable to increase its national income enough to pay its debts to foreign lenders at previously negotiated rates. (Put another way, if the debts were to be repaid at the agreed rates, the debtor nation would substantially wipe out its annual margin of economic growth or, in extreme cases, even suffer a decline in national income.) Developing countries have been pressing for payments moratoria on such accumulated external debts.

The main argument for such additional concessions to developing countries is that without them the purposes of the original loans—to allow the recipients to generate development investments that would be unavailable out of current earnings—would be negated, and they would be unable to sustain their economic growth; worse yet, they might fall into total bankruptcy. The main arguments against debt moratoria are (1) that they would constitute, in fact, an additional loan by those who had already extended help at concessionary rates of interest, and that these lenders (including many nongovernmental contributors to the resources of financial institutions) would be driven away from future lending to developing countries if this becomes the pattern; (2) that debt moratoria tend to reinforce weak economic performance; and (3) that better risk borrowers, therefore, will have less funds available to them.

Although there is no agreement among United States policymakers on debt moratoria as a general policy, there is a consensus that the issue should be approached on a country-by-country basis to determine both the legitimate need and the consequences of a moratorium in each particular case. This, of course, provides just one more entry point for injecting political considerations into development financing, especially when the question is about debts owed the United States government directly.

Closely related to the debt problem are the severe balance of international payments deficits frequently incurred by developing countries, which are caused largely by their export earnings dropping far below their expenditures on imports. There is general support among United States policymakers for helping developing countries overcome temporary balance-of-payments deficits so that they can continue to purchase needed imports during a period of declining exports; the normal source for obtaining such additional financial reserves is the International Monetary Fund or regional multigovernmental financial facilities. Controversy, however, surrounds proposals to allocate Special Drawing Rights (SDRs) against the IMF funds to developing countries with balance-of-payments difficulties—that is, to have the needy countries obtain a larger share of IMF credits than they would have under normal IMF criteria. Some policymakers favor this SDR-development link, while others are against mixing development issues with the main purpose of SDRs—namely, to provide sufficient liquidity to tide high levels of international trade over the reserve depletions suffered periodically by major trading countries.

Opponents of the SDR link argue that a diversion of SDRs to development purposes may reduce their availability for this primary role of avoiding severe international recessions that might accompany constrictions in trade when there are liquidity bottlenecks in the system. Advocates of the SDR link to development aid contend that the amounts of SDRs transferred to developing countries need not be of such magnitude to detract from the larger liquidity providing functions of the IMF and that the principle problems with the SDR link are technical and administrative and can be overcome if the moral commitment is there.

THE POLITICAL INTERVENTION TRILEMMA*

When it comes to the issue of whether, under what circumstances, and how the United States should intervene to affect

*The material in this section is adapted from my essay, "The Trilemma of U.S. Foreign Policy," *AEI Foreign and Defense Review,* Vol. II., No. 5 (1980), pp.2-4.

the *political* conditions in Third World countries, the debates become most intense for they reach to the very essence of what the United States stands for in the world. Three alternative philosophies contend for basic acceptance as U.S. policy:

1. *Help friendly regimes secure themselves against U.S. adversaries.* This policy—reflected in the 1984 report by President Reagan's Commission on Central America, headed by Henry Kissinger—rests on the geopolitical premise that the most important determinants of United States support are a country's international alignments in the big power games of vital interest to the U.S.: the U.S.-Soviet rivalry and the efforts of the industrialized countries to maintain access to the world's energy resources and other critical raw materials. A regime's domestic characteristics are of little account when it is on our side in these international power games. Dictators and democrats, conservatives and reformers, fascists and communists—all are, in principle, equally acceptable as allies of the United States as long as their international interests converge with ours.[9]

In practice, this policy normally inclines the United States more toward rightist than leftist regimes. Leftist governments are suspected of having a basic animus against the United States as the leading capitalist power and of being supported by movements hostile to the United States. Rightist governments are presumed to be motivated more purely by practical considerations of power and thus will be more grateful for whatever tangible assistance the United States can provide them against their internal and external opponents. They are believed to be dependent for their political survival on domestic, commercial, and military classes, and deathly afraid of what would befall them if the leftists, especially those friendly to the Soviet Union, gained control. In the Reagan administration's lexicon, rightist regimes of an undemocratic character warranting U.S. support are called "authoritarian" while leftist regimes of an undemocratic character are called "totalitarian" and normally would not warrant U.S. support (China being a glaring exception).[10]

United States assistance to regimes warranting U.S. support on the above grounds takes several forms: generous financial credits, technology transfers, military and police training programs, and a permissive weapons sales policy—all of which constitute in fact, if not by explicit design, a rather significant intervention into the domestic affairs of the client country to help keep the existing regime in power. Occasionally this policy—appropriately called "conservative *realpolitik*"—can take the form of U.S. attempts to destabilize potentially shaky leftist governments. (These attempts might be overt through highly restrictive lending and commercial policies or covert through assistance to opposition groups.)[11]

The main problem with the conservative *realpolitik* policy is that a United States-supported regime, such as the autocracy of the Shah of Iran, may lose credibility with its own people and succumb to a sudden coup or a long germinating swell of popular discontent. In such cases, the United States may find its reputation sullied by its close association with the deposed government. Moreover, the elements engineering the coup or directing the revolution might have aligned themselves with our major international rivals to counterbalance U.S. support for the established government.

Defenders of the conservative *realpolitik* policy grant these risks but argue that the world political arena, particularly the volatile Third World, is by its very nature an uncertain field of competition. Either we accept the risks and participate vigorously on behalf of our friends, or we leave the field open to our major rivals who will intervene to tip local balances in favor of themselves and their friends—cumulatively, the global balance of power as well.

2. *Identify the United States with "progressive" regimes and political movements.*[12] The basic premise of this policy is that the dominant forces in world politics are those working to equalize the distribution of wealth, broaden political participation, and expand human rights. This is assumed to be the outgrowth of the universal spread of literacy and the accompanying exposure of the world's peoples to Lockean and Marxist ideas; namely, that all persons are to be regarded as equal in their basic rights to life, opportunity for economic betterment, and political activity; that governments are legitimate only to the extent that they rest on the consent of the governed; and (in some socialist variants) that disparities in wealth and socioeconomic class are to be eliminated.

From this point of view, United States success in the global rivalry with the Soviet Union, and U.S. international influence in general, will depend on the resourcefulness of this country in championing *two* movements—those for liberty and those for equality. The United States, because of the philosophical roots of its independence movement and constitutional system, the evolution of its humane domestic social welfare policies, and the main thrust of its best foreign policy traditions of anticolonialism and antiautocracy, can credibly identify its basic liberal ethos with the reformist forces of the contemporary world.

Proponents of the policy like to emphasize that they are not motivated primarily by altruism or even idealism. The policy is designed, they contend, to drive a wedge between the communists and the democratic progressives by providing the latter with sufficient financial, organizational, and military resources to allow them to operate separately from communist-organized leftist coalitions. If the United States were to provide hope and concrete assistance to the noncommunist left, then this country—not the Soviet Union and Cuba—would be the reformers. In addition to reducing the U.S.SR's prospects of gaining new clients and satellites, such a policy, if it were well executed, presumably would gain the United States long-term access to petroleum resources, other raw materials, and important geopolitical bases in the Third World.

There are problems, however, with this "progressive" interventionary policy also: To be successful it requires almost omniscient knowledge about who's who and what's what in the political life of complex and unfamiliar societies. Despite our best efforts, the regimes or movements supported might fail. Equally important, political leaders whom we may believe to be "progressive" might, once they assume power, turn out to be autocratic and brutal. The ideologies they express concerning human rights, economic egalitarianism, and democratic constitutionalism may be nothing more than instruments to garner popular support on the march to power, only to be discarded for instruments of oppression designed to eliminate their opponents once they are in control. Moreover, a posture of nationalist nonalignment vis-à-vis the U.S.-Soviet rivalry might also prove to be little more than a temporary expedient to gain international support, whereas the deeper commitments of Marxist elements in a "progressive" regime might incline it toward the Soviet Union.

The United States certainly has the option of withdrawing its support from those who have betrayed our faith in them. But unless such withdrawal of support is accompanied by an active policy of destabilizing the regime in power—with all the risks that entails—it will be viewed as a futile gesture, only increasing the opportunities for our major rivals to make the regime more completely dependent on them. Furthermore, if such second-thought reversals tend to become characteristic of U.S. policy, the global influence of the United States will be weakened by an embarrassing reputation for inconstancy and incompetence.

3. *Maintain a posture of scrupulous neutrality toward indigenous rivals for power in other countries.*[13] This policy does not prevent the United States from assisting those currently in power in worthwhile projects nor from vigorously objecting to policies that might injure U.S. interests or seriously offend basic American values. Nor does it deny the United States the option of counterintervention when our international rivals have intervened in regional or local conflicts. But it does attempt to preserve a clear-cut distinction between projects and policies on the one hand and other personalities and parties on the other. Official and unofficial contacts with various elements of the opposition would be regarded as a normal feature of U.S. relations with other countries. In the event that internal turmoil erupts in countries with which this country has diplomatic relations, the United States would insist on keeping communications open with persons and groups that do not necessarily have the government's official sanction.

Under such a noninterventionist policy, the United States government would not support political activity or cause anti-regime groups to agitate. It would be official U.S. policy, however, to encourage foreign governments to allow transnational organizations, such as labor unions, churches, human rights groups, that support their fellow members across nation-state lines. Furthermore, the United States could make it clear that it would be strongly biased against funding or promoting projects of regimes that systematically suppressed dissent or political opposition.

The United States need not dispense with a capacity to change a local political situation that is detrimental to important U.S. interests or to affect the outcome of an ongoing local conflict whose results, in the absence of such intervention, would substantially injure important U.S. interests. Nevertheless, the basic policy would be one of nonintervention in the affairs of other countries. The advocates of intervention would have to demonstrate that a situation requires U.S. intervention and that the costs and risks of such action are less than the costs and risks of no action at all.

The problem with such a noninterventionist stance is that it could well tempt major adversaries of the United States (the Soviet Union in particular) to intervene first in situations that are below the threshold of a U.S. interventionist reponse, to establish a *fait accompli,* and to thrust on to the United States the awesome responsibility of choosing between initiating or avoiding a large-scale confrontation.

Advocates of this policy, therefore, usually are also advocates of international conflict control mechanisms, international peacekeeping forces, UN-supervised (or other international or regional agency) cease-fires and elections, international arbitration, and the like to prevent deteriorating local and regional situations from giving our adversaries the pretext for unilateral intervention. Even if the international presence does not succeed in settling a conflict or stabilizing a deteriorating situation, it can provide a buffer against competitive outside interventions of the type that could spark a larger conflagration.

NOTES

1. Ronald Reagan, Address to the Organization of American States, February 24, 1982, U.S. Department of State, Current Policy, No. 370.
2. Ronald Reagan, Address to the Board of Governors of the International Monetary Fund and the World Bank, September 29, 1981, *Weekly Compilation of Presidential Documents,* Vol. 17, No. 4, pp. 1052-1055.
3. *North-South: A Program for Survival* (Cambridge, Massachusetts: MIT Press, 1980), p. 75.
4. *Ibid.*, the whole report.
5. *Ibid.*, p. 18.
6. Department of State, "Law of the Sea: January-February 1982," *Current Policy,* No. 371.
7. Ronald Reagan, Address of September 29, 1981, *Weekly Compilation of Presidential Documents,* Vol. 17, No. 4, pp. 1052-1055.
8. On the responses in the U.S. policy community to specific demands of the Third World countries, see Richard N. Cooper, "A New International Order for Economic Gain," *Foreign Policy,* No. 26 (Spring 1977), pp. 65-120; and Roger D. Hansen, "North-South Policy—What's the Problem?" *Foreign Affairs,* Vol. 58, No. 5 (Summer 1980), pp. 1084-1103.
9. The archpractioner of the conservative *realpolitik* approach toward the Third World was Henry Kissinger during the period 1969-1975. See his retrospective defense of the U.S. support for the Shah of Iran in his *The White House Years* (Boston: Little, Brown, 1979), pp. 1258-1264. See also my book, *The Crises of Power* (New York: Columbia University Press, 1979), pp. 107-140.
10. Jeane Kirkpatrick's "Dictatorships and Double Standards," *Commentary,* Vol. 68, No. 5 (November 1979), pp. 34-35, developed the distinction between "authoritarian" and "totalitarian" regimes and so pleased President-elect Reagan that he appointed her ambassador to the United Nations.
11. Justifications for U.S. interventions to destabilize leftist governments are found in the following policy statements by the Reagan administration: Ronald Reagan, Address to the Organization of American States, February 24, 1982, Department of State, *Current Policy,* No. 370; Ronald Reagan, Address before the British Parliament, June 8, 1982, *Current Policy,* No. 399; Richard Halloran, "Reagan Aide Tells of New Strategy on Soviet Threat," *New York Times,* May 22, 1982.
12. The principal Third World development initiatives of the Kennedy administration were an expression of the "progressive" interventionist stance, although the public presentation of these policies tended to stress the purely economic objectives. The political interventionary premises are detailed in Arthur M. Schlesinger, Jr., *A Thousand Days: John F. Kennedy in the White House* (Boston: Houghton-Mifflin, 1965), pp. 195-196.
13. The aloof noninterventionist rationale is most clearly articulated by J. William Fulbright, *The Arrogance of Power* (New York: Vintage Books, 1967). It also finds articulation in George F. Kennan, *The Cloud of Danger: Current Realities of American Foreign Policy* (Boston: Little, Brown, 1977). A pragmatic version of this approach, fused somewhat with interventionist reformism, was advocated in the Carter administration by Cyrus Vance. See his *Hard Choices: Critical Years in America's Foreign Policy* (New York: Simon and Schuster, 1983).

The U.S. and Third-World Dictatorships: A Case for Benign Detachment

The U.S.'s current foreign policy "tragically identifies the U.S. and—even worse—its capitalist democratic system with the most reactionary elements around the globe."

Ted Galen Carpenter

Mr. Carpenter is a foreign policy analyst at the Cato Institute, Washington, D.C.

IT is a central dilemma of contemporary American foreign policy that the world's leading capitalist democracy must confront an environment in which a majority of nations are neither capitalist nor democratic. U.S. leaders have rarely exhibited ingenuity or grace in handling this delicate and often frustrating situation.

The current turmoil in Central America is illustrative of a larger problem. American officials assert that this vital region is under assault from doctrinaire communist revolutionaries trained, funded, and controlled by the Soviet Union. Danger to the well-being of the U.S. is immediate and serious, Administration spokesmen argue, and it is imperative that the Marxist-Leninist tide be prevented from engulfing Central America. Accomplishing this objective requires a confrontational posture toward the communist beachhead (Nicaragua) combined with massive support for all "friendly" regimes, ranging from democratic Costa Rica to autocratic Guatemala. Washington's Central American policy displays in microcosm most of the faulty assumptions underlying America's approach to the entire Third World.

The current strategy of the U.S. betrays a virtual siege mentality. It was not always thus. Throughout the 19th century, U.S. policymakers exuded confidence that the rest of the world would emulate America's political and economic system, seeing the U.S. as a "beacon on the hill" guiding humanity to a better future. As late as the 1940's, most Americans and their political representatives still believed that democracy would triumph as a universal system. The prospective breakup of the European colonial empires throughout Asia and Africa was generally viewed as an opportunity, not a calamity. Scores of new nations would emerge from that process, and Americans were confident that most would choose the path of democracy and free enterprise, thus isolating the Soviet Union and its coterie of Marxist-Leninist dictatorships in Eastern Europe.

The actual results were acutely disappointing. No wave of new democracies occurred in this "Third World"; instead, decolonization produced a plethora of dictatorships, some of which appeared distressingly friendly to Moscow. This development was especially disturbing to Washington since it took place at a time when America's Cold War confrontation with the U.S.S.R. was at its most virulent. The nature and magnitude of that struggle caused American leaders to view the Third World primarily as another arena in the conflict. Consequently, the proliferation of left-wing revolutionary movements and governments seemed to undermine America's own security and well-being.

Washington's response to this adversity has been a particularly simplistic and unfortunate one. American leaders increasingly regarded any anti-communist regime, however repressive and undemocratic it might be at home, as an "ally," a "force for stability," and even a "friend." At the same time, they viewed leftist governments—even those under democratic procedures—as little more than Soviet surrogates, or at least targets of opportunity for communist machinations.

A portent of this mind-set among the U.S. policymakers surfaced during the earliest stages of the Cold War. Pres. Harry Truman's enunciation of the so-called Truman Doctrine in 1947 proclaimed the willingness of the U.S. to assist friendly governments resisting not only external aggression, but also "armed minorities" in their own midst. It was an ominous passage, for the U.S. was arrogating the right to intervene in the internal affairs of other nations to help preserve regimes deemed friendly to American interests. Although Washington had engaged in such conduct throughout Central America and the Caribbean for several decades, those incidents were a geographical aberration in what was otherwise a noninterventionist foreign policy. The Truman Doctrine raised the specter that America's meddlesome paternalism in one region might now be applied on a global basis.

Although Truman stressed that the *status quo* was not "sacred," his doctrine soon made the U.S. a patron of repressive, reactionary regimes around the world. It was a measure of how far that trend had developed by 1961 that Pres. John F. Kennedy could proclaim in his inaugural address America's determination to "support any friend, oppose any foe" in the battle against world communism. Today, leading foreign policy spokesmen such as Henry Kissinger, Alexander Haig, and Jeane Kirkpatrick express a fondness for "friendly" authoritarian regimes that would have seemed incomprehensible to most Americans only a few decades ago.

A false realism as well as moral insensitivity characterize American policy toward Third World dictatorships. There is a disturbing tendency to view such regimes in caricature, regarding right-wing governments as valuable friends whose repressive excesses must be ignored or excused, while perceiving leftist insurgent movements and governments as mortal threats to America's national interest, justifying a posture of unrelenting hostility. For example, the Reagan Administration pursues a confrontational policy toward the Marxist government of Nicaragua, terminating all aid programs, imposing a trade embargo, and supporting rebel guerrillas. At the same time, Washington lavishes economic and military aid upon equally repressive "allies" in South Korea, Taiwan, Zaire, and elsewhere.

The consequences of this simplistic and morally inconsistent strategy are highly unfortunate. America finds itself involved far too often in futile or mutually destructive confrontations with left-wing regimes. Even worse is the evolution of a cozy relationship between Washington and a host of right-wing authoritarian governments. A pervasive perception of the U.S. as the sponsor and protector of such dictatorships has undermined America's credibility as a spokesman for democracy, caused Third World peoples to equate both capitalism and democracy with U.S. hegemony, and established a milieu for rabidly anti-American revolutions. It is an approach that creates a massive reservoir of ill will and, in the long run, weakens rather than strengthens America's national security.

A flawed policy

Washington's policy toward Third World dictatorships is seriously flawed in several respects. One fundamental defect is the tendency to view largely internal struggles exclusively through the prism of America's ongoing cold war with the Soviet Union. Secretary of State John Foster Dulles was an early practitioner of this parochial viewpoint during the 1950's, when he insisted that the emerging nations of Asia and Africa "choose sides" in that conflict. Nonalignment or neutralism Dulles viewed as moral cowardice or tacit support for the U.S.S.R. Such an attitude only antagonized nonaligned leaders who were concerned primarily with charting a postcolonial political and economic course for their new nations and cared little about an acrimonious competition between two alien superpowers. The chilly relationship between India, the Third World's leading democracy, and the U.S. throughout this period was due in large part to Washington's hostility toward Prime Minister Jawaharlal Nehru's policy of nonalignment.

American policymakers have learned few lessons from Dulles' errors in the subsequent quarter-century. During the 1960's, Washington still saw internal political conflicts in nations as diverse as Vietnam and the Dominican Republic exclusively as skirmishes in the larger Cold War. A decade after the victory of one faction in the complex tribal, linguistic, and economic struggle in Angola, former Secretary of State Henry Kissinger describes that war as part of "an unprecedented Soviet geopolitical offensive" on a global scale. Kissinger's former boss, Gerald Ford, likewise interprets the episode purely as a struggle between "pro-Communist" and "pro-West" forces. Former UN Ambassador Jeane Kirkpatrick views such countries as Mozambique and Nicaragua not as nations in their own right, but as components of the Soviet empire. Similarly, Pres. Reagan's bipartisan commission on Central America describes the multifaceted conflicts of that troubled region as part of a Soviet-Cuban "geo-strategic challenge" to the U.S.

This failure to understand the complexities and ambiguities of Third World power rivalries has impelled the U.S. to adopt misguided and counterproductive strategies. One manifestation is an uncritical willingness to embrace repressive regimes if they possess sufficient anti-communist credentials.

At times, this tendency has proven more than a trifle embarrassing. During a toast to the Shah of Iran on New Year's Eve, 1977, Pres. Jimmy Carter lavished praise on that autocratic monarch: "Iran, because of the great leadership of the Shah, is an island of stability in one of the more troubled areas of the world. This is a great tribute to you, Your Majesty, and to your leadership, and to the respect and admiration and love which your people give to you." Apparently concluding that America's vocal enthusiasm for the Shah and his policies during the previous quarter-century did not link the U.S. sufficiently to his fate, the President emphasized: "We have no other nation on earth who [sic] is closer to us in planning for our mutual military security."

Barely a year later, the Shah's regime lay in ruins, soon to be replaced by a virulently anti-American government. Carter's assumption that the Shah was loved by the Iranian people was a classic case of wishful thinking. CIA operatives in the field warned their superiors that the American perception was a delusion, but those reports were ignored because they did not reflect established policy. Blind to reality, the Carter Administration identified itself and American security interests with a regime that was already careening toward oblivion.

One might think that American leaders would have gained some humility from the wreckage of Iranian policy and at least learned to curb vocal expressions of support for right-wing autocrats. Unfortunately, that has not been the case. Less than four years after Carter's gaffe, Vice Pres. George Bush fawned over Philippine dictator Ferdinand Marcos: "We stand with you sir. . . . We love your adherence to democratic principle [sic] and to the democratic processes. And we will not leave you in isolation."

It is a considerable understatement to suggest that the burgeoning Philippine opposition (which contained many legitimate democrats, such as Salvador Laurel and Butz Aquino) did not appreciate effusive praise for the man who suspended the national constitution, declared martial law, governed by decree, and imprisoned political opponents to perpetuate his own power. From the standpoint of long-term American interests (not to mention common decency and historical accuracy), Bush should have considered how a successor Philippine government might perceive his enthusiasm for Marcos. During his second presidential campaign debate with Walter Mondale, Reagan not only defended this nation's intimate relationship with the Marcos regime, but also implied that the only alternative to Marcos was a communist takeover—which proved to be a gross distortion of reality.

Ill-considered hyperbole with respect to right-wing autocratic governments places the U.S. in an awkward, even hypocritical posture. Equally unfortunate is the extensive and at times highly visible material assistance that Washington gives such regimes. For more than three decades, the U.S. helped train and equip the military force that the Somoza family used to dominate Nicaragua and systematically loot that nation. Similarly, the American government provided lavish military hardware to the Shah of Iran as well as "security" and "counterinsurgency" training to SAVAK, the Shah's infamous secret police. Throughout the same period, Washington gave similar assistance to a succession of Brazilian military governments, a parade of Guatemalan dictatorships, the junta that ruled from 1967 to 1974, and several other repressive governments. Most recently, the U.S. gave the Marcos regime economic and military aid totaling more than $227,000,000, plus millions more in payments for the military installations at Clark Field and Subic Bay. Despite ample signs of that government's increasingly shaky tenure, the Reagan Administration asked Congress to increase aid by nearly 20%. Congress exhibited little enthusiasm for that approach, approving instead a significantly smaller sum and attaching various "human rights" restrictions.

Warm public endorsements of autocratic regimes combined with substantial (at times lavish) material support produce an explosive mixture that repeatedly damages American prestige and credibility. Many of those governments retain only the most precarious hold on power, lacking significant popular support and depending heavily upon the use of terror to intimidate opponents. When repressive tactics no longer prove sufficient, the dictatorships can collapse with dramatic suddenness—as in Iran. American patronage thus causes the U.S. to become closely identified with hated governments and their policies. The domestic populations see those regimes as little more than American clients—extensions of U.S. power. Consequently, they do not view the ouster of a repressive autocrat as merely an internal political change, but as the eradication of American domination.

Moreover, there is a virtual reflex action to repudiate everything American—including capitalist economics and Western-style democracy. The U.S. unwittingly contributes to that process. By portraying corrupt, autocratic rulers as symbols of the "free world," we risk having long-suffering populations take us at our word. They do not see capitalism and democracy as those systems operate in the West, enabling people to achieve prosperity and individual freedom. Instead, Third World people identify free enterprise and democratic values with the corruption and repression they have endured. Historian Walter LaFeber, in *Inevitable Revolutions*, describes how that reasoning has worked in Central America: "U.S. citizens see [capitalist democracy] as having given them the highest standard of living and the most open society in the world. Many Central Americans have increasingly associated capitalism with a brutal oligarchy-military complex that has been supported by U.S. policies—and armies."

Hostility to the left

The flip side of Washington's promiscuous enthusiasm for right-wing autocrats is an equally pervasive hostility toward leftist Third World regimes and insurgent movements. There have been occasional exceptions to this rule throughout the Cold War era. For example, the U.S. developed a cordial relationship with communist Yugoslavia after Premier Josef Tito broke with the Soviet Union in 1948. A similar process occurred during the early 1970's, when the Nixon Administration engineered a rapprochement with China, ending more than two decades of frigid hostility. These achievements are instructive and should have demonstrated to American policymakers that it is possible for the U.S. to coexist with Marxist regimes. However, that lesson has not been learned, and such incidents of enlightenment stand as graphic exceptions to an otherwise dreary record.

More typical of America's posture is the ongoing feud with the Cuban government of Fidel Castro. The campaign to oust or, failing that, to make him a hemispheric pariah, was shortsighted, futile, and counterproductive from the outset. It served only to give him a largely undeserved status as a principled, courageous revolutionary and to drive his government into Moscow's willing embrace. Soviet defector Arkady Shevchenko recalls a 1960 conversation with Nikita Khrushchev in which the latter viewed America's hostility toward Cuba with undisguised glee. Describing U.S. efforts to "drive Castro to the wall" instead of establishing normal relations as "stupid," Khrushchev accurately predicted that "Castro will have to gravitate to us like an iron filing to a magnet."

Apparently having learned little from the Cuban experience, the Reagan Administration seems determined to make the same errors with the Sandinista government of Nicaragua. Washington's attempts to isolate the Managua regime diplomatically, the imposition of economic sanctions, the "covert" funding of the contra guerrillas, and the use of apocalyptic rhetoric to describe the internal struggle for power in that country all seem like an eerie case of *deja vu*. Reagan's depiction of the contras as "the moral equal" of America's own Founding Fathers constitutes ample evidence that U.S. policymakers have not learned to view Third World power struggles with even modest sophistication. One need not romanticize the Sandinista regime, excuse its suppression of political dissent, or rationalize its acts of brutality (*e.g.*, the treatment of the Miskito Indians), as the American political left is prone to do, to advocate a more restrained and detached policy. Administration leaders fear that Nicaragua will become a Soviet satellite in Central America; Washington's current belligerent course virtually guarantees that outcome. As in the case of Cuba nearly three decades ago, the U.S. is creating a self-fulfilling prophecy.

The American government's hostility toward left-wing regimes in the Third World has even extended to *democratic* governments with a leftist slant. An early victim of this antipathy was Iranian Prime Minister Mohammed Mossadegh. Evidence now clearly shows extensive CIA involvement (including planning and funding) in the 1953 royalist coup that enabled the Shah to establish himself as an absolute monarch. Mossadegh's "crime" was not that he was communist, but that he advocated policies inimical to powerful Anglo-American economic interests. A year later, the left-leaning reformist government of Jacobo Arbenz in Guatemala suffered the same fate. This time, American complicity in the overthrow of a democratically elected government was even more blatant. The U.S. Ambassador to Guatemala reportedly boasted that he had brought the counterrevolution to a successful conclusion barely "forty-five minutes behind schedule." Even Reagan's bipartisan commission on Central America concedes U.S. assistance in the coup, and Washington's role has been amply documented elsewhere.

Buoyed by such successes, the U.S. helped oust Patrice Lumumba, the first elected Prime Minister of the Congo (now Zaire), in 1960. Like Mossadegh and Arbenz, Lumumba had committed the unpardonable sin of soliciting communist support. There is also some evidence of American complicity in the 1973 military coup that toppled the government of Chilean Pres. Salvador Allende. We do know that the Nixon Administration sought to thwart Allende's election in 1970, discussed a coup with disgruntled elements of the military immediately following that election, and ordered steps to isolate and destabilize the new government economically. No less a figure than Henry Kissinger, then serving as National Security Advisor, concedes that the U.S. authorized covert payments of more than $8,800,000 to opponents of the Allende government during the three years preceding the coup. Given the relatively modest size of the Chilean economy and population, an infusion of such an amount of money certainly created a considerable political impact, but Kissinger and Nixon both blame Allende's downfall entirely on internal factors. The Marxist president's pursuit of disastrous economic programs together with his systematic attempts to undercut the conservative middle class and harass political opponents undoubtedly galvanized the opposition, weakening his already precarious political position. Nevertheless, it would be naive to accept at face value the Nixon Administration's protestations of innocence regarding the coup, especially in light of Kissinger's ominous assertion that Allende was "not merely an economic nuisance or a political critic but a geopolitical challenge."

It is reprehensible for a government that preaches the virtues of noninterference in the internal affairs of other nations to have amassed such a record of interference. The level of shame mounts when American meddling undermines a sister democracy and helps install a repressive autocracy. Yet, in Iran, Guatemala, Zaire, and Chile, that was precisely what happened. Post-Mossadegh Iran endured the Shah's corrupt authoritarianism for 25 years before desperately embracing the fanaticism of the Ayatollah Khomeini. Guatemala after Arbenz has witnessed a dreary succession of military dictatorships, each one rivaling its predecessor in brutality. The ouster of Patrice Lumumba facilitated the rise to power of Mobuto Sese Seko in Zaire. His regime is regarded as one of the most corrupt and repressive on any continent.

Perhaps Chile is the saddest case of all. Although deified by Western liberals, Allende had his unsavory qualities. His enthusiasm for Marxist economic bromides pushed his nation to the brink of disaster. He also exhibited a nasty authoritarian streak of his own, including an intolerance of political critics. Nevertheless, his actions remained (although sometimes just barely) within constitutional bounds. Moreover, he was the last in an unbroken series of democratically elected rulers stretching back more than four decades—an impressive record in Latin America. The Pinochet dictatorship that replaced Allende is conspicuous for its brutal and systematic violation of individual liberties. Yet, Kissinger can assert that the "change in government in Chile was on balance favorable—even from the point of view of human rights." Such a view reflects either willful blindness or an astounding cynicism.

Strategic, economic, and ideological justifications

Those individuals who justify America's existing policy toward the Third World cite strategic, economic, and ideological considerations. On the strategic level, they argue that the U.S. must prevent geographically important regions from falling under the sway of regimes subservient to the Soviet Union. Otherwise, a shift in the balance of global military power could jeopardize American security interests, perhaps even imperil the nation's continued existence. Economically, the U.S. must maintain access to vital supplies of raw materials and keep markets open for American products and investments. It is not possible, this argument holds, for an economy based upon free enterprise to endure if the world is dominated by state-run Marxist systems. Finally, beyond questions of strategic and economic self-interest, the U.S. must thwart communist expansionism in the Third World to ensure that America and its democratic allies do not become islands in a global sea of hostile, totalitarian dictatorships.

All these arguments possess a certain facile appeal, but they hold up only if one accepts some very dubious conceptions of America's strategic, economic, and ideological interests. Moreover, proponents have often employed these arguments as transparent rationalizations for questionable foreign policy initiatives.

The notion that the United States must assist and defend right-wing regimes while opposing leftist insurgencies or governments for its own strategic self-interest depends on several important subsidiary assumptions. Those who justify America's Third World policy on this basis generally define "strategic interests" in a most expansive manner. In its crudest form, this approach regards Third World states as little more than bases or forward staging areas for American military power. Such a rationale is convincing only if one assumes that the United States truly possesses "vital" strategic interests in regions as diverse as Southeast Asia, the Persian Gulf, Central Africa, and South America, and that successor regimes in regional "keystone" nations would be hostile to those interests.

One can and should question whether the U.S. actually has strategic interests, vital or otherwise, in areas thousands of miles removed from its own shores. How a plethora of small, often militarily insignificant nations, governed by unpopular and unstable regimes, could augment U.S. strength in a showdown with the Soviet Union is a mystery. One could make a more plausible argument that attempts to prop up tottering allies weaken America's security. These efforts drain U.S. financial resources and stretch defense forces dangerously thin. Worst of all is the risk that a crumbling Third World ally could become an arena for ill-advised American military adventures. As we saw in Vietnam, the entrance to such quagmires is easier to find than the exit.

The inordinate fear of successor governments is equally dubious, for it assumes that such regimes would inevitably be leftwing and subservient to Moscow. Neither assumption is necessarily warranted. The ouster of a right-wing autocracy does not lead ineluctably to a radical leftist government. Vigorous democracies succeeded rightist dictatorships in Portugal and Greece. Moreover, even in cases where a staunchly leftist government does emerge, subservience to Moscow can not be assumed. Such pessimism may have had some validity in the bipolar ideological environment of the late 1940's and early 1950's, but, given the diffusion of power away from both Moscow and Washington in the past 30 years, it is now dangerously obsolete. When China and the U.S.S.R. are mortal adversaries, Yugoslavia charts a consistently independent course, and such a country as Rumania—in Moscow's own geopolitical "backyard"—dares exhibit maverick tendencies on selected foreign policy issues, the assumption that a Marxist Third World state will be merely a Soviet stooge is clearly unwarranted.

Economic factors

The economic thesis for current U.S. foreign policy is no more persuasive than the strategic rationale. Assumptions that rightist governments serve as pliant instruments of American economic objectives or that left-wing regimes become commercial adversaries can not be sustained as a general rule. It is true that countries ruled by right-wing autocrats tend to be friendlier arenas for U.S. investment, but the price in bureaucratic restrictions and "commissions" (*i.e.*, bribes) to key officials is often very high. Moreover, governments of whatever ideological stripe usually operate according to principles of economic self-interest, which may or may not correspond to American desires.

Washington received a rude awakening on that score in the 1970's, when its closest Middle East allies—Iran and Saudi Arabia—helped engineer OPEC's massive oil price hikes. Neither U.S. client was willing to forgo financial gain out of any sense of gratitude for political and military support. Much the same situation occurred in 1980, when the Carter Administration invoked a grain embargo against the Soviet Union for the latter's invasion of Afghanistan. The U.S. encouraged, even pressured, its allies to cooperate in that boycott. Nevertheless, the Argentine military junta, a regime that the U.S. had routinely counted upon to stem the tide of leftist insurgency in Latin America, promptly seized the opportunity to boost its grain sales to the U.S.S.R.

Just as right-wing regimes exhibit a stubborn independence on economic matters, revolutionary leftist governments are not inherent commercial enemies. When the U.S. has allowed trade with leftist countries to occur, that trade has usually flourished. The lucrative oil and mineral commerce with the Marxist government of Angola is a case in point. Similarly, once the emotional feud with mainland China ceased in the 1970's, commercial and investment opportunities for the United States also began to emerge. Although a Marxist state dominating the global market in some vital commodity might conceivably attempt to blackmail the U.S., that danger is both remote and theoretical.

Economic realities exert a powerful influence that often transcends purely political considerations. Most Third World governments, whether right-wing or left-wing, benefit from extensive commercial ties with the industrialized West, particularly the U.S. America is often the principal market for their exports and is a vital source of developmental capital. Revolutionary rhetoric, even when sincerely believed, can not change that fundamental equation. It is no coincidence that Third World governments have rarely instituted economic boycotts; most embargoes originate as a deliberate U.S. policy to punish perceived political misdeeds.

Rather than adopting economic sanctions as a device for political intimidation, the U.S. should relish the prospect of promoting commercial connections to the greatest extent possible. Nothing would more readily provide evidence to left-wing leaders that a system based on private property and incentives is vastly superior to the lumbering inefficiencies of Marxist central planning. On those rare occasions when the U.S. has pursued a conciliatory, rather than a truculent and confrontational, approach, the results have been gratifying. The Marxist regime in Mozambique, for instance, first looked to the Soviet bloc for economic as well as ideological guidance, only to confront arrogant Russian imperialism and a recipe for economic disaster. The disillusioned leadership now has begun to turn away from the U.S.S.R. and open its country to Western trade and investment, a process that is likely to accelerate in the coming years.

The most misguided justification for America's attachment to right-wing Third World states lies in the realm of politics and ideology. Proponents assume an underlying ideological affinity between authoritarian systems and Western democracies. They insist that, while rightist regimes may be repressive, such governments are natural U.S. allies in the struggle against world communism. Conversely, revolutionary leftist movements are "totalitarian" in origin and constitute accretions to the power of that global menace.

No one has advanced this thesis more passionately and at greater length than former U.S. Ambassador to the United Nations Jeane Kirkpatrick. While conceding that "traditional" autocracies sometimes engage in practices that offend American "sensibilities," Kirkpatrick clearly finds those regimes more palatable than their leftist adversaries. She asserts that "traditional authoritarian governments are less repressive than revolutionary autocracies," are "more susceptible to liberalization," and are "more compatible with U.S. interests." That being the case, American aid to keep such friendly regimes in power is not only justified, but becomes something akin to a moral imperative.

Even if one concedes that the repression practiced by leftist dictatorships is more pervasive and severe than that of right-wing dictatorships, a more fundamental issue still exists—American complicity. The U.S. has neither the power nor the requisite moral mandate to eradicate injustice and oppression in the world. At the same time, as the most powerful and visible symbol of democracy, America does have an obligation not to become a participant in acts of repression and brutality. Our sponsorship of right-wing autocracies violates that crucial responsibility. Assisting dictatorial regimes makes the U.S. government (and by extension the public that elects it) an accomplice in the suppression of other people's liberty. In a profound way, such complicity constitutes a stain on our democratic heritage.

Kirkpatrick's contention that traditional autocracies are more susceptible to liberalization likewise misses a fundamental point. She asserts that autocratic regimes sometimes "evolve" into more democratic forms, whereas no analogous case exists with respect to revolutionary socialist governments. Yet, her own examples—Spain, Greece, and Brazil—do not involve evolutionary transformations, but, rather, the *restoration* of democratic systems that right-wing elements had destroyed. History demonstrates that, while communist revolutionaries oust competing repressive systems, rightist insurgents habitually overthrow democratically elected governments. There is only one instance of a successful communist uprising against an established democracy—the takeover of Czechoslovakia in March, 1948. Conversely, right-wing coups and revolutions have erased numerous democratic regimes. Spain (1936), Guatemala (1954), Brazil (1964), Greece (1967), the Philippines (1972), Chile (1973), and Argentina (1976) represent only the most prominent examples. It may be more difficult to eradicate leftist (especially totalitarian) systems than it is to replace rightist regimes, but right-wing autocratic movements pose the more lethal threat to functioning democracies. No fact more effectively demolishes the naive notion of an underlying affinity between democracies and rightist dictatorships. The two systems are not allies; they are inherent adversaries.

An alternative

A new foreign policy must eschew inconsistent moral posturing as well as amoral geopolitics. The most constructive alternative would stress "benign detachment" toward *all* Third World dictatorships, whatever their ideological orientation.

The concept of benign detachment is grounded in the indisputable reality that, for the foreseeable future, the U.S. will confront a Third World environment in which a majority of nations are undemocratic. It would unquestionably prove easier to function in a community of capitalist democracies, but we do not have that luxury. Democracy and capitalism may emerge as powerful doctrines throughout the Third World, but such a transformation would be long-term, reflecting indigenous historical experiences. We certainly can not hasten that process by abandoning our own ideals and embracing reactionary autocrats. In the interim, the U.S. must learn to coexist with a variety of dictatorships. Benign detachment represents the most productive and least intrusive method of achieving that objective.

This approach would reject the simplistic categorization of right-wing regimes as friends and Marxist governments as enemies. It would require redefining America's national interests in a more circumspect manner. No longer should Washington conclude that the survival of a reactionary dictatorship, no matter how repressive, corrupt, and unstable it might be, somehow enhances the security of the U.S. A policy of benign detachment would likewise repudiate the notion that there is an underlying kinship between rightist autocracies and Western democracies. Right-wing dictatorships are just as alien to our values as their left-wing counterparts.

America's primary objective should be a more restrained and even-handed policy toward repressive Third World regimes. Cordial diplomatic and economic relations should be encouraged with *all* governments that are willing to reciprocate, be they democratic, authoritarian, royalist, or Marxist. This would require normalizing diplomatic and commercial relations with such countries as Cuba, Nicaragua, and Vietnam while curtailing aid to so-called allies.

Conservatives invariably protest that this position is a manifestation of a liberal double standard. It is not. In fact, conservatives ignore the actual effects such policies have had in the past. Take the case of mainland China. Throughout the 1950's and 1960's, Washington's attempts to isolate the People's Republic of China only caused that nation to turn inward and fester, producing a particularly oppressive and regimented system. Since the U.S. abandoned its misguided strategy in the early 1970's, China has become a far more open and progressive nation. Deng Xiaoping and his followers now eagerly welcome Western trade and investment, particularly in the field of high technology. Equally important are the changes sweeping the domestic economy. Chinese officials are dismantling crucial elements of Marxist central planning, decentralizing production, creating incentives, and even legalizing certain forms of private property. All those developments should be gratifying to Americans who believe in the virtues of a market economy. Moreover, the first, albeit hesitant, signs of political liberalization in China are beginning to emerge. Prominent Chinese spokesmen even assert publicly that Karl Marx was not infallible and that many of his ideas are irrelevant in the modern era—sentiments that would have merited the death sentence only a few years ago.

While the U.S. initiative in establishing cordial political and economic relations with China can not account entirely for this movement toward liberalization, there is no question that it helps facilitate progressive trends. Conservatives who advocate isolating Cuba, Vietnam, Nicaragua, and other Marxist nations would do well to ponder that point. Liberals who endorse economic sanctions against South Africa should consider whether their suggested strategy is not counterproductive as well.

A policy of benign detachment is not isolationist—at least insofar as that term is used to describe a xenophobic, "storm shelter" approach to world affairs. Quite the contrary, it adopts a tolerant and optimistic outlook, seeing Third World states not merely as pawns in America's cold war with the Soviet Union, but as unique and diverse entities. Extensive economic relations are not merely acceptable, they are essential to enhancing the ultimate appeal of capitalism and democracy. There is even room for American mediation efforts to help resolve internecine or regional conflicts, provided that all parties to a dispute desire such assistance and our role harbors no danger of political or military entanglements. The U.S. need not practice a surly isolation. America can be an active participant in Third World affairs, but the nature of such interaction must be limited, consistent, and nonintrusive.

A policy of benign detachment would bring numerous benefits to the U.S. No longer would America be perceived as the patron of repressive, decaying dictatorships, or as the principal obstacle to indigenous change in the Third World. Our current foreign policy tragically identifies the U.S. and—even worse—its capitalist democratic system with the most reactionary elements around the globe. This foolish posture enables the Soviet Union to pose as the champion of both democracy and Third World nationalism. It is time that America recaptured that moral high ground. If the U.S. allowed the people of Third World nations to work out their own destinies instead of trying to enlist them as unwilling combatants in the Cold War, Russia's hypocritical, grasping imperialism would soon stand exposed. Moscow, not Washington, might well become the principal target of nationalistic wrath throughout Asia, Africa, and Latin America. Moreover, the inherent inequities and inefficiencies of Marxist economics would soon become evident to all but the most rabid ideologues.

Equally important, a conciliatory non-interventionist posture toward the Third World would reduce the risk of U.S. military involvement in complex quarrels generally not relevant to American security. Savings in terms of both dollars and lives could be enormous. Our current policy threatens to format a plethora of "brush fire" conflicts with all the attendant expense, bitterness, and divisiveness that characterized the Vietnam War.

Finally, and not the least important, reducing our Third World commitments would put an end to the hypocrisy that has pervaded U.S. relations with countries in the Third World. It is debilitating for a society that honors democracy and fundamental human rights to embrace regimes that scorn both values. A nation that believes in human liberty has no need for, and should not want, "friends" who routinely practice the worst forms of repression. A policy of detachment would restore a badly needed sense of honor and consistency to American foreign policy.

Five Myths About the Third World

REFLECTIONS ON U.S. POLICY

Delivered to the Institute on World Affairs, Iowa State University, Ames, Iowa, November 10, 1987

ERNEST W. LEFEVER, *President, Ethics and Public Policy Center*

. . . "The Third World" is a delightfully ambiguous but useful phrase. It embraces a wide diversity of countries and regimes that do not fall easily into the *First World* (largely Western countries that have democratic political systems, market economies, and a developed industrial system, e.g., the United States, Britain, West Germany, and Japan).

The *Second World:* The Communist world dominated by the U.S.S.R. and other totalitarian political systems with centrally run economies and severely limited human rights. They tend to be expansionist. Eastern Europe, Cuba, Angola, Ethiopia, and Vietnam are run by Moscow, and Nicaragua may not be far behind.

The *Third World:* Most countries in Asia, Africa, and Latin America. They have authoritarian regimes; a few are fledgling democracies. They tend to be underdeveloped economically, and have semi-feudal systems. Poverty and disease are widespread. Political rights are frequently limited. They tend to be politically unstable and the normal way they change governments is by a bloody or a bloodless coup.

During the past twenty-five years, I have visited some sixty Third World countries in Africa, Asia, and Latin America, many of them several times. My views toward them are instructed by my political philosophy made more vivid by actual observation.

As a citizen of a democratic superpower and the leader of the First World, I speak as a morally concerned realist. I am concerned about security, peace, prosperity, and the full range of human rights.

With this brief introduction, I will present five myths about U.S. policy toward the Third World and answer each myth with what I regard as salient facts, assertions based on verifiable empirical information.

Myth 1: Third World poverty is the result of First World wealth. This myth asserts that the United States and other "capitalist" powers, in their quest for raw materials and political power, have exploited the underdeveloped areas for private profit. The chief culprit in this exploitation is the multinational corporation.

Facts: Poverty never needs to be explained. It has existed since man's earliest days. Only the absence of poverty requires an explanation. The real question is: Why and how have some societies worked their way out of scarcity and want?

Until they were colonized by the Western powers, these areas in Asia, Africa, and Latin America were primitive and traditional societies based on kinship authority structures and barter economies. During the colonial period and since, many traditional ways have persisted. Feudalism has characterized South and Central America. But now most Third World countries have mixed economic systems.

Their poverty is a result of their tradition, feudalism, primitive science and technology, and the absence of modern ways of thought and the work ethic.

In virtually every case, the colonial power increased productivity and developed some infrastructure for communication and commerce. Britain, for example, made a tremendous contribution to the modernization of India.

In the post-colonial period, foreign investment and multinational corporations have further developed the economies. The multinational corporations have been engines of productivity and economic development. The late Anwar Sadat of Egypt understood this. When he made peace with Israel, the United States offered him substantial government aid. He said: Forget the aid. Send me your multinationals; they know how to get things done.

Third World regimes should welcome multinational corporations. At the same time, they should control them. Foreign businesses do not fight their way into El Salvador, Ecuador, or Zaire. They go where they believe they can make a reasonable profit, enough to compensate for the risk of expropriation and war. A recent study found that these so-called profit-hungry corporations have made about 12 percent profit in their foreign investments compared to approximately 11 percent in the United States.

In short, perhaps the best way for a Third World country to develop economically is to create an environment that attracts foreign investment and multinational operations.

Myth 2: Socialism is the best path to political liberation, prosperity, and economic justice.

By socialism I mean the doctrine and practice of the Soviet Union, Cuba, or Communist China, or some mixture of Marxist doctrine and Leninist practice applied to Third World conditions.

Facts: The application of socialist or Marxist practices by any Third World country has always led to economic stagnation and political repression. In some cases like Cuba, the political structure has moved from authoritarian to totalitarian; most human rights have been snuffed out. Grim examples of the "socialist model" include North Korea, Vietnam, Ethiopia, and Angola. Unless the West responds vigorously, Nicaragua and Afghanistan will fall into this tragic category. Communist China is still more totalitarian than authoritarian, but the chances for change there are better than in the U.S.S.R.

Conversely, the rejection of the Marxist model and the adoption of a market economy, i.e., democratic capitalism, has led

From *Vital Speeches of the Day*, Vol. 54, No. 9, February 15, 1988, pp. 286–288. Reprinted by permission.

both to economic prosperity and to greater political freedom and respect for human rights. The most dramatic though less-than-perfect examples are South Korea, the Republic of China on Taiwan, and Singapore.

The clear message for those with eyes to see is that socialism leads to disaster while democratic capitalism can lead to greater adundance and respect for human dignity. There is a profound difference in quality of life possible under totalitarian North Korea on one hand and South Korea on the other.

Myth 3: Third World regimes can be reformed by U.S. preaching or economic sanctions.

According to this view, the United States should attempt to overthrow or modify "undemocratic" or otherwise distasteful regimes by withholding economic aid or imposing economic sanctions. These actions should be accompanied by public condemnation of the unacceptable policies of the target regimes.

Facts: Economic sanctions (boycotts, forced disinvestment, export controls, etc.) have never succeeded in their proclaimed objectives. In most cases they have been counterproductive. South Africa is a good example: The net effect of U.S. sanctions has been less employment for local and foreign black workers, a negative impact on the economy, and a slowing of reforms toward greater racial justice and wider political participation.

The best that even the mighty United States can do in the vast external realm is to nudge history in the right direction. Our most powerful weapon is our example of a democratic and humane society. As secretary of state, John Quincy Adams expressed this approach to American responsibility in 1821; "Wherever the standard of freedom and independence has been or shall be unfurled, there will be America's heart, her benedictions, and her prayers. But she goes not abroad in search of monsters to destroy. She is the well-wisher to the freedom and independence of all. She is the champion and vindicator only of her own."

We must avoid the danger of "reform intervention," conscious of our own shortcomings and recognizing that each society must earn its own human rights and pay the price of self-determination and independence. Mao Tse-Tung once said that revolution cannot be exported. He is right. Democracy and human rights cannot be exported. They must be won by hard work and sacrifice. Revolution and tyranny, however, can be imposed. Democracy by definition cannot be imposed. But we must acknowledge that the United States under the legitimacy of an occupation statute did a good job in Japan after World War II.

In dealing with less-than-perfect regimes, we can combine our example with quiet (not silent) diplomacy and appropriate policies. We must, however, speak out against gross evils like terrorism, aggression, and genocide. Totalitarian brutality by the Soviet Union against its own people and in Afghanistan deserves public outcry.

In the Third World, where repressive regimes have been sponsored, imposed, or supported by Moscow, we have an obligation to help the forces of freedom, specifically in Afghanistan, Angola, and Nicaragua.

Myth 4: The United States always supports right-wing dictatorships. The flip side of this myth is that Washington fails to support liberation movements and just revolutions in the Third World. This myth assumes that Third World countries can be liberated only by revolution, and usually revolution is defined in Marxist or socialist terms.

Facts: First, the United States has no preference for right-wing, authoritarian regimes. It has a strong preference for democratic governments that respect human rights and encourage economic development.

But, alas, Washington has to be accredited to the existing regime, good, bad, or somewhere in between. Or, it can choose to wash its hands and have no contact. Rarely do we take this drastic step.

In dealing with the regimes as they are, we are limited by history, custom, and circumstance. At best we can nudge things in the right direction. We can, as the diplomats say, "keep in touch with the next government," as indeed we were during the recent transition of power in the Philippines.

Taking into account the profound difference between right-wing authoritarian regimes and left-wing totalitarian regimes, we have made some mistakes in our policies toward Cuba, Iran, and Nicaragua. No totalitarian regime of the left or right has ever made a peaceful transition to a more democratic government. In contrast, many right-wing authoritarian regimes have evolved into more democratic ones. You see this movement clearly in South Korea and Taiwan.

Getting back to Batista, Somoza, and the Shah of Iran, the United States may have been too hasty in discrediting the old regime (corrupt and repressive) and in welcoming the "revolutionaries," who in short order became more corrupt and repressive than the antecedent regime. We helped to cast out one devil and seven new devils came to take his place. Politics and ethics are concerned with the lesser of two evils, not with the easy choice between light and darkness.

The United States wisely has not enlisted in "revolutions" supported by those liberation theologians who insist that revolutionary violence alone will bring earthly salvation to the repressed. Some even say that a combination of Marx and Christ is essential to earn eternal salvation. As far as I can ascertain, no violent revolution in our century has created greater justice or freedom than the "old order" it replaced. Can you name a single example of where the post-revolutionary situation delivered a better quality of life than the previous regime?

By all measures, including millions voting with their feet and millions of boat people, human beings have stated emphatically their repugnance of revolutionary regimes. During the darkest days of the Vietnam War, when the United States was being castigated by the blame-America-first chorus, there were no boat people fleeing the cruel war there. Only after they were "liberated" did millions of Vietnamese risk their lives for freedom. And the Berlin Wall was not built to keep West Germans from fleeing into "liberated" East Germany. This leads to the final myth.

Myth 5: U.S. military power, military assistance, foreign bases, and military action reinforce repression and block revolution and reform. Or, as the World Council of Churches put it, U.S. militarism and capitalism go hand in hand in stifling progress toward justice and liberation.

Facts: Of the five myths, this comes closest to being the celebrated big lie. As far as I can ascertain, every major use of U.S. military power since Pearl Harbor has increased the chances of security, freedom, and human rights. This does not mean that every specific action, or every bit of military aid, or every expenditure was wisely used. But consider the record:

(1) If it were not for U.S. military power, Hitler and the Japanese militarists may have prevailed and be running the world today.

(2) U.S. military occupation of Japan and Germany has advanced the cause of freedom and democracy.

(3) In Vietnam our cause was just — to prevent the Communist North from conquering the South. When we left, the revolutionaries took over. Now Hanoi, with the support of Moscow, has brutalized its people and millions have fled to sea in leaky boats.

(4) U.S. military action liberated Grenada.

(5) U.S. military action diminished Libyan support of international terrorism.

(6) U.S. military assistance (including a quarter of a million troops in Germany and the nuclear deterrent) has protected Western Europe from a Soviet attack.

(7) The U.S. military response to North Korea's attack against the South has enabled the Republic of Korea to be free and independent. Our continued presence there of some 35,000 troops has defended South Korea against the expansionist North, and provided the security that enabled the country to develop economically and politically toward greater democracy.

(8) U.S. military assistance to more than fifty countries in the Third World has helped these regimes withstand external and internal revolutionary pressures that are encouraged, supported, or sponsored by the U.S.S.R.

In short, with rare exceptions, U.S. military assets have been employed to make a more peaceful and secure world, thus enabling Third World countries to go about the peaceful pursuit of building a viable economy and a more open political system. Security is a prerequisite for the development of institutions to guarantee human rights.

Conclusion

Let me close on a note of caution and humility. We live in a very dangerous world. Freedom and security are gravely threatened by the predatory utopianism of the Soviet Union. Third World chaos and instability exacerbate the problems of economic and political development.

The United States has a responsibility commensurate with its capacity to affect external developments. I fear that we are not fully prepared to use our moral, economic, and military assets to deal with the threats that confront us.

We have not yet shaken off the shroud of self-doubt that our defeat in Vietnam has draped over our shoulders. I worry far more about the paralysis of American power than I do about the alleged arrogance of American power.

America is a great society, but we are not without flaws. The democratic experiment is never complete. Yet we cannot wait until we reach perfection to act. Abraham Lincoln once said: No man is good enough or wise enough to be president, but someone has to be. Similarly, no country is good enough nor wise enough to be the leader of the Free World, but we have no choice. He who has much given to him will have much required of him.

Quagmire in the Making

In El Salvador, only the names have been changed

FRANK SMYTH

Frank Smyth is writing a book about U.S. policy in El Salvador to be published by Westview Press.

"Only last year," said the U.S. official, was the army "willing to move more than nine to five." I'd heard those same words two years before in the same room deep within the walls of the heavily guarded embassy in San Salvador.

Transforming the Salvadoran armed forces into an effective counterinsurgency force has been a perennial problem for U.S. officials. After seven years of training and more than $3 billion in U.S. aid to El Salvador, American policy is in shambles.

Army commanders have learned to mimic the rhetoric of "low-intensity warfare" but not the execution, and the U.S.-advocated strategy of winning hearts and minds has been abandoned for more primitive methods.

When the forces of the Farabundo Marti National Liberation Front (FMLN) took the initiative this year, a growing movement within the Salvadoran officers' corps demanded a ruthless response. El Salvador's lame-duck Christian Democratic government of José Napoleón Duarte was in no position to object. The newly ascendant right-wing ARENA party, which took over the legislature in March, gave the green light for a crackdown.

The military command has warned that organizations which "try to exploit the basic needs of people" will be equated with the armed combatants of the FMLN. Since October, killings and disappearances of civilian activists have doubled.

El Salvador is returning to the days when civilian sectors of the population were the primary targets of the war. More carnage is to come.

Civic-action programs have been an integral part of U.S. counterinsurgency strategy since Vietnam. Pentagon advisers describe the task of getting the Salvadoran military to rethink its notorious policy toward civilians as the most important aspect of the counterinsurgency campaign.

Writing in a U.S. Army War College report dated January 1, 1985, Colonel John D. Waghelstein outlined three objectives for El Salvador: "*balanced development* to negate the causes of the insurgency; *neutralization* to destroy the guerrillas armed element; and *mobilization* of the national resources (human and material) for popular involvement in progress."

But even Waghelstein was less than sanguine about the prospects. "Whether El Salvador *and* the United States have the vision and stamina to pursue this difficult task remains to be seen," he wrote.

By mid-1986, the Salvadoran military seemed to be following the U.S. blueprint. Not surprisingly, its strong suit was "neutralization." The Salvadoran army and air force completed a series of massive ground sweeps and aerial bombings designed to penetrate and destroy the FMLN's traditional zones of control—at much cost to civilian lives. The population in and around these zones was forcibly resettled.

At the same time, the Salvadoran military launched a civic-action program to win popular support. It was called "United to Reconstruct."

"Especially important to the campaign," the Salvadoran army said, "are psychological operations, the organization and training of civil-defense units, civic/

The most comprehensive attempt to implement U.S. counterinsurgency in the Americas is a failure.

military programs, and the active participation of the local population."

Echoing the words of the Waghelstein report, "United to Reconstruct" was to unfold in three stages: clean-up operations, consolidation, and reconstruction. The government, private business, trade unions, the Church, and the general population would all participate—under military supervision—in the last two stages of the plan.

"United to Reconstruct" was heavily supported by both the U.S. embassy and the U.S. Agency for International Development, which diverted funds designated for such private voluntary organizations as Save the Children.

U.S. officials wholeheartedly endorsed the program, boasting that the Salvadoran military had finally come around to their way of thinking. The embassy pointed to the prominent role of young Salvadoran army officers in the plan as evidence that U.S. training and assistance had finally made a difference.

But neither U.S. advisers nor Salvadoran army commanders were able to explain how civic-action programs were supposed to work. They failed to demonstrate that psychological operations, civil-defense units, and "the participation of the local population" would offset joblessness, inequitable land tenure, infant mortality, or malnutrition.

The government was to provide social services, and the private sector was to provide jobs. Yet two years have passed, and no progress has been made. Besides constructing a dozen ill-equipped and understaffed health clinics, "United to Reconstruct" has little to show for itself.

"United to Reconstruct" is still "the factor to attack the crisis," says Colonel Mauricio Ernesto Vargas, chief of operations for El Salvador's military command. But U.S. officials admit that except on paper, the plan no longer exists. This is a tremendously embarrassing concession: The most comprehensive attempt to implement U.S. counterinsurgency in the Americas is a failure.

The reasons are not hard to come by. In theory, "United to Reconstruct" purported to recognize the "structural" roots of the crisis. But it did not address the link between poverty and high concentrations of economic and political power. The much-heralded 1980 land reform, for instance, remains stalled; fewer than 18 per cent of peasant families have been affected.

The ultimate goal of civic action, however, is not social reform but the improvement of civilian-military relations. In this regard, the architects of "United to Reconstruct" were hopelessly naive. It is hard to imagine how an army clown passing out balloons in a small pueblo in war-torn Chalatenango would be able to make up for a century of institutionalized violence.

While the plan has failed to win support from the civilian population, it has swelled resentment in the ranks of the military. The Salvadoran armed forces have watched uneasily as the guerrillas succeeded in organizing a wider rural and urban base. Predictably, as the army has found U.S.-advocated civic action to be ineffective, soldiers have increased their abuses of civilians.

Many of the same officers who initially supported "United to Reconstruct" are now demanding more independence from U.S. military strategists. Bolstered by the overwhelming victory of the ultraconservative ARENA party in March, the hardliners within the military may soon have their way. Most of these officers are associated with *La Tandona*, the Salvadoran War College class of 1966, the largest ever to graduate from the military school. Members of the class now command 90 per cent of El Salvador's field brigades. Within the past year, the *Tandona* has moved farther away from U.S. policy and the Duarte government.

The turning point came Monday, September 28, 1987. In an all-day meeting at the National Palace, members of the *Tandona* threatened President Duarte with a military coup. The hardliners were unhappy with a proposed amnesty for leftist

Make Them Disappear

On March 11, 1988, the commander of the National Guard headquarters in the Salvadoran city of Zacatecoluca issued an order to his subordinates to maintain strict surveillance on two members of the labor union representing Ministry of Interior employees.

"At the opportune moment, proceed against them using any type of maneuver until they are made to disappear," said the order.

Typewritten on an official form available only to commanders and high officials of the National Guard, the order was made available to friends of the two intended victims, apparently by an officer of the local post. Salvadoran news organizations were prohibited from publishing copies of the order but one newspaper in the capital published ads placed by two Salvadoran unions, which created a national controversy.

To date, the intended victims have not been harmed. But they were sent for by the same commander who had signed their "disappearance" order.

He met them in his office on March 18. Appearing nervous, he told the two he was their friend and had been for years. He said the incident had caused him a lot of trouble, and that he was being transferred because of it. He also asked them who had given them the document.

He said he was surprised that the incident had created so much concern, and that he had not known the two were so important. He said he thought they were only simple union members and Interior employees.

—David L. Silk

(David L. Silk is a free-lance writer in Stonington, Connecticut.)

political prisoners and upset about an impending trial against two military officers implicated in the massacre of nineteen peasants in 1983. The Salvadoran president was not deposed, in part because he pardoned (with only two exceptions) military officers and members of El Salvador's rightist death squads for more than 40,000 documented killings of noncombatants since 1979.

"We no longer need a coup because we already have power," said Juan Orlanda Zepeda, chief of intelligence for the military command and a *Tandona* member.

The influence of the hardliners is now completely unchallenged. Still, a crude military approach to the insurgency is unlikely to succeed. From January 1986 to October 1987, the Salvadoran military launched wave after wave of counterinsurgency sweeps. With such reminiscent names as "Operation Phoenix" and "Operation Concord," these offensives involved up to 40,000 troops—80 per cent of armed-forces personnel. But except for breaking the FMLN base camp on Guazapa Volcano near the capital city, these operations have failed.

The military did succeed in inflicting 7,879 casualties by its count. Nearly all of those involved civilians living in contested zones.

Massive forced displacement of civilians was the only other "success" of the 1986-1987 counterinsurgency operations. The army subsequently could not understand why the population did not embrace "United to Reconstruct."

When government troops cross into FMLN-dominated territory in the northeastern province of Morazán, they enter as an occupying force. The rebels' civilian support network is extensive and well organized, although it is disguised to avoid detection. Government battalions rarely find or engage the enemy, and the guerrillas have learned to leave deadly mine fields in their wake.

In the north central province of Chalatenango, the FMLN has followed the Morazán model. It cannot stop the army from penetrating into rebel-controlled territory, but it prevents the army from maintaining a stationary presence.

East of the province capital in Chalatenango, the massive military presence which permeates much of the rest of the country suddenly disappears. I encountered only one heavily armed government patrol on a two-hour hike into the interior. The only other sign of war was an occasional white flag tied to a bamboo pole flapping in the breeze.

Eight kilometers east of the town of Chalatenango is the village of Los Ranchos, home of 585 settlers. They are part of a group of 4,200 Salvadorans repatriated from the U.N. refugee camp in Mesa Grande, Honduras, last October, after fleeing military repression in 1980. Villagers explain that the white flags flying above Los Ranchos are intended to impress the government.

Yet the residents of Los Ranchos refuse to accept aid distributed by the armed forces, and they receive no help from the government. Officials of the Duarte government are busy, however, trying to document the settlers. Jorge Alberto Caravantes from the Ministry of the Interior was present in March, preparing to issue identity cards to every resident. "If they don't have their card," he said, "they will be taken for guerrillas."

The residents at Los Ranchos are afraid of the armed forces. An elderly woman said that soldiers frequently enter the camp and planes fly overhead once in a while. "They haven't dropped any bombs yet," she added, "but we're scared."

Can we get it right this time?

THE PANAMA PERPLEX

TINA ROSENBERG

Tina Rosenberg is a writer living in Santiago, Chile.

Panama City
It was a rainy Sunday in Panama and the 30th day of Ramón Eskildsen's new career. On August 15 Eskildsen, who drives a BMW and lives in one of Panama City's nicer neighborhoods, quit his job as a Xerox executive. Today he was crouched in the doorway of a Minimax supermarket while bullets whizzed by outside. Eskildsen was at his new full-time job protesting the regime of Gen. Manuel Antonio Noriega.

Eskildsen was part of a four-hour march in pouring rain to commemorate the second anniversary of the decapitation of Dr. Hugo Spadafora, a Noriega critic who had accused the general of drug trafficking and was last seen alive in the custody of the Panamanian Defense Force, which Noriega controls. For the first few hours the march was a parade, with about 2,000 Panamanians in symbolic anti-Noriega white clothing or black "Justice" headbands singing, eating Popsicles, waving white banners, and chanting, "Noriega is a murderer." But it scattered abruptly when goon squads, including military and government officials, began throwing fireworks and shooting at the crowd.

In the evening Eskildsen went to mass. Planned for Spadafora, the mass was also said for Carlos Ephrain Guzmán, the 49-year-old owner of a small bakery killed during the march. The Spadafora family passed out cards with a painting of an angel carrying the head of St. John the Baptist. "Perhaps in Nicaragua or El Salvador such decapitations are normal, but not here," said Eskildsen, exhausted and soaked. "Here we are not accustomed to seeing bodies with no heads."

Panama is a different country today than it was a few months ago. On June 6 Col. Roberto Díaz Herrera, the second most important man in the Panamanian Defense Force, and therefore in all of Panama, spurred by his conscience and forced retirement, announced to an astonished nation what it had suspected all along. The Defense Force had stolen the 1984 election (indeed, much of the fraud had taken place in Díaz Herrera's house); its leaders were fat with corruption; and Noriega had ordered the 1985 murder of Spadafora. The day after Díaz Herrera's confession, while political opposition leaders were debating what to do, a hundred thousand people—a tenth of the population of Panama City—went into the streets at noon. Since then a spontaneous wave of revulsion has gripped the country. For months afterward, Panama City's main street was filled with the ranks of the "seditious," as Noriega calls them, the "Civic Crusade," as they call themselves, who emerged each day from their banks and their office buildings into the sticky heat of noon in "I ♥ Sedition" T-shirts to honk horns, throw confetti, and scream, "Down with the pineapple!" an allusion to Noriega's pockmarked complexion.

Although the events of recent months have not brought about a change in Panama's government, they have changed Panama. A country of two million people at the southernmost tip of Central America, Panama has never considered itself part of Central America and has never shared in the regional heritage of politicization and protest. "For a Panamanian to pick up a rock is the same as a Central American picking up a machine gun," said Ricardo Arias Calderon, leader of the Christian Democratic Party. Now the headlines sound ominously familiar: government-sponsored paramilitary troops shoot at protesters, politicians receive death threats in the form of animal entrails smeared on their office door, and "Dobermans," as riot police are called, throw tear gas bombs into houses in the slums. What had been a relatively unrepressive military dictatorship has hardened, and this peaceful country is learning fear and violence. Panama has joined Central America.

This is exactly what the United States, through years of support for General Noriega, has been trying to prevent. Historically so close to the United States that its currency is the U.S. dollar, Panama is probably the most strategically important country south of Mexico. Under the Panama Canal Treaties of 1977, the United States must cede the Canal to complete Panamanian control on December 31, 1999. Panama is also home until that date of the Southern Command, headquarters for U.S. military and intelligence operations in Latin America. The Canal and the command depend on the stability and goodwill of Panama's government. Before June 6, Noriega seemed to offer both. As Franklin Roosevelt said of Nicaragua's Anastasio Somoza, "He might be an SOB, but he's our SOB." Today, hoping to arouse international support and Panamanian nationalism, Noriega is accusing the United States of directing the protests, straining the old ties.

The United States is no longer Noriega's protector. After the attack on the U.S. Embassy on June 30, the State Department suspended all U.S. aid and Secretary of State George Shultz endorsed the Civic Crusade. This decision to shift support from a corrupt, unloved dictator to a peaceful, democratic, popular protest movement has, bizarrely enough, won the United States the official condemnation of every government in Latin America, with both Castro's Cuba and Pinochet's Chile siding with Noriega against U.S. interventionism. The diplomatic situation in Panama today is a giant French farce in which each party, having woken up in a new bed with a different partner, is choosing to pretend that nothing has changed.

THE PUBLIC PROTESTS have diminished with time, as the initial expectation that they would bring down Noriega has worn off. But opposition to Noriega has not decreased. A recent Gallup Poll found that 75 percent of all Panamanians want Noriega to give up control of the country. It seems hard to believe that even a quarter of the country supports him. No matter whom I talked with—anti-U.S. students, poor families in the countryside, blacks in the San Miguelito district, or wealthy bankers—the only support I heard for Noriega came from the military or officials of his party.

The Panamanian government says that the opponents of Noriega are *rabiblancos*—"white tails"—and his supporters are poor blacks. Not really. Panama today is an uneasy marriage of the Jetsons and the Flintstones, a place where facsimile machines whir in carpeted offices a few blocks from a hospital to which surgical patients must bring their own thread. There are two Panamas, but Noriega enjoys the support of neither.

There are few *rabiblancos* in San Miguelito, a city of 250,000 mostly poor people outside the capital. Despite government promises, residents said that there are no books or paper in the schools, roads and bridges are rarely repaired, and in the entire city there is no hospital. I asked if people had work—official unemployment is 10.6 percent here, but analysts say that underemployment and unemployment is really about 45 percent. Maria, a housewife in rubber thongs, laughed and pointed to her children's high school diplomas on the wall. "One of my five has a job," she said.

Only a few miles from Maria's house, downtown Panama City looks more like Miami than San Miguelito. The cashier in a supermarket scans microwave popcorn and Bartles and Jaymes wine coolers on her electronic register. On the traffic circle outside is a Hardee's, a Dairy Queen, and a McDonald's. The skyline is defined by mirrored office towers and gleaming white 20-story apartment complexes, about half of which are owned by the Colombian drug mafia. The protests at noon each day are run from the Chamber of Commerce. If news about Panama appears in the foreign press, Crusade supporters in Miami and Washington fax copies to about 40 local law firms and businesses, where they are copied by the thousands and passed out on the street. And this wealthy Panama suffers as well. Four different families showed me tapes of marches or funerals on their VCRs, stopping the tape to check the angle of a gunshot or to point out a prominent figure.

THE SAME historical developments that built a revolution run by fax machine also produced the base for what Panamanians are protesting against: corruption. The service economy, which today accounts for three-quarters of Panama's GNP, has its base in the Canal, but also includes the world's second-largest duty-free zone after Hong Kong, a fleet of 12,500 Panama-registry ghost ships, an oil pipeline, and the offshore banking center. Since the banking center was established in 1970, about 120 international banks have come here, bringing with them modern communications, financial professionals from around the world, and a huge quantity of dirty money. "The secrecy clause is the secret of success here," said one Panamanian banker. Panama offers depositors tax-free, numbered, anonymous accounts, has no controls on bringing cash into the country, and unlike the United States, does not require banks to report cash transactions of more than $10,000. The U.S. Treasury Department guesses that $600 million of the $1 billion that passes through Panama every year is laundered drug money.

It is virtually impossible to trace money in a Panamanian account, but particularly nervous depositors can form a dummy corporation for $1,000 with almost any lawyer in Panama City. The company's "profit" then goes into the bank account for a double veil of secrecy. Steven Samos, a Panamanian corporation vendor, testified in Miami that when a client once scolded an office boy for spilling coffee on him, Samos advised him: Better not complain. He's the president of your company. Three of Lt. Col. Oliver North's companies, Lake Resources Inc., Udall Research Co., and NRAF Inc., were Panamanian corporations.

"The Panama Defense Force is the axle around which the wheel of corruption turns," said a U.S. House Foreign Affairs Committee study in 1985. The Defense Force controls the police, narcotics police, forestry, civil aviation, currency customs, and migration agencies. It came to power in a 1968 coup when a group of officers pushed aside a civilian president-elect. Omar Torrijos, later to appoint himself brigadier general, emerged as the leader of the group. A handsome, charismatic man who liked women and drink, Torrijos was Panama's answer to Juan and Evita Perón combined. Like Juan Perón, he created a party and ran his country on a kind of demagoguery and populism that resisted a political label. Like Evita, he was a showman. He traveled with a suitcase full of money and loved to arrive in a small town, knock on the door of a house, and press dollars into the startled housewife's hand. On borrowed money he built schools, libraries, and bridges (some of which functioned), and he died in 1981 in a mysterious plane crash before the Latin economies collapsed and the bills came due.

Noriega's brother was one of a group of officers who had once led a coup attempt against Torrijos. Noriega, then a captain in the Chiriquí province, backed Torrijos, earning the post of intelligence chief. Noriega rose quickly in the Torrijos regime by compiling dossiers on his rivals, and after Torrijos died, following the brief tenure of two other generals, he became the new strongman.

Noriega's empire is diverse. A 1976 series of articles by Seymour Hersh in the *New York Times* reported that Noriega was a double agent, on the payroll for years of both the CIA and Fidel Castro. Ramon Milian Rodríguez, a Cuban accountant who worked for both the CIA and the Medellín, Colombia, cocaine cartel, told a Senate panel that Noriega had a long-term relationship with the Medellín traffickers, a charge also made by a Panamanian pilot cooperating with a federal investigation in Miami. Milian Rodríguez said he brought Noriega $10 million a month from the cartel, and that Noriega took 1.5 percent of the cartel's Panama operations. Three U.S. government agencies have begun to investigate Noriega on charges of drug trafficking, money laundering, and selling high-technology equipment to Cuba.

PANAMANIANS HAVE KNOWN of Noriega's activities for years. But people put up with it. Thanks to Panama's base in services instead of agriculture, it was never divided into landed oligarchs and oppressed peasants. There is poverty here, but also social mobility, and a large middle class that thought about business, not politics. It must have seemed to Noriega that the system could go on forever—until the death of Hugo Spadafora.

Like the deaths of Benigno Aquino in the Philippines, Steve Biko in South Africa, and Pedro Joaquin Chamorro in Nicaragua, the murder of Hugo Spadafora produced not only a corpse—in this case, a headless corpse—but also a ghost that continues to haunt the Noriega regime. Spadafora had been Torrijos's vice minister of health, but he was no admirer of Noriega.

On September 13, 1985, Spadafora, who was living in Costa Rica, took a bus from Costa Rica to Panama. When the bus reached Panama, two Defense Force officials took Spadafora off the bus. It was the last time he was seen alive. The next day a Costa Rican man found his body under a bridge on the Costa Rican side of the border. The body showed bruises, fingernails black from torture, three broken ribs, and evidence of handcuffs. Scratched on his back was the inscription F-8, the signature of a Panamanian paramilitary group. Spadafora had been killed, the Costa Rican autopsy showed, by three surgically sophisticated vertical cuts that severed his head. The head was never found.

Then-President Nicolas Ardito Barletta, visiting the United Nations, promised to investigate the death. When he returned to Panama, Defense Force officers met him at the airport and took him to Noriega's office. He spent 14 hours there. After that, there was no more talk of investigation. No investigation was needed to galvanize the country. The brutality of the death and Díaz Herrera's confession did that.

NORIEGA IS now trying to turn the situation around with new spending, repressive measures, and accusations against the United States. Due to Torrijos's borrowing, even before the protests Panama had by far the highest external debt per capita in Latin America. Since the crisis began, the State Department has cut off current aid and Congress has voted to condition this year's aid—set for $33 million—on human rights improvements that do not appear likely. Crusade participants have withdrawn their money from Panamanian banks. Most important, the crisis has shaken global confidence in Panama's stability. Due to the crisis and a secrecy scare from a U.S. Drug Enforcement Agency operation in May, local deposits have dropped 13 percent since June.

With no currency of its own, Panama cannot finance deficits by printing money. Its only recourse is to cut spending. The government has canceled all new development projects, and in October President Eric Delvalle announced that the government would not pay salaries on time or meet its debt interest payments. To fight off a local bank collapse, which would topple the house of cards that is Panama's economy, banks have canceled new loans. Such measures, of course, have made the government even less popular.

Unable to quell discontent with new spending, Noriega has used repression. On June 11, five days after Díaz Herrera's confession, the government declared a state of emergency and suspended the constitution. On June 27 the three opposition daily newspapers, two weeklies, and four radio stations were closed, and soldiers arrested Díaz Herrera after attacking his house with bazookas, helicopters, and tear gas. He recanted his charges in jail. In October the government proposed new laws prohibiting statements that "offend the dignity" of Noriega and other officials, and excessive honking of horns, among other things. Three people have been shot to death since the protests began, and police truncheons, bullets, and tear gas have wounded dozens of others.

Noriega's third tactic is to paint himself as the victim of U.S. aggression, charging that the United States is trying to take back the Canal and punish Panama for its role in the Contadora peace process. Each new day in Panama seems to bring a new twist on the charge of U.S. interventionism. Posters on the streets show U.S. Ambassador Arthur Davis and Noriega with the headline: "Panamanian! Choose between the Panamanian patriot and the Yankee invader!" When some members of a U.S. Air Force school paid a call on the embassy, Delvalle charged that U.S. soldiers had invaded Panama City. On June 30 about 40 men, among them Revolutionary Democratic Party (the PRD) ministers, threw trash, stones, and paint at the U.S. Embassy and consulate, creating damage for which the Panamanian government later paid $106,000. Campaigns in the press have targeted the ambassador, deputy chief of mission, the economic attaché, and even the ambassador's daughter as meddlesome directors of the demonstrations. During the march commemorating Spadafora's death, David Miller, the economic attaché who was observing the march, was made to lie on the floor at gunpoint for half an hour, then arrested and held incommunicado overnight. In 1950s terminology, the United States has "lost" Panama. "Noriega isn't your SOB anymore," said Tomás Herrera, a lawyer who opposes the government. "Now he's just an SOB."

The U.S. government's position is rich with irony. President Carter heaped praise on Torrijos to encourage the Senate to ratify the Canal treaties. The United States had said nothing when officers overthrew the president-elect in 1968, or in 1984 when the same hapless politician was again denied office through fraud, even though the U.S. Embassy had proof that the military had stolen the election. Shultz even attended the inauguration of Ardito Barletta, the military's candidate.

Relations between the two militaries have been especially close. Ten thousand U.S. troops and their families still live in Panama, adding $200 million a year to the Panamanian economy. They can join the Balboa YMCA, go to their sons' junior high football games, and watch Johnny Carson or the Miss America pageant on Southern Command Network TV. The Southern Command needs Panamanian Defense Force acquiescence for its operations here, which include training and supply of the *contras*, and as Hersh reported, a listening post that covers all of Central America and much of South America. Indeed, Panama had only a police force until the United States created its military in 1956, named and designed after the dubious model of Somoza's National Guard. (The name was changed to the Defense Force in 1983.) At the U.S. School for the Americas, a training center for Latin military officers that was moved to the United States from the Canal Zone in 1978, Panamanian officers made up the third-largest group of graduates.

THE ROMANCE has certainly soured in the last few months. Why did the United States change its position? If punishing Panama for its role in Contadora were the purpose, there would be far subtler and more effective methods. There is more evidence that some U.S. critics are motivated by a desire to keep the Canal. "Our biggest problem is that our first supporter in the United States was Jesse Helms," said Gabriel Lewis, referring to the conservative North Carolina senator not previously distinguished by his concern for human rights. Helms led a move this October to keep control of the Canal if Panama does not allow the United States to defend it after 2000. The measure was defeated in the Senate by a vote of 50 to 39. But liberal senators and State Department officials pledge to adhere to the Canal treaties.

"The United States continues to hold the security of the Canal as a priority," said Christian Democratic leader Arias Calderon. "For that you need the stability of Panamanian society. What has changed is all these years the U.S. thought stability was independent of democratization and the military was the most important factor. Now it's obvious that democracy is not an independent variable."

U.S. SUPPORT for the Civic Crusade has mixed effects. Inside Panama, it seems to have helped. "We feel we're not alone," said Carlos Ernesto Gonzalez de la Lastra, a Crusade spokesman. But it lends credibility to the "interventionism" charge Noriega was making even while enjoying U.S. backing. It has helped Noriega abroad. If there is one issue that unites Latin America, it is opposition to U.S. interventionism. Not a single government in Latin America has spoken up for the Crusade; in September the Mexican government even gave Noriega a medal. "The United States has done him a great favor, it has made him a victim of the giant," said one Latin ambassador in Panama City. Although many ambassadors privately expressed their government's distaste for Noriega, their opposition to U.S. action against a sitting government is stronger. Some have had to perform astonishing contortions to support Noriega. Although the Sandinistas had often charged that the *contras* were being supplied and trained from U.S. bases here—impossible without a nod from Noriega—the charges vanished when Noriega came under U.S. attack. "We have no proof Noriega was sending arms to the *contras* or that he knew about U.S. training of them here," said a Nicaraguan government official.

The left in Panama, like everywhere else in Latin America, has little love for the United States, but Panama, so accustomed to U.S. support for a military government, struck me as the least likely country in the hemisphere to get excited about this new kind of Yankee interventionism. "Everyone has a sister or a cousin married to an America," said one Panamanian woman with a husband in the U.S. Air Force. Many Panamanians, especially the poor, said they did not want the U.S. bases to leave. On a dirt road outside of Chitré, near where a military base had been until four years ago, families said they wished the gringos would return. The Defense Force had promised to build a seawall to keep their homes from being flooded, but after years of delay, the families asked the U.S. soldiers to build it. "Things they built stayed built," said a woman, as I sat with her family on a Sunday morning, reminiscing about the soldiers. "They weren't just out to line their pockets. We cried so when they left." Her husband said that the soldiers gave the family a present to remember them by that he still keeps on his dresser. He showed it to me proudly. It was an empty bottle of mosquito repellant.

Rancor Aside, Trade Ties Grow Between South Africa, Black States

William Claiborne

Washington Post Foreign Service

Johannesburg—While sabre rattling continues to overshadow South Africa's relations with its black-ruled neighbors, behind-the-scenes attempts to expand economic ties and solidify South Africa's role as the dominant power in southern Africa are being intensified, according to senior government officials and leading economists.

Despite the public contentiousness, the climate for regional economic cooperation has never been more promising, according to Glenn Babb, deputy director general of South Africa's Ministry of Foreign Affairs.

Babb said that in one week this month, four delegations from black African states—a record number—visited Pretoria to discuss expending economic ties. But he refused to identify the countries, saying that the delegates came with the understanding that their hosts would not embarrass them by disclosing their identities.

"The lobbying is coming from their side, not ours," said Babb, suggesting that Pretoria's intensified government trade initiative was encouraged by this increased interest of black African states.

Officials said it not only provides South Africa with a cushion for its reduced export outlets, but helps make western sanctions appear meaningless when it is seen—at the same time the U.S. Congress is considering tighter sanctions—that South Africa and its black neighbors are increasing trade.

While the government keeps details of trade with African states secret, independent trade analysts noted that the partners include some of the most outspoken critics of South Africa, such as Mozambique and Zimbabwe. Both countries have been attacked by South African military forces for allegedly harboring guerrillas of the African National Congress.

Zambia, headquarters of the exiled ANC, and Tanzania, the base for the outlawed Pan Africanist Congress, also trade actively with South Africa and send people here for specialized training in the fields of science, technology, health and industry. Zaire maintains economic ties with South Africa as well, the analysts said.

Officials of some of the "front-line" states neighboring South Africa said that Pretoria tends to overstate the extent of the existing economic ties and that its optimism over prospects for future trade expansion is not realistic. They maintain that they conduct only as much business with South Africa as necessary and are constantly seeking alternative partners.

Nevertheless, a cooling of the revolutionary ferment that swept South Africa from 1984 to 1986, coupled with signs that the Soviet Union may want to shift from confrontation to local resolutions of conflicts in southern Africa, is leading the rulers of many black states to try to revive their stagnant economies by dealing openly with South Africa, according to economic analysts here.

The analysts' theory holds that if Moscow reduces pressure on the front-line states to resist dealing with South Africa, it will lead to more practical business decisions and further trading.

"No country wants to admit that it is economically dominated by another," said John Barratt, director of the South Africa Institute of International Affairs. "But more and more African countries are beginning to realize that economic cooperation with South Africa could be a means to an end, a way of pulling themselves together until the day they can seek economic independence."

Many black African states already maintain strong but low-profile economic ties with white-ruled South Africa.

South Africa had $1.5 billion worth of trade with African countries in 1986, excluding trade figures for Botswana, Swaziland and Lesotho, with which it has formal customs agreements. There is only one African country, Guinea Bissau, with whom South Africa does not trade, according to officials in Pretoria.

Moreover, South African investment plays a major function in the economies of seven of the nine member states of the Southern African Development Coordination Conference (SADCC), whose purpose is to reduce economic dependency on South Africa, according to the group's executive secretary, Simba Makoni.

Although Malawi is the only African country with which South Africa maintains formal diplomatic relations, Pretoria has trade missions in five of the SADCC countries.

The trade mission in Mozambique is one of the most active. South Africa exports a wide range of goods to Mozambique, sells it electricity and maintains its fleet of commercial airliners, which provide service at Johannesburg's Jan Smuts International Airport.

Export executives said that Mozambique has one of the best on-time payment records in the region, and that traders think nothing of granting $250,000 open credit accounts to Mozambican importers.

South Africa, according to one trade analyst, has become Mozambique's second or third largest trading partner.

South Africa also has a trade mission in Zimbabwe, where President Robert Mugabe has maintained a hard-line stance against Pretoria and has advocated tough sanctions. South African goods, ranging from sophisticated med-

From *The Washington Post*, April 1, 1988, pp. A15, A18. © The Washington Post.

ical equipment to the popular Lion Lager beer, are readily available in Harare, the Zimbabwean capital.

Trade experts here said that even Angola, with which South Africa is virtually in a declared state of war, imports South African food, mining equipment and other products through neutral middlemen.

South Africa's biggest economic development projects in southern Africa include rebuilding power lines in Mozambique so that South Africa can import electricity from a huge hydroelectric facility at Cahora Bassa on the Zambezi River, and an ambitious highlands water and power project in Lesotho.I

Also, Eskom, the state-owned utility company, is engaged in negotiations for power projects in Swaziland, Malawi and Botswana, all SADCC members.

Ian McRae, chief executive of Eskom, said he envisions an industrial network stretching from the Cape of Good Hope to the Equator, powered by a cooperative electricity grid.

"The subcontinent has a simple choice: economic stagnation caused by political division, with growing unemployment and worsening poverty, or economic dynamism stemming from cooperation in the nonpolitical sphere," McRae warned recently in Business Day, a financial daily.

In addition, Pretoria recently granted export credit guarantees to a new $450 million soda ash project in Botswana, the largest single industrial venture in that country's history. It will be funded, in part, by private South African capital and by the Botswana government.

When complete, the project will assure South Africa of a guaranteed supply of soda ash, a strategic product important in the arms industry and in manufacturing. Botswana, in return, expects 600 permanent jobs. The project also will help offset the severe trade imbalance that comes from Botswana's annual purchase of about $600 million in South African goods.

Businessmen and government officials in Botswana are far more candid about their business dealings with South Africa than their counterparts in many front-line states.

"In this part of the world, the one place where private capital tends to be readily available is South Africa," said Louis Nchindo, chief executive of Debswana, the company that markets Botswana's most valuable resource, diamonds. The company is half owned by the Botswana government and half by De Beers Consolidated Mines.

"Because of the rhetoric of [Zambian President Kenneth] Kaunda and Mugabe, they are ashamed to admit that they, too, are trading with South Africa," said Nchindo. "So they trade under the table."

Although government officials will not disclose details about it, South Africa also has agricultural and industrial development projects under way or on the drawing boards in a number of West African countries, reportedly including Equatorial Guinea, Gabon, and Ivory Coast.

In addition to talking with the African delegations that come here, South African officials from several different ministries and private sector trade experts regularly travel to the capitals of black states, looking for open doors.

Sally Gallagher, former head of African trade for the South African Foreign Trade Organization and now a trade consultant, said she regularly attends trade meetings in hostile front-line states and has never thought about changing her business card to disguise the fact that she is South African. She said she was welcomed at a SADCC trade convention last month in Harare.

Pretoria and the private sector also sponsor numerous training programs for visiting Africans in such fields as science, industry and trade.

Publicly, leaders of many of the countries cooperating with Pretoria have intensified their condemnation of South Africa for its apartheid policies and have even demanded mandatory international sanctions, of which they would presumably be in violation.

But even if neighboring states were to apply sanctions against South Africa, they would still be dependent on its rail network in order to transport their export goods and raw materials to ships at the port of Durban.

"No matter what is done to affect trade, nothing will change because of the rail transportation network. It always comes back to that," said Gallagher.

She noted that besides Durban, the only ports available to the southern African states are at far-distant and inefficient Dar es Salaam, in Tanzania, and in Mozambique by way of the Beria corridor from Zimbabwe to the Indian Ocean, which is under near-constant attack by right-wing rebels seeking to overthrow the Marxist government in Maputo.

South Africa's critics charge that Pretoria continues to support the guerrillas in order to impede the rehabilitation of the Beira corridor and perpetuate its neighbors' dependency. South African officials deny the allegation, saying they would encourage export shipments through Mozambique to relieve the pressure on their own rail system.

Front-line nations also will continue to import South African goods, Gallagher said, because of need and availability.

"If you have a product that is of acceptable quality and price, you are going to sell that product. Countries don't trade, businessmen trade," she said, adding that the alternative of importing European-made goods would be costlier because of the distance.

The increase in economic ties between South Africa and its neighbors has led to suspicions by critics inside and outside the country that Pretoria is trying to spread its tentacles and dominate the region in the colonialist tradition.

But Barratt, of the private Institute of International Affairs, disagreed. "This problem of domination would continue even if there were a black government here," he said. "South Africa would still have the main say in the region." Government officials estimate that 40 percent of all of Africa's manufacturing capability is centered in South Africa.

Barratt said that in the case of South Africa's immediate neighbors, Pretoria's motives could include a desire for leverage in security matters. "I think there's a pattern to try to draw these countries closer to South Africa to give them more to lose if they allow [guerrilla] infiltration," he said.

Babb, of the foreign affairs ministry, admitted that one motive has been a desire to reduce South Africa's isolation in the world community, and he predicted that increased economic ties eventually would lead to diplomatic recognition by some black African countries.

Human Rights and Democratic Rule

In recent decades, the world community has become increasingly aware of and concerned about the extent and severity of human rights violations in the Third World. These abuses—which take sundry forms—are instituted in order to isolate or eliminate actual or potential political opponents who may pose a threat to the ruler or regime.

Since 1975, Third World governments have either ordered or condoned the political killings of hundreds of thousands of people by the army and police, other regular security forces, special units, and "death squads" sanctioned by official authorities. Typically, these killings occur outside the legal or judicial process; the victims are denied all constitutional protections. Political dissidents are frequently abducted, illegally detained, and/or tortured before they are murdered.

In some cases, the killings are orchestrated at the highest levels of the government. In others, the government either refuses to investigate the murders or refuses to adopt concrete measures to prevent further killings. When these murders are revealed, the governments usually deny that they occurred, blame their political opponents, or insist that they were the result of violent confrontations with government forces or of attempts by the victim to escape from official custody.

According to Amnesty International, political killings can be defined as "the unlawful and deliberate killings of persons by reason of their real or imputed political beliefs or activities, religion, other conscientiously held beliefs, ethnic origin, sex, color, or language, carried out by order of a government or with its complicity." These killings are committed in blatant violation of national and international law, and take place throughout the world, irrespective of political ideology. They range from individual assassinations to the indiscriminate slaughter of either members of opposition movements or ethnic groups.

In addition to political killings, many Third World governments also engage in the systematic violation of basic civil liberties, including freedom of speech, press, religion, assembly, and petition. In the case of political dissidents, governments regularly violate the constitutional safeguards of individuals who, in their view, pose a threat to their survival. Typical targets include politicians, government officials, judges, lawyers, military officers, unionists, journalists, teachers, students, and clerics. For example, in South Africa, the white government of President Pieter W. Botha illegally imprisoned black activist Nelson Mandela, who has now been incarcerated for over 25 years. Freedom fighters like Mandela are routinely jailed in South Africa and elsewhere, not because they are convicted criminals, but because of what they represent—namely, a potent opposition voice, with widespread popular support.

Government opponents who succeed in escaping imprisonment are frequently subjected to intimidation, harassment, and violence. Many are forced to adopt disguises, travel secretly, and find living quarters free of government surveillance. In many cases, opposition leaders are also forced to abandon their families, give up their careers, live in poverty, and survive as outlaws in their own land. In these instances, the government hopes to isolate the dissidents, discredit their reputations, and destroy their followings.

In many Third World nations, particularly those ruled by the gun, government officials employ even harsher measures, including kidnapping, torture, blackmail, death threats, and violence. Freedom fighters are denied the right to speak, write, organize, travel, and work. The courts exist in name only—they merely rubber-stamp the actions of high-level officials, who exert political pressure on judges to legitimize their conduct. Unless the judges acquiesce, they will be replaced, punished, or killed.

In many developing countries, the rights to life, liberty, and property exist only on paper—to be abridged at will by government officials. Freedom is permitted only to the extent that it serves the objectives of the government. Despots fear democratic rule because it encourages popular participation, which could ultimately bring down the government. This explains, in part, why many Third World governments are quick to silence opposition newspapers, suspend political parties, close churches, and impose martial law.

Looking Ahead: Challenge Questions

Why does the United States support many governments that deny democracy and abuse freedom?

What can and should the United States do to protect human rights in the Third World?

Does present American policy promote respect for human rights in the developing world?

Unit 5

What factors contribute to the politics of detention in Somalia?

Why do many Third World nations, like Somalia, tolerate repression and intimidation?

What impact has South Africa's press ban had on the quality and quantity of news coverage in that nation?

What, if anything, can be done to offset government press censorship in South Africa?

Why has the South Korean government failed to adopt strict measures to outlaw the sale of babies?

What explains the demand for black market babies in the United States?

Is baby-selling wrong, even if it may mean a better life for the children in question?

How did the murder of Hugo Spadafora contribute to Panamanian General Manuel Noriega's fall from grace?

How has the regime of Ayatollah Khomeini altered the social, political, and economic fabric of Iranian society?

What factors have made post-colonial Iran a strong and effective power?

THE HUMAN RIGHTS IMPERATIVE

Cyrus R. Vance

CYRUS R. VANCE *was secretary of state from 1977 to 1980.*

The last 5 years have not been easy for those who believe that a commitment to human rights must be a central tenet of American foreign policy. The concept and definition of human rights have been twisted almost beyond recognition. Long-standing principles of international law and practice have been chipped away. Doublespeak has too often been the order of the day. Yet the time may be coming when Americans will be able to sweep aside the illusions and myths that have been used, often deliberately, to fog the human rights debate. The time may be coming when the opportunities presented by a strong human rights policy can again be seized.

These signs do not presage merely a belated recognition that former President Jimmy Carter was correct in committing U.S. foreign policy to human dignity and freedom. One can sense a rising desire among Americans to see a return to the fundamental beliefs on which their country's human rights policy must rest and from which it draws its strength. If so, and if their leaders will respond to this desire, Americans will be able again to pursue their ideals without sacrificing their traditional pragmatism.

President Ronald Reagan is fond of calling America a "city upon a hill." But the Puritan leader John Winthrop, who first uttered those words in the 17th century, intended them as a warning about the importance of adhering to the values that eventually shaped America's founding and development—particularly those later reflected in the U.S. Constitution in the Bill of Rights—not as a boast about military or economic power. As a country, America cannot be, as Reagan suggests, the "last, best hope of man on earth" unless it is prepared to restore to its rightful place in American national life respect for and protection of human rights at home and abroad.

Let me define what I mean by human rights. The most important human rights are those that protect the security of the person. Violations of such rights include genocide; slavery; torture; cruel, inhuman, and degrading treatment or punishment; arbitrary arrest or imprisonment; denial of fair trial; and invasion of the home. In the United States, many of these protections are enshrined in the Bill of Rights.

Second is that bundle of rights affecting the fulfillment of such vital needs as food, clothing, shelter, health care, and education—in the scheme of President Franklin Roosevelt's four freedoms, the freedom from want. Americans recognize that fulfilling these rights depends largely on the stage of a country's economic development. But the United States can and should help others attain these basic rights. Americans must never forget those whose empty stomachs and grinding poverty dominate their daily lives. Nor must they forget that governmental inaction, governmental indifference, and governmental corruption can threaten these rights just as seriously as the most dramatic acts of God.

Third, there is the right to enjoy civil and political liberties. These include not only freedom of speech, freedom of the press, freedom of religion, and freedom to assemble and to petition the government to redress grievances, which are guaranteed by the First Amendment to the Constitution, but also the right that most Americans take for granted—the freedom to move freely within and to and from one's own country.

Civil and political rights also must include the liberty to take part in government, the affirmation of Thomas Jefferson's declaration that the only just powers of a government are those derived from the consent of the governed. By exercising this freedom, citizens may insist that their government protect and promote their individual rights.

Finally, there is a basic human right to freedom from discrimination because of race, religion, color, or gender.

Almost all of these rights are recognized in the United Nations Universal Declaration of Human Rights, a document that the United States helped fashion and that draws heavily on the American Bill of Rights, the British Magna Carta, and the French Declaration of the Rights of Man and of the Citizen. Each of these documents has played a vital role in the historical evolution of respect for human rights. But after World War II, the world witnessed an unprecedented human rights revolution, including measures to institutionalize the international enforcement of human rights.

A genuine reversal of the administration's human rights policy could change profoundly the way America is seen in the world.

Until then, the idea that a regime could be held accountable to international standards and to the world for the treatment of its people was regarded largely as an idiosyncrasy of the democratic West, invoked only when it served a Western power's interests. A sovereign government, tradition held, could rule its people or its territory as it saw fit.

Even countries like the United States and Great Britain, which professed to follow higher standards, did not seem to believe that those standards applied to treatment of people without white skins. There was no international outcry when the United States used harsh methods to subdue opposition forces in the Philippines at the turn of the century or brutally drove native Americans onto reservations. The British could employ the most extreme tactics in repressing native populations around the globe, and few whites thought the worse of them for that. And countries without the respect for law were even less concerned about others' rights.

Such attitudes changed radically after World War II, principally because of the horror felt around the world when the Holocaust was exposed and when the full extent of Joseph Stalin's purges became clear. Individuals and countries suddenly realized that without standards, there were also no limits. The war also revealed that the far-flung colonial systems were bankrupt. Great powers could no longer hold sway over peoples they had for so long considered, in the English writer Rudyard Kipling's words, "lesser breeds without the Law."

Against this historical background, substantial progress has been made over the last 40 years. Since 1945, the world has codified a wide range of human rights. That process is in itself an enormous achievement. The power of these codes is demonstrated when movements like Poland's outlawed independent trade union Solidarity cite international norms to justify popular demands for greater liberty. Even countries that show little respect for human rights feel a need to pay lip service to them. But codes alone are not enough. It also has been necessary to develop international institutions to implement them.

First, in 1945, the United Nations Charter was adopted, enshrining human rights both as a basic objective of the newly created body and as a universal obligation. Article 55 of the charter states that the United Nations shall promote "human rights and fundamental freedoms for all without distinction as to race, sex, language, or religion." Article 56 obliges member countries "to take joint and separate action in co-operation with the Organization" to achieve those purposes.

In 1946, the Commission on Human Rights was established in the United Nations; Eleanor Roosevelt, the former U.S. first lady, was elected its first chairman. In 1948 came the Universal Declaration of Human Rights, a basic though nonbinding declaration of principles of human rights and freedoms. The 1940s and 1950s also saw the drafting of the Convention on the Prevention and Punishment of the Crime of Genocide and the preparation of two separate human rights covenants—one on political and civil rights and the other covering economic, social, and cultural rights.

During much of the 1950s, Washington stood aloof from treaties furthering those rights and limited itself to supporting U.N. studies and advisory services. But during the 1960s, America resumed its leadership, and in 1965–1966, the two covenants were finally adopted by the United Nations and presented for ratification by member states.

Largely in response to American pressure, the world moved to implement these codes more effectively. To this end, Western Europe, the Americas, and later, Africa, established their own human rights institutions. On another front, the U.N. system for several years confined its public human rights activities to only three cases: Chile, Israel, and South Africa. But beginning in the Carter years, further U.S. prodding led the international community to broaden its concern to include the examination of human rights violations in many countries, including communist countries. Progress, though sometimes halting, has been made in a process that has no precedent.

Dangerous Illusions

Many opportunities and obstacles lie ahead. But first the illusions that cloud, and fallacies that subvert, American human rights policy must be dispelled. Only then can a coherent and determined course be charted.

The first and most dangerous illusion holds that pursuing values such as human rights in U.S. foreign policy is incompatible with pursuing U.S. national interests. This is nonsense. As Reagan stated in March 1986: "A foreign policy that ignored the fate of millions in the world who seek freedom would be a betrayal of our national heritage. Our own freedom, and that of our allies, could never be secure in a world where freedom was threatened everywhere else."

Moreover, no foreign policy can gain the American people's support unless it reflects their deeper values. Carter understood this when, as president, he championed human rights. In addition to enabling millions of people to live better lives, this commitment helped redeem U.S. foreign policy from the bitterness and divisions of the Vietnam War. It reassured the American people that the U.S. role abroad can have a purpose that they could all support.

Human rights policy also requires practical judgments. Americans must continually weigh how best to encourage progress while maintaining their ability to conduct necessary business with countries in which they have important security interests. But the United States must always bear in mind that the demand for individual freedom and human dignity cannot be quelled without sowing the seeds of discontent and violent convulsion. Thus supporting constructive change that enhances individual freedom is both morally right and in America's national interest.

Freedom is a universal right of all human beings. America's own national experience, as well as recent events in Argentina, Haiti, and the Philippines, attests to the power of the drive for freedom. In a profound sense, America's ideals and interests coincide, for the United States has a stake in the stability that comes when people can express their hopes and build their futures freely. In the long run, no system is as solid as that built on the rock of freedom. But it is not enough simply to proclaim such general principles. The more difficult question remains: What means of support should be provided to those whose rights are denied or endangered? And to answer this question, two underlying groups of questions must be addressed.

First, what are the facts? What violations or deprivations are taking place? How extensive are they? Do they demonstrate a consistent pattern of gross violations of human rights? What is the degree of control and responsibility of the government involved? Will that government permit independent outside investigation?

Second, what can be done? Will U.S. actions help promote the overall cause of human rights? Can U.S. actions improve the specific conditions at hand, or could they make matters worse? Will other countries work with the United States? Does America's sense of values and decency demand that the country speak out or take action even where there is only a remote chance of making its influence felt?

If the United States is determined to act, many tools are available. They range from quiet diplomacy, to public pronouncements, to withholding economic or military assistance from the incumbent regime. In some cases, Washington may need to provide economic assistance to oppressed peoples and, in rare instances like Afghanistan, limited military aid. Where appropriate, the United States should take positive steps to encourage compliance with basic human rights norms. And America should strive to act in concert with other countries when possible.

A second illusion that must be exposed is one pushed by many critics of Carter's human rights focus. Wrapping themselves in a rhetorical cloak of democracy and freedom, these critics pursue a curious logic that leads them to support governments and groups that deny democracy and abuse freedom. They insist on drawing a distinction for foreign-policy purposes between "authoritarian" countries that are seen as friendly toward the United States and "totalitarian" states seen as hostile. Authoritarian governments, the argument continues, are less repressive than revolutionary autocracies, more susceptible to liberalization, and more compatible with U.S. interests. Generally speaking, it is said, anticommunist autocracies tolerate social inequities, brutality, and poverty while revolutionary autocracies create them.

Sadly, this specious distinction, rooted in America's former U.N. representative Jeane Kirkpatrick's November 1979 *Commentary* article "Dictatorships and Double Standards," became a central element of the new human rights policy set forth at the start of the Reagan administration. Kirkpatrick's thesis damaged America's image as a beacon of freedom and a wise and humane champion of human rights. If it were simply an academic exercise, this version of the authoritarian-totalitarian distinction might cause little mischief. But it has a deeper political purpose. The implication that such a distinction provides a basis for condoning terror and brutality if committed by authoritarian governments friendly to the United States is mind-boggling.

The suggestion that America should turn a blind eye to human rights violations by autocrats of any stripe is unacceptable. Such thinking is morally bankrupt and badly serves U.S. national interests. To the individual on the rack it makes no difference whether the torturer is right- or left-handed—it remains the rack. In short, a sound and balanced human rights policy requires condemnation of such conduct, no matter who the perpetrator is.

Recent events give some hope that this cruel and insensitive philosophy is being buried. In his March 14 message to Congress, Reagan stated that America opposes "tyranny in whatever form, whether of the left or the right." Debate over whether this statement reflects a policy reversal will continue until the new posture inspires a pattern of concrete actions. But it must not be perverted into a ploy to gain votes in Congress for increased military aid for the Nicaraguan *contra* rebels. A genuine reversal of the administration's human rights policy could change profoundly the way America is seen in the world and also unleash powerful forces that would encourage truly democratic alternatives. Such a policy surely would have strong bipartisan support.

A third human rights illusion, deriving from the second, is the fallacy inherent in the so-called Reagan Doctrine enunciated in the president's 1985 State of the Union address. Speaking about U.S. policy toward armed insurgencies against communist regimes, he declared: "We must not break faith with those who are risking their lives—on every continent, from Afghanistan to Nicaragua—to defy Soviet-supported aggression and secure rights which have been ours from birth.... Support for freedom fighters is self-defense."

No doubt there will be situations in which the United States should aid insurgencies—as in Afghanistan, where such aid promotes human rights and clearly serves American interests. There, the Soviet Union invaded a small neighboring country with overpowering military force, deposed the existing government, and imposed its own hand-picked government that, with the support of massive Soviet firepower, slaughtered tens of thousands of Afghans and turned millions more into refugees. It is critical to note that in supporting the Afghan rebels, Americans are not merely supporting an anticommunist rebellion. The United States is vindicating universal principles of international law and helping the Afghan people to determine their own future.

Yet the Reagan Doctrine, taking shelter under the banner of human rights, commits America to supporting anticommunist revolution wherever it arises. By implication, the doctrine offers no such assistance to opponents of other tyrannies. As the case of Nicaragua shows, the support the doctrine promises can include American arms. Consequently, despite repeated administration denials, the doctrine clearly holds out the possibility of ultimate intervention by U.S. forces.

This policy is both wrong and potentially dangerous to America's interests and its standing in the world. As with virtually all doctrines, it is automatic and inflexible by nature. That inflexibility blinds policymakers in a double sense. It blinds them to the realities and available alternatives in individual situations, and it blinds them to the principles of respect for national territorial sovereignty and nonintervention—cornerstones of international order.

The Reagan Doctrine's evident bias toward military options could easily prompt Washington to overlook better ways to achieve worthy goals. Even where economic incentives or restrictions may be sufficient, and even where U.S. policy may lack regional support and might work against broader U.S. interests, the Reagan Doctrine suggests that, at a minimum, America should fund military forces.

Beyond this strategic misconception, the Reagan Doctrine obscures the hard but essential questions of means and consequences. To avoid self-delusion, Americans must recognize that anticommunism cannot always be equated with democracy. Nor is anticommunism a shield against the consequences of unrealistic and imprudent action. At the very least, the United States must ask whom it intends to support. Do they believe in democratic values? Can they attract sufficient support in their country and region to govern if they take power? How would such a change affect the citizens of their country? Does America risk raising hopes or expectations that it cannot or will not fulfill? Can America deliver enough aid to decisively affect the outcome? Finally, will such a policy have the domestic support needed to sustain Washington's chosen course of action?

Ironically, many champions of the Reagan Doctrine call themselves realists. Yet any policy that tempts the country to ignore these basic questions cannot be called hardheaded or realistic. The doctrine's dogmatism and seductive ideological beckoning to leap before looking, are, in fact, strikingly unrealistic. So systematically ignoring the principles of sovereignty and nonintervention is not in America's national interest.

New Hope for Progress

A key strength of this country has always been its respect for law and moral values. To follow the Reagan Doctrine would undermine America's moral authority. What the United States and the Soviet Union have to offer the world must be distinguished by more than the simple declaration that, by definition, whatever Washington does is right and whatever Moscow does is wrong.

President John Kennedy once said that the United States is engaged in a "long, twilight struggle" in world affairs. But if that is so, America's principles and interests both are more likely to thrive if the country keeps faith with the ideals for which it struggles.

Principle must be the foundation of America's course for the future, but policy will be sustained only if it is also pragmatic. That must not mean that pragmatism should dominate. U.S. foreign policy must never become realpolitik unconnected with principle. Yet promoting ideals that have no chance of being put into practice risks becoming mere posturing. Nor should Americans focus simply on the great issues and ignore the fact that, at heart, human rights concern individual human beings. Indeed, it matters greatly what America can do in concrete cases, in individual countries, for any one person to live a better life.

The charge to U.S. human rights policy has rarely been put more clearly than by Felice Gaer, executive director of the International League for Human Rights. Testifying before a subcommittee of the House Committee on Foreign Affairs in February 1986, she said: "The United States needs to do more than make declarations and to provide free transport for fleeing dictators. . . . The U.S. Government has leverage to use—if it chooses to use it. It has the power to persuade governments."

The United States has many opportunities, and faces many problems, in trying to advance human rights abroad. In a few countries, there is reason to give thanks for recent progress. In others, recent shifts in stated U.S. policy provide hope for future progress.

Chile is a case in point. The regime of General Augusto Pinochet recently has increased pressure on Chilean defenders of human rights. Members of the Chilean Commission for Human Rights, the country's most important secular human rights organization, face almost daily threats, physical intimidation, and overt violence. Last November, the commission's office was invaded and ransacked. Its documents, compiled for a U.N. investigation, were confiscated by armed plainclothes police. The intruders beat the office caretaker with their fists and a revolver, causing a concussion. When the caretaker's daughters tried to help her, they were threatened with death. Before leaving, the invaders shouted, "Now you will know the hand of CNI [the Chilean national intelligence agency]."

On January 15, 1986, two commission officers were attacked and stoned in front of a police station by a mob of progovernment protesters while the civilian police stood idly by. The victims were the commission's president, Jaime Castillo, a founder and past president of the Christian Democratic party and former minister of justice in the democratic government of Eduardo Frei in the 1960s, and the commission's vice president, Maximo Pacheco, a former minister of education in the Frei government. The windows of the car in which they were riding were shattered by rocks, and Castillo was struck in the head with a rock and lacerated in the face and back by splintering glass. Fortunately, the two men were able to keep the car moving and escaped with their lives. Since then the pressure has continued. Pacheco has been harassed, his household servant kidnaped, and his daughter and her child subjected to threats of kidnaping and violence. The Chilean government has brushed aside all protests.

Despite such brutalities, there is still reason for hope. Chile does have a long tradition of popular rule before 1973—when Pinochet seized power in a bloody military coup—on which to build. A foundation for human rights does exist beneath the rubble created by the military dictatorship. Moreover, U.S. policy toward Chile has begun to change. From the outset, the Reagan administration opposed a U.N. resolution condemning Chile for human rights abuses. In March 1986, however, the administration changed its position and sponsored its own resolution condemning Chile. Much credit must go to America's courageous ambassador, Harry Barnes, Jr., to Secretary of

State George Shultz, and to those members of Congress who have long pressed the Chilean government to restore respect for human rights and to hold early, free, and fair elections.

In future dealings with Chile, the United States must make its views on human rights clear. Washington must stress that U.S.-Chilean relations will be affected by Santiago's conduct. America must state bluntly that unless Chile's human rights policies and conduct change, the United States will, among other actions, vote against all future international bank loans to Chile.

In Argentina, meanwhile, promise has become reality. Under the leadership of President Raúl Alfonsín, respect for freedom and for individual dignity has been restored to that country. As the publisher Jacobo Timerman—who was tortured under Argentina's old military regime—and others have pointed out, the Argentine people can be thankful to Americans who kept faith in the dark days of the late 1970s, when thousands of Argentines "disappeared" and many were murdered at the hands of the military.

Above all, Argentina's return to democracy is truly a triumph of popular courage and determination, a victory of the faith and will of the oppressed over their oppressors. Americans must continue to support the Alfonsín government both politically and economically as it confronts massive economic difficulties. Washington should be forthcoming and steady in providing help, bilaterally and through the international financial institutions.

Encouraging news recently has come from the Philippines and Haiti as well. In Haiti, the heir to one of the world's worst traditions of government finally was driven from power. This island country remains desperately poor and faces a difficult future. But at least its destiny is being determined largely by men and women who seek a better life for all Haitians. America can and must help, beginning with immediate emergency food aid, while it urgently assesses Haiti's longer-term needs. In the Philippines, the problems are even more complex, but the victory achieved is even more inspiring. All Americans have marveled at the magnificent commitment of the Filipino people to freedom, at the physical and moral courage of President Corazon Aquino, at the support of the Roman Catholic church under the leadership of Jaime Cardinal Sin, and at the unforgettable sight of peaceful, unarmed men and women facing down tanks and guns with their "prayers and presence." The United States should offer whatever support it can as that country seeks to rebuild both politically and economically.

One of the most striking developments of the 1980s has been the answer to Stalin's question concerning how many divisions the pope has. From Poland to the Philippines, the world has heard the answer: Quite a few. Much remains to be done in the Philippines, and the doing will not be easy. But what has been shown in Buenos Aires, in Port-au-Prince, and in Manila is that peaceful, democratic change is possible in today's world, that such change carries with it great promise, and that there is much that American human rights policies can do to promote it.

In many other countries the pace of change has been maddeningly slow, and in some, nonexistent. Both opportunities and pitfalls abound. This is particularly true in Central America, and nowhere more so than in Nicaragua. Furnishing military aid to the *contras* is a disastrous mistake. The United States should listen to the virtually unanimous advice of its Latin American neighbors who urge it not to give such aid and to give its full support instead to the Contadora process. Despite temporary setbacks, this regional peace effort provides a framework for ending Central America's agony while safeguarding the hemisphere's security interests. But whatever their viewpoint, Americans all should be able to agree that human rights are denied and abused in Nicaragua, and have been for decades—by the late dictator Anastasio Somoza Debayle and his supporters and by the Sandinistas. Americans must continue to demand an end to all such abuses.

To avoid self-delusion, Americans must recognize that anticommunism cannot always be equated with democracy.

In the Pacific, human rights are of special importance in South Korea. The United States has major national interests in South Korea and its future. Americans fought side by side with the South Korean people in defending the country. Seoul is an important ally, America's seventh largest trading partner, and a critical force for stability in Northeast Asia. And South Korea's future will be vitally affected by the way its government responds to popular demands for greater pluralism and respect for the rights and dignity of all of its citizens. America must exert its influence to that end. The next 3 years will be especially important as international attention to South Korea increases when Seoul hosts the Asian

Games in fall 1986 and the summer Olympic Games in 1988.

South Korea differs from the Philippines in its political traditions and cultural heritage. The Filipino people have democratic roots several decades long, while South Korea's slow movement toward more open government is a relatively recent development. These differences should caution Americans in drawing conclusions and predicting how each government will act to open up its society. Failure to be realistic can lead to false hopes and expectations.

This does not mean playing down human rights issues in U.S. relations with South Korea. Quite the contrary, as a friend and ally, the United States must speak more candidly and forcefully than it has about the need for South Korea's leaders to open up the political process more rapidly and to recognize and respect the right of all its citizens to be free from repression and secure from arbitrary arrest, imprisonment, and the invasion of their homes. A pragmatic as well as principled policy also would make clear that the United States will continue to help South Korea defend itself against the threat of attack from North Korea, while maintaining America's strong interest in South Korea's economic development and prosperity.

The Soviet Union clearly presents the most difficult problems in balancing human rights principles and pragmatism. Two critically important truths must always be kept in mind. First, human rights must always be on America's agenda with the Soviet Union. On that there can be no compromise. Second, human rights almost never can be on the agenda alone. The facts of the nuclear age require dealing with Moscow on matters that can determine the fate of the planet—avoiding nuclear war and preventing regional conflicts that could lead to nuclear war. No American government can honor its commitment to the human family if it fails to pursue human rights with Soviet leaders; it cannot honor its commitment, however, if it does not also pursue the cause of peace.

The United States must continue to prod the Soviet Union to honor its commitment to the human rights provisions of the Helsinki Final Act. America must also prod the Soviets to relax their grip on those people, from the dissident scientist Andrei Sakharov to thousands of unknown individuals, who are most oppressed by Soviet rule. America must do so because those individuals have few other advocates in world councils. America must do so because, in speaking out, it reminds the world of the difference between the vision of Jefferson and the perverse outlook of Stalin. And America must do so because it can have an effect. Sometimes America may act through quiet diplomacy; at other times, through forceful public statements. Still other situations may call for the use of incentives or rewards on the one hand and threats and punishments on the other.

Americans must also remember the special plight of Soviet Jewry. Specifically, Moscow must be pressed to increase the level of Jewish emigration at least to that achieved in the mid- and late 1970s. It was possible then; it should be possible now.

Since martial law crushed the Solidarity movement in December 1981, human rights conditions have been a major problem in Poland. American economic sanctions that initially were imposed have been dismantled step by step as the Polish government met certain conditions: Martial law was lifted and many political prisoners were released. The calibrated American response has been, on the whole, an intelligent application of U.S. human rights policy.

Yet despite what some take as normalization of the situation, the last year has seen severe incursions on academic freedom and purges, together with the harassment and even imprisonment of some of Solidarity's leading figures. Further U.S. assistance to help Poland overcome its economic catastrophe should be keyed to Warsaw's willingness to reverse the setbacks of the last year and to move toward genuine national reconciliation involving the Polish government, the Roman Catholic church, and Solidarity.

Finally, there is South Africa. The United States has maintained diplomatic relations with South Africa for many years. During World War II, although many of the strongest advocates of apartheid were pro-Nazi, the South African government itself fought with the Allies to free the peoples of Europe from fascist tyranny. South Africa is a source of important raw materials, occupying a strategic position along the sea routes running from the Indian Ocean and the Middle East into the Atlantic Ocean. Yet productive relations with South Africa are impossible because of sharp differences over apartheid, over the right of South Africa's blacks to live decent lives, and over their right to participate as full citizens in governing their country.

South Africa has institutionalized discrimination of the most vicious sort and resists fundamental change of this abhorrent system. What the United States seeks in the near term is clear: the dismantling of apartheid, root and branch, and the sharing of political power among whites, blacks, mixed-blood "Coloreds," and Asians alike.

The United States should make unmistakably clear to President P. W. Botha and all South Africans that Americans are committed to the total abolition of apartheid and to genuine power sharing. The U.S. government must underscore that South Africa cannot adopt one policy for worldwide public consumption and a second, less stringent policy for private discussion in Pretoria. America must make unmistakably clear that time is running out and that major steps must be taken now. The South African government also must be told that, without prompt action, the United States will impose more stringent economic restrictions than those approved by Reagan in September 1985. And America should work with like-minded countries to pressure South Africa to make those decisions that are necessary now to stop further repression and a bloody civil war later.

The world has a long agenda in the pursuit of human rights. There will be, I fear, no final victory over tyranny, no end to the challenge of helping people to live decent lives, free from oppression and indignity. But this generation has set the highest standards for human rights in human history. It has achieved much; it has proved repeatedly that no idea is so compelling as the idea of human freedom. America was "conceived in Liberty, and dedicated to the proposition that all men are created equal." It is America's task, a century and a quarter after Abraham Lincoln spoke, to do its utmost to help redeem that promise for men and women everywhere.

What Price Political Prisoners?

Somalia

RICHARD GREENFIELD

Richard Greenfield, a member of Oxford University's International Development Centre, was political adviser to the Somali government from 1977-86.

The long-awaited trials of several former government ministers and officials detained since 1982 are scheduled to take place in February. Their outcome may prove decisive in resolving the ongoing "Somali succession" crisis, as well as in unifying opposition to the aging Siad Barre's regime.

Though once an outspoken opponent of tribalism and an inspiration to most Somalis, President Mohamed Siad Barre is now visibly aging and ill. On October 21, the anniversary of his 1969 coup d'état, hundreds demonstrated against his regime in many cities throughout the world.

But septuagenarian autocrats are seldom easily led to relinquish power. Rather, they tend to clamp down on human rights and encourage uncertainty by petty, devious, arbitrary, and often vindictive decisions and frequent government reshuffles. Sadly, at such times, the fate of possible successors—all too often maligned as political opponents and incarcerated in wretched political prisons—hangs on the finest of threads.

In Somali culture, few things are more admired than an alliterative verse or an apt proverb. It is said, for example, that "a desire for perfection in kinsmen will foster isolation"—in other words, when assessing one's relatives, one should relax normal standards of evaluation. The aging president of Somalia, many argue, is doing just that.

Siad Barre's eldest son, Maslah Mohamed Siad, a comparatively inexperienced soldier fond of the good life, has recently been propelled to unparalleled prominence. It is barely a year since Maslah was promoted brigadier-general. Although a successful and wealthy contractor, he has very little military or political command experience. Even so, at the probable instigation of the president's influential senior wife, Khadidja Ma'alin, a formidable new command has been created for him.

The structure of the 77th Sector, which controls all units in the capital and the surrounding region, has been revised and expanded, endowing it with maximum influence over national security—and indeed potentially over the whole government. This move is clearly designed to protect the position and wealth of Siad's family and leading members of the small Marehan clan currently in power, but a corollary has been considerable resentment, expressed by others interested in the wider but not unrelated issue of the "Somali succession."

All the President's Clan

Since the fateful car accident in May 1986, Siad Barre's health has remained problematic. It is quite remarkable that he recovered at all, but doctors insist that he will never again enjoy the stamina to singlehandedly balance the varied clans and interests in the Somali nation, which he has done with consummate skill and often ruthlessness for many years. Today government decisions are fiercely contested by rival groups and families and are by no means invariably initiated by him. Increasingly they reflect local rivalries and more generally, a dangerously narrowing power base.

As predicted in *Africa Report* (May-June 1987), Siad's constitutional successor, Lt.-Gen. Mohamed Ali Samatur, and those who support him, including Brig.-Gen. Ahmed Sulayman Abdulla, minister of interior, have lost some of their previously considerable influence. Samatur is no longer referred to on Radio Mogadishu as first vice-president, but only as "first" or "prime" minister, nor has he retained the vital portfolio of defense. A new minister has yet to be announced, but Siad has appointed three vice-ministers. Neither Samatur nor Abdulla are Marehan, although the latter is the president's son-in-law.

The Marehan are seriously divided and factionalism is rife even within the president's own family. Siad's first wife bore him four sons and his second gave birth to 10 children. Then there are uncles and in-laws. Inside the extended family circle, powerful men and a few women—including the two wives—eye each other with the gravest suspicion. Siad's half-brother, Dr. Abdurahman Jama Barre, minister of foreign affairs since 1977, also aspires to leadership of the family, the clan, and the nation.

Outside, most leaders of other, often much larger clans and subclans are apparently content to look on for the time being. But several harbor resentment at being dispossessed and persecuted in the past. If economic stagnation worsens, as seems likely, and tension rises, the passing months will present a built-in dynamic for instability.

Siad is nearly 80 years old and as with most military regimes, there is no clear successor. The potential for civil disturbance is very apparent—witness outbreaks of stone-throwing in Mogadishu last August, which greatly alarmed the government, not to mention foreign missions, some of which counseled against the customary violent reaction.

The Politics of Detention

Several formerly prominent ministers and national leaders languish in Somalia's primitive prisons. The best known is probably Mohamed Aden Sheikh, who is reputedly in one of the worst—Labatan Jirow. A medical doctor by profession, he was president of the Somali Academy of Sciences and sometime minister of information and national guidance, and is often considered the intellectual behind Siad's "scientific socialism" period.

A Marehan himself, he fell from favor, was arrested with five other parliamentarians in June 1982, and charged with treason. It is currently rumored that he will be made out to have been a Soviet agent. That Sheikh for a period was close to the Italian Communist Party, which has unsuccessfully lobbied for his release, is well known. But Sheikh has never been to the Soviet Union, and any such charge will lack popular credence, the more so since several of his alleged fellow "conspirators" were much more right-wing in their views.

Although feared by his secretaries for a few outbursts occasioned by high blood pressure, Sheikh is more usually remembered as a genial, popular, and articulate nationalist. Many Somalis are watching his fate with foreboding. He and his colleagues have been adopted by Amnesty International as "prisoners of conscience," and the Council of the American African Studies Association has recently included his name and that of Abdi Ismail Yunis, formerly dean of education at the National University, in an appeal relating to imprisoned African academics.

"Siad is nearly 80 years old and as with most military regimes, there is no clear successor. The potential for civil disturbance is very apparent."

Another imprisoned Marehan is Maj.-Gen. Omar Haji Mohamed, formerly minister of health and also acting minister of defense and chief of staff of the armed forces. A man of considerable status, his detention illustrates that much of the "palace politics" in Mogadishu revolve around attempts to free or to incarcerate potential allies or political opponents.

Perhaps the best known of the prominent prisoners—because he once stood for secretary-general of the OAU—is Omar Arteh Ghalib. Now 58 and unfortunately for him, an Isaak by clan, his health is failing under the rigor of his imprisonment. The Isaak are the mainstay of the rebellion in the north led by the Somali National Movement (SNM).

Ghalib was a long-serving minister of higher education and then of foreign affairs. He was displaced in the early stages of the Ogaden war by Dr. Abdurahman Jama Barre. A tall and articulate man, Ghalib served in the presidency and was elected member of Parliament. At the time of his arrest in June 1982, he was first deputy speaker of the National Assembly. A devout Muslim and a nationalist, the charge that he too was guilty of treason and espionage for an unspecified foreign government borders on the ludicrous.

More senior even than Ghalib is another detainee, Maj.-Gen. Ismail Ali Abokor. Abokor, an outspoken, efficient, and incorruptible administrator, was a graduate of Sandhurst Military Academy, assistant secretary-general of the ruling Somali Revolutionary Socialist Party, and third vice-president. He, too, is Isaak.

Ghalib, Abokor, and others anticipated the present crisis over succession and privately suggested that it might be prudent for their aging president to consider giving up that office, or at least secretary-generalship of the party, to make way for a younger man. That is widely believed to have been the real cause of their arrest.

Sheikh, Mohamed, Ghalib, Abokor, Col. Osman Mohamed Ghelle (a former minister of livestock), Mohamed Yusuf Weiran (a former minister of finance), and 14 other officials are now said to be charged on counts varying from "organizing a subversive organization" to "conspiracy against the state," "banditry," and "possession of seditious material," all of which carry a mandatory death sentence.

Forty young persons—doctors, professionals, and students, all Isaak—who had founded a self-help organization and were arrested in 1982 around Hargeisa, are also to be tried. It has at last been announced that trial of the parliamentarians will commence on February 1, 1988, at 9 a.m. sharp. It is not clear, however, whether members of other clans will be tried at the same time as the Isaak.

The Unsettled North

The number of security incidents in northern Somalia has increased in recent months. Demonstrations have led to curfews in the towns of Hargeisa,

Berbera, and Burao and more recently, Borama. The military, under the command of Maj.-Gen. Mohamed Saeed Hirsi, nicknamed Morgan, is greatly extended by the demands of a deteriorating security situation. He has ordered his troops to destroy Isaak settlements if it seems the inhabitants are in support of the SNM. Wells have been sealed and crops burnt. Nomads have been harassed.

In the townships, suspected persons and curfew breakers have been arbitrarily arrested and released, if at all, only on the payment of a "ransom." Merchants suspected of sympathizing with the SNM have had their property and vehicles sequestered and their bank balances frozen—although some have been able to cash checks through friends of the regime, albeit at a ten or greater percentage discount.

Following the embarrassing leakage early last year of a secret policy paper advocating oppressive political and economic measures, Morgan may be hard put to fend off his rivals' efforts to have him transferred from command of the 26th Sector northwest. Maj.-Gen. Mohamed Hashi Gani, before his appointment as vice minister of defense, Morgan's predecessor as "viceroy" of the north, is a particular critic.

Several meetings have recently taken place between leading members of the "Marehan committee" and the Isaak elders, although the latter, of course, admit no connection with the SNM. Filial relationships being what they are, however, the Isaak elders will be in a difficult position if Siad is planning, as is strongly rumored, to demand their cooperation against the SNM in return for commuting death penalties on their political leaders and their articulate youth—flavored, doubtless, by the promise of development projects financed by Western agencies.

Economic Paroxysm

More significant, however, is the fact that neither World Bank officials nor the IMF have waxed sympathetic over the economic crises which are the day-to-day experience of all but a few Somalis. Nor have repeated devaluations of the Somali currency and the introduction of currency auctions proven the hoped-for palliative. Indeed, the exchange rate has again been pegged and auctions recently stopped. Officials close to the government report that as a further economy measure, a number of civil servants are to be suspended and certain embassies abroad closed.

In January, the cabinet is also expected to be reshuffled again and much reduced in size—perhaps to some 10 or 12 ministers. While relatives of the ruling Marehan families still manage to maintain villas in Washington and other capitals, such is the shortage of foreign exchange that Somali diplomats in many countries have remained unpaid for long periods and one frustrated landlord even locked up the offices of the Somali Mission to the United Nations in New York.

Indeed, the state of the national economy remains quite desperate. In a paragraph of unusual candor in a confidential briefing paper issued in August, the Somali government frankly admitted that "annual debt service payments stand at 167 percent of export earnings." Somalia's crippling debts are by no means all owed to OECD countries and multilateral agencies. Among others, they include commercial borrowing from Credit Lyonnais at high repayment rates. Such debts were neither wisely incurred nor properly utilized and do not prove easy to reschedule.

Not only have climatic factors and the crisis in the north disturbed the livestock industry, but there is mounting competition in Somalia's traditional meat markets. The Gulf war also continues to disrupt the import of essential petroleum products, causing sudden shortages which by themselves are politically unsettling. Over the years, such difficulties have often been resolved by "begging trips" to Saudi Arabia and the Gulf states.

Aid in the form of cash grants is preferred by the regime, only partly because the civil service, although improved over the years, still lacks the infrastructure to process the quantity of supporting paperwork demanded by most donors. However, when Siad attended the emergency Arab summit on the Gulf war in early November, his request for a substantial handout was rejected as untimely, even tactless.

"Opposition in Somalia is clearly fraught with hazard, but opposition movements have yet to establish a wide enough platform to provide an alternative to the ruling regime and Marehan plans for a 'dynastic succession.' "

Blood Money

In mid-1987, in a supposed good will gesture for the Muslim festival of Id al-Ahda—but actually in recognition of Saudi interest in the case—Siad commuted death sentences passed secretly by the National Security Court on nine mullahs accused of possessing anti-government literature. He substituted indefinite imprisonment. In Somalia, the preventative detention law of 1970 legalizes indefinite detention without charge or trial.

If they are found guilty as expected, it is rumored that an attempt will soon be made to barter the lives of the accused high officials in return for aid from the Gulf states. As architect of Somalia's joining the Arab League, Omar Arteh Ghalib is particularly well-liked by several Gulf leaders. Survival aid and an economic package may again be requested, despite recent negative responses.

There is no doubt that execution of respected figures can prove a last straw. Many prayers are being offered for political prisoners in Somalia today. For their friends—and for all friends of the Somali people—these are anxious times. For even if a stay of execution is granted, and the Somali government is once again bailed out financially by the Arab states, the impression may well remain in the West that only time has been bought. Future patterns remain obscure.

Opposition in Somalia is clearly fraught with hazard, but opposition movements have yet to establish a wide enough platform to provide an alternative to the ruling regime and Marehan plans for a "dynastic succession." The Somali National Movement is active, but although it has made several attempts to appear truly national, it is still largely associated in the public mind with the Isaak. Moreover, based in Ethiopia, it is facilely accused of being completely in the hands of the Ethiopian intelligence services.

Siad has also successfully played off the Ogadeen clan, who are still fairly powerful in the Somali military, against the Isaak, even while himself subtly degrading Ogadeen power as an obstacle to any unpopular deal he may feel pressured to make with Addis Ababa.

Against such a scenario, the vexing but delicate issue of human rights may yet provide a common platform for the growing number of Somalis who are demanding that their country return to democracy, free elections, and consensus politics. The February trials, if they are not once again postponed, cannot but provide a focus for the many strands and tensions in the unstable Somali political scene.

Indeed, there is another Somali proverb that says that if one's sandals become seriously fouled, it may be wise to discard them completely. One false move could prove disastrous for the family, and likewise for many of the factions currently jockeying for position in and around the ailing regime in Mogadishu.

South Africa: Where Did the Story Go?

American media coverage of the South African crisis has diminished in both quantity and quality since the press restrictions under the state of emergency. This *Africa Report* exclusive examines why and what can be done about it, talking with the editors and journalists who make the news.

BY DANNY SCHECHTER
with research by ANDRE ASTROW
and DAPHNE TOPOUZIS

Danny Schechter is a television network news producer who has written about southern Africa for 20 years. Research for this article was conducted by Africa Report *assistant editor André Astrow and acting managing editor Daphne Topouzis.*

On the night after Thanksgiving, CBS News viewers may have been startled to see a few minutes of an evening news report about apartheid devoted to the pulsating beat of black American rappers chanting "A.F-R.I.C.A." in a music video about southern Africa. Correspondent Bruce Morton cited the song, along with other anti-apartheid films and albums, as evidence that the entertainment industry seems to be doing more to raise awareness about the issue than the news media.

Where has the apartheid story gone? Is it being covered less because less is happening? Has the international press packed up and moved on? Or has South Africa's press ban been so successful that coverage has been effectively curtailed? Could the American media be doing more?

These questions raise important issues about the politics and practices of news coverage. To explore them, *Africa Report* surveyed South Africa coverage in major American newspapers and reviewed Vanderbilt University's TV News Index and Abstracts, looked at what the "alternative press" in South Africa covers that we may not, and spoke with editors and correspondents, in the U.S. and South Africa.

On average, the Americans interviewed tended to have a more sanguine view of the problem than the South Africans. The editors of prominent American newspapers defended their coverage as adequate. TV journalists tended to be a bit more unhappy because of their need for visual images and their problems getting the stories they do file on the air.

But South Africans opposed to apartheid and activists who support them in this country are far more dissatisfied, arguing that the American media has been essentially complicit in Pretoria's media restrictions. One conclusion was undebatable: There has been less coverage of South Africa overall, especially since the various press bans went into effect starting in late 1985.

"The dominant pre-emergency news frame of rebellion, if not open warfare, has vanished."

Using my own non-scientific "bathroom scale test," I weighed the TV News Index and Abstracts on South Africa from July-October 1985, a time of intense unrest, comparing it with the same period in 1987, a period of continuing labor unrest which included the strike in the gold mines. There is a three-pound difference. In August 1987, there were 102 citations of TV news stories on South Africa; in August 1985, several hundred. A survey of newspaper clips tells the same story.

No one disputes that South Africa's emergency regulations have had an effect in limiting coverage of unrest, particularly those dramatic confrontations between the army and the community in the townships. The dominant pre-emergency news frame of rebellion, if not open warfare, has vanished.

In August 1985, the three networks—ABC, CBS, and NBC—ran 60 South Africa stories between them. In November, after the first month of the press restrictions, there were only 20. At that time, the violence had not abated. A month later, ABC's principal news anchor, Peter Jennings, acknowledged that the restrictions had "worked." Marc Kusnetz, foreign news producer for NBC's nightly news recently echoed the same theme: "Has the censorship been effective? Sure it has. Is that even a question?"

There is no doubt that media coverage of the violence fueled protests overseas, including calls for disinvestment and sanctions. Media attention turned the battle inside South Africa into a global cause, one which was forcing Pretoria to consider reforms, however modest. Predictably, the South African government's response—given the nature of that government and the way it sees its interests—was to clamp down on coverage, so as to drive "the pictures," particularly vivid white-cops-beating-black-kids pictures, off the air.

Pretoria's press regulations appear calculated to keep the media off balance: They are deliberately vague, calculated to impose caution, restraint, self-censorship. *New York Times* foreign editor Joseph Lelyveld, who won a Pulitzer Prize for his book about South Africa, told us "the press clampdown has had some success."

"But there is no formal censorship system. I don't think we have ever submitted a line of copy. It's a system of self-censorship. They lay down guidelines and the correspondents have to decide how close they want to come to those guidelines. Some use the government's pressure of close scrutiny as an excuse for not doing a hell of a lot."

Adds Paul van Slambruck, international news editor of *The Christian Science Monitor*: "The burden of proof is on you. There are a bunch of laws and if you break them, you'll be prosecuted."

CBS senior producer Richard Cohen, formerly Dan Rather's foreign producer, says: "They've spun a web around us," of the ban prohibiting direct coverage of security personnel and all "unrest." "They've kept us from covering the story because of the fear that by breaking the rules, we'll get tossed out."

"Those journalists who have been ousted seem to have been ejected as 'examples' for domestic political reasons—to assuage the hard-right critics of the ruling National Party—rather than for specifically cited infractions."

Cohen's response was to pen an op-ed article asking the networks to "seriously consider" pulling out of South Africa. "We play an insidious game of video appeasement with the government," he wrote in *The New York Times*. "Walk up to the line. Don't cross it. Show as much as you think you can get away with, never more." His pull-out proposal, however, was not a popular one among journalists who generally contend that some coverage is better than none, and that to leave would be to do voluntarily what the South African authorities want. Cohen, however, has not backed down.

"The idea deserves an open and honest debate," he told me in February from his post in Iowa where he was directing the network's political coverage. "Nothing really has changed. The story is not being seen. By staying there, the public thinks we are covering the story—but we're not. That's the dirty little secret that journalists don't want to discuss."

Many American journalists we spoke with will discuss the issue, but tend to place the blame on a lack of commitment at the network level, which in turn, is justified because of a perceived lack of interest by the public. Martha Teichner, the CBS correspondent in South Africa, told us, "Half the problem is in South Africa, and half is in the interest in the U.S. Right now, our news organizations pay lip service to being interested in South Africa, and certainly claim they are interested in the analytical stories. But they are not making air. They are simply being eclipsed by other events."

NBC's bureau chief in South Africa, Heather Allan, seems more upbeat about her network's productivity. Of 150 stories shot in 1987, she says, 80 percent were aired. That is a good batting average, but it is not clear how many were shown on the premiere news shows, and how many in early morning slots or less watched weekend news times.

"You do not see violence on TV every night from South Africa," Allan says. "So in that respect, the government has been successful. But we are doing three stories a week, and more in-depth." Those "in-depth" stories though don't seem to have the power of the earlier coverage, in the same way that nothing NBC has done about the miserable famine in Mozambique has equalled the impact of its first footage out of Ethiopia.

There seems to be a clear link between air time allotted a story and public interest—remove the former and you reduce the latter. When viewers don't see the story, legislators and policymakers don't hear about the issue. According to *The Washington Report on Africa*, the lack of news media coverage has affected the prospects of tougher sanctions legislation.

"Congressional aides on both sides of the issue agree that curtailed press coverage from South Africa has already been an important, if not decisive, factor in this year's debate," says the newsletter. The House of Representatives Subcommittee on Africa is planning to hold hearings on the media black-out.

Most news people agree that an issue's popularity or lack of it should not affect coverage, but that handful of news producers who assign stories and decide what runs are undeniably influenced by what is hot and what isn't. The *New Republic*'s weekly "Zeitgeist" column, which charts issues as if they were on a best-seller list, offers a good illustration of the way news stories tend to flame in and out of media fashion. Apartheid hasn't "made" the list for a long time.

News organizations are also bureaucratic institutions where issues need "champions" in decision-making circles or they are given little priority. ABC's

Ken Walker told a Nieman Foundation conference on South Africa and news censorship last April that the U.S. news media is guilty of a failure of will and a failure of nerve.

He says that *Nightline*'s celebrated 1985 programs from South Africa followed years of lobbying by black employees and the growth of the Free South Africa Movement. He said Pretoria only granted *Nightline* visas after *60 Minutes* carried a Morley Safer report considered flattering by the government there. It expected a repeat performance.

Walker believes that the news media doesn't care about the South Africa story and the coverage reflects that. He believes that the absence of regular black network correspondents in the field—none have ever been assigned to South Africa—is another indicator of an unwillingness to challenge the system.

One South African journalist I spoke with (who asked to remain anonymous) said a reporter's political openness is as important as racial sensitivity. "South Africa is viewed as one of us, as a Western democracy, and the correspondents operate as if it was one," he said angrily. "Western reporters cover South Africa from the point of view of the people who run it, not from the point of view of the people who suffer it."

Can hard-hitting journalists cover South Africa? Brian Ellis, who produced the outspoken CBS documentary, "Children of Apartheid," with Walter Cronkite, says it is difficult to work there "but not impossible." "There is a certain amount of risk to bending or working outside the restrictions, but it can be done."

Ellis took some risks in having Cronkite enter the country as a tourist, not a journalist. The documentary was reportedly delayed for six months so that CBS's South African lawyers could vet it for problems because of a South African government complaint. The script was modified somewhat to avoid provoking a confrontation.

For one of the children interviewed, the CBS exposure may have triggered a confrontation, a fatal one. Eighteen-year-old Godfrey Dhlomo's story of being tortured by police while in detention was featured in the report. On January 24, Dhlomo was found shot to death shortly after being questioned by police.

His funeral on February 6 was described in *The New York Times* as "one of the most emotional and politically charged events" in Soweto since June 1986. Yet it was played down and treated with only five paragraphs on page six of the Sunday paper. The featured story on that page dealt with a U.S. government official criticizing Romania's human rights record. That story was given twice as much space.

Angry anti-apartheid demonstrators marched outside CBS on the day of the young man's funeral protesting the lack of coverage and demanding a public statement by CBS itself. They called on CBS and the rest of the networks to do more about the issue. Only CBS's local station in New York covered their protest. The written press did not.

After Dhlomo's death, the Johannesburg *Star* carried a report listing more than 20 incidents of similar unexplained deaths of militant black youths. "Yet none of them were reported in the States," says Jim Cason of the Africa Fund. "Surely the media here can't claim that the information isn't available. Despite all the media restrictions, South Africans can read about it. It's only Americans who are being kept in the dark. Why?"

Part of the reason one hears over and over again is that if American journalists challenge the government's press regulations, they will be tossed out. Yet those who have been ousted—print journalists primarily—seem to have been ejected as "examples" for domestic political reasons—to assuage the hard-right critics of the ruling National Party, rather than for specifically cited infractions.

New York Times editor Lelyveld said that the ouster of correspondent Alan Cowell and the refusal to accredit his replacement, Serge Schmemann, was not attributed to what *The Times* wrote, only that it was writing too much. Critics say it was not doing enough.

ABC's Walker links the lack of video footage available to TV news also to the fear of expulsion. Yet he asserts that the same fear is not present in Eastern bloc countries where government restrictions are routinely challenged, and where expulsion is often a badge of honor. CBS's Cohen seconds this point. "We smuggle pictures out of the wilderness of Afghanistan. We could do the same in South Africa."

Anti-apartheid activists question news organizations who cite a lack of video footage as reason for reduced coverage, pointing out that there are well-known alternative sources of video inside South Africa—footage shot by independent crews whose work is distributed by such agencies as Afravision, which covers demonstrations, union meetings, and other dissident activity.

Afravision's London-based distributors tell me that they have a hard time selling their stuff to the American networks unless a story is on the wires or has lots of action. ABC, for example, did run excerpts from an Afravision interview with Govan Mbeki, the ANC leader released from prison, but such interactions are rare.

These alternative media outlets also define "the story" somewhat more broadly than most American journalists. They see it in regional terms, as a southern African story, not just a South Africa one. It apparently took the expulsion of a *Times* reporter inside South Africa to prompt *The Times* to add more regional coverage, although the paper does not plan to open a bureau in Harare.

For the first time in years, front-page stories appeared from the frontline states with correspondents Serge Schmemann stopping in Maputo and James Brooke writing from Angola. That coverage has continued sporadically. Brooke was able to tour the war zones in southern Angola in late 1987, while Sheila Rule reported from Mozambique's shattered provinces.

Yet curiously, news of South African troops fighting alongside Unita in Angola only followed an uncharacteristic admission by the South African military. Earlier claims by the Angolan government to that effect appear to have been dismissed as propaganda. Likewise, reports in the British press of a mutiny in Angola by black South African soldiers were hard to find in the U.S. media.

Angola coverage often appears skewed by a cold war frame. U.S. support for Unita has been justified by the administration with the same arguments that support aid to the Nicaraguan contras. A January 27, 1988 *Washington Post* dispatch by William Claiborne from Johannesburg was most revealing. The story reported a claim by Unita of a key victory inside southern Angola. The source was a Unita representative in Washington whose statements made up the first 10 paragraphs of the story.

The Post also checked with the Pentagon which would not fully confirm it. That was played in paragraph seven. The South African presence in Angola only surfaced in paragraph twelve as a claim by the Angolan government which the South Africans, a paragraph later, would not respond to. A day later, Reuters in Luanda reported Angolan military sources as saying that the town in question had not been overrun.

A tendency to take Unita claims at face value is mirrored inside South Africa by the American media's lack of serious monitoring of South Africa's alternative press. That media has a reputation for being the best informed about the state of the liberation movements, the people in detention, and the suffering in the black community. The same news organizations which continually seek out refusniks and their samizdat publications in the Soviet orbit seem to steer clear of regular contact with South Africa's alternative press.

"There is not consistent day-to-day contact with the alternative press," admits CBS's Martha Teichner. Heather Allan of NBC says the same: "We are not in close contact, but we use them as interview subjects if we need their comments." *The Washington Post*'s foreign editor, Michael Getler, also says: "I don't see the alternative press."

Are newspapers such as *The Sowetan, New Nation,* or *Weekly Mail* read in the TV newsrooms? It does not appear that their viewpoint exerts much influence over the analysis pursued by American reporters.

For example, a February 4, 1988 NBC news report by Mike Boetcher on conditions in neighboring Mozambique began, "People are dying as a result of a Marxist-Leninist government, a drought, and a civil war." "Nowhere in the report do they mention who is behind the civil war," argued Josh Mamis, associate editor of *Africa News,* an American independent press service. "There was no mention that South Africa is behind Renamo which is carrying out horrible atrocities against the populace."

"Pretoria's press regulations appear calculated to keep the media off balance: They are deliberately vague, calculated to impose caution, restraint, self-censorship."

South Africa's alternative media reports regularly on the destabilization policy its government is carrying out in the frontline states—they see it as the dominant issue—yet recent news reports on NBC and in *The New York Times* and *The Washington Post* downplay and minimize the South African role. The British press is not similarly inclined. On January 14, the London *Guardian Weekly* headlined a report from Maputo: "Mozambique blames Pretoria for wrecking health care."

If Mozambique has not received the play it deserves, Namibia has been all but ignored, except when the South African military runs its annual press tour, prompting a flurry of similar articles. When 4,000 black miners went on strike last year, the story received scant attention. Yet inside Windhoek, *The Namibian,* a professionally edited weekly, had all the details available.

American newspapers can't use a lack of video footage as an excuse. In fact, they make no excuses and reveal little self-criticism. Michael Getler of *The Washington Post* has said his newspaper has been able to report everything of significance in South Africa. Nothing major was missed, he claims.

Joe Lelyveld of *The Times,* who was himself ousted from South Africa in 1966 but returned for a second stint a decade later, is disappointed because the newspaper has not been able to assign a full-time correspondent of its choice. Instead, the paper has hired a white South African journalist, John Battersby, who may not, Lelyveld concedes, have the proper distance to be a *Times* correspondent. "It's awfully tough to be a foreign correspondent in your own country," he says. "It's hard to see the stories as your audience needs to see them."

John F. Burns, a former *Times* reporter in South Africa, was dispatched to fill in for Battersby during a recent vacation. "Burns is the first staff correspondent we've been able to get a visa for," Lelyveld explains. Briefly in the news himself for getting in trouble and then for being tossed out of a country—China, not South Africa—Burns' orientation seems to particularly crystallize what critics find lacking.

"For Burns, the story seems to be upbeat, one of apartheid withering away," says the Africa Fund's Cason. "The headline one day is 'South African Blacks Moving to White Areas,' and the next is 'A Non-White Gets a Finger on the Lever of Power.' Burns spent his time writing about housing bias eroding, the anguish of Afrikaners, blacks going to amusement parks with whites, and how racial divisions are forgotten during a carnival in Cape Town. All of this in a country that is a virtual racial dictatorship!"

To be fair, Burns did not only file features. A long takeout on "black versus black violence" did describe the political nature of the fighting between Gatsha Buthelezi's Inkatha movement and the multi-racial anti-apartheid activists of the United Democratic Front. However, Burns did not investigate external support for Inkatha nor did his articles include any reference to government regulations limiting press coverage. That practice seems to have been dropped, although the restrictions haven't been.

At least two American papers devote considerably more space to the South Africa issue. *The Washington Times,* a conservative outlet owned by the Rev. Sun Myung Moon, carries more stories on the region than *The Washington Post,* but most of them reflect hard-right biases and support for Unita, Renamo, and critics of the ANC.

The Christian Science Monitor, on the other hand, features extensive coverage, including a recent piece—not seen elsewhere—on a press ban imposed by the U.S. Embassy in Pretoria which limits journalists' access to what most American officials are doing and saying.

Not many media outlets can make the same kind of claim as that of *The Monitor*'s Van Slambruck: "The kind of coverage we were doing two years ago is the same kind of coverage we had five years ago is the same kind of coverage we have now," he says.

"We're looking at South Africa as a page one possibility every single day. . . it requires much more cunning and ingenuity on the part of the writer to get at stories, to give them a dynamic and some life so they don't begin to sound like features. And that's a tougher brand of journalism."

In South Africa, the critics contend that as the going got tough, the tough got going—away from challenging the regulations, away from the story itself. At the time the regulations were imposed, there was a lot of heady talk about news organizations sustaining a commitment to South Africa reporting. Peter Jennings denounced South Africa's news policy on the air. Writing in *The New York Times*, Anthony Lewis, who has probably done more than any single American journalist to keep the information flow going, said that the press ban won't work.

"This is a test for American journalism, but also for the public," he opined on December 10, 1985. "It will influence future editorial judgment if the results show that people aren't interested unless they see shocking pictures, or if they show they can't be hoodwinked by the blackout and understand its purpose."

Have we passed or failed the test? In this election year, when even candidate Jesse Jackson doesn't list South Africa in a mass mailing as one of his principal issues, apartheid seems to "have gone away," to use a TV term about stories assignment editors are hot on one minute and cool the next. The story is on the back burner. A few overseas reporters have been tossed out of South Africa, but others carry on, business as usual. In the "beloved" country, brave black editors like Zwelakhe Sisulu rot in prison, while his newspaper is threatened with official reprisals again and again. How many Americans even know his name?

Babies for Sale

South Koreans make them, Americans buy them

MATTHEW ROTHSCHILD

Matthew Rothschild is the managing editor of The Progressive. Research for this article was supported by a grant from the Fund for Investigative Journalism.

Seoul, South Korea. Five pregnant women sleep on blankets on the tile floor of a small room. They keep their personal belongings in three wooden closets on one wall above their feet. This is home, at least until the babies come.

The dormitory is called Ae Ran Won, and it is one of a dozen homes for unmarried pregnant women in South Korea. Ae Ran Won can hold fifty pregnant women in its ten rooms, but when I was there in November, it had only thirty-five.

These women supply the raw material for a peculiar South Korean business: the export of babies to the United States.

U.S. families are adopting 6,000 Korean children a year, most of them infants, at a price of about $5,000 a head. Korea is by far the largest supplier of foreign babies for the U.S. adoption market; 62 per cent of all babies adopted from abroad are South Korean. That amounts to 10 per cent of the total adoptions in the United States by families unrelated to the adoptees.

Many of the babies come from unwed mothers' homes, about 250 a year from Ae Ran Won alone. At first, the women do not want to give up their babies.

"According to the questionnaire that we distribute at the orientation interview, 90 per cent want to keep the babies," says Kim Yong Sook, the director of Ae Ran Won. But after counseling, "maybe 10 per cent will keep them."

"We suggest that it's not a good idea to keep the baby without the biological father," explains Kim Yong Sook, "and if the unwed mother and biological father are too young or too weak financially, we suggest that they give the baby up for adoption. We can't push, but we can suggest."

After delivery at a hospital, the baby is taken from the mother and given to one of four adoption agencies licensed by the South Korean government. The agencies then place the baby with a foster mother until an American or European family can be found to adopt it.

For some of the Korean mothers, the experience hurts. "Just after delivery, they are very upset," says Kim Yong Sook, who was a social worker and an unwed mothers' counselor for eleven years for Holt Children's Services, the largest adoption agency in Korea, before joining Ae Ran Won. "They have guilt feelings and avoidance feelings. 'I'd like to see my baby again,' they say. Sometimes they have bad dreams. They miss the baby and have a lot of pain."

Most of the mothers are poor women from low-paying factory or clerical jobs. They do not receive payment for their babies, though medical expenses—including delivery costs—are picked up by the adoption agency that takes the baby. Ae Ran Won provides free room and board for up to a year, free vocational training, and as much as $100 to help the mother adjust when she leaves Ae Ran Won.

Like most of the homes for unwed expectant mothers, Ae Ran Won is supported by the Korean government, the adoption agencies, and charitable donations.

On the other side of Seoul, at the end of a narrow open-air fruit and vegetable market in a poor section of town, a two-year-old boy pees in the street and a mangy white dog prowls about. Two houses down is Sung Ro Won Babies' Home, an orphanage for infants under three.

It, too, is a supplier for the U.S. market. The orphanage, which had 106 infants when I visited, turns over at least that number each year to Holt and other agencies for foreign adoption.

"Almost all are abandoned and brought here by the Seoul police," says Kim Chong Chan, the superintendent of the babies' home. "Some kids are waiting now, in jail or some other place."

Son Mi Gu was born on December 8, 1986, and was abandoned in a motel that same day. She has a pony tail standing straight up on the top of her head. Dressed in a pink frilled shirt and white thermal stockings, she sits up in one of the twenty-four white crated cribs that crowd the room. All are occupied. In one month, Son Mi Gu will go to her American family.

In a nearby room, eleven girls who are two-and-a-half sing "Kum Ba Ya, My Lord." Some clutch my blue blazer. Ten boys in the next room greet me in unison, then some call me "appa" or dad. They bring out brown envelopes with pictures of Americans. Kim Chong Chan goes over the photos with them, explaining about their new parents.

Kim Chong Chan takes me to his office. On his desk, under the glass top, is a long

From *The Progressive,* January 1988, pp. 18-23. Reprinted by permission from *The Progressive,* 409 East Main Street, Madison, Wisconsin 53703.

'For the agencies, it's a business. It's time for us to stop it.'

—Nam Kyong Hyun, an instructor of social work at the Methodist Theological Seminary in Seoul

poem from a grateful American couple, praising God for sending such a wonderful child:

"He picked up our baby
Our daughter so fine
And delivered her to us
Via Northwest Airlines."

Adoptions from South Korea began in 1955 when Harry Holt, a born-again Christian from Eugene, Oregon, went to Korea and adopted eight war orphans. For the next decade, most of the children adopted from Korea were fathered by American soldiers who fought in the Korean war. But Amerasians now account for fewer than 1 per cent of the adoptees. Today, Korea is exporting its own.

Korean babies are "high-quality commodities," says one observer, who opposes the practice of foreign adoption but wants to remain anonymous so that he won't be persecuted by the Korean government.

Nam Kyong Hyun is less timid. "It's time for us to stop it," she says. An instructor of social work at the Methodist Theological Seminary in Seoul, Nam headed the Tai-Wha Christian Social Center for twelve years. She has dealt with the private nonprofit adoption agencies first hand, and she claims they care more about money than about the babies or the mothers.

"For the agencies, it's a business," she says.

The four agencies, in order of size, are Holt Children's Services, Eastern Social Service, Social Welfare Society, and Korea Social Service. Beside adoption work, they all provide care for handicapped children. But it is the foreign adoptions that keep the agencies going.

Holt and Eastern are avowedly Christian organizations, and they make every effort to place Korean babies in Christian homes. Holt especially stresses its fundamentalist, evangelical faith.

"We like to place with a Christian family, but we don't enforce that," says the Reverend Yoon Jae-Sung, secretary general of Holt Children's Services in Korea.

Holt International Children's Services in Eugene, Oregon, is a legally separate entity from Holt Korea. The Korean organization split from the parent organization more than ten years ago, but it still maintains close ties. According to Holt International's 1986 annual report, the American agency provided $2 million in financial support to its Korean namesake. And in 1986, Holt Korea placed 924 children in American families through Holt International—accounting for 90 per cent of Holt International's placements from foreign countries.

Holt International also emphasizes the importance of Christian families. "If you adopt a child through Holt International, you will be asked for your statement of faith," states a Holt booklet, *Adoption—A Family Affair.* "It is our personal desire that these children go into Christian homes. . . . We want to let these children we serve come to know Jesus."

One out of four persons in Korea is Christian, and the Korean adoption law requires adoptive parents to "recognize the freedom of religion of the adoptive child."

The Korean government closely regulates the adoption agencies. Indeed, they are quasi-governmental institutions. The government approves their budgets, scrutinizes each adoption application, sets informal quotas on the number of children to be adopted through each agency, and helps select the heads of the three largest agencies.

Foreign adoptions serve many purposes for the government. First, they bring in needed hard currency—roughly $15 to $20 million a year. Second, they relieve the government of the costs of caring for the children, which could be a drain on the budget. Third, they help with population control, an obsession of the Korean government. And finally, they solve a difficult social problem: What to do with orphans and abandoned children?

Birth control is inexpensive and accessible in Korea, and abortions—though technically illegal—are widespread and accepted. Still, the problem of unwanted children persists. In 1986, South Korea had 18,700 orphaned or abandoned children. Almost half were sent abroad for adoption, 70 per cent of these to the United States, the rest to Canada, Australia, and eight European nations.

"We have many children from unwed mothers, but few families who want to adopt," says Park Yon-Soo, director general of the Bureau of Family Affairs in the Ministry of Health and Social Affairs. "That's why we send our children to foreign families."

Critics and proponents alike agree that Korea's patrilineal culture is hostile to domestic adoption and discriminates against unwed mothers and their offspring. Unwed mothers are stigmatized by family and community, and they may not be able to get a job or find a husband. This is the social spur to foreign adoptions.

"Korea is a very blood-oriented society," says Park, who oversees the adoption program for the Korean government. "Koreans do not want to adopt a child unrelated by blood, and if they do, they don't want anyone to know."

For the last several years, the Korean government has urged the adoption agencies to increase domestic adoptions. From 1976 to 1978, it even imposed quotas on the agencies. But the program did not succeed. "Domestic adoptions are not that active," Park says. About 3,000 children were adopted in Korea in 1986.

Park has some misgivings about the volume of foreign adoptions, especially since it has handed the North Koreans a propaganda bonanza.

"We are very concerned about the numbers," he says. "In the 1970s, the North Koreans spoke ill about the numbers, about Korea selling its children abroad. We don't want to be involved in that again."

Yet the numbers have increased dramatically. In fiscal 1981, American families adopted 2,444 Koreans, according to the U.S. Immigration and Naturalization Service (INS). In fiscal 1986, they adopted 6,254.

The demand from the United States is fueling the business. One out of every twelve married couples in the United States is infertile, the U.S. Center for Health Statistics reports. The domestic supply of babies up for adoption simply cannot keep up with the demand.

"Two million couples would like to adopt in this country," says Jeffrey Rosenberg, the director of public policy for the National Committee for Adoption. "And there are only 20,000 healthy children available for adoption. That's a 100-to-1 ratio."

The supply is so coveted that the Community Adoption Center in Madison, Wisconsin, has sponsored a "Healthy White Infant Lottery." The entry fee is $300, but the winner still has to pay $5,000.

Because of the tight domestic market, Americans are increasingly looking abroad for children, and foreign adoptions are booming. "It's the highest it's ever been," says Rosenberg. "It's the fastest area of adoption growth in this country."

Nowhere is it faster than in South Korea.

"You got big bucks here. You're talking dollars," says Robert Ackerman, the INS officer in charge at the U.S. embassy in Seoul. "I see much potential for hanky-panky."

The adoption agencies in Korea collect about $2,000 a child right off the top. Then they charge American families $1,000 for transportation of the child to the United States. (A one-way coach fare from Seoul to Chicago costs $700, and the agencies receive a discount from the airlines. They also collect a donation of between $250 and $400 from each "escort" who travels with the baby on the plane; the agency picks up the airfare for the escort.) The adoption-placement agency in the United States then charges about $1,500 for its services. Add another $500 for legal paperwork and miscellaneous processing, and the total comes to $5,000. Often, it is several hundred dollars more.

Ackerman combs each adoption application to make sure everything is on the up and up. He is a direct and forceful man, and he's been known to terrify social workers from the adoption agencies with his gruff manner.

"He rejects too many applications," complains Dr. Kim Do-Young, executive director of Eastern Child Welfare Society, the second largest adoption agency in Korea.

The adoption business troubles Ackerman. "I get bothered by it," he says. "Five hundred kids a month is an incredibly high number for just a humanitarian issue. One has to question where humanitarianism stops and business begins."

He has heard allegations of mothers being bribed to give up their babies, but in his five years at the embassy he's never been able to confirm them. "It would be very disturbing if they were buying babies from the parents," he says.

But Korea is not like El Salvador, Mexico, or Sri Lanka, where a black market in babies seems to flourish. In Korea, it is more institutionalized, efficient, and above board.

Virtually from conception, the adoption agencies have established a system of guaranteeing a steady supply of healthy children. They support pregnant-women's homes; in fact, three of the four agencies run their own. One of the agencies has its own maternity hospital and does its own deliveries. All four provide and subsidize child care. All pay foster mothers about $80 a month to care for the infants, and the agencies provide the food and clothing and other supplies free of charge. And they support orphanages, or operate them themselves. When the time for departures arrives, the babies are flown off to their foreign families, escorted by strangers who wait in line for their discounted airfares.

"I've had to ask myself, do we really have baby factories here?" Ackerman says.

> **'It's really like dealing with a product. Our weekly staff meetings were all about numbers: How many babies did we get that week?'**
>
> *—A Korean social worker who quit her job with an adoption agency*

He also has asked himself whether some of the religiously oriented agencies were viewing adoptions as a quick means of spreading the gospel, a head start on proselytizing. "It's crossed my mind," he says, but the agencies don't insist on strict applications of their religious standards. "There is a broad cross-section of adoptive parents, as far as a variety of religion goes."

For all his doubts, Ackerman comes out in favor of the adoption agencies. "On balance, it's probably more humane to allow them to stay in business," he says. "They are probably doing a service to the baby, the mother, and the adoptive parents." What's more, he says, adoptions from Korea are more regulated and less expensive than adoptions from other foreign countries.

To a great extent, the social workers are the heavies. They are hired by the adoption agencies and the pregnant-women's homes to persuade mothers to give up their children.

Most mothers are relieved, "but some have a guilty sense their whole life," says Chun Byung-Hoon, president of Social Welfare Society, one of the four adoption agencies. "It's a very sad story, you know. Some girls want to keep their children, but the social worker persuades her that that's impossible, so she gives up the child."

One social worker couldn't take it any longer. She was employed by one of the four adoption agencies for several years, and she was appalled by the increasing callousness and the competition.

"It's really like dealing with a product instead of taking care of the mother and child," the social worker told me, speaking on condition that she would not be identified. "Our weekly staff meetings were all about numbers: How many babies did we get that week? The numbers were the most important thing."

It never used to be so bad, she says. Before, agencies would work hard on their "sponsorship" programs; they would solicit charitable donations from Koreans and foreigners to care for the child in Korea. Not any longer.

"What's really happened is there is no interest in the sponsorship program," she says. "There's too much competition for babies."

This social worker had the unenviable task of taking the baby from the mother right at the hospital. "I was assigned to seven hospitals and clinics, and I was supposed to cultivate them," she says. "Any time there were children available for adoption, I was notified and I'd go to the hospital. I would talk to the mothers, and ask them to sign the papers."

Money did change hands. "I would pay the doctor for her medical fees and ask the doctor to pay the mother," she says. "In some cases, the doctor would tell me to give the money directly to the mother." The amount varied widely; sometimes it was just enough to pay the mother's bus fare back home.

Finally, she quit. "As a trained social worker," she says, "I could no longer continue to work in an agency where the basic concern was economic, with very little thought about the mother and the child and what was happening to them."

Payments are routine to maternity hospitals, midwives, and obstetricians, officials at each of the four agencies acknowledged. The agencies will cover the costs of the delivery and of the medical care for any woman who gives up her baby for adoption.

"We pay for our girls," says the Reverend Yoon Jae-Sung, secretary general of Holt, referring to the women Holt sends to the hospital from its counseling service or from its affiliated pregnant-women's home. And if hospitals send other babies over to Holt, "we'll give them a little help."

The agencies also use their influence with hospitals, and with the police, to acquire abandoned children. "The agencies have all the connections with the hospitals and the police stations," says Dom Yano Park, who helps run Seoul Boystown with Father Aloysius Schwartz. Seoul Boystown is one of the largest orphanages in Korea, housing 2,500 children between the ages of three and fifteen.

Under photographs showing Nancy Reagan visiting Seoul Boystown, Dom Yano Park explains how the agencies work. "They constantly try to get the babies from hospitals and the police," he says. "They

'Babies want to grow up, and when they get to be pubescent and adolescent, some people throw them away.'

—Lou Simmons, assistant director of the Lane County juvenile department in Eugene, Oregon

are so desperate to get babies to meet the demand, to fill the demand from the American side."

Hospitals and the police oblige, Dom Yano Park says, by handing over abandoned children to the agencies. Then, when mothers come to Boystown looking for their children, they are nowhere to be found.

Dom Yano Park opposes foreign adoption and objects to the practices of the adoption agencies. "If charity work is carried out so perfectly and mechanically in the business style," he says, "it loses the essence of charity."

Father Benedict Zweber sees things differently. He is the director of St. Vincent's Orphanage in Inchon, one hour west of Seoul. He lives and works out of a tiny office, just barely six feet high and with room for only a desk, a small filing cabinet, and a single bed. These are his temporary quarters while a new building is being completed.

A tennis racket dangles from the ceiling, a crucifix stands above his bed, and a WE LOVE FATHER BEN poster hangs over his desk. As I talk to him, three young boys enter. One sits on his lap and one on mine.

"I work with hard-to-place kids and try to place them," he says, as five more boys squeeze in. "Babies are in high demand. It doesn't take any work to place them."

He accepts any children between the ages of three and fifteen. His only condition is that they come with the documents freeing them up for adoption.

"It's better for those kids to get into homes than to raise them in orphanages in Korea," he says. "It's so much better that they go."

On this point, the genial priest becomes emphatic. "In Korea, a kid who is raised in an orphanage is considered a second-class citizen," he says. "It's very difficult for them to succeed in life here."

Father Zweber has taken on the toughest tasks of adoption: placing older children and sibling groups. "We make it a policy not to break up siblings," he says, adding proudly that he has placed up to five siblings with a single family in the United States. Every year, he visits the United States and Canada to see how the children are doing.

"We've probably sent 1,200 kids," he says, "and there isn't one who's having a lot of problems. They have problems—all kids have problems—but they fit in pretty well."

He knows that the adoption program is controversial, but he supports it enthusiastically. "I find it hard to criticize anybody who's placing a kid overseas," he says.

One thing does bother him, however. "I don't like an agency giving out money to hospitals and clinics," he says. "That's inviting people to abandon kids. It could lead to very big corruption."

Father Zweber was assigned to Korea in 1959, and he has been working with children in the Inchon area since 1965. He feels a personal tie to the country, since his brother, who fought in the Korean War, drowned in the Han River shortly afterward. "Koreans were very good to my mother and the family," he says.

In a way, he sees himself repaying that debt of kindness. "It's very, very rewarding work," he says softly, "to take street kids whose chances of surviving the prison gates for more than five years are very, very small and then to see them go to college in the United States. Some of these kids come in as very rough diamonds."

Molly Holt is founder Harry Holt's oldest living daughter. She still works at Ilsan, the home for handicapped children that her father established in 1964. It has 300 permanent residents now. Though her primary concern is with these handicapped children and the institution run by Holt Korea, she strongly supports the international adoptions.

"Those who are opposed to these adoptions are people from the upper strata of society," she says. "Of course, it's better if a child stays with its own family. Of course, it's better if a child is adopted by a Korean family. But as yet, we don't have enough families, and it's better for a country to allow its children to seek families abroad than to have the children warehoused."

Once they get to the United States, some Korean adoptees face problems. Like other adopted children, they have to come to terms with their identity. But these identity problems are compounded for children adopted from abroad.

"Youngsters who come from different countries, who speak different languages and belong to different races, have several more hurdles to clear," says Lou Simmons, assistant director of the Lane County juvenile department in Eugene, Oregon, home of Holt International Children's Services.

"When they're young, they're cute and cuddly. When they grow up, they're going to have problems with discrimination," says Simmons, who eighteen years ago adopted an Eskimo when the child was two-and-a-half.

The Eugene area, because of the presence of Holt, has had an unusually high number of Korean children. "We've seen some of them fail," Simmons says. "Oftentimes, parents adopt kids because they want a baby. But babies want to grow up, and when they get to be pubescent and adolescent, some people throw them away."

Marjorie Hendrickson has been a social worker for twenty-three years for the Lane County children's services department. She, too, has seen many Korean adoptees.

"By and large, they've assimilated well," she says. "It's been a good life for them."

Racism is an issue, Hendrickson acknowledges. The irony, though, is that it affects American black adoptees more severely than adopted Koreans.

"The Korean kids do have some problems, but not as much as the black kids," says Hendrickson. "This society is more accepting of Korean children than blacks. It's too bad; there's something terrible in this society the way it views blacks. I kept hearing from adopting parents when they were applying for a child: 'Any race but black,' 'Any race but black.' The general rule is, the lighter the skin, the easier the time the kid has."

Black social workers in the United States strongly oppose the adoption of black children by white families. They view it as a form of cultural genocide.

"We are opposed to transracial adoptions," says Janice Shindler, associate director of the Association of Black Social Workers Child-Adoption and Referral Service. "We feel black children should be placed with black families in order to maintain their cultural identity and develop mechanisms to survive in this country."

Some Koreans have similar concerns. "As a nation, we must look after the children who are born in this land," says Kim Oknah, president of the Korean Association for Volunteer Effort. "It is very, very disturbing" that Korea allows its children to be sent off to foreign countries, she says.

The human-rights organization for children, Defense for Children International, is split on this issue. "It's a crazy area," says Mike Jupp, the executive director of the U.S. branch. "The North American, Swedish, and Finnish people say there are kids who are being abandoned and neglected and need a home, whereas the representatives from Third World countries view it as a further example of exploitation of their natural resources. The West, they say, took their sugar, their coal, their bauxite, their gold, and their silver, and now it is taking their babies."

Certainly, the cultural identity of the adopted children tends to be sopped up by the sponge of American society. "One of the miracles of this program is the rapid and good adjustment of these kids into American culture," says Michael Short, an adoption specialist with Lutheran Social Services in Milwaukee, which places Korean children with U.S. families. "In six months, they have some language skills. In a couple of years, they are grade appropriate and Americanized."

Adoption-placement agencies in the United States differ as to how much time American adopting parents should devote to stressing Korean culture. For instance, the National Committee for Adoption promotes a book called *Oriental Children in American Homes*, by Frances Koh, which offers eight tips on how to handle this issue. Among Koh's suggestions:

"Teach her about her country's history and heroes—but don't overemphasize them. After all, you're rearing her as an American, and her big holiday, like yours, will be the Fourth of July.

"Wear a perfume that includes the flowers of her country and keep a potpourri of native spices in a basket on her bureau. Cooking with these spices will also carry the smells through the house.

> 'The Korean kids do have some problems, but not as much as the black kids. The general rule is the lighter the skin, the easier time the kid has.'
>
> *—Marjorie Hendrickson, social worker for the Lane County children's services department*

"Buy her a Rice Paddy Baby, a sort of Asian Cabbage Patch doll. She won't care that it comes with its own passport, but she will like having a doll that looks like she does."

The U.S. Government has a double standard. While it allows Americans to adopt babies born in foreign countries, it does not allow foreigners to adopt babies born in the United States.

Not every Third World country places its babies on the export ramp. North Korea, for instance, prohibits it. And some First World countries don't let their citizens adopt from abroad: Great Britain and Japan have laws against it.

In South Korea, however, the adoption business is so efficient that it perpetuates itself. It serves as a sort of safety valve for the social problems of unwed mothers and abandoned children. Rather than address the discrimination against unwed mothers and orphans, the society simply strips the one and exports the other.

That's why some Korean social workers want to put a stop to foreign adoptions. As alternatives, they say, unwed mothers could be supported by the government instead of shunned. And the government could make a more aggressive effort at promoting in-country adoptions.

"I haven't heard the government appeal to the people to adopt Korean children," says Kim Oknah of the Korean Association for Volunteer Effort. "I haven't seen anything on television, radio, or in the newspapers, and I've lived in this country all my life. If the government had a special campaign on this issue, the Korean people would follow gradually."

The babies are crying. United Flight 876 from Kimpo International Airport to San Francisco and Chicago is taking off with five Korean infants aboard, ranging from three to eight months old. They come from Holt Children's Services, and they are headed for Baltimore.

"I'm just the escort," says Kim J.D., who seems frazzled by the responsibility of keeping track of the infants with two other Korean adults. "This is my third time." Kim gave Holt a donation of about $250, and the agency paid for his one-way ticket. He just met the five infants that afternoon at Holt's headquarters in Seoul.

Many of the women passengers take turns consoling and cuddling the infants. "She's so cute," one woman says. "I wish I could keep her."

"Don't fall too much in love," the stewardess responds. "They already belong to someone." ■

HUGO SPADAFORA'S LAST DAY

A murder in Panama undoes a regime

Guillermo Sánchez Borbón

Guillermo Sánchez Borbón is a columnist for La Prensa, *a Panamanian newspaper closed by the government last summer. He is now living in exile in Miami. His report "Panama Fallen Among Thieves" appeared in the December 1987 issue of* Harper's Magazine.

The story's the same, only the details vary. Belshazzar had to drink from the temple vessels, Nixon had to record himself on tape. One little luxury, one extra nibble, and after that the fellow's days are numbered, down he comes. So it will be with General Manuel Antonio Noriega. His days, too, are numbered, and no longer much fun—all because of one measly self-indulgence. He had an enemy murdered—but not discreetly. And now the murdered man is taking revenge. He, Noriega, will wind up in exile, if not in prison or the next world.

I know, I know! Why go to all the trouble of becoming a despot if you can't have an enemy tortured and beheaded? What can I tell you? Life's unfair.

Here is how his excess undid him: In the fall of 1983, Noriega flew to Washington to help Secretary of State George Shultz and CIA Director William Casey pick the next puppet president of Panama, the fig leaf of democracy that squeamish Uncle Sam absolutely required to mask the gross facts of military dictatorship. The choice fell on a former student of Shultz's, Nicolás Ardito Barletta. His election was put through by fraud the following May. For the most part, Barletta proved an obedient puppet, but even he couldn't stomach what happened to Dr. Hugo Spadafora in September 1985. When Spadafora's family called for the creation of a special commission to investigate the crime and bring the murderers to justice, Barletta agreed to name one. Which Noriega could not tolerate, so he tossed Barletta out of office. But Barletta the fig leaf was also the forbidden fruit. Noriega could traffic in drugs and arms, torture to his heart's ease, murder whom he cared to, and his protector, the United States, would look the other way; but he must not touch Nicky Barletta, the choice of Bill Casey and George Shultz. When he did, Noriega began his fall from grace. Soon he was the darkest of evils to Washington—a drug-dealing dictator.

There you have it, the same old story, the whole enterprise lost for one moment of fun—or, in Noriega's case, one afternoon and maybe Hugo's head to keep as a trophy. How often Noriega must replay that day in his mind, the day he went too far, the day my friend Hugo died the awful death that would come to haunt a country and its tyrant.

On the day they were going to kill him—Friday the thirteenth of September 1985—Dr. Hugo Spadafora got up at six in the morning to do his yoga. Later, after his shower, he put on a striped, long-sleeved shirt and coffee-colored trousers and had breakfast with his wife

Ariadne. Then he packed a bag, a canvas sports bag, placing in it his diary (it was book-size, bound in vinyl, with a page for each day, the sort professionals keep for noting appointments) and some copies of the memoir he'd published in 1980. He'd been living in San José, Costa Rica, and commuting to the war in Nicaragua, but today he was going home to Panama.

He was then in his forty-sixth year, and fourth revolution. At twenty-five, when other graduates of the Facoltà di Medicina in Bologna were thinking of setting up practice and getting ahead, he joined the struggle for independence in Portuguese Guinea (now Guinea-Bissau) and served two years as a *guerrillero* medic. Next came the bogus revolution in Panama proclaimed by Brigadier General Omar Torrijos Herrera, after he and a group of officers seized power in October 1968 and established the dictatorship that endures to this writing. Hugo opposed it at first and landed in prison. Later he joined the government, seduced by Torrijos's populist rhetoric; for a time he was the vice minister of health.

Then, in 1978, weary of being a bureaucrat and privately disillusioned by the corruption around him, he raised a band of resolutes and went off to Nicaragua to fight Somoza, staying on until the fall of Managua the following year. By 1982 he was back in Nicaragua, this time with the *contras*—a restless man, operatically handsome, haunted by compassion for the downtrodden and the lust to have a cause, to be in action.

Hugo's intention was to get back into politics. He had already accused Noriega of trading in cocaine

Now, in the late summer of 1985, he was disillusioned again—and at the same time drawn to a new adventure. Early in September he'd met with agents of the U.S. Drug Enforcement Administration at the American embassy and offered them information about *contra* drug dealings with Noriega. He'd already accused Noriega publicly of being a tyrant as well as trading in cocaine; and in August he'd announced his intention to return to Panama and get back into politics. The trip he was making today, September 13, was preparatory to a permanent relocation.

The route he chose was somewhat circuitous: light plane south from San José to a rural airstrip near the border; taxi eight miles from there to the frontier; minibus from Paso Canoa on the Panamanian side to David, the capital of Chiriquí Province; long-haul bus from David to Panama City. A precaution of sorts, but not a particularly unusual one: he'd gone the same way several times before. And anyway, caution wasn't Hugo's method. His brother Winston remembers him at age ten, taking a dare and jumping from the bridge over Río La Villa, something no other boy in the town of Chitré would do. His life thereafter demonstrated much the same attitude. He wasn't fearless. He simply didn't let fear affect his behavior.

He left his house in San José around nine and crossed into Panama a bit before noon.

Into Panama. The words have taken on a sinister resonance. Once a fortunate country, remarkably civilized, where *carnaval* was said to be the only thing people took seriously, Panama had become a place of darkness. It had fallen among thieves, then come into the clutch of an interesting monster. But you know him.*

Understanding him is something different, though his early life seems to offer some hints. No father, mother a servant. Abandoned by her at age five, dumped in a foster home. Here were the makings of a frightful insecurity, later transposed into a towering will to power. And a bottomless envy. There is the motive, I think, for what happened to Hugo—more than the disclosures Hugo was making or the threat he posed as a political rival—and for how he was murdered if not why. Hugo was a doctor. Noriega wished to study medicine but missed the chance. Hugo was handsome. Noriega is, in the kindest term, grotesque. And Hugo had the daily beauty in his life that the General envied, the gift of health, the gift of youth (that is to say, of enthusiasm), the capacity to care for things outside himself. Noriega, on the other hand...

But there are many disadvantaged orphans. Not all become monsters, much less world-class. Nor was Noriega entirely deprived. He had good schooling, for instance. Panama once provided good public education, spent a larger portion of the budget on it than did any other country in the region. Noriega and Hugo went to the same high school. Both received sufficient preparation to win scholarships for study abroad, in Noriega's case to Peru's military academy. But you know about Noriega, his military life. In my part of the world the military fulfills no function (unless abuse of the citizenry be considered one).

Into Panama—a conquered country; a subject people; an occupying force so corrupt and brutal it came within an eyelash of being indicted by a Miami grand jury as a continuing criminal enterprise; and a pitiless despot with the CIA wrapped round his finger, with Washington's blessing and support, with no restraints whatsoever on the gratification of his several lusts. This was the Panama Hugo crossed into.

He had lunch in Paso Canoa before board-

**Since then his corrugated face has blotched your TV screens, his résumé has stained your newspapers and the pages of this magazine. Trafficker in drugs, trafficker in weapons. Spy for the CIA and Cuba and God knows who else. Thief, assassin, and torturer. Oppressor of his people, vendor of his country, distributor of terror and despair. Time was when all this was known only in Panama, and in the inner circles of the U.S. government, where he was considered a pearl without price. Now, the rock, as it were, has been lifted, and the slimy thing wriggling underneath... As I've said, you know him.*

ing the minibus—rabbit stew with rice and potato salad at a place called Los Mellos, a shack with tables beside it under a metal roof set up on posts, behind the bus station a few yards from the border. The owner, Iván García, remembers. He remembered later that month, when Panamanian authorities maintained that Hugo never crossed the border, and when other witnesses were intimidated. García, whose friends call him "El Guapo" ("Gutsy"), did honor to his nickname by coming forward and telling the truth. Yes, Hugo was in Panama. Hugo lunched at his café. Hugo ate quickly, was in a hurry. (And, yes, Hugo was in a hurry to get to Panama City. He was supposed to meet his wife at the airport when she flew in from San José.) Before he left, he gave "El Guapo" a copy of his memoirs.

At 12:15 P.M. Hugo got onto a green and white Toyota Coaster minibus, owned and run by the David-Frontera bus line, plate number 4B-52. It was driven that afternoon by Alexis Baules, with Edwin Nuñez as his assistant. A man in dark glasses got on behind Hugo. This was Francisco Eliécer González, a sergeant in the Panama Defense Forces (PDF) and an agent of the G-2, the intelligence service, stocked by Noriega with men of his own character and loyal to him. González is a short, stocky man with Indian features and skin the color of mahogany. He wore dark trousers with a black sleeveless jersey and a cream-colored corduroy cap with little buckles on the sides. González knows some karate and is said to have a violent nature, and for these traits goes by the nickname of "Bruce Lee." The bus pulled out as soon as they were seated.

A man in dark glasses got on the bus behind Hugo: an agent of the G-2, the intelligence service

It would help to know where, exactly—which seats they rode in. I would like to talk to more people. But I cannot go to Panama. I face a five-year prison term, a death sentence really, for the "crime" of looking into my friend Hugo's murder and publishing some of what I found out. Nor would it be prudent as things stand now, in the turbulent spring of 1988, for anyone acting for me, no matter how secretly, to interview *señores* Baules and Nuñez. But it is my duty to relive those last hours of Hugo's, and every minor detail is helpful.

I know what he saw from the bus window: low hills, very green at that time of the year, broken each mile or so by *quebradas* that flow southwest into the Chiriquí River (which, in its turn, flows southeast into the Pacific)—Quebrada Gapacho, Quebrada Jacú, Quebrada La Conga. The sun I am sure was fierce, the day hot and humid, suffocatingly so, whenever the bus stopped. I just wish I knew where Hugo and González sat.

I'll make a guess. I'd have gone as far to the rear of the bus as I could, so as not to have González sitting behind me—G-2 agents are notorious louts. But since Hugo didn't let fear affect his behavior, I'll guess he sat toward the front of the bus, on the right side. In that bus the right-side seats are single. If so, González sat in the row behind him, sprawled across two seats, on the left.

At Jacú, two miles south of the border, is the first of several checkpoints set up by the PDF to control immigration. Here a guard boarded the vehicle to check the passengers' documents. He asked Hugo to get off the bus, treatment normally reserved for those whose documents are not in order. But Hugo had received this treatment on previous occasions, and so he remained calm. He went into the guard post, sat down, took a newspaper from the desk there, and began reading. González got off the bus behind him, without being asked, and paid Nuñez, the assistant, forty cents—the fare from Paso Canoa to Jacú—as if he had reached his destination. Shortly after that Nuñez heard a guard say, "Go ahead, Hugo, it's all right." Hugo got back on the bus. And so did González. As Nuñez turned to get on, he heard someone behind him in the guard post say, "The great Hugo Spadafora!" When the bus started up, he whispered to Baules, "We've got Hugo Spadafora with us."

At the second checkpoint, eight miles further on, Hugo was again asked to get off, then again allowed back on board to continue his journey. This time, though, González stayed put. The bus continued another eight miles to the town of Concepción, halting first at the outskirts, then at the bus stop beside the park, a short walk from the PDF *cuartel*—the barracks, that is, and district headquarters. Here, as passengers were getting off, González got up and went beside Hugo and, gesturing toward the door, said, "Come with me." According to Nuñez's declaration (made after "El Guapo" had set an example for him), Hugo looked at González with a kind of laugh, as if to say, "Who are you to be making this kind of invitation?" Then González took Hugo's bag from the rack, and saying, "Allow me," as one might to a lady or an old man, carried it off the bus. Hugo followed.

Hugo followed González past Nuñez, who stood at the door of the bus, then turned round and took his identity card out of his shirt pocket and showed it to the bus man. "So you'll know who I am. I'm Dr. Hugo Spadafora." Then he turned back to González, who had stopped a few paces off, and said, "Give me the bag, I'll go with you."

As Hugo and González walked toward the corner, Baules reminded Nuñez that Hugo hadn't paid. Nuñez ran after him.

"Are you staying, señor?"

"I'm being detained by this member of the Defense Forces."

"Then the driver says to please pay me the fare."

Hugo paid Nuñez one dollar twenty. When the bus pulled away, he and González were on the corner opposite the Montero Dental Clinic by the park in Concepción. That was the last time any civilian saw Dr. Hugo Spadafora alive.

It was one o'clock in the afternoon or thereabouts when Francisco Eliécer González and Omar Vega Miranda brought Dr. Hugo Spadafora into the *cuartel* at Concepción. Vega Miranda, too, was a PDF sergeant. He'd been on duty that day at the first checkpoint, and the likelihood is that he followed bus 4B-52 in a PDF vehicle to back up González in case of trouble. There was none. The openness of the surveillance and arrest no doubt calmed Hugo, suggested petty harassment, nothing grave. But when the door of the *cuartel* closed behind him, he was lost utterly, as if the waters of the deep had closed over his head. He still had seven hours or so to suffer, though, which my duty now is to relive and relate.

Hugo Spadafora was made to suffer in the towns of Concepción and Alanje, and near the villages of Canto Gallo, Santo Tomas, and Estero Rico in Chiriquí Province. He was murdered in a place called Corozo, not even a village—once an agricultural station, then a PDF outpost, today totally razed, wiped from the earth. The officer in charge that day at the *cuartel* in Concepción was Sublieutenant Edgardo Jaramillo. Major Luis Córdoba was in command in Chiriquí Province. The puppet President of Panama was Nicolás Barletta. The country's *de facto* ruler was Manuel Noriega.

In Concepción, probably, Hugo was simply beaten

In Concepción, probably, Hugo was simply beaten. The PDF abuse everyone they take into custody, insult them, threaten them, shove them around. Hugo had an irascible nature. He would have resisted. That would have meant blows. Not too many, however. It would never have done to damage him before his suffering could be properly administered—carried out and savored by people of greater refinement in such matters than are likely to have been on hand. The autopsy performed on Hugo's corpse in Costa Rica found evidence of severe and prolonged beating, but I doubt that he got much of it in Concepción. My guess is he was thumped once or twice on the kidneys with a truncheon or rifle butt, then stuffed in a cell while the joyful news of his capture was relayed to higher-ups. I don't mean to say I think the news *surprised* them. The "operation" that followed wasn't an impromptu affair. I'm sure the PDF knew exactly when Hugo left San José, probably knew it the moment he booked his passage.

In Alanje, ten miles southwest along the Pan-American Highway, then another six miles due south on a secondary road, Hugo's suffering may have been entirely mental. Panama's chief torturer was in Alanje that day. And why shouldn't he be, the town was his birthplace? I cannot name him here because I do not know *for sure* that he took part in what happened to Hugo. But I can't imagine his having missed it. He'd have never forgiven himself. More importantly, he'd have never forgiven those who left him out of the fun. What's certain is that Hugo passed through Alanje that day in a military vehicle. If the gentleman I've alluded to joined him, Hugo would have experienced severe mental suffering. He'd have known then and there that he was going to be tortured.

By mid-afternoon it was already evening in Paris. Why bring up Paris? Because General Manuel Noriega was there. Nine days earlier he'd been in Cuzco, Peru, for a meeting with Bolivian drug lord William Pizarro—this according to the Council on Hemispheric Affairs in Washington, which says the subject discussed was Hugo Spadafora, his declarations to the DEA, and what should be done with him. Now Hugo had been taken by the PDF and was about to be horribly tortured and murdered, yet General Manuel Noriega was out of the country. Odd, don't you think? No, not really. Noriega had been similarly out of Panama when Dr. Mauro Zúñiga, another physician who'd criticized Noriega, was kidnapped by the paramilitary gang known as F-8*; they smashed one of his ribs and carved a two-inch-high "F-8" in his shoulder. And out of sight doesn't always mean out of mind. That afternoon—or evening, if you were in Paris—the National Security Agency of the United States monitored a conversation between Major Luis Córdoba in Chiriquí Province and General Manuel Noriega in Paris, part of which went as follows:

He'd have known then and there, in Alanje, that he was going to be tortured

CORDOBA: We have the rabid dog.
NORIEGA: And what does one do with a dog that has rabies?

And now I will tell you what they did to Hugo near the villages of Canto Gallo and Santo Tomas and Estero Rico. These are tiny villages near the sea, and they took Hugo from one to another, like a band of carousers dragging the groom from cantina to cantina on the last night of his bachelorhood. The land there is swampy, low fields and, toward the sea, great clutches of mangroves from which one emerges as from a tunnel onto the beach—lovely, long,

**F-8 is composed of members of the military, absolutely trustworthy men. But no more punctual than other Panamanians. In June 1985, they were supposed to murder Dr. Zúñiga; they kidnapped him cleanly enough in Veraguas Province, but a few hours late, after he'd left Chiriquí Province, where the military commander was Luis Córdoba, a Noriega resolute. The commander in Veraguas didn't want corpses littering his district, so Zúñiga's life was spared.*

white-sand beaches pounded gently by the unsoilable Pacific. According to the local *campesinos*, Hugo's murderers took him down to the various beaches and away from the houses, no doubt so that his howling would not be heard. A beach party then, a perambulating fiesta, with a fresh salt breeze and warm sunlight and the beat of gentle surf.

Who were they? Members of F-8. Military men. Noriega's men.

And General Manuel Noriega himself, don't forget him. He was there in spirit. And there via the telephone too, it wouldn't surprise me. He doesn't get around much anymore, now that he's a fugitive from United States justice, but back then he traveled all the time, yet managed to stay in touch. His communications hookup included an open satellite line and a "repeater" in his house in Panama City, so that all one had to do was dial the number there to get Manny anywhere in the world. (Cost: $5,000 a day.) Did they patch a line to a two-way radio so that Noriega could listen to Hugo's howling and get a running commentary? It wouldn't surprise me.

The cook hurriedly sawed off Hugo's head, amid sprays of blood

And what did they do to Hugo? They jabbed sharp objects under his fingernails, the blade of a knife or bamboo slivers or something similar. That, I think, was the first course, though they were beating him all the while, and vilifying him and screaming threats and insults, and laughing at him, making fun of his pain. I say "first course" because although the pain is exquisite—as anyone knows who's done it by mistake, driven something sharp underneath a fingernail—there's no sense of being mutilated. Stick something under a nail, and it hurts very badly, but you know it will heal up and you'll be all right. The real horror is in knowing that one is being smashed permanently, busted up, wrecked for good.

Did they question him? I think they did. Not because he had secrets they wanted, but to give what they were doing a semblance of necessity. I suppose they asked him what he'd told the DEA, whom had he met with, and so forth; and this, sooner or later, he told them. That didn't matter. They tortured Hugo to calm Noriega's envy, and because they enjoy torturing people.

At one point Hugo was stripped naked. With appropriate tweaks and pinches, I imagine, degrading little prods and feels. And then someone took a sharp knife and made two careful, deep, symmetrical cuts, one along the inside of each of his legs, from just above his knee to mid-thigh. The point here was to disable Hugo's leg muscles, so that he'd be unable to close his legs, and thus unable to disturb the pleasure they meant to take of him next. Of everything I've learned about Hugo's sufferings, this is what troubles me most. It argues that Hugo's ordeal was nothing special, that many others had suffered similarly at the hands of the degenerate who now rules Panama. Those neat, symmetrical cuts show anatomic knowledge and practical experience. Without them someone would have had to hold Hugo's legs, a tiresome thing in our tropical climate. And think of the added torment to Hugo, the incapacity, the hideous helplessness. Perhaps the expertise implicit in those cuts was what General John Galvin, then of the Southern Command, and other U.S. officials were referring to in their repeated praise of the PDF's professionalism.

Aside from those cuts, the proceedings followed more long-standing tradition. For instance, something was rammed up Hugo's rectum, a pole of some sort or perhaps just a piece of driftwood, for the autopsy showed that his rectum was badly deformed. The act is commonplace, expressive of what seems to be a widespread pathology. Damage to the prostate gland means permanent sexual impairment. And I guess it makes cowardly perverts feel brave and manly. I don't know what they used on Hugo. I know he screamed, I know his tormentors chortled. Reliving the scene as clearly as I dare to, I also know why people invented the concept of Hell. There ought to be a place for those tormentors. That they are in Panama fills me with shame and fury.

As for the rest . . . they beat him. On the back. Blows to the kidneys are especially painful. I see him lying face down in the sand, with the pole or whatever it was being worked by one of them while others beat him on the kidneys. And on the genitals. The autopsy found his testicles monstrously swollen. For Hugo the world became an endless howl.

Then I see them, winded by exertion and pleasure, flop down on the sand beside and around their obscenity—panting, chuckling to one another as they prod it with sticks, then heave themselves up and drag it to the vehicle, dump it inside, get in, and go off with wan smiles to another beach for another round of fun.

When they were finished, spent or sated if you like, they broke two of his ribs, perhaps with a rifle butt. (This has some ritual meaning for them.) And then, like honest craftsmen, they signed their work, using a needle of some sort and indelible ink to tattoo "F-8" on Hugo's shoulder. And the sun went down, as on any other evening, hovering splendidly, then dunking itself in the ocean. And the stars came out, and maybe the moon also. I could look that up, find out if the moon shone that night, and if so, if it was full or half or quarter, but I'm sick of reliving that day, I've had enough.

There is one last station in Hugo's calvary: between seven and eight on the evening of September 13, 1985, Dr. Hugo Spadafora was brought to the PDF outpost at Corozo in a military vehicle—he was very badly battered but still alive. They put him on the cement floor of the barracks, which had been the director's house when the place was still an agricultural station. The cook in the detachment sat down astraddle Hugo's chest and plunged a butcher knife into his throat. Hugo made a spasmodic movement. At that, the cook hurriedly sawed off Hugo's head, amid sprays of blood and horripilating gurgles.

Hugo Spadafora's head was buried in the yard in front of the barracks. His headless body was put into a U.S. mailbag—how it was obtained, I don't know—and loaded back onto the vehicle that had brought him. It was then driven into Costa Rica, convoyed by another vehicle. The border in that region runs along a road. Crossing back and forth is no problem. At a place in Costa Rica called El Roblito the body was dumped in a ravine. On their way back, the soldiers stopped at a banana-packing station called Balsa and washed both vehicles. Like Corozo, the PDF outpost, Balsa has since been demolished, razed, swept from the earth.

At Corozo, soldiers heated water and scrubbed the floor. Then they got infernally drunk.

Another drinking party was held on Coiba Island, in an area called Playa Hermosa—the area, ironically enough, where seven years earlier the volunteer force raised by Hugo Spadafora received training before going off to Nicaragua to fight Somoza. A great celebration was held that night; it went on loudly till early morning.

On Monday, September 16, a yellow dog began whining and scraping nervously near the spot where Hugo's head was buried. The soldiers shot the dog. That night they dug up Hugo's head and took it I don't know where.

ALONG THE STREETS OF TEHRAN

Life under Khomeini

John Simpson

John Simpson is the diplomatic editor of BBC television news. His book Inside Iran *will be published later this year by St. Martin's Press.*

We shook hands in the dark, my friend and I, standing on the doorstep of his house. Behind him, in the passageway, carpets glowed in the faint golden light of a lamp, and books glimmered on the walls as we said our good-byes. We had passed an enjoyable evening talking about the state of the outside world, and he had given me the latest news of our friends in Iran. The dinner had been good, too: *chelo kebab* and a pomegranate sorbet, in a quiet restaurant not far away. It would be months, perhaps longer, before I would be back in Tehran, and we would see each other again. But my friend was not one to parade his emotions: having shaken my hand, he turned and went inside. The lock clicked audibly before I was five yards down the road.

Like most people who go by car around a city, I had no idea how long it would take to walk to where I wanted to go. The journey to his house from my hotel—the Intercontinental, now renamed the Laleh, *laleh* meaning tulip, the flower of martyrdom—had taken twenty minutes by taxi in Tehran traffic earlier that evening; but I didn't want to taxi back. I wanted to walk in Tehran, and do some observing and thinking.

My friend thought it would take me an hour to walk to the hotel, a poor estimate, as it turned out. I headed off optimistically, walking fast and sampling the warm night air—air laced with that faint, agreeable savor I think of as characteristic of Iranian cities: the smell of heat and sun-dried brick and cow dung. Around me in the darkness was the sound of voices.

Persians are among the most sociable people on earth, and at midnight they are still to be found on the Tehran streets, chatting to acquaintances, parading up and down, driving slowly around to see what's going on. It was this way at the time of my first visit, in the months before the Shah quit Iran in January 1979. And it remains so, despite the Islamic Revolution and all that the revolution has changed. Since the revolution, I have visited Iran a number of times. I believe I have come to know the country as well as anyone can without actually living there; I have traveled around Iran freely and at will, and have established a network of friends and contacts—supporters and opponents of the regime alike. I have developed an abiding love for the people of Iran, which no amount of fanaticism or cruelty, and there has been much of both, has altogether killed.

It is impossible for me, and perhaps any non-Muslim of the West, to accept the revolution in Iran entirely on its own terms: it constitutes too much of a challenge to Western values. The Islamic Republic of Iran is not a Western democracy, and the country's leaders have no intention of creating one. The republic, established after the overthrow of the Pahlavi monarchy, is based not on Enlightenment principles but largely upon Islamic principles formulated in the seventh century and little understood, much less accepted, in the West. The revolution was consolidated brutally. All political parties that opposed the Islamic Republic were eventually banned. There were executions not only of former members of the Shah's army and secret police but of many who had participated in the Shah's overthrow—members of moderate and left-wing parties, intellectuals, and so on. No one is sure how many men and women were executed in the first years of the revolution; Amnesty International has learned of 2,444 executions in the second half of 1981 alone.

I cannot simply accept this. But I have found it equally impossible to accept the demonization of Iran that has taken place in the West, and in the United States in particular: the caricature projected by politicians and commentators who imagine Iran to be a crazed wasteland of fanatics and their victims, a country governed by madmen and peopled by their unquestioning followers. The truth is, as always, much more complicated. No matter how some among the Shi'ite mullahs—who are still the political driving-force of the country—might wish to return Iran to the seventh-century ethic of the Holy Koran, it has not proved possible in practice; the complex, subtle-minded culture of the Persians has ensured that. People obey the rules outwardly, because the penalties for disobedience are considerable; but men and women in Iran and in particular Tehran, which I have come to know best during my stays, live in a variety of ways, guided by a variety of desires, values, and interests. In this way, they are not so different from you and me.

And this is especially true now—now that the post-revolution terror appears to have run its course, and since Ayatollah Khomeini's twelve-point declaration, made at the end of 1982, that people are to be allowed to lead lives in private as they wish. Families split by the revolution are beginning to coalesce again. Some exiles are trying to make their peace with the authorities, returning if only for a visit. Among the middle class, at least, there is less praying, fewer visits to the mosque. Everywhere, there are signs that the early revolutionary fervor has waned.

The caricaturing of Iran not only blurs the complexity of the country but serves to erase its history, and our role in it. What extremism there has been must be understood—perhaps chiefly understood—as a response to the way the West once behaved in Iran. The revolution of 1978–79 was largely a reaction to the corruption and the impatient Westernization that had characterized the last half-dozen years under the Shah; but beyond that, it was a rebellion against a century of virtual colonialism by Britain, and later by the United States, who together gave Iran its rulers and governed through them from London and then Washington. In Iran before the revolution, the press was muzzled, as were independent political parties; and SAVAK, the fearsome secret police, was responsible for countless tortures and deaths. Over the years both Britain and the United States helped the Shah defeat the more moderate forms of opposition to this state of affairs. And that made the emergence of Khomeini's far fiercer Islamic opposition something of an inevitability.

Who on either side of the Atlantic now remembers that the British joined with Stalin to dismember Iran during World War II, deposing Reza Shah in 1941 and placing his son Mohammad Reza on the Peacock Throne? Or that the CIA, with British help, engineered the overthrow of the lawful government of Mohammad Mossadeq in 1953 and brought back the Shah after he had fled the country? Or that Washington demanded and received for its military personnel legal immunity in Iranian courts if they committed crimes in the country? Or—to take just one example of everyday arrogance—that American employees used to ride their motorcycles around the center of at least one major city at night, threatening and scattering the locals? Americans (and the British too) have a tendency to react to the history of their doings in other people's countries like drunks about some spectacularly dreadful scene at a party the night before: *O God, did I really do all that?* And however much we ourselves may try to excuse our embarrassing behavior or put it out of our minds, the resentful hosts do not. We cannot begin to understand Iran—"Iranian anti-Americanism" most of all—until we understand this, that we are not innocent.

Outside in the warm, pungent, sociable darkness, I left my friend's house behind me. In many ways Tehran has changed not much at all in the past ten years. In the mornings, streets are still clogged with Paykans, the popular car built from kits exported by a British car manufacturer. The Tehran bazaar, the great block of shops and businesses at the center of the city, remains Iran's economic heart: a stock exchange, banking system, and commodities market masquerading as a collection of hucksters' stalls. There was no planning in the Shah's days, and there is none now—the city sprawls. But the Shah's road-building schemes have been continued, as has his program to afforest the city's edge.

There are differences, however, some of them noticeable at once. The city is more crowded: the population of Tehran has gone from 6 million in 1978 to more than 10 million today, swelled by those searching for work or social-welfare payments; by refugees who lost their homes along the border areas when Iraq invaded in 1980; by Afghans who fled the Soviet invasion of their country. The city has decayed too. Tehran was drab and dirty under the Shah, but it looks worse now—one sees more rusted metal, more dirt, more shops with broken signs, more shops closed up for good. Boom businesses, like everywhere in the world it seems, are in video rentals and fast-foods. During my previous walks and rides around the city, I had seen an old Colonel Sanders's sign changed to one of a smiling Iranian ("Our Fried Chicken") and even a MacAli's. And I had seen too what Americans used to see each night, the American Embassy. It is well guarded, and the sign says, in approximated English: "Center of Publication for U.S. Espionage Den of Documents."

My way now took me close to a barracks that belonged to the Revolutionary Guards, the *pasdaran*, and there was a roadblock at the end of this street. A couple of bored *pasdars* in yellowish green uniforms sat on upturned boxes, talking and playing with the worry beads that are called *tasbih* in Farsi. I had a *tasbih* of my own in my pocket, and I fiddled nervously with its silver beads as I walked toward the *pasdars*. The Revolutionary Guards, formally established by Ayatollah Khomeini in May 1979, are the eyes and ears, and the avenging hands, of the Islamic regime; they bear the brunt of the fighting in the Gulf war with Iraq (the *pasdaran* form a separate force from the regular army). The *pasdars*, together with their civilian counterparts, the local revolutionary committees or *komitehs*, control the country and provide the regime with protection against a possible uprising or military coup. The *komitehs* sprang up throughout the country after the revolution. In 1979, there were 1,500 such committees in Tehran alone. The *komitehs* serve both as local security forces and as the agents of revolutionary authorities: they might guard buildings, confiscate property, or hustle someone off to prison. The committees still exist in every place of work and in every section of the town or city, checking on the way people behave.

But nowadays the *komitehs* and the *pasdaran* have done their work so effectively that there are no perceptible challenges to the authority of the regime, and they don't appear to be interested in the movements of wandering foreigners. The two *pasdars* at their roadblock took no notice of me, beyond waving me past. I said my thank-yous, and one of them placed his hand politely over his heart by way of reply.

Out in the main part of the street, despite the late hour, half-a-dozen boys and girls, eight-year olds by my reckoning, were playing soccer with a tin can. A beefy girl stormed past and scored a goal, and the others, their attention momentarily relaxed, stared at me as I walked past. The *pasdars* might not have been interested in me, but the fact is that Westerners are almost as rare as an unveiled woman in Iran today; there are probably fewer than two hundred Westerners in the entire country, leaving aside the European or American wives of Iranian citizens. The children may have been seeing a first.

The noise of the soccer game faded behind me as I turned right into a narrow side street, and started climbing the slow gradient northwards. I was emulating the movement of the city itself, which began in the plain and had shifted gradually during the course of the twentieth century toward the north, into the foothills of the magnificent Elburz Mountains that separate Tehran from the Caspian Sea. Or rather, I was emulating the movement of the well-to-do, since the city itself has spread across the plain in less attractive directions too. Only the rich have been able to head up toward the cool, green hill villages; and North Tehran has become a continuous string of pleasant suburbs, linked by noisy roads to the city proper.

The streetlights were on, but they were few in number and faint. I leaped across an open ditch—one of the *jubs* characteristic of Tehran. The *jubs* bring water from the mountain streams down into the center of the city; they provide everything from drinking water to ready trash cans. As I leaped, I immediately cursed myself for my carelessness. The paving stones were broken and uneven, and in the semi-darkness I could have broken my ankle if I had landed badly.

That was, however, the only danger to which I exposed myself by walking through the Tehran streets that night. Tehran is not Beirut, a wild, lawless, Hobbesian nightmare of a place, where there is continual fear and danger of violent death, and where gangs of kidnappers roam the streets. And although we are sometimes inclined to imagine that Iran, too, is a wild lawless place because of the things its leaders say in their country (and its exiles say in ours), it is in fact a strictly ordered society. This was so under the Shah, while he had authority, and the far greater control exerted by the *komitehs* since the revolution has ensured that violent street crime is rare.

Iran's system of justice is, of course, one of the things we feel we know most about in Iran: the whipping, the cutting off of hands and feet, the stoning to death. There is no question but that political repression in Iran was fierce in the early 1980s. Faced with separatist movements in various parts of the country, and with an armed insurrection by the left-wing People's Mojahedin movement in which dozens of leading clerics and hundreds of government officials—

including the country's president, secretary general, and four cabinet ministers—were assassinated, the regime instituted its own campaign of terror: arbitrary arrests; beatings and torture; summary trials; public hangings and firing squads. Harsh punishment for those who oppose the regime continues, though not on the previous scale. In 1986, Amnesty International recorded 115 executions (though it believes this figure to be well below the true total).

Facts about harsh punishments meted out by Iranian courts for non-political offenses are more difficult to obtain. Supporters of the regime are inclined to play down the extent of such punishments. An ayatollah who was also a judge—the judiciary has been almost completely taken over by the clerics, and Islamic penal codes have been written into the statute books—told me that there were so many conditions that had to be fulfilled before a thief's hand could be severed that in practice it was almost impossible to impose amputation as a punishment; the same applied to execution by stoning. And yet the Iranian newspapers have reported a couple of dozen cases of amputation and a number of executions by stoning since the revolution in 1979—perhaps ordered by judges who were less particular than the ayatollah I spoke with. Drug peddling has been the crime most likely to result in grisly sentences. (Drug use, a problem under the Shah, continues to be a problem, particularly now that the drug of choice is no longer opium but heroin.)

Whipping is a more routine punishment. Someone who had been whipped for possessing alcohol told me that in Iran it is as commonplace as the fine for a driving offense is in the West. You are taken to court, and if found guilty are escorted to the courthouse basement where two rather bored men tie you onto a low table and proceed to carry out the sentence—in the case of the man I spoke to, twenty-five painful lashes with a cane, which started at the neck and traveled progressively down to the ankles, before moving upwards to the neck again. Such punishments—amputations, stonings, whippings—are difficult to accept or justify. But it should be said that they are carried out not only in Iran but in such "moderate" states as Saudi Arabia and the United Arab Emirates.

As I toiled up the hill, my earlier enthusiasm fading into mere determination, many of the walls I passed were smothered with posters of men's faces: smiling faces, serious faces, blurred faces, dead faces. These are the last offerings of parents and friends to the memory of those who had died in the war with Iraq, a war now more than seven years old. Respectful death notices, recalling little more than age, regiment, place of death, and the certainty of religious reward:

> The parents of Ali Tabrizi of the 521st infantry regiment announce the martyrdom of their son on the southern war front in the *Val-Fajr-8* offensive. His death, at the age of 28, was for God and the cause of religion.

Perhaps 300,000 like him have died, the victims of amateur tactics and of the knowledge that Iran's advantage lies in its overwhelming, squanderable manpower. (Iran's population of more than 46 million people is three times that of Iraq.) Aerial bombings of Tehran and other cities have also taken lives. There are economic costs as well: by 1984, the war and war-related activities were estimated to be absorbing one-third of the budget, or $10 billion a year. Oil refineries have been bombed and revenues have fallen. Gasoline, fuel, and staple foods are rationed, and in Tehran, one now sees people queuing, ration books in hand, for rice, meat, and butter.

Yet aside from the queues and the posters—and the occasional sandbagged emplacement—there are few signs in the streets of Tehran that Iran is fighting one of the bloodiest wars in history. The working class, which strongly supported the Islamic Revolution, supports the war still, if with less zeal. The bulk of those doing the fighting continue to be volunteers, though a haphazard draft system is in place. There is opposition to the war, some of it coming from within the regime, but it is neither loud nor effectively organized. Perhaps the strongest signs of opposition to the war are to be read in the faces of the middle-class people of Tehran. Their living standards have declined dramatically. They are most affected by the shortages the war has brought about. They are war weary.

A motor scooter passed me, with a man and two young women on it, their black *chadors* flapping in the wind. Scooters and motorbikes rarely seem to carry fewer than two or three people in Iran, but they have been given a faint protection in the difficult circumstances of the Tehran traffic: if you hit one with your car, it is automatically your fault. After the scooter had passed, the gurgling of the water in the *jub* was the only audible noise, apart from my own footfalls and the faint layer of sound that any city gives out at nighttime.

I passed the sandbagged entrance to a government building, and sized-up an attractive printed banner with the stern face of Ayatollah Khomeini, which hung outside. It occurred to me to take it, part of the spoils of my trip: but I changed my mind as the night watchman inside glanced up, alerted by the sound of my step on the uneven pavement. He was an elderly man with a beard: he could have been Khomeini's distant relative. The banner stayed where it was.

I looked ahead, toward the mountains. Somewhere up there, in the village of Jamaran, the head reproduced on the banner lay asleep on a Spartan pillow, surrounded by hundreds of guards and a million dollars' worth of security equipment. The Ayatollah, now eighty-five, is the Islamic Revolution's most valuable possession: its architect, its avatar, its final court of appeal. He takes little part in the day-to-day business of the government or the conduct of the war, but he sees his leading ministers regularly and is prepared, if he disagrees, to condemn their decisions in public. Khomeini's disapproval means political death for an aspiring politician; this may explain why, after seven years of a bloody and exhausting war, no group has surfaced to suggest the possibility of a negotiated end to the fighting. In other fields, where Khomeini does not have strong feelings, as he does about defeating Iraq, the political debate is intense and sometimes rowdy: within the narrow confines of the Islamic agenda there is something akin to democracy among the political leadership of Iran, and its parliament, the *majlis*, broadcasts its proceedings live on television.

"You Westerners," a senior figure in the official hierarchy had said musingly as I sat on the floor of his modest flat in East Tehran and emptied my plate of rice and *zereshk*, the sharp red berries that flavored it. "Why do you always talk about us as having power struggles while you yourselves merely have politics?" Now I thought that perhaps he had a point: we have the impression in the West that numerous obscure clerics are pressing round the aging form of Khomeini, waiting to take over power from him the moment death snatches it away. The reality is more complex. Khomeini's political power is based on his immense personal influence as leader of the revolution. But his constitutional position as supreme authority, or *faqih*—making him the court of last resort on all matters that touch upon Islamic law—derives from the Shi'ite concept of an Islamic jurisprudent who will be in overall charge of affairs until such time as the twelfth Imam returns to earth. When Khomeini dies, his position as supreme jurisprudent will be filled by another Grand Ayatollah or, if no single jurist is universally recognized as Khomeini came to be, by a council of jurists. In 1985, the special Council of Experts designated Ayatollah Hosain-Ali Montazeri as the successor to Khomeini as *faqih*—though some have interpreted the execution of Mehdi Hashemi, the relation of Montazeri's who leaked the news of the mission to Tehran by Oliver North and Robert McFarlane, as a sign that all may not go as smoothly as constitutionally planned.

The chances are that things will not change suddenly when Khomeini dies (and since his elder brother died in his mid-nineties Khomeini may well be with us for some time yet). A new *faqih* will be installed, or a council appointed. Day-to-day power will no doubt continue to be wielded by much the same loose, competing coalition of figures (Speaker of the Parliament Rafsanjani, President Khamene'i, Prime Minister Musavi, and so on) who wield it at present. But what will disappear with his death—and may be a factor down the road—will be his position as the nation's chief referee, the one person whose verdicts, because of his enormous political power, are universally accepted. Without him to keep the various political figures in check, power struggles may indeed overtake politics in Iran.

Khomeini today is not how Americans remember him from the days of the Shah's overthrow, which is when I first spoke with him. He is white, frail, his compelling voice now little more than a whisper. He has, somehow, an air of transparency, like a ghost in Shakespeare. Yet his words can still reduce a crowd of soldiers to tears, and rouse a group of businessmen to noisy defiance of Iraq and the United States. If he is frail, his power is not.

I passed an unfinished apartment building. In the first years after the revolution, there was little building construction, but now the government is starting to encourage it. Housing, especially for the urban poor, remains the problem it was under the Shah. The poor, who continue to stream to the city, often make do in shantytowns.

The window of a ground-floor flat in the unfinished building was open, and I stopped to peer in. Beneath the light of a bare bulb a couple lay fully clothed on a mattress. The woman was asleep, her black *chador* around her like a sleeping bag. The man rested on his back, his eyes open, staring at the light bulb as it moved slightly in the night air. He switched his gaze to me as I stood there: it was a frank, neutral look, not hostile in any way, but I muttered an apology and moved on. What right had I to intrude in his life, staring into his poverty as a visitor at a zoo might stare into an animal's cage? I heard him say something to the woman, and she groaned sleepily as I moved out of earshot.

There is poverty in Iran, as there was before the revolution, though beggars in the streets are rare, and even among the people living in the shantytowns in South Tehran there are few if any signs of actual malnutrition. The population in Iran is increasing by one of the highest rates in the Middle East, and this is making it worse for the poor. The dramatic oil-price decline that hit in the winter of 1985–86 jolted the economy; annual oil revenues, which reached an estimated $21 billion in 1983, plummeted to $10 billion in 1986. The official unemployment rate is 14 percent even with the buildup of the armed forces. But the regime has placed a moderate emphasis on welfare programs, despite revenue losses and war costs. And there have been stabs at land reform. Moreover, the poor have no doubt benefited psychologically from the fact that there has been a certain leveling throughout society of economic status—and have benefited as well from the fact that Iran's leaders are relatively modest men now.

The real victims of the revolution have been the average-income middle class: the officeworkers and teachers and civil servants. Hundreds of thousands, especially those with technical skills, left Iran after the mullahs came to power. For those who stayed, a single job is often insufficient to provide enough money to cope with the naggingly high inflation. I have met teachers who are taxi drivers in their spare time, and taxi drivers who double as night porters, and night porters who are training as teachers. All of them had the distracted look of men who guessed that they would not be able to stay afloat much longer.

A car moved sclerotically up the hill and was suddenly surrounded by the yellow beams of torches: the *basijis* had set up a roadblock to check for stolen cars or signs of drunkenness. *Basijis* are army volunteers, often trained for only a month or so before they are sent off to the war: Iran has some two million such volunteers and 200,000 of them are said to be at the front at one time. The *basijis* are the kind of men whom Western television news reports like to show on the parade ground beating their breasts in unison and chanting *Marg bar Amrika!*—Death to America! It gives them an air, in Western eyes, of manic dedication and malevolence, and it produces a frisson of horror and revulsion in us.

In fact, the *basijis* I've encountered tend to be mild enough fellows. I have never been shouted at or attacked in Iran in the years since the revolution took place. I have scarcely even been criticized there, except by government officials who disliked my reporting—officials of Western governments of course do likewise. Which is to say that there exists in Iran a sophisticated awareness that not every individual can be held responsible for the actions of his government. (I should also say that there are cruel exceptions to this rule: there are two Americans and an Englishman in Iranian jails. John Pattis has been sentenced to ten years' imprisonment for espionage on grounds that were clearly absurd; another American is being held on unspecified charges. Roger Cooper, a British journalist, is also being held as a spy but is likewise clearly innocent.)

"What were you looking for?" I asked a bespectacled *basiji* in my best Farsi. He had just waved the car driver on, and in the light of the torches I could see he had a pleasant face, smiling under his heavy mustache.

"Oh, the usual things," he said.

"You mean booze?"

He laughed. "Everything."

"What happens if you find something?"

"We don't often find anything." He laughed again.

A Jewish carpet dealer, a friend of a friend of mine, was stopped recently, not by the *basijis* but by the Revolutionary Guards—a more serious matter. It was on the main freeway out of Tehran to the west, and when they searched his car they found a bottle of homemade vodka under the front seat.

What's this? they asked, starting to get nasty. The small Jewish population of Iran (20,000–30,000), like the rather large Armenian one, has to be careful: the Revolutionary Guards don't like Jews or Armenians much. But I have neither seen nor heard of any routine persecution of these minorities as there has been of the Baha'is, decent and devout people who regard their faith as an improvement on Islam, a dangerous belief in Iran.

"I'm glad you asked me that," the carpet dealer said, thinking fast. "It's a bottle of vodka. Unopened, you notice."

The point was an important one; possession of an unopened bottle of alcohol could incur a penalty of twenty-five lashes from the courts, whereas indications that he had been drinking from the bottle would lead to a much heavier punishment: seventy-five lashes, at least.

And what do you think you're doing, carrying a bottle of vodka around with you?

"My friends," said the man, his years of carpet dealing standing him in good stead, "I'll be frank with you. I am not, as you may have realized, a Muslim. As a Jew, it is not against the law for me to drink alcohol. I bought this bottle of vodka—not something I often do, you understand—in order to be able to drink to the continuing health and lasting success of the great Imam Khomeini."

On your way, said one of the guards. They even handed him back the bottle.

The manufacture of vodka is one of the great underground achievements of modern Iran. It is not, as the carpet dealer pointed out, an offense for the non-Muslims to drink alcohol, or even to make it for their own consumption: it is simply an offense to make it for other people. But crime or not, the production and marketing of alcohol remains an industry in Iran, and an efficient one: the price of a liter of vodka, made from the best raisins, remains today what it was in 1979—a thousand rials, the equivalent of ten dollars in purchasing power. The ordering is done in coded terms, and the required number of containers will be delivered to your door.

Poured out in generous proportions and mixed with orange juice, a veritable Persian screwdriver, it has a memorable, slightly nutty taste.

Ahead of me, a couple wandered out of a small darkened *kucheh* or alley, holding hands. As they reached the better-lit street they relinquished their hold on one another and walked demurely up the hill, side by side. They seemed moderately well-to-do, and the girl wore jeans and high heels under her *chador*. A little farther on, they crossed the road and walked toward the entrance to a restaurant. A couple of Mercedes were parked outside, and there was a general sense of discreet money.

The rich in Iran are not as rich as they once were, but times are not exactly hard for them. The shops in the expensive parts of North Tehran still display gold Rolexes and Piagets set with diamonds, and the after-shaves and perfumes carry the best European names. The common complaint is less about money than about the boredom of life under the Islamic Republic. "This isn't living, it's just existing"—so many people said that to me when I visited North Tehran that it seemed they must have read it somewhere. Such people often make the best company for a Westerner in Iran. But when there is real hardship and real sacrifice in the air it is hard to sympathize with people whose main concern appears to be to stay out of the army and to get their hands on the latest expensive cars.

As I watched the couple enter the restaurant, I saw that the young man stood politely aside, allowing the girl to go in ahead of him, Western fashion. I saw, too, her partially covered head turn in the light of the doorway, and a suggestion of rouge on the lips that smiled at him.

Women are expected to cover their hair and the contours of their body with either a *chador*, a *maghne'eh* (a hooded garment), or a scarf and a cloak, and this—the oppression that Westerners believe it symbolizes—has led to strong criticism abroad of the Iranian attitude toward women. But the role of women in Iran is quite complex. Women have always played an important part in Persian life; and after the revolution, as before it, they own property, run businesses, and hold positions in the civil service. In Tehran it is not unusual to see a woman driving a car—women have been dragged from their cars and beaten for this in Saudi Arabia. And although on previous visits I have seen women wearing a bit of eye makeup approached on the street and lectured by members of a *komiteh*, I noticed on my last visit that things had become more lax, at least for now. A few women wore makeup in the streets, and in many cases the *chadors* were shorter and less than all-embracing.

I had reached the crossroads at the foot of Val-ye-Asr Avenue; when I first visited Tehran, it was Pahlavi Avenue, and led northwards to the Shah's magnificent palaces in the foothills of the Elburz. In the daytime, with the police on duty, crossing the vast extent of the Val-ye-Asr circle is bad enough; but at night, with cars swerving fast around the curve of the circle, it can be terrifying. Now, however, the old imperialist came out in me as I marched across the roadway, determined to look neither to the left nor right. Twice large Mercedes charged by within a few feet, but Iranians are skilled at missing one another on the road and quite often do so. I reached the other side, fifty yards away, unscathed.

Here, a large wooden hoarding hid one of the building sites for the Tehran Metro—a curious act of faith for a country at war and desperately short of foreign currency. The plans for the Metro began under the Shah with the assistance of the French, but it was dogged by incompetence and corruption and lapsed before the revolution. Construction got underway again in October 1986, much against the better judgment of a number of figures in the religious hierarchy, who doubted that the capital investment would—as supporters of the Metro claimed—cut unemployment and lead eventually to a regeneration of Iranian industry. (Economic issues of all kinds have been among the most contentiously debated in Iran: in the bazaar, the newspapers, the *majlis*, everywhere.) This time the Japanese were there to give advice and technical assistance, and the plans were far more elaborate than before: one line, twelve miles long, from north to south of the city, and a second, even longer, from east to west. Not many weeks before my recent visit, Speaker of the Parliament Rafsanjani had examined the work for himself. A pragmatic, rather raffish figure, second in political influence only to Khomeini, Rafsanjani told those on hand: "A lot of people have said we were wrong to build this Metro. Well, who knows? But just think what a great air-raid shelter it will make, when the Iraqis come over."

I continued walking and passed a little park beside a hospital. On a seat among a group of bushes two patients in pajamas—God knows why they were out so late—were talking earnestly, too immersed in their argument to look up at me. The bushes had a tart, clean smell to them, as though they had been planted by nurses. The two men were talking about the war, arguing and reminiscing by turns. One of them, he was perhaps twenty-two, had rested his crutches against the back of the bench. The end of his blue-striped pajama trousers stirred slightly in the night breeze: his leg had been amputated above the knee.

I was close to my hotel now, and could see the massive T it formed on the ridge above me, as I toiled up the broken pavement of what had been Los Angeles Road and was now Hejab ("Islamic Dress") Avenue. I saw the light shining from the window of my room, one of the few lights still on in the hotel, and turned into the courtyard.

A dark figure detached itself from the shadow of a pillar, where other dark figures were gathered, and walked across to me. Recognizing him, I put my arm around his shoulder: "Reza, how are you?"

"Is it quite good, Simpson," he said.

Reza was my driver; he was timid by nature, and inclined to complain if we went filming illicitly, without an official government "minder" from the Orwellian-sounding Ministry of Islamic Guidance. He spoke English, but habitually transposed the words "is" and "it," thereby creating spurious questions out of statements he made; and he had never quite been able to work out what my first name was, so that in an effort to be free and easy with me he called me by my surname, which gave an imperious touch to everything he said: "Look there, Simpson," or "Simpson, open the door."

"Time to go home now, Reza," I said, feeling guilty about having kept him waiting so long (though he was paid by the hour, and seemed to relish the work at this time of few visitors).

"Is it no problem, Simpson," he replied, grandly.

Up in my familiar room, which sentiment suggested was the one in which I had stayed during the months that led up to the revolution, I looked out at the view to the south of Tehran, toward the great plain that opens up there and leads eventually to the desert, to Qom, and to Isfahan, one of the loveliest cities on earth. A thousand miles beyond that, U.S. navy ships were plowing grimly through the waters of the Gulf, protecting the sea lanes at tremendous cost and, perhaps, looking for an opportunity to wreak vengeance on Iran for all the attacks and indignities it has inflicted on Americans in recent years. It is hard to avoid seeing in all this the anger of a great power against a smaller one that refuses to behave itself as a good client state should: the response, in effect, of the colonialist.

The old center of Tehran was spread out below me in the darkness, the few lights of its buildings and streets blurring in the dirty night air. I could never look at this view, either at the time of the Shah's last days or now, without experiencing the feeling that something would crack this quiet. Iran has settled down, and its religious fervor has moderated since the early 1980s; but the system is still too extreme for it to last in quite its present form. It must change. But Iran will change only if it changes itself. The Islamic Republic does not—as the West so often assumes complacently—face collapse. Far from it; it has weathered a seven-year war, the drop in oil prices, the hostility of the West. The country is well administered, and intelligently—if often cynically—governed. Post-colonial Iran is a strong and effective power; sooner or later, the United States will have to come to terms with it.

Easing the Debt Crisis

Most political scientists and economists believe that the present international debt crisis represents a potential powder keg in the Third World, one that threatens to wreak havoc and instability in the developing nations. The situation is particularly acute in Latin America, where many nations face insurmountable problems in repaying their debts. For example, in the wake of a series of devastating earthquakes, Ecuador's president, Léon Febres Cordero, suspended—for the remainder of 1987—$1.3 billion in payments due on Ecuador's $8.2 billion foreign debt. In announcing the suspension, Cordero stated that Ecuador was incapable of both rebuilding that country's all-important oil pipeline and repaying the mounting interest on its escalating debt.

Ecuador is but one example of the increasing number of Latin American nations that have either unilaterally suspended their interest payments or requested the International Monetary Fund to reschedule those payments. In Latin America, the debt crisis has exacerbated an ever-widening economic crisis that dates back to the 1930s. Indeed, Latin America's population is now three to four times larger than it was in the 1930s, its social problems have increased geometrically, and the purchasing power of its exports has plummeted to a record low.

The debt crisis has been fueled by a sharp decline in the terms of trade, high interest rates, the flight of capital, and unprecedented inflation. These and other developments have precipitated a dire economic crisis. To repay their debts, many Latin American countries will be forced to curtail badly needed programs and services, at enormous social costs.

It is questionable whether some of these nations can tolerate further sacrifices. For example, in the Dominican Republic—a more or less stable country—immediately following the implementation of the first of the IMF's measures, a spontaneous rebellion occurred. The army and police were summoned to quash the revolt, in which 50 people were killed and hundreds more were wounded. In Panama, measures aimed at balancing the budget brought hundreds of thousands of people into the streets. And in Bolivia—which has been virtually paralyzed by the debt crisis—inflation soared to over 2,300 percent in 1986.

Twenty-five years ago, Latin America was practically debt-free. Today, its debt amounts to over $400 billion. How was the money spent? Part of it was invested in weapons. In Argentina, for example, tens of billions of dollars was spent on military hardware. The same was true of Chile and other Latin American countries. Another part was either embezzled, stolen, or misappropriated. Still another part was returned to the United States and Europe as a result of the flight of capital. And last, another part was squandered on unnecessary or wasteful projects. Only a small part of the money was spent on essential programs and services.

As a result, many Latin American leaders argue that they cannot and should not be required to repay their debts, which they view as immoral. They ask: What benefits did the people derive from these expenditures? They contend that it would be much more moral to cancel the debt, which would benefit billions of people in Latin America, Africa, and Asia, 70 percent of the world's population. To do otherwise, they insist, would be to invite massive social upheaval.

Obviously, the lender nations disagree with this analysis. In March 1987, 44 countries assembled to discuss the deepening debt crisis in Latin America. At this conference, financial representatives from those nations debated a proposal which, its critics maintain, would give the United States veto power over how billions of dollars in new loans to Latin America will be allocated. Specifically, the debate focused on a U.S. proposal to exclude debtor countries from decisions on loans granted by the Inter-American Development Bank, which channels approximately $3 billion a year in loans to Latin America and the Caribbean.

The debt crisis has not only adversely affected the struggling masses in Latin America, but has seriously hurt American automobile workers in Detroit and farmers in Kansas. Some U.S. officials, like Senator Bill Bradley (D-NJ), believe that it is necessary to reduce both the principal and interest payments to banks and international lending organizations. For instance, in the two years after Mexico nearly defaulted in 1982, sales of U.S. construction equipment to Latin America experienced a sharp decline. During the 1980s, living standards have dropped 8 percent in Mexico, 14 percent in Peru, 17 percent in Argentina, and 19 percent in Venezuela.

At the present time, the solution to the debt crisis rests with the industrialized world. Unless the lender nations propose bold new initiatives, they are likely to aggravate the situation and force the debtor nations to adopt extreme measures. They cannot afford to turn a deaf ear to the problem, as the crisis promises to grow increasingly worse. Before too much longer, Latin America and other Third World countries will impose their own solution, which could seriously jeopardize future relations. Clearly, both sides have made legitimate claims. The problem cannot be solved by rhetoric. It will require compromise,

Unit 6

cooperation, and consensus. Both sides must rise to the challenge.

Looking Ahead: Challenge Questions

What are the principal causes of the international debt crisis?

Who are the main winners and losers in the debt crisis?

How has the debt crisis affected the Third World?

Can the developing world repay its debts without mortgaging its future?

What are the major options for resolving the debt crisis?

Will debt swapping prevent economic catastrophe in the Third World?

Does the developing world have the right to default on its debts?

How is the debt crisis contributing to environmental degradation?

Are there signs that economic prospects are starting to brighten in the developing world?

Is Brazil's debt pact a possible solution to the debt problems of other Third World nations?

MORTGAGING A HOUSE OF CARDS

THE ETHICS OF INTERNATIONAL DEBT

KENNETH P. JAMESON

KENNETH P. JAMESON *is professor of economics at the University of Notre Dame. This article is adapted from a talk given at the Woodstock Forum, sponsored by the Woodstock Theological Center at Georgetown University.*

During the humid summer of 1983, an unenviable Midwestern bank found itself at the center of the international debt crisis. That August, the Michigan National Bank sued Citibank. Michigan National had bought $5 million of a loan to Pemex, the Mexican state oil company. Pemex was unable to repay, even after the loan had been extended three times. Finally the bank, whose president was a fervent Mormon, decided that principle prohibited throwing bad money after good and refused to renew. Citibank attempted to renew the Pemex loan without permission. Michigan National Bank sued, thereby breaking the unity of banks in "muddling through" the crisis of unpayable loans.

Michigan National may have been correct legally. But the bank lost, and lost big. Observers said that the bank was going to feel a lot of heat. As one put it, "I wouldn't be surprised if the auditors are there tomorrow." Later, ostensibly for other reasons, Michigan National's president was forced to step down, and he at one point faced penalties in the six-figure range for irregularities subsequently uncovered. Perhaps his problems are unrelated to the loan affair, but the story illustrates very clearly that there are big stakes in the debt game, that it is a political game, and that the whole structure resembles more a house of cards than a Gibraltar of financial security.

The basic facts on debt are clear: third-world debt now amounts to around $1 trillion, about half of which is in Latin America; the Latin American countries are now exporting capital to the U.S. to the tune of some $30 billion per year as a result of the debt; many major U.S. banks have third- world loans greater than their capital base, meaning that nonpayment would threaten the banks' survival. For example, one *Washington Post* article indicated that Chemical Bank's loans to Mexico were 48.6 percent of its primary capital in 1986. Rather than dwell on these rather well-known matters, however, I would like to deal with three issues which relate to the moral issues and obligations that are posed by the current third-world debt crisis.

First is the question of who is to blame. In Catholic terms, what about sin, guilt, and punishment? I could make the case that the banks are to blame, that the third-world governments are to blame, that the elites of the third-world are to blame, that the OPEC countries are to blame, and probably that you and I are to blame as well. But that would not be a particularly useful approach. A better way might be to ask who is benefiting at this point from the operation of the debt game? If we could ascertain that, and if we could agree that there is something wrong with the game, then we could move to deal with it.

There are some clear winners in the present situation. The banks are the biggest winners, for although they would rather be out from under the loans, they are still collecting something on what were bad loans, what should have been clear losses. And even if they end up selling the loans at a discount of 30 percent for Chilean loans or of 75 percent for the Peruvian loans, they are getting back more than they should have expected had the firms they loaned to gone under and the loans simply been written off, or had the respective governments simply declared the loans unpayable.

Other winners are the private individuals and government officials of third-world countries who now have real estate or bank accounts outside of their own country as a result of their take from these loans. One study by Morgan Guaranty Trust estimated that the net debt of many of the Latin American countries would essentially be zero if extreme capital flight had not occurred.

There are clear losers as well. The poor and middle classes of the Latin American countries have seen twenty years of growth and development stripped away, as their governments have undertaken the recessionary steps the international structure requires of them. Their access to services such as education and health is being diminished, and there is evidence that malnutrition and infant mortality are increasing.

So presumably any steps to deal with the debt problem must make an assessment of who is to pay the cost, and it should be those who are benefiting from the continued existence of this house of cards.

My second point is to examine the various ways that the debt problem can be confronted. There are five general approaches.

● *Muddling through.* The argument is that the system has functioned since the 1982 Mexican debt crisis, and that policy should concentrate on continuing this experience with or without augmented financial flows. Perhaps the industrialized countries should stimulate their economies to aid third-world exports. Perhaps there should be new flows of capital from the banks and international institutions, as in the Baker Plan. Perhaps changes in commodity prices will begin to aid the debtors. Perhaps a decline in real interest rates will relieve the debt burden in some degree. But don't do anything to pull out one of the cards. This past August, Swiss Bank Corporation balked at putting up the money for the Mexican "rescue." As the headlines read: "Swiss Bank Jeopardized Mexican Rescue but Relented after Pressure by the IMF" (*Wall Street Journal,* August 13, 1986). If I were president of the bank, I'd be looking over my shoulder!

● *Redefinition of assets.* The loans could be sold to a new international bank at a discount, and that bank would then be the collecting agency, insulating present lender banks from the illiquidity problems of debtors. Or the loans could be swapped for assets such as plants and equipment. For example, in Bolivia, the most valuable asset is the national oil company. It could simply be sold to pay off the debt. The comic strip *Bloom County* actually anticipated this scenario some time ago, when Opus became dictator of Bolivia, and showed how ludicrous such an option is. Whether the loans were sold or swapped for assets, there would presumably be a write-down of the loans to reflect their current value. However, there would be no substantial change in the situation of the debtor countries; in the first case they would still have to pay the international bank, presumably on the full value of the debt; and in the second, they would lose control over the most profitable assets in their economy.

● *Share the cost.* Another approach would share the current adjustment costs among the banks, the debtors, and the beneficiaries of capital flight. Senator Bill Bradley's plan calls for a write-down of the loans by 3 percent per year over three years, so that the actual principal amount debtors have to pay is reduced, i.e., so that there is debt relief. Interest rates on the debt are also to be reduced, which would give liquidity relief. This would share adjustment between banks and countries. Some have suggested that the debtor countries, with the collaboration of the international banking system, simply call in the foreign assets of their nationals, as England and France did during World War I. Their citizens would be paid in bonds, but would certainly bear some of the costs of the adjustment. This would call upon the beneficiaries of capital flight to bear a portion of the burden.

● *Link to domestic performance.* Alan Garcia, the president of Peru, has declared that his country's payments will be dependent upon Peru's ability to pay, i.e., that payments will not exceed 10 percent of export earnings in a given year. The Cartagena Group of Latin American debtors will meet in April in search of a coordinated plan to limit the payment in some such way. Such an approach deals with the solvency and liquidity problems, and clearly indicates that the poor and middle classes of debtor countries will no longer pay the costs of adjusting. President Garcia's approach has not been particularly popular internationally, and Peru is an international pariah at this point. Nor does this solution solve the real long-term problem, for the unpaid interest is simply being added to the overall debt bill that remains. Nonetheless, the tying of payments to domestic economic performance is clearly going to become more common. The recent Mexican renegotiations for example, made some concessions to Mexico, taking into account the low price of oil and a low domestic growth rate.

● *Repudiation.* This has been the traditional way of dealing with the issue, going back in Latin America to the 1820s and 1830s. Until a few years ago, Peru's railroads were owned by the holders of bonds defaulted on in the 1860s. Fidel Castro has suggested this approach for Latin America, while at the same time paying his own debts. Even orthodox economic advisors have questioned whether new democratic governments should be required to pay debts contracted by military-civilian dictatorships. However, repudiation is a direct affront to the international banking system, and has not become an avowed policy, though Bolivia quietly quit paying in 1984 simply because it did not have the resources, and Nicaragua currently is not paying.

Which of these options might be most desirable and effective in dealing with this massive problem, particularly in light of the moral obligations that are involved? My criteria for choosing are two: first, that those who have benefited should bear the costs; and second, that the disruption of the structure should be minimized, if not avoided.

I dismiss muddling through, a process which at present allows the banks to benefit while the poor continue to pay. Redefining the assets would be preferable, only because it would increase the stability of the financial structure. But redefinition of assets has the same problems as muddling through. Repudiation, on the other hand, would be too disruptive, focusing the cost too completely on the banks, or on the American public, the lenders of last resort.

I would suggest that a combination of cost sharing and linkage to domestic performance would be the most effective and fairest approach. The present system is simply pyramiding added debt on top of the existing debt. As such, it is neither fair nor realistic: the debts themselves are unlikely ever to be paid, and their cost to the poor is unfair. Some write-down of the obligations of the debtors is therefore essential. A combination of lower interest rates and their linkage to the actual possibilities of a debtor country to pay in terms of its exports, would confront both the liquidity and solvency problems at a cost which would be more acceptable to the people of the indebted countries. Finally, there is no reason that a major beneficiary group, such as those who engaged in capital flight, should be protected from the required adjustments. Perhaps they stole it fair and square, to paraphrase former Senator Hayakawa, but there is no justification for allowing them to hide behind the faceless "international capital system." Clearly, this is a very good reason to interfere with capital markets and to bring them an order that will allow third-world countries to undertake development efforts with some assurance they won't be frustrated by capital drain to the safe haven of the U.S. Nor should the banks benefit from such deposits.

The debt problem is clearly a major challenge of the next several years. This is most acutely felt by the debtors whose economies are, for the most part, in disarray. But it should also be felt in the U.S. on moral grounds. The Catholic bishops pointed this out quite clearly in their recent pastoral on the economy when they called for systemic change of international economic institutions. But the need for change must be recognized by a much broader economic and political constituency. The economic interest of the United States lies with a prosperous and progressing third world, particularly in Latin America. This will occur only if meaningful steps for dealing with the debt problem are undertaken.

SWAPPING THIRD WORLD DEBT

Richard S. Weinert

RICHARD S. WEINERT *is president of Leslie, Weinert & Co., Inc., a New York-based investment banking firm active in debt swapping.*

Markets work. So President Ronald Reagan and his backers have taught legions of skeptics, and examples keep popping up in unlikely places. One is Third World debt. When the debt crisis arrived in 1982, many analysts—including this writer—foretold dire consequences if forceful action was not taken to write down the value of the debt and give relief to debtor countries. This did not happen. To date no public entity—creditor-country governments, debtor-country governments, the International Bank for Reconstruction and Development (World Bank), or the International Monetary Fund (IMF)—has taken any specific initiative to reduce debt-service burdens.

Yet markets have not been idle. Despite, or because of, the public policy vacuum, capital markets have begun to adjust. A new secondary market in discounted Latin American and other Third World debt has developed, with big discounts regularly applied to the debt's face value. In fall 1986, for example, Brazilian government debt could be bought for about 75 per cent of its face value; Mexican government debt for about 57 per cent; Philippine, 60 per cent; Argentine, 65 per cent; Chilean, 67 per cent; and Peruvian, 22 per cent. Bolivian and Nicaraguan debt, by contrast, each sold for less than 10 per cent of their face values. These steep discounts belie the claim that the loans are still good, that the debtor countries are merely experiencing some temporary illiquidity. The claim may be true, but the market does not believe it.

Understanding how and why this debt swapping developed and how it works will help reveal whether the practice should be encouraged or restrained. Even more important, it can show how swapping can serve as a model for a lasting and politically acceptable solution to the debt crisis that will help debtors and creditors alike.

As debt swapping expands and develops further, it will profoundly influence debtor-creditor negotiations.

The secondary market in debt serves three purposes that feed off each other. First, it enables private banks to readjust their portfolios by shuffling loans around, much as children trade baseball cards. Second, debtor countries encourage investors to use discounted debt to make investments. Third, debtors use the market to retire debt. Shuffling loans reduces risks to the international financial system by permitting individual banks to strengthen their balance sheets. Debtors have benefited by encouraging investment flows and by starting to lighten their debt burdens.

No one knows exactly how big the market for debt swaps has become. No transactions are publicized, and most banks are very secretive about them. It is clear, however, that the market is still small but growing quite rapidly. It may have totaled about $1 billion in 1984, $3 billion in 1985, and $6 billion in 1986. This trend is likely to continue and presents some challenges and opportunities to the world economy.

Initially, swapping was stimulated by some banks' desires to modify their exposure to troubled debtors. This could be done in several ways. The simplest would be for a bank to sell off its loans to a given country at a discount and register the loss suffered against its earnings. This tack was eventually taken by smaller banks to the extent that they had sufficient profits to absorb the loss or had already written the loans down to the market's discounted values. At first, however, such transactions were modest simply because there were no buyers, even at discounted prices.

Major creditors could not sell loans for two additional reasons. Financially, they could not afford to take the implicit losses. For example, large private banks typically held Latin American debt equal to two to three times their capital. To register a loss of even 25 per cent of that portfolio would imply wiping out one-half to three-fourths of their capital. This was clearly impossible. Moreover, the political consequences would have been unbearable. The world's big banks had painstakingly forged cooperative links on the debt issue that served all of their interests. For one bank to break ranks and try to dump its debt would have threatened those links and shaken international banking and capital markets.

Accounting gimmickry came to the rescue. By exchanging, or swapping, the debt of one country for that of another, banks could reduce or even eliminate their exposure in some countries without registering any loss. The key to this sleight of hand was what banks call "historical cost accounting." That is, some debt was on their books at its historical cost, or par, although its secondary-market value was far less. Through intricate swaps involving higher-value debt for lower-value debt, the latter could be made to disappear with no loss registered. In this way, some large banks eliminated such countries as Nicaragua and Bolivia from their portfolios while taking on larger amounts of Mexican and Brazilian debts.

Some banks swapped debt not to reduce or eliminate loans to weak countries but to balance their portfolios. A bank with too much Mexican exposure could exchange it for some other comparable risk, such as Brazil or the Philippines, where its loans were relatively modest. Or a bank might wish to reduce the number of countries in its portfolio to simplify its administration—for example, by exchanging Chilean for Argentine debt. Such transactions could also be structured to avoid any losses—or gains—even though the secondary-market valuations of the loans being exchanged differed.

In addition, debtor countries swapped loans to alter the foreign-debt exposure of their overseas branches. During the heyday of expanded international lending in the 1970s, many Third World countries entered global capital markets not only as borrowers, but also as lenders. Today this seems absurd, but at the time it was quite fashionable for public and private Latin banks to set up branches in the Bahamas, London, New York, and elsewhere, and to participate in the lending boom side by side with the major multinational banks. Predictably, banks from the larger countries such as Brazil and Mexico were the most numerous and the most active. But Argentine, Colombian, and Venezuelan banks played a significant role, and even Chilean and Peruvian banks dabbled in the Eurodollar market.

When the music stopped in 1982, these Latin banks found themselves in the awkward, not to say farcical, role of holding one another's debts. They were obliged to participate in each other's rescheduling efforts even while claiming hardships of their own. The situation cried out for a remedy.

The remedy was provided by the secondary market. Through swapping, banks of one country could exchange debts of other countries for their own country's debt. Thus Latin banks could shed their foreign loans and end up with what for them were domestic loans. From the debtor countries' point of view, even when carried out by private banks, this process in effect nationalized some of their debt. Although the debt was not retired, it no longer represented the same claim on foreign exchange. All the overseas Latin bank branches have swapped debts this way, and by the end of 1986 most of them will have reduced sharply, if not eliminated, their loans to other countries.

Debt Capitalization

But a market limited to these kinds of swaps would have stagnated at very low levels. Real growth was stimulated when cash buyers appeared. Where did this money come from? It did not come from nontraditional lenders, such as insurance companies or pension funds, which some thought could be lured into the Third World. Having avoided these countries during the boom, these institutions not surprisingly maintained their distance during the bust. Nor did the cash come from private speculators, who have yet to join this drama to any significant degree.

Enter the debtors. For countries, retiring debt through direct purchases at discounted prices was problematical. How could a government plead with banks for lower interest rates and extended maturities while simultaneously prepaying debt through secondary-market purchases? Yet ways were found through imaginative programs of "debt capitalization." In December 1982, Brazil became the first country to adopt a debt capitalization scheme. Chile followed in June 1985 and Mexico announced its own version in mid-1986. Argentina, Bolivia, Costa Rica, and Ecuador are thought to be working on plans. Outside Latin America, the Philippines permitted three deals on an experimental basis and then formulated its program. Nigeria reportedly has also expressed interest. But Latin America is the source of most Third World debt and where most of the debt capitalization remains.

Debt capitalization schemes served two quite different purposes. One was to stimulate new investment by converting debt to equity. The second was to retire debt. For either purpose, a buyer would purchase foreign debt at a discount and obtain local currency. The debtor country thereby succeeded in retiring some of its foreign debt without using up any scarce foreign exchange.

The basic concept of converting debt to equity is quite simple. It borrows from the process of reorganizing bankrupt corporations with a view to revitalizing them. In corporate reorganizations, a common technique is to convert part of the debt owed to capital stock of the corporation. The result: lower corporate debt and thus lower interest burdens. Lenders receive some stock in the corporation in lieu of their loans, and if the company survives and prospers, they may see some return. The well-publicized Chrysler Corporation bailout scheme employed this technique, and lenders eventually benefited.

Countries, of course, are not corporations, and this concept could not be applied directly. However, debt capitalization was conveniently married to another notion that became commonplace as bankers pondered with hindsight the origins of the debt crisis. Countries had acquired too much debt and not enough direct investment, they solemnly intoned. Debt, they observed, saddled countries with very high interest payments that had to be paid irrespective of changes in the world economy, such as plunging commodity prices, which rendered unprofitable some of the uses to which the borrowed funds had been put. In addition, borrowing countries were deprived of the discipline of the marketplace, which might have reined in some of the public investments made with borrowed funds.

Converting some of the existing debt to equity—capitalizing it—met this criticism. Governments devised schemes under which debt could be used to make an investment. This practice led to two types of transactions. First, banks might convert some of their own debt into local investment. Bankers Trust did this in Chile, converting some of its Chilean loans to shares in a pension management company. In Brazil, its loans were turned into shares in an investment bank. The National Commercial Bank of Saudi Arabia converted some of its Chilean loans into shares in industrial companies, and the American Express Company converted some Philippine debt into shares in a commercial bank.

The more common type of transaction, however, involved multinationals and used the secondary market. Fiat, for example, used Brazil's capitalization scheme to expand its plant there. It bought Brazilian debt at a discount and delivered it to the central bank. The central bank registered the debt as if it were a new investment and gave Fiat the cruzado equivalent of the face value of the debt. Nissan Corporation has arranged a similar deal in Mexico, and the Dow Chemical Company has entered one in Chile. Nissan and Dow shared the discount with the Mexican and Chilean central banks, respectively, receiving less than the peso equivalent of the face value of the debt. Whether used by banks or by multinationals, however, these schemes retired debt and transformed it into an equity investment. Moreover, debt capitalization stimulates new investment. The secondary market is an essential element in making this possible.

A second type of capitalization scheme aims directly at retiring debt. The idea is to permit someone to purchase foreign debt at a discount and to obtain payment in local currency. Chile has instituted the most ambitious and most successful program of this type to date. An enterprising investor, or a firm with a local operation, can purchase Chilean dollar debt at a discount and receive payment in pesos, which it can then use as it wishes. The central bank shares the benefit of the discount and succeeds in retiring foreign debt with local currency. Although anyone can use this scheme, it is designed for wealthy Chilean nationals. They may use some of their assets to buy Chilean debt and obtain pesos, which they might then use either to pay off local debts or to make new investments. By the end of 1986, Chile will have retired about $1 billion—about 5 per cent of its foreign debt—this way.

Large-scale debt swapping would overcome a fatal weakness of the Baker plan—its insufficient incentives to carry out economic change that could be painful in the short run.

This form of capitalization scheme might induce Latin Americans who have transferred their holdings abroad to bring them back home, or at least prevent some of this flight capital from leaving. The sums involved are widely believed to represent a substantial percentage of Latin debt, and their return—even in part—would both alleviate the burden of debt service and stimulate growth through local investment.

Such schemes created a steady demand for cash purchases of Brazilian and Chilean foreign debt by companies that could use them locally. Because of these programs' technical complexities, they also generated a steady demand for more swapping. Generally, only certain types of Brazilian or Chilean debt are eligible. Often the holder of the eligible type is not willing to sell because of accounting or other considerations. The holder might, however, swap for some other similar debt or for debt of another country. Hence market dealers often have to construct a daisy chain of several swaps to produce a single purchase. For instance, a dealer might purchase Philippine debt, swap it for Brazilian, swap that for ineligible Chilean, and swap that for the eligible Chilean debt, which the dealer can sell. Some transactions have involved up to 20 steps. These cash purchases keep the secondary market expanding, and, through swapping, create cash purchases of the debt of countries lacking such schemes. For instance, Argentine debt might be sold by swapping it for Chilean debt, which could then be sold for cash.

Debtor countries benefit from these activities since they reduce their debt. But these countries have another option in the secondary market—to purchase their own debt directly. Direct, open purchases by debtor countries were not officially acknowledged as of late 1986, but several have come close. One large Argentine private bank, for instance, purchased substantial amounts of Argentine government debt at discounts and then used that debt to settle its own obligations with multinational banks. This step could only have been taken with Buenos Aires' knowledge and approval. A Venezuelan government bank has been active in purchasing at discounts debt of other Venezuelan government entities. There have been substantial purchases of Peruvian debt under circumstances that suggest governmental involvement, though officially they have been private transactions. This last case is especially interesting, since Peru has been behind on interest payments since October 1984 and since its debt commands only about 22 cents on the dollar. Peru may well have concluded that using, say, $22 million to retire $100 million in debt makes more sense than using this sum at face value to make a small dent in overdue interest, which now exceeds $600 million. It is only a matter of time before this use of the secondary market spreads.

Debt swapping is not a panacea for the debt crisis. Capitalization schemes and direct purchases can chip away at the debt mountain, but these transactions can substantially reduce debt overhang only over a very long period. To begin with, the market is relatively small. The few billion dollars' worth of swaps in 1986 is dwarfed by the several hundred billion dollars or so in total debt of the countries whose debt is traded in the secondary market. Moreover, structural limitations inhibit the use of the secondary market to retire debt. First, direct foreign investment in Latin America never exceeded more than a few billion dollars annually during the lending boom. Total foreign investment in Mexico, for example, is estimated at only $15 billion, compared with a total debt of some $100 billion. Even if capitalization schemes were to restore the investment flow to earlier levels, these would amount to only a small fraction of the debt service. Second, many of the largest creditors could not bear the financial or the political cost of liquidating their loans at substantial discounts. Therefore, much of the debt probably will not become available on the secondary market.

Retiring debt through capitalization schemes will be helpful at the margin, but will probably never amount to more than a few per cent per year of a country's debt, if that. Some flight capital may be seduced back (or inhibited from leaving), but political and economic uncertainties will continue to crimp that flow. Direct purchases will also help, but will be constrained by the very foreign-exchange limitations that produced the discounts in the first place.

Implications of Debt Swapping

The market has a significance beyond its size. As debt swapping expands and develops further, it will profoundly influence debtor-creditor negotiations. Bank creditors simply cannot continue solemnly to negotiate full-interest payments and multiyear reschedulings with debtor governments while dealing in the secondary market for the same debt at substantial discounts. Debtors will point to the market valuations of their loans to legitimate larger concessions, and banks will find it hard to insist on full market terms for rescheduling when the secondary market provides such different signals.

Thus far, only the market's benefits are apparent, but swapping poses a serious dilemma for U.S. bank regulators and accountants. Loans traded at deep discounts in the secondary market are carried at substantially higher values on banks' balance sheets. American banks still carry most of them at par. Canadian, Japanese, and West European banks have taken write-downs against many of these loans, but rarely to the levels applicable in the secondary market. How should banks account for loans traded at deep discounts? Should more write-downs be required? Does debt swapping require special accounting treatment?

There are good reasons to avoid wholesale write-downs. First, they could cause heavy losses at some banks and thus shake confidence in the financial system. Second, forcing banks to write down the debt to secondary-market values would undercut the prevailing strategy of dealing with the debt crisis. Since 1982, banks have been rescheduling and lending new money. At the 1985 IMF meetings, Secretary of the Treasury James Baker unveiled a plan that essentially called for more of the same—more rescheduling and more new lending in exchange for economic policy reforms by debtor countries. Cajoling banks to lend new money is difficult enough in today's circumstances; it would be impossible if combined with forced debt write-downs. No lender would willingly make new loans knowing that those loans would be immediately marked down below face value.

Yet the concern for conservative, prudent balance sheets argues for sharp write-downs in light of the economic deterioration of the borrowers, as signaled by secondary-market valuation. The accounting profession, backed by the Securities and Exchange Commission, has a strong institutional interest in large write-downs and disclosures, since accountants can be sued by disgruntled shareholders. Accountants therefore favor the largest write-downs and disclosures possible. Bank regulators, however, are more concerned with maintaining confidence in the financial system and facilitating banks' ability to raise capital. Consequently, they are torn between their support for conservative balance sheets and their fear of weakening banks and jeopardizing the rescheduling of Third World debt. The accounting profession examined debt swaps in 1985 and produced a set of accounting guidelines vague enough to permit significantly differing interpretations. Bank regulators have been looking hard at the secondary market but have yet to take a firm stand.

No one has suggested that banks immediately write down all or most of their debt to secondary market values, but many accountants feel that any secondary-market trade should trigger a write-down of the traded debt to its discounted value. These write-downs, however, can cause banks to record losses they would otherwise not have to record. Thus some banks are wary of the secondary market. Others are not participating at all for fear of accounting or regulatory disapproval. Banks that do swap battle continually to persuade their auditors and regulators to approve completed or proposed transactions.

But the secondary market helps everyone and should be encouraged by regulatory authorities. Creditors benefit because they can reduce or adjust their portfolios as they see fit. Debtors benefit because they reduce their foreign debt, gaining either an investment or the return of flight capital in the bargain. The financial system is strengthened as banks adjust and as debt burdens are lowered. Banks must continue to build their loan loss reserves but should not be required to register specific losses as a result of swapping debt.

Although swapping per se is no panacea for the debt crisis, the secondary market does contain the seeds of a more profound solution. As numerous analysts have suggested, the most promising approach to easing the crisis involves a partial assumption of the debt by public-sector entities in exchange for substantial interest-rate relief. The secondary market both suggests the basis for doing this and provides a mechanism. The basis would be to use the secondary-market valuation to determine the amount of interest-rate relief provided. The mechanism would be a swap: government bonds for Third World debt.

Suppose some public entity—the World Bank, developed-country governments, or some combination of the two—offered to swap its bonds for debts of troubled debtors. The swap would be voluntary and would be conditioned on a range of economic and political reforms. Obviously, the interest rate on these bonds would be lower than the rates on the debt, and the savings could be passed on to the debtor countries.

The main problems would involve determining the savings and avoiding offering relief to stronger countries. A solution could be based on the market valuation of a given country's debt. For example, Brazil's debt is currently offered at around 75 per cent of face value. In today's market, a government-entity 15-year dollar bond with an interest rate of 4.9 per cent would have a similar price. Mexico's debt goes for roughly 57 per cent of face value—approximately equivalent to a government-entity 15-year bond with an interest rate of 2.75 per cent. Hence, the government entity could issue bonds with those interest rates and offer to swap them on a one-for-one basis with banks. It would offer the 4.9 per cent bonds for Brazilian debt and the 2.75 per cent bonds for Mexican debt.

The rate on the government bonds, then, would depend on the value of the specific country debt for which they are swapped. This policy preserves differences among countries and concentrates assistance where it is needed most. Relatively well-off countries whose debt sells for relatively higher prices in the secondary market would receive bonds with correspondingly higher interest rates. A country whose debt commanded a very low market price would receive bonds with lower interest rates, and possibly longer maturities, to equalize their value with the value of that country's debts in the secondary market.

Debt swapping on this grand scale would not be a substitute for the economic and political reforms needed in debtor countries. On the contrary, only reforming debtor countries would be eligible to participate. Thus large-scale debt swapping would overcome a fatal weakness of the Baker plan—its insufficient incentives to carry out economic change that could be painful in the short run.

Moreover, this approach provides incentives in the right proportions. The least solvent countries probably need the most thoroughgoing reforms, and will have the greatest difficulty adopting them. They therefore need the strongest incentives. This form of debt swapping provides them through lower interest rates on bonds. Economically healthier countries would qualify for and receive less interest-rate relief through the bond swap.

Banks that accepted this swap would suffer reduced interest income in future years, but they would also strengthen their balance sheets by replacing uncertain assets with riskless ones. Regulators should facilitate the swap by not requiring any write-down, permitting banks to swap if they wished with no immediate effect on their balance sheets. Passing on the interest savings to debtors would strengthen the banks' financial situation and make repayment more likely. And because repayment would be more likely, there should be no cost to the bond-issuing government entity, which would be able to collect enough from Brazil and Mexico to make the necessary payments on the bonds it had issued.

The broader political and economic gains would probably exceed the financial gains. Such swapping could defuse a smoldering crisis. It could avert a political confrontation that threatens to sour relations between the United States and many Third World countries. In fact, it would enable the United States to exercise leadership to alleviate severe financial strains in a way that would benefit all concerned. The resulting improvements for both debtors and creditors would facilitate economic growth worldwide and would increase trade—which would mean greater purchases of U.S. goods. Therefore, swapping would contribute to raising living standards in both debtor and creditor countries. Finally, this approach is consistent with free markets, whose emergence and valuation provide its very framework.

DEBT-EQUITY SWAPS

Here Comes The Repo Man

WAYNE CURTIS

Wayne Curtis is a Washington-based writer specializing in Latin American affairs.

In August 1982, Mexico threatened international financial calamity by announcing that it was no longer able to pay interest on its debt. Since then, alarmist newspaper headlines notwithstanding, the "debt crisis" has been calmly and quietly managed because both debtors and creditors have found it convenient to maintain certain fictions: the debt will be paid off; new loans will be repaid in full, with interest; through growth, Latin America will be able to honor its obligations. Because of a peculiar etiquette that kept either party from allowing reality to intrude on its discussions, banks could post profits and debtors could retain access to trade credits and other necessary funds.

That state of affairs ended on Friday, February 20, when Brazil's President, José Sarney, announced on national television that he was suspending interest payments indefinitely on $68 billion worth of commercial bank loans. U.S. bankers defused the panic by insisting that Brazil was simply using a time-honored negotiating tactic, much as a professional wrestler eats a beer bottle before climbing into the ring. But Brazil's challenge is more far-reaching than the banks would have us believe.

Brazil's action may signal the first, long-overdue, step toward fashioning a new international debt order. Finance Minister Dilson Funaro has explained to creditors and government officials of the industrialized world that although debt management may have served as an interim measure for four-and-a-half years, solutions, not palliatives, are now urgently needed. In short, Brazil has startled the financial world by indecorously stating the obvious.

There is growing consternation among commercial bankers and Reagan Administration officials about how to respond to Brazil's defiance. It is even uncertain whether the two forces will make a joint stand against this common adversary, because they have increasingly disagreed on debt issues. The banks never embraced the Baker plan, unveiled by Treasury Secretary James Baker in October 1985, which called for extensive new loans by both the multilateral and the commercial banks. Mexico was promised the first Baker loan in September 1986, $7.7 billion of which came from commercial lenders. Executives of the major banks voice support but have extreme misgivings about throwing good money after bad. They are especially nervous about more broad-based plans, such as Senator Bill Bradley's proposal to make the banking world contend with tougher regulations.

Whether the timorous Treasury Department will eventually distance itself from the banks and support some form of limited debt relief remains to be seen, but the bankers are wasting no time in promoting a free-market alternative of their own. Banks have the same fondness for debt relief that most people have for cholera. If regulations force them to write off portions of their Latin American debt, their profits—which continue to be registered on paper—will fall, perhaps dramatically. They will also have to put up with more meddling government regulators, a situation adverse to their sensibilities. Naturally, they don't offer those arguments when assailing debt relief. Instead, bankers frequently assert that if they are forced to discount their loan portfolio to reflect its actual value, they will lose all incentive to extend further credit to Latin America. They find it convenient to ignore the fact that they have little incentive anyway, and offer loans only under extreme duress.

When a domestic loan goes bad, the banks have three choices: provide new loans in the hope of rejuvenating the debtor, offer some form of debt relief or repossess assets. Although international and domestic loans are not directly comparable, the choices in the event of default are essentially the same, and it is apparent that the banks have tried the first, rejected the second and are now looking for a polite way to undertake the third. In delicate international situations, however, a bank cannot foreclose on, say, a Brazilian coffee plantation in lieu of payments, as it could on a Nebraska farm. There are legal niceties, not to mention sovereignty issues, that prevent such crude action. But the banks have devised a quiet and roundabout equivalent as an alternative to debt relief. In fact, such a mechanism, known as a debt-equity swap, has been in active use for several years. Familiar to bankers and finance managers of large corporations, it is nevertheless generally unknown to the public. That may soon change.

The principle behind debt-equity swaps is simple: in exchange for debt relief the debtor hands over ownership of a tangible asset. The basic swap involves shares of local companies instead of debt payments. Banks have completed direct swap transactions in recent years in Chile, Brazil and the Philippines, retiring limited amounts of debt and gaining an equal amount of stock ownership in local financial corporations. But banks are not in the business of managing companies and prefer to sell their debt quickly and painlessly to someone who is interested in running a company abroad. Therefore, they have required an active secondary market.

The financial community is never slow to respond when a need is identified. An informal market for Third World debt surfaced in 1983 and has flourished in the past two years. Estimates of the size of this market vary widely, but it is a safe guess that about $3 billion was converted from bank debt to foreign ownership of assets in 1985, and $6 billion was converted last year. That is likely to increase this year. The rapid growth can be attributed partly to the development of programs to aid swaps in several debtor countries, including Brazil, Argentina, Chile and Mexico. There is virtually only one source of capital that can provide adequate funding to pay back the banks, and that is the banks themselves. Cut off from international loans, and with reserves at dangerously low levels, the debtors have had to search for alternatives to lure investment and hard currency. The debt-equity swap is an easy alternative. Just as the Reagan Administration has sold off government property for a one-time reduction in the budget deficit, the debtors are finding that selling off local assets to foreigners in exchange for debt relief provides a tidy short-term gain.

Debt swaps involve two transactions and work basically like this. First, a multinational company considering an investment in a country with an active debt-swap program asks its financial advisers if they know of any debt for sale. If the advisers locate a bank that wishes to reduce its troubled debt exposure, they bring the two together. A sale price is then negotiated. Simply put, the corporation gets tag-sale prices on secondhand loans. Chilean and Brazilian debt has been selling for about 70 cents on the dollar recently, and Mexican debt can be picked up for less than 60 cents. Nicaraguan and Bolivian debt obligations have reportedly been selling for less than 10 cents on the dollar.

Next, the buyer takes the debt to the central bank of the host country, which buys back the obligation in local currency at close to full value. Chile generally pays back about 92 cents on the dollar; Mexico pays between 70 and 100 cents on the dollar, depending on how important the authorities rate the intended investment. Most host countries restrict the use of the new money. In Chile purchasers of debt must use the funds for investment, rather than for day-to-day operating costs, and cannot repatriate any of the capital for at least ten years. In Argentina investors must put up new capital equal to the swapped funds.

Chile is the acknowledged pioneer and leader of the debt-equity swap program. The Chilean Central Bank has been its principal practitioner, and its regulations are the least restrictive. *Euromoney* calls Chile's program "the most successful so far." Since it was launched, in June 1985, the Central Bank has swapped $1.3 billion, or about 6 percent of the country's total $20 billion foreign debt. Nations with nonauthoritarian regimes are destined to remain Chile's inferiors in the finance game. Favorable rates are easier to obtain in a country where independent labor organizations have been systematically destroyed.

The $6 billion secondary market may seem huge to the uninitiated, but it is considered small and untapped among international financiers well acquainted with Latin America's total external debt of about $370 billion. The market has so far been limited mainly because of U.S. banking regulations. Under current accounting rules, banks claim the face value of their loans, formally maintaining the fiction that the loan will be fully paid off: they are required to record a loss only when selling the loan. If the big banks were required to register the loss on just a single loan sale, then they might be willing periodically to "take a hit" on the sale of a $50 million or a $200 million loan, nibbling down their overall Latin American exposure.

But the accounting rules are fuzzy here, leaving bankers uneasy. Many accountants maintain that only the loss on the specific loan sale should be written off, but government bank regulators do not agree. There is always the chance that Federal regulators will rule that the sale of one loan to, say, Argentina reflects the value of all the bank's loans to that country. The bank would then be required to mark down its entire outstanding Argentine debt. (As one U.S. government official put it, banks fear that one discount sale might spread a "contagion to the rest of their portfolio.") The potential impact is enormous: Citicorp, for example, has $2.8 billion in outstanding loans to Mexico. If the bank sold a $10 million Mexican loan discounted to 58 cents on the dollar, and regulators decided that this should reflect the value of Citicorp's entire Mexican portfolio, it would register an immediate $1.2 billion loss. The stockholders would not approve.

To date, most of the banks that have been selling their debt are relatively small. They can afford to write off all loans to a particular country because, having come in at the end of the loan-syndication bonanza of the late 1970s and early 1980s, their exposure was always limited. As both debtors and creditors have discovered, swap agreements offer clear short-term benefits. Banks rid themselves of some of the bad debt that often requires reserves to be set aside and attracts the attention of nosy regulators. Indebted nations slow the accumulation of debt (since reschedulings and rollovers increase their debt annually even if they don't get new loans), and in some cases even reduce the overall debt while doubling or tripling investment flows. Multinationals get cheap investment capital.

As Donald Lessard of the Massachusetts Institute of Technology said at a recent conference on debt conversions, swaps are the "public relations person's dream"—something for everyone. But common wisdom warns that if a deal seems too good to be true, it probably is. For one thing, host governments cannot simply swap a debt obligation for an investment. It defies the laws of finance and logic. When the central bank repurchases the debt in local currency from a foreign investor, it must get the money from somewhere, generally through local borrowing. The debt servicing costs, therefore, rise considerably, because local interest rates are steep in most severely indebted nations, which must offer substantial returns to retain domestic capital inclined to seek out more financially stable shores. Short-term interest rates in Brazil, for instance, soared to more than 1,000 percent in February, after the economic-stabilization plan unraveled.

Thus, to play the game, governments must stoke budget deficits through increased payments on the domestic debt. In Brazil and Mexico burgeoning domestic budget deficits already impede economic stability, and Argentina's budget is becoming more unmanageable daily. Swapping external for internal debt is obviously not a miracle cure. Pragmatists note that costs are even higher than is immediately apparent because debtors are paying back no principal and little interest on the external debt anyway.

It is also uncertain how much of the investment will be devoted to new production. The swap programs are still young, but it seems likely that many of the investments will involve the acquisition of already existing factories and plants from local owners who are pinched by credit shortages, rather than the creation of new productive facilities. Although some of the swapped funds may be recycled into the economy, a large chunk is sure to take flight to havens abroad. The result: net capital inflows remain roughly the same, but foreign companies gain an increasing stake in local operations. Inflation is also given an unwelcome boost, as more money is introduced into the system without an increase in overall production. And at best, as in Chile, swaps can reduce the total debt by only a few percentage points annually.

In 1981, Walter Wriston, then chair and chief executive officer of Citibank and one of the identifiable culprits in the debt crisis, said: "Bankruptcy is a procedure developed in Western law to forgive the obligations of a person or company that owes more than it has. Any country, however badly off, will 'own' more than it 'owes.'" Placed in that context, the transfer of ownership through debt-equity swaps seems the logical next step in the saga of the debt crisis. History's largest loan has gone bad, and the repo man is on his way.

As the evolution of the debt crisis over the past several years has made abundantly clear, the banker's primary concern is for short-term profits. As long as interest payments keep coming in, they prefer to avoid discussion of payments on the principal. Their willingness to acknowledge that the debt is not worth full value and to sell that debt on the secondary market (if accounting rules are softened) might be interpreted as a step in the right direction because the full debt, not just the interest, is at least being discussed. But the short-term prospect again dominates. If debt-swap programs are broadly expanded, as the banks have suggested, the economies of participating countries will be further weakened, reducing demand for discount debt and causing the living standards of debtor countries to fall even more sharply. The crisis will intensify with a vengeance.

A resolution of the debt crisis probably can be postponed for another five years if the accounting rules are changed to favor the banks and to expand debt swapping and encourage new loans, but only at the expense of Latin America, which will suffer as it continues to fight a losing economic battle. Brazil may knuckle under and accept a new "emergency loan" at the urging of creditors, and possibly of other debtors worried about upsetting the apple cart. But a new international debt order is inevitable, and significant debt relief is the only way out of the current financial mess. Any other approach, including the expansion of debt-equity swap programs, is just stalling.

LATIN AMERICA: WHY NOT DEFAULT?

Arthur MacEwan

Arthur MacEwan, a frequent contributor to Monthly Review, *teaches economics at the Boston campus of the University of Massachusetts.*

Why do the governments of debtor nations generally continue to meet their payment schedules with the banks? Why do the people of the debtor nations accept the austerity programs imposed upon them so that the debts can be paid?

Within the debtor nations—in particular, within Latin America—the costs of the debt crisis have been horrendous. Between 1980 and 1985, while not all countries in Latin America have fared equally badly, per capita income in the region fell by about 9 percent. As unemployment has risen and governments have cut back social spending, the incomes of the poor have suffered disproportionately. In Mexico, for example, the purchasing power of the minimum wage dropped by 30 percent between 1981 and 1984. In Brazil the fall in real wages was not quite so extreme; the decline from 1980 to 1984 was 17 percent.

Declining wages, however, have not meant good times for business. In recent years, Brazil and Mexico, for example, have been turning over some five percent of national income to foreign creditors. The costs of such a huge transfer cannot be confined to the bottom segments of society.

So far, governments of capitalist countries in Latin America have failed to offer any alternative to austerity and have attempted to solve their economic problems by relatively orthodox means. They have, in general, attempted to shape programs that would allow them to pay the debt. All profess a desire for economic growth and an improvement of living standards; but, judged by their actions, it would seem that all accept the subordination of domestic concerns to the continued payment of the debt. There has been a great deal of rhetoric and some limited actions which challenge the absolute necessity of paying the debt. Bolivia suspended debt payments in 1985 and has since been in a state of de facto if not de jure default; Peru has also severely limited its payments. Even some of the large debtors have fallen briefly behind on their payments. These actions, however, have been presented as temporary and limited responses to emergency conditions. (Bolivia is the possible exception, where a 27 percent decline in income between 1980 and 1984—Bolivia was already the poorest nation in Spanish America—has left the economy in chaos and made payment virtually impossible.)

HETERODOX AUSTERITY

Many would challenge the generalization that Latin American governments have used orthodox means to deal with their problems. Current policies in Argentina and Brazil, in particular, are presented as new alternatives for Latin America and are often referred to among economists as "heterodox programs." In each case, programs introduced by post-military, elected governments depart from the sort of orthodoxy usually imposed by the International Monetary Fund (IMF).

The difference between IMF orthodoxy and the new "heterodoxy" is important. Nonetheless, both approaches share the fundamental commitment to paying the debt. Both are orthodox in that they define the problem as one of finding a way to simultaneously pay the debt and solve domestic economic problems. Paying the debt means continuing to transfer a large amount of resources out of Latin America into the hands of bankers in the United States, Europe, and Japan. To one degree or another, this has to mean austerity.

The "heterodox" programs adopted in 1985 in Argentina and in 1986 in Brazil were dominated by a concern with inflation. In Argentina, prices had risen by 164 percent, 344 percent and 627 percent during the three years preceding the program's implementation. In Brazil, the three years before the new program's introduction had seen price increases of 211 percent, 224 percent, and 235 percent. Inflation was seen as both a principal symptom and a cause of the economies' instability. The basic idea behind the new policies was that if inflation could be controlled the economies would begin to expand.

The most striking common feature of the programs is monetary reform, involving the substitution of a new currency for the old—the *austral* for the *peso* in Argentina and the *cruzado* for the *cruseiro* in Brazil. The monetary reforms were designed as dramatic moves which would put the governments in a position to greatly reduce the rate of growth of their countries' money supplies. Both programs have also included moves to reduce government spending so as to reduce the government deficit.

Where these programs depart from IMF orthodoxy is in the imposition of wage and price controls. The wage and price controls involve direct government intervention in the economy, a rejection of reliance on unfettered markets. Moreover, the introduction of wage and price controls is accompanied by a commitment, at least a rhetorical commitment, to limiting the impact of austerity measures upon the poor. In Brazil, for example, the new program promised that the government would guarantee the supply of basic staple food.

The Argentina and Brazilian programs do represent a change in Latin America, a change away from reliance on the free market and the ideology of monetarism towards acceptance of an interventionist role for governments and a resurgence of developmentalist ideology. Developmentalism rejects the "devil take the hindmost" approach of monetarism and the IMF because it is so destructive. The devastation wrought by monetarist policies—for example in Chile and Argentina during the 1970s—meant extensive bankruptcies and raised the threat of serious social turmoil. Never accepted in Brazil, even by the military governments, monetarism now seems to be on the defensive in much of Latin America.

The conflict between monetarism and developmentalism in Latin America is parallel to the conflict between monetarism and Keynesianism in the United States. They do represent significantly different approaches, both on the practical and the ideological levels, to how capitalist economies should be run. Neither, however, calls into question the basic principles of capitalism, and in Latin America this means that neither calls into question the basic commitment to pay the debt.

In their early implementations, the programs in Argentina and Brazil appear to have had mixed success. Both have greatly reduced the rate of inflation. At least in Argentina, however, the reduction of inflation has not been translated into successful growth; national income continued to decline through 1985 and into 1986. (It is not yet possible to say anything about the effect of the new program on growth in Brazil.)

With regard to wages, the "heterodoxy" of the Argentinian and Brazilian programs does not seem to be an alternative to traditional orthodoxy. Reliable data are not yet available, but according to the *Latin American Weekly Report (LAWR)* for April 11, 1986, one source suggests that wages in Argentina fell 20 percent in the first year of the *austral* program. An early forecast (reported in *LAWR* for March 14, 1986) of the impact of the Brazilian program indicates that workers there could expect an initial 12 percent decline in their real wages.

Yet, even within the social and political framework that prevails in most of the region, one can certainly conceive of real alternatives. The option of defaulting appears, at least on the surface, particularly attractive. In Argentina, Brazil, and Mexico, debt service annually takes up in excess of $10 billion (though such figures are continually subject to renegotiation and change). Defaults would release huge quantities of funds which could be used to expand much needed imports and provide a basis for growth. The magnitude of the funds now going to service the debts stands out in comparison to the countries' current merchandise imports, which for these countries in 1984 had fallen to $4.2 billion, $13.9 billion, and $10.3 billion respectively.

Debtor nations have defaulted before. The crisis of the 1930s led to defaults throughout Latin America. In the current crisis, the Cuban government as well as many nationalists—those of the left and others—have advocated a cessation of debt payments. Why do the governments of Latin America abjure such action?

THE COSTS OF DEFAULT

Default is sometimes viewed as an unreasonable alternative because creditors could supposedly impose extremely costly sanctions on a defaulter. An interesting book, *The Costs of Default* by Anatole Kaletsky (The Twentieth Century Fund, N.Y., 1985), however, argues convincingly that sanctions do not constitute a deterrent to default. To begin with, Kaletsky, a correspondent for London's *Financial Times*, points out that were default to take place the banks could achieve very little if anything through judicial processes. Chase Manhattan cannot foreclose on Brazil in the same way that the local savings and loans can seize the car of a delinquent debtor. Even though most international loans are signed subject to the laws of either the United States or Britain, the courts provide very limited recourse for a bank in its actions against a sovereign defaulter. The doctrine of sovereign immunity, by which governments cannot be sued even for their commercial activities, has been modified in recent decades, but only to a limited extent. In important cases, courts have ruled that to pass judgment on acts of a foreign state would encroach on the making of foreign policy, a function outside the role of the judiciary. In at least one case, even where the foreign debtor was a private concern, the court ruled that default resulted from the acts of a foreign sovereign and refused to make a judgment in favor of the creditors.

Moreover, the "veil of incorporation" protects the assets of state controlled enterprises with their own legal—i.e., corporate—identities from being held responsible for the debts of their governments. For example, a shipping company wholly subject to the control of a debtor government could not, if it were a legal entity in its own right, have its ships confiscated to fulfill the obligations of its government to foreign banks. Also, a defaulting country could arrange that its exports would become the property of the buyer before they crossed its own border. Kaletsky provides the example of Mexican oil exports which become the legal property of a foreign purchaser the moment they pass the flange of the customer's tanker.

Legal doctrine in this area remains in flux, and some of the legal decisions noted above are being contested. There is, however, no reason to believe that potential legal action by creditors is sufficient to dissuade governments from defaulting.

Kaletsky also dismisses the idea that commercial sanctions imposed by private interests—the banks in alliance with other corporations—would be an effective deterrent to default. Default would not mean the abrogation of all financial and commercial relations, and there is little likelihood that foreign enterprises not directly harmed by a default would join action against a government which defaulted on debts to the banks. Past cases of defaults and even nationalizations have not brought any effective imposition of private commercial sanctions. Kaletsky notes: "Managers of multinational companies point out that bankers have rarely refused to do business with countries which had expropriated industrial, oil or mining companies—for example, in Libya, the Middle East, Peru and even Cuba."

Indeed, were default to recreate a basis for economic expansion in Latin America, many multinational firms would probably welcome it, in spite of public protestations to the contrary. Growth would mean market expansion which, after all, has been the primary attraction for multinationals operating in Latin America. Even the banks themselves would not want to give up their lucrative local operations in Brazil just because the Brazilian government defaulted on its international loans. During the early 1930s, Citicorp, the example cited by Kaletsky, was earning over 20 percent of its worldwide profits in Brazil, with a net return on assets five times the U.S. level.

There is a danger that default would make it impossible for a country to obtain new loans, not because of some organized sanctions but simply because it would be viewed as a bad risk in international capital markets. While the specter of being cut off from international capital markets may have inhibited defaulters prior to 1982, it is hardly a credible threat today. To a very large degree the debtor nations of Latin America have *already* been cut off from capital markets. New loans have been forthcoming in recent years to finance payments on old loans, but there has been virtually no net increase in funds provided.

The most serious potential problem for defaulting nations would not lie in the realm of private action, whether judicial or nonjudicial, actively planned or simply through the blind operation of the market. The real question, as Kaletsky emphasizes, is what the reaction of the creditor governments—particularly the U.S. government—would be. There are of course many things which the United States and other governments could do, ranging from curtailing trade with the defaulting nation to military intervention. Yet there is little reason to believe that such actions would be taken.

In the age of Reagan, one may believe that Kaletsky is overly sanguine when he asserts that "the use of armed might against a defaulter is unthinkable today." Nonetheless, it is hard to imagine that even the hawks who currently control policy in Washington would attempt an invasion of Argentina, Brazil, or Mexico in response to a default.

In case of a default, it is likely that there would at least be a small chorus raised in Congress for some sort of action—trade restrictions or aid cutoffs, for example. Yet those responsible for foreign policy would be unlikely to view the U.S. "national interest" as well served by the implementation of sanctions. The government would probably see its primary task as one of containing the default, of preventing it from disrupting the international financial system and threatening other economic interests, such as those of industrially based multinationals operating in the defaulting nation. Escalating political conflict through sanctions would be unlikely to serve the end of containment. Modern history certainly supports this view. During the last 50 years, since the end of the era of "dollar diplomacy," governments of the advanced capitalist countries have generally taken no action in response to defaults by debtor nations.

Kaletsky's analysis points toward the conclusion that it is in the interest of governments in debtor nations to default. What's more, he argues that those who make policy in the debtor nations will probably reach the same conclusion, and thus: "A default . . . appears quite likely in the foreseeable future."

WHY THE RELUCTANCE TO DEFAULT?

Kaletsky's book has been out for a while now and, although one might extend "the foreseeable future" a good deal further, there have been as yet no true defaults. Why not?

Even if a default were to occur tomorrow—and of course one could occur at any point—it would still be necessary to explain why the governments of debtor countries have been so reluctant to default. Kaletsky's argument and the history of the 1930s and earlier eras would lead us to believe that there should have been defaults by now.

I think there are three mutually supporting explanations for why Latin American governments have been reluctant to default, for why they have attempted to deal with the debt crisis through relatively orthodox means.

The first of these explanations concerns the particular nature of today's debt as compared to the debt of the 1930s. In that earlier era much of the third world debt was in the form of bonds widely dispersed among private individuals in the creditor countries. In the 1930s, when a government could not meet its payments, it was forced into default: there was simply no mechanism by which the many bondholders could be organized to negotiate a rescheduling. Today, with the debt highly concentrated in the hands of large money-center banks, negotiated reschedulings are readily organized. Options to outright default exist which did not exist in the 1930s. Also, today's concentration of debt means that the potential consequences of default for the international financial system could be much more severe (I shall return to this point shortly).

A second explanation for the reluctance to default emerges from a closer look at Kaletsky's argument. Kaletsky accepts the concept of "national interest," and he argues that it is in the national interest of debtor countries to default. The problem is that in class societies there is no such thing as the national interest. What is important in explaining the actions of a government on any particular issue is the interests of the dominant class or classes. On the matter of alternative ways to deal with the debt crisis, it would appear that *the orthodox programs being followed in Latin America do in fact serve the interests of the ruling groups.*

Even though businesses in Latin America are experiencing hardships in the current era, the private wealth and incomes of rich individuals have not suffered so greatly. In his last speech before leaving office at the end of 1982, Mexican President Lopez Portillo made the point when he referred to "poor enterprises with rich entrepreneurs." From Mexico particularly, but also from other large debtor countries in Latin America, there has been a huge flight of capital to safe havens in the advanced countries, particularly the United States. Thus wealthy Latin Americans have protected themselves against the crisis by acquiring foreign assets. Also, as adjustment programs have devalued Latin American currencies, the value of these foreign assets measured in terms of home currencies has risen sharply. Rich Latin Americans have not totally disconnected themselves from the fortunes of their enterprises in their own countries, but they have succeeded in insulating themselves—and may even have gained—from the adjustment processes.

In addition, the adjustment processes in Latin America may serve a positive long-run function from the point of view of capital. Governments throughout the region are rolling back costly social programs and pushing wage rates through the floor. Organized labor appears ineffective in the face of the onslaught and is likely to suffer a long-run loss of political strength. Thus the debt crisis is providing a convenient rationale for an offensive by capital. This approach is, of course, by no means an automatic winner: attempting to create a basis for expansion in this way can precipitate a worse crisis. Yet it is an approach which has obvious attraction for capital. (One should note the similarity to the aggressive actions of U.S. capital in recent years.)

A third explanation of the reluctance to default lies in the larger implications of such actions. Major defaults would threaten a possible international financial collapse, which would do drastic harm to the system generally and within the defaulting nation as well. Of course a default, even by a Mexico or a Brazil, would not necessarily precipitate a financial collapse. The U.S. government and the governments of the other creditor nations have the means to provide banks with the funds necessary to prevent collapse in the face of default. Yet the injection of funds in this way would itself be disruptive to international finance, and there is always the possibility that the creditor powers would not act sufficiently rapidly and appropriately. So the first line of defense against international financial turmoil is the prevention of default.

Kaletsky's analysis does not ignore the possibility of international financial turmoil, but he apparently believes that such larger concerns are beyond the scope of third world rulers. He analyzes their actions from a narrow economistic point of view that focuses on direct and tangible costs and benefits while ignoring larger interests. In contrast, we might better understand the actions of Latin American ruling groups if we view them as junior partners in the operation of international capitalism. True, they do not have the same global responsibilities as do their counterparts in the imperial centers, but they do share in the burdens (and benefits) of power. The well developed complex of ties to international business, of rewards through military and development aid, and of direct political pressure has integrated them into an imperial system and taught them that it serves their own larger interests to avoid disruptive actions.

The situation with regard to maintaining the system is substantially different now than it was in the 1930s. The changed nature of the debt, as noted above, means that default today would more likely be disruptive. While defaults in the 1930s were costly for those who held the bonds, today they would directly threaten the viability of major banks; and through the banks, the impact of defaults could have rapid and deleterious effects on the general availability of liquidity.

Furthermore, the ruling groups in Latin America have a different relation to international capitalism now than in the 1930s. In that earlier era, the state in Latin American nations was not a modern capitalist state, representing as it did an alliance of traditional landed groups, a commercial elite, a semi-autonomous military, and a distinctly junior and emerging industrial capitalist class. The Latin American state was a subordinate state within the international system and operated in alliance with foreign capital; but it was also separate from that system, representing the dominant interests in a society that was still being integrated into world capitalism. The half century since that earlier round of defaults has seen dramatic changes in the sociopolitical structure of Latin American states and in the relation of those states to international capitalism. Especially in the larger nations of the region—most obviously Brazil, Mexico, Argentina, Venezuela—the state has become much more a capitalist state. Accordingly, with this national development of capitalism in Latin America, the relation with international capital has been more firmly and completely established.

CAPITALISM OR BARBARISM?

The reluctance of Latin American governments to default is, then, not so hard to understand. There may still be defaults, the debt crisis is far from over. Yet one should expect that the dominant groups in Latin America will continue to pursue "alternatives" which remain within the confines of accepting the debt and the austerity that goes with it. What remains to be explained is why the peoples of Latin America continue to tolerate the situation.

6. EASING THE DEBT CRISIS

Nowhere in Latin America has the debt crisis led to the upsurge of a movement challenging the basic orthodoxy of the governments' economic programs. Trade unions in Brazil and Argentina have formally opposed the continued imposition of austerity in those countries, but their ability to carry off actions has not been impressive. In the spring of 1986, for example, the Argentinian *Confederacion General del Trabajo* (CGT) called two general strikes. According to the *Latin American Weekly Report* (April 4, 1986), however, the March strike failed completely to shut down transportation and retail stores. The April strike was then called off when the government made some minimal compromises toward the CGT's demands (*LAWR*, April 25, 1986). In Brazil some trade union leaders spoke strongly against the government's actions, but generally the new program's introduction seems to have been favorably accepted (*LAWR*, March 14, 1986). Among the large debtors, Mexico's government has probably faced the most substantial challenges, but these have come from the right, not the left. They reflect a reaction against the government's failures by both middle-class groups and some segments of the business elite. But the economic program of the right calls for less government intervention in the economy and does not challenge the basics of austerity.

Perhaps it would be unrealistic to expect a strong popular protest movement to have developed at this point in Latin America's crisis. Economic downturns do not lead to popular opposition the way turning on the spigot starts the flow of water. In fact, at least under some circumstances, as things get worse workers may become less ready to protest. After the failure of the March strike in Buenos Aires, the *Latin American Weekly Report* (April 11) offered this explanation from a private-sector manager: "It has been a hard time for workers; since the *austral* was introduced they have seen their wages reduced by 20 percent, and they do not want to lose their attendance bonus now."

For a popular opposition to develop, people need to believe that a viable alternative exists—not simply in the sense of an alternative economic program, but in the sense of an alternative political force. Especially in Argentina and Brazil, and elsewhere where military regimes have recently been ousted, experience of the last few years has greatly limited popular conceptions of alternatives. Instead of viewing protest as the route to a progressive economic program, many are undoubtedly afraid of a return to military rule. Current governments are not unaware of this fear. In response to CGT threats of action against the Argentinian government, the Interior Minister "reminded the public that confrontations of the sort pursued by the CGT had led to the ouster [by the military], in 1966, of President Arturo Illia" (*LAWR*, March 14). Thus, on the one hand, people see the current elected regimes with their programs of austerity. On the other hand, they have lived through the brutality and economic hardships of military rule. The choice then may appear as one between the current austerity or a return to military rule—capitalism or barbarism.

The vivid memory of military rule not only provides current governments with an effective lever in persuading people that programs of austerity are the best that can be hoped for. In addition, military regimes destroyed or greatly weakened popular opposition movements. Whether this took the form of murder and disappearances or simply harassment and severe restrictions of left political activity, the military successfully prevented the left from becoming a viable alternative political force today.

There are of course important differences among the countries which have recently emerged from military rule. In Mexico where a progressive opposition is no more apparent than in Brazil or Argentina, a relatively stable, formally democratic civilian regime has held power for decades. Yet, in spite of differences, in most of Latin America the ruling groups have succeeded in preventing progressive forces from presenting themselves as a viable political alternative. Whether the strategy has been brutal military repression or extensive bureaucratic control or a combination of both, the organized left has, at least up to the present, been effectively marginalized.

This is not a counsel of despair. It is a recognition of the objective limits which oppositional forces face in Latin America. Change often comes much faster than we would anticipate in an era of economic crisis, but it seldom comes simply as a spontaneous response to the economic hardships of the crisis. In building and rebuilding the political bases for change it is essential to recognize that economic circumstances per se do not generate a progressive response. An alternative to austerity is possible, but it will be realized only if it is politically created.

WILL THE PLANET PAY THE PRICE FOR THIRD WORLD DEBT?

The battle against the earth's destruction pits world leaders against an intractable foe: Poverty

The demonstrations in West Berlin last month stretched from the conference hall of the World Bank and the International Monetary Fund conclave to the golden arches of a McDonald's restaurant. Among the gripes: environmental destruction wreaked by projects financed by the World Bank, including the destruction of rain forests to make room for cattle grazing. By pushing hamburgers, chains like McDonald's Corp. must share part of the blame, the protesters said. They weren't the only ones concerned. In his address to the bankers, West German Chancellor Helmut Kohl warned darkly that unconstrained development "could prove disastrous for mankind."

In a year when a thinning ozone layer, a warming globe, and floating medical garbage have vied for front-page coverage, the politics of ecology has secured its place as a mainstream issue. But the battle against the earth's destruction pits world leaders against a foe much tougher than terrorists, drug-traffickers, or nuclear stockpiles: Third World poverty. As the planet warms partly from the effects of depleted rain forests from Indonesia to Brazil, the industrialized world is starting to feel the cost of Third World development as never before. The traditional paths to growth—building big dams, roadways, and the other megaprojects favored by international lending agencies—are thus coming under increasing scrutiny.

LOUDER VOICE. Just as the industrialized world is waking up to the consequences of such growth policies, poor countries are staggering under mountains of debt. Their desperation for cash—at any environmental cost—is only adding to the growing ecological crisis. Says José Lizárraga, Latin America director of the U. N. Environmental Program: "The debt crisis puts countries in a short-term frame of mind."

Even if the world's bankers were to forgive much of the debt, governments until recently had little incentive to devote scarce resources to saving forests and streams. Now, for the first time, they find themselves confronted with environmental movements at home. In Mexico, ecology activists supported opposition candidate Cuauhtémoc Cárdenas. In September environmentalists in São Paulo, Brazil, draped around the fence of the governor's palace a 2,500-meter-long petition calling for a new national preserve. Meanwhile, in Taiwan, strong support for the opposition Democratic Progressive Party forced the ruling Kuomintang to form an environmental protection agency and spend more money on cleanup projects. The broad shift toward pluralism that has swept from Brazil and Argentina to Korea and the Philippines in this decade is giving environmental groups a louder voice.

Still, neither the First nor Third World can deny that the developing countries' ability to support their mushrooming populations is increasingly dubious. In the next 60 years the world will grow from today's 5 billion people to between 11 billion and 14 billion, according to a U. N. report. Some 90% of this growth will occur in poor countries. Countries that are now hard-pressed to provide for their people will have to feed, clothe, house, and transport billions more within several decades. In preparing to face this task, they must make optimum use of their precious natural resources.

Yet throughout Africa and Latin America, debtor countries are cutting down forests, overusing fertilizers, and exhausting groundwater supplies in efforts to produce cash crops. In debt-ridden Brazil, for example, streams of impoverished settlers head west, hoping to cash in on abundant gold, tin, and land in the vast Amazon jungle. In the past decade settlers have slashed and burned enough forest to cover France. Each year, Brazilian scientists say, the cutting and burning of trees in the Amazon alone contributes as much as one-tenth of all the planet's principal greenhouse gas, carbon dioxide. As the world's largest rain forest shrinks, it absorbs less carbon dioxide and produces less oxygen. Worse yet, all of the world's rain forests are located in poor southern countries: Brazil, Zaire, Indonesia, and the Philippines.

In Central America, farmers douse their fields with megatons of pesticides long outlawed in the U. S. The result: Poisoned waters annually kill three of every 1,000 inhabitants, according to the U. S. Agency for International Development. Overuse of pesticides in Central America is also certain to affect the region's agricultural exports, three-quarters of which end up in the U. S.

'GREENING PROCESS.' With its enormous power over economic development—approving $17.5 billion for 217 projects this year—the World Bank is a highly visible target for environmental critics. Throughout its postwar history, the multination lending organization has enraged conservationists by funding ecologically unsound megaprojects. At the Berlin meeting, environmentalists from 20 nations presented a list of the World Bank's "dirty half-dozen"—six major projects that they say have damaged local environments. The projects range from a cattle-raising program in Botswana that has led to overgrazing to bank-backed overuse of pesticides in the Sudan.

Long before the meeting, however, attitudes had begun to change if slowly. Over the past five years the World Bank and its regional subsidiaries have begun what bank officials call "a greening process." A 60-person environmental department within the bank now oversees new projects. Still, environmentalists contend that ecology remains a mere tag-on item at the bank. "The types of projects coming out of the pipeline—the real test—have not changed significantly," says Brent Blackwelder, vice-president of the Environmental Policy Institute in Washington. Blackwelder claims that more than 90% of the bank's lending still goes to huge coal projects and big dams, such as the $10 billion Yangtze River Dan now under consideration for financing, which would force large-scale relocation.

QUANDARY. After getting an earful of suggestions at the Berlin meeting, World Bank Environmental Director

Kenneth Piddington urged patience. "It's not a question of an institution like the bank turning green overnight," he said. "It's a long process." Other officials stress that the bank has limited clout in development financing. "A number of these [controversial] projects would have gone on with or without World Bank intervention," says Jeremy Warford, senior adviser in the bank's environmental department. "Environmentalists don't want to hear that."

Indeed, a World Bank report in September called on Brazil to curtail tax and agricultural incentives that are luring settlers and big farmers into the Amazon. Ironically, one of the problems mentioned in the report was the Brazilian Polonoroeste project, which features a large road through the jungle's southern rim. The World Bank has already invested $617 million in it. The Amazon controversy puts Brazil in a quandary. The country has a financial disaster on its hands: It pays more than $10 billion a year in interest on its $120 billion foreign debt, and inflation is nearing 1,000% annually. Rio de Janeiro just declared bankruptcy. Famine claims lives throughout the country's northeast.

Yet an accidental find of rich tin deposits deep in the Amazon has made Brazil a world leader in tin production. Now that it has found a source of precious revenue, the country is being told that for the good of the planet it must rein in Amazon development.

Worse, according to analysts at the World Wildlife Fund in Washington, Brazil needs to spend some $3 billion to $4 billion a year to protect the jungle and clean up the mess in its southern industrial region. Should Brazil be left to sort out the problems by itself? No way, says José Goldemberg, rector of the University of São Paulo. "If you leave industrializing countries alone, they will do nothing."

JAPAN'S ROLE. So desperate are they for cash that many leaders will look elsewhere for loans, despite warnings of dire ecological consequences. Many controversial projects are funded by the richest new power in international aid, Japan. The country is pouring aid into dams, roads, and railways from rain forests in Asia to the Brazilian Amazon. "The problem with Japan's aid," says Jonathan Holliman, a spokesman for Friends of the Earth Japan, "is that there is no environmental assessment."

In several cases, Japan has offered to pick up loans that other lending agencies have dropped for environmental reasons. In Thailand, critics say, Japan's Overseas Economic Cooperation Fund (OECF) was prepared to finance the Nam Choan Dam even after the World Bank backed away from the controversial project last spring. In the end, the Thai government shelved the project under pressure from environmentalists. Counters a Japanese Foreign Ministry official: "We try to improve the well-being of the recipient country, and instead we are accused of destroying the environment."

For decades, Chinese leaders have worried far more about industrial production than about the environment. One result is a green-brown smog that envelops Chinese cities. Citizens cover their mouths with scarves or masks on particularly thick days. Like London in the 1950s, Beijing suffers from extensive coal-burning: more than 20 million tons a year. More worrisome from a greenhouse perspective is China's plan to quadruple its coal consumption by the turn of the century.

With increased smog, environmental awareness is growing in China. In July the Beijing city government finally passed regulations to limit air pollution. And the *Guangming Daily* complained that China's pollution was "as heavy as that in the developed countries in the 1950s and 1960s."

DEBT SWAPS. Elsewhere, a few ingenious conservation schemes are sprouting. Last year several environmental groups, led by the World Wildlife Fund, began to finance conservation projects with debt-for-equity swaps. These swaps, now in vogue among investors in debtor countries, allow the environmental group to buy the countries' debt at a discount and cash it in for local currency. Rather than invest the money in a hotel or a factory, the environmentalists finance local conservation projects, thereby attacking both crushing problems of debt and environment at once. So far, several million dollars worth of such debt-for-nature deals have been done in Bolivia, Costa Rica, Ecuador, and the Philippines.

Exploding populations and stagnant economies threaten to turn Haiti and El Salvador into woodless wastelands

In Mexico City, dozens of bureaucrats work late hours in the Environmental Secretariat to complete the country's first set of environmental regulations before the new presidential administration takes office on Dec. 1. And for more than a year, public pressure forced the government to postpone loading the first reactor of the $3.5 billion Laguna Verde nuclear facility in the state of Vera Cruz. Meanwhile, environmentalists flexed their muscles before the recent presidential elections, reaping loads of promises from the candidates to attack the thick layer of smog that chokes the Valley of Mexico's approximately 20 million residents.

But in other regions of Mexico, as the population grows and the economy stagnates, once-great forests in the states of Michoacán and Chiapas are succumbing to a combination of small-time wood gatherers and lumber companies. This process, brought on by economic need and greed, already threatens to turn Haiti into a woodless wasteland and has turned formerly lush El Salvador into semi-desert. Those countries serve as grim reminders of the cycle of poverty that leads to environmental abuse. As the land fails, social tensions grow, sometimes exploding into war. Refugees flock to greener pastures, often chopping down trees along the way.

Cleaning up world development is too big a task for any one institution or country to handle alone. Even without the debt crisis, experts say, an environmental crisis would exist in the Third World, just as it does in the First. Treaties vowing cooperation to battle the greenhouse effect and ozone depletion are a promising start. But while leaders sign documents, peasants from Indonesia to Zaire continue to hack farm plots out of rain forests. The challenge at hand is not to preach to those people of the jungle's importance, but to offer them jobs that will leave it intact.

By Stephen Baker in Mexico City, with Jeffrey Ryser in Sao Paulo, William Glasgall in Berlin, Vicky Cahan in Washington, and bureau reports

The Third World smiles

Gloom has been so common in the Third World for the past five years that few people have noticed the first hint of a reason for a smile. Nonetheless, economic prospects for the nearly 4 billion people in developing countries are starting to brighten. If their governments seize the chance, they will soon be striking back at man's ancient enemies of poverty, ignorance and disease.

Those three sentences of sweeping generalisation need to be qualified, and will be. But the necessary complications should not obscure one broad truth: that the third world's economic progress can be judged by whether its real gross domestic product grows by more than 5% a year, or less. Between 1965 and 1980, its annual GDP growth averaged 6%. Since 1980 it has slowed to 3¼%. As the first half of the 1980s brought the roughest economic times in half a century, the chances of a big improvement are good. Look around to see why.

Northern cheer

The rich industrial democracies in the northern hemisphere buy about 80% of the Third World's exports and provide almost all its foreign capital. When they are sick, they are infectious; healthy, they are strong enough to pull many developing countries along with them. The OECD economies now have several reasons for feeling chipper. They are gaining greatly from cheaper oil, which has already raised their expected GDP growth this year to 3-3¼%. Inflation in rich industrial countries is low and still falling; interest rates are coming down; exchange rates are no longer as wildly out of kilter as they were a year ago, so pressures for trade protectionism should soon start to ease. These are big achievements, which are making the remaining and familiar weaknesses—America's budget deficit, the shakiness of many bank assets—seem less menacing than they once were.

The poor south has it own reasons for optimism. Roughly 70 developing countries are net oil importers, and more than 3 billion people live in them. Cheaper oil means more foreign exchange to spend on other things: machinery, fertiliser, school books, medicines. Or it means a chance to rebuild foreign reserves or pay off loans, both measures that will improve their creditworthiness. In the longer run, the indirect benefits of cheaper oil will be even greater. If American interest rates come down and stay there; if the OECD countries reduce their unemployment and become less protectionist; if world trade picks up—all those ifs are no longer fanciful, and together they promise faster and steadier growth.

Habitual pessimists will choose to dwell on how this new world harms the 20 or so developing countries (with their 600m people) that are net exporters of oil. For them, economic life has indeed become tougher as the dollar price of a barrel of oil has tumbled towards $10—in real terms back to where it was in 1973, when OPEC just looked like a typing error. A few oil exporters have wisely tended the riches of a dozen years. They have something useful—competitive farms and factories at home, bigger investment income from abroad—that they did not have before. The others have frittered the money away.

There lies the biggest moral for the Third World as it seeks to push GDP growth above 5% a year again. Money is not what counts, but how it is used—and that depends on the economic policies of governments, and how businesses and farmers respond to them. Nothing could be more irrelevant than the idea proposed by Israel's prime minister last week. He wants the West to finance a Marshall plan for the Middle East, a region which had about an extra 3% of gross world product thrown at it for most of an OPEC-dominated decade. Largesse is often lethal, disguising the consequences of bad economic policies until it is too late. The developing world's most successful economies in the past 25 years have not had a drop of their own oil: Singapore (where GDP per person grew by 7½% a year), Taiwan (7%), South Korea (6½%) and Hongkong (6%).

Lest that list seem to suggest that the secret of growth is to have a yellow skin and live near the Pacific, add Botswana (7¼% a year). Its example is a valuable antidote to the usually justified pessimism about Africa. While Asians have increased their average real incomes by some 170% in the past 25 years and Latin Americans by only slightly less, the average African is now poorer than in 1960. Wars, drought, pestilence—the Old Testament horrors have plagued Africa, but they matter less than some crass government errors. Most African governments have done the opposite of their Asian counterparts: they have gone for import substitution rather than exports, let their exchange rates become uncompetitive, shunned foreign investment, held down farm prices, preferred fancy hospitals and universities to local clinics and schools.

This message, repeated hundreds of times (most recently by the World Bank, see page 68), may slowly be getting through. Ghana and Zambia have been converted to competitive exchange rates. Cameroon has shown that being an oil exporter need not be the death of agriculture (Nigeria, please note). Botswana is not alone in having fine natural resources; it owes its rapid growth mainly to the fact that it has encouraged foreign investors to come and develop them.

That is a lesson that much of the Third World is starting to heed. Northern bankers, scarred by Latin America and scared of a repeat performance, will not lend much. Northern governments are trying to cut public spending, and will not recapture their aid generosity of the 1960s. But direct investment from northern multinationals and fund managers would double if they thought they were welcome in the reviving south, and double again if poor countries' annual GDP growth were to get back to 6% or so. The conditions that attract foreign investors—unbossy politicians, sound finance, free-market policies—are also those that encourage domestic entrepreneurs and farmers. China and India have switched their economic policies not mainly to attract foreign investment, but because it was good for their own growth. The other side of that coin is that governments of small and poor countries are wrong to assume that they cannot attract foreign investment. If they do what is best for local economic growth, foreigners will not be slow to invest.

Nobody should doubt that many developing countries face big challenges. Three years ago, with the world in recession and oil costing more than $30 a barrel, those challenges seemed overwhelming. The difference today is between hope and despair, between a smile and a frown. Now is the time to start smiling.

Brazil Debt Pact Called Innovative

ERIC N. BERG

The agreement between Brazil and its foreign creditor banks to reduce sharply the interest Brazil pays on more than $60 billion of debt and to provide it with $5.2 billion in new loans was described yesterday as innovative and significant by a number of experts on third-world debt.

"This is a new approach that focuses on giving the debtor country lower interest rates and more time," said Antonio Villamil, the chief economist at the Bank of the Southeast in Miami. "We have moved away from short-term austerity. To me, it's a whole new ball game."

Final terms of the accord remain to be hammered out, but Citibank, which heads the committee of Brazil's bank creditors, said yesterday that agreement had been reached on several important points.

Brazil's Finance Minister, Maílson Ferreira da Nóbrega, announced some details of the agreement in Brasília on Tuesday.

Under the agreement, Brazil, in the next few days, will pay $350 million to cover overdue interest from March, and another $1 billion on June 30 to cover its arrears for April and May. That will make Brazil, the largest debtor in the developing world, current on its obligations.

In turn, the banks will sharply reduce the interest rate they have been charging on Brazil's $60 billion in medium-term loans. The banks will also provide $5.2 billion in new loans: $4 billion by Oct. 31, another $600 million by year-end and $600 million more in the first quarter of 1989.

That schedule of payments represents a victory for Brazil, several debt experts said. They noted that the first $4 billion will be disbursed well before Brazil is asked to meet certain fiscal and monetary targets under a proposed economic-adjustment program with the International Monetary Fund.

The arrangement marks the first time that the banks have agreed to provide a big debtor such a large loan without linking it to I.M.F. conditions.

Such terms would seem to fly in the face of Treasury Secretary James A. Baker 3d's debt plan, which calls for new bank financing accompanied by economic adjustments.

Another debt expert, who asked not to be named because he does consulting work for some of Brazil's bank creditors, said, "The Brazilians will be getting the bulk of their new financing without doing much of anything."

But William Rhodes of Citibank, who is chairman of the creditors' committee, insisted that the Brazilians were meeting certain conditions.

By the time the first new loans are provided in October, he said, "the board of directors of the I.M.F. will have approved Brazil's economic program."

Variety of Options

The banks will have several options in dealing with Brazil, including the right to participate in co-financing agreements with the World Bank; buying so-called exit bonds, which allow a bank to roll over existing loans rather than extend new credit, and participating in debt-equity swaps, in which a bank exchanges its loans for ownership stakes in local industry.

"The menu of options is the most extensive and innovative since the debt crisis began in 1982," Mr. Rhodes said.

Other experts said the bankers had agreed to provide money early because of a growing conviction that a less-rigid approach to the debt crisis might be beneficial. For the last few years the approach has essentially been that the banks would disburse money gradually, timing the loans to coincide with achievement by the debtor nation of economic goals set by the I.M.F.

In some ways the agreement is a victory for the banks, some experts said.

The most immediate impact of the accord will be to end the interest moratorium that Brazil imposed in February 1987. In a statement issued by Citibank, Mr. Nóbrega said the accord would allow Brazil "to regularize interest payments to commercial banks within the next few months."

The Moratorium's Results

The moratorium produced a war of words, with Brazil saying it would miss interest payments for an extended period and the banks threatening to cut off Brazil from trade lines of credit.

In the end, the banks prevailed: Brazil's reserves fell, and the banks carried on business as usual, notwithstanding a big drop in their profits.

"The results of the moratorium were disastrous for Brazil," said Mr. Villamil of the Bank of the Southeast. He said it increased Brazil's cost of borrowing and produced a slowdown in domestic investment.

Under the new agreement, Brazil's interest rate has been set at 13/16 of a percentage point more than the banks' cost of funds. That is less than half the 1¾ percentage points differential set under previous agreements.

The lower interest will help Brazil service all $118 billion of its debt, not just the $60 billion owed to foreign commercial banks.

A World in Change

Sadly, the Third World—far more than the industrialized world—faces a host of urgent social problems. These include malnutrition, poverty, illiteracy, disease, pollution, overpopulation, and war. To a large extent, these ills stem from social, political, and economic inequality. Despite numerous efforts, the developing world has failed to close the ever-widening gap between the have and have-not nations.

Like its industrialized counterpart, the Third World is extremely pluralistic. Obviously, one cannot compare such "poor countries" as Nigeria and Mexico to the "poor, poor nations" of Haiti and Bangladesh. Indeed, some developing countries have proven far more successful than others in achieving stability, unity, and economic progress. As such, it is difficult, if not impossible, to make sweeping generalizations about the status of the Third World.

With this caveat in mind, it is still possible to identify the principal challenges facing the developing world, chief of which is the problem of war and civil strife. In several Third World nations, one can easily discern any number of organizations, states, and private individuals who are actively engaged in fomenting or supporting violent campaigns to accomplish their objectives. This is clearly the case in the Philippines, Nicaragua, Lebanon, South Africa, and elsewhere. The problem has grown increasingly acute due to the widespread manufacture and proliferation of armaments, which has become an important industry in some Third World countries.

The developing world also faces numerous economic problems, fueled in recent years by the banks and multinational corporations which have fostered increased financial dependency. These institutions wield significant power in many Third World countries, often to the detriment of the people they seek to serve. In some cases, these international organizations function independently of their parent governments, with little accountability or responsibility. This situation is due, in part, to the dismal economic conditions in many developing nations, which possess inadequate resources, limited technology, and fragile political institutions.

Equally important is the problem of resources—that is, their control, conservation, and distribution. Third World nations, like many other countries, have squandered precious resources, ignored environmental warnings, failed to develop alternative energy sources, and refused to impose strict limits on population growth. Reckless disregard for the environment—in the form of air, land, and water pollution—could pose a major disaster. Moreover, future industrial development in the Third World threatens to intensify the problem.

The battle for human rights represents yet another threat to the future of the Third World. Countless developing countries practice widespread political repression. Today, many Third World peoples live in a permanent state of tyranny and oppression. The number of dictatorships has multiplied, and with them the use of kidnapping, torture, imprisonment, and assassination, which are commonplace in many developing nations.

The Third World is also plagued by problems of immigration, emigration, and statelessness. In some countries, the lack of economic opportunity and political freedom has encouraged many talented young people to migrate to other nations where life appears more rewarding. In addition, the intensification of racial, religious, and ethnic rivalries has produced a new wave of problems, causing some developing nations to impose tight new immigration restrictions or order mass expulsions.

In summary, one must ask: In what direction is the Third World headed? What new problems will it confront in the future? Is it reasonable to expect these nations—given their present economic conditions—to solve such critical problems as hunger, poverty, unemployment, and overpopulation? Clearly, solving the problems of the Third World will demand unprecedented resolve and ingenuity. The challenges of the future will require a major commitment of human and material resources. The developing world cannot continue to bury its head in the sand; it must meet the challenges of the twenty-first century head-on. Unless they act now, Third World nations may well lose many of the benefits of their hard-won independence and face a hostile world which has little if any interest in their future.

Looking Ahead: Challenge Questions

What are the short- and long-term effects of malnutrition?

Unit 7

Why is malnutrition so common in the Third World?

What factors explain the rise of the world's refugee population?

Why have many nations refused asylum to millions of refugees?

What obstacles prevent a permanent solution to the refugee problem?

Why have many developing nations become arms merchants?

What dangers, if any, does the acquisition of ballistic missiles pose to the future of the Third World?

Why is narco-terrorism on the rise in the developing world?

To what degree is the Western world responsible for the increase in international drug trafficking?

In what sense have drugs become a potent political weapon, both in terms of destabilization and revolution?

What are some solutions to the crisis in health care in the Third World?

Why has AIDS reached epidemic proportions in the developing world, particularly in Africa?

What, if anything, can be done to combat the AIDS crisis in Africa?

Should international corporations, like Union Carbide, be held more accountable for their actions in the Third World?

Does the developing world need a new international economic order?

What major challenges are most likely to confront the Third World in the twenty-first century?

THE HIDDEN MALICE of Malnutrition

EVEN IF WORLD hunger ended tomorrow, the long-term effects of famine would linger for more than eight generations

PHOTOGRAPH: IRENE PEARLMAN

Robert N. Ross

Robert Ross *is a Brookline-based freelance writer.*

Images of starving children are all too familiar: dull eyes, listless expressions, spindly limbs and protruding bellies. Images of their parents have also become commonplace: their faces similarly impassive, except perhaps for the hint of frustration and fear in their eyes.

Throughout history famine has affected young and old alike. An estimated 10 million people died in the great Bengal famine of 1769; perhaps as many as three million people died in the great Irish potato famine; and the civilian deaths during World War II

From *Bostonia*, February/March 1987, pp. 49-57. Reprinted with permission of *Bostonia* magazine.

caused by food shortages in Russia are beyond all accurate reckoning. The count is also unknown for the famine we have witnessed most recently in the Sahel region of West Africa and in Ethiopia.

But despite the horror of famine and starvation, the effects of these disasters pale by comparison with the effects of the chronic undernutrition from which most of the world's population continually suffers. Short-term starvation, as after an earthquake or during a state of siege, is relatively easy to cure—all it takes is more food. The young are especially likely to survive and recover. The physical, mental and emotional effects of long-term malnutrition, due to an inadequate supply of nutrients, unfortunately do not all respond to short-term fixes. The simple solution of more food might remedy the initial problem, but it cannot fix the physical and physiological effects of malnutrition on future generations.

Malnutrition is more likely to occur as a chronic problem than a single devastating episode. The way of life for undernourished people of the impoverished Third World has been perpetuated for generations. In fact, recent research on the effects of undernutrition in human beings and laboratory animals shows that adults who have a condition of deficient body nutrition from an inadequate intake of food (undernutrition), bear mentally and physically weakened offspring whose newborns are likewise impaired, and so on. This pattern is closer to a downward spiral than a cycle. For surviving becomes increasingly difficult with each new generation of chronically undernourished animals — whether they are laboratory animals deliberately underfed in an experimental setting or poor people trying to get by with meager resources.

Some effects of malnutrition are painfully obvious in children. As parents are well aware, hungry infants can be irritable, restless and difficult to calm. Even trying to feed them seems to make them more irritable. Hunger and starvation, of course, are two very different states. Hunger is a normal signal to start looking for food. Starvation (the word itself derives from the Old English word meaning to die) is all too common; but it is not natural. Although malnutrition that accompanies long-term starvation causes a variety of physical problems, it may also cause much more subtle mental and emotional difficulties. Language skills develop more slowly in malnourished children. Motor skills are retarded. Crying patterns suggest that something is not right in the central nervous system.

> "In real life, malnutrition is a chronic, long-term problem of surviving. For animals and humans alike, the process of malnutrition is intergenerational."
>
> Dr. Janina Galler

Much of the research on malnutrition has been carried out on laboratory animals. "But starving experimental animals for short periods of time is not a realistic model of malnutrition," according to Janina R. Galler, M.D., director of the Center for Behavioral Development and Mental Retardation at Boston University School of Medicine. "In real life, malnutrition is a chronic, long-term problem of surviving. For animals and humans alike, the process of malnutrition is intergenerational."

Galler has studied the intergenerational effects of malnutrition on long-term growth and behavior of animals and human beings. In one study that has continued for 18 years, she and her co-principal investigator Dr. Frank Ramsey, Director of the National Nutrition Center in Barbados, have watched Barbadian children grow up. The most disquieting conclusions to be drawn from her Barbados study are that ongoing under-nutrition affects long-term learning and behavior. More critical is the fact that the effects of malnutrition on learning and behavior may not disappear when the child is eventually fed a normal diet. Even after children have supposedly "recovered" from the most obvious physical effects of malnutrition, their mental and emotional growth remains impaired. Scores on tests of abstract reasoning, logical and relational thinking, language development, IQ and social relations remain well below normal. Reading and writing difficulties persist.

Low scores on achievement tests, poor grades in school, social difficulties and other problems never go away for some children.

In the Barbados study, Galler and Ramsey have been following 314 children since their first year of life. Of these children, 185 were severely malnourished in their first year of life and were later rehabilitated. The comparison group was a group of their classmates with no histories of malnutrition. The children are now grown.

"We were able to document that among the girls suffering from protein-energy malnutrition, there was a delay of about one and one-half years in menarche and sexual maturation." The girls in the study group were undernourished in the first year of their lives but were then provided with a nourishing diet. Nonetheless, as Galler says, "something went awry in the programming of their development and the girls' sexual maturation was delayed."

The delay is interesting because, surprisingly, it shows that the *brain* is severely affected by chronic undernutrition. A poorly understood "clock" in the brain is set to trigger production of hormones that stimulate changes in the reproductive organs and secondary sexual characteristics. Whatever damage the undernutrition did to the girls' brains during that first year of life must have remained dormant until, 10 or 12 years later, that part of the brain was needed to orchestrate the complex events of sexual maturation.

Many growth factors play a role in

a process as complicated as sexual maturation. One of these factors, which can be measured in the blood, is a good reflection of brain processes controlling growth and maturation. The measured substance is an insulin-like growth factor called somatomedin-C/IGF—1. Galler and her co-workers have found that in adolescents with histories of early malnutrition, levels of somatomedin-C/IGF-1 were significantly lower than one would have expected for children at that age. Lower levels of this growth factor alone did not explain the delays in sexual maturation. The abnormally low levels of the growth factor in children who had been malnourished many years earlier suggested how insidious are the long-term effects of such undernutrition.

The Barbados study has also shown that undernutrition disturbs at least one of the brain's hormonal functions. Undernutrition will also disturb how the brain processes information. In particular, undernutrition disturbs attention, even after children have been rehabilitated with a normal diet.

Galler's long-term studies have shown that a person or animal with a previous history of undernutrition has difficulty adapting to new situations. Whatever unknown neuroanatomic, neurophysiologic or neurochemical lesion is produced in the brain by undernutrition, that lesion is responsible for a wide range of subtle problems in the adult. Among the long-term consequences is attentional deficit disorder, or hyperactivity, in school-age children. A hyperactive child has a hard time settling down and is easily distracted.

And chronically malnourished children look very much like certain brain damaged children. Children with the brain condition known as attentional deficit disorder are sometimes hyperactive, impulsive, emotionally labile, subject to temper tantrums and victims of panic attacks. Some children with attentional deficit disorder have one or more of these symptoms; others may have none of them. One symptom they all share, however, is a failure to concentrate in certain settings. Not surprising, children who cannot concentrate adequately also have learning disabilities.

"The damage to the brain does not simply occur at the time of malnutrition. Rather, there appears to be some impact on the programming of the brain," noted Galler. Even after relieving the brain, the damage continues to occur in a sequential way. "We have measured this by looking at the brain at certain periods when particular populations of cells should be developing. We are finding that certain cells that do not even appear until later in development are adversely affected by earlier malnutrition."

In the United States, these children are diagnosed as having "attentional deficit disorder." "The conditions of attentional deficit disorder and nutrition-related attentional deficits may be similar; but they are not identical." When, for instance, she compared the exploratory behaviors of malnourished animals, hyperactive animals and a comparison group, Galler found subtle but interesting differences among the groups. She found that animals experimentally made hyperactive by depleting the neurotransmitter dopamine in their brains were consistently more hyperactive than the comparison group regardless of what sort of setting they were placed in. In contrast to truly brain damaged hyperactive animals, malnourished animals were not hyperactive as long as they were in a familiar environment.

Unlike the truly brain damaged animals, the malnourished animals eventually settled down to approximately normal behavior. But when placed in a new situation, these chronically malnourished animals became hyperactive. Stress seems to be an important trigger. "If the demands are not made on the animal or the person, we may not see the behavior consequences of chronic malnutrition. When a new situation demands a new adaptive response, however, the signs of abnormal behavior are patently clear."

To understand the long-term effects of undernutrition requires carefully controlled laboratory experiments. The body of an adult animal, including the human animal, will do everything it can to maintain a steady supply of energy to the brain. Between meals, when sugar and nutrient levels in the body normally fall, and when they rise after eating, the brain's supply of nutrients remains remarkably constant. Even in occasional times of starvation and other stresses, the adult body will sacrifice its supplies of fat, muscle, water and oxygen to keep the brain satisfied.

In babies, a lack of the critical chemical building blocks (specific nutrients) and the energy (calories) needed to fuel the biological processes of life during the critical period of the brain's growth spurt (just before birth and through infancy) is known to distort normal brain growth and development. Scientists have recognized for many years that overall brain size, the number of brain cells, the density of interconnections among the approximately one hundred billion cells in the human brain and the DNA content of those brain cells are all lower than normal in children who have been undernourished during their earliest years of life. Human beings, for instance, are highly vulnerable from the last three months of gestation through the second year of life.

To establish an experimental model of undernutrition, Galler used descendants of a colony of undernourished rats begun in the mid-1960s at the London School of Tropical Hygiene. On July 4, 1973, Galler stepped off an airplane at Logan Airport with 125 rats she had flown first-class from London to her laboratory at MIT. Using this colony as a model of chronic undernutrition typical of most impoverished human populations, Galler was able to study what happens when we stop the cycle of malnutrition and decline by providing adequate nutrition.

The logical question was whether feeding rats coming from a culture of undernutrition would reverse the deficits. According to Galler, that depends on when rehabilitation is begun, how long the animals had been undernourished, what type of malnutrition they suffered and how severe it was. Malnutrition is an insidious process. It breeds problems that make it more difficult for the succeeding generation to survive. Animals born of undernourished mothers are smaller, have a lower birth weight, have increased behavioral problems and suffer such physical problems as increased infectious diseases and a variety of failures to cope adequately with the environment. If the animals are not fed adequately, the decline continues unabated until about the eighth generation.

"At that point," says Galler, "at least as far as we can observe, generations no longer decline. The 10th generation, for example, is not observably worse off than the eighth generation."

"One of the more frightening findings," continues Galler, who followed these animals for 25 generations, "is that when we provided adequate diet after several generations of undernutrition, certain deficits persisted for as long as four generations after rehabilitation."

A person's normal mental and physical growth depends on the fine regulation of literally thousands of metabolic processes by another set of thousands of chemical regulators. In this way, the body makes itself. The genes supply the information, the blueprint that establishes the body plan and the sequence of events by which the plan will be realized. The actual substance of the body, however, comes from outside the body in the form of food.

If the nourishment is not available, the lack can disrupt the body plan as well as the sequence of events. Says Galler, "I have always marveled at how, at a certain point in time, a flower blooms or pubescence presents itself in an individual. It happens like clockwork. It is predictable. The process is set forth at the time of conception, or earlier if we consider the parental impact on the process. Malnutrition probably has the capacity to alter particular programs."

Galler's research is demonstrating conclusively that malnutrition disturbs the organism at a very basic cellular level and that these upsets endure for a long time, perhaps throughout the organism's life. This research suggests that there is no easy remedy for the effects of human malnutrition, especially for the effects of generations of undernutrition. Bringing food into an impoverished region to feed the hungry is, of course, a humanitarian gesture. It goes without saying that adequate nutrition is better than not having enough.

But we now see from research like Galler's that it would be a mistake to believe that supplying adequate food will, in itself, solve the problems associated with chronic undernutrition. The Bible and Greek tragedies recognized a truth that we in the 20th century prefer to ignore: Some problems take generations to work out.

The 'Fourth World'

Ten million refugees with nowhere to go

WILLIAM SHAWCROSS

The Spectator

There are at least 10 million refugees scattered around the world. They are in many senses a Fourth World, far less able to speak for themselves than is the Third World, from which the vast mass of them come and in which many of them linger.

One of their problems is that classical definitions no longer fit. Refugees are defined by the 1951 United Nations Convention as individuals fleeing well-founded fears of persecution. The question is whether they too should be accorded refugee status.

The principal international responsibility for refugees lies with the UN High Commissioner for Refugees, based in Geneva. In recent years this organization has grown considerably to meet unhappy demands. It has also become a flabby, badly run bureaucracy unable to keep pace with refugee movements. But in January a new High Commissioner, Jean Pierre Hocké, was appointed and things are changing.

Among the most pressing crises he faces is the increasing reluctance of American and European governments to continue to grant asylum to those arriving at their ports. Now that American culture is global, it seems that half of the world would like to live in the U.S. Tamil or Filipino peasants now can watch *Dallas* or similar offerings on television in their huts so their visions of Western affluence may not be realistic but they are often alluring.

This is excerpted from the weekly "Spectator" of London.

Refugees can still get to the U.S., but it is easier for those fleeing Communist countries. In 1985 there were 70,000 refugees — 59,000 from the U.S.S.R., Eastern Europe and Indochina.

In the late 19th century the U.S. detained aliens who did not have proper papers on Ellis Island, usually briefly. Those detentions were ended in 1954, when such aliens were released on parole pending the hearing of their cases. In 1958, the Supreme Court said, "This policy reflects the humane qualities of an enlightened civilization." It has now been abandoned by the Reagan administration. Instead of releasing people on parole, it locks them up.

Since May, 1980, about 1,800 Cuban boat people have been held in a U.S. federal prison. Some, but not all, have records of crime or mental instability. They have been locked up because the U.S. believes they have no right to asylum, and Cuba will not take them back.

The U.S. Immigration and Naturalization Service has built a new detention center for refugees in Oakdale, La. This is in the middle of nowhere. There are only five attorneys in the entire county — which means that the refugees will find it hard to get legal assistance. By the end of 1986 the U.S. will have the facilities to detain up to 10,000 aliens, including asylum seekers.

Conditions of detention centers vary, but in all of them boredom, despair and hunger strikes are commonplace. There have been suicides. Processing often takes a year.

Most refugees or asylum seekers in the U.S. come from Central America, where more and more people have been displaced by conflict or political persecution. The Reagan administration has not dealt kindly with them. More than a million people have fled El Salvador and Guatemala, but in 1984 only 93 Salvadorans — 2 percent of those seek-

"The Fourth World," by William Shawcross, *The Spectator* (London), as it appeared in *World Press Review*, September 1986, pp. 35-36. Reprinted by permission.

ing asylum — were admitted to the U.S. No Guatemalans were allowed.

The government argues that Hispanic asylum seekers are "economic migrants" and that poverty, political oppression and civil unrest are not legal grounds for granting asylum. As a result, a strong "sanctuary" movement has grown among American churches — especially in the South, where most Hispanics first arrive.

A similar crisis and similar restrictions have developed in Europe. Last year about 165,000 people came to Europe seeking asylum or refugee status — compared with less than 20,000 10 years earlier. The largest number, almost 74,000, came to West Germany. After that came France and Sweden. Fewer than 5,000 arrived in Britain.

These people represent less than 2 percent of the refugee problem worldwide, but they are arriving at a time of growing concern about unemployment. European governments have reacted by trying to close borders, imposing visa requirements, applying sanctions against airlines and carriers and locking up asylum seekers at ports of entry.

Two of the largest groups seeking asylum in Europe are Tamils and Iranians. Since the beginning of civil strife in Sri Lanka in 1983, more than 125,000 Tamils have fled to India and more than 50,000 have made it to Europe. Most are in West Germany.

The Tamils went there because the Soviet airline Aeroflot and East Germany's Interflug offered them cheap flights to East Berlin plus transit on the train under the Berlin Wall, so they became West Germany's responsibility.

Conditions for refugees in West Germany are deplorable. They are locked up in old hospitals and abandoned barracks. They may linger for years through an unending appeal process. Acute depression is common and suicide frequent. West German officials have made it clear that this is part of the government's policy to deter refugees and to keep Germany white.

Iranians are the other large group of asylum seekers in Europe. About 19,000 arrived in 1985, more than half in West Germany and about 1,000 in Britain. Many are young males seeking to avoid the Iran-Iraq war.

They fly to Europe in a variety of ways. Some get false visas in Syria. Others travel through Rumania, where almost anyone seems to be able to get on any flight. Others come by way of Vienna, which has a transit lounge suitable to Austria's ambiguities: Friends visiting the airport can drop tickets and papers over a balcony to transit passengers.

Last year the Swiss government, responding to public disquiet over too many black faces in the clean white streets, forced more than 50 Zairians out of Geneva and back to Zaire. Each of the Zairians was flown home handcuffed to a policeman. There was some Swiss opposition. The canton of Geneva tried to resist Bern's orders, and some policemen complained about the violence done to the deportees and refused to go on the handcuffed flight. As in the U.S., Swiss churches denounced the government and declared that they would become places of asylum for refugees.

> "By the end of 1986 the U.S. will have facilities to detain up to 10,000 aliens."

The man who now has to try to alleviate these problems is Jean Pierre Hocké, a Swiss, who was previously the operations director of the International Committee of the Red Cross. Hocké believes that the UN High Commission for Refugees (UNHCR) must get involved in politics and dare to tackle the root cause of people's flight.

To many officials and politicians, this is anathema. They want organizations to deliver aid to the victims and not question the causes. That has certainly been the UNHCR way until now. But Hocké insists that aid often merely assuages our consciences and does nothing to help the people at whom it is directed.

He aims to persuade European governments to act in unison with each other and with UNHCR instead of leaping to unilateral restrictions. The Europeans have begun to listen to him in a way they never listened to his predecessor. The Swiss are no longer sending refugees back, and Britain has agreed to allow about 3,000 Tamils who arrived before the end of May, 1985, to stay.

Hocké and his aides will eventually have to confront the detention policies of the Reagan administration. The Commission's internal memoranda have frequently criticized such policies as being in breach of U.S. and international law, but until now the Commission has not intervened on a high level with its principal donor.

A second urgent task for Hocké is to extend his protection to the quarter-million Cambodians who for six years have been scandalously denied anyone's protection along the Thai-Cambodian border. He has good relations with Thailand and Vietnam, so he has a chance to succeed. No one else has tried, because for all the governments concerned the refugees are a politically and militarily convenient buffer.

European countries want the Commission to insist upon "regional solutions," which were the norm before the mass settlement of Indochinese in the West. They argue that Kurds and Iranians should be assimilated in the Middle East and Tamils in the subcontinent — just as most Africans are given refuge in Africa. But the question remains: What if no one in the region will do it?

It is worth remembering the contribution that refugees have made to most societies, and that the idea of international protection for them grew out of Europe. After World War I, Fridtjof Nansen, the arctic explorer, was given the task of rescuing refugees from Russia. He coined the slogan, "To love one's neighbor is Realpolitik." Now Europeans have to decide how far the neighborhood stretches.

REFUGEES A fact of life?

The world's refugee population is on the rise. Some 12 million people have been granted 'refugee' status. This gives them certain protections and rights. But nations are slowly closing their doors to asylum seekers. Resettlement officials say the world community appears unable – or unwilling – to mitigate the underlying causes of refugee movements. Thus, they see a need for greater public understanding of refugee issues.

Shannon A. Horst
Staff writer of The Christian Science Monitor

Boston

In 1951, there were 1½ million refugees. Today there are almost 12 million, according to the office of the UN High Commissioner for Refugees.

The steady rise in this population is the result of protracted civil wars and foreign occupations – the Afghanistan war alone has created more than 4 million refugees.

According to the official definition of "refugee" by the UNHCR, the world body vested with the authority of establishing, promoting, and policing refugee policies, they are people have proved to officials in the countries to which they have fled that they have a "well-founded fear of being persecuted for reasons of race, religion, nationality, membership of a particular social group or political opinion . . ." if they return to their homeland.

Refugees often find that their status is the same as that of foreigners living in the country illegally. But this figure of 12 million does not include some 16 million people who live lives as undocumented aliens in a foreign land or displaced persons in their own countries. (No agency is capable of, or responsible for, tracking internally displaced persons. The latter figure is a "conservative worldwide estimate" by the United States Committee for Refugees – a US-based resettlement organization.)

Although it was established in 1951 for a three-year period only – to meet the needs of the World War II refugees – the UNHCR's mandate has been renewed for five-year periods ever since. Its current mandate extends to Dec. 31, 1988. Each year, the need for its services increases.

To fulfill its mandate – to provide refugees with international protection and assist them toward durable solutions – the UNHCR depends on the cooperation of 99 nations that have signed the 1951 UN Convention, the 1967 Protocol Relating to the Status of Refugees, or both.

As signatories of these documents, these nations have agreed to protect refugees within their borders from *refoulement* – "deportation or expulsion of a refugee, against his will, in any manner whatsoever to a territory where he fears persecution."

Protection and basic rights

Under the 1967 Protocol, the 99 nations grant refugees favorable legal status – freedom from discrimination and the enjoyment of economic and social rights. Among these guarantees are:

- The same status as a national in access to courts and legal assistance.
- Treatment at least as favorable as that of nationals with respect to freedom to practice their religion and freedom in the religious education of children.
- The right to identity papers and travel documents to facilitate movement.
- The same access to public assistance as that of nationals.

In turn, a refugee is required to conform to the laws and regulations of a country, and to measures taken for the maintenance of public order.

The UNHCR works with federal governments and a plethora of national and international refugee agencies to provide material assistance – food, shelter, and medical aid – to new refugees, and to find sound solutions for them.

Solutions come in one of three actions: voluntary repatriation to the home country; integration into the country where the refugee first sought asylum; resettlement to a third country.

It is not uncommon for refugees to live three or more years – often in detention-like conditions – before a durable solution is found. Some are now viewed as "legitimate tools for the advancement of state policies," says the UNHCR.

Dangers of temporary care

In its 1986 status report, the UNHCR pinpoints the key concerns of its staff in attempting to protect refugees and find solutions to the world's steadily growing refugee population. These concerns, particularly the obstacles to resettlement, have been echoed by refugee agency officials in many different nations.

Armed attacks on refugee camps. Once very uncommon, armed attacks have become "distressingly" common. The UNHCR recommends that nations do everything possible to maintain a purely civilian and humanitarian character within all camps, to protect them from being seen as party to any conflict.

Protection of women and girls. Abduction of and physical violence against female refugees, including sexual abuse, are common during overland flight and armed attacks on refugee camps.

More common within refugee settlements and in urban settings that are void of traditional family ties is discrimination against women and girls that leads many of them to be exploited (in the workplace, for example), to become prostitutes, and even to participate in sexual abuse for pay to meet their own and their family's needs. Fear of reprisal and ostracism often keeps them from reporting anything.

Detention-like settings. In many countries, asylum seekers and refugees are kept in detention-like settings where the UNHCR often has no access to them.

Obstacles to permanent solutions

Western nations tightening their borders. Economic instability and insecurity in dealing with third-world asylum seekers and illegal aliens have spurred many nations to tighten their borders.

The United States, the world's leading country for resettlement, has had a three-year downward trend in refugee admissions – 71,113 in 1984, 68,045 in 1985, and 62,450 in 1986. But it has, for the first time since 1980, increased its admission ceiling. For 1987, it will be 70,000.

Many nations have begun using discouragement tactics to ward off asylum seekers – longer waiting periods for employment rights, rejection at border crossings, and punishment of airlines that bring in dubious asylum seekers.

Lack of cooperation among receiving nations. The UNHCR is increasingly concerned about the lack of cooperation among signatories of the refugee protocal. Uncoordinated activity causes both multilateral and bilateral strains.

When one nation decreases the number of refugees it will accept in a year, other nations must pick up the overload. When nations put into place new or toughened rules concerning illegal aliens, refugees often find themselves unjustly counted among the "alienated." And, because of geographic locations, many nations that

Refugees in relation to indigenous population

Resettlement country	1975-1984	1985	Population (in millions)	Ratio (refugees/ population)
Namibia	40,000	N/A	1.1	1/28
Australia	114,100	9,680	15.5	1/125
Canada	157,700	16,456	5.5	1/146
Sweden	30,500	6,241	8.3	1/226
US	949,500	70,583	239.0	1/234
Switzerland	17,400	936	6.5	1/354
Denmark	5,550	8,962	5.2	1/358
France	132,700	13,259	55.0	1/377
New Zealand	6,900	871	3.3	1/425
Austria	14,100	71	7.6	1/536
Norway	6,500*	763	4.2	1/578
West Germany	53,100	11,124	61.3	1/1,130
Netherlands	9,800	907	14.5	1/354
Spain	25,500	206	38.8	1/1,509
Belgium	3,200*	642	9.9	1/2,577

*Statistics unavailable for 1975-1981. These totals reflect 1982-1984 entries.

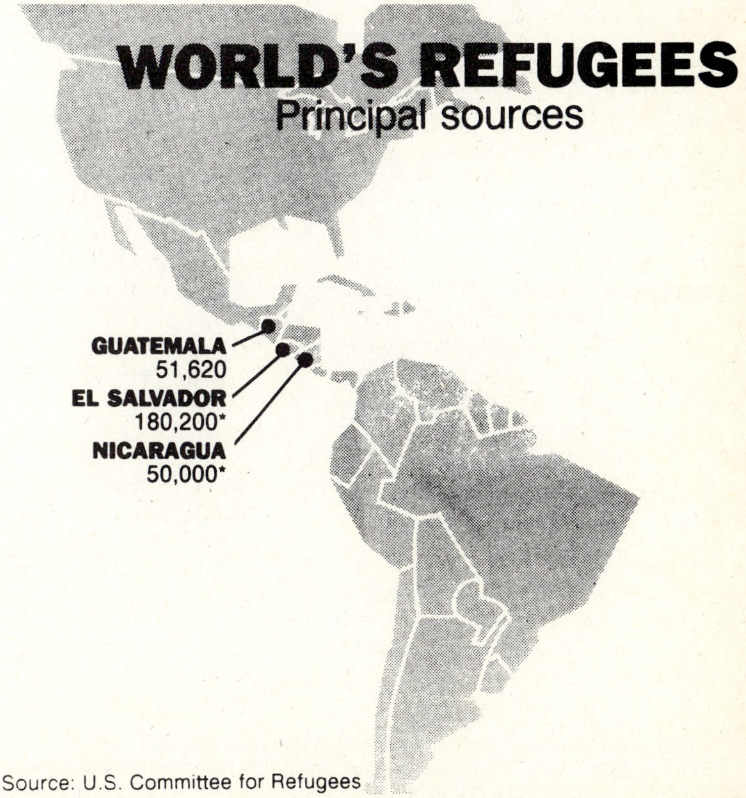

Source: U.S. Committee for Refugees

are least able to care for refugees take in the greater flow of asylum seekers.

Institutionalized and politicized refugee policy. The UNHCR contends that the world community has been unable – or unwilling to mitigate the underlying causes of refugee movements. There is grave danger, it warns, in believing that "as long as humanitarian intervention takes care of the victims, the underlying political situation can be disregarded."

1986 funding for international refugee agencies

Country	Contribution Per capita	Population (in millions)	Contributions (in millions)	GNP Per capita
Norway	$5.87	4.2	$24.60	$13,990
Denmark	4.24	5.1	21.60	11,490
Sweden	3.12	8.4	26.20	12,440
Switzerland	2.36	6.5	15.40	16,250
Netherlands	1.11	14.5	16.10	9,870
Canada	1.11	25.6	28.30	12,280
United States	0.96	241.0	232.10	14,080
Finland	0.84	4.9	4.10	10,710
Germany	0.79	60.7	47.70	11,400
Kuwait	0.61	1.8	1.10	16,200
United Kingdom	0.57	56.6	32.40	9,180
Japan	0.54	121.5	65.50	10,100
Australia	0.51	15.8	8.00	11,460
Qatar	0.45	.3	.14	21,160
Italy	0.45	57.2	25.70	6,390

Source: US Committee on Refugees; US State Department

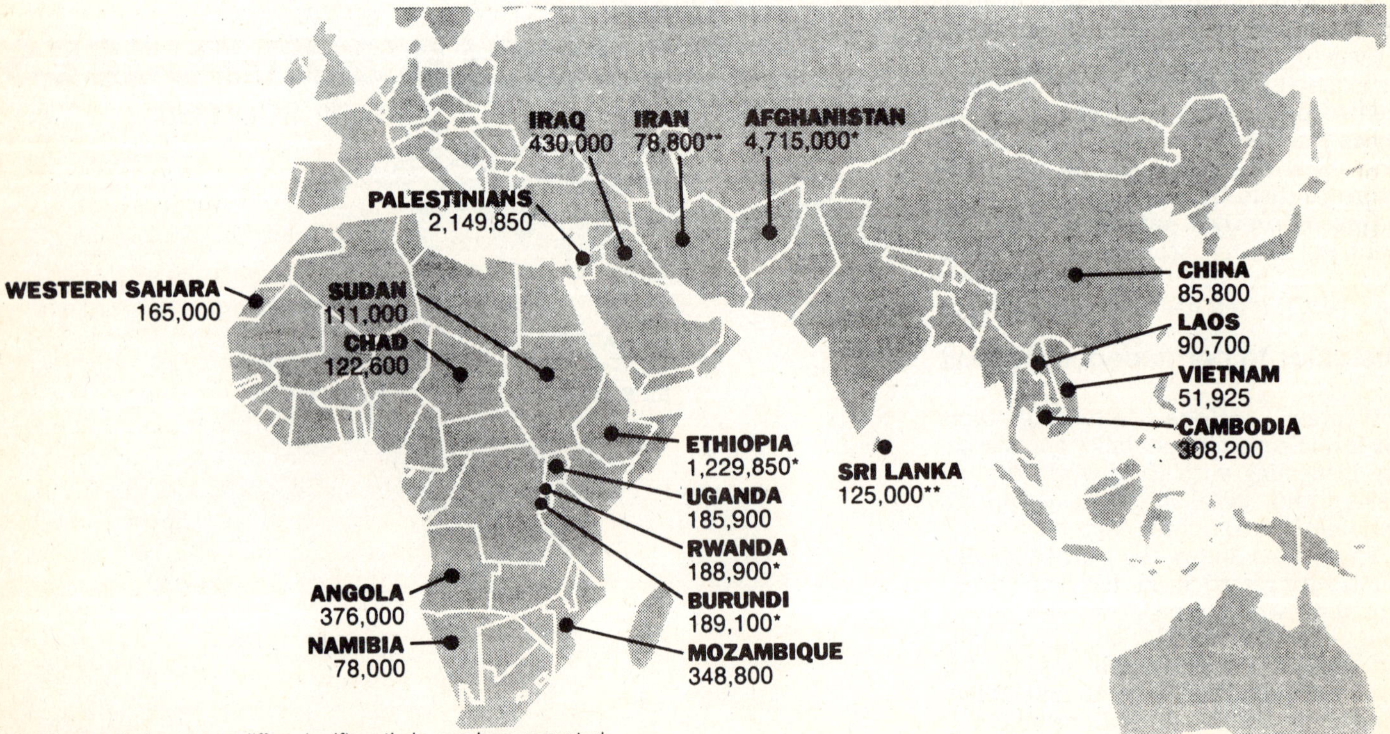

*Indicates that sources differ significantly in numbers reported
**Figures reflect only refugees accorded asylum. Substantial additional numbers are in refugee-like circumstances.

The frantic Third World quest for ballistic missiles

Belatedly, Western nations are trying to staunch the flow of technology that has helped create a number of new ballistic missile forces in the Third World. While some are being used in war, others are ominously combined with nuclear programs.

Aaron Karp

Aaron Karp is arms trade project leader at the Stockholm International Peace Research Institute (SIPRI).

ON FEBRUARY 25 INDIAN Prime Minister Rajiv Gandhi announced that his nation had successfully tested a ballistic missile with a range of at least 240 kilometers (149 miles). The missile, named Prithvi, which is Hindi for "earth," has sufficient power to carry large warheads and will, according to Gandhi, eventually be part of the Indian military forces. Although such deployment lies in the future, the Prithvi alters New Delhi's relationship with Islamabad because it has the range to strike almost any target in Pakistan.

Three weeks after Gandhi's announcement, the U.S. State Department said China had sold Saudi Arabia an unspecified number of CSS-2 medium-range missiles. The Chinese missile has a range of 2,200 kilometers and can reach nearly any part of the Middle East. Like the Prithvi, Saudi Arabia's CSS-2, when it is finally deployed, will alter the regional military balance, particularly Riyadh's relationship with Israel and Iran.

Ballistic missiles already are being used in one Third World conflict. Since the end of February, Iran and Iraq have fired more than 100 short-range, inaccurate missiles at each other's cities, causing thousands of casualties.

These events illustrate that ballistic missiles are becoming an ominous reality in the Third World. Indeed, 20 Third World countries, including Israel and Brazil, currently possess ballistic missiles or are striving to develop them. On one level, these missiles—which are propelled by rockets into the upper atmosphere, travel in a ballistic trajectory, and are pulled by gravity to their targets—are for these nations a logical step in building up their military forces. While the missiles vary in range and accuracy, they can reach many targets in regional conflicts. Unlike manned aircraft, they do not require large, vulnerable bases. They are not as easily intercepted as slow bombers. And they are easier to develop because they are less sophisticated than modern cruise missiles such as the U.S. air-launched cruise missiles.

In terms of global security, the most worrisome aspect of Third World ballistic missiles is their potential as nuclear weapons delivery systems. They typically have a payload capacity of over 500 kilograms and thus could carry nuclear warheads. Recognizing this danger, many of the world's leading economic powers began meeting secretly in 1983 to develop a protocol restricting missile technology exports. After four years of negotiation, the international Missile Technology Control Regime was unveiled on April 16, 1987. The new regime is the first multilateral effort to include potential delivery systems under nuclear nonproliferation controls and thus represents a significant nonproliferation step. It was signed by the United States, Britain, Canada, France, Italy, Japan, and West Germany.

The regime comes at a critical moment, just as many Third World missile programs near maturity. The regime will complicate their work, but as currently structured it is too weak to do much more than slow their progress. If Third World ballistic missile programs are to be prevented from evolving into effective nuclear delivery systems, the regime must be strengthened considerably. And there is no time to waste.

Less than four months after unveiling the regime—which also covers cruise missile technology—the world learned that Israel had already tested its nuclear-capable Jericho II. This medium-range ballistic missile has a range of over 1,400 kilometers, equal to the old U.S. Jupiter missile. Such a missile is most likely intended as a nuclear delivery vehicle. The magnitude of this development is such that Moscow has threatened to retaliate against any Israeli threat to Soviet territory.

BALLISTIC MISSILES HAD made their way to the Third World many years before the idea for the Missile Technology Control Regime emerged. In the early 1960s, for example, German technicians developed crude missiles for Egypt; Israel tested its French-designed Jericho I in 1968; by the mid-1970s, Moscow had transferred nuclear-capable but conventionally armed surface-to-surface missiles to a half dozen Middle East nations and North Korea, and Washington had sold counterparts to its regional allies. From a superpower perspective these transfers were a relatively safe way of cementing relationships with friends and allies. The quantities involved were small, and none of the recipients, with the possible exception of Israel, were in a position to arm them with nuclear warheads.

But in the late 1970s Third World nations began developing their own ballistic missiles and these weapons no longer looked stabilizing. The dangers to international security were heightened when these programs were unfolded in direct combination with obvious nuclear weapons programs.

This combination became unmistakable in 1978 as the Carter administration, trying to restructure Washington's foreign policy toward East Asia, presented plans for withdrawing U.S. troops and nuclear forces from South Korea and withdrew diplomatic recognition of Taiwan in favor of the People's Republic of China. Both Seoul and Taipei reacted furiously; both dropped loud rumors about nuclear weapons research and ballistic missile development. The South Korean missile, which apparently is now operational although Seoul has no nuclear warheads to arm it with, was a highly modified Nike-Hercules surface-to-air missile. Taiwan deployed a copy of the U.S. Lance missile while hinting that another model with a range of 600–1,000 kilometers was in development. (Taiwan recently closed down a secret installation being built to extract plutonium, a prime ingredient of nuclear weapons, from spent nuclear fuel, after an informant revealed the plant's existence to U.S. officials.[1]) If this was not enough, a group of German engineers, the Orbital Transport und Raketen Aktien Gesselschaft (Otrag), was working in Zaire and Libya developing a commercially available space launcher with abundant military potential.

In the 1980s, more Third World nations have entered the ballistic missile business via space-launch programs. These programs benefited from the maturation of the technology and the rising sophistication of Third World aerospace industries. The major difference between a space-launch vehicle and a ballistic missile is the payload they carry, and the inherent similarities have not passed unnoticed. Brazilian and Indian space launchers can, with only slight modification, be used to deliver nuclear warheads and do not require a sophisticated guidance package to hit cities. Recall that U.S. Atlas and Titan rockets and the Soviet SS-6 were used almost interchangeably as space launchers and intercontinental missiles; Third World missile makers can easily do likewise.

Now India has the Prithvi. A Brazilian company, Avibras, will soon begin testing missiles with ranges up to 300 kilometers, and Brazil plans to develop longer-range missiles. Otrag has conducted rocket development programs in Libya, and other countries, including Argentina, Egypt, and Pakistan, have announced programs of their own.

The missile threat intensified when Iraq developed chemical weapons and began using them in 1983 against Iran. Often called the "poor man's atom bomb," chemical weapons could easily be adapted to missiles already in a dozen Third World arsenals. U.S. Defense Department and British Ministry of Defence reports stated in 1986 that some 14 to 20 nations, including Syria and North Korea, had chemical arsenals, and the combination of chemical weapons with surface-to-surface missiles means that nations with no known nuclear capability can still field threatening arsenals.

INFORMAL RESTRICTIONS ON the transfer of missile technology were in place by the end of 1985. As announced by the White House in 1987, a missile technology control regime essentially coordinates Western restrictions on the transfer of key technologies to most countries. Since the regime is not a treaty its authority rests exclusively on the consent of the signatories. The regime represents an agreement to align national policies and consult in cases of uncertainty and in this regard it resembles the Coordinating Committee on East-West technology transfer (CoCom) or the 1974 London Nuclear Suppliers Group. But unlike the London group, which can rely on the International Atomic Energy Agency, the missile control regime has no international agency to monitor compliance and no mechanisms to enforce restraint.

The agreement is not a total embargo. Its language, which specifies an intent "to limit the risks of nuclear proliferation by controlling transfers that could make a contribution to nuclear weapons delivery systems other than manned aircraft," leaves exporters with considerable latitude. The guidelines distinguish between military missile and civilian space-launch programs and "are not designed to impede national space programs . . . as long as such programs could not contribute to nuclear weapons delivery systems."[2]

Unable to establish an embargo, the regime codifies a prejudice. It sets restrictions under two categories, the first of which covers the most immediately dangerous items—those that could be assembled into working missiles in a matter of weeks or months. This includes complete rocket systems with a payload of at least 500 kilograms (1,100 pounds)—thought to be the minimum weight for a crude nuclear weapon—and a range of over 300 kilometers. Category one also covers major subassemblies such as whole rocket stages, rocket engines, guidance systems, reentry vehicles, and warhead parts. The regime notes that for these items, "there will be a strong presumption to deny such transfers."

Category two covers less immediately threatening technologies, principally production technologies that would aid a nation aspiring to mass produce missiles many years in the future. This list is much longer and includes propellant production equipment, structural materials, avionic equipment, ground support equipment, test equipment, and computer software. While category one items generally will not be transferred without explicit government-to-government assurances between buyer and seller, category two items will be routinely transferred unless there are outstanding concerns. In that case, category two items may be transferred if official reassurances are supplied.

ONE PRACTICAL EFFECT of the missile technology control regime is to internationalize U.S. policy. The United States has since 1972 enforced restrictions similar to those of the regime. The United States implemented these curbs largely to protect its space-launch industry from foreign competition. According to State and Defense Department officials, the United States began applying them in the late 1970s for national security reasons as well.

As middle level officials in Washington focused their attention on the worrisome situations in South Korea and Taiwan they confronted the fact that a unilateral U.S. policy was ineffective. The United States, although undoubtedly the world's leader in space-launch and missile technology, had no monopoly on it. Now that Washington refused to export key missile technologies, other nations were filling the gap. Their technical wherewithal might not carry as much prestige, but it served nascent Third World programs just fine. British, French, German, and Israeli experts were welcomed abroad like evangelists for the missile age.

From this perspective the missile regime was a genuine success for Washington. Six other nations, all active or potentially significant suppliers, agreed to adopt the U.S. position. But this singular success conceals serious shortcomings that need to be addressed in the near future. Foremost, the agreement fails to include many of the most profligate technology exporters. China, which had already earned a poor reputation by selling Silkworm cruise missiles to both Iran and Iraq, recently entered the longer-range missile export business with the Saudi sale. Israel is widely suspected of helping Taiwan copy the U.S. Lance surface-to-surface missile and develop a family of shorter-range weapons. Israeli influence is also apparent in the design of South Africa's missiles. Brazil has made millions of dollars exporting artillery rockets and is developing missiles with ranges up to 1,000 kilometers that it also plans to export. Argentina clearly would like to enter the business.[3] Before any missile technology regime is complete it must include these current and potential suppliers.

The Soviet Union poses a special problem, for while it does not appear to share individual missile technologies with anyone—not even with India, its favorite Third World ally—it has been exceptionally generous in exporting surface-to-surface missiles. Since the late 1960s, about 1,000 Soviet FROG and Scud missiles have been shipped to the Middle East and North Korea, and these missiles are being used for attacks against cities by both Iran and Iraq. The United States, of course, has furnished Honest John rockets to South Korea, Greece, and Turkey, and Lance missiles to Israel. But while Soviet missile sales burgeoned throughout the decade the United States has licensed no new sales since 1974. In 1983, for example, Moscow sent Syria a new generation of much improved SS-21s.[4] Although these missiles

Choosing what to control

One of the most difficult questions faced in negotiating the [Missile Technology Control] regime was to determine what items are necessary in the development of missiles, and therefore important to control. In the case of ballistic missiles, the very difficulty of their development made the task easier. Structures, propellants, engines, control devices, and particularly guidance systems, must all be developed and integrated. Since the landing point of a ballistic missile warhead is determined early in flight, all course corrections must be completed by the end of powered flight, which is usually only about 10–20 percent of total flight time. At the end of powered flight, many miles from its ultimate destination, the missile must be travelling in the right direction at exactly the right velocity. This requires a sophisticated, computer-driven guidance and control system adequate to position the missile as desired, exact knowledge of the coordinates of the launch site and target, and the ability to program a computer to achieve the desired flight path. Even if the guidance and control is sufficient, successful assembly and launch of volatile solid or liquid-fueled rocket systems cannot be taken for granted. Consequently, there are a number of significant technology items which lend themselves to restrictions.

The framers of the regime realized that it would be necessary to control the technology for space launch vehicles as well as ballistic missile technology, since they are essentially interchangeable. The US TITAN II, for example, was used for early Gemini space vehicle launchers, yet it was in the U.S. Air Force inventory as an ICBM for 25 years. The only major difference between the space and missile variants is that the final boost stage of the ICBM is terminated earlier, before the payload has achieved enough velocity to enter orbit, resulting in its return to earth.

The one major component of a ballistic missile system that is not part of a space system is the reentry vehicle. Therefore, the regime includes all items associated with ballistic reentry vehicles as Category I items. Of particular importance are heat shields, heat sinks, and other items designed to permit a vehicle to withstand the heat of reentry. Similarly, warhead safing, arming, fuzing, and firing mechanisms are not required for peaceful satellites, and these are also Category I items. Just as there are payload related items that clearly have application only for missiles, the same applies for space vehicles. □

—U.S. Arms Control and Disarmament Agency, *World Military Expenditures and Arms Transfers 1987*, p. 26.

are, in NATO parlance, battlefield weapons, they have a range of 120 kilometers and can reach strategic targets in many Third World environments.

Yet Moscow may eventually be a party to the new regime. During the 1977–78 conventional arms limitation talks, Soviet negotiators seemed especially enthusiastic about the possibility of controlling missile sales. And Moscow has demonstrated some export restraint. Despite widespread rumors in 1984, there is no evidence that the Soviet Union ever exported its 900-kilometer-range SS-12. And according to the July 24, 1987, *Manchester Guardian*, Moscow apparently refused to furnish Syria with highly accurate SS-23s, which have a range of 500 kilometers. But ending missile sales will not be painless or easy for the Kremlin; its regional allies have grown accustomed to these regular infusions and will not take a cutoff lightly. Nor is it clear that the regime's category one restraints apply to Moscow's highly popular Scuds, which have a range just under the 300-kilometer threshold.

A second shortcoming is that the regime, as an agreement on principles, gives each member full authority over implementing and interpreting its stipulations. There is no guarantee that members will apply equally strict definitions in their regulations of missile exports nor any assurance that they will not use grandfather clauses to perpetuate all contracts. Verifying compliance is catch-as-catch-can—there is nothing similar to the safeguarding and inspection procedures of the 1968 nuclear Non-Proliferation Treaty.

Third, the agreement ignores the most important category of technology: human knowledge. Many leading Third World countries such as Argentina, Brazil, Egypt, Pakistan, the Koreas, and Turkey can acquire the physical accoutrements necessary to build ballistic missiles. Through their aerospace industries, they have many of the basic resources; what they lack is design skills, managerial experience, and manufacturing confidence. Their physical resources are not state-of-the-art, but talented foreign consultants can use these resources to generate powerful military results.

Egypt's missile program in the 1960s and Otrag's rogue activity today show what nations can achieve with surprisingly little hard technology. The regime's failure to regulate the work of expatriate engineers is a major, and perhaps irremediable, flaw; laws can be passed making it illegal to assist missile research in specific countries, but restricting travel is not a strength of free societies.

MOST IMPORTANT, the agreement does nothing to reduce the military incentives nations have for acquiring ballistic missiles. Third World nations may be turning to ballistic missiles for nuclear delivery missions just as the major powers did before them. All five of the existing nuclear weapons states initially relied on piloted aircraft to deliver nuclear weapons and later shifted greater emphasis to missiles. In all likelihood nuclear proliferators will follow a similar pattern, relying initially on their air forces and gradually converting to missile forces. Nations such as Israel and Pakistan are believed to have instituted nuclear training for their forces.[5]

This conversion could be hastened as Third World air forces lose the initiative to the defender. Improved and cheaper missiles, ground radars, and airborne early warning systems make aerial penetration ever more difficult and dangerous, even for the most dedicated attacker. The rising capability of surface-to-air missiles illustrates the trend vividly. Over North Vietnam, it took about 60 Soviet SA-2 missiles to down a single U.S. aircraft: today an Afghan rebel carrying a U.S.-made Stinger missile has at least a one-in-three chance of destroying an attacking Soviet aircraft. The difference in cost—$1.2 million for an SA-2 versus $35,000 for a Stinger—means defenders can easily saturate their airspace. The attacker's job will get progressively harder.

Of course there will always be methods to get around even the best defenses and a sky jammed with guns, missiles, planes, and radars cannot guarantee that no attacker will get through. But an attacker considering anything so consequential as nuclear war will probably try to find another way and ballistic missiles are the obvious alternative. It is no accident that even Israel, with arguably the world's best air force and less than the best opponents, has consistently invested in ballistic missiles.

Aside from the strategic imperatives, ballistic missiles are international status symbols. The prestige of having long-range missiles is enough to motivate many governments to pursue these weapons. This was illustrated in its most ludicrous form last summer as Iran and Iraq each announced they had indigenously developed missiles able to reach each other's capital cities. Tehran's claim in June that it was producing a missile called Oghab (eagle) was followed in August by Baghdad's claim that it had tested a better missile with a range of 600 kilometers (372 miles).[6] Considering that neither country has the metallurgical, chemical, or electronics industries essential for missile building, their claims can safely be dismissed. Both countries still must rely on foreign missiles for long-range attack. The claims of the two countries regarding their missile industries stand, rather, as testimony to the powerful incentives the new regime must overcome.

Against the powerful incentives for missile proliferation, the regime's restrictions, although better than nothing, are woefully inadequate. In general, the regime serves to keep Third World countries from getting Western missiles the easy way, by buying them. This is less of a constraint than it appears, however, since Western nations rarely sell such equipment and Third World countries rarely seek it. Most Third World decision makers are aware that Moscow remains the sole supplier for complete ballistic missile systems.

Restrictions on manufacturing technology could be more significant, however, because the most serious long-term danger is that Third World countries will mass produce missiles; tight control of key technologies could significantly retard this. While Third World efforts cannot be stopped entirely because much missile technology is now publicly available, any delay can be used to ameliorate regional conflict and weaken the incentives for missile proliferation.

Unfortunately, the category two restrictions on manufacturing technology are little more than a symbolic gesture

Third World ballistic missiles

Country	Designation	Range[1] (kilometer)	First flight[2]	Comments
Algeria	Soviet FROG-5/7	50–70	1975	
Argentina	IIAE Castor	300	1970	For research only
	IIAE Condor	150	Imminent	Reportedly offered to Iran or Egypt
	IIAE Alacran	850	Planned	Reportedly offered to Egypt
Brazil	Orbita EE-150	150	Imminent	Orbita is designing larger missiles
	Avibras SS-300	300	Imminent	May be a copy of Soviet Scud
	Avibras SS-1000	1,200	Planned	
	INPE Sonda IV	940	1984	Research rocket
	MECB VLS	1,500	Planned	Space launcher
Egypt	Al Zafir	378	1963	German designers
	Al Kahir	604	1963	German designers
	Al Ared	950	—	German designers, never tested
	Soviet FROG-5/7	50–70	1968	Used in 1973 Arab-Israeli War
	Soviet Scud-B	280	1973	
Greece	U.S. Honest John	37	1959	
India	ISRO SLV-3	800	1980	Space launcher
	ISRO ASLV	1,200	1987	Space launcher
	ISRO Polar SLV	2,000	Planned	Space launcher
	Prithvi	240	1988	Scheduled for mass production in 1988.
Iran	Soviet FROG-7	70	1984	Received from Libya and Syria, used against Iraq
	Soviet Scud-B	280	1984	Received from Libya and Syria, used against Iraq
	Oghab	?	1987?	Unsubstantiated claim
Iraq	Soviet FROG-7	70	1969	Used against Iran
	Soviet Scud-B	280	1974	Used against Iran
	"Tehran rocket"	650	1987?	Possibly imported from Brazil, China, or Soviet Union
Israel	Jericho I	480	1968	French design
	U.S. Lance	130	1975	U.S. supplied instead of Pershing I
	Jericho II	1,450	1981?	Disclosed July 1987
Libya	Soviet FROG-7	70	1978	
	Soviet Scud-B	280	1976	
	Otrag rocket	300	1980	German firm left in 1981 but work continues; latest test in 1987
North Korea	Soviet FROG-5/7	50–70	1969	
South Korea	U.S. Honest John	37	1959	
	U.S. Nike-Hercules	140	1978	Locally upgraded air defense missile
Kuwait	Soviet FROG-7	70	1978	
Pakistan	Designation unknown	?	Planned	Design studies in progress
Saudi Arabia	CSS-2	2,220	—	Received from China
South Africa	Designation unknown	?	Planned	Design studies in progress
Syria	Soviet FROG-5/7	50–70	1973	
	Soviet Scud-B	280	1974	
	Soviet SS-21	120	1983	
Taiwan	U.S. Honest John	37	1960	
	Ching Feng	130	1979?	Copy of U.S. Lance with Israeli aid
	Designation unknown	1,000	—	Pursued 1977–1981?
Turkey	U.S. Honest John	37	1960	
South Yemen	Soviet FROG-7	70	1979	
	Soviet Scud-B	280	1979	

Other Third World nations including Indonesia, Mexico, Peru, and the Philippines have experimented with suborbital sounding rockets.

1. Range in surface-to-surface mode
2. For imported missiles, date is for initial deliveries.

—Aaron Karp

and can easily be circumvented by a determined government. A potential proliferator merely has to assure the exporting government that it will use the technology for its civilian space-launch program. While some of the regime's members will interpret category two restrictions rigorously, it is reasonable to assume, based on scores of disputes over other Western technology export restrictions, that a determined buyer will inevitably find an unscrupulous seller.

DESPITE THESE BAD omens, the regime offers a sound formula for controlling missile technology exports and can still have a bright future. What is needed now is a sustained effort to strengthen the regime's terms and vigorously enforce its provisions.

Of course there are critics of the regime who doubt whether it has much of a future at all. On one side are Third World advocates who suspect that it is too tight and who condemn the agreement as a discriminatory device that unfairly penalizes their civilian space programs.[7] They see the regime, like the Non-Proliferation Treaty and the attempts to control the international arms trade, as a conspiracy to keep them powerless and dependent and will try to circumvent its regulations. On the other side are rising voices in the West, including some who participated in the negotiations, who argue that the regime is weak; diplomatic initiatives, they believe, cannot offer as much security as new military programs to counter the missile threat. Instead of relying primarily on the regime these critics call for accelerating the development and deployment of antitactical ballistic missiles (ATBMs).

The demand for ATBMs, which are missiles designed to shoot down short-range ballistic missiles, is especially troublesome since it could erode the Western resolve to strengthen the accord. While the ATBM option is an important alternative that must not be foreclosed, it is no panacea for missile proliferation. ATBMs are no less vulnerable than strategic antiballistic missiles, may not be cost-effective against nuclear or chemically armed missiles, and probably will be ineffective.[8] In any case, the cost of full-scale development and procurement will be very high, almost certainly much higher than the cost of protecting an entire nation with passive defenses such as shelters and protective gear.

Instead of jumping into controversial countersystems, nations should concentrate on making the new regime work. Several specific steps will greatly strengthen its potential:

• *More suppliers of missile technology must be brought into the regime.* The most important holdouts are China and the Soviet Union, but all nations with significant export possibilities must be brought in as well. Argentina, Brazil, Israel, and Sweden are also high priorities. In the long run other nations with advanced aerospace industries must be included, among them Belgium, India, the Netherlands, South Africa, South Korea, and Taiwan.

• *The regime's restrictions must be broadened and translated into national laws for strict enforcement.* As a general policy, more items of technology should be included under category one, the mandatory export ban. The discretionary restrictions of category two should be amended from their present bias favoring exports of development and production technology to a bias against such exports. The burden of proof must rest on buyer and seller alike to assure that the technology will be used for peaceful purposes only. Sales must be conditioned on positive assurances—preferably including on-site inspection—that the technology is used exclusively for approved purposes.

• *Exporters should condition the sale of space-launch technology on adherence to the Non-Proliferation Treaty.* Since the threat posed by Third World missiles is primarily nuclear, nonnuclear missiles are considerably less worrisome. A Non-Proliferation Treaty signatory that fully upholds the treaty cannot arm its missiles with nuclear warheads. Adherence to the treaty should not be seen as a green light for selling missile technology, however, since even conventional or chemically armed missiles are far from harmless. But supplying missile technology to a government that rejects the treaty, such as Argentina, Brazil, India, or Israel, is the height of irresponsibility.

• *Nations must press for a universal ban on testing ballistic missiles.* Because no new missile system can become operational without a series of test flights, a test ban would make it impossible for any country to develop new missile systems. A universal missile test ban can emerge only from negotiations between Washington and Moscow, the owners of the largest existing ballistic missile forces. Once they agree on a basic plan, it could be expanded to include other governments. But it is not essential for the rest of the world to wait on the vagaries of superpower relations. Similar test bans can be established regionally and could be equally effective.

Attentive policy making can transform a weak foundation into a strong, enduring structure. With measures such as these, the Missile Technology Control Regime could constitute an important addition to the nonproliferation system and enhance regional security worldwide.

1. Stephen Engelberg with Michael R. Gordon, "Taipei Halts Work on Secret Plant to Make Nuclear Bomb Ingredient," *New York Times*, March 23, 1988, p. 1.
2. White House press release, "Missile Technology Control Regime," April 16, 1987; White House press release, "Equipment and Technology Annex," April 16, 1987.
3. Arthur F. Manfredi et al., *Ballistic Missile Proliferation of Non-Major Military Powers: An Update*, report no. 87-654 (Washington, D.C.: Congressional Research Service, 1987), pp. 19–32, 23–48.
4. Peter Adams, "Israeli Military Experts Predict Increasing Threat," *Defense News* (June 1, 1987).
5. Leonard S. Spector, "Foreign-Supplied Combat Aircraft: Will They Drop the Third World Bomb?" *Journal of International Affairs*, vol. 40, no. 1 (summer 1986), pp. 143–58.
6. James Bruce, "Iran Building Up Its Own Arms Industry," *Jane's Defence Weekly* (June 20, 1987), p. 1302; "Iraqi Missile," *Defense and Foreign Affairs Weekly* (Aug. 17–23, 1987).
7. Ravi Shastri, "The Missile Technology Regime: An Extension of the Old Order," *Strategic Analysis*, vol. 11, no. 4 (July 1987).
8. Benoit Morel and Theodore A. Postel, *A Technical Assessment of Potential Threats to NATO from Non-Nuclear Soviet Tactical Ballistic Missiles* (Stanford, Calif.: Center for International Security and Arms Control, Feb. 1, 1987).

With cash from global drug trafficking bankrolling the agendas of governments and insurgents bent on destabilizing democracies, spawning anarchy and exporting revolution, the specter of narco-terrorism is a powerful threat on the international stage as dope becomes the newest political weapon

NARCOTICS: TERROR'S NEW ALLY

■ It is the unholiest of alliances, a malevolent marriage between two of the most feared and destructive forces plaguing modern society—terror and drugs.

Tapping the Croesus-like profits available from the international drug trade, "narco-terrorism" is fraying the social and political fabric of dozens of nations around the world. It is helping to underwrite bloody insurgencies on four continents. And even more insidious, the combination of drugs and terror has become an unofficial new weapon of national policy of several Soviet-bloc nations bent on destabilizing the West.

Perhaps the most frightening description of this deadly new threat on the international stage comes from one of the principal links between narcotics and revolution, Carlos Lehder Rivas, the swaggering Colombian drug lord, who was arrested in February and extradited to the United States. Declaring that drugs are the Third World's "atomic bomb," Lehder further boasts that: "Coca has been transformed into a revolutionary weapon for the struggle against American imperialism. The Achilles' heel of imperialism are the *estimulantes* [drugs] of Colombia."

There is, no doubt, as much bluster as there is substance in Lehder's sloganeering, but the proliferation of narco-terrorism imbues his words with a discomfiting ring of truth and underscores the fact that Latin America has evolved as the focus of the new menace in this hemisphere. Conversely, America's enormous drug appetite—estimated at well over $30 billion a year and possibly even triple that amount—indirectly supports the terrorists who attack U.S. citizens and institutions.

As narco-terrorism erodes the social and political foundations of democracies and other American allies worldwide, combatting the emerging phenomenon presents new and perplexing difficulties for law enforcement. Part of the problem is that the United States has been slow to recognize the threat, and develop strategies to deal with it. "Nobody worried about narco-terrorism—particularly the State Department—because it was a dirty business," complains Carlton Turner, until December the White House drug-policy adviser. "It took a long time to realize what was happening. No one looked at the big picture. It was disheartening. Because of our ignorance and failure to learn from history, we're now playing catch-up."

A TAMIL ATROCITY

Consider these examples of narco-terror's diverse and deadly harvest:

• Last week, more than 150 persons were killed in Sri Lanka when a powerful car bomb, believed set by Tamil guerrillas, exploded at a bus terminal in the capital of Colombo, destroying at least six buses filled with homebound commuters. The Tamils, an ethnic minority seeking a separate homeland, have increasingly financed their bloody campaign with heroin sales in Canada, West Germany and in France where authorities have arrested close to 200 Tamil drug couriers in the past two years. Last week's atrocity follows the murder of 145 civilians two weeks ago by Tamil militants.

Reprinted from *U.S. News & World Report,* May 4, 1987, pp. 30-37. Copyright 1987, U.S. News & World Report.

• Last January in Budapest, the Colombian ambassador to Hungary was seriously wounded in an assassination attempt outside his residence. Enrique Parejo González, a former Justice Minister in Bogotá, had been under a death threat for his uncompromising hard-line stance toward drug traffickers. The irony is that because his predecessor had been murdered by drug bosses, Parejo was quietly slipped into the overseas diplomatic post on the badly flawed assumption that 6,134 miles, the Atlantic Ocean and the iron curtain would be sufficient protection from the threatened vengeance of Colombian terrorist *narcotraficantes.*

• On June 24, 1984, a C-123 aircraft landed at Los Brasiles airport northwest of Managua, Nicaragua. With military guards surrounding the aircraft, 1,500 kilos of cocaine in duffel-type bags being transshipped from Colombia were hoisted aboard and flown to Miami. The loading operation was secretly photographed by a federal informant, and two of the smugglers were later identified as Pablo Escobar, a major Colombian trafficker and Lehder associate, and a Nicaraguan named Federico Vaughan. A few months ago, according to Washington sources, Vaughan and his boss were overseeing the setting up of cocaine-refining labs in remote coastal areas of Nicaragua. The boss was identified as Tomás Borge, the Sandinistas' Minister of the Interior.

• After the 4,600-ton Soviet merchantman *Kapitan Tomson* steamed into Rotterdam harbor last May 30, Dutch authorities searched the vessel and found 200 kilograms of Afghan heroin, which they valued at some $20 million, hidden among cases of raisins. The manifest showed that the cargo had been loaded at the port of Riga in Latvia. Unable to make a solid case against the captain or his crew, Dutch officials allowed the ship to sail on. Scholars of Soviet subterfuge say that it is naïve to think that lowly crew members on a Russian rust bucket would have the money, connections or wherewithal to broker such a massive narcotics shipment. Their suspicion: Another example of official Soviet involvement in drug trafficking.

Until recently, the dope trade was largely the province of greedy criminals who were intent mostly on accumulating wealth and power. What began as a relative trickle of drugs into the U.S. during the 1960s has grown into an annual multibillion-dollar tidal wave of heroin, hashish, cocaine and marijuana. About six or seven years ago, various terrorist groups around the world began to recognize the potential opportunities offered by the drug trade. According to the U.S. Drug Enforcement Administration, in the early '80s narcotics deals increasingly began to provide the financial underpinning for "rural insurgents, urban terrorists, liberation movements, arms traffickers, subversives, left and right-wing political groups and high-level officials acting on behalf of their governments."

Until they began utilizing drug profits, the groups cited by the DEA used to depend on bank robberies, kidnap for ransom and similar crimes for the money needed to buy weapons and sustain their operations. But even small slices of the megaprofits produced by narcotics can provide far greater infusions of cash. "A drug-deal profit of $20 million, not large by current international standards, can buy an election or finance major arms purchases," notes Mark Dion of the State Department's Bureau of International Narcotics Matters. Adds Dion's boss, Secretary of State George Shultz: "Money from drug smuggling supports terror-

THE WORLDWIDE SPREAD OF NARCO-TERRORISM

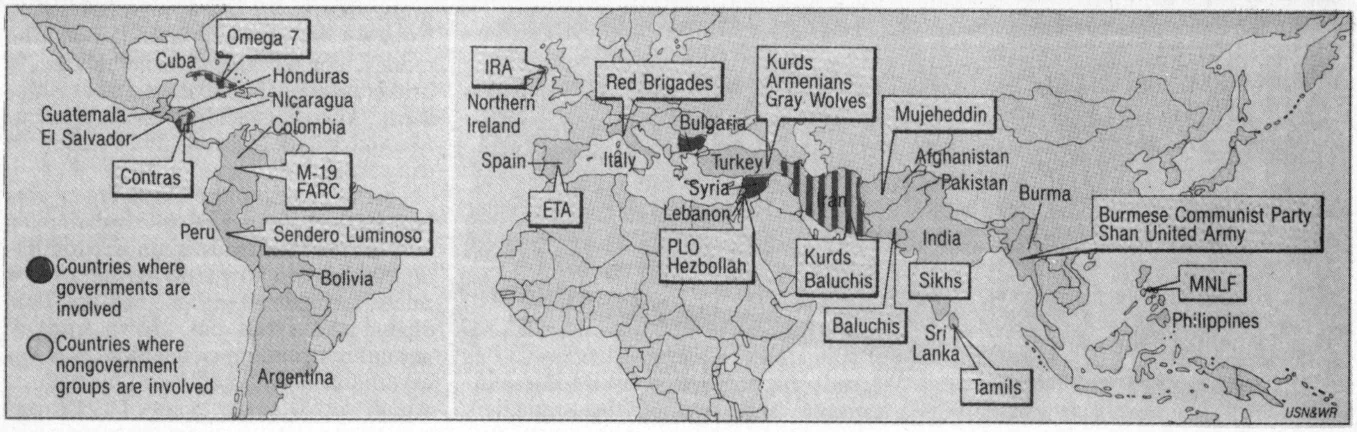

Colombia

M-19: Formed 1973, 2,000 members, Marxist, extremely violent urban-rural, with ties to Cuba, Nicaragua, Libya

FARC: Formed 1966, 4,000-7,000 members, also Marxist, very violent, similar political connections

Peru

SENDERO LUMINOSO: Formed 1969, 2,000-7,000 members, Maoist, unaligned, seeks peasant-backed overthrow

Nicaragua

CONTRAS: Formed 1979, 12,000-15,000 U.S.-funded rebels seeking overthrow of Sandinista regime

Ireland

IRA: Formed 1956, aims to drive British from Ulster, reunite Ireland. Uses urban violence in Northern Ireland, U.K.

Spain

ETA: Formed 1959, 500 members, seeks independent nation for Basque minority, killed Prime Minister 1973

Italy

RED BRIGADES: Formed 1968; targets judiciary, police, business; links with other anti-NATO terrorists

Lebanon

PLO: Formed 1964, umbrella organization for eight groups, seeks independent Palestinian homeland, main target Israel

HEZBOLLAH: Formed 1985, 4,000 members, umbrella for groups seeking Lebanese Islamic republic, close ties to Iran

Afghanistan

MUJEHEDDIN: Formed 1979 by seven urban and rural Moslem tribal groups, seeking ouster of Soviets in protracted guerrilla war, gets limited U.S. and Iranian support

India

SIKHS: 16-million-strong minority, want separate homeland in Punjab, killed Prime Minister Indira Gandhi

Sri Lanka

TULF: 8,000 members, formed 1972 by Tamil ethnic minority seeking a separate homeland. Violent, urban, Socialist

Burma

BCP: Formed 1946, seeks Communist rule, 10,000 well-armed rural insurgents based in the Golden Triangle region ists. Terrorists provide assistance to drug traffickers. It's the modern version of piracy."

How do the modern pirates operate? Three Americans are scheduled to go on trial this week in Boston, charged with illegally exporting 7 tons of automatic rifles, submachine guns, ammunition, grenades and explosives for the Irish Republican Army, and two months later with importing 35 tons of marijuana that was seized from a ship in Boston harbor. Authorities note that the weapons were purchased with cash and are convinced that this was a narco-terror connection.

The Sikh rebellion provides another variation on the narco-terror theme. In 1984, when Indian troops stormed the Golden Temple in Amritsar in an attempt to crush Sikh militants, local newspapers reported that the soldiers found "huge quantities" of heroin and hashish destined to be sold to finance arms purchases—much like the Tamils in neighboring Sri Lanka.

In the nether world of narco-terrorism, there are three main protagonists: The insurgent groups such as the IRA, the Tamils and the Sikhs; the intelligence services and officials of governments bent on exporting revolution such as Cuba and Iran, and finally, dope gangsters like Lehder who use political violence and classic terror tactics to further their aims. The three types of narco-terrorists invariably traffic in weapons, launder money, share intelligence, trade false passports, provide each other with safe havens and render mutual assistance in a loose global alliance.

The first group—the revolutionaries—represents a Baedeker of terror. It includes Colombia's 19th of April Movement, or M-19; the Revolutionary Armed Forces of Colombia, or FARC; Sendero Luminoso, or "Shining Path," in Peru; Nicaraguan Contra rebels; the anti-Castro Omega 7; Argentine right-wing dissidents; the Palestine Liberation Organization and a viper's nest of terrorist factions in the Mideast; Italy's Red Brigades; the ETA Basque separatists in Spain; Kurdish and Armenian rebels and the right-wing Gray Wolves in Turkey; Baluchi ethnic separatists in the Iran-Pakistan border area; Moslem insurgents in the Philippines; the Shan United Army (see story at right) and the Burmese Communist Party in the Golden Triangle area of Southeast Asia, and the Moslem mujeheddin who are fighting the Soviets in Afghanistan.

The second group of narco-terrorists is made up of officials and quasi officials of Soviet-bloc and other nations who regard Western democracy as a threat to their global or theocratic ambitions. While there is no smoking gun directly linking Moscow to narco-terror (see next page), the evidence against its surrogates—Bulgaria, Nicaragua and Cuba—is incontrovertible. U.S. officials have publicly accused all three Soviet proxies of trafficking in drugs and taking a nod-and-wink attitude when narcotics bound for the U.S. or Western Europe pass through their territories. "The directions of the flow are ideologically attractive," points out Michael Ledeen, Georgetown University terrorism expert and former consultant to the National Security Council. "Drugs go to the bourgeois countries where they corrupt and where they kill, while the arms go to pro-Communist terror groups in the Third World."

Outside of the Soviet sphere, intelligence sources in the Mideast believe that officials of Syria and Iran are also deeply involved in the drug trade and are funneling most of the profits into revolutionary activities as well as into shoring up their shaky national economies.

THE VIOLENCE ESCALATES

The final element of narco-terrorism's unholy trinity: The dope grandees whose propensity for violence has escalated in recent years from simple gang-

S. E. ASIA'S GOLDEN TRIANGLE

Reign of an opium warlord

In the rogues' gallery of world-class criminals, Khun Sa is unique—a cutthroat freebooter from a "Terry and the Pirates" comic strip, with the brooding menace of a character in a Joseph Conrad novel. The spiritual father of narco-terrorism, Khun Sa rules his remote domain in the rugged 60,000-square-mile Golden Triangle area of Burma, Laos and Thailand with feudal brutality. Deserters from his army are tracked down and shot, informants buried alive. One tale has Khun Sa ordering wrongdoers hanged, drawn and quartered in the marketplace of Ban Hin Taek, his former Thai headquarters village. Another has him killing a barber who had given him a bad haircut.

Long before many of today's Kalashnikov-toting terrorists were even born, the opium warlord had started to build a narcotics empire that today makes him the world's biggest heroin trafficker. For almost 25 years, Khun Sa and his Shan United Army (SUA) ostensibly have fought the Burmese government in order to establish a separate independent homeland state for the Shan ethnic minority. But while waging his intermittent guerrilla war with Rangoon, Khun Sa gradually has come to dominate the enormously productive and profitable opium-heroin trade in the Golden Triangle.

The U.S. Drug Enforcement Administration believes that Khun Sa controls 80 percent of the 90 or more tons of heroin that will be produced this year from Golden Triangle opium. He also has some 15,000 well-equipped, highly disciplined men under arms. Both Burmese and Thai military forces make periodic attempts to dislodge Khun Sa from his nearly inaccessible redoubt. All have failed.

Regarded as an astute, crafty politician with a keen sense of public relations, the 54-year-old warlord tries hard to cloak his reputation as a drug kingpin beneath the mantle of freedom fighter. Some drug experts believe Khun Sa has shed his separatist political ambitions and now functions solely as a drug trafficker—if for no other reason than to support his army and maintain a lavish personal lifestyle that includes sending his six children overseas for college educations in England, Singapore and the United States.

Khun Sa's search for respectability has taken some unusual turns. In 1977, a U.S. congressional negotiating team went to Ban Hin Taek after he offered to sell that year's entire Golden Triangle opium crop to Washington for $20 million, thus removing a huge chunk of potential heroin from the market. Hearings were held on Capitol Hill, but the bizarre proposal eventually ran into a wall of skepticism.

Five years later, Khun Sa tried again and sent a letter to Ronald Reagan offering to suppress the opium trade in return for cash and a crop-substitution program. The response: The President said "No" to drugs.

by Michael Satchell

sterism to political atrocities. Mexican marijuana smugglers in November, 1985, for example, ambushed, tortured and killed 22 policemen during a single incident. In Colombia, scores of incorruptible public officials, dozens of crusading antidrug journalists and some 300 police officers have been murdered. The chief suspects: Members of the so-called Medellín cartel, reported to be responsible for 75 percent or more of all the cocaine smuggled into the United States.

Ideologies and motives may vary among the insurgent groups and governments in narco-terrorism's fold, and while money and weapons are the principal payoff, dope's deleterious effects on American or Western European society are a bonus.

Former Nicaraguan diplomat Antonio Farach, who defected to the United States in 1983, has testified on Capitol Hill on the complicity of Sandinista officials in transshipping cocaine to the United States. Nicaragua became involved at Cuba's instigation, Farach related, following a September, 1981, meeting in Managua between Raúl Castro and Humberto Ortega, the brothers of the two countries' leaders. "The drugs were used as a political weapon because in that way we were delivering a blow to our principal enemy," Farach explained. "The drug trafficking produced a very good economic benefit which we needed for our revolution. We wanted to provide food to our people with the suffering and death of the youth of the United States."

Other opportunists who are seeking to force change in Latin America have also been drawn into the drug-terror fold. Persistent reports—some alleging CIA involvement—charge that Nicaraguan Contra rebels based in Costa Rica and Honduras have shipped cocaine to the U.S. to pay for weapons and matériel for their fight to overthrow the Sandinistas. Senator John Kerry (D-Mass.) has pressed the inquiry but any hard evidence has yet to be publicly disclosed. The Contra-drug connection allegations have prompted investigations by two congressional committees and the independent counsel probing the Iran-Contra affair.

A November, 1984, plot to stage a coup in Honduras was foiled when the FBI arrested eight people in Florida who had planned to assassinate Honduran President Roberto Suazo Córdova. Agents seized $10 million worth of cocaine, the conspirators' bankroll to buy airplanes, tanks, explosives and other military hardware for the planned takeover of the close U.S. ally.

THE SOVIETS: PROXY POWER

What is the Kremlin's role?

Just how deeply is the Soviet Union involved in narco-terrorism? A definitive answer is impossible, but some Kremlin watchers subscribe to the theory of a well-orchestrated, Soviet-inspired plot reaching back more than two decades to undermine the West with the help of narcotics.

They point to Moscow's history of fostering terrorism and see a Soviet role in the plague of heroin and marijuana that enervated many GI's during the Vietnam War. Also cited is the well-documented complicity of government officials of three Soviet satellites—Bulgaria, Cuba and Nicaragua (see main story). Seasoning the conspiratorial stew are such incidents as last year's 200-kilogram heroin seizure from a Soviet cargo vessel in Rotterdam and the testimony of Soviet-bloc defectors.

Gen. Jan Sejna was secretary of the Czechoslovak Defense Council and chief of staff at the Ministry of Defense when he sought political asylum in the West in 1968. Now living in the Washington area, Sejna recalls attending a secret 1962 Moscow meeting of top Warsaw Pact leaders, chaired by Nikita Khrushchev. The Soviet Premier, Sejna tells *U.S. News,* urged the satellite nations to exploit drugs to destabilize Western societies while generating foreign exchange.

Sejna says he recalls well the Soviet Premier's closing remarks, which he reconstructs as follows: "When we discussed this strategy," he quotes Krushchev as saying, "there were some who were concerned that this operation might be immoral. But we must state categorically that anything that speeds the destruction of capitalism is moral."

In 1971, Stefan Sverdlev, a colonel in KDS, the Bulgarian Committee for State Security—the equivalent of the Soviet KGB—defected to Greece and brought with him some 500 secret documents. Among them was KDS directive M-120/00-0050 dated July 16, 1970. Sverdlev has told Nathan Adams, a *Reader's Digest* senior editor who has done extensive research on the Bulgarian drug-terror connection, that the document was drafted after a 1967 meeting in Moscow of the heads of Warsaw Pact security services. Its subject: Destabilization of Western society through the use of various methods, including drugs.

"We all knew what it meant," Adams quotes Sverdlev. "The movement of narcotics from the Middle East through Bulgaria to Western Europe and North America was well-known to us. It was, of course, illegal, and drugs were seized when found. Now it would be a weapon."

The final result of directive M-120/00-0050 was the use of Kintex, the Bulgarian state trading organization, to smuggle drugs and weapons—a practice well documented by Western intelligence agencies. In the face of strong public condemnation by the United States, Bulgaria has adopted a lower profile in the past two years, while Cuba and Nicaragua have expanded their involvement.

"It's important to recognize that the Soviet Union has had a major role in the growth of international narcotics trafficking," maintains Joseph D. Douglass, Jr., a national-security analyst. "They are employing drugs as a political weapon."

Others don't see any Soviet master plan but acknowledge that Moscow has certain objectives and much to gain. "I don't subscribe to the Wurlitzer theory where some guy in the Kremlin is twisting knobs and pulling levers all the time," says Jon Thomas, former head of the State Department's Bureau of International Narcotics Matters. "But there's no doubt they and their proxies provide support for international drug criminals and underworld organizations. It's to their benefit: They know we have to expend huge amounts of resources to handle drug problems and enforcement."

by Michael Satchell

CUBA'S INVOLVEMENT

Until this decade, there were only two well-established connections between drugs and terror: The PLO in the Middle East and the opium warlords of Southeast Asia's Golden Triangle. Narco-terrorism's expansion to this hemisphere began in the late 1970s when the DEA began to pick up intelligence reports of growing ties between Cuban officials and Colombian drug bosses. What brought the two groups together was geography. Prior to 1975, Colombian ships carrying U.S.-bound marijuana and cocaine had to thread carefully through the Windward Passage between Cuba and Haiti. A slight navigational error could put the ships into Cuban territorial waters where they would be in danger of being seized, the drugs confiscated, and the crews imprisoned. But in late 1975, a clan of Colombia's principal dealers—anxious to negotiate freedom for their ships and crews—were reportedly summoned to a secret meeting in Bogotá with Cuban Ambassador Fernando Ravelo-Renedo, who offered them a deal they couldn't resist.

The ambassador's proposal: For a fee of up to $800,000 a boatload, Cuba would not only allow the drug vessels to ply its territorial waters but also would provide refueling and repair service at its ports. The boats would be allowed to fly Cuban flags and gunboats would escort these "mother ships" to rendezvous with small Florida or Bahamas-based boats that would sneak the drugs into the United States. The profits, conservatively estimated at $10 million a month, went to purchase hundreds of tons of weapons and supplies to support the Sandinistas in Nicaragua and Marxist insurgencies in El Salvador and Guatemala. Cuba was now in the narco-terror business.

Eventually, the Cubans saw a further opportunity to export revolution. A federal indictment details how Jaime Guillot-Lara, a Colombian drug dealer with close ties to the small but growing band of M-19 guerrillas, was dealt in on the arrangement. For the next two years, Guillot-Lara's ships moved large quantities of marijuana and cocaine through Cuban waters to the United States. Arms and explosives purchased in the U.S. or elsewhere would be loaded aboard the vessels in Havana and then carried to the M-19 insurgents in Colombia.

A confidential U.S. government report obtained by *U.S. News* states that the Guillot-Lara case "is only the tip of the iceberg of Cuba's ultrasecret involvement in the drug trade." Citing DEA intelligence sources, the document says that there have been more than 50 recorded cases of Cuban government involvement in drug trafficking since 1982. Among these is a 1984 report that Carlos Lehder, under increasing pressure from Colombian authorities, actually moved his cocaine-processing operations to Cuba. Castro's officials not only provided equipment and chemicals to refine the cocaine, but the operation was set up on an unnamed military base, affording maximum security.

Today, according to other sources, the Cubans now operate their own highly profitable cocaine-refining labs near Havana. Smugglers' aircraft are permitted to fly the north-south Maya air corridor over the eastern part of the island, and Havana continues to provide fuel and protection for drug boats using its waters.

Also involved in the Cuban connection is U.S. renegade Robert Vesco, who lives in Havana under Castro's protection and was a pivotal figure in a Colombia-Nicaragua-Cuba axis that shipped cocaine to Europe and the United States. Profits went to purchase high-tech equipment for the Castro government and arms for Colombian rebels. Last year, the fugitive financier was reported to have set up a large-scale money-laundering operation for favored traffickers. Vesco also was said to be directing his own drug conspiracy in Costa Rica from his downtown Havana office.

After the overthrow of the Somoza regime in Nicaragua, the enterprising Cubans saw still another opportunity to foster the growth of narco-terrorism in Latin America.

SANDINISTA CONNECTION

Pressed for hard currency and eager for a share of profits from the dope trade, the Sandinistas—at Raúl Castro's specific direction—eagerly established their own transshipment routes for Colombian cocaine. At the helm of the operation was Interior Minister Tomás Borge. With a steady pipeline of chemicals obtained in Europe and shipped through Havana, the Sandinistas, following the example of their Marxist cohorts in Cuba, decided to maximize profits by vertically integrating their drug business, which meant opening their own refineries.

As these drug plots widened, M-19 and FARC guerrillas in Colombia began raising large sums to finance their insurgencies by extorting protection money from growers and traffickers. In return for their payoffs, the drug network—from the farm to the processing labs and the airstrips—was allowed to operate in remote areas under rebel control.

Perhaps nothing better illustrates the frightening potential of narco-terror than the actions of M-19 in November of 1985. Some 60 guerrillas seized the Palace of Justice in Bogotá and took more than 300 persons hostage, including judges from Colombia's highest court. The purpose: To destroy the records of some 200 important narcotics offenders threatened with extradition to the United States, the most prominent being Lehder himself.

During the savage fighting to regain control, scores of persons were killed or murdered, including 11 of the Justices, and the palace was gutted by fire. Colombian drug traffickers—almost certainly the Medellín cartel—financed the assault. A check of serial numbers on some of the M-19 weapons proved that they had been obtained from the Sandinistas, who originally had been given them by the Venezuelan government during the Sandinista struggle to oust Nicaraguan President Anastasio Somoza. A leading Bogotá newspaper later reported that reputed billionaire Lehder—buying fireworks with pocket change—paid $4 million to M-19 to mount the attack.

In Peru, Maoist Shining Path insurgents follow the example of their revolutionary brethren in Colombia and tax coca growers in return for protection. As in Colombia, drug-related violence is fostering a state of near anarchy that the Lima government finds difficult to quell. Significantly, the 19 victims in a Shining Path massacre in the coca-producing Upper Huallaga Valley region were workers employed in a U.S.-funded program to destroy coca plants.

But it is in the Middle East where narco-terrorism has been woven most deeply through the political fabric. In war-torn Lebanon, for instance, the annual 1,500-ton, multibillion-dollar hashish trade—recently supplemented by opium and heroin—has for years supported terrorists with ideologies ranging from Communism to Islamic fundamentalism, and has helped foment the civil anarchy that has torn the country apart. Lebanese hashish helps pay for everything from hijacking and bombing spectaculars in Europe and the Middle East to a simmering revolt by Moslem insurgents in the Philippines. The Syrian government, intelligence agencies say, is deeply involved in the heroin-and-hashish trade at the highest levels through the activities of Rifat Assad, the Paris-based brother of Syrian President Hafez Assad. Without the annual injection of some $500 million or more in drug profits, the threadbare Syrian economy would be in even worse shape, according to these sources.

So important have narco-profits become to Damascus that there is growing evidence of Iran's seeking an increased share of the drug action. Ignoring Syrian objections, the 4,000-strong pro-Iranian Shiite militia Hezbollah—at the direction of central-government officials in Teheran—has recently established its own smuggling routes from Lebanon's Syrian-controlled Bekaa Valley into Europe. Middle East intelligence sources say Iran is using drug profits not only to export the Islamic revolution and finance pro-Iranian terror rings, but also to help defray the crippling costs of its war with Iraq. Syria has also replaced Bulgaria as the leader of state-sponsored narco-terrorism in that region, with Iran following closely behind.

The Soviet hand influencing Cuba and Nicaragua is also clearly visible in the operations of Kintex, the state import-export trading organization of Bulgaria. Western intelligence agencies have detailed a flourishing, long-term trade in dope and weapons by Kintex. Heroin and hashish are funneled into Western Europe hidden among legitimate cargoes. Profits are used to purchase weapons shipped to various European and Middle East terror groups and to Kurdish and Armenian rebels in Turkey. The benefits: Hard currency for the Bulgarian economy, support for Western European urban terrorists like Italy's Red Brigades and Spain's ETA, and destabilization in key NATO countries.

GLOOMY PREDICTIONS

The Kintex network also involved Mehmet Ali Agca, the Turk convicted of trying to assassinate Pope John Paul II. Agca was guided in the plot by Abuzer Ugurlu, a Turkish crime boss who worked closely with the Bulgarian drugs-and-weapons-smuggling operation. Agca testified that Bekir Celenk, another Turkish drug runner with Kintex ties, introduced him to the Bulgarian secret service, which allegedly financed the papal assassination conspiracy.

What does the spread of narco-terrorism imply? For the American drug user—an addict mainlining heroin, a student sharing a marijuana joint, a partygoer snorting cocaine—there could be a connective thread to events far removed from narcotic reverie: An American kidnapped, a European airport bombed, a Latin American election disrupted, an Asian official assassinated.

For law-enforcement agencies that combat international drug trafficking, it is another difficult element in an already dangerous business. Overwhelmed by the volume of dope flowing into this country, the U.S. can seemingly do little but bluster and threaten when sovereign states facilitate the movement of drugs across our borders.

And for those who worry about terrorism's increasing worldwide reach, the phenomenon looms with frightening implications. Narco-profits present a raft of new opportunities for those bent on destabilizing democracies, spawning anarchy and exporting revolution. "The amounts of money to be made in international drug trafficking are staggering," offered one federal official. "As bad as terrorism has been so far, I don't think we've seen anything yet."

by Michael Satchell with Richard Z. Chesnoff and Maia Wechsler in Paris, Joseph P. Shapiro in Rome, Robert Rosenberg in Tel Aviv, Carla Anne Robbins in Bogotá and Sharon Golden in Washington

A LOW-TECH APPROACH
Prescriptions for Third World Health

DARRYL D'MONTE

DARRYL D'MONTE *often writes for the* NL *on Indian and Third World affairs.*

HALFDAN T. MAHLER

BOMBAY

DR. HALFDAN T. MAHLER, who in July will be stepping down as Director General of the World Health Organization (WHO) after 15 long years in that position, can at times sound like the arrogant Western expert armed with all the answers to the Third World's problems. Declaring that he is about to become a "development terrorist," he told a recent interviewer: "Drop me in Africa or Asia or Latin America, give me $20 for each member of the population I'm going to serve, and I'll show you we can produce a miracle."

Brave new words? Actually, the 62-year-old Danish physician would spend his money in a rather old-fashioned, unspectacular way—not on exotic medicines or futuristic technologies, but on primary health care. That, in fact, is the approach the WHO has been energetically promoting as part of its ongoing "Health for All by the Year 2000" program, conceived a decade ago at a conference in the Soviet city of Alma-Ata. (Oddly, the Heritage Institute, an ultra-conservative Washington think tank, smells something subversive in this effort. See my "Undermining the WHO," NL, July 14-28, 1986.)

Of course, there is not much chance that the WHO will succeed in totally eradicating diseases as prevalent as malaria and bilharziasis in the mere dozen years remaining before the deadline it has given itself. Yet despite the bluster of the "Health for All" slogan, one cannot help being impressed by the strategy behind it.

At the most basic level, the WHO is trying to convince those living in developing countries that their health is to a large degree in their own hands—and not dependent on some elusive white-coated doctor, or on the powders and liquids peddled by the international drug industry. Such is the mystique of modern medicine in the Third World that people there tend not to realize how much they can accomplish on their own initiative, without the help of professionals.

Take the case of infant mortality. In India, one in every three babies is stillborn, and some 65 out of every 1,000 who survive birth die in the crucial first week of life. These statistics are a grim index of underdevelopment, and a shocking reflection of the medical system's failure to protect human existence in its vulnerable beginning stage.

What makes India's infant mortality rate all the more distressing is the extent to which it is due to simple ignorance. As this writer can attest from his observations at rural health projects throughout India, families here find it difficult to discard the belief that the "weakness" besetting a woman during pregnancy must be "cured" before she gives birth or else it will be transferred to the offspring. That means an unnecessary trip to the doctor—either a full-fledged medical graduate who visits the village from time to time or perhaps a less well-trained practitioner who has set up shop locally. Invariably these well-meaning individuals prescribe one or more of the "tonics" produced by pharmaceutical firms in bewildering variety to ameliorate every "ailment" under the sun—including pregnancy.

Scarce household money spent on such useless commercial preparations could be much more prudently used by prospective mothers to assure themselves healthier diets. Pulses, leafy vegetables and other foodstuffs that furnish nutrients essential to the developing fetus are affordable even by rural families on tight budgets. Moreover, the simple home remedy of a little sugar and salt in a glassful of water will remove the threat of dehydration posed by infant diarrhea—a major killer in the Third World, where medicine is not always available when an emergency occurs.

In the fourth century B.C., Hippocrates wrote that "to investigate medicine properly, one must take into account the seasons, the winds, water, orientation of the city, topography, and the customs and occupations of the people under observation." The father of medicine was thus well aware that health is holistic in character. Modern physicians, who still take Hippocrates' oath upon completing their medical school training, have too often lost sight of this. Indeed, Christiaan Barnard—arguably the world's most famous doctor —was not expressing a terribly heterodox attitude when he said just prior to the Alma-Ata conference, "malnutrition is not a medical problem." The WHO, striving to correct this way of thinking, has defined good health as "a state of complete physical, mental and social well-being."

In a farewell interview, Dr. Mahler discussed some of the measures outside the usual purview of the medical establishment that have enormous potential to raise the standards of health in poor countries. One of these involves, quite simply, increasing the availability of clean water. The magnitude of the suffering in the Third World caused by diseases attributable to contaminated water can perhaps be most vividly expressed by putting the problem in terms of First and Second World equivalents: Imagine, for instance, a part of the globe where those urinating blood as a result of bilharziasis equal virtually the entire population of the United States, those in the grip of gastroenteritis add up to all the residents of Western Europe, and those afflicted with swollen legs due to elephantiasis could replace every citizen of the Soviet Union.

At present, access to a safe supply of water is a relative luxury in much of the world. In the majority of developing countries, only a small minority is served by piped water, even in urban areas. Indian municipal authorities suggest that drinking water be boiled in the summer months to prevent typhoid, cholera and other diseases. That precaution requires fuel, however; in a city like Bombay, over half the population lives in slums and cannot afford the "luxury."

Providing clean water wherever it is not now available would, by the WHO's estimates, cost as little as $15 billion annually—or a paltry $5 for every man, woman and child. (As a point of comparison, the world's military outlays total approximately $500 billion, or $150 for every Third World inhabitant.) It is not necessary, "alternative technologists" have been pointing out, to reproduce the conventional water supply and purification systems that have become standard in the West. Several cheaper substitutes are available that could be built and operated with local labor and materials in the less advanced countries.

Another of Dr. Mahler's parting prescriptions for improving the world's health would make greater use of "barefoot doctors"—traditional quasi-medical personnel with roots in their communities—to deliver health care. Although many developing nations pay lip service to this concept, few other than China have done much to put it into effect. In India in the early '70s, for example, then Prime Minister Indira Gandhi toyed with the idea of drafting the services of practitioners of Indian folk medicine, but her primary interest was in having them promote family planning. The short-lived Janata Party government (1977-79) did train some 15,000 community health workers at 700 centers throughout the country, and their ranks were supposed to swell to 500,000 by 1981. Unfortunately, this project was abandoned in the subsequent political turmoil, and the government's stirring motto, "People's health in people's hands," vanished into thin air.

Where one does see signs of the barefoot principle at work here is in the cooperation between village midwives, or *dais*, and nongovernmental voluntary health groups. The *dais*, though entirely illiterate, have extensive rapport with the people in their communities—unlike visiting doctors and paramedics—and can perform such simple yet significant tasks as monitoring the weight of babies. Many health groups have trained the village midwives to follow more scientific methods when they assist at a delivery, and supply them with kits containing sterile materials at a modest cost.

Innovations such as the provision of clean water and the marshaling of community health resources to extend preventive techniques can in a vast number of cases make a difference between life and death. That is not to suggest medicines have no role to play in raising Third World health standards, Dr. Mahler says. At the same time, the retiring WHO head emphasizes that a small number of basic drugs, possibly as few as 200, would be adequate for primary health care. In India, over 60,000 pharmaceutical concoctions are on the market—most at prices only the rich can easily afford.

AIDS in Africa: Ravager of the nation builders

An epidemic threatens a continent's future

Poverty and malnutrition have long been the lot of sub-Saharan Africa. Wars exact a terrible toll. The ancient scourges of malaria, tuberculosis and cholera outlast all who fight them. Three of every 10 babies born do not survive their first four years. Now, AIDS threatens to destroy Africa's best and brightest, worsening the odds already stacked against its future.

The story is told in the obituary columns of newspapers in the hardest-hit nations of central Africa. Notices record the "untimely deaths" of young nation builders: Doctors, lawyers, bankers, writers, politicians and army officers. The cause is never given, but in the capitals of Zambia, Uganda, Rwanda, Burundi, Zaire, Tanzania, Congo and the Central African Republic, everybody knows instantly.

Although only 11,474 AIDS cases have been reported to the World Health Organization from Africa, the actual total is clearly much higher. Some experts say the HIV virus has already spread to upward of 1.5 million, but African leaders in a recent summit admitted that the figure may be closer to 10 million. No relief is in sight: At the fourth international conference on AIDS in Stockholm last week, some 7,000 delegates heard of slight progress in control of the disease, but nothing approaching a cure.

In Africa, AIDS is a heterosexual disease of the cities, striking young men and women in equal numbers—a pattern far different from that in Europe and the United States, where it mainly affects male homosexuals and intravenous drug users and the male-to-female ratio is 13 to 1. Central Africa is the epicenter. AIDS leaps borders with truckdrivers and the prostitutes who serve them on roads from Lake Victoria to the ports of Dar es Salaam in Tanzania and Mombasa in Kenya. One faint glimmer of hope in a bleak picture is that education may be reducing the rate among these carriers.

But AIDS is killing so many of the best educated in their most productive years that the World Bank predicts "highly negative" consequences for national economies. In countries that count themselves lucky to have a dozen qualified engineers, the loss of even one is deeply felt. A study by Harvard researchers suggests that by 1991 losses due to the epidemic will more than offset total foreign aid in some countries.

Infection among young adults in Kinshasa, Zaire's capital, is estimated at 20 percent. Half the staff of one Kinshasa bank has died. Uganda reports only 2,639 confirmed AIDS cases, but doctors in Kampala say the real figure is much higher and doubling every six months. A quarter of the pregnant women in Kampala's main hospital recently tested positive. Most of their babies died within days of birth. Unchecked, experts say, the disease could cut population growth in half. In Tanzania, Fred Mhalu, head of the government's task force on AIDS, says that 3,255 Tanzanians already have the disease, and he estimates that 120,000 will be dying of it within five years—a doomsday scenario for a poor country already short of doctors, medicine and money.

"Dante's inferno must have looked like this," said one doctor at Lusaka's University Teaching Hospital, where AIDS patients fill most of the 2,000 beds, dying in agony because there are no painkilling drugs. The hospital staff is not immune. Thirty percent of its members are HIV positive; one department lost a quarter of its workers in the past year. They caught the disease from sexual partners, not patients. The head of the hospital's blood-screening unit, asked if he would take a transfusion from his own stocks, responds with an emphatic no.

A fearful choice

His fear is shared by small communities of foreign diplomats, businessmen, aid workers and their families throughout the region. Injury could force them to choose between a quick death without a transfusion or a slow one with it. Random testing—regular screening is too expensive—indicates between 10 and 20 percent of blood donors carry the virus.

Fear is one reason governments have been so slow to admit the extent of the epidemic: Fear of losing the foreigners who run aid programs; fear, in Kenya, of seeing tourist dollars evaporate. There have been cases of personal courage. President Kenneth Kaunda of Zambia, breaking with Africa's speak-no-evil attitude toward the disease, acknowledged that a son died of AIDS. But such candor does not crack the wall of official secrecy around reports revealing, for example, that in Zambia's vital copper center of Kitwe, 44 percent of all females hospitalized tested positive. Or that two of nine provincial medical officers had died of the disease.

Where fear does not explain silence, anger and shame do. The anger is driven by what many see as a conspiracy to portray Africa as the birthplace of AIDS, an early theory now being questioned by researchers. The shame comes from recognition that the only remedy is education—public talk of sex in traditionally modest societies. In Swahili, AIDS is said to stand for *aibu imeingia duninani sasa,* or "shame has fallen on the earth."

But silence cannot contain the unfolding tragedy. "If we don't take the right steps," says Dr. Sam Nyaywa, who heads Zambia's AIDS Surveillance Committee, "it's possible that quite a large population will be wiped out."

by John Barnes in Lusaka
with Steven Findlay in Stockholm

Union Carbide and the Devastation of Bhopal

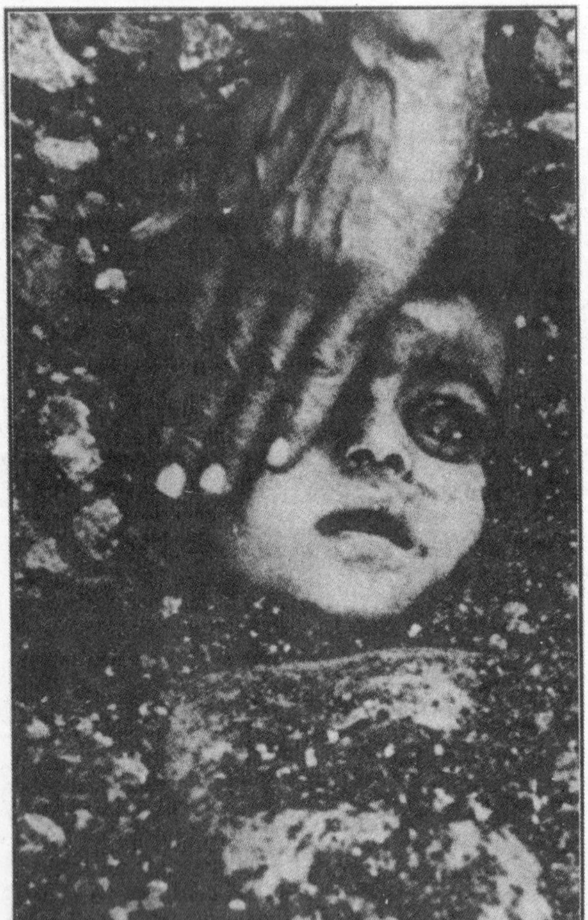

Partially buried victim of Union Carbide disaster in Bhopal, India.

At 2:30 a.m. on December 3, 1984, 40 tons of deadly gases spewed from the Union Carbide India Ltd. (UCIL) plant in Bhopal, India. In the next several hours thousands died, hundreds of thousands were injured and both UCIL and its U.S. parent company, Union Carbide, attempted damage control.

Praful Bidwai, a chemical engineer and journalist, described the situation three days later at a hospital in Bhopal, a city of 800,000. "No one is counting numbers any longer," Bidwai said. "People are dying like flies. They are brought in, their chests heaving violently, their limbs trembling, their eyes blinking from photophobia. It will kill them in a few hours – more usually minutes."

"It" was methyl isocyanate (MIC), a toxic chemical used at UCIL's factory in Bhopal to manufacture pesticides. UCIL was 50.9 percent owned by Union Carbide Corporation, the Danbury, Connecticut-based multinational. The MIC production facility at the Bhopal plant had been shut down for two months, but on the night of December 2, workers conducting routine maintenance noticed a leak. At 12:30 a.m. on December 3, the ground around one of the MIC storage tanks began to rumble. Water had entered the tank, triggering a chain reaction that created heat and pressure and led to the release of 40 tons of toxic gases into the atmosphere over Bhopal.

The release of gas from the Union Carbide plant killed from 2,000 to 5,000 people by conservative estimates, and injured another 200,000 people, at least 30,000 to 40,000 of them seriously, making it the world's worst industrial disaster.

Many of the severely injured suffer from respiratory ailments, permanent eye problems, and mental disorders. Medico Friend Circle, a Bhopal-based citizen's group, conducted a survey in 1985 which found that rates of spontaneous abortions were higher among women who conceived shortly after the gas disaster.

On December 4, the day after the gassing, former Union Carbide Chairman, Warren Anderson, accompanied by other company officials, flew from the United States to India to personally inspect the disaster. Upon arrival in the Bhopal area, Andersen and two local Union Carbide officials were arrested and charged with criminal negligence. Six hours after their arrest, the three were released, ordered to pay $2,000 bail, and Anderson was ordered to leave the country, which he planned to do in any event. The charges, an attempt by the Indian government to quell public outrage at the corporation and at the government — which was widely perceived as ineffective in bringing medical relief to the victims, were never pursued. Upon returning to the United States, Anderson told reporters that the purpose of his trip to India was to provide medical aid and seek information on the cause of the accident. But Carbide's offer of $1 million in disaster relief came to about $5 per victim, and the week after the accident, Carbide sent only one shipment of medicine, sufficient for 300 to 400 people.

Perhaps the more important reason Anderson went to India was to see that the company wouldn't be dragged into a costly legal battle. Anderson had good reasons for wanting to avoid litigation. Even though Union Carbide repeatedly claimed that the company was not at fault and that "the Indian company has nothing to do with the U.S. company," the facts point to a close and structured relationship between the two companies. While the Bhopal plant was operated by UCIL, it was controlled by Union Carbide's U.S. management.

The UCIL plant in Bhopal was storing MIC, a highly volatile and deadly gas. Although the plant had a refrigeration unit which was designed to keep the MIC storage tank at a temperature low enough to prevent a runaway chemical reaction, the unit was not working at the time of the accident. The MIC in the storage tank therefore was warmer than allowed by the plant's operating manual. "The refrigeration unit had been down over five months," Union Carbide officials admitted to a crowded March 20, 1985 press conference at Carbide's world headquarters in Danbury, Connecticut. The shutdown was a violation of plant procedure rules.

With the refrigeration unit out, it was crucial that instruments designed to measure the temperature and pressure of the gas in the storage tank be in good operating order. But the Temperature Indicator Alarm had been giving faulty readings for years. The Pressure Indicator Control was similarly faulty.

The plant also had an emergency scrubber system to neutralize gas in the event of a leak. But the scrubber system had been out of use for six weeks. The flare tower, designed as the final line of defense to burn off excess MIC, also was closed down 10 days before the fatal leak. Due to neglected maintenance, the line to the flare tower had corroded.

To make matters worse, the workers operating this faulty equipment at the Bhopal plant were inadequately trained. The leak was apparently triggered when an untrained worker attempted to wash a pipe that was not sealed. It was the mixture of water and gas that triggered the chemical reaction and caused the gas leak.

"Everything that could possibly go wrong had gone wrong," said Bruce Agnew, editor of *Safety and Risk Management*, the magazine of the British Safety Council. "Machinery failed; workers panicked; managers either took no decisions or took the wrong decisions."

If the cases against UCIL and Union Carbide ever to to trial, either in the United States or India, the evidence indicating reckless operation of the Bhopal plant could mean a verdict that would quickly deplete the assets of UCIL, estimated at $100 million. As half owner of UCIL, the loss of the Bhopal plant's assets is of concern to the parent, Union Carbide. Of much greater concern to Carbide, however, is the threat of losing its own assets. If a judge makes a legal determination that Union Carbide exercised control over its Indian subsidiary, then Carbide's entire net worth is open to the claims of the victims. And the evidence condemning Carbide's relations with its subsidiaries indicates strict authority and control by the parent company. UCIL is listed on Union Carbide's consolidated balance sheet. Through its majority holding, Union Carbide had direct representation on the board of UCIL.

More importantly, Union Carbide was directly involved in the design and operation of the Bhopal plant. According to a report on December 27, 1984 in the *Times of India* by chemical engineer and investigative reporter Praful Bidwai, Union Carbide designed the Bhopal plant and was responsible for approving and inspecting all major equipment installed in the factory. The Bhopal plant was "grossly underdesigned," according to Bidwai.

"Thus even if each piece of equipment had functioned as designed and the plant as a whole had been properly maintained and operated — which it evidently was not — it would still not have been possible to avert the disaster," Bidwai concluded.

In February, 1985, Edward Munoz, a retired Union Carbide official and former managing director of UCIL, claimed in a sworn affidavit that in the early 1970s Union Carbide insisted that large amounts of MIC be stored in Bhopal despite UCIL's objection. In the early 1970s, Munoz "represented the Union Carbide India Ltd. position that only token storage (of the chemical at Bhopal) was necessary, preferably in small individual containers, based both on economic and safety considerations," according to the affidavit. But Union Carbide's corporate engineering group "imposed the view and ultimately made to be built (at Bhopal) large bulk storage tanks patterned

UNION CARBIDE

Sales: $9 billion
Assets: $10.5 billion
Net Income: $581 million
Employees: 91, 459
Rank in Sales: 39
Headquarters: Danbury, CT
CEO: Robert D. Kennedy
Products: Prestone Antifreeze, Eveready Batteries, Glad Plastic Wrap

Source: Union Carbide and *Fortune Magazine*.

on similar Union Carbide facilities at Institute, W. Va.," Munoz asserted in his affidavit.

In the wake of the Bhopal disaster, a growing chorus of critics joined Munoz in disputing Union Carbide's view that "the Indian company (UCIL) has nothing to do with the U.S. company." A wide-ranging, seven-week investigation of the Bhopal disaster conducted by *The New York Times* in January, 1985 concluded that Union Carbide "had the authority to exercise financial and technical control over its affiliate (UCIL) and the American parent used that right."

"Union Carbide had its finger on the pulse of the Bhopal plant all the time," Kamal K. Pareek, senior project engineer during the building of the Bhopal plant's methyl isocyanate installation, told *The New York Times*. "They just didn't appreciate the information they were getting."

An internal Union Carbide report supports this view. Dated May 1982, the report, submitted to Union Carbide by a team of American experts, points out major safety concerns at the Bhopal plant, including deficiencies in instrumentation and safety valves, lax maintenance procedures, and high turnover of operating and maintenance staff. The report, stamped "Business Confidential," warned that the plant presented "serious potential for sizeable releases of toxic materials." The U.S. team made numerous recommendations to rectify the deficiencies at the plant, but according to reports from union activists, not one of the recommendations was ever implemented.

After this report was sent from Union Carbide corporate headquarters to the Bhopal plant, union organizers appealed to U.S. management to improve safety conditions.

There were other warnings. Three months prior to the Bhopal gas leak, an internal Union Carbide memo warned that "a real potential for a serious incident exists" at Bhopal's sister plant in Institute, West Virginia, and that efforts to control the problem "would not be timely or effective enough to prevent catastrophic failure of the [storage] tank." The memo warned of a "runaway reaction" at the West Virginia facility.

Union Carbide's culpability in the Bhopal gas leak is compounded by a history of serious accidents at the Bhopal plant. Between 1978 and 1984, there were six accidents at the plant that should have tipped off corporate executives at world headquarters in the United States that something was wrong in India. On November 24, 1978 a fire at the alpha-napthol storage area burned out of control for 10 hours, resulting in $5 million in property damage. Plant operator Mohammed Ashraf was killed by a phosgene gas leak on December 26, 1981. Another phosgene leak in January 1982 seriously injured 28 persons. Three electrical operators were severely burned while working on a control system panel on April 22, 1982. On October 5, 1982, methyl isocyanate escaped from a broken valve and seriously injured four workers. Several people living in nearby communities also experienced burning in the eyes and breathing trouble due to the exposure. Two similar incidents were also reported in 1983.

Despite the number of serious accidents at the UCIL plant, few Bhopal residents knew that pesticides were being produced at the factory nor did they know of MIC's dangers. Even after the leak, Carbide took two hours to warn Bhopal's residents, many of whom lived in shanty towns surrounding the plant. The leak occurred about 12:30 a.m. on December 3, but the first alarm failed to warn most Bhopal residents until between 2:00 and 2:30 a.m.

"If they had [sounded the sirens] before or just after the gas leaked out, we would have known what to do," said one survivor. "We'd at least have had a chance to run. I lost my wife and two sons only because they didn't warn us. These people are criminals, butchers, worse than murderers."

Immediately after the accident, UCIL officials in Bhopal denied that MIC was hazardous. "The gas that leaked is only an irritant, it is not fatal," one UCIL official told reporters immediately after the leak, but the MIC operating manual used at the Bhopal plant and adapted from a similar manual used at Bhopal's sister MIC plant in Institute, West Virginia tells another story. The authors of the manual, five Indian engineers, make abundantly clear the dangers of MIC: "MIC's limited exposure can be fatal. The chemicals involved in its production are highly toxic and hazardous in nature. Even the big corporations have refrained from making this lethal chemical due to the complexity involved in the operation."

Immediately following the Bhopal disaster, lawsuits were filed across the United States against Union Carbide on behalf of the victims and the government of India. But on May 12, 1986, Federal Judge John F. Keenan ruled that the lawsuits belonged not in the United States, but in India. The judge concluded that it would be more convenient and save U.S. taxpayer's money to have the Bhopal cases tried in India. That decision was appealed by lawyers for the victims.

In the year preceding his decision, Judge Keenan, in his words, "labored long and hard" to promote a settlement, all "to no avail." Indeed, Robert Hager, a lawyer representing 20 religious and public interest groups, argued, in appealing the judge's decision, that the Bhopal victims had been "seriously prejudiced because Judge Keenan labored for a settlement too hard and too long." Arguing that "Carbide and its powerful Wall Street owners stood to lose probably $5 billion or more if the Bhopal case reached an American jury," Hager reasoned that "Carbide had to settle the case cheap, hide its assets, or get the case out of the U.S. courts to avoid or at least postpone potential bankruptcy."

Hager charged that by permitting a year-long delay before making his decision, Judge Keenan allowed Union Carbide the time to liquidate substantial assets and make extraordinary payouts to its shareholders reducing its equity available to pay for any judgment awarded the Bhopal victims. The payouts reduced equity from around $5 billion before the disaster to less than $700 million on the books by the end of 1985.

"Carbide's depleted equity will now enable it to defend by means of bankruptcy, against any Indian judgment substantially in excess of its settlement offer ($350 million) without significant loss to the company's pre-Bhopal owners," Hager said.

Hager's appeal was denied and the case against Union Carbide is slowly proceeding through the Indian courts.

WHERE THE FUTURE BEGINS

Amadou-Mahtar M'Bow
Director-General of Unesco

SINCE Unesco was created thirty-seven years ago as a result of its founders' determination to provide mankind, in the sphere of activities of the mind, with the means for influencing its own future development, the world has changed profoundly. The international community has expanded considerably with the emergence of new nations, and mankind has constantly strengthened its control over the planet and increased its mental and material powers. Scientific and technological advances, the successive stages of which have conspicuously marked development in the last quarter of a century, for instance, enabling man even to explore space, have considerably improved the lives of a certain number of peoples and have now given the whole human race, for the first time in its history, the means of ridding itself of the major concerns that have preoccupied it since the dawn of time—food, health, shelter, protection against natural calamities, security.

The spread of education has given more and more people access to the most varied and advanced forms of knowledge, thus greatly enhancing the capacity for innovation, and hence the well-being of many societies. The achievement of political sovereignty by almost all nations has made possible an extraordinary widening of the scope for human initiative and liberty and has given each of them the opportunity to play an active role in a history that will henceforth be worked out by a collective effort. Exchanges of goods, capital, knowledge and know-how are becoming more and more numerous; intellectual and cultural intermixing proceeds apace; and anxieties, hopes and fears are beginning to converge, transcending the demarcation lines drawn by history or established by geography. As all communities are more and more gathered together within one and the same network of vital relationships and even mutual dependence, the prospect at last gleams ahead of a world community joined in unity of purpose and finally reconciled with itself, where all will be sure of the means to live a better life, unhampered by fear, and where there will be an ever fuller flowering of freedoms and creative faculties.

But entire populations are still living in absolute poverty. Profound inequalities continue to divide peoples and individuals and the pursuit of progress itself frequently gives rise to contradictions, uncertainties and doubts. Disturbing harm is being done to the natural environment. There is mounting tension between countries and within some countries; life in many societies is troubled by violence. Instruments of destruction are being further developed and stockpiled. Nuclear weapons, by their quantity and destructive capacity, are already capable of annihilating all that mankind has constructed through thousands of years of effort, and even mankind itself. Overarming is not only an expression of the mutual distrust which is advanced to justify it; but it accentuates the trend towards division of the world into spheres of influence and leads to military, economic and cultural interference in the lives of others; and it diverts an enormous volume of resources from the satisfaction of societies' urgent needs.

One world

From whatever angle one approaches the major questions which mankind has to answer, one realizes that the future of modern societies will be enacted in a context now expanding to worldwide scale.

As a result, societies which had been able to live in almost total ignorance of each other up to a few decades ago are now in increasingly regular contact. Reciprocal influences are becoming ever more numerous and interdependence is becoming a multidimensional reality. While interdependence is doubtless a source of mutual enrichment, receptivity, initiative and creativity, it also leads to frustrations when accompanied by a deterioration in the lot of some people, a reduction in the scope for manœuvre, increased unpredictability and greater vulnerability.

The image that emerges from any analysis or effort of reflection is therefore that of an increasingly complex world in which sources of friction are on the increase just as the reasons for co-operating and the means for communicating are becoming stronger.

Reproduced from the *Unesco Courier,* January 1983, pp. 5–9, by permission.

Asymmetries and inequalities

Economic statistics provide blunt evidence of the scale of the disparities between nations and groups of nations. But inequalities also persist within most societies and are in some cases even becoming more pronounced. The prosperity of many industrialized countries may conceal an uneven distribution of income, and some sections of the population in those countries lead a difficult, sometimes even precarious existence. In the Third World, vast populations frequently enjoy none of the benefits of progress and towns and cities—in many cases and at least as regards certain social categories—are like islands of modernity cut off from the hinterland.

The picture of destitution, concentrated for the most part in countries of the Third World is a familiar one. An age-old word—poverty—has today become a central concept of economics. It betokens serious deficiencies in food, housing, health and education and an extremely low income level. Depending on the criteria adopted, it may be reckoned that there are some 800 million people in the world living in a state of absolute poverty (World Bank) or about 1,100 million poor (International Labour Office). Other equally impressive figures have to be taken into account to form a more detailed picture of various categories of unfulfilled needs: 430 million people severely undernourished, 1,000 million badly housed, 1,300 million without adequate access to drinking-water, and, according to statistics established by Unesco, 814 million adult illiterates and 123 million children of school age not attending school.

The international economic system

The present situation is really only the most recent stage in a process that began in the distant past. The rise of certain countries, the creation of vast colonial empires for their benefit and the dawning and development within those same countries of the industrial revolution had the effect of placing them in a position of economic dominance, which has finally reduced many other parts of the world to the state described by the concept of "dependence" set forth in certain economic theories.

Whether politically colonized or not, most "dependent" countries served as reservoirs of raw materials or specially favourable markets for the manufactured goods of the dominant countries. The economies of these countries have thus developed basically under the pressure of demands originating elsewhere rather than in accordance with their own needs.

Even today, with the exception of petroleum, the Third World countries have no control over the prices of the products which constitute the basis of their exports, nor over the prices of products which they must import. Many of them are faced with a steadily deteriorating balance of payments, while their borrowing capacity is shrinking.

Notwithstanding the different constraints to which they are subjected and the specificity of their situations, the development of Third World countries has been conceived, given its basis in theory and directed, in most cases, by reference to the international economic situation which has been imposed on them. Underdevelopment has been interpreted as essentially a time-lag in the various branches of socio-economic activity, as compared with the situation obtaining in the so-called developed countries, while development has been seen as a universal process occurring in all places and at all times in the same sequence of successive "phases". A progression has thus been envisaged, leading necessarily from the traditional, predominantly agricultural society towards "modern" society, frequently described as the "age of consumption", and inevitably involving, sooner or later, an "economic take-off". This seems to have been the premiss, explicit or otherwise, behind the efforts made in the last few decades, an approach which at times failed to perceive the crucial importance of the constraints imposed on the developing countries by the international economic system.

It appears, however, that genuine development has to be elicited from within, willed and conducted by all the vital forces of a nation. Accordingly, it should encompass all aspects of life and involve all the energies of a community within which each individual, each occupational category and each social group has its part to play in the general effort and its share in the resulting benefits.

Development cannot therefore be considered solely from the standpoint of economic performance and the growth of material goods. No doubt economic growth and the production of material goods will always be vitally important because of the essential contribution they alone can make to the general welfare; but they should serve purposes consciously accepted by all, that enrich everyone's life, increase the creative capacities of the entire population and have their roots in culture, with all that it implies of truth to self and receptivity to progress.

A growing awareness of the importance of the cultural dimension of development thus emerges as one of the salient facts of our time.

Peace and the arms race

The face of war has changed today. The quantity and destructive potential of modern nuclear weapons and of chemical and biological weapons, are such that a conflict between the great powers, in which such weapons would inevitably be used, would result in the destruction of the human race. The feature that makes the present era radically different from previous eras is this capacity of the human race for self-annihilation. It is a state of affairs unique in the history of mankind, and one that must be constantly borne in mind at a time when it is sometimes asserted that with tactical nuclear weapons, a nuclear conflict could remain localized and its consequences be surmounted. In practice there is no guarantee that, once set off, a nuclear conflagration could ever be contained. The after-effects of atomic explosions would be so extensive that there would be a strong likelihood of the threshold being quickly reached where the scale of destruction would prove lethal for the whole of mankind.

It is against this background that the many localized conflicts that have occurred since the end of the Second World War, involving developing countries for the most part and causing the deaths of millions of people, must be set. Several of those conflicts have stemmed from the will of the colonized or formerly colonized peoples to win their independence or to withstand external pressures that imperil their freedom. Others, admittedly, have more complex origins—confrontations within nations or disputes between nations—but all of them are inevitably aggravated, if not brought on, by the antagonisms within the world community.

The arms race, originating in many cases from the will to predominate or from a sense of insecurity which, far from mitigating, it aggravates, accelerates under its own momentum. It has undeniably become a phenomenon which, by virtue of its scale and implications, dominates the international scene. Total military expenditure in 1980 may be estimated at over $500 thousand million—a sheer waste of these colossal resources, it may be said, since they do not enhance the security of those who foot the bill, the balance tending simply to establish itself at an ever higher level.

It should also be pointed out that the arms race at present ties up valuable human resources and, especially, very large numbers of top scientists. If this huge research and development potential were used for purposes of human welfare, considerable progress could be made towards solving some of man's major problems, such as those in the fields of health, education or agricultural production. Quite obviously, such a redeployment has an ethical dimension and is one of the major issues in the current debate on the ultimate purposes of science and technology.

On a more general level, ethical concerns cannot be dissociated from attempts to build peace, which means considerably more than the absence of war. Peace has a positive content, demanding as it does justice in relations between societies and recognition of the equality in dignity of all peoples and all cultures. It is hence more

particularly synonymous with respect for fundamental human rights and the freedom of the peoples to make their own decisions.

Human rights

Massive violations of human rights continue; foremost among them, mention must be made of the apartheid regime that still prevails in South Africa, despite repeated condemnations by the international community. That regime continues to institutionalize racism and to deny, by its very existence, the most fundamental principle on which human rights are based: the oneness of the human race and the equal worth of all human beings.

The right of peoples to self-determination is also seriously flouted. Some peoples are still politically subjugated, as a result of long-standing, or in some cases recent, historical circumstances. Many communities are still deprived of the right to an identity.

There are some ten million refugees in the world today; their situation is particularly grave because of the precariousness of their living conditions, the fact of their having been uprooted and the difficulty of finding viable solutions in the prevailing political and economic circumstances.

No less disquieting is the trend with regard to individual freedoms, which are jeopardized in various ways, either by blind terrorism that strikes even at the totally innocent in the name of particular aspirations or principles, or by the established authorities. Authorities in many countries have curbed political liberties and freedom of association and put down opposition movements. In some cases, the law itself is used to redouble the attacks upon human rights, for instance by retroactive, repressive legislation, the widening of the interpretation of national security, or the institutionalization of emergency measures. There is a disquieting tendency to "criminalize" opposition by bringing mere political disagreement within the scope of the penal code. Furthermore, normal legal safeguards are often set aside, with the resultant development of various forms of detention without trial.

No less serious, and perhaps even more serious, is the tendency to adopt, parallel to official and legal repression, procedures beyond the pale of legality and State power, involving undercover operations of kidnapping or murder whose perpetrators enjoy a sort of impunity.

Moreover, although prohibited by legislation in most States, torture and, more generally, humiliating and degrading treatment are still practised. In some places they are inflicted, seemingly on a systematic basis, when suspects are arrested and during their interrogation and detention.

But not even the denunciation of violations of human rights is unaffected by the political rifts in the world. For instance, the very people who habitually express indignation at certain actions tend to minimize others that are equally serious, because the regimes responsible for them share their view of the world or serve their interests. The danger with such attitudes to violations of human rights is that they may lull consciences into acquiescence; they must be countered by an unconditional insistence on respect for human rights, irrespective of the political judgements that may be passed on particular situations. Individual freedoms and the freedom of peoples are two sides of the same coin. These problems, like those of development and peace, concern each human being and the entire human race.

The environment and natural resources

There is another area in which complex networks of interactions now appear to bind the fate of the individual inextricably to the collective future of mankind: this is the relationship between man and nature. Attention is now also focused, as the result of a new awareness which has become especially marked over recent decades, on the pressure that man's activities, based on technological advance, exert on the environment, either through the unchecked eating-up of resources and of space, or through the production of wastes that the natural environment can no longer absorb without suffering far-reaching effects. The major risks emerging in the relationship between man and nature are the exhaustion or scarcity of certain non-renewable resources essential for human activities and irreversible damage that might jeopardize the balance of the biosphere.

These concerns must be seen in the context of problems of society and development which are of decisive importance as regards the environment. Underlying all these problems, in fact, are the forms of production and consumption of the industrial societies. In the purely technical and economic logic of industrialization as it has generally been conceived, the environment and natural resources are treated simply as instruments serving economic growth. The pursuit of quick and high returns means that the cost of environmental damage is overlooked. Society as a whole, considered either nationally or internationally, then has to bear costs which are entirely neglected in any economic reckoning. This type of behaviour, which leads to unrestrained and what might fairly be termed unscrupulous exploitation of natural resources, gives rise to serious damage. In many Third World countries, it entails an overworking of natural resources that is detrimental in the long term, whether they be living resources, like forests and fish stocks, or mineral resources occurring in finite quantities.

But situations of underdevelopment, in themselves, also have unfortunate implications for the environment. Poverty leads to over-use or irrational use of the productive capacities of ecosystems, of soil, water and wood. It also leads to uncontrolled extension of urbanization, which has today become a major problem in many countries.

Environmental problems can never be considered apart from the present forms of the international division of labour and the constraints imposed by the international economic system. Control by the developing countries over their own natural resources is, incidentally one of the main lines of emphasis in efforts to bring about a new international economic order.

But this objective cannot be dissociated from the idea of a global environmental ethic based on wise use of the resources that the planet offers to men and that human ingenuity succeeds in discovering and turning to account.

Such an aim may in the long term imply changes in the manner in which resources are used in most countries of the world, eventually involving far-reaching changes in behaviour and recognition of the primacy of such values as solidarity and equity, in application not merely to people alive today but to those who will come after us, as opposed to behaviour guided solely by immediate self-interest.

Communication between people and between cultures

Recent developments have made the world more and more one as regards communication and exchanges between people and between cultures. Countless communication networks have grown up as production, management and organization technologies have spread throughout the world, with the intensive circulation of products and people, the rapid strides made by telecommunications and data processing, and the huge increase in the volume of messages put out all over the world by the mass media.

These technologies are playing a part in transforming societies and causing them to move towards ever greater complexity. Communication and information may in fact be regarded as the nervous system of contemporary societies: they are essential to their activities, particularly in economic matters, and play an essential part in financial transactions and banking and in the development of trade, of land, sea and air transport, of health or public administration systems, and of military systems. Any political power is of necessity placed at the centre of a complex communication and information system, since decision-making increasingly necessitates consideration of more and more constantly changing items of information, and since, furthermore, any policy needs to be explained and commented on if it is to gain acceptance. Some people consequently consider that tomorrow's economy will be one based mainly on information, and that information is in the process of becoming the key resource marked out for a major role still more decisive than that of raw materials and energy.

This makes the very great disparities in the different countries' situations as regards their communication and information capacity all the more serious. The least well equipped countries, especially the developing countries, are deprived of some of the most effective means of controlling the various aspects of the development process. The development of communication and information in the developing countries, which is generally recognized to be necessary by the international community today, is therefore a prime prerequisite for the advent of a world of greater equity and solidarity and for the free development of democracy within the various societies. If they were better able to communicate and to acquire and impart information, the developing countries could not only make their voices heard more effectively in international affairs but could also make more progress in education—particularly in the struggle against illiteracy—and could develop their scientific and technological potential, improve their health systems, promote rural development, and be in a better position to deal with natural disasters. Communication and information can also help those countries, and indeed all others, to consolidate national unity, preserve their cultural identity and make provision for greater participation by the public in the changes currently taking place.

It seems essential, therefore, to do away with the obstacles that prevent people and nations from gaining access to all sources of information and from directly expressing their own points of view, as also to avoid the distortions which compromise the dignity and independence of peoples. In this context, it is clearly important to foster the development of all forms of communication and information in all countries, and particularly in the developing countries, and to encourage efforts to discover and apply innovations which will allow of readier adaptation of structures and content for the purposes of different categories of users, the compiling of information with broader participation by the public, and greater diversification in cultural expression.

Science, technology and society

Existing modern technologies already confer enormous powers upon man, and their potential is such that many of the problems confronting human societies could be solved if they were systematically employed. The prospects opened up by modern science are therefore full of new promise.

To obtain a clearer picture of these prospects, it is important to note that very profound upheavals have reshaped the map of the scientific world and the relations between the various sciences. This development and its practical implications are bound to exert a strong influence on scientific and technological strategies. A new configuration of fields of knowledge could be said to be forming, in which the branches of the future appear to be biology, data processing, systems theory and the communication and information sciences. We are thus witnessing nothing less than a scientific and technological revolution, which seems capable of transforming not only methods of production and patterns of consumption but mentalities and social practices as well. It is even tending to efface, to some extent at least, the old-established demarcation lines between the natural sciences and the social and human sciences. We are perhaps living in an era in which cross-over points are emerging between the major fields of human creativity: among the various scientific disciplines and between them and culture.

Although considerable efforts have been made, much more remains to be done in order to find appropriate solutions to the problems of energy supply, food, housing, transport, leisure or the management of the environment still encountered in all societies in different forms and degrees. The bulk of scientific and technological potential is still concentrated in a limited number of countries which alone possess the means for conducting research in certain fields, especially the advanced fields, and therefore hold the keys, so to speak, to the major advances of the future. Moreover, the lines of emphasis in research and the choice of fields in which it is applied are determined primarily by the needs and problems of the countries that are already best provided for—which adds to their accumulated wealth of scientific and technological knowledge, while the existing stock of knowledge and know-how is still inaccessible to most developing countries.

Science must be used to increase the well-being of all peoples. This presupposes a freer and more intensive flow of information and knowledge concerning both science and technology, a worldwide concerted effort to make scientific research more relevant to the needs of the whole of mankind, and to ensure in all countries, the developing countries in particular, their own development of science and technology. On this last point, it should be stressed that scientific and technological development must come about as a result of a set of complex interactions between the need for scientific and technological solutions to economic and social problems, on the one hand, and, on the other, efforts to train researchers and specialists and to organize scientific research and experimental development programmes.

Cultural identity

The need to rethink development, and to invent new strategies to take account of what is distinctive in each nation's way of life and culture and to call into play the enterprise of all the individuals and groups that go to make it up, is becoming all the more urgent today because of the tendency towards uniformity that is developing and, in many countries and among many sections of the population, impinging upon life-styles and modes of thought and on the organization of the social, individual and family environment. This tendency results less from a convergence of the different values of civilization than from the predominance of certain centres propagating the knowledge, know-how and social usages specific to the best endowed societies. The very fact of the growing oneness of the world in economic, social and cultural matters is bringing certain needs and aspirations to the fore, in more and more environments and within various societies, and causing them all to follow the same model, based on goods and services produced and distributed throughout the world. In every area of life—from food to clothing, from transport to leisure—the same patterns of consumption are tending to spread. This tendency is enhanced by the media and the cultural industries which are extending it into cultures, ideas and ways of seeing or depicting the world.

This logic of growing uniformity favours certain lines in the pursuit of knowledge to the detriment of other forms; it imposes certain aesthetic or ethical values; it stimulates the growth of certain areas of activity, encourages certain talents and modes of feeling—and ignores others. Whole sectors of creativity are thus repressed, societies mutilated in their individuality and their distinctive structure. Carried to the extreme, this logic could lead to mankind's becoming ossified, since diversity, if accepted on a footing of complete equality, is indeed an essential and fertile source of vitality alike for individual societies and for the whole world.

The growing homogeneity that world uniformity based on a single model would produce could well leave all humankind bereft of the means to face unknown or new dangers. Who can say whether a given culture or a given genetic feature, now lost beneath the ruins of traditional societies, may not have been an integral part of a heritage and perhaps essential to the further progress of

humanity? Nor can we rule out the possibility that one day the global technological society might perish from entropy, for lack of a sufficient differentiation between cultures.

These would appear to be the historical implications—in reaction to the growing globalization of fundamental social processes and the pressures towards uniformity brought to bear on the individual or collective mentality—of the reawakening of specificities, which is the manifestation of a now overriding demand, that of identity, which can be seen everywhere in the world and which in some countries links up with the efforts successfully carried out or more recently undertaken to enhance the status of the national culture.

In this respect, it is significant that the demand for cultural identity, first voiced in certain parts of Europe in the nineteenth century and which crystallized the aspirations of the young nations formerly under colonial rule—for whom the conquest or reconquest of their mutilated past represented the most precious achievement in the struggle for independence—should now be raised again in the industrialized societies, where the need to preserve or to revitalize regional or ethnic identities is increasingly felt. In all regions, cultural identity appears now as one of the chief driving forces of history, representing neither a fossilized heritage nor a mere collection of traditions, but an internal dynamic, a process whereby a society continually creates itself, nourished by internal diversities consciously and voluntarily accepted, and welcoming, assimilating and if necessary transforming contributions received from elsewhere.

Far from coinciding with withdrawal into an immutable, self-enclosed past, it promotes a lively, original and constantly renewed synthesis. Identity thus appears increasingly to be the *sine qua non* of progress for individuals, groups and nations, for it is the force that animates and underpins the collective will, that gathers to itself the internal resources for action, and that turns necessary change into creative adaptation. More and more linguistic, religious, cultural and occupational groups are accordingly asserting their individuality and strengthening their internal bonds. The protection of their specific identities seems to be the first step towards the regaining of their creative faculties, their inventiveness and ability to participate in a world that has tended to efface them. It should in no way be interpreted as a mere revitalization of former values, but betokens chiefly a search for new cultural designs whereby to carry on from rehabilitation of the past by an awareness of increased responsibility for the future.

Uncertainties and the renewal of values

While it is now clearly appreciated that economics cannot be the only criterion in development, that other objectives must be defined and that new methods, modelled more closely on the requirements and aspirations of the community must be invented, the striking feature of many contemporary societies is extreme diversity in the behaviour, demands and aspirations of individuals and groups, and the juxtaposition, at times, of different scales of values. This diversification in systems of standards is no doubt connected with the development of societies and changes within them but it is also connected, in part, with the increasing flow of goods, services, technologies and messages from one part of the world to another.

In most countries of the Third World, a host of needs and new motivations are appearing, based on the systems of standards and values specific to certain industrialized societies. The combination of new aspirations and traditional loyalties produces divided values in certain regions, within certain families and even in the hearts of more and more individuals. The sharp division between modernity and the underlying cultures appears in many countries to be opening a gulf between those who have integrated into the new world and those to whom it remains foreign, thus aggravating the polarization between groups, between town and country and between the industrialized and rural sectors.

In the past few years, however, there have in a number of countries been attempts to rebuild society on the basis of a revival of its most deeply rooted cultural values. It is this aspiration that is imparting fresh impetus to the spiritual, religious or mystic movements through which part of the population in those countries is seeking to re-establish links with an ethic of solidarity and mutual assistance. It is this, too, that is inspiring certain peoples with the determination to build their own version of modernism, by reinterpreting tradition so as to identify its creative features. This ambition calls for an endeavour to renovate social standards and practices by drawing on those cultural traditions and traditions of work, and aesthetic or moral values, that will enable the society to make room for progress without self-betrayal, and by rejecting all those traditions and values that would shut it into a past offering no way forward.

Questionings and new approaches are also appearing, for different reasons and in other forms, in a number of industrialized societies where more and more groups, particularly among the young, are tending to adopt new attitudes towards income and social success, work and leisure, and the man-made and natural environments. New aspirations are emerging and giving rise to a greater demand for decentralization and participation; to an attempt to find a new, settled place in small communities, whether geographical, professional, religious or linguistic; to a lesser emphasis on order and even on economic security, and to a desire for emancipation *vis-à-vis* anything that may have a centralizing function. Are these changes the forerunners of an imminent transformation in the axiological systems of certain industrialized societies? It is difficult to assess either their scope or their precise significance because of the extreme diversity of the attitudes involved, their uncertain and often ambiguous or contradictory nature, and the heterogeneity of the aspirations they reveal.

In some countries social movements of a new kind are emerging, bringing into the political arena and the sphere of collective action matters hitherto regarded as strictly private, like birth, old age, housing, environment and communication. Associations that cut across the usual social barriers are being set up—women's groups or clubs for "senior citizens", neighbourhood co-operatives, consumer or user associations, and groups getting together for leisure activities or work—which are experimenting with novel types of cultural activity and often introducing new relationships between the economic and political spheres. As a result, new issues now have their spokesmen in society, while cultural production is linked once more with social production as in the past.

All these ventures show that people are radically challenging the established order and exploring new avenues in a great variety of ways, which may denote a revival of social creativity.

Between breakdown and renewal, therefore, a fundamental challenge arises and will no doubt face a large number of societies and the international community itself in the coming years: how, with the growing complexity of forms of organization and production systems, to reconcile the demand for the cohesion and effectiveness needed both nationally and internationally for action to promote development with the demands for a share in initiative and creativity that are often voiced? The movement towards a diversification of systems of references, in reaction against the trend towards uniformity and conditioning, is undoubtedly indicative of the intrinsic vitality of contemporary cultures. It may herald a regeneration, on condition however that more appropriate forms of communication and exchange are established, within a context of greater justice, among societies and within those very societies, among social groups separated by their differing loyalties and aims, and among nations which must arrive at mutual understanding and reach agreement on the co-operative actions which are called for and indeed demanded by the world today.

Index

Credits/ Acknowledgments

Cover design by Charles Vitelli

1. Understanding the Third World
Facing overview—United Nations.

2. People, Power, and Leadership
Facing overview—United Nations photo by S. Jackson.
57—Ministry of Information and Propaganda, Mexico. 59, 63, 66, 68—Photos by Jeffrey Elliot.

3. Stability, Crisis, and Revolution
Facing overview—United Nations.

4. The Limits of American Power
Facing overview—United Nations photo by Kate Truscott.

5. Human Rights and Democratic Rule
Facing overview—United Nations.

6. Easing the Debt Crisis
Facing overview—United Nations photo by Jongen.

7. A World in Change
Facing overview—United Nations photo by Paul Heath Noeffel.
210—Photo by Irene Pearlman. 234—APPEN.

We Want Your Advice

Annual Editions revisions depend on two major opinion sources: one is our Advisory Board, listed in the front of this volume, which works with us in scanning the thousands of articles published in the public press each year; the other is you—the person actually using the book. Please help us and the users of the next edition by completing the prepaid article rating form on this page and returning it to us. Thank you.

ANNUAL EDITIONS: THIRD WORLD 89/90

Article Rating Form

Here is an opportunity for you to have direct input into the next revision of this volume. We would like you to rate each of the 46 articles listed below, using the following scale:

1. Excellent: should definitely be retained
2. Above average: should probably be retained
3. Below average: should probably be deleted
4. Poor: should definitely be deleted

Your ratings will play a vital part in the next revision. So please mail this prepaid form to us just as soon as you complete it.
Thanks for your help!

Rating	Article	Rating	Article
	1. The Third World		22. Quagmire in the Making
	2. Second Thoughts About the Third World		23. The Panama Perplex
	3. "We Are Told . . . We Must Have More of the Disease"		24. Rancor Aside, Trade Ties Grow Between South Africa, Black States
	4. Ethnocentrism and Third World Development		25. The Human Rights Imperative
	5. Third World War: The Global Conflict Over the Rights of Indigenous Nations		26. What Price Political Prisoners?
	6. Industrial Development—A Natural Growth if Rooted in Agricultural Demand		27. South Africa: Where Did the Story Go?
	7. Gorbachev's New Politics: Soviet Third World Policy		28. Babies for Sale: South Koreans Make Them, Americans Buy Them
	8. When Leaders Fall: Succession Systems in the Non-Industrial World		29. Hugo Spadafora's Last Day
	9. Mobutu Sese Seko: "I Have a Clear Conscience"		30. Along the Streets of Tehran: Life Under Khomeini
	10. Savimbi: Warrior Poet		31. Mortgaging a House of Cards: The Ethics of International Debt
	11. Playboy Interview: Imelda and Ferdinand Marcos		32. Swapping Third World Debt
	12. A Pioneering Democracy Struggles With Disillusion		33. Here Comes the Repo Man
	13. Do the Sandinistas Want Democracy? Nicaragua at a Crossroads		34. Latin America: Why Not Default?
	14. The Arab World: Its Own Worst Enemy		35. Will the Planet Pay the Price for Third World Debt?
	15. Ayatollah Realpolitik		36. The Third World Smiles
	16. Collective Violence in India		37. Brazil Debt Pact Called Innovative
	17. The RENAMO Menace: Hunger and Carnage in Mozambique		38. The Hidden Malice of Malnutrition
	18. South Africa and Its Neighbors		39. The "Fourth World"
	19. Policies Toward the Third World		40. Refugees: A Fact of Life?
	20. The U.S. and Third-World Dictatorships: A Case for Benign Detachment		41. The Frantic Third World Quest for Ballistic Missiles
	21. Five Myths About the Third World: Reflections on U.S. Policy		42. Narcotics: Terror's New Ally
			43. A Low-Tech Approach: Prescriptions for Third World Health
			44. AIDS in Africa: Ravager of the Nation Builders
			45. Union Carbide and the Devastation of Bhopal
			46. Where the Future Begins

(Continued on next page)

ABOUT YOU

Name ______________________________ Date ____________
Are you a teacher? ☐ Or student? ☐
Your School Name ______________________________
Department ______________________________
Address ______________________________
City ____________________ State __________ Zip __________
School Telephone # ______________________________

YOUR COMMENTS ARE IMPORTANT TO US!

Please fill in the following information:

For which course did you use this book? ______________________________
Did you use a text with this Annual Edition? ☐ yes ☐ no
The title of the text? ______________________________
What are your general reactions to the Annual Editions concept?

Have you read any particular articles recently that you think should be included in the next edition?

Are there any articles you feel should be replaced in the next edition? Why?

Are there other areas that you feel would utilize an Annual Edition?

May we contact you for editorial input?

May we quote you from above?

No Postage Necessary if Mailed in the United States

ANNUAL EDITIONS: THIRD WORLD 89/90

BUSINESS REPLY MAIL

First Class Permit No. 84 Guilford, CT

Postage will be paid by addressee

The Dushkin Publishing Group, Inc.
Sluice Dock
DPG **Guilford, Connecticut 06437**